AQA

advanced
Economics

AQA

advanced
Economics

Ray Powell

Philip Allan Updates
Market Place
Deddington
Oxfordshire
OX15 0SE

tel: 01869 338652
fax: 01869 337590
e-mail: sales@philipallan.co.uk
www.philipallan.co.uk

© Philip Allan Updates 2005

ISBN-13: 978-0-86003-761-3
ISBN-10: 0-86003-761-4

This textbook has been written specifically to support students studying AQA Advanced Economics. The content has been neither approved nor endorsed by AQA and remains the sole responsibility of the author.

All website addresses included in this book are correct at the time of going to press but may subsequently change.

All photographs are reproduced by permission of TopFoto, except where otherwise specified. Front cover (Comstock Images/Alamy), p. 1 (Jackson Smith/Alamy), pp. 47, 121, 209 (Ingram), p. 382 (David Norton Photography/Alamy).

Printed by Scotprint, Haddington

Environmental information
The paper on which this title is printed is sourced from managed, sustainable forests.

Contents

Introduction viii
Using this book *viii* ● How to use the book at AS *ix* ● How to use the book at A2 *x*

Part 1   Markets and the price mechanism

Chapter 1   The economic problem and economic systems 2
Economics and the economic problem *3* ● Economic systems *3* ● Capital goods and consumer goods *3* ● The economic problem on a production possibility diagram *4* ● Opportunity cost *4* ● Economic growth *5* ● The difference between economic growth and economic development *5* ● Full employment and unemployment *6* ● Types of economy or economic system *6* ● The UK as a mixed economy *8* ● The sectors of an economy *9* ● How the sectors of an economy change over time *10* ● Developed and developing economies *13*

Chapter 2   Supply and demand and the price mechanism 16
The functions of prices in a market economy *17* ● Goods markets and factor markets *17* ● Demand and supply curves *17* ● Functional relationships *18* ● Market plans and market action *19* ● The equilibrium price *19* ● Maximum price laws or price ceilings *21* ● Minimum price laws or price floors *23* ● Shifts of demand *23* ● Shifts of supply *25* ● Shifts of demand and supply curves, and adjustments along demand and supply curves *26* ● The problem of agricultural prices *27*

Chapter 3   Elasticity 34
The elasticities you need to know *35* ● Price elasticity of demand *35* ● Price elasticity of supply *39* ● Income elasticity of demand *42* ● Cross elasticity of demand *43* ● Elasticity case study: shifting the incidence of an expenditure tax *43*

Part 2   Production

Chapter 4   Production and cost theory 48
Production and costs *49* ● Short-run production theory *49* ● Short-run costs *52* ● Long-run production theory *55* ● Long-run costs *57*

Chapter 5   Perfect competition and monopoly 62
Market structures *63* ● Profit-maximising behaviour *64* ● Perfect competition *65* ● Monopoly *68* ● Evaluating perfect competition and monopoly *73*

Chapter 6   Oligopoly 83
What is oligopoly? *84* ● Competitive oligopoly *85* ● Collusive oligopoly *97* ● Game theory and oligopoly *98*

Chapter 7   Further aspects of the growth of firms 102
What is a firm? *103* ● Types of private firm *103* ● Plant and firms *105* ● Economies of scale *105* ● Internal and external growth of firms *109* ● Small firms *111* ● The capital market and the growth of firms *113* ● The growth of venture capital or private equity finance *115* ● The trade-off facing public companies *115* ● Entrepreneurs and the divorce between ownership and control *116* ● Alternative theories of the firm *117*

Part 3   Government and markets

Chapter 8   Industrial policy...122
A short history of UK industrial policy *123* ● Competition policy *123* ● Private versus public ownership of industry *132* ● Economic liberalisation *137*

Chapter 9   Market failure..147
Equity and efficiency in markets *148* ● Public goods and public 'bads' *149* ● Externalities *152* ● Merit goods and demerit goods *161*

Chapter 10 Cost–benefit analysis and government failure...........................168
Why cost–benefit analysis is needed *169* ● The use of cost–benefit analysis *169* ● Private sector investment appraisal *170* ● The differences between private sector investment appraisal and CBA *172* ● Some difficulties involved in CBA *173* ● Government failure *175*

Part 4   Labour markets

Chapter 11 Labour markets..180
Price theory and the labour market *181* ● Perfectly competitive labour markets *182* ● Monopsony labour markets *191* ● Wage equalisation in a perfectly competitive market economy *192* ● Explanations of different wage levels *193* ● Methods of pay determination in the UK *201* ● The decline of trade unions in the UK *204*

Part 5   Macroeconomic theory

Chapter 12 The growth of modern macroeconomics..................................210
Keynesian macroeconomics *211* ● The monetarist and free-market counter-revolution *219* ● Monetary policy in recent years *223*

Chapter 13 National income, standards of living and economic growth............227
Measuring national income *228* ● Measuring economic welfare and standards of living *230* ● Economic growth *237*

Chapter 14 Aggregate demand...251
Aggregate demand *252* ● Consumption and saving *255* ● Investment *264*

Chapter 15 The aggregate demand and aggregate supply macroeconomic model......275
The *AD/AS* model: two cautionary notes *276* ● Macroeconomic equilibrium *276* ● The aggregate demand curve *277* ● Aggregate supply *278* ● The *AD/AS* model and economic policy: some fundamentals *286*

Chapter 16 Unemployment and inflation...289
Unemployment *290* ● Inflation *299*

Part 6   Macroeconomic policy

Chapter 17 Money, banking and monetary policy.......................................320
What is money? *321* ● The functions of money *321* ● The development of modern money *322* ● Banks and bank deposits *323* ● Money, money substitutes and near money *325* ● The problem of defining the money supply *326* ● Why bank deposits are the most important form of money *327* ● Portfolio balance decisions *328* ● The Bank of England and monetary policy *329* ● Objectives and instruments of monetary policy *329* ● Monetary policy objectives *330* ● Monetary policy instruments *331* ● Current and recent monetary policy in the UK *332* ● The transmission mechanism of monetary policy *335*

Chapter 18 Taxation, government spending and fiscal policy 339

Taxation and other sources of government revenue *340* ● Public expenditure *344* ● The aims of taxation and public spending *346* ● Fiscal policy *348*

Chapter 19 Supply-side economics 366

The meaning of supply-side economics *367* ● Supply-side economic policy *368* ● Supply-side microeconomic theory and the supply of labour *370* ● Supply-side macroeconomic theory *371* ● The roles of fiscal policy and monetary policy in supply-side macroeconomics *374* ● Supply-side economics, New Keynesianism and New Labour *375* ● Examples of supply-side economic policies *376*

Part 7 International economics

Chapter 20 International trade and globalisation 382

The case for international trade *383* ● The case for import controls and protectionism *389* ● International trade and welfare *391* ● The changing pattern of world and UK trade *393*

Chapter 21 The balance of payments 404

The structure of the balance of payments in the UK *405* ● Equilibrium and disequilibrium in the 'balance' of payments *412*

Chapter 22 Exchange rates 422

Measuring the exchange rate *423* ● The different types of exchange rate system *424* ● Freely floating exchange rates *424* ● Fixed exchange rates *430* ● Managed exchange rates *431* ● Fixed and adjustable peg exchange rates and monetary policy *433* ● The development of a single currency in the EU *434* ● Reserve currencies *439*

Part 8 Markets at work and the European Union

Chapter 23 Markets at work 444

Housing markets *445* ● The environment *454* ● Sport and leisure markets *463*

Chapter 24 The European Union 472

Special features of the Unit 4W case study examination paper *473* ● Origins and history of the EU *474* ● The EU as a trading bloc *481* ● The EU as an economic and monetary union *483* ● The EU as a possible future political union *484* ● The EU, trade creation and trade diversion *485* ● The common agricultural policy (CAP) *486* ● The common fisheries policy *488* ● Labour mobility in the single market: the Bosman case *490* ● EU competition policy *491* ● EU regional problems and regional policy *493* ● EU transport problems and transport policy *496* ● Macroeconomic performance in the EU *498* ● 'Old Europe', 'New Europe' and different models of capitalism *500* ● EU fiscal policy, tax harmonisation and the Stability and Growth Pact *502*

Index 506

Introduction

This book has two main objectives. The first and most important is to help you achieve the highest possible grades in the AS and A-level economics examinations.

The second objective is to turn you into a good economist. For those of you who are not intending to study economics at university, I hope that reading the book will enable you to contribute thoughtfully and informatively when discussing economic issues with family or friends, or with prospective employers you need to impress. And for those of you who decide to study economics or an economics-related subject at university, I hope the book reinforces this decision, provides you with an enjoyable period of study and prepares you for studying the subject at a higher level.

Since 2000, when the current AS and A2 economics specifications were introduced, many teachers have complained about the modular nature of the A-level curriculum. These teachers argue that modularity causes students to study topics in 'bite-sized chunks' in order to pass an examination, and then to forget what they have learnt as they move on to study the next module. According to this view, students become much better economists when taught the whole of an A-level course over 2 years, with one set of examinations at the end of the course.

In my view, the present examination system suffers a second disadvantage, stemming from the 'dumbing-down' of subject content at AS. Too many AS topics are taught and examined in a rather superficial way, simply because this is all the AS specifications demand. Teachers then find themselves in the A2 part of the course having to re-teach, in greater and more accurate depth, topics they had taught much less rigorously a year earlier.

To try to tackle these weaknesses in the current AS and A2 economics course, I have written a traditional economics textbook that proceeds in an orderly way from microeconomics to macroeconomics. I have tried also to explain each topic in the depth it deserves, regardless of whether the topic is examined at AS or at A2. On occasion, I have deliberately gone beyond the AQA economics specification in order to include information I consider interesting and necessary if a student is to become a good economist rather than just a grade achiever at A-level. The additional topics I have included are:

- the cobweb theory of agricultural price fluctuations (Chapter 2)
- the nature of firms, the capital market and the stock exchange (Chapter 7)
- different forms of money and the nature of the banking system (Chapter 17).

Using this book

The chapters deal with modularity in two ways. First, each chapter begins with a specification coverage that states whether the chapter content is AS, A2, or a mix of both, and that indicates the sections of each AS or A2 specification covered in the chapter. Second, **examiner's voice** inserts are scattered through each chapter. Many of these indicate whether the adjacent information is relevant for AS or A2. On other occasions, the examiner's voice notes that the text includes useful background information, but that examination questions will not be set on it.

The AQA economics specification requires candidates to 'have developed a good knowledge of the recent trends and developments in the UK economy and government policies which have taken place during the past 10 years'. Examination questions do not require knowledge of earlier events (though candidates are sometimes asked to describe or to compare data series extending back more than 10 years). Nevertheless, I firmly believe that students benefit from a basic knowledge of economic history and of different schools of economic thought, such as Keynesianism and monetarism. Where I think it helps, I have adopted a historical approach, particularly in the explanation of macroeconomic topics such as theories of inflation and unemployment, and in the way monetary policy, fiscal policy and supply-side economics have developed over the years.

At the end of each chapter, there are a number of **self-testing questions**. These can be used by teachers to reinforce understanding of chapter content, or by students testing their own knowledge. The book does not provide answers to the self-testing questions, though answers are given, along with a selection of European Union case-study questions and answers, in the *AQA Advanced Economics Teacher Answer Guide*, available from Philip Allan Updates.

Examination-style questions have not been included in this book. However, objective test, data-response and essay questions relevant to the different unit exams are available, along with summary specification coverage, in the following Student Unit Guides published by Philip Allan Updates:

AQA AS Module 1: Markets and Market Failure (2nd edn)

AQA AS Module 2: The National Economy (2nd edn)

AQA AS Module 3: Markets at Work

AQA A2 Module 5: Business Economics and the Distribution of Income

AQA A2 Module 6: Government Policy, the National and International Economy

How to use the book at AS

If you are starting an AS course in economics, you should begin by reading Chapter 1. This explains the economic problem and the nature of economic systems and provides a good introduction to the course. How you then use the book should depend on whether you are studying the course module by module (in which case you will probably study Module 1 before Modules 2 and 3) or whether you are studying Modules 1 and 2 'side-by-side'. As you read each chapter or section of a chapter, answer the self-testing questions at the end of the chapter that are relevant for AS economics. Then check your answers against the chapter content.

The chapters relevant for **Module 1** are:

Chapter 2 Supply and demand and the price mechanism

Chapter 3 Elasticity

Chapter 5 Perfect competition and monopoly (only the sections on the meaning of monopoly and the concepts of productive efficiency and allocative efficiency)

Chapter 9 Market failure (the diagrams showing marginal cost and benefit curves can be ignored)

Chapter 10 Cost–benefit analysis and government failure (only the sections on government failure)

Chapter 20 International trade and globalisation (only the section on specialisation and the division of labour)

The chapters relevant for **Module 2** are:

Chapter 13 National income, standards of living and economic growth (only the sections on the various measures of national income, and a first look at economic growth)

Chapter 14 Aggregate demand (the meaning of aggregate demand, and the determinants of consumption and investment)

Chapter 15 The aggregate demand and aggregate supply macroeconomic model (concentrate on macroeconomic equilibrium and the causes and effects of a shift of the *AD* curve, the *SRAS* curve and the *LRAS* curve)

Chapter 16 Unemployment and inflation

Chapter 17 Money, banking and monetary policy (only the sections on monetary policy)

Chapter 18 Taxation, government spending and fiscal policy (only the sections on fiscal policy)

Chapter 19 Supply-side economics

Chapter 21 The balance of payments (only the sections on the current account of the balance of payments)

Note that these chapters cover the requirements of A2 as well as AS economics.

The chapter relevant for **Module 3** is:

Chapter 23 Markets at work

How to use the book at A2

Much of the content of Module 5: Business Economics and the Distribution of Income is significantly different from that of AS Module 1: Markets and Market Failure. By contrast, with the exception of parts of the specification which cover international economics, most of Module 5: Government Policy, the National and International Economy simply develops in more detail and rigour topics already studied in the AS course.

Both the Unit 5 and the Unit 6 examinations are synoptic. Synopticity may be vertical, horizontal or diagonal. A Unit 5 examination question is vertically synoptic when it tests knowledge learnt in Module 1. Two examples are supply and demand

and elasticity. Likewise, a Unit 6 examination question testing knowledge learnt in Module 2 is vertically synoptic. Examples include national income, the multiplier and *AD/AS* analysis.

Horizontal synopticity requires the application of a macroeconomic concept or theory learnt when studying Module 6 to answer a microeconomic question in the Unit 5 examination (or vice versa). For example, a question on poverty (in Unit 5) may test knowledge of how fiscal policy (a Module 6 topic) may reduce poverty. Diagonal synopticity requires the use of Module 2 terms and concepts to answer a Unit 5 question, or the use of knowledge learned in Module 1 to answer a Unit 6 question.

At A2, as well as at AS, it is a good idea to answer the relevant self-testing questions at the end of each chapter. You should check your answers against the chapter content.

Before starting the A2 course, read Chapter 1 again. If you haven't already read Chapter 12, read this as a general introduction to Module 6 macroeconomics.

The chapter relevant for **Module 4W** is:
Chapter 24 The European Union (together with the sections of Chapters 2 and 22 that respectively cover government intervention in agriculture and the single European currency or euro)

The chapters relevant for **Module 5** are:
Chapter 4   Production and cost theory
Chapter 5   Perfect competition and monopoly
Chapter 6   Oligopoly
Chapter 7   Further aspects of the growth of firms
Chapter 8   Industrial policy
Chapter 9   Market failure (the chapter develops the AS coverage of market failure, particularly in terms of marginal cost and benefit diagrams and the application of the concept of allocative efficiency)
Chapter 10 Cost–benefit analysis and government failure (concentrate particularly on cost–benefit analysis which is an A2 but not an AS topic)
Chapter 11 Labour markets

The chapters relevant for **Module 6** are:
Chapter 12 The growth of modern macroeconomics
Chapter 13 National income, standards of living and economic growth (concentrate on the use of national income as a measure of economic welfare, business cycles, the causes of economic growth and the costs and benefits of economic growth)
Chapter 14 Aggregate demand (this chapter is well worth reading again before studying the *AD/AS* model in the depth required at A2)
Chapter 15 The aggregate demand and aggregate supply macroeconomic model (although the *AD/AS* model must be studied in more detail at A2, especially the relationship between *SRAS* and *LRAS* curves, detailed knowledge of the derivation of the *AD* and *AS* curves is not really needed)

Chapter 16 Unemployment and inflation (concentrate on the causes of unemployment, the natural rate of unemployment, the Phillips curve, and the costs and benefits of inflation)

Chapter 17 Money, banking and monetary policy (monetary policy must be understood in greater detail than at AS)

Chapter 18 Taxation, government spending and fiscal policy (A2 requires knowledge of the levels and patterns of taxation and government spending, as well as greater knowledge of fiscal policy than is required at AS)

Chapter 19 Supply-side economics (a greater knowledge of supply-side economics and supply-side policies is needed at A2)

Chapter 21 The balance of payments (capital flows as well as the current account, and the links between the balance of payments and exchange rates)

Chapter 22 Exchange rates (fixed, managed, but especially floating exchange rates, together with the relationships between exchange rates, the balance of payments and monetary policy)

It now remains for you to use the book, to become an economist, and to pass your exams with flying colours. I wish you every success.

Ray Powell

Part **1**

Markets and the price mechanism

Chapter 1
The economic problem and economic systems

Specification focus

This chapter introduces themes and concepts that are relevant throughout an economics course, both at AS and at A2. The chapter is particularly relevant for:

AS **Module 1 Markets and Market Failure**
The Economic Problem

Module 2 The National Economy
Performance of the UK Economy and Government Policy Objectives

A2 **Module 5 Business Economics and the Distribution of Income**
Government Intervention in the Market

Module 6 Government Policy, the National and International Economy
Growth of the Economy and Cyclical Instability

A2 **Synoptic coverage**
Knowledge of the concepts introduced in this chapter, such as the economic problem, opportunity cost, and the meaning of a market, may be tested synoptically in the A2 examination.

Introduction

This first chapter introduces the economic problem and asks you to think about the nature of the UK economy and of types of economic system that are very different from the UK. The chapter then describes different ways of classifying economic systems, and explains how the main types of economic system attempt to solve the economic problem. The concluding part of the chapter examines how economic systems, including the UK mixed economy, have been changing in recent years.

Economics and the economic problem

> Economics is the science which studies human behaviour as a relationship between ends and scarce means which have alternative uses.

> Lionel Robbins, *Essay on the nature and significance of economic science*, 1932

Professor Robbins' long-established definition provides perhaps the best-known starting point for introducing and understanding what economics is about. Economics is literally the study of **economising** — the study of how human beings make choices about *what to produce*, *how to produce* and *for whom to produce*, in a world in which most resources are limited. How best can people make decisions about the allocation of scarce resources among competing uses, so as to improve and maximise human happiness and welfare? This is the **economic problem**.

Economic systems

> An economic system is a set of institutional arrangements whose function is to employ most efficiently scarce resources to meet the ends of society.

> *The United Nations Dictionary of Social Science*

Although the problem of scarcity is fundamental and common to all forms of human society — from humble tribal groupings of hunter-gatherers in the Amazonian forest to rich nations such as the USA — different societies have produced different institutional frameworks and methods for allocating scarce resources among competing uses. The set of institutions within which a community decides what, how and for whom to produce is called an **economic system**.

Capital goods and consumer goods

Before we examine the economic problem in greater detail, and how different economic systems attempt to solve it, we shall briefly introduce a number of key economic concepts. This section explains the distinction between capital goods and consumer goods.

Capital goods, which are also known as producer goods, investment goods and intermediate goods, are not bought by households for final consumption; instead they are bought by other firms as raw materials or inputs for the purpose of production. The capital goods industries, many of which are 'heavy' industries, include the iron and steel, mechanical engineering and chemical industries.

As their name suggests, **consumer goods** or final goods are bought by persons or households for the purpose of final consumption, to satisfy wants and needs. Cars, television sets, washing machines and similar goods purchased by individuals or households for ordinary consumer use are examples of **consumer durables** — consumer goods with a long average life, during which they deliver a 'stream' of consumer services. By contrast, a non-durable consumer good, such as a packet of soap powder, needs replacing after it has been used. Some consumer durable goods, especially housing, are bought for investment purposes as well as for the consumer services that they deliver to households.

The economic problem on a production possibility diagram

The **production possibility frontier** (or production possibility curve) in Figure 1.1(a) shows the various combinations of capital goods and consumer goods that can be produced, assuming that inputs of labour, capital and land are fully used, with no spare capacity. Given that resources and capacity are limited, a choice has to be made about which type of good to produce.

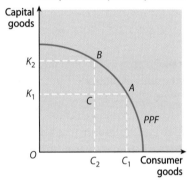

(a) The economic problem illustrated on a production possibility frontier

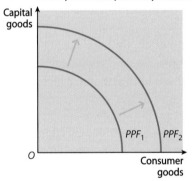

(b) Economic growth illustrated by a shift of the production possibility frontier

Figure 1.1

e*xaminer's voice
You must learn to draw and interpret production possibility diagrams, which are very important in AS and A2 economics. In this chapter, we use production possibility diagrams to illustrate opportunity cost, economic growth, full employment and unemployment. Later chapters will show you how to use these diagrams to illustrate and analyse other terms and concepts that are likely to be tested in the AS and A2 examinations.

For example, point A on the production possibility frontier shows K_1 capital goods and C_1 consumer goods. But if the country's inhabitants want faster economic growth, more of society's scarce resources will have to be devoted to capital goods and fewer to consumer goods. This can be shown by the movement from point A to point B on the production possibility frontier. Capital good production rises to K_2, but at the expense of a fall in consumer good production to C_2.

Opportunity cost

The movement from point A to point B on the production possibility frontier in Figure 1.1(a) illustrates a very important aspect of the economic problem, namely the principle of **opportunity cost**. The opportunity cost of any choice, decision or course of action is measured in terms of the *alternatives* that have to be given up. Hence the opportunity cost of increasing the production of capital goods from K_1 to K_2 is the fall in consumer goods from C_1 to C_2.

We can develop the concept of opportunity cost a stage further. In economics we always assume that **economic agents** (for example, individuals, households or firms) behave rationally. This means that people try to make decisions that are in their self-interest and that maximise their private benefit. When a choice has to be made, the best alternative is always chosen, which means that the *second best* or *next best* alternative is rejected. Providing people are rational, the opportunity cost of any decision or choice is the *next best alternative sacrificed or forgone*.

Economic growth

A decision to sacrifice *current* consumption in favour of a higher level of *future* consumption means that more of society's scarce resources go into investment or the production of capital goods, enabling the country's capital stock to grow larger. Over time, the production possibility frontier shifts outward, as illustrated in Figure 1.1(b). This outward movement indicates an increase in the *potential* level of output that the economy can produce, or economic growth. Strictly speaking, the shift shown in Figure 1.1(b) is *long-run* economic growth. Some economists argue that a movement from a point inside the production possibility frontier (such as *C* in Figure 1.1(a)) to a point on or closer to the frontier shows *short-term* economic growth. The difference between short-term and long-term growth is that the former makes use of spare capacity and takes up the slack in the economy, whereas the latter requires an increase in total productive capacity.

The difference between economic growth and economic development

Economic growth measures changes in the physical quantity of goods and services that an economy actually produces, or has the potential to produce. As later chapters explain, growth does not *necessarily* improve the economic welfare of all or most of the people living in a country.

Economic development is a better indicator of improved human welfare, and the ability to continue to improve welfare, than economic growth. Economic development, which includes the quality and not just the quantity of growth, is measured by:

- a general improvement in living standards which reduces poverty and human suffering
- greater access to resources such as food and housing that are required to satisfy basic human needs
- greater access to opportunities for human development (for example, through education and training)
- environmental sustainability and regeneration, through reducing resource depletion and degradation

Resource depletion occurs when finite resources such as oil are used up, and when soil fertility or fish stocks irreversibly decline. By contrast, **resource degradation** is best illustrated by pollution of air, water and land. To benefit people

in the long run, growth (and development) must be sustainable. **Sustainable economic growth** requires the use of:

- *renewable* rather than *non-renewable* resources
- technologies that minimise pollution and other forms of resource degradation

Full employment and unemployment

All points on an economy's production possibility frontier (such as points *A* and *B* in Figure 1.1(a)) represent full employment of the economy's available resources. However, a point such as *C* inside the production possibility frontier is associated with unemployment. At point *C*, it is no longer true that the opportunity cost of increasing the output of consumer goods is the sacrifice of some production of capital goods. In this situation, production of capital goods and consumer goods can both be increased by employing previously idle resources.

Types of economy or economic system

Classification by allocative mechanism

Perhaps the most widely used method of defining and classifying economic systems is according to the type of **allocative mechanism** by which scarce resources reach the people who eventually consume or use them. Although there are a variety of ways in which wealth and purchasing power can be allocated among individuals, including inheritance and other types of gift, theft and chance (such as winning a fortune on the National Lottery), the two allocative mechanisms by which economic systems are defined are the **market mechanism** (or price mechanism) and the **command mechanism** (or planning mechanism). An economic system in which goods and services are purchased through the price mechanism in a system of markets is called a **market economy**, whereas one in which government officials or planners allocate economic resources to firms and other productive enterprises is called a **command economy** (or planned economy).

Market economies

In a pure market economy, the **market mechanism** (the price mechanism and market forces) performs the central economic task of allocating scarce resources among competing uses. A market economy comprises a large number of markets varying in the degree to which they are separated from and interrelated with each other.

A **market** is a meeting of buyers and sellers in which goods or services are exchanged for other goods or services. Occasionally, the exchange is direct and is known as **barter**. More usually, however, the exchange is indirect with buyers and sellers using money. One good or service, such as labour, is exchanged for money, which is then traded a second time for other goods or services, sometimes immediately but often some time later. The exchange must be voluntary; if one party forces a transaction upon the other, it is not a market transaction.

Transport costs and lack of information may create barriers that separate or break up markets. In past centuries, such barriers often prevented markets from operating outside the relatively small geographical areas of a single country or even a small region within a country. However, while some markets exist in a particular geographical location – for example, a street market and until quite recently the London Stock Exchange – many markets do not. In recent years, modern developments have allowed goods to be transported more easily and at lower cost, and have helped in the transmission of market information via telephone, fax and increasingly the internet. This has enabled many markets, especially commodity and raw material markets and markets in financial services, to become truly global or international markets functioning on a worldwide basis.

Command economies

A complete command economy is an economy in which all decisions about what, how, how much, when, where and for whom to produce are taken by a central planning authority, issuing commands or directives to all the households and producers in the society. Such a system could only exist within a very rigid and probably totalitarian political framework because of the restrictions on individual decision making that are obviously implied.

In fact, in much the same way that a pure market economy, in which the price mechanism alone allocates resources, is a theoretical abstraction, so no economy in the real world can properly be described as a complete or pure command economy. Before the collapse of the communist political system around 1990, the countries of eastern Europe were command economies. However, they were not pure command economies. Production but not consumption was planned. Consumers often had to queue to get consumer goods, whose prices were fixed by the planners. Shortages resulted, which, together with the generally inferior quality of consumer goods, contributed to the breakdown of the command economies. Some communist countries still exist, namely the People's Republic of China, North Korea, Vietnam and Cuba. However, all these countries, with the exception until very recently of North Korea, have encouraged the growth of markets to a greater or lesser extent. They have communist political systems, but they have moved away from being pure command economies.

Classification by ownership

So far we have defined economic systems in terms of the allocative mechanism (the market mechanism or the planning mechanism) used to solve the economic problem. Economic systems can also be defined in terms of who owns the **means of production**: private individuals or the state.

Capitalist economies

Capitalism is a system in which the means of production are privately owned by individuals (or capitalists), who employ labour to operate the capital they own, so as to produce output for sale at a profit.

Socialist economies

In contrast to capitalism, in a **socialist** economic system the means of production are owned by the state on behalf of the people.

Classification by allocative mechanism and ownership

Mixed economies

Many economies, particularly those of the developed countries of western Europe such as the UK, are called **mixed economies**. A mixed economy, as the name suggests, is a mixture of different types of economic system. Figure 1.2 shows how a mixed economy can be defined both in terms of the mechanism for allocating resources and in terms of ownership. The upper panel of the diagram shows that a mixed economy is intermediate between a market economy and a command economy. Defined in this way, a mixed economy contains a large market sector and a large non-market sector. The lower panel of the diagram shows that a mixed economy contains a large public sector and a large private sector.

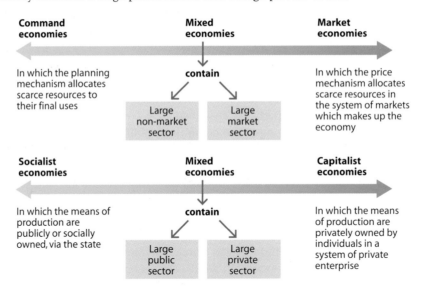

Figure 1.2 Different types of economic system

The UK as a mixed economy

The development of the mixed economy

A mixed economy developed quickly in the UK in the 1940s, when a number of important industries such as coal, rail and steel were nationalised and taken into public ownership. At the same time, the 1944 Education Act and the creation of the National Health Service extended state provision of education and healthcare.

For about 30 years after the end of the Second World War, from the 1940s to the 1970s, the majority of UK citizens (and the major political parties) agreed that the mixed economy was working well. Most people believed that certain types of economic activity, particularly the production and distribution of consumer goods and services, were best suited to private enterprise and the market economy. But people also accepted that some industries, the utility industries, which at the time were natural monopolies, ought to be nationalised, and that important services such as education, healthcare and roads should be provided by government 'outside the market' and financed through the tax system. In short, a consensus existed around the belief that the mixed economy was 'about right' for the UK.

**e*xaminer's voice*

Examiners expect candidates to know what has happened in the UK economy in the 10 years before the examination. While you are not required to know about earlier events, you should appreciate that change is a continuous process, and that recent events often have their origins in changes which took place many years ago.

Recent changes in the mixed economy

From the 1960s onward, however, a growing minority (and perhaps eventually a majority) of economists and politicians blamed the mixed economy for the UK's deteriorating economic performance, relative to that of its main competitors in western Europe and Japan. Critics argued that the public and non-market sectors of the economy are very often inefficient and wealth *consuming* rather than wealth *creating*. The public and non-market sectors had become too big and needed cutting down to size. Critics of the mixed economy argued that a concerted effort should be made to change fundamentally the nature of the UK economy by increasing private ownership and market production.

During the 1980s and early and mid-1990s, Conservative governments implemented policies that succeeded in changing the nature of the mix in favour of private ownership and market forces, at the expense of public ownership and state planning. The UK economy is now much closer to being a pure market and private enterprise economy than it was 25 years ago. The three main policies used to change the nature of the UK economy have been:

■ **privatisation** — selling off state-owned assets such as nationalised industries to private ownership
■ **marketisation or commercialisation** — charging a market price for goods and services that the state previously provided 'free'
■ **deregulation** — removing barriers to entry and government red tape and bureaucracy from the operation of markets

These policies of **economic liberalisation** were first introduced by Margaret Thatcher's Conservative governments. Thatcher believed that the mixed economy she inherited in 1979 was actually a mixed-up economy, performing inefficiently and uncompetitively. To a large extent, she established a new agenda that Tony Blair's New Labour governments have also accepted, continuing the process of reform (or reaction?) that they inherited.

The sectors of an economy

A **sector** is simply a division or part of the economy. We have already introduced two methods of dividing an economy into sectors: first, into the market and non-market

sectors; and second, into the private and the public sectors. A third method of division is based on the type of economic activity or industry involved. On this basis, the economy can be divided into primary, secondary and tertiary industrial sectors.

Primary sector

The **primary sector** contains extractive industries, also known as basic industries, such as agriculture, fishing, forestry and mining and quarrying. Primary industries literally extract raw materials and foodstuffs from the resources of the earth's surface. Raw materials produced by the primary sector then serve as the inputs of the secondary sector.

Secondary sector

The **secondary sector** contains manufacturing, processing and construction. Secondary industries eventually convert raw materials into finished or final goods that satisfy consumer wants and needs. Oil refining, gas works, power stations and water works are processing industries, while car plants and factories making computers provide examples of manufacturing.

Tertiary sector

The **tertiary sector** contains service industries, such as financial services, administration, transport and entertainment industries.

Figure 1.3 illustrates the relative sizes of the primary, secondary and tertiary sectors in the UK economy today, and provides examples of industries in each of the three sectors.

The service industry is now the largest part of the UK economy

	Extractive industries	Manufacturing, processing, construction	Service industries
Examples:	**Primary sector** Farming Fishing Forestry Mining, quarrying, oil extraction	**Secondary sector** Iron and steel making Car manufacturing Assembling mobile phones Generating electricity Building shopping malls	**Tertiary sector** Administration Education Healthcare services Police and armed forces Leisure and tourism Communication Financial services

Figure 1.3 Primary, secondary and tertiary sectors in the UK economy

How the sectors of an economy change over time

At different stages of economic development and growth, the primary, secondary and tertiary sectors of an economy assume a different relative importance and size.

Figure 1.4 illustrates how the relative sizes of the primary, secondary and tertiary sectors change as an economy grows and develops. Different countries have, of course, grown and developed in different ways, particularly when growth and development have taken place at different times in history. Figure 1.4 is a *general* guide to the historical stages of growth and development, but the diagram is not necessarily accurate for any particular country.

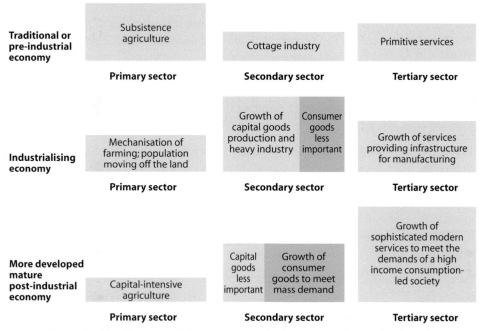

Figure 1.4 The changing relative importance of primary, secondary and tertiary sectors

The upper panel of Figure 1.4 illustrates the structure of a **pre-industrial or traditional society,** such as the UK some time before Britain's industrial revolution, or a country in sub-Saharan Africa at the present day. Agriculture and sometimes other extractive activities form the largest part of the economy. Primary production dominates economic activity and the secondary and service sectors are relatively small. Indeed, in true traditional societies, the secondary sector is restricted largely to village crafts such as shoe repairing and weaving, the economy not yet having developed the factory or industrialised production typical of the manufacturing sector in more advanced economies. Large numbers of people live and are employed on the land. Production is labour intensive, and much of the foodstuff produced is consumed by the farmers and their families. This is **subsistence farming**. Output per worker is very low and people are poor and unable to save. In this phase of development (or lack of development), economies stagnate and generally lack the conditions, such as a supply of savings and an entrepreneurial culture, to foster economic growth and development.

In the process of **industrialisation**, the secondary or manufacturing sector grows to become the largest and dominant sector of the economy. During the earlier

stages of industrialisation, capital goods and heavy industry are usually more important than the production of consumer goods. This phase of growth is illustrated in the middle panel of Figure 1.4. As the economy matures and develops a wider range of manufacturing industries, consumer goods usually become more important.

For much of the twentieth century, manufacturing and services both grew in the UK economy, but services grew faster than manufacturing and processing. In the UK, this phase lasted until the 1970s, when **deindustrialisation** began significantly to affect the structure of the economy. Deindustrialisation means different things to different people. If defined as the *relative* decline of the manufacturing industry, deindustrialisation has affected the UK economy for more than 100 years. Usually, however, deindustrialisation is defined as the *absolute* decline of manufacturing, with some economists extending the definition to include the decline of primary activities such as coal mining and fishing.

Defined in this way, deindustrialisation has severely affected the UK economy since the 1970s. Manufacturing output has at times declined at a rapid rate and is now below 17% of UK output. The decline has been particularly marked when the economy has been in recession. (A **recession** is a fall in national output, or negative growth, for 6 months or more.) Manufacturing output generally recovers in the upswing of the business cycle, but not always by enough to offset the decline in the previous recession.

Even when manufacturing *output* has grown, manufacturing *employment* has fallen. This is because, to recover from recession, surviving manufacturing firms need to reorganise and restructure, which means adopting more capital-intensive ways of producing output. Likewise, new manufacturing firms which replace firms that close down generally have to adopt state-of-the-art automated methods of production.

Deindustrialisation means that the previously mature industrialised economies in western Europe and North America have entered a new **post-industrial phase of development**, which is illustrated in the lower panel of Figure 1.4. A generally thriving service sector now dominates, so personal incomes remain high. The demand for consumer goods is now largely met by imports from countries such as South Korea, Malaysia, Singapore and especially China. These countries are called **newly-industrialising countries** (NICs), or **newly-industrialised countries** in the case of countries that have already reached a mature stage of development. Indeed, some of the older NICs are now themselves suffering deindustrialisation as manufacturing jobs move to China. The People's Republic of China has become the world's leading manufacturing country.

examiner's voice
Make sure you understand that the UK is now a post-industrial economy, dominated by service sector activity.

As manufacturing industries generally produce internationally tradable goods, they are especially vulnerable to competition from NICs and eastern Europe, where wage and other labour costs are lower than in the UK. Until recently, many services were much less internationally tradable. This has now changed, especially for services delivered via the telephone and the internet. Four factors are now contributing to a shift of services such as call centres to countries like India. These are:

- **The 'death of distance'.** The internet and satellite technology create instant and almost cost-free communication.
- **The growing role of English as the language of international business.** Millions of overseas workers speak good English and perform service jobs previously undertaken by UK-based office workers.
- **Overcoming the problem of different time zones.** Firms use shift work throughout a 24-hour day to communicate with UK customers at a time convenient (or sometimes inconvenient) to the customer.
- **Skilled workers earning low wages.** English-speaking service workers in NICs are usually graduates, who are prepared to work for lower wages than their UK counterparts.

> *e***xaminer's voice**
>
> All these changes contribute to globalisation. You should understand how virtually all the world's economies, including the UK's, are part of a globalised economy.

Developed and developing economies

Countries such as the USA, Japan and those in western Europe are generally called **developed economies**, or sometimes **more developed countries** (MDCs). Other countries are then classified as **developing countries** – a rather unsatisfactory and 'catch-all' label. It includes on the one hand countries with very great poverty, which lack almost any form of modern development and, at the other extreme, NICs that are more industrialised and urbanised than any country in the 'developed' world. Countries in the developing world are called **less developed countries** (LDCs). The United Nations divides LDCs into high-income, upper-middle-income, lower-middle-income and low-income developing countries.

Other labels used to describe a country's state of development, and sometimes also its political system, include **North** and **South**, and the **first**, **second** and **third worlds**. Because they are mostly in the northern part of the northern hemisphere, developed countries are in the 'North'. By contrast, the countries of the 'South' are the tropical and sub-tropical LDCs, lying mostly to the south of the developed world. The 'North' includes countries such as Australia and New Zealand, which are further south than any developing country apart from the southern parts of Argentina and Chile! (Argentina and Chile are middle-income developing countries, whereas many NICs and Persian Gulf oil-producing countries are high-income developing countries.)

The 'first' and 'second' worlds are part of the 'North'. The 'first world' comprises the developed 'western' market or capitalist economies of North America, western Europe and Japan. Before their disintegration, the socialist and command economies of the Soviet Union and other Eastern Bloc countries formed the 'second world': a group of countries described – semi-jokingly – as combining a 'first world' military-industrial complex with a 'third world' economic infrastructure. Living standards were generally lower, the agricultural populations were larger, there was

greater reliance on 'heavy' secondary manufacturing industries, and service industries were less developed than in the 'first world' market economies of the West. These and other factors led to the collapse of the political and economic systems in 'second world' countries in the late 1980s and early 1990s. The countries of the 'second world' are now **transitional economies**, in the process of change to western-style market and mixed economies. In some former Eastern Bloc countries, the change has not been smooth, giving way at times to what has been called **gangster capitalism**.

*e*xaminer's voice

Although knowledge of development economics is not required by the AQA specifications, you must understand how the UK economy is affected by changes in poorer countries, such as the movement of manufacturing industries to countries like China.

In contrast to the 'first' and 'second' worlds, the label 'third world' is not based on a political division between non-communist and communist political regimes. The 'third world' is just another name for the developing world and the 'South'. This includes both market and capitalist economies such as South Korea, Singapore and Malaysia, and socialist and command economies such as the People's Republic of China and Cuba. While most 'third world' countries have benefited from at least some significant development, there are a number of low-income developing countries where this has not occurred. Economists sometimes identify a 'fourth world' of backward, undeveloped and poverty-stricken countries, for the most part located in sub-Saharan Africa.

Summary

In this chapter we have seen how economic systems are defined in terms of the method by which resources are allocated within the economy (market economies and command economies), or in terms of ownership (capitalism and socialism). None of these labels describes accurately the modern UK economy, which is a mixed economy containing large market and non-market sectors and large private and public sectors.

Economic systems do not exist in a timeless vacuum; rather they continuously evolve. The UK mixed economy was remarkably stable and unchanged from the late 1940s to the 1970s. Since then, however, the nature of the 'mix' has changed, with the economy moving closer to a pure private enterprise and market economy. In the 1980s, Margaret Thatcher's Conservative governments reduced the size of the public and non-market sectors of the economy, using the instruments of

privatisation, marketisation and deregulation to achieve these objectives. In the 1990s and early 2000s, the process of economic liberalisation has generally been continued by post-Thatcherite governments. However, the recent New Labour governments have been more committed than previous Conservative administrations to state provision of a safety net for the poor.

Most people are now familiar with global divisions of economies into 'North' and 'South' and first and third worlds, based on the extent to which previously very poor countries have developed, or failed to develop, their economies. The growth of newly-industrialised countries (NICs) such as China has impacted upon the UK economy, primarily by accelerating the deindustrialisation process (mainly the decline of manufacturing) and the growth of the service sector of the economy.

Self-testing questions

1 What is the central economic problem?

2 What are the two main methods by which resources are allocated between competing uses?

3 Define consumer and capital goods.

4 What is meant by economic growth?

5 What is a market?

6 Distinguish between a market economy, a command economy and a mixed economy.

7 Distinguish between capitalism and socialism.

8 Explain the difference between the primary, secondary and tertiary sectors of an economy.

9 List three secondary sector activities and three tertiary sector activities.

10 How has the UK mixed economy changed over the last 30 years?

11 Distinguish between privatisation and marketisation (or commercialisation).

12 What are LDCs, NICs, the 'North' and the 'South'?

13 How has the growth of NICs affected the structure of the UK economy?

Chapter 2
Supply and demand and the price mechanism

Specification focus

This chapter introduces and explains one of the most important parts of microeconomics: how a market functions within a market or mixed economy. The chapter is particularly relevant for:

AS Module 1 Markets and Market Failure
Allocation of Resources in Competitive Markets

Module 3 Markets at Work
The Housing Market; The Economics of Sport and Leisure

A2 Module 4 Working as an Economist
Case Study on the European Union

Module 5 Business Economics and the Distribution of Income
Competitive Markets; The Labour Market; Government Intervention in the Market

A2 Synoptic coverage
The whole chapter is relevant for the Unit 5 examination, particularly for understanding and analysing labour markets.

Introduction

Chapter 1 explained that a market economy is an economic system made up of a large number of interrelated markets. In a pure market economy, prices and markets alone perform the central economic task of allocating scarce resources between competing uses, but markets are also important, and usually dominant, in mixed economies. This chapter explains how a market functions, and then looks at some of the characteristics of leisure markets and agricultural markets. The chapter concludes by explaining why governments intervene in agricultural markets: to try, for example, to stabilise farmers' incomes or the price of food.

The functions of prices in a market economy

A **market** is a voluntary meeting of buyers and sellers who trade or exchange goods or services. Within a market, prices perform the important functions of:

- *signalling* the information that allows all the traders in the market to plan and co-ordinate their economic activities
- *creating incentives* for buyers and sellers to behave in a manner that allows the market to operate in an orderly and efficient way
- *rationing* and *allocating* scarce resources between competing uses

In the case of rationing and allocating resources, suppose, for example, that the price of apples increases. Apples are now more expensive relative to other goods in the economy. On the one hand, the higher relative price causes households to reduce their demand for apples, substituting, for example, pears in their place. But, on the other hand, a higher relative price may indicate that growing apple trees is a very profitable activity. If this happens, farmers increase production of apples. In this way, the information signalled by changing relative prices creates incentives for economic agents to alter their market behaviour, and changes the way scarce resources are rationed and allocated between competing uses.

> **examiner's voice**
> It is important to recognise that when markets perform well, prices convey accurate information and create suitable incentives for economic agents to respond to. But when one or more of the three functions of prices performs unsatisfactorily, or in extreme cases breaks down completely, market failure occurs.

Goods markets and factor markets

Although a market economy contains a very large number of markets, many of the markets can be grouped under the heading of either **goods markets** (also called product markets) or **factor markets**. These markets are respectively markets for **final goods and services**, or outputs, and markets for the **factors of production**, or inputs necessary in the process of production.

Households and firms operate simultaneously in both sets of markets. In goods markets, households exercise demand for consumer goods and services produced and supplied by firms. For household demand in the goods market to be an **effective demand** (i.e. demand backed up by an ability to pay), households must sell their labour, or possibly the services of any capital or land they own, in factor markets. In these markets, it is the firms that exercise the demand for the factor services sold by the households, as inputs into the production process.

> **examiner's voice**
> Unit 1 exam questions at AS are likely to be on goods markets, but Unit 5 A2 questions may be on the labour market.

Demand and supply curves

The rest of this chapter largely ignores factor markets (the labour market is explained in some detail in Chapter 11), examining instead the process of price determination within a single market in the goods market of a market economy.

The essential features of such a market are shown in Figure 2.1.

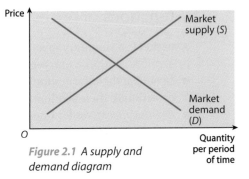

Figure 2.1 A supply and demand diagram

As its name indicates, the graph in Figure 2.1 contains two curves: a demand curve and a supply curve. The **demand curve** is a market demand curve, which shows the quantities of the good or service that all the consumers in the market would like to purchase at different prices during a particular period of time. In a similar way, the **supply curve** is a market supply curve, showing the quantities of the good or service that all the firms in the market would like to supply at different prices in the same time period.

It is important to note two things about demand and supply diagrams:

- Later diagrams in this chapter label the demand and supply curves *D* and *S*, respectively, and the horizontal axis 'Quantity'. *D*, *S* and 'Quantity' are shorthand for market demand, market supply and quantity per period of time.
- Don't confuse *market* demand and supply curves, such as those illustrated in Figure 2.1, with *individual* demand and supply curves. An individual demand curve shows how much a single consumer within the market wishes to purchase at different prices, whereas the market demand curve maps the demand decisions of all consumers. The relationship between the two is quite straightforward: to obtain the market demand curve, simply add up horizontally the demand curves of each of the consumers in the market. Likewise, to obtain the market supply curve, add up horizontally the supply curves of each firm in the market.

Functional relationships

The market demand and supply curves in Figure 2.1 illustrate two very important functional relationships. A **functional relationship** exists between two variables whenever a change in one variable, known as the **independent variable**, causes a change in a second variable, which is the **dependent variable**. The demand function illustrated by the demand curve in Figure 2.1 can be written as:

$$Q_d = f(P)$$

This means that the quantity demanded of a good is a function of the good's price. The symbol 'f' indicates that a change in the value of the independent variable (shown inside the brackets) causes a change in the dependent variable (on the left-hand side of the equals sign). In a demand function, changes in the good's price are assumed to *cause* changes in the quantity demanded.

$Q_d = f(P)$ does not indicate the precise nature of the functional relationship, but as the demand curve slopes downward to the right, the usual relationship is *negative* or *inverse*: an increase in price causes a decrease in the quantity demanded.

In a similar way, the supply curve in Figure 2.1 maps a functional relationship represented by the equation:

$$Q_s = f(P)$$

But in contrast to the demand function, the supply function usually depicts a *positive* functional relationship. On the diagram, this means that the supply curve slopes upward to the right, showing that at higher prices firms are prepared to supply larger quantities of the good or service.

Market plans and market action

Demand and supply functions are examples of **behavioural functions**: they embody theories of how human beings behave. Households are assumed to respond to a price fall by demanding more, while firms are assumed to react by supplying less. It is also very important to understand that demand and supply functions represent how consumers and firms *intend* to behave in the market rather than how they necessarily end up behaving. In short, demand and supply functions depict market plans rather than market action.

examiner's voice

Many students never really get to grips with microeconomic analysis because they fail to understand the difference between market plans and market action. Your market plans are what you *want* to do when you go shopping; your market action is what you *end up* doing.

A demand curve, such as those drawn in Figures 2.1 and 2.2, shows the quantities of a good that households would like to purchase at different prices. This is called **planned demand**, **intended demand** or **ex ante demand**. Similarly, the supply curve shows how much the firms would like to supply at different prices: **planned supply**, **intended supply** or **ex ante supply**.

Whatever the price at which goods are traded, the amount bought (**actual** or **realised demand**) always equals the amount sold (**actual** or **realised supply**). Students often confuse planned or intended demand (and supply) with actual or realised demand (and supply). (Actual or realised demand is also called **ex post demand**, and actual or realised supply is called **ex post supply**.)

The equilibrium price

The concepts of equilibrium and disequilibrium are of very great importance in economic theory and analysis. Essentially, **equilibrium** is a state of rest or a state of balance in which an economic agent, such as a household or firm, is able to fulfil its market plans. Conversely, **disequilibrium** exists when market plans are not fulfilled or realised.

It is impossible at most prices for both households and firms simultaneously to fulfil their market plans. In Figure 2.2, P_1 is a disequilibrium price because firms would like to supply Q_2, but households are only willing to purchase Q_1. Likewise, the market is in disequilibrium at price P_2 because households cannot buy as much as they wish to at this price.

examiner's voice

It is important to understand the concepts of equilibrium and disequilibrium in economics. You will come across many examples besides the market equilibrium and disequilibrium explained in this chapter. In your later studies, look out for the equilibrium firm, macroeconomic equilibrium and balance of payments equilibrium.

To explain this further, it is useful to divide the market into two 'sides', the **short side** and the **long side**. When the price is P_1, households are on the short side of the market and firms are on the long side. Economic agents on the short side can always fulfil their market plans, but those on the long side cannot! Thus, when the price is P_1, households can purchase exactly the amount they wish to, namely Q_1. Firms, however, are in a different situation. They would like to sell Q_2, but can only sell Q_1, as long as the price remains at P_1. The difference between Q_2 and Q_1 is **excess supply** or unsold stock.

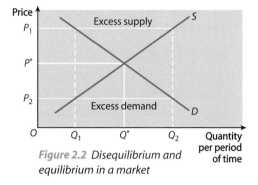

Figure 2.2 *Disequilibrium and equilibrium in a market*

At P_1, as at any other price, actual demand equals actual supply. However, this is largely irrelevant: the key point is that at price P_1, planned supply exceeds planned demand. By contrast, at a price such as P_2, households are on the long side of the market, with firms on the short side. Households would like to buy Q_2, but they can't because at this price firms are only willing to supply Q_1. In this case, the difference between Q_2 and Q_1 is **excess demand** or unfulfilled demand. Households end up buying Q_1 because this is the maximum that firms are prepared to sell at this price. Once again, actual demand equals actual supply (namely Q_1), but planned supply is now less than planned demand.

We now introduce a most important assumption about economic behaviour, which recurs throughout economic theory and analysis. We assume that whenever an economic agent, such as a household or firm, fails to fulfil its market plans, it changes its market behaviour. When excess supply exists in the market (as at P_1), the price mechanism acts to reduce supply. By doing so, the price mechanism moves the market towards equilibrium. Firms are assumed to react to stocks of unsold goods by accepting a lower price. Eventually the price falls until the amount that households wish to buy equals exactly the quantity that firms are prepared to supply. Equilibrium is reached at price P^*.

In the case of excess demand, it is useful to divide households into two groups of customers. The first group, shown by the distance from O to Q_1, are the lucky consumers who manage to buy the good at price P_2. By contrast, unlucky households, shown by the distance from Q_1 to Q_2, cannot buy the good at P_2, possibly because they turned up too late. In order to be able to purchase the good, unlucky consumers bid up the price until, once again, equilibrium is reached at P^*.

The equilibrium price P^* is the *only* price that satisfies both households and firms, which consequently, once this price is reached, have no reason to change their market plans. At P^*, planned demand equals planned supply and the market clears.

To summarise the main conclusions of this very important part of the chapter, there is *disequilibrium* in the market when:

- planned demand < planned supply, in which case the price falls
- planned demand > planned supply, in which case the price rises

Equilibrium occurs when:

- planned demand = planned supply, in which case the price does not change

Maximum price laws or price ceilings

Figure 2.3 illustrates a situation in which a maximum price law prevents the price rising above P_1. Because the price ceiling has been imposed *below* the free market equilibrium price of P^*, it creates excess demand, shown by the distance between Q_1 and Q_2. In a free market, the price would rise to a point where there is no excess demand (P^*). But because the price ceiling prevents this happening, there is no mechanism in the market for reducing excess demand. Rather than being rationed by price, households are rationed by quantity. Queues and waiting lists occur — and possibly bribery and corruption, through which favoured customers obtain the good, but others do not.

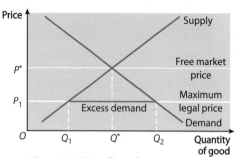

Figure 2.3 The effect of a maximum price law or price ceiling

The emergence of a **secondary market** (sometimes called a **black market**) is also likely. Secondary markets emerge when **primary markets** (or **free markets**) are prevented from working properly. A secondary market is a meeting place for lucky and unlucky customers. In the secondary market, some lucky customers, who bought the good at price P_1, resell at a higher price to unlucky customers who were unable to purchase the good in the primary market. Secondary markets, particularly when illegal, are characterised by imperfect market information and trading through middle men such as spivs, touts and racketeers. Nevertheless, economists believe that secondary markets can perform a very useful economic function, reducing excess demand in a primary market constrained by the price ceiling.

Note that a price ceiling imposed *at* or *above* the free market equilibrium price has no effect on the market. To distort free markets, price ceilings must be imposed *below* the free market price.

Secondary markets in tickets for sports events

The secondary markets that occur when governments impose maximum price laws or price ceilings are of course illegal, although criminalised trading still takes place in such markets. However, some secondary markets are perfectly legal, such as markets in tickets for popular sports events such as the FA Cup final. In these cases, the secondary market emerges because the agency promoting the event under-prices tickets. This is illustrated in Figure 2.4(a). The supply curve for tickets is vertical, reflecting the capacity of the stadium in which the event takes place. The

Some fans are willing to pay large amounts to see their team in the FA Cup final

number of seats in the stadium is 70,000. Given the position of the demand curve, if tickets were priced at £150, the primary market would work efficiently. There would be no excess demand, and hence no need for a secondary market. But if the Football Association prices tickets at £50, then 150,000 fans will want to see the match. Excess demand is 80,000. In this situation, a secondary market enables 'unlucky' supporters, who are prepared to pay more than £50, to watch the match. They can buy tickets from 'lucky' fans, who are prepared to sell at a price above £50.

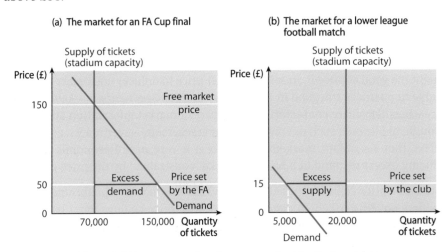

Figure 2.4 Excess demand and excess supply at football matches

Figure 2.4(b) shows a situation more common in lower league football, and in other less popular sports. Because of the position of the demand curve, only 5,000 tickets are sold at the price set by the club, even though stadium capacity is 20,000. There is an excess supply of 15,000 seats at the price set by the football club. Indeed, in this example, some seats would remain empty even if tickets were given away free. To fill the stadium, the club would have to pay people to watch the match!

Minimum price laws or price floors

Sometimes governments impose minimum price laws or price floors. For a minimum price law to affect a market, the price floor must be set *above* the free market price. Figure 2.5 illustrates the possible effect on a labour market of the national minimum wage imposed in the UK. A national minimum wage rate set at W_1 (which is above the free market wage rate of W^*) creates an excess supply of labour, thereby causing unemployment equal to the distance between L_1 and L_2. It may also cause 'rogue' employers to break the law — for example, paying 'poverty wages' to illegal immigrants. Note too that a national minimum wage set *below* the free market wage rate has no effect on unemployment. This is the situation in many UK labour markets.

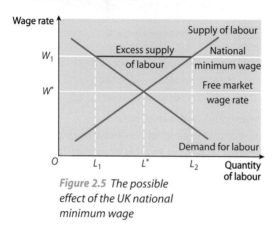

Figure 2.5 The possible effect of the UK national minimum wage

examiner's voice

Maximum and minimum price laws are examples of government intervention in the economy. You need to understand *why* governments intervene in markets, and how intervention can lead to government failure. Remember also that maximum and minimum prices may distort price signals, alter incentives and interfere with the allocative or rationing function of prices.

Shifts of demand

When a market demand curve is drawn to show demand at various possible prices, it is assumed that all the other variables influencing demand are held unchanged or constant. This is the ceteris paribus assumption. **Ceteris paribus** means 'other things being equal'. Among the variables whose values are held constant or unchanged when we draw a demand curve are disposable income and tastes or fashion. Collectively, the variables other than the good's own price, whose values determine planned demand, are called the **conditions of demand**.

The main conditions of demand are:
- the prices of substitute goods (or goods in competing demand)
- the prices of complementary goods (or goods in joint demand)
- personal income (or, more strictly, personal disposable income: that is, income after tax and receipt of benefits)
- tastes and preferences
- population size

If any of the conditions of demand change, the *position* of the demand curve changes, shifting either rightward or leftward. Figure 2.6 illustrates a rightward shift of the demand curve, which is also called an **increase in demand**. Following

a rightward shift of demand, more of the good is demanded at all prices. For example, at a price of P_1, the quantity demanded increases from Q_1 to Q_2. Conversely, a leftward shift of demand (known as a **decrease in demand**) causes the quantity demanded to fall at all prices.

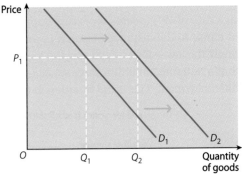

Figure 2.6 The effect of a rightward shift of demand

*e***xaminer's voice**

Exam questions at AS ask you to illustrate equilibrium in a market, and then to identify from data a reason why the demand curve or the supply curve shifts. You must then illustrate the new equilibrium, and explain how excess demand or excess supply is eliminated in the adjustment to the new equilibrium.

Among events that might cause a rightward shift of demand are:

- an increase in the price of a substitute good or a good in competitive demand
- a fall in the price of a complementary good or a good in joint demand
- an increase in personal disposable income (but see the qualification below this list)
- a successful advertising campaign, making people think more favourably about the good
- an increase in population

When disposable income increases, a demand curve shifts rightward, but only if the good is a **normal good**. A normal good is a good for which demand increases as income increases. However, some goods are **inferior goods**. In the case of an inferior good, demand decreases as income increases, and an increase in income shifts the demand curve leftward.

An increase in the price of a complementary good has the opposite effect to an increase in the price of a substitute good. For example, CD players and compact discs are complementary goods in joint demand, but CD players and mini-disc players are in competing demand, being substitutes for each other. Following a significant rise in the price of CD players, demand for CD players falls, which in turn reduces the demand for compact discs. The demand curve for compact discs shifts leftward. However, the demand curve for mini-disc players shifts rightward, providing consumers switch to the substitute good.

Shifts of demand in leisure markets

When two leisure activities are substitutes or complementary goods, a change in the price of one leisure activity causes the demand curve for the other to shift. Suppose, for example, there is a fall in the price of tickets to see soccer matches (association football). This might lead to a leftward shift of the demand curve for tickets for rugby football matches. This is shown in Figure 2.7(a) below. The size of the leftward shift will depend on the extent to which, from a spectator's point of view, the two types of football are substitutes for each other.

However, a fall in the price of tickets for soccer matches will trigger a rightward shift in the demand curve for complementary goods, such as the replica shirts worn by many spectators. This is shown in Figure 2.7(b).

examiner's voice

This is relevant for the Economics of Sport and Leisure option in the AS Unit 4 examination. If you are studying for this option, make sure you can explain and illustrate relationships in markets for complementary and substitute goods in sport and leisure markets.

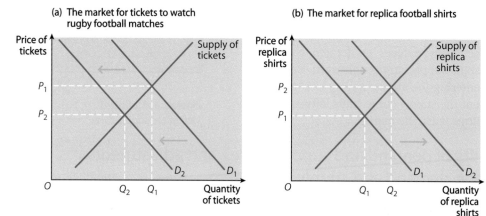

Figure 2.7 Shifts of demand for substitute and complementary goods, following a fall in admission prices to soccer matches

Shifts of supply

Just as a change in the conditions of demand shifts the demand curve, so a change in the **conditions of supply** leads to a shift of the supply curve. The main conditions of supply are:

- costs of production, including wage costs, raw material costs, energy costs and the costs of borrowing
- technical progress
- taxes imposed on firms, such as VAT, excise duties and the business rate
- subsidies granted by the government to firms

If any of the conditions of supply change, the supply curve shifts to a new position. A rightward shift of supply is also known as an **increase in supply**, whereas a leftward shift is known as a **decrease in supply**.

An increase in wage costs, which for many firms are the most important cost of production, shifts the supply curve leftward (or upward). Firms reduce the quantity of the good they are prepared to supply because production costs have risen. For example, when the price is P_1 in Figure 2.8, a leftward shift of supply from S_1 to S_2 causes the quantity that firms are prepared to supply to fall from Q_1 to Q_2.

An **expenditure tax** imposed on firms has a similar effect to an increase in production costs, shifting the supply curve upward or leftward. Expenditure taxes are also known as **indirect taxes**. Consumers indirectly pay some or all of the tax through the higher prices they pay for the goods on which the tax is levied. In the UK, value added tax (VAT) and customs and excise duties levied on tobacco, alcoholic drinks and petrol and diesel fuel provide examples of indirect expenditure taxes. Production **subsidies** paid by the government to firms have the opposite effect to expenditure taxes, shifting the supply curve rightward or downward.

Supply curves also shift when technical progress occurs, or when firms enter or leave the market. Technical progress generally reduces production costs and shifts supply curves rightward. New firms entering the market have a similar effect, but the supply curve shifts leftward when firms leave the market.

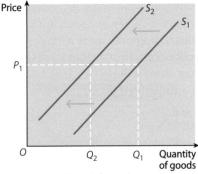

Figure 2.8 A leftward shift of the supply curve

Shifts of demand and supply curves, and adjustments along demand and supply curves

The extent to which price or output changes following a shift of demand or supply depends upon the slope and **elasticity** of the curve that has not shifted. (Elasticity is explained in the next chapter.) Figure 2.9 shows a demand curve shifting rightward, along a gently sloping supply curve in part (a) of the diagram, and along a much more steeply sloping supply curve in part (b). Prior to the shift of demand, equilibrium occurs at point X in both parts of the diagram. In each case, the rightward shift of demand induces an adjustment along the supply curve to a new equilibrium depicted at point Z. With the gently sloping supply curve shown in

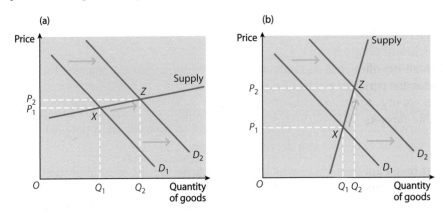

Figure 2.9 The adjustment to a new equilibrium following a shift of demand

Figure 2.9(a), the quantity adjustment is greater than the price adjustment. The reverse is true in Figure 2.9(b), where the supply curve is much steeper. The diagram shows how the adjustment to a new equilibrium, following a shift of demand (or supply), depends on the slope (and elasticity) of the curve that has not shifted.

> **examiner's voice**
> Make sure you can distinguish between a *shift* of a supply or demand curve, and the adjustment to a new equilibrium along the curve that does not shift.

The problem of agricultural prices

Throughout recent history, agricultural markets for foodstuffs and primary products such as rubber have experienced two closely related problems. First, there has been a long-run trend for agricultural prices to fall relative to those of manufactured goods; and second, prices have fluctuated considerably from year to year. Agricultural markets are prone to disequilibrium and random shifts of the supply curve from year to year, caused by climatic factors. This leads to unacceptable fluctuations in agricultural prices that may require government intervention to stabilise them.

The long-run downward trend can be explained by shifts of the demand and supply curves for agricultural products over extended periods of time. This is shown in Figure 2.10, where the equilibrium price for an agricultural product in an earlier period is P_1. Over time, *both* the demand and supply curves have shifted rightward. Rising incomes and population growth have shifted the demand curve, while improved methods of farming have increased supply. But for many farm products, the shift of supply brought about by improved crop yields and increased agricultural productivity has greatly exceeded the shift of demand. The result has been a fall to the lower equilibrium price P_2.

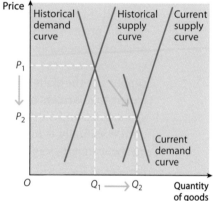

Figure 2.10 The long-run fall in the price of agricultural products

Short-run fluctuations in agricultural prices

Agriculture often has a relatively long production period compared, for example, with many types of manufacturing. Arable farmers make decisions to grow crops several months before the harvest, while, in a similar way, livestock farmers must breed animals for meat production many months before slaughter. As a result, farmers may plan how much to supply on the basis of *last year's prices*

Farmers have to plan what to produce several months before the supply reaches the market

rather than on the *prices current this year*. The length of the production period means that there is a supply lag between the decision to produce and the supply actually coming on to the market. A possible effect of a supply lag can be explained by the **cobweb theory** illustrated in Figure 2.11.

The diagram shows a stable cobweb in the turkey market, in which the market price eventually converges to equilibrium at price P_1, located where the long-run demand and supply curves

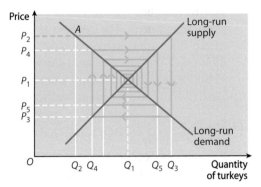

Figure 2.11 Farm price fluctuations illustrated on a cobweb diagram

intersect. Suppose an outbreak of fowl disease reduces turkey supply from Q_1 to Q_2 in year 1 (but does not affect the position of the demand curve, or the supply of healthy turkeys, in future years). In the current year (year 1), the maximum number of turkeys that can be sold on the market is shown by a vertical line drawn through Q_2. The vertical line is the short-run supply curve for year 1. This means that the price rises to P_2, determined at point A on the vertical line. The now higher price of P_2 encourages farmers to breed Q_3 turkeys for slaughter in year 2. When year 2 arrives, the vertical line drawn through Q_3 depicts maximum possible supply. But the slaughter of Q_3 turkeys causes the market price to fall to P_3, which means that farmers breed fewer turkeys (Q_4) for slaughter in year 3. In subsequent years, price and output continue to oscillate in a series of decreasing fluctuations until eventually — in the absence of any further shock hitting the market — the market converges again to a long-run equilibrium.

In Figure 2.11, the cobweb eventually converges to a long-run equilibrium because the long-run demand curve has a gentler slope than the long-run supply curve. This is a **stable cobweb**. However, an **unstable cobweb** is also possible. Instability occurs if the long-run demand curve is steeper than the long-run supply curve. In this case, the market diverges in a series of yearly oscillations further and further away from the long-run equilibrium.

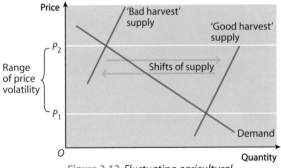

Figure 2.12 Fluctuating agricultural prices caused by shifts of supply

The need for price-support policies

Figure 2.12 provides another explanation of fluctuating farm prices, where price volatility is caused by random shifts of the short-run supply curve in response to fluctuations in the harvest. The diagram shows two short-run supply curves: a 'good harvest' supply curve and a 'bad harvest' supply curve. Weather conditions and other factors outside the farmers' control shift the position of the supply curve from year to year, between the limits set by the two supply curves. As a result, market prices fluctuate from year to year within the range of P_1 to P_2.

Governments often wish to stabilise the prices of agricultural goods, believing this to be in the interest of farmers, or consumers, or possibly both. A method of intervention is illustrated in Figure 2.13. This diagram is similar to Figure 2.12, except that a third supply curve, the 'normal harvest' supply curve, is located midway between the 'bad harvest' and the 'good harvest' supply curves. Suppose that the government, or an agency of farmers, decides to stabilise the good's price at the 'normal' year price, P_3. Following a good harvest, the government buys quantity $Q_4 - Q_3$ to prevent the market price falling below P_3. But next year, following a bad harvest, the government supplements supply by releasing the product on to the market from the previously accumulated stock. The sale of $Q_3 - Q_5$ prevents the price rising to P_2, and stabilises the price at P_3.

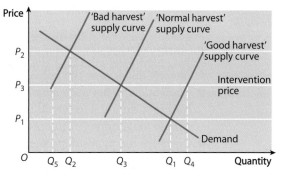

Figure 2.13 Government intervention to stabilise the price of an agricultural commodity

The policy just described is an example of a **buffer stock** policy. The government, or an association of producers, accumulates a buffer stock when the harvest is good, for releasing on to the market in the event of a crop failure. Figure 2.14 illustrates a slightly different form of buffer stock intervention. In this case, rather than completely stabilising the price, buying and selling *reduces* rather than eliminates the fluctuations resulting from free market forces. Two **intervention prices** are set: a lower intervention price

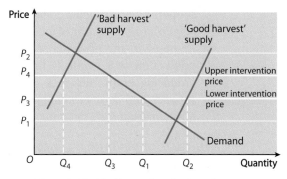

Figure 2.14 A buffer stock policy based on upper and lower intervention prices

at P_3 and an upper intervention price at P_4. Following a good harvest, the market price falls towards P_1. As the price falls through P_3, the buffer stock agency steps into the market and purchases a buffer stock. This prevents any further fall in the price, which stabilises at P_3.

Suppose that the next year, following a bad harvest, market forces cause the price to rise towards P_2. When the price reaches the upper intervention price of P_4, the government once again steps into the market, selling $Q_3 - Q_4$ from the buffer stock. The release of the buffer stock prevents the price rising above P_4.

By purchasing a buffer stock when the price falls to the lower intervention price of P_3, and selling from the buffer stock when the price rises to the upper intervention price of P_4, support-buying is meant to be self-financing. In theory, costs of management and administration are financed from the margin between the lower and upper intervention prices. In practice, however, buffer stock agencies often run out of money. Farmers who previously grew other crops, for which there is no guaranteed price, often decide to enter the market. They know that if they over-produce, the buffer stock agency will purchase their output. As a result, the entry of a large number of new producers causes the crop's supply curve to move permanently to the right, whatever the state of the harvest.

Problems resulting from buffer stock policies

Buffer stock policies can cause a number of problems, which harm and can ultimately undermine the policy. The problems include the following:

- Good and bad harvests may not alternate. A succession of bad harvests could lead to a situation in which the government's buffer stock is exhausted and it can no longer prevent the price from rising.
- However, the opposite problem of over-production is more likely. A succession of good harvests could result in continuous over-production, with the government accumulating an ever-growing buffer stock.
- As a result, the fund used to finance the purchase of the buffer stock may then run out. A few years ago, the tin producers support-buying scheme collapsed, basically because it ran out of money.
- As noted in the previous section, over-production will occur if farmers stop producing crops that lack government support, and start producing crops that are supported.

*e**xaminer's voice***

Exam questions at AS may be set on causes of price fluctuations of agricultural goods, or on how buffer stock intervention can try to reduce fluctuations, or on the difficulties involved in buffer stock intervention. Sometimes a question requires knowledge of more than one of these.

Fluctuations in farmers' incomes

From a farmer's point of view, fluctuations in income are more serious than fluctuations in price. Figure 2.15 shows two possible situations. A gently sloping (and

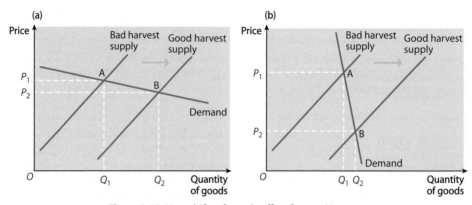

Figure 2.15 How shifts of supply affect farmers' incomes

elastic) demand curve is shown in Figure 2.15(a), and a steeply sloping (and inelastic) demand curve has been drawn in Figure 2.15(b). (See the next chapter for an explanation of slope and elasticity.) Following a bad harvest, when the price is P_1, farmer's incomes are shown by the area OQ_1AP_1 (quantity sold × price). Following a good harvest, the price falls to P_2. Now consider how this affects farmers' incomes. In Figure 2.15(a), farmers' incomes *increase* to the area OQ_2BP_2. Contrast this to the situation shown in Figure 2.15(b). In this case, farm incomes *decrease* in the event of a good harvest and rise when the harvest is poor. In these demand and supply conditions, farmers benefit from an increase in income when the crop fails, providing they have at least some of the crop to sell at the high prices ruling in the market.

Farm support policies in the UK and the European Union

In 1973 the UK joined what is now called the **European Union** (EU) and a fundamental change took place in UK agricultural policy. UK farmers are relatively high-cost producers when compared to farmers in such countries as the USA, Canada and Australia, but they are efficient within the constraints imposed by the UK climate and average farm size. And compared with many European farmers employed on even smaller and less mechanised farms, UK farmers are relatively low-cost producers.

Before the UK joined the EU, **deficiency payments**, which were a form of producer subsidy, were the main form of agricultural support. Deficiency payments provided cheap food for the UK population, while ensuring the incomes of domestic farmers. Imports of food were allowed into the UK at the world price and subsidies were paid to UK farmers to keep them in business.

By contrast, the EU's **common agricultural policy** (CAP) results in relatively expensive food for consumers. The CAP imposes an external tariff or levy, which brings the price of imported food up to the level of European costs of production. The levy has increased EU food production, but has done so by increasing the price of food imports.

The levy on food imports is tied in with a **support-buying policy** based on minimum price guarantees, similar to the intervention prices described on page 29. However, the minimum price guarantees have often been set too high, resulting in the accumulation of

The political power of French farmers has made reforming the CAP difficult

butter and wheat 'mountains', wine 'lakes' and over-production in general. Prices can be sustained only if the CAP intervenes continuously to purchase excess supply.

So far, the political power of farmers, particularly in France, has prevented significant reform of the system. Over-production has generally continued, at great expense to EU taxpayers who finance the CAP. Poor developing countries outside the EU also suffer. They are denied free access to the rich EU market and suffer from the EU **dumping** stocks (selling surplus production at below cost) in their markets, which destroys indigenous agriculture in poor countries.

Summary

In this chapter we have examined how, by conveying information (signalling) that creates incentives for buyers and sellers to alter their market behaviour, the price mechanism allocates scarce resources between competing uses. Market transactions are voluntary transactions, and a market brings buyers and sellers together. Within a market, the demand and supply curves respectively show effective demand and supply at different prices. The curves also map the market plans or intended market behaviour of households and firms, showing planned demand and supply at different prices. However, there are other determinants of demand and supply beside price. These are known as the conditions of demand and supply. For each demand or supply curve, the conditions of demand or supply are held constant, under the ceteris paribus assumption. When we relax the ceteris paribus assumption and change the conditions of demand or supply, the demand or supply curve shifts to a new position.

This chapter has introduced the key economic concept of equilibrium. Market equilibrium is a state of rest or balance, in which the market plans of buyers and sellers are consistent with each other and can be fulfilled. Planned demand equals planned supply in equilibrium, and there is no excess demand or excess supply. By contrast, in disequilibrium the market fails to clear, in which case either the buyers or the sellers cannot fulfil their market plans. If the market is competitive and prices are flexible and free to adjust, market disequilibrium should be self-correcting. If the price is initially too high (in which case planned demand is less than planned supply), the price falls to eliminate excess supply. Conversely, if the price is initially too low (in which case planned demand is greater than planned supply), the price rises to reduce excess demand. Either way equilibrium is restored. However, government intervention in markets — for example, by imposing maximum or minimum legal prices — may prevent the automatic adjustment process from working.

Sometimes shifts of supply and demand result in highly unstable markets, particularly in primary product markets. Agricultural markets are especially prone to disequilibrium caused by climatic extremes shifting supply curves from year to year. Governments (or farmers' agencies) may try to stabilise agricultural prices — for example, by operating a buffer stock scheme. However, such intervention schemes suffer a number of problems, including permanent over-production and insufficient finance.

Self-testing questions

1 List and explain the three functions that prices perform in a market.

2 Distinguish between the goods market and the factor market.

3 What is effective demand?

4 Distinguish between planned demand and realised demand.

5 Explain why, when planned demand equals planned supply, a market is in equilibrium.

6 Explain the difference between market equilibrium and disequilibrium.

7 Distinguish between excess demand and excess supply.

8 Explain how a maximum legal price (a price ceiling) may distort a market.

9 Using a supply and demand diagram, explain how a national minimum wage may increase unemployment in labour markets.

10 Why may a demand curve shift?

11 Why may a supply curve shift?

12 Why are agricultural prices often unstable?

13 What is a buffer stock scheme?

14 Explain why buffer stock intervention often fails.

Chapter 3
Elasticity

Specification focus

This chapter explains one of the most important of all the microeconomic concepts that AS and A2 examination candidates need to know. The chapter is particularly relevant for:

AS **Module 1 Markets and Market Failure**
Allocation of Resources in Competitive Markets

Module 3 Markets at Work
The Housing Market; The Economics of Sport and Leisure

A2 **Module 5 Business Economics and the Distribution of Income**
Competitive Markets; Concentrated Markets; The Labour Market

A2 **Synoptic coverage**
Questions on perfect competition, monopoly and oligopoly in the Unit 5 examination require application of elasticity concepts learnt at AS.

Introduction

Whenever a change in one variable (such as a good's price) causes a change to occur in a second variable (such as the quantity of the good that firms are prepared to supply), an elasticity can be calculated. Elasticity measures the proportionate responsiveness of the second variable to the change in the first variable. For example, if a 5% increase in price were to cause firms to increase supply more than proportionately (say by 10%), supply would be elastic. In this example, a change in price induces a more than proportionate response by producers. But if the response were less than proportionate (for example, an increase in supply of only 3%), supply would be inelastic. If the change in price were to induce an exactly proportionate change in supply, supply would be neither elastic nor inelastic — this is called unit elasticity of supply. Elasticity is a useful way to analyse the relationship between two variables because it is independent of the units, such as price and quantity, in which the variables are measured.

The elasticities you need to know

Although, in principle, economists could calculate a great many elasticities — indeed, one for each of the economic relationships in which they are interested — the four main elasticities you must know are:

- price elasticity of demand
- price elasticity of supply
- income elasticity of demand
- cross elasticity of demand

The following formulas are used for calculating these elasticities:

$$\text{price elasticity of demand} = \frac{\text{proportionate change in quantity demanded}}{\text{proportionate change in price}}$$

$$\text{price elasticity of supply} = \frac{\text{proportionate change in quantity supplied}}{\text{proportionate change in price}}$$

$$\text{income elasticity of demand} = \frac{\text{proportionate change in quantity demanded}}{\text{proportionate change in income}}$$

$$\begin{array}{c}\text{cross elasticity of demand} \\ \text{for good A with respect to} \\ \text{the price of B}\end{array} = \frac{\text{proportionate change in quantity of A demanded}}{\text{proportionate change in price of B}}$$

examiner's voice

Make sure you don't confuse the four main elasticities. It is very easy to confuse the price elasticities of demand and supply, and price and income elasticity of demand. You must also avoid writing the formulas 'upside down'.

Price elasticity of demand

Price elasticity of demand measures consumers' responsiveness to a change in a good's price. (Price elasticity of demand is sometimes called an **'own price' elasticity of demand** to distinguish it from cross elasticity of demand, which measures the responsiveness of demand for a particular good to a change in the price of a completely different good.)

A simple rule for detecting whether demand is elastic or inelastic

As an alternative to using the formula stated above to calculate price elasticity of demand between two points on a demand curve, a simple rule can be used to determine the elasticity between any two points on the demand curve:

- If total consumer expenditure increases in response to a price fall, demand is *elastic.*
- If total consumer expenditure decreases in response to a price fall, demand is *inelastic.*
- If total consumer expenditure remains constant in response to a price fall, demand is neither elastic nor inelastic: in other words, elasticity is *unity* (1).

Elasticity and slope

It is important not to confuse *absolute* response, indicated by the slope of a curve, with the *proportionate* response measured by elasticity. Take a careful look at the two demand curves drawn in Figure 3.1. In Figure 3.1(a), a straight-line (or linear) demand curve has been drawn. Quite obviously, a straight line has a constant slope. But although the slope is the same at all points on the curve, the elasticity is not. Moving down a negatively sloping linear demand curve, price elasticity of demand falls from point to point along the curve. Demand is elastic (or greater than 1) at all points along the top half of the curve. Elasticity equals 1 exactly half way along the curve, falling below 1 and towards 0 along the bottom half of the curve. **Point elasticity of demand** measures elasticity at a point on the demand curve. **Average (or arc) elasticity of demand** measures elasticity over a range of the curve, though strictly the range should be quite small.

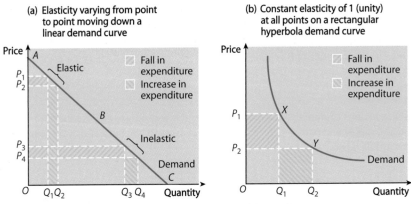

Figure 3.1 *Price elasticity of demand*

Unitary elasticity of demand

If elasticity *falls* from point to point moving down a linear demand curve, it follows that a non-linear curve (i.e. a *curved* line) is needed to show the *same elasticity* at all points on the curve. Figure 3.1(b) shows a demand curve with a constant elasticity of 1 at all points on the curve: that is, elasticity equals unity at all points on the curve. Mathematicians call this a **rectangular hyperbola**. Whenever the price falls, the proportionate change in quantity demanded equals the proportionate change in price. In this case, consumer expenditure remains unchanged following a rise or fall in price.

Infinite and zero price elasticity of demand

Horizontal and vertical demand curves have constant elasticities at all points on the curve. A horizontal demand curve, such as the demand curve in Figure 3.2(a), is infinitely elastic or perfectly elastic. At the other extreme, the vertical demand curve in Figure 3.2(b) is completely inelastic, displaying zero price elasticity of demand, at all points on the curve. When the price falls, for example from P_1 to P_2, the quantity demanded is unchanged.

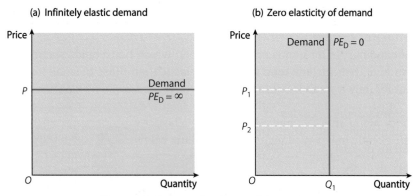

Figure 3.2 Horizontal and vertical demand curves

Negative elasticities

Usually demand curves are neither horizontal nor vertical, but have a negative slope, showing that as the good's price falls, quantity demanded rises. In this situation, elasticity and slope are both negative. However, economists usually ignore the minus sign of the elasticity. Ignoring the minus sign, all elasticities larger than 1 are elastic and all less than 1 are inelastic.

To summarise, the five main types of demand curve and their respective elasticities are shown in Figure 3.3.

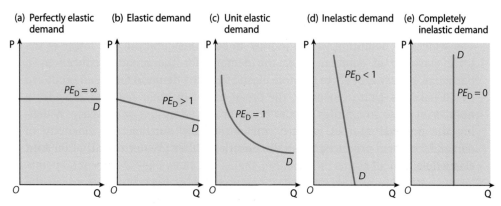

Figure 3.3 The five main demand curves

The factors determining price elasticity of demand

The determinants of price elasticity of demand are as follows.

Substitutability

Substitutability is the most important determinant of price elasticity of demand. When a substitute exists for a product, consumers respond to a price rise by switching expenditure away from the good, buying instead a substitute whose price has not risen. When very close substitutes are available, demand for the product is highly elastic. Conversely, demand is likely to be inelastic when no substitutes are available.

Percentage of income

The demand curves for goods or services upon which households spend a large proportion of their income tend to be more elastic than those of small items that account for only a small fraction of income.

Necessities versus luxuries

It is sometimes said that the demand for necessities is inelastic, whereas demand for luxuries is elastic. However, this statement should be treated with caution. When no obvious substitute exists, demand for a luxury good may be inelastic. While at the other extreme, demand for particular types of basic foodstuff is likely to be elastic if other staple foods are available as substitutes. It is really the existence of substitutes that determines price elasticity of demand, not the issue of whether the good is a luxury or necessity.

Storing goods means firms can quickly adapt to a change in prices

The 'width' of the market definition

The wider the definition of the market under consideration, the lower is the price elasticity of demand. Thus the demand for the bread produced by a particular bakery is likely to be more elastic than the demand for bread produced by all bakeries. Quite obviously, the bread baked in other bakeries provides a number of close substitutes for the bread produced in just one bakery. Widening the possible market we are considering still further, the elasticity of demand for bread produced by all the bakeries will be greater than that for food as a whole.

Time

The time period in question will also affect the elasticity of demand. For many goods and services, demand is more elastic in the long run than in the short run because it takes time to respond to a price change. For example, if the price of petrol rises relative to the price of diesel fuel, it will take time for motorists to respond because

> ### examiner's voice
>
> Examination questions are much more likely to focus on the *causes* of elastic or inelastic demand than on the mathematical properties of demand curves. The existence (or lack of existence) of close *substitutes* is the main determinant you must understand.

they will be 'locked in' to their existing investment in petrol-engined automobiles. However, in certain circumstances, the response might be greater in the short run than in the long run. A sudden rise in the price of petrol might cause motorists to economise in its use for a few weeks before 'getting used to the price' and drifting back to their old motoring habits.

Price elasticity of supply

Whereas demand curves are generally downward sloping, supply curves usually slope upwards. A rise in price causes firms to respond by supplying more of the good. The mathematical properties of upward-sloping (or positive) supply curves are different from those of downward-sloping (or negative) demand curves. As with demand curves, the 'flatness' or 'steepness' of a supply curve is a misleading indicator of elasticity. The key point is not the slope of the supply curve, but whether it intersects the price axis or the quantity axis.

examiner's voice
It is useful to understand why the elasticity of upward-sloping supply curves differs from the elasticity of downward-sloping demand curves.

Linear supply curves

Upward-sloping straight-line (linear) supply curves display the following price elasticities:

■ If the supply curve intersects the price axis, the curve is elastic at all points, although elasticity falls towards unity moving from point to point up the curve (Figure 3.4(a)).
■ If the supply curve intersects the quantity axis, the curve is inelastic at all points, although elasticity rises towards unity moving from point to point up the curve (Figure 3.4(b)).
■ If the supply curve passes through the origin, elasticity equals unity (+1) at all points on the curve (Figure 3.4(c)).

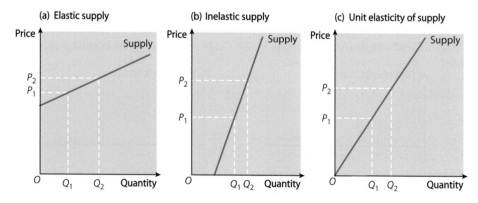

Figure 3.4 *Price elasticity of supply and linear supply curves*

The five main types of linear supply curve and their respective elasticities are shown in Figure 3.5.

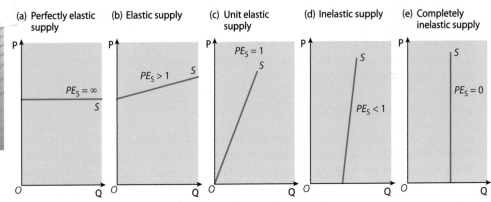

Figure 3.5 The five main linear supply curves

Non-linear supply curves

Figure 3.6 shows how elasticity can be observed at any point on an upward-sloping non-linear supply curve. This is done by drawing a tangent to the point and noting the axis that the tangent intersects. Because the line drawn tangential to point *A* intersects the price axis, supply is elastic at point *A*. The tangent to point *B* intersects the origin, so supply at point *B* is unit elastic. Finally, the tangent to point *C* intersects the quantity axis, so supply is inelastic at point *C*. With this supply curve, elasticity falls moving from point to point up the curve. Supply is elastic in the lower section and inelastic in the upper section of the curve.

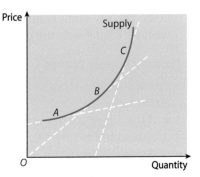

Figure 3.6 Price elasticity of supply and a non-linear supply curve

A closer look at perfectly elastic demand and supply

A perfectly elastic demand curve and a perfectly elastic supply curve are shown in Figure 3.7. Although the two panels of the diagram appear to be identical (apart

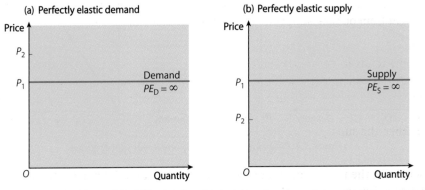

Figure 3.7 Perfectly price elastic demand and supply curves

from the labels), this is very misleading. The apparent similarity disguises a significant difference between perfectly elastic demand and supply. In Figure 3.7(a), demand is infinitely elastic at *all prices on or below the demand curve*, although if the price rises above the demand curve (for example, from P_1 to P_2), the amount demanded immediately falls to zero. This is because perfect substitutes are available when demand is perfectly price elastic. Customers cease to buy the good as soon as the price rises above the demand curve, switching to the perfect substitutes whose prices have not changed.

By contrast, in Figure 3.7(b), supply is infinitely elastic *at all prices on or above the supply curve*, although if the price falls below the supply curve (for example, from P_1 to P_2), the amount supplied immediately drops to zero. P_1 is the minimum price acceptable to firms. If they are paid this price (or any higher price), firms stay in the market, but at any lower price the incentive to stay in the market disappears. Firms leave the market, unable to make sufficient profit.

*e**xaminer's voice***
Make sure you understand the difference between a perfectly elastic demand curve and a perfectly elastic supply curve.

The factors determining price elasticity of supply

The determinants of price elasticity of supply are as follows.

The length of the production period
Supply will tend be more elastic if firms can convert raw materials into finished goods very quickly (for example, in just a few hours or days) than if several months are involved, as with many agricultural goods.

The availability of spare capacity
When a firm possesses spare capacity, and if labour and raw materials are readily available, production can generally be increased quite quickly in the short run.

The ease of accumulating stocks
When stocks of unsold finished goods are stored at low cost, firms can respond quickly to a sudden increase in demand. Alternatively, firms can respond to a price fall by diverting current production away from sales and into stock accumulation. Likewise, the ease with which stocks of raw materials or components can be bought from outside suppliers and stored has a similar effect.

The ease of switching between alternative methods of production
Supply tends to be more elastic if firms can quickly alter the way they produce goods (for example, by switching between the use of capital and labour) than if there is little or no choice. In a similar way, if firms produce a range of products and can switch raw materials, labour or machines from one type of production to another, the supply of any one product tends to be elastic.

The number of firms in the market and the ease of entering the market
Generally, the more firms there are in the market, and the greater the ease with which a firm can enter or leave, the greater is the elasticity of supply.

Time

We have already observed that demand is more elastic in the long run than in the short run because it takes time to respond to a price change. The same is true for supply. Figure 3.8 shows three supply curves of increasing elasticity, S_1, S_2 and S_3, which illustrate respectively market period supply, short-run supply and long-run supply.

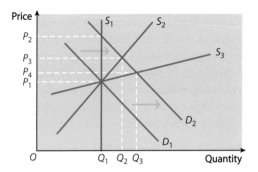

Figure 3.8 The effect of the time period upon price elasticity of supply

- **Market period supply.** The market period supply curve S_1 is shown by a vertical line. Following a sudden and unexpected rightward shift of demand from D_1 to D_2, supply is completely inelastic and the price rises from P_1 to P_2 to eliminate the excess demand.
- **Short-run supply.** The higher price means that higher profits can be made, creating the incentive for firms to increase output. In the short run, firms increase output by hiring more variable factors of production, such as labour. The short-run increase in output is shown by the movement up the short-run supply curve, S_2. The short-run supply curve is more elastic than the market period supply curve, S_1. In the short run, supply increases to Q_2 and the price falls from P_2 to P_3.
- **Long-run supply.** If firms believe that the increase in demand will be long-lasting and not just a temporary phenomenon, they may increase the scale of production by employing more capital and other factors of production that are fixed in the short run, but variable in the long run. When this happens, firms move along the long-run supply curve, S_3. Output rises to Q_3 and the price falls once again, in this case to P_4.

In a competitive industry with low or non-existent barriers to entry, elasticity of supply is greater in the long run than in the short run because in the long run firms can enter or leave the market. Short-run supply is less elastic because supply is restricted to the firms already in the industry.

examiner's voice

You should remember that, for most goods, both the demand curve and the supply curve are more price elastic in the long run than in the short run.

Income elasticity of demand

The nature of income elasticity of demand — which measures how *demand* responds to a change in income — depends on whether the good is a **normal good** or an **inferior good**. Income elasticity of demand is always *negative* for an inferior good and *positive* for a normal good. This is because the quantity demanded of an inferior good falls as income rises, whereas the quantity demanded of a normal good rises with income.

Normal goods can be further divided into **superior goods** or **luxuries**, for which the income elasticity of demand is greater than +1, and **basic goods**, with an income elasticity lying between 0 and +1. Although the quantity demanded of a normal good always rises with income, it rises more than proportionately for a superior good (such as a luxury car). Conversely, demand for a basic good such as shoe polish rises at a slower rate than income.

Cross elasticity of demand

Cross elasticity of demand measures how the demand for one commodity responds to changes in the price of another good. The cross elasticity of demand between two goods or services indicates the nature of the demand relationship between the goods. There are three possibilities: joint demand (or complementary goods); competing demand (or substitutes); and an absence of any discernible demand relationship. (Don't confuse goods in joint demand with goods in composite demand, which have two or more distinct uses.)

Joint demand or complementary goods

Complementary goods, such as computer games consoles and computer games, have negative cross elasticities of demand. If the manufacturer increases the price of games consoles (the hardware), demand for the consoles falls. This causes demand for games to use in the consoles (the software) also to fall. A rise in the price of one good leads to a fall in demand for the other good.

Competing demand or substitute goods

The cross elasticity of demand between two goods that are substitutes for each other is positive. A rise in the price of one good causes demand to switch to the substitute good whose price has not risen.

No discernible demand relationship

If we select two goods at random (for example, pencils and bicycles), the cross elasticity of demand between the two goods is likely to be zero. A rise in the price of one good will have no measurable effect upon the demand for the other good.

Elasticity case study: shifting the incidence of an expenditure tax

We saw in Chapter 2 that taxes imposed on firms by the government shift supply curves leftward. How the supply curve shifts depends on whether the tax that firms are forced to pay is an ad valorem tax or a specific tax.

- An **ad valorem tax**, such as value added tax (VAT), is levied at the same percentage rate (for example, 17.5%) on whatever the price would be without the tax. The new supply curve with the tax is steeper than the old supply curve. This is shown in Figure 3.9(a).
- But in the case of a **specific tax** or **unit tax**, such as the excise duty levied on tobacco, alcohol or petrol, the tax is a specified amount levied on each unit

of the good and is not affected by the good's price before the tax was imposed. Because of this, the new and old supply curves are parallel to each other, as Figure 3.9(b) shows.

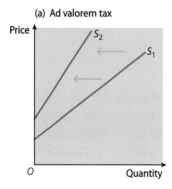

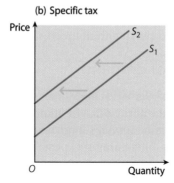

Figure 3.9
How ad valorem and specific taxes shift the supply curve

From the firms' point of view, an expenditure tax has the same effect as a rise in costs of production, such as wage costs or raw material costs. As is the case with cost increases, firms try to raise the price charged to customers by the full amount of the tax. However, their ability to do this depends on the elasticity of demand (note that the demand curve has not shifted).

Figure 3.10 shows that when demand is relatively elastic, consumer resistance means that some, but not all, of a tax (in this case, a specific tax) is passed on to consumers as a price rise. The tax per unit (labelled T in Figure 3.10) is measured by the vertical distance between S_1 (the supply curve before the tax was imposed) and S_2 (the supply curve after the tax was imposed). Immediately after the imposition of the tax, firms may try to raise the price to $P_1 + T$, passing all the tax on to consumers. However there is excess supply at this price. Via the market mechanism, the price falls to P_2, thereby eliminating the excess supply. In the new equilibrium, part, but not all, of the tax has been passed on to consumers as a price rise. When demand is relatively elastic, as in Figure 3.10, the amount passed on to consumers is less than 50% of the tax.

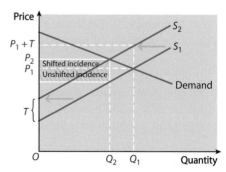

Figure 3.10 *Shifting the incidence of a tax when demand is price elastic*

The part of the tax passed on to consumers as a price rise is called the **shifted incidence** of the tax. The rest of the tax (the **unshifted incidence**) is borne by firms or producers. In Figure 3.10, the total tax revenue paid by firms to the government is shown by the shaded rectangle. The part of the tax rectangle above the previous equilibrium price (P_1) shows the shifted incidence of the tax. The part of the tax rectangle below P_1 shows the unshifted incidence.

You should now draw diagrams similar to Figure 3.10, but with perfectly elastic, unit elastic, relatively inelastic and completely inelastic demand curves. The diagrams will show that firms' ability to pass the incidence of a tax on to consumers as a price rise is greatest when demand is completely inelastic and non-existent when demand is perfectly elastic.

Students often confuse the effect of an indirect tax imposed on firms with the effect of a direct tax such as income tax imposed on individuals. Whereas a tax imposed on firms shifts the supply curve of a good, income tax shifts the demand curve for a good by reducing consumers' incomes. An increase in income tax shifts the demand curve for a normal good leftward, but if the good is an inferior good, the demand curve shifts rightward.

Finally, note that subsidies granted to firms have the opposite effect to indirect taxes imposed on firms. Subsidies shift the supply curve rightward or downward, showing that firms are prepared to supply more of the good at all prices.

examiner's voice

You should apply elasticity analysis when answering exam questions on the effects of a shift of a demand or a supply curve. The extent to which the good's price or the equilibrium level of output changes depends on the price elasticity of the curve that has not shifted. For example, when the supply curve shifts leftward, the price elasticity of the demand curve determines the extent to which the good's price and quantity change.

Summary

Whenever the value of one variable responds to that of another variable, elasticity can be measured. Elasticity is a useful analytical concept for measuring responsiveness because it is independent of the units, such as quantity and price, which are used to measure the values of the variables. The four main elasticities studied in microeconomic theory are price elasticity of demand, price elasticity of supply, income elasticity of demand and cross elasticity of demand.

Demand (or supply) is price elastic when a change in price induces a more than propor-tionate change in demand (or supply). Average elasticities can be measured between any two points on a demand or supply curve, but because the elasticity often varies from point to point on a curve, elasticities should only be measured for small changes along the curve. Alternatively, point elasticity can be calculated at a particular point on a supply or demand curve. Price elasticity of demand is usually negative and price elasticity of supply is generally positive, but income elasticity of demand can be positive or negative depending on whether the good is normal or inferior. The cross elasticity of demand, which measures the strength of a demand relationship between two goods, is positive for substitutes and negative when the goods are in joint demand. The size of the cross elasticity indicates the strength of the demand relationship.

Information about elasticities is useful both for firms and for the government. Knowledge of price elasticity of demand indicates to a firm whether a price increase will cause total sales revenue to rise or fall. For the government, price elasticity of demand determines the effect on total tax revenue of a higher sales tax. Cross elasticity of demand determines the extent to which consumers switch expenditure away from taxed goods such as cigarettes, towards untaxed or lower-taxed goods.

Self-testing questions

1 Distinguish between the elasticity of a curve and the slope of a curve.

2 State the formulas for demand and supply elasticities.

3 What is meant by elastic demand?

4 How does price elasticity of demand affect total consumer spending when a good's price falls?

5 Comment on the price elasticity of demand of a rectangular hyperbola demand curve.

6 Contrast perfectly elastic demand with perfectly elastic supply.

7 Distinguish between point elasticity and average elasticity.

8 What is the most important determinant of price elasticity of demand?

9 List the other determinants of price elasticity of demand.

10 List the determinants of price elasticity of supply.

11 Contrast the income elasticity of demand of normal and inferior goods.

12 What can be inferred about the demand relationship between two goods with a cross elasticity of (+)0.3?

13 If demand is inelastic, what effect will a price fall have on a firm's total sales revenue?

14 If demand is elastic, what effect may a good harvest have on farmers' total incomes?

15 If demand is inelastic, what effect might a unit sales tax have on (a) the price of the good; (b) the quantity bought and sold?

Part **2**

Production

part 2

Chapter 4
Production and cost theory

Specification focus

This is the first of four chapters devoted to the core of the A2 Module 5 specification covering the theory of the firm. The chapter is particularly relevant for:

A2 Module 5 Business Economics and the Distribution of Income
Theory of the Firm

A2 Synoptic coverage
This chapter is not generally relevant for AS, although the chapter introduces students to the Module 1 concepts of specialisation, the division of labour, production, economies of scale and unit costs, which are also tested in the Unit 5 exam at A2.

Introduction

Throughout this book you will be reminded that the ultimate purpose of economic activity is to increase economic welfare. (The economic welfare enjoyed by consumers is sometimes called utility.) For most people, most of the time, increased welfare means higher levels of demand and consumption of consumer goods and services. But before goods and services can be consumed, they first have to be produced. This chapter explains two important parts of microeconomic theory: production theory and cost theory. The latter is concerned with how firms incur costs of production when purchasing labour and the other factor services necessary for production to take place.

Production and costs

Production, which is depicted in Figure 4.1, involves processes that convert inputs into outputs. The inputs into production processes (land, labour, capital and enterprise) are also called **factors of production**. The nature of production depends to a great extent on the time period in which production is taking place. Chapter 3 (on elasticity) explained the difference between three time periods that economists identify when undertaking microeconomic analysis: the market period, the short run and the long run. The market period is a period so short that production cannot be changed at all. This chapter examines how firms can increase production, and thence incur **costs of production**, in the short run and in the long run.

Figure 4.1
Production

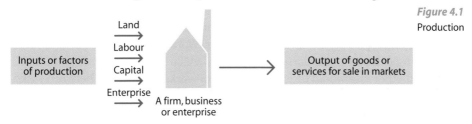

examiner's voice

Economists often use the terms *short run* and *long run*. Be careful with these terms because they sometimes have a different meaning in macroeconomics to their meaning in microeconomics. In micro-economics, at least one factor of production is fixed and cannot be varied in the short run, whereas in the long run the *scale* of all inputs can be varied. By contrast, when we are looking at the future impact of government macroeconomic policies, the short run stretches ahead for about a year, the medium term lasts from about 1–3 years and the long run refers to any period longer than about 3 years in the future.

Short-run production theory

In microeconomic theory, the **short run** is the time period in which at least one of the inputs or factors of production is fixed and cannot be changed. (By contrast, in the long run, the scale of all the factors of production can be changed.) As a simplification, we shall pretend that only two inputs or factors of production are needed for production to take place – capital and labour. We shall also assume that in the short run, capital is fixed. It follows that the only way the firm can increase output in the short run is by adding more of the variable factor of production, labour, to the fixed capital.

Table 4.1 Short-run production with fixed capital

Number of workers (with fixed capital)	0	1	2	3	4	5	6	7	8	9
Total output, product or returns	0	1	4	9	16	25	32	35	36	34
Average output, product or returns	0	1	2	3	4	5	5.3	5	4.5	3.8
Marginal output, product or returns		1	3	5	7	9	7	3	1	−2

Table 4.1 shows what might happen to car production in a small luxury sports car factory when the number of workers employed increases from 0 to 9. The first worker employed builds 1 car a year, and the second and third workers respectively add 3 and 5 cars to total production. These figures measure the marginal product (or marginal returns) of the first three workers employed. **Marginal product** is the addition to total output brought about by adding one more worker to the labour force.

In Table 4.1, the first 5 workers benefit from increasing marginal productivity (or increasing marginal returns). An additional worker increases total output by *more* than the amount added by the previous worker. Increasing marginal productivity is indeed very likely when the labour force is small. In this situation, employing an extra worker allows the workforce to be organised more efficiently. By dividing the various tasks of production among a greater number of workers, the firm benefits from **specialisation** and the **division of labour**. Workers become better and more efficient in performing the particular tasks in which they specialise, and time is saved that otherwise would be lost as a result of workers switching between tasks.

But as the firm adds labour to fixed capital, eventually the **law of diminishing marginal productivity** (or **law of diminishing marginal returns**) sets in. In this example, the law sets in when the sixth worker is employed. The fifth worker's marginal product is 9 cars, but the sixth worker adds only 7 cars to total output. Diminishing marginal productivity sets in because labour is being added to fixed capital. When more and more labour is added to fixed plant and machinery, eventually the marginal product of labour must fall, though not often at a labour force as small as 6 workers.

Note that the law of diminishing marginal productivity does not set in because the extra worker joining the labour force is any less hardworking or motivated than his or her predecessors. It is because the benefits resulting from any further specialisation and division of labour eventually become exhausted as more labour is added to a fixed amount of capital or machinery.

e*xaminer's voice

In production theory, students often confuse the law of diminishing returns, which is a short-run law, with returns to scale, which relate to the long run when firms change the scale of *all* the factors of production. You must avoid making this mistake. The law of diminishing returns is important for explaining short-run cost curves, and likewise, returns to scale help explain long-run cost curves and the concepts of economies and diseconomies of scale.

Product curves

Figure 4.2 illustrates the law of diminishing marginal returns. In the upper panel of the diagram, the law sets in at point *A*, where the slope of the total product curve begins to change. With increasing marginal productivity, the slope of the total product curve increases, moving from point to point up the curve. When diminishing returns set in, the total product curve continues to rise as more workers are combined with capital, but the curve becomes less steep from point to point up the curve. Point *Y* shows where *total* product begins to fall. Beyond this point, additional workers begin to get in the way of other workers, so the marginal product of labour becomes negative. However, you must avoid explaining negative marginal productivity in terms of workers' bloody-mindedness or their tendency to throw a spanner in the works.

The total product curve in the upper panel of Figure 4.2 plots the information in the top row of Table 4.1. By contrast, the lower panel of the diagram plots the marginal product of labour (from the information in the bottom row of Table 4.1) and the average product of labour (from the information in the middle row of Table 4.1).

It is important to understand that all three curves (and all three rows in Table 4.1) contain the same information, but used differently in each curve (and row). The total product curve plots the information cumulatively, adding the marginal product of the last worker to the total product before the worker joined the labour force. By contrast, the marginal product curve plots the same information non-cumulatively, or as separate observations. Finally, at each level of employment, the average product curve shows the total product of the labour force divided by the number of workers employed.

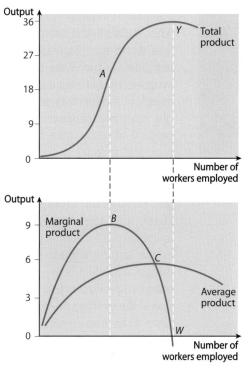

Figure 4.2 *Total, marginal and average product curves*

In the lower panel of Figure 4.2, the law of diminishing marginal productivity sets in at point *B*, at the highest point on the marginal product curve. Before this point, increasing marginal productivity is shown by the rising (or positively sloped) marginal product curve, while beyond this point, diminishing marginal productivity is depicted by the falling (or negatively sloped) marginal product curve. Likewise, the point of diminishing *average* productivity sets in at the highest point of the average product curve at point *C*. Finally, marginal product becomes negative beyond point *W*.

The relationship between marginal product and average product
The relationship between the marginal productivity and the average productivity of labour is an example of a more general relationship that you need to know. Shortly, we shall provide a second example, namely marginal cost and its relationship to average cost.

Marginal and average curves plotted from the same set of data always display the following relationship:
- When the marginal is greater than the average, the average rises.
- When the marginal is less than the average, the average falls.
- When the marginal equals the average, the average is constant, neither rising nor falling.

It is vital to understand this relationship. It does not state that an average will rise when a marginal is rising; nor does it state that an average will fall when a marginal falls. As we have explained, the numerical example illustrated in Table 4.1 and the marginal and average product curves drawn in Figure 4.2 show that marginal product begins to fall as soon as the law of diminishing marginal productivity sets in. Nevertheless, as long as the marginal product is greater than the average product of labour, the latter continues to rise. When marginal product is greater than average product, it 'pulls up' the average, even when the marginal product curve is falling. But when the marginal product falls through the average product curve (at point *C* in Figure 4.2), the average product begins to fall. The marginal product curve cuts the average product curve at the latter's highest point. Beyond this point, the marginal product curve continues to fall, and because marginal product is less than average product, it 'pulls down' the average product curve.

*e***xaminer's voice**
It is essential at A2, though not at AS, to understand the relationship between the marginal and average values of economic variables. You must understand the relation-ship between marginal and average *product*, between marginal and average *cost* (covered later in this chapter), and between marginal and average *sales revenue*, which is explained in the next chapter.

Short-run costs

Cost curves measure the costs that firms have to pay to hire the inputs or factors of production needed to produce output. In the short run, when the inputs divide into fixed and variable factors of production, the costs of production can likewise be divided into fixed and variable costs. This can be written as:

total cost = total fixed cost + total variable cost

or:

$TC = TFC + TVC$

Likewise, average total cost per unit can be written as:

average total cost = average fixed cost + average variable cost

or:

$ATC = AFC + AVC$

To explain how total costs of production vary with output in the short run, we shall look first at fixed costs and then at variable costs.

Fixed costs

Fixed costs of production are overheads, such as the rent on land and the main-tenance costs of buildings, which a firm must pay in the short run. Suppose, for example, that a car manufacturing company incurs overheads of £1 million a year from an assembly plant it operates. We can represent these costs both as the horizontal total fixed cost curve in Figure 4.3(a) and as the downward-sloping average fixed cost curve in Figure 4.3(b). If the plant only managed to produce

High output reduces average fixed costs in the VW car plant

1 automobile a year, *AFC* per car would be £1 million — the single car would bear all the overheads. But if the company were to increase production, average fixed costs would fall to £500,000 when 2 cars are produced, £333,333 when 3 cars are produced and so on. Average fixed costs per unit of output fall as output increases, since overheads are spread over a larger output.

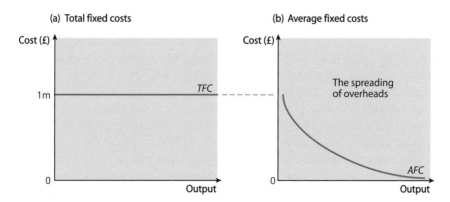

Figure 4.3
Fixed costs of production

Variable costs

Variable costs are the costs that the firm incurs when it hires variable factors of production such as labour and raw materials. For simplicity, we shall assume that labour is the only variable factor of production. The upper panel of Figure 4.4 shows the marginal and average productivity of labour. Diminishing marginal returns begin at point *A*. Increasing marginal productivity of labour (or increasing marginal returns) is shown by the positive (or rising) slope of the marginal product curve, while diminishing marginal returns are represented, beyond point *A*, by the curve's negative (or falling) slope.

When labour is the only variable factor of production, variable costs are simply wage costs. If all workers receive the same hourly wage, total wage costs rise in exact proportion to the number of workers employed. However, with increasing marginal labour productivity, the total variable cost of production rises at a slower rate than output. This causes the marginal cost (MC) of producing an extra unit of output to fall. In Figure 4.4, the increasing marginal productivity of labour (shown by the positive slope of the marginal product curve in the upper of the two diagrams) causes marginal cost (shown in the lower of the two diagrams) to fall.

But once the law of diminishing marginal productivity sets in, marginal cost rises with output. The wage cost of employing an extra worker is still the same, but each extra worker is now less productive than the previous worker. Variable costs rise faster than employment, so marginal cost also rises.

Just as the *MC* curve is derived from the marginal returns or marginal productivity of the variable inputs, so the average variable cost (*AVC*) curve (illustrated in the lower panel of Figure 4.4) is explained by the average returns or productivity (shown in the upper panel). While increasing average returns are experienced, with the labour force on average becoming more efficient and productive, the *AVC* per unit of output must fall as output rises. But once diminishing average returns set in at point *B*, the *AVC* curve begins to rise with output.

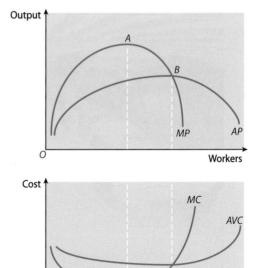

Figure 4.4 Deriving the MC and AVC curves from short-run production theory

e*xaminer's voice*

Figure 4.4 illustrates how a firm's short-run marginal and average cost curves are derived from short-run production theory. Make sure you understand the relationship between product curves and cost curves.

Average total costs

The firm's average total cost (*ATC*) curve is obtained from the addition of the *AFC* and *AVC* curves, as shown in Figure 4.5(a). Figure 4.5(b) shows the *ATC* curve on its own, without its two components separated (*AFC* and *AVC*). You should note that the *ATC* curve is typically U-shaped, showing that average total costs per unit of output first fall and later rise as output is increased. In the short run, average total costs must eventually rise because, at high levels of output, any further spreading of fixed costs becomes insufficient to offset the impact of diminishing returns upon variable costs of production. Sooner or later, rising marginal costs (which, as we have seen, result from diminishing marginal returns) must cut through and 'pull up' the *ATC* curve.

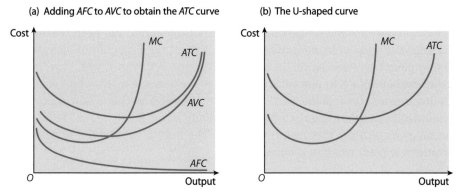

Figure 4.5 *The average total cost (ATC) curve*

Applying the rule on marginal and average curves

In the left-hand panel of Figure 4.5 the *MC* curve cuts both the *AVC* and the *ATC* curves at their lowest points. If you are unsure as to why this is so, read again the earlier section in the chapter covering the relationship between marginal and average product. You learnt there that a falling marginal product curve cuts the 'dome-shaped' average product curve at its highest point.

Long-run production theory

The only way a firm can increase output in the short run is by adding more variable factors of production (such as labour) to its fixed capital. But eventually the law of diminishing productivity sets in, which causes short-run marginal costs to rise. When the *MC* curve rises through the firm's *ATC* curve, average total costs of production also rise.

To escape the adverse effect of rising short-run costs upon profit, the firm may decide to change the scale of its operations in the economic long run. In the economic long run there are no fixed factors of production. The firm can change the scale of all its factors of production, including its capital or production plant, which is normally assumed to be fixed in the short run.

Returns to scale

Figure 4.6 illustrates the important distinction between returns to a variable factor of production, which occur in the short run, and **returns to scale**, which operate

only in the economic long run. Suppose that initially a firm's fixed capital is represented by plant size 1 in the diagram. Initially, the firm can increase production in the short run, by moving along the horizontal arrow *A*, employing more variable factors of production such as labour. However, the only way the firm can further increase profits once the short-run profit-maximising output has been reached is to change the scale of its operations, assuming that the firm cannot operate its existing plant more efficiently. In the long run, the firm can invest in a larger production plant, such as plant size 2, shown as the move along the vertical arrow *X* in the diagram. Once plant size 2 is in operation, the firm is in a new short-run situation, able to increase output by moving along arrow *B*. But again, the impact of diminishing returns may eventually cause the firm to expand the scale of its operations to plant size 3 in the long run.

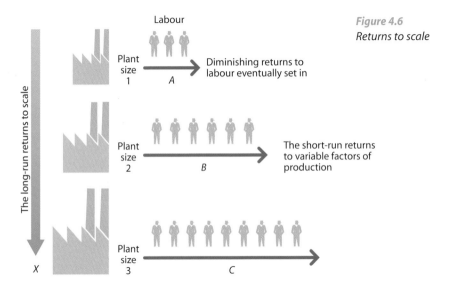

Figure 4.6
Returns to scale

The law of diminishing marginal productivity, explained earlier in the context of short-run production, is a short-run law that does not operate in the long run when a firm increases the scale of all its inputs or factors of production. With returns to scale there are three possibilities:

- **Increasing returns to scale.** If an increase in the scale of all the factors of production causes a more than proportionate increase in output, there are increasing returns to scale.
- **Constant returns to scale.** If an increase in the scale of all the factors of production causes a proportionate increase in output, there are constant returns to scale.
- **Decreasing returns to scale.** If an increase in the scale of all the factors of production causes a less than proportionate increase in output, there are decreasing (or diminishing) returns to scale.

It is important not to confuse *returns to scale*, which occur in the long run when the scale of all the factors of production can be altered, with the *short-run returns* that occur when at least one factor is fixed. We have already seen how short-run returns affect the shape of a firm's short-run cost curves. We shall now explain how returns to scale affect the shape of a firm's long-run average costs (*LRAC*) of production.

Long-run costs

In the long run, a firm can change the scale of all its factors of production, moving from one size of plant to another. Figure 4.7 shows a number of short-run average total cost (*SRATC*) curves, each representing a particular size or scale of firm. In the long run, a firm can move from one short-run cost curve to another which is associated with a different scale of fixed capacity. The line drawn as a tangent to the family or set of *SRATC* curves is the long-run average cost (*LRAC*) curve.

examiner's voice

Short-run production is affected by the law of diminishing returns (or diminishing marginal productivity). No similar 'law' affects long-run production: in the long run, increasing returns to scale, constant returns to scale and decreasing returns to scale may all occur, but not all of them have to occur.

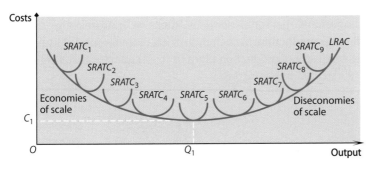

Figure 4.7
A U-shaped LRAC curve and its related SRATC curves

Economies of scale and diseconomies of scale

Just as it is important to avoid confusing short-run returns or productivity with long-run returns to scale, so *returns to scale* must be distinguished from a closely related concept: *economies and diseconomies of scale*. Returns to scale refer to the technical relationship in production between inputs and outputs measured in physical units. For example, increasing returns to scale occur if a doubling of a car firm's factory size and its labour force enables the firm to more than double its output of cars. There is no mention of *money* costs of production in this example of increasing returns to scale. Returns to scale are part of long-run *production* theory, but economies and diseconomies of scale are part of long-run *cost* theory. Economies of scale occur when long-run average costs (*LRAC*) fall as output increases. Diseconomies of scale occur when *LRAC* rise as output increases.

examiner's voice

A firm's *long-run* average cost curve *may* be U-shaped, but it does not have to be U-shaped. As Figures 4.8–4.10 show, the *LRAC* curve may be U-shaped but *skewed* to the left or right, or it may be L-shaped, or possibly horizontal.

There is, however, a link between returns to scale and economies and diseconomies of scale. Increasing returns to scale lead to falling long-run average costs or economies of scale, and likewise decreasing returns to scale bring about rising long-run average costs or diseconomies of scale.

examiner's voice

Examination candidates must know about economies and diseconomies of scale at AS and also at A2. AS candidates must know that economies of scale reduce a firm's long-run average costs, and they should also have basic knowledge of types of economy of scale (see Chapter 7). AS candidates are not expected to know about average cost curves. However, A2 candidates must thoroughly understand cost curves, especially the difference between short-run and long-run cost curves.

The shape of the long-run average cost curve

Figure 4.7 illustrates a U-shaped long-run average cost curve in which economies of scale are eventually followed by diseconomies. An increase in all the inputs or factors of production causes $LRAC$ to fall to C_1, at output Q_1, but after this point, diseconomies of scale set in.

However, the long-run average cost curve need not be U-shaped, in which economies of scale are followed symmetrically by diseconomies of scale. Some industries, including many personal services such as hairdressing, exhibit **economies of small-scale production**. In such industries, diseconomies of scale may set in at a relatively small size of production plant or fixed capacity, resulting in the rising $LRAC$ curve illustrated in Figure 4.8.

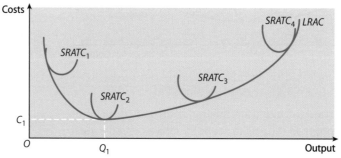

Figure 4.8
Economies of small-scale production

In other industries, which lack significant economies or diseconomies of scale, the horizontal $LRAC$ curve depicted in Figure 4.9 may be more typical, allowing firms or plants of many different sizes to exist within the same industry.

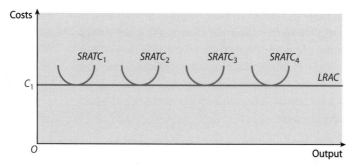

Figure 4.9
A horizontal LRAC curve

In much of the manufacturing industry, however, statistical studies suggest that the $LRAC$ curve is L-shaped, as illustrated in Figure 4.10. Beyond output Q_1 the $LRAC$

AQA Advanced Economics

Aircraft building firms are limited by market constraints rather than by diseconomies of scale

curve is horizontal. No further economies of scale are possible, but likewise there are no diseconomies of scale. In industries such as automobile and aircraft building, for which the L-shaped curve may be typical, size of firm is limited by market constraints rather than by the onset of diseconomies of scale.

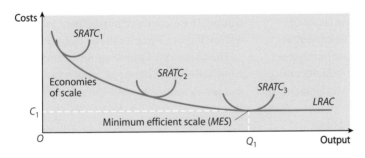

Figure 4.10
An L-shaped LRAC curve and the minimum efficient scale (MES)

The optimum size of firm and minimum efficient scale

The size of plant at the lowest point on the firm's $LRAC$ curve is known as the **optimum plant size**. When the long-run average cost curve is U-shaped, as in Figure 4.7, we can identify a single optimum plant size level of output, occurring after economies of scale have been gained, but before diseconomies of scale set in. In Figure 4.7, optimum plant size is shown by the short-run cost curve $SRATC_5$, with optimum output at Q_1. In the case of the horizontal $LRAC$ curve illustrated in Figure 4.9, where there are no economies or diseconomies of scale, it is not possible to identify an optimal plant size.

However, when the $LRAC$ curve is L-shaped, as in Figure 4.10, no further substantial economies of scale can be gained after plant size 3, located where long-run average costs 'flatten out'. Plant size 3 is therefore known as the **minimum efficient scale** (*MES*), indicating the smallest size of plant that can gain all the available scale economies.

The different types of economy and diseconomy of scale

As we have seen, economies of scale occur when a firm's long-run average cost (*LRAC*) curve falls as its scale of operations increases. Likewise, diseconomies of scale occur with rising long-run average costs. To learn more about the many different causes or types of economy and diseconomy of scale, you must read Chapter 7. This chapter explains the difference between internal and external economies and diseconomies of scale, and between the various types of plant-level and firm-level economy and diseconomy, such as technical, managerial and finance-raising economies and diseconomies.

Summary

This chapter has introduced and explained the first two 'building blocks' of the theory of the firm. These are production theory and cost theory. The chapter's main messages are that a firm's short-run cost curves derive from short-run production theory and that, similarly, a firm's long-run cost curves derive from long-run production theory.

In microeconomic theory, the short run is the time period in which at least one factor of production (or input) is fixed and cannot be varied. A firm can increase output in the short run only by adding more variable factors of production (e.g. labour) to its fixed factors (e.g. capital). In the short run, the law of diminishing marginal returns (or diminishing marginal productivity) operates. The firm's short-run costs of production divide into fixed cost (the cost of hiring the fixed factors of production) and variable cost (the cost of hiring labour and other variable inputs). As soon as diminishing marginal returns set in, the firm's marginal cost of production begins to rise. When marginal cost rises above average variable cost (and later above average total cost) the *AVC* and *ATC* curves also rise. This means that the *AVC* and *ATC* curves are U-shaped.

The short-run marginal returns to a variable factor of production such as labour must eventually diminish because of the conditions in which production is taking place, namely at least one factor of production is assumed to be fixed. In microeconomic theory, the long run is the time period in which all the factors of production can be changed. When firms increase production in the long run, they experience returns to scale. It is vital not to confuse short-run marginal returns with long-run returns to scale. Returns to scale relate changes in output to changes in all the inputs (i.e. capital and land, as well as labour). There are three possibilities: increasing, decreasing or constant returns to scale.

The shape of a firm's long-run average cost curve reflects the nature of returns to scale. Increasing returns to scale cause long-run average costs to fall. A falling *LRAC* curve displays economies of scale. Likewise, a rising *LRAC* curve (displaying diseconomies of scale) results from decreasing returns to scale as the firm increases production in the long run. The *LRAC* curve may be L-shaped, U-shaped, symmetrical, skewed or horizontal, depending on the nature of the scale economies and diseconomies experienced by the firm. However, the short-run *ATC* curve will be U-shaped, providing the law of diminishing returns operates.

The next two chapters bring together the cost theory covered in this chapter with the sales revenue curves of firms operating in three different market structures: perfect competition and monopoly (in Chapter 5) and oligopoly (in Chapter 6).

Self-testing questions

1 Define production.

2 What are the factors of production?

3 Distinguish between a fixed factor and a variable factor of production.

4 Distinguish between the short run and the long run.

5 Give two examples of fixed costs.

6 Explain the law of diminishing returns.

7 How does the law of diminishing returns affect the marginal product curve and the average product curve of labour?

8 How do marginal returns affect marginal costs?

9 Why is a short-run *ATC* curve U-shaped?

10 Distinguish between short-run returns and returns to scale.

11 What is the relationship between returns to scale and economies of scale?

12 Distinguish between economies and diseconomies of scale.

13 Must the *LRAC* curve be U-shaped?

Chapter 5
Perfect competition and monopoly

Specification focus

This chapter links production theory and cost theory to competitive markets and monopoly in the A2 Module 5 specification. For AS, the chapter expands and develops two parts of the Module 1 specification: Allocation of Resources in Competitive Markets; and Monopoly. The chapter is particularly relevant for:

AS **Module 1 Markets and Market Failure**
    Allocation of Resources in Competitive Markets; Monopoly; Production and Efficiency

A2 **Module 5 Business Economics and the Distribution of Income**
    Competitive Markets; Concentrated Markets (Monopoly); Government Intervention in the Market

A2 **Synoptic coverage**
    Basic knowledge of competitive markets and monopoly learnt at AS is relevant for the Unit 5 A2 examination.

Introduction

Chapter 4 explained how production takes place, and how the nature of production affects a firm's costs of production, in both the short run and the long run. This chapter introduces two further elements in the theory of the firm, namely the revenue that the firm earns when it sells its output, and the profit (and sometimes the loss) that the firm makes as a result of the sale. The chapter starts by explaining the market structures of perfect competition and monopoly. The latter part of the chapter uses the concepts of economic efficiency and consumer surplus to analyse and evaluate the desirable and less desirable features of these opposing market structures.

Market structures

Perfect competition and **monopoly** are opposite extremes, which separate a spectrum of market structures known as **imperfect competition**. The main forms of market structure are illustrated and defined in Figure 5.1.

Pure monopoly, in which a single firm produces the whole of the output of a market or industry, is the most extreme form of imperfect competition. Indeed, a pure monopolist faces no competition at all, since there are no other firms to compete against. Usually, however, monopoly is a *relative* rather than an *absolute* concept. Until quite recently, the British Gas Corporation was the single producer of piped gas to households and most industrial customers, but it experienced competition from other sources of energy such as electricity and oil. British Gas's monopoly power was further reduced in 1998 when other companies, including electricity companies, were allowed to sell gas to customers via the pipelines previously owned by British Gas. Monopolists do, therefore, face competitive pressures, both from substitute products and sometimes also from outside firms trying to enter the market to destroy their monopoly position.

> **examiner's voice**
>
> For the Unit 5 A2 examination, candidates must expect data-response or essay questions to be set on perfect competition, monopoly or oligopoly. Questions will *not* be set on monopolistic competition. AS candidates must understand how competitive markets operate, and the meaning of monopoly, but they don't need to know the detailed theory and the diagrams explained in this chapter.

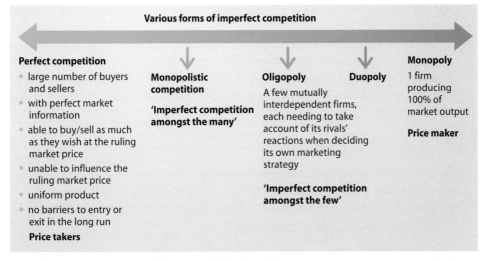

Figure 5.1 The main market structures

> **examiner's voice**
>
> While you should know the six conditions of perfect competition listed in Figure 5.1, it is seldom if ever relevant to regurgitate this list in an examination answer. Rather, you must learn the skills of applying one or more or the conditions of perfect competition to explain, analyse or evaluate the characteristics of a perfectly competitive market, or to compare perfect competition with monopoly or oligopoly.

Although this chapter covers only perfect competition and monopoly, you should not conclude that either of these market structures is typical or representative of the real economy. Even ignoring competition from substitute products, pure monopoly is exceedingly rare; in the past, the **state monopolies** or **public monopolies** provided perhaps the best examples. These were nationalised industries such as the Royal Mail. In the last 25 years, government policy in the UK has reduced the role of the state monopolies, both by introducing competition and by transferring nationalised industries to the private sector in a process known as **privatisation**.

At the other end of the spectrum, **perfect competition** is actually non-existent. It is best to regard perfect competition as an unreal or abstract economic model defined by the conditions listed in Figure 5.1. As we shall see shortly, real-world markets cannot display simultaneously *all* the conditions necessary for perfect competition. Since any violation of the conditions of perfect competition immediately renders a market imperfectly competitive, even the most competitive markets in the real economy are examples of imperfect competition rather than perfect competition.

Despite the lack of perfect markets in the real world, the theory of perfect competition is perhaps the most important and fundamental of all conventional economic theories. Critics of orthodox microeconomic theory strongly argue that economists pay undue attention to perfect competition as a market form and that this encourages a false belief that a perfect market is an attainable ideal. As you read this chapter, remember at all times that perfect competition is an unrealistic market structure. (It would be clearer for students if perfect and imperfect competition were respectively called *unrealistic competition* and *realistic competition*.) Nevertheless, perfect competition performs a very useful function. It serves as a standard or benchmark against which we may judge the desirable or undesirable properties of the imperfectly competitive market structures of the world we live in.

Profit-maximising behaviour

The assumption of profit-maximising behaviour on the part of firms or producers is fundamental to the traditional (or neoclassical) theory of the firm which is explained in this and the next chapter. A firm's total profit is given by the formula:

total profit = total revenue − total cost

Providing we assume that a firm wishes to make the largest possible profit, it aims to produce the level of output at which $TR - TC$ is maximised. The maximisation of $TR - TC$ is the **equilibrium condition** (or **optimising condition**) for a profit-maximising firm, since if the firm produces and sells the output yielding the biggest possible profit, it has no incentive to change its level of output.

However, it is generally more convenient to state the equilibrium condition for profit maximisation as:

marginal revenue = marginal cost

MR = *MC* means that a firm's profits are greatest when the addition to sales revenue received from the last unit sold (**marginal revenue**) equals exactly the addition to total cost incurred from the production of the last unit of output (**marginal cost**). Imagine, for example, a market gardener producing tomatoes for sale in a local market, but unable to influence the ruling market price of 50p per kilo. At any size of sales, average revenue is 50p, which also equals marginal revenue. Suppose that when she markets 300 kilos of tomatoes, the cost of producing and marketing the 300th kilo is 48p. If she decides not to market the 300th kilo, 2p of profit is sacrificed. Suppose now that total costs rise by 50p and 52p respectively when a 301st kilo and a 302nd kilo are marketed. The marketing of the 302nd kilo causes profits to fall by 2p, but the 301st kilo of tomatoes leaves total profits unchanged: it represents the level of sales at which profits are exactly maximised.

The ruling market price and costs of production will dictate how many tomatoes are sent to market

To sum up, when marginal costs are rising, disequilibrium conditions are as follows:

■ If *MR* > *MC*, profits rise when output is increased.
■ If *MR* < *MC*, profits rise when output is reduced.
■ Therefore only when *MR* = *MC* are profits maximised.

Perfect competition

Revenue curves in perfect competition

Perfect competition is defined by the market conditions or characteristics listed in Figure 5.1 at the beginning of this chapter. In Figure 5.2, these conditions are used to derive the revenue curves facing a firm in a perfectly competitive market. The assumption that a perfectly competitive firm can sell whatever quantity it wishes at the ruling market price P_1, but that it cannot influence the ruling market price by its own action, means that the firm is a **price-taker**. Demand for the firm's output is infinitely elastic (or perfectly elastic) at the price ruling in the whole market. The horizontal price line is also the perfectly competitive firm's average revenue (*AR*) and marginal revenue (*MR*) curve. This price line is determined in Figure 5.2(b), where the market demand curve intersects the market supply curve in the market as a whole.

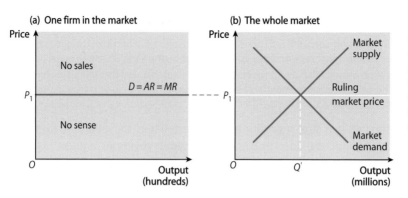

Figure 5.2
Deriving a perfectly competitive firm's average and marginal revenue curves

Notice that the labels 'no sales' and 'no sense' have been placed on Figure 5.2(a), respectively above and below the price line P_1. 'No sales' indicates that if the firm raises its selling price above the ruling market price, customers desert the firm to buy the identical products — or perfect substitutes — available from other firms at the ruling market price. 'No sense' refers to the fact that although a perfectly competitive firm can sell its output below the price P_1, doing so is irrational. No extra sales can result, so selling below the ruling market price inevitably reduces both total sales revenue and profit. Such a pricing policy therefore conflicts with the profit-maximising objective that firms are assumed to have.

Normal and supernormal profit

Before explaining the profit-maximising or equilibrium firm in perfect competition, we must first introduce normal profit and above-normal profit. **Normal profit** is the minimum level of profit necessary to keep incumbent firms (that is, firms that are in the market already) in the market. However, the normal profit made by incumbent firms is insufficient to attract new firms into the market. Because a firm must make normal profit to stay in production, economists treat normal profit as a cost of production, including it in a firm's average cost curve. In the long run, firms that are unable to make normal profit leave the market.

*e***xaminer's voice**

It is easy to confuse normal *profit* with a normal *good*. Remember, from Chapter 2, that a normal good is one for which demand rises as income increases. By contrast, normal profit is the minimum level of profit that keeps a firm in the market, while being insufficient to attract outside firms into the market.

Supernormal profit (also known as **abnormal profit** and **above-normal profit**) is extra profit over and above normal profit. In the long run, and in the absence of entry barriers, supernormal profit performs the important economic function of attracting new firms into the market.

Short-run equilibrium in perfect competition

In the short run, the equilibrium level of output of a perfectly competitive firm can be shown by superimposing the firm's horizontal average and marginal revenue curves upon its average and marginal cost curves. Point *A* in Figure 5.3(a) (at which $MR = MC$) locates the profit-maximising level of output Q_1. At this level of output,

AQA Advanced Economics

total sales revenue is shown by the area OQ_1AP_1. Total cost is shown by the area OQ_1BC_1. Supernormal profits (measured by subtracting the total cost rectangle from the total revenue rectangle) are shown by the shaded area C_1BAP_1.

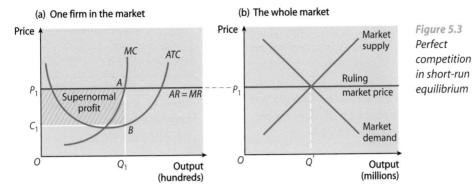

Figure 5.3
Perfect competition in short-run equilibrium

Long-run equilibrium in perfect competition

If you refer back to the conditions of perfect competition listed in Figure 5.1, you will see that although firms cannot enter or leave the market in the short run, they can in the long run. Suppose that in the short run, firms make supernormal profit, as illustrated in Figure 5.3. In this situation, the ruling market price signals to firms outside the market that supernormal profits can be made, thus providing an incentive for new firms to enter the market.

Figure 5.4 shows what might happen next. Initially, too many new firms enter the market, causing the supply curve in Figure 5.4(b) to shift rightward to S_2. This causes the price to fall to P_2, which lies below each firm's ATC curve. When this happens, firms make a loss (or subnormal profit). But just as supernormal profit creates the incentive for new firms to enter the market, subnormal profit provides the incentive for marginal firms to leave the market. The market supply curve shifts leftward and the market price rises. Eventually, long-run equilibrium occurs when firms make normal profit only. For the market as a whole, this is shown at output Q''' and price P_3 in Figure 5.4(b).

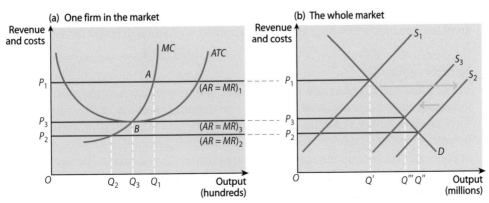

Figure 5.4 *Perfect competition in long-run equilibrium*

In Figure 5.4(a), each firm produces the output Q_3. This represents long-run or true equilibrium. Total revenue equals the total cost of production, and there is no incentive for firms to enter or leave the industry. As it depicts the whole market, and also a particular firm within the market, Figure 5.4 is a rather complicated diagram. By contrast, Figure 5.5 shows the essential points you need to know about a perfectly competitive firm in long-run equilibrium.

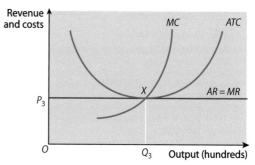

Figure 5.5 A perfectly competitive firm in long-run equilibrium minimising average costs of production

Monopoly

Pure monopoly means that there is only one firm in a market. Before we examine the equilibrium pricing and output conditions of a market in which there is only one firm, we shall first survey the market conditions that favour the emergence of a monopoly supplier.

The causes of monopoly

An effective monopoly must be able to exclude rivals from the market through barriers to entry. However, even when a firm is a monopoly producer of a particular good or service, the monopoly position is weak if close substitutes exist, produced by other firms in other industries. The closer the substitutes available, the weaker is the monopoly position. A monopoly is therefore strongest when it produces an essential good for which there are no substitutes — or when demand for its good is relatively inelastic. There are several causes of monopoly.

Natural monopoly

In the past, utility industries such as water, gas, electricity and the telephone industries have been regarded as natural monopolies. Because of the nature of their product, utility industries experience a particular marketing problem. The industries produce a service that is delivered through a distribution network or grid of pipes and cables into millions of separate businesses and homes. Competition in the provision of distribution grids is extremely wasteful, since it requires the duplication of fixed capacity, therefore causing each supplier to incur unnecessarily high fixed costs in relation to the firm's market share.

Until quite recently, utility industries were generally monopolies. However, governments had to choose whether utilities should be publicly owned monopolies (nationalised industries) or privately owned monopolies, possibly subject to public regulation. For historical reasons, most UK utility industries were nationalised industries. In the 1980s and early 1990s, utilities such as the British Gas Corporation and British Telecom (BT) were privatised, becoming privately owned utilities. Immediately following privatisation, they remained monopolies, protected from competition but subject to a certain amount of state regulation: for example, BT was regulated by OFTEL (now called OFCOM). However, as Chapter 8 explains, the government has now successfully removed barriers to entry to many utility industries and opened them up to competition. Most utility markets (except water) are now much more contestable than they used to be.

Geographical factors

A *pure* natural monopoly is rather different from the natural monopolies described in the previous paragraph. It occurs when, for climatic or geological reasons, a particular country or location is the only source of supply of a raw material or foodstuff. Monopolies of this type are quite rare, but geographical or spatial factors quite commonly give rise to another type of monopoly. Consider the case of a single grocery store in an isolated village or a petrol company that owns all the land around a busy road junction on which it has built a filling station. In the former case, entry to the market by a second store is restricted by the fact that the local market is too small, while in the second example the oil company uses private property rights to exclude immediate competition. In both these examples, no monopoly exists in an *absolute* sense, since the villagers can travel to the nearest town to buy their groceries, or motorists can drive on to the next convenient filling station. Nevertheless, the grocery store and the petrol station can still exercise considerable market power, stemming from the fact that for many villagers and motorists it is both costly and inconvenient to shop elsewhere. Prices charged are likely to be higher than they would be if competition existed in the immediate neighbourhood.

Economies of scale

Many manufacturing industries, such as the aircraft building industry, benefit from economies of large-scale production. However, the size of the national market, and in extreme cases the world market, limits the number of firms that can coexist in an industry and continue to benefit from full economies of scale. Economies of scale thus help to explain the existence of natural monopoly; a natural monopoly occurs when there is room in the market for only one firm benefiting from full economies of scale.

Government-created monopolies

Governments sometimes create monopolies in industries other than utility industries or those with natural monopolies. In the UK, industries such as coal, rail and steel were nationalised in the 1940s by a Labour government and turned into *state-owned monopolies*. At the time, the Labour government believed, on the one

hand, that these industries were the commanding heights of the economy, and were essential for the well-being and planning of the whole economy; and on the other hand, that state ownership was required for the industries to operate in the public interest, rather than in the narrower interests of their previous private owners.

In other instances, government may deliberately create a *private monopoly*. Examples include the granting of a broadcasting franchise to a commercial television company or a gambling franchise to a casino. Both of these are examples of the state using monopoly to regulate the consumption of a good or service. State monopolies can ensure standards of supply of a merit good such as public service broadcasting, or prevent the worst excesses of consumption of a demerit good such as gambling. (See Chapter 9 for an explanation of **merit** and **demerit goods**.)

Patent law provides another example of government-created monopoly. Patents and other forms of intellectual copyright give businesses, writers and musicians exclusive rights for many years over new products or creative work in art, music and literature.

Control of market outlets and raw materials

Firms may try to obtain exclusive control over market outlets in order to deny access to their competitors. UK examples have included oil companies buying up garages and petrol stations, and breweries acquiring public houses. In a similar way, firms may obtain exclusive control over sources of raw materials or components for their products, starving their competitors of a source of supply, or charging artificially high prices.

Advertising as a barrier to entry

Monopolies and other large firms can prevent small firms entering the market with methods such as **saturation advertising**. The small firms are unable to enter the industry because they cannot afford the minimum level of advertising and other forms of promotion necessary to persuade retailers to stock their products. The mass advertising, brand-imaging and other marketing strategies of large established firms effectively crowd out newcomers from the marketplace.

The demand for a monopolist's output

The demand curve facing a monopolist differs from the demand curve facing a firm in a perfectly competitive market. Because the monopoly *is* the industry, the industry demand curve and the demand curve for the monopolist's output are the same. This means that a monopolist faces a downward-sloping demand curve, whose elasticity is determined by the nature of consumer demand for the monopolist's product.

The downward-sloping demand curve affects the monopolist in one of two different ways. If the monopolist is a price-maker, choosing to set the price at which the product is sold, the demand curve dictates the maximum output that can be sold at this price. For example, if the price is set at P_1 in Figure 5.6, the maximum quantity that can be sold at this price is Q_1. If the monopolist raises the price to P_2, sales fall to Q_2, unless the monopolist successfully uses advertising or other forms of marketing to shift the demand curve rightward. Alternatively, if the monopolist is a quantity-setter, the demand curve dictates the maximum price at which the chosen quantity can be sold. The fact that the demand curve is downward-sloping means that the monopolist faces a trade-off. A monopoly cannot set price and quantity independently of each other.

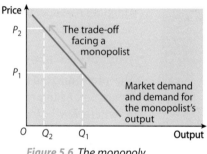

Figure 5.6 The monopoly demand curve

Revenue curves in monopoly

Because the demand curve shows the price that the monopolist charges at each level of output, the demand curve is the monopolist's average revenue curve. However, unlike in perfect competition, marginal revenue and average revenue are *not* the same in monopoly. To explain this, we shall reintroduce the mathematical relationship explained in Chapter 4, between a marginal variable and the average to which it is related:

- If the marginal is greater than the average, the average will rise.
- If the marginal is less than the average, the average will fall.
- If the marginal equals the average, the average remains constant.

Since the monopolist's average revenue curve falls as output or sales rise, marginal revenue *must* be below average revenue. This relationship is shown in Figure 5.7, which depicts a monopolist's AR and MR curves, with the MR curve drawn twice as steep as the AR curve. This is always the case whenever the AR curve is a straight line or linear. This mathematical property does not apply, however, when the AR curve is non-linear, although the MR curve will always be below the AR curve as long as the AR curve is falling.

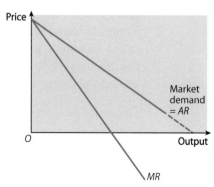

Figure 5.7 Monopoly average revenue and marginal revenue curves

The next diagram, Figure 5.8, explains the relationship between a monopolist's AR and MR curves. Because the demand curve (or AR curve) facing the monopolist is downward sloping, the firm can only sell an extra unit of output by reducing the price at which *all* units of output are sold. Total sales revenue increases by the area k in Figure 5.8, but decreases by the area h. Areas k and h respectively show the revenue gain (namely the extra unit sold multiplied by its price) and the revenue loss resulting from the sale of an extra unit of output. The revenue loss results from the fact that in order to sell 1 more unit of output, the price has to be reduced for *all* units of output, not just the extra unit sold.

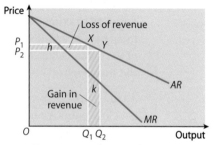

Figure 5.8 Explaining the monopolist's MR curve

Marginal revenue, which is the revenue gain minus the revenue loss (or $k - h$), must be less than price or average revenue (area k).

Equilibrium in monopoly

The profit-maximising or equilibrium level of output in monopoly is shown in Figure 5.9. As in perfect competition, the equilibrium output Q_1 is located at point A, where $MR = MC$. It is worth repeating that, providing the firm is a profit-maximiser, the equilibrium equation $MR = MC$ applies to any firm, whatever the market structure. However, in monopoly, point A does *not* show the equilibrium price, which is instead located at point B on the demand curve or AR curve above point A. The equilibrium price is P_1, which is the *maximum* price the monopolist can charge and succeed in selling output Q_1.

You will notice that Figure 5.9 does not distinguish between *short-run* and *long-run* equilibrium in monopoly. This is because a monopoly is protected by barriers to entry, which prevent new firms entering the market to share in the supernormal profit made by the monopolist. Entry barriers enable the monopolist to preserve supernormal profits in the long run as well as in the short run. By contrast, in perfect competition, supernormal profits are temporary, being restricted to the short run. Indeed, in monopoly, supernormal profits are often called **monopoly profit**. A monopolist has the market power to preserve profit by keeping competitors out.

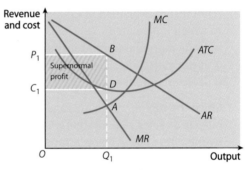

Figure 5.9 Monopoly equilibrium

Elasticity of demand in monopoly

It is often said that a monopolist's ability to exploit consumers is greatest when demand is price inelastic and consumers are captive, in the sense that no substitutes are available. While it is true that a monopolist can produce under the inelastic section of the AR curve to maximise profit, a monopoly must produce under the elastic section of the demand curve or AR curve facing the firm. Figure 5.10 shows why.

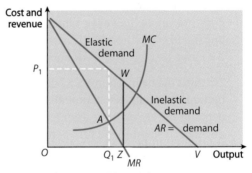

Figure 5.10 Monopoly equilibrium and elasticity

As in Figure 5.9, profit maximisation in Figure 5.10 occurs at output Q_1. Output Q_1 is below point A on the diagram, where $MR = MC$. Now, because marginal cost is positive at all levels of output, marginal revenue also has to be positive at Q_1 where $MR = MC$. Yet, whenever MR is positive, demand is price elastic. As already explained, when the demand curve (or AR curve) is linear and downward sloping,

the monopolist's *MR* curve is twice as steep as the *AR* or demand curve. In Figure 5.10, the *MR* curve intersects the quantity axis at point *Z*, which is exactly half way between the origin and point *V*, where the *AR* curve meets the quantity axis. The vertical line above point *Z* cuts the average revenue curve at point *W*, which is also half way along the *AR* curve. We know from Chapter 3 that demand is elastic at all points on the top half of a linear downward-sloping demand curve, and inelastic at all points on the bottom half. Bringing all these points together, the profit-maximising level of output Q_1 must lie under the top half of the average revenue curve. If it wishes to maximise profit, the monopoly must produce under the elastic section of the demand curve, even though monopoly power may appear to be greater when demand is inelastic.

*e*xaminer's voice

Questions in the Unit 5 examination on perfect competition, monopoly or oligopoly may be synoptic, testing your understanding of and ability to apply the concept of elasticity introduced in the AS course.

Evaluating perfect competition and monopoly

We shall use two different sets of concepts to answer questions such as: is perfect competition preferable to monopoly; and are there any circumstances in which monopoly can be justified? First, we shall introduce and apply efficiency concepts, before making use of the concepts of consumer surplus and producer surplus to examine the effects of perfect competition and monopoly on economic welfare.

Economic efficiency

You must always remember that a fundamental purpose of any economic system is to achieve the highest possible state of human happiness or welfare. Within a market economy, perfect competition and monopoly must ultimately be judged on the extent to which they contribute to improving human happiness and well-being, while remembering, of course, that perfect competition is an abstract and unreal market structure.

In order to judge the contribution of a market structure to human welfare, we must first assess the extent to which the market structure is efficient or inefficient. We shall now explain some of the meanings that economists attach to the word 'efficiency', before discussing the extent to which perfect competition and monopoly can be considered efficient or inefficient.

Technical efficiency

A production process is technically efficient if it maximises the output produced from the available inputs or factors of production. Alternatively, we may say that at any level of output, production is technically efficient if it minimises the inputs of capital, labour, etc. needed to produce that level of output.

Productive efficiency or cost efficiency

Productive efficiency represents the translation into money costs of technical efficiency. To achieve productive efficiency, a firm must use the techniques and factors of production that are available, at the lowest possible cost per unit of output. In the short run, the lowest point on the relevant short-run average total cost curve

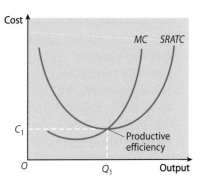

Figure 5.11 Productive efficiency in the short run

locates the most productively efficient level of output for the particular scale of operation. Short-run productive efficiency is shown in Figure 5.11.

However, *true* productive efficiency is a long-run rather than a short-run concept. A firm's long-run average cost curve shows the lowest unit cost of producing different levels of output at all the different possible scales of production. The most productively efficient of all the levels of output occurs at the lowest point on the firm's *long-run* average cost curve. This is shown at output Q_N in Figure 5.12. Output Q_1 is also productively efficient, but only for the short-run cost curve $SRATC_1$.

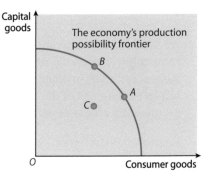

Figure 5.13 Productive and technical efficiency illustrated on a production possibility frontier

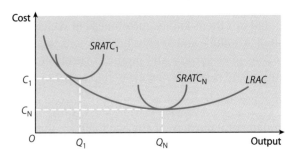

Figure 5.12 Short-run and long-run productive efficiency

Figure 5.13 illustrates another application of the concept of productive efficiency. All points such as *A* and *B* on the production possibility frontier drawn for the whole economy are productively (and also technically) efficient. When the economy is on its production possibility frontier, it is only possible to increase output of capital goods by reducing output of consumer goods (and vice versa). By contrast, a point such as *C* inside the frontier is productively and technically inefficient. Output of capital goods could be increased by using inputs in a technically more efficient way, without reducing output of consumer goods.

X-efficiency

In the 1960s, the US economist Harvey Leibenstein argued that, due to organisational slack resulting from the absence of competitive pressures, monopolies are always likely to be technically and productively inefficient. This happens at all levels of output. Leibenstein introduced the term **X-inefficiency** to explain organisational slack.

Consider the short-run average total cost curve illustrated in Figure 5.14, which shows the lowest possible unit costs of producing various levels of output. This curve assumes such conditions of production as the scale of the firm's fixed capacity and the prices of the factors of production used to produce the good. According to the cost curve, it is impossible for the firm to produce output Q_1 at a level of unit costs or average costs below C_1. A point such as A, at which average costs are C_2, cannot be reached, unless the cost curve shifts downward over time. Conversely, if factors of production are combined in a technically inefficient way, unit costs greater than C_1 would be incurred when producing output Q_1. In this case, the firm would be producing off its cost curve, at a point such as X, at which average costs are C_3 rather than C_1.

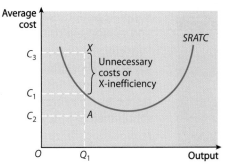

Figure 5.14 *X-inefficiency occurring when a firm incurs unnecessary costs*

Point X, and indeed any point above or off the cost curve, is said to be X-inefficient. All points on the cost curve (including the productively efficient point where unit cost is lowest) are X-efficient. X-inefficiency occurs whenever, for the level of output it is producing, the firm incurs unnecessary production costs: in other words, if the firm wished, it could reduce costs.

There are two main causes of X-inefficiency. First, a firm may simply be technically inefficient: for example, employing too many workers (over-staffing) or investing in machines that it never uses. Second, X-inefficiency can also be caused by the firm paying its workers or managers unnecessarily high wages or salaries, or buying raw materials or capital at unnecessarily high prices. X-efficiency requires that the lowest possible prices are paid for inputs or factors of production.

Allocative efficiency

This rather abstract concept is of great importance to the understanding of economic efficiency. Allocative efficiency occurs when $P = MC$ in all industries and markets in the economy. To explain this further, we must examine closely both P and MC. The price of a good, P, is a measure of the value in consumption placed by buyers on the last unit consumed. P indicates the utility or welfare obtained at the margin in consumption. This is the good's opportunity cost in consumption. For example, a consumer spending £1 on a bar of chocolate cannot spend the pound on other goods. At the same time, MC measures the good's opportunity cost in production: that is, the value of the resources that go into the production of the last unit, in their best alternative uses.

Suppose that all the economy's markets divide into two categories: those in which $P > MC$ and those in which $P < MC$. In the markets where $P > MC$, households pay a price for the last unit consumed which is greater than the cost of producing the last unit of the good. The high price discourages consumption, so we conclude that at this price the good is under-produced and under-consumed. Conversely, in the second set of markets in which $P < MC$, the value (P) placed on the last unit consumed by households is less than the MC of the resources used to produce the last unit. The price is too low, encouraging too much consumption of the good; thus at this price the good is over-produced and over-consumed.

Suppose resources can be taken from the second group of markets where $P < MC$ and reallocated to the former group of markets in which $P > MC$. Arguably, total consumer welfare or utility will increase as reallocation of resources takes place. As the reallocation proceeds, prices tend to fall in those markets *into which* resources are being shifted and prices tend to increase in the markets *from which* resources are being moved. Eventually, as prices adjust, P equals MC in all markets simultaneously. Beyond the point at which $P = MC$ in all markets, no further reallocation of resources between markets can improve consumer welfare (assuming, of course, that all the other factors which influence welfare, such as the distribution of income, remain unchanged). The outcome in which $P = MC$ in all markets is allocatively efficient.

In summary, allocative inefficiency occurs when $P > MC$ or $P < MC$. For any given employment of resources and any initial distribution of income and wealth among the population, total consumer welfare can increase if resources are reallocated from markets where $P < MC$ into those where $P > MC$, until allocative efficiency is achieved when $P = MC$ in all markets.

Dynamic efficiency

All the forms of efficiency so far considered are examples of **static efficiency**: that is, efficiency measured at a particular point in time. By contrast, **dynamic efficiency** measures improvements in technical and productive efficiency that occur *over time*. Improvements in dynamic efficiency result from the introduction of better methods of producing existing products (including firms' ability to benefit to a greater extent from economies of scale), and also from developing and marketing completely new products. In both cases, invention, innovation and research and development (R & D) improve dynamic efficiency. (**Invention** refers to advancements in pure science, whereas **innovation** is the application of scientific developments to production.)

ℯxaminer's voice

For AS exams, you must know that any point on a production possibility frontier is productively efficient, and that allocative efficiency is achieved only when the goods and services produced in the economy match people's needs and preferences. For A2 exams, you should know much more about productive and allocative efficiency, together with the difference between static and dynamic efficiency. Despite the fact that neither exam requires knowledge of technical efficiency or X-efficiency, these concepts may well be useful when analysing and evaluating market structures for Unit 5 questions on market structures.

Perfect competition and economic efficiency

Figure 5.15 (which is similar to Figure 5.5) shows the long-run equilibrium of a perfectly competitive firm. The diagram clearly demonstrates that a perfectly competitive firm achieves both productive and allocative efficiency in the long run, provided there are no economies of scale. The firm is productively efficient because it produces the optimum output at the lowest point on the *ATC* curve, and it is allocatively efficient because $P = MC$. (Strictly, we should qualify this conclusion by stating that the firm is allocatively efficient only if *all* markets in the economy are perfectly competitive and in long-run equilibrium, which means that every firm in every market is producing where $P = MC$.)

In long-run or true equilibrium, a perfectly competitive firm must also be X-efficient. The reason is simple. If the firm is X-inefficient, producing at a level of unit costs above its *ATC* curve, the firm could not make normal profits in the long run. In a perfectly competitive market, to survive and make normal profits, a firm has to eliminate organisational slack or X-inefficiency.

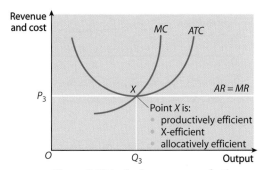

Figure 5.15 In the long run, a perfectly competitive firm is productively, allocatively and X-efficient

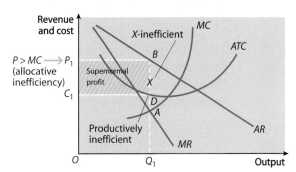

Figure 5.16 A monopoly is productively and allocatively inefficient, and it is likely to be X-inefficient

Monopoly and economic efficiency

In contrast to perfect competition — and once again assuming an absence of economies of scale — monopoly equilibrium is both productively and allocatively inefficient. Figure 5.16 (which is similar to Figure 5.9) shows that at the profit-maximising level of output Q_1, the monopolist's average costs are above the minimum level and $P > MC$. Thus, compared to a firm in perfect competition, a monopoly produces too low an output, which it sells at too high a price.

The absence of competitive pressures, which in perfect competition serve to eliminate supernormal profit, means that a monopoly is also likely to be X-inefficient, incurring average costs at a point such as X which is above the average cost curve. A monopoly may be able to survive, perfectly happily and enjoying an 'easy life', incurring unnecessary production costs and making satisfactory rather than maximum profits. A monopolist is protected by market entry barriers. As a result, the absence of competitive forces means there is no mechanism in a monopoly to eliminate organisational inefficiency.

Natural monopoly and economies of scale

On the basis of the above analysis, it seems we can conclude that perfect competition is both productively and allocatively efficient whereas monopoly is neither. Monopoly is also likely to be X-inefficient. However, the conclusion that perfect competition is

productively more efficient than monopoly depends on an assumption that there are no economies of scale. When substantial economies of scale are possible in an industry, monopoly may be more productively efficient than competition.

Figure 5.17 illustrates a natural monopoly where, because of limited market size, there is insufficient room in the market for more than one firm benefiting from full economies of scale. The monopoly may, of course, be producing above the lowest point on short-run average cost curve $SRATC_N$, hence exhibiting a degree of productive inefficiency. However, *all* points on $SRATC_N$ incur lower unit costs – and are productively *more* efficient – than any point on $SRATC_1$, which is the relevant cost curve for each firm if the monopoly is broken into a number of smaller competitive enterprises.

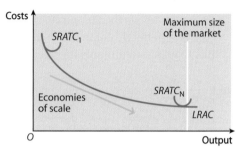

Figure 5.17 The justification of monopoly when economies of scale are possible

Dynamic efficiency in monopoly

Under certain circumstances, monopolies may also be more *dynamically efficient* than a perfectly competitive firm. Protected by entry barriers, a monopoly earns monopoly profit without facing the threat that the profit disappears when new firms enter the market. This allows an innovating monopoly to enjoy, in the form of monopoly profit, the fruits of successful research and development (R & D) and product development. The Austrian-American economist, Joseph Schumpeter, argued that firms with considerable market power, including monopolies, may be prepared to take risks, innovate, and introduce new technologies, in a process of 'creative destruction' of old technologies and ways of producing goods. By contrast, in highly competitive markets there may be little or no incentive to innovate because other firms can 'free ride' and gain costless access to the results of any successful research. This argument justifies **patent** legislation, which grants a firm the right to exploit the monopoly position created by innovation for a number of years before the patent expires.

However, there is a counter-argument that monopoly reduces rather than promotes innovation and dynamic efficiency. Protected from competitive pressures, as we have noted, a monopoly may *profit-satisfice* rather than *profit-maximise*, content with satisfactory profits and an easy life.

Perfect competition, monopoly and economic welfare

To explain how market structures affect economic welfare, we must first introduce the concepts of **consumer surplus** and **producer surplus**. Consumer surplus and producer surplus are measures of welfare, as their names imply, respectively for consumers and firms. Both are illustrated in Figure 5.18.

Consumer surplus is the difference between the *maximum price* that a consumer is prepared to pay and the *actual price* he or she needs to pay. In a competitive market such as Figure 5.18(a), the total consumer surplus enjoyed by all the consumers in the market is measured by the triangular area P_1EA. Consumer welfare increases whenever consumer surplus increases — for example, when market prices fall. Conversely, however, higher prices reduce consumer surplus and welfare.

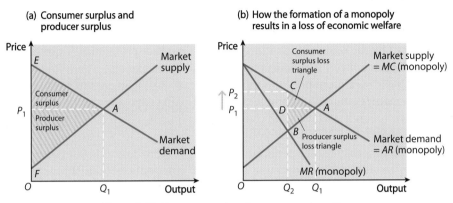

Figure 5.18 *How monopoly reduces economic welfare*

Producer surplus, which is a measure of producers' welfare, is the difference between the *minimum price* that a firm is prepared to charge for a good and the *actual price* charged. In Figure 5.18(a), the producer surplus enjoyed by all the firms in the market is measured by the triangular area FP_1A.

Figure 5.18(b) illustrates what happens to economic welfare when monopoly replaces perfect competition (assuming there are no economies of scale). Market equilibrium in perfect competition is determined at point A; output is Q_1 and price is P_1. However, monopoly equilibrium is determined at point B, where $MR = MC$. *(Note that the marginal cost curve in monopoly is the same curve as market supply in perfect competition.)* The diagram illustrates the standard case against monopoly, namely that compared to perfect competition, monopoly restricts output (to Q_2) and raises price (to P_2).

But we can take the analysis one stage further and investigate how *consumer surplus* and *producer surplus* (and hence *economic welfare*) are affected. Raising the price from P_1 to P_2 transfers consumer surplus equal to the rectangular area P_1P_2CD to the monopoly. This means that producer surplus (in the form of monopoly profit) increases at the expense of consumer surplus. Over and above this transfer, however, there is a *net loss of economic welfare* caused by the fact that the amount bought and sold falls to Q_2. The welfare loss is shown by the two shaded triangular areas in Figure 5.18(b), which depict the loss of consumer surplus (the top triangle) and the loss of producer surplus (the bottom triangle).

*e***xaminer's voice**

It is important to understand consumer surplus and producer surplus in order to analyse how economic welfare may be affected by events that raise or lower the price of a good. The next chapter uses consumer and producer surplus in the analysis of price discrimination, and Chapter 20 applies the concepts when analysing free trade and the effect of tariffs.

Consumer sovereignty and producer sovereignty

Perfect competition has the advantage of promoting **consumer sovereignty**, which means that the goods and services produced in a perfectly competitive market economy are those that consumers want. Firms and industries which produce goods other than those for which consumers are prepared to pay, do not survive in perfect competition. By contrast, a monopoly may impose **producer sovereignty** on to consumers. The goods and services available for consumers to buy are determined by the monopolist rather than by consumer preferences expressed in the marketplace. Even if producer sovereignty is not exercised on a 'take-it-or-leave-it' basis by a monopoly, the monopolist may still possess sufficient market power to manipulate consumer wants through persuasive advertising.

Why firms like to become monopolies

Economists generally regard perfect competition as more desirable than monopoly. However, the desirable properties of perfect competition (namely, economic efficiency, welfare maximisation and consumer sovereignty) do not result from any assumption that business people or entrepreneurs in competitive industries are more highly motivated or public spirited than monopolists. Economic theory assumes that everyone is motivated by self-interest and by self-interest alone. This applies just as much to firms in competitive markets as it does to monopolies. Entrepreneurs in competitive industries would very much like to become monopolists, both to gain an easier life and also to make bigger profits. Indeed, from a firm's point of view, successful competition means eliminating competition and becoming a monopoly. But in perfect markets, market forces (Adam Smith referred to the **'invisible hand'** of the market), and the absence of barriers to entry and exit, prevent this happening.

Imagine, for example, a situation in which a firm in a perfectly competitive industry makes a technical breakthrough that reduces production costs. For a short time, the firm can make supernormal profits. But because, in perfect competition, perfect market information is available to all firms, other firms within the market and new entrants attracted to the market can also enjoy the lower production costs. A new long-run equilibrium will soon be brought about — at the lower level of costs resulting from the breakthrough — with all firms once again making normal profits only.

Ultimately, of course, consumers benefit from lower prices brought about by technical progress and the forces of competition. However it is market forces, and not some socially benign motive or public spirit assumed on the part of entrepreneurs, that accounts for the optimality of perfect competition as a market structure.

How competitive is perfect competition?

Although perfect competition is an abstract and unreal market structure, it is interesting to consider how competition might take place in a perfectly competitive market economy. The first point to note is that price competition, in the form of price wars or price cutting by individual firms, would not take place. In perfect competition, all firms are passive price-takers, able to sell all the output they produce at the ruling market price determined in the market as a whole. In this situation, firms cannot gain sales or market share by price cutting. Other forms of competition, involving the use of advertising, packaging, brand-imaging or the provision of after-sales service to differentiate a firm's product from those of its competitors, simply destroy the conditions of perfect competition. These are the forms of competition which are prevalent, together with price competition, in the imperfectly competitive markets of the real economy in which we live.

So the only form of competition that is both available to firms and compatible with maintaining the conditions of perfect competition is cost-cutting competition. Cost-cutting competition is likely in perfect competition because each firm has an incentive to reduce costs in order to make supernormal profit. But even the existence of cost-cutting competition in a perfect market can be questioned. Why should firms finance research into cost-cutting technical progress when they know that other firms have instant access to all market information and that any super-normal profits resulting from successful cost cutting can only be temporary?

Think also of the nature of competition in a perfect market, from the perspective of a typical consumer. The choice is simultaneously very broad and very narrow. The consumer has the doubtful luxury of maximum choice in terms of the number of firms or suppliers from whom to purchase a product. Yet each firm is supplying an identical good or service at exactly the same price. In this sense, there is no choice at all in perfect competition.

Summary

This chapter began by explaining how the theoretical models of perfect competition and pure monopoly are located at opposite ends of the spectrum of market structures. Pure monopoly is rare, while perfect competition is non-existent in the real economy. However, both market structures should be regarded as abstract models or benchmarks against which to judge the properties of the imperfectly competitive markets of the world we live in.

A profit-maximising objective on the part of firms is the starting assumption for the theory of the firm. This gives rise to the concept of an equilibrium firm producing the output at which $(TR - TC)$ is maximised, and at which $MR = MC$. For all market structures, profit maximisation occurs at the level of output at which $MR = MC$.

In perfect competition, we distinguish between short-run and long-run equilibrium,

and note that only in the long run can new firms enter the industry, attracted by supernormal profits made in the short run by firms already in the market. By contrast, in pure monopoly, barriers to entry prevent new firms entering the market in the long run. Monopoly equilibrium is the same in the long run as in the short run, except when economies of scale enable a monopoly to move in the long run to a new, and more productively efficient, average cost curve.

In terms of productive efficiency, perfect competition is more efficient than monopoly, provided there are no economies of scale. Because the price charged equals the marginal cost of production $(P = MC)$, perfect competition is allocatively efficient too, whereas in monopoly $P > MC$. To survive, perfectly competitive firms must also eliminate

X-inefficiency. By contrast, protected by entry barriers, monopolies can end up X-inefficient, incurring unnecessary costs. Other advantages of perfect competition include consumer sovereignty — as distinct from the producer sovereignty of the monopolist — and greater consumer surplus because output is higher and the market price is lower than in a monopoly. Again, the last conclusion depends on an absence of economies of scale.

Two arguments can be used to justify some monopolies. These are economies of scale, which lead to greater productive efficiency in the long run, and improvements in dynamic efficiency. Monopolies may be dynamically efficient because the prospect of future monopoly profit favours R & D and the introduction of improved methods of production and new products. However, the reverse is true for those monopolies protected by entry barriers, which simply prefer an 'easy life'.

Self-testing questions

1 Why is perfect competition an unreal market structure?

2 Explain why profit is maximised when $MR = MC$.

3 Why is a perfectly competitive firm's average revenue curve horizontal?

4 Distinguish between normal and supernormal profit.

5 Draw a diagram to show short-run equilibrium in perfect competition.

6 What happens to supernormal profit in the long run in perfect competition?

7 State four causes of monopoly.

8 Explain the relationship between average revenue and marginal revenue in monopoly.

9 Draw a diagram to show monopoly equilibrium.

10 How does elasticity of demand affect monopoly?

11 Briefly explain the main types of economic efficiency.

12 Is perfect competition efficient?

13 Is monopoly efficient?

14 How do economies of scale affect productive efficiency?

15 How does monopoly affect consumer surplus compared to perfect competition?

16 Is monopoly necessarily more dynamically efficient than perfect competition?

Chapter 6
Oligopoly

Specification focus

This chapter centres solely on the A2 Module 5 specification, covering one of the main areas of advanced microeconomics. Besides explaining the market structure known as oligopoly, the chapter explains pricing strategies undertaken by monopolies as well as by oligopolistic firms.

A2 **Module 5 Business Economics and the Distribution of Income**
Concentrated Markets; Government Intervention in the Market

A2 **Synoptic coverage**
Basic knowledge of markets learnt at AS is relevant for Unit 5 A2 examination questions on oligopoly and firms' pricing.

Introduction

Almost all real-world markets are imperfectly competitive, lying between the extremes of monopoly and perfect competition. Imperfect competition is a wide-ranging term, covering all market structures from duopoly (two firms only in a market) to highly competitive markets that are very close to being perfectly competitive. This chapter explains one of the most important forms of imperfect competition: oligopoly. We shall look first at competitive oligopoly, in which a relatively small number of firms compete against each other. We shall then examine conditions in which competitive oligopolists may be tempted to collude or cooperate with each other, and form cartels.

What is oligopoly?

Oligopoly is a form of *imperfect competition.* Remember that *perfect* and *imperfect competition* are both misleading labels. The word 'perfect' suggests a state of competition that cannot be bettered. Likewise, imperfect competition implies inferior or second-rate competition. But imperfect competition is *realistic* competition, accurately portraying real-world markets and firms' behaviour in such markets. By contrast, perfect competition is *unrealistic* competition: indeed, a theoretical abstraction.

Oligopoly can be defined in terms of both market structure and market behaviour.

Oligopoly and market structure

Market structure refers to the number of firms in a market. **Oligopoly**, which is a market structure in which there are a relatively small number of firms, is sometimes called *imperfect competition among the few.* **Duopoly** is a special case of oligopoly in which there are only two firms. Oligopolistic firms are not pure monopolies, but they possess monopoly power. You must avoid confusing *monopoly power* with *monopoly.* Pure monopoly is a precise market structure, but firms in all imperfectly competitive markets can exercise a greater or lesser degree of monopoly power — for example, by imposing entry barriers that enable firms to raise the price of a good. Whenever firms exercise producer sovereignty in this way, monopoly power exists.

Concentration ratios provide a good indicator of oligopolistic market structures. For example, a **four-firm concentration ratio** shows the percentage of output in an industry produced by the four largest firms in the industry. The four-firm concentration ratio in the UK supermarket industry shown in Table 6.1 is 94.3. Since 2003 the supermarket industry has become even more concentrated, partly through market leaders such as Tesco buying up large numbers of small stores.

Table 6.1 Market concentration in the UK supermarket industry, year to January 2003

Supermarket group	Market share (%)
Tesco	31.3
Sainsbury's	21.9
Asda	21.5
Morrisons/Safeway	19.6
Others	5.7

Source: *Financial Times,* 27 September 2003.

examiner's voice

The compulsory data-response question in the Unit 1 exam may include a table showing the number of firms in the market. Practise calculating concentration ratios and writing about evidence of concentration in the market.

Tesco: imperfect competition among the few

Oligopoly and market behaviour or conduct

Oligopoly is best defined, however, not by market structure or the number of firms in the market, but by **market conduct**, or the behaviour of firms within the market. An oligopolistic firm affects its rivals through its price and output decisions, but its own profit can also be affected by how rivals behave and react to the firm's decisions. Suppose, for example, that the firm reduces its price in order to increase market share and boost profit. Whether the price reduction increases the firm's profit depends on the likely reactions of the other firms. So, when deciding whether to lower its price, the firm must make assumptions about likely responses by other firms.

Perfect and imperfect oligopoly

Perfect oligopoly exists when the oligopolists produce a uniform or homogeneous product such as petrol. One brand of petrol is really a perfect substitute for any other brand, although a petrol company such as Shell may use advertising to try to persuade motorists that Shell petrol is different from and better than other brands. By contrast, **imperfect oligopoly** exists when the products produced by the firms are by their nature differentiated and imperfect substitutes: for example, automobiles.

Competitive oligopoly

Competitive oligopoly exists when the rival firms are *interdependent* in the sense that they must take account of the reactions of one another when forming a market strategy. But they are *independent* in the sense that they decide their market strategies without cooperation or collusion. The existence of uncertainty is a characteristic of competitive oligopoly — a firm can never be completely certain of how rivals will react to its marketing strategy. If the firm raises its price, will the rivals follow suit or will they hold their prices steady in the hope of gaining sales and market share?

> **examiner's voice**
> Examination questions may ask you to explain why inter-dependence and uncertainty exist in markets dominated by a few firms. Oligopoly itself may not be mentioned in the question.

The kinked demand curve theory

The kinked demand curve theory can be used to illustrate how a competitive oligopolist may be affected by rivals' reactions to its price and output decisions. The theory was originally developed to explain alleged price rigidity and an absence of price wars in oligopo-listic markets.

Suppose an oligopolist initially produces output Q_1 in Figure 6.1, selling this output at price P_1. In order to anticipate how sales might change following a price change, firms need to know the position and shape of the demand and revenue curves for their products. But in imperfectly competitive markets, firms lack accurate information about demand and revenue

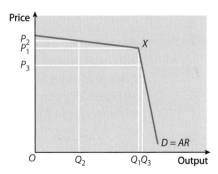

Figure 6.1 The kinked demand curve

curves, particularly at outputs significantly different from those currently being produced. This means that the demand curve or *AR* curve in Figure 6.1 is not necessarily the correct or *actual* demand curve for the oligopolist's output. Instead, it represents the firm's *estimate* or guess of how demand changes when its selling price changes.

When *increasing* price from P_1 to P_2, the oligopolist expects rivals to react by keeping their own prices stable and not following suit. By holding their prices steady, rivals try to gain profit and market share at the firm's expense. The oligopolist expects demand to be *relatively elastic* in response to a price increase. The rise in price from P_1 to P_2 is likely to result in a *more than proportionate fall in demand* from Q_1 to Q_2.

Conversely, when *cutting* its price from P_1 to P_3, the oligopolist expects rivals to react in a very different way, namely by following suit immediately with a matching price cut. In this situation, because the market demand curve for the products of all the firms slopes downward, each firm will benefit from some increase in demand. However, the oligopolist fails to gain sales from rivals within the market. This means that the oligopolist expects demand to be less elastic, and possibly *relatively inelastic* in response to a price cut. The fall in price from P_1 to P_3 may result in a *less than proportionate increase in demand* from Q_1 to Q_3. The oligopolist therefore expects rivals to react *asymmetrically* when price is raised or lowered.

In Figure 6.1, the oligopolist's initial price and output of P_1 to Q_1 intersect at point *X*, or at the 'kink' at the junction of two demand curves of different elasticity. Each part of the curve reflects a different assumption about how rivals may react to a change in price. In this situation, the oligopolist expects both a price increase and a price cut to reduce total profit. Given these assumptions, the best policy may be to leave the price unchanged.

The theory provides a second reason why prices may tend to be stable in oligopoly. As Figure 6.2 illustrates, there is a vertical section in the *MR* curve at output Q_1. This links the marginal revenue curves associated respectively with the relatively elastic and relatively less elastic demand (or average revenue) curves. Suppose initially the firm's marginal cost curve is MC_1, intersecting the *MR* curve at point *A* in its vertical section. The diagram shows that the *MC* curve can rise or fall within the vertical section of the *MR* curve, without altering the profit-maximising output Q_1 or price P_1. But if marginal costs rise above MC_2 at point *B* or fall below MC_3 at point *C*, the profit-maximising output changes. The oligopolist would have to set a different price to maximise profits, providing of course that the *AR* curve accurately measures demand for the firm's product at different prices. Nevertheless, the oligopolist's

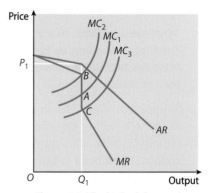

Figure 6.2 The kinked demand curve and stable prices in oligopoly

selling price remains stable at P_1 as long as the marginal cost curve lies between MC_2 and MC_3.

Criticisms of the kinked demand curve theory

There are a number of weaknesses in the theory of the kinked demand curve. Although at first sight it offers a neat and apparently plausible explanation of price stability in conditions of oligopoly, few economists now accept the kinked demand theory of oligopoly pricing.

First, it is an *incomplete* theory. It does not explain how and why a firm chooses in the first place to be at point X. Secondly, the evidence provided by the pricing decisions of real-world firms gives little support to the theory. Competitive oligopolists seldom respond to price changes in the manner assumed in the kinked demand curve theory. It is more reasonable to expect a firm to 'test the market': that is, to raise or lower its selling price to see if rivals react in the manner expected. If they do not, then the firm must surely revise its estimate of the shape of the demand curve facing it. Research has shown fairly conclusively that oligopoly prices tend to be stable or sticky when demand conditions change in a predictable or cyclical way. However, oligopolists usually raise or lower prices quickly and by significant amounts, both when production costs change substantially and when unexpected shifts in demand occur.

examiner's voice
Students often wrongly believe that the kinked demand curve provides a complete theory of oligopoly. It is actually a very doubtful theory, but it does illustrate how oligopolists are interdependent and affected by uncertainty.

Other aspects of pricing in oligopolistic markets

The ways in which prices are set in oligopolistic markets can be quite complicated. Some of these pricing methods are explained below.

Cost-plus pricing

Cost-plus pricing, also known as **mark-up pricing** and **full-cost pricing**, is the most common pricing procedure used by firms in imperfectly competitive markets. It means that a firm sets the selling price by adding a standard percentage profit margin to average or unit costs:

$$P = AFC + AVC + \text{profit margin}$$

When customers are captive and willing to pay high prices, the profit mark-up can be high — for fashionable goods that may quickly go out of style, often over 100%. But when markets are more competitive, firms may find it much more difficult to charge a mark-up. Indeed, in a very competitive market, the mark-up may be limited to a size that gives firms normal profit only, which then deters or limits the entrance of new firms into the market.

examiner's voice
Firms in real-world markets seldom use the $MR = MC$ rule when setting prices. They are much more likely to undertake cost-plus pricing.

Price parallelism

Price parallelism occurs when there are identical prices and price movements within an industry or market. It can be caused by two different sets of circumstances, which make it difficult to decide whether the market is highly competitive

or collusive. On the one hand, price parallelism can occur in a very competitive market, resembling perfect competition, where firms all charge a ruling market price determined by demand and supply in the market as a whole. But on the other hand, price parallelism results from price leadership in tightly oligopolistic industries, where overt or tacit price collusion occurs.

Price leadership

Because overt collusive agreements to fix the market price, such as cartel agreements, are usually illegal, imperfectly competitive firms often use less formal or tacit ways to coordinate their pricing decisions. An example of covert collusion is **price leadership**, which occurs when one firm becomes the market leader and other firms in the industry follow its pricing example.

Three different types of price leadership have been identified:

- **Dominant price leadership.** When there is just one large firm in a market, the dominant firm can set a price to satisfy its own needs, taking into account also the anticipated reactions of a large number of small competitors that are each too small to have a noticeable effect on price. The smaller firms in effect behave like perfect competitors, adjusting their output decisions to the 'market price' set by the dominant price leader. The dominant firm might in principle be able to use its cost advantages to reduce prices and force the smaller firms out of business. However, fear of government intervention and knowledge that the small firms might easily re-enter the market once profit margins were restored can explain why the dominant firm tolerates the survival of smaller firms.

- **Collusive price leadership.** When several large firms together dominate the market, different firms may set the price at different times. It is usually easiest for one of the firms to set a price which its rivals will follow when: there are only a few firms; the firms produce close substitutes; the firms' cost curves are similar; there are barriers to entry; demand is relatively inelastic.

- **Barometric price leadership.** On occasion, however, the price leader acts as a barometer of market conditions, indicating the various pressures on price. Within the market, the barometric price leader may change over time, but it is likely to be a firm monitored by the other firms because of its ability to respond to market conditions rather than because it is necessarily larger or more efficient. If, in the view of its rivals, the barometric price leader makes a wrong assessment of the market, its price may not be followed and the firm may have to change its decision if it is to keep its market share.

Limit pricing

When natural barriers to market entry are low or non-existent, incumbent firms (that is, firms already in the market) may set low prices, known as **limit prices**, to deter new firms from entering the market. Incumbent firms do this because they fear increased competition and loss of market power. With limit pricing, firms already in the market sacrifice short-run profit maximisation in order to maximise long-run profits, achieved through deterring the entry of new firms.

Should limit pricing be regarded as an example of a competitive pricing strategy, which reduces prices and the supernormal profits enjoyed by the established firms in the market? Or is limit pricing basically anti-competitive and best regarded as an unjustifiable restrictive practice? The answer probably depends on circumstances, but when limit pricing extends into predatory pricing, there is a much clearer case that such a pricing strategy is anti-competitive and against consumers' interests.

Predatory pricing

Whereas limit pricing deters market entry, successful **predatory pricing** removes recent entrants to the market. Predatory pricing occurs when an established or incumbent firm deliberately sets prices below cost to force new market entrants out of business. Once the new entrants have left the market, the established firm may decide to restore prices to their previous levels.

Price discrimination

Price discrimination is charging different prices to different customers based on differences in customers' ability and willingness to pay. Those customers who are prepared to pay more are charged a higher price than those who are only willing to pay a lower price. In the main form of price discrimination, the different prices charged are not based on any differences in costs of production or supply. However, in one form of price discrimination, **bulk buying**, consumers are charged lower prices when buying larger quantities than when purchasing smaller quantities of the good. When this happens, different costs of supply may be involved. Bulk purchases generally have lower average costs of production than smaller purchases.

> **examiner's voice**
> It is only usually necessary to learn about one form of price discrimination, but you must also learn how to illustrate it on a diagram.

A closer look at price discrimination

The case of two sub-markets or market segments

In Figure 6.3 *a nightclub* divides its market into male and female customers, each with a different price elasticity of demand. At any price charged to enter the club, female demand is more elastic than male demand, indicating perhaps that women are less enthusiastic about the entertainment offered by the club. For both men and women, the demand curves shown in Figure 6.3 also show average revenue (*AR*), but not marginal revenue (*MR*). In each case, the *MR* curve is twice as steep as the

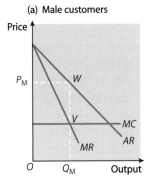

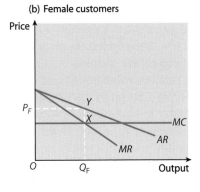

Figure 6.3
Price discrimination when a firm charges different prices to two groups of customers

AR curve. The diagrams also assume that the marginal cost (*MC*) incurred when an extra person enters the club is always the same. This is shown by the horizontal *MC* curve.

To maximise profit, *MR* must equal *MC* in both male and female sub-markets. As the diagrams show, this results in men paying a higher price than women for admission to the club. Men pay P_M, while women pay the lower price of P_F, and Q_M males and Q_F females are admitted. The different prices charged result from different male and female price elasticities of demand. Profit is maximised when more price-sensitive female customers pay less to enter the club than the less price-sensitive males. Note that the *MR* received from the last man and woman admitted are the same. If this were not the case, the club could increase profit by changing the numbers of men and women admitted.

The conditions necessary for successful price discrimination

Successful price discrimination requires that the following conditions are met:

- It must be possible to identify different groups of customers or markets for the product. This is possible when customers differ in their knowledge of the market or in their ability to 'shop around'. Some customers may have special needs for a product, and competition among oligopolists may vary in different parts of the market. In some geographical areas and for some products a firm may face many competitors, whereas in other parts of the market the firm may be the sole supplier.

- At any particular price, the different groups of customers must have different price elasticities of demand. Total profits will be maximised by charging a higher price in a market in which demand is less elastic. However, demand will never be inelastic, since this would require negative marginal revenue and this cannot occur at the profit-maximising level of output.

- The markets must be separated to prevent **seepage**. This takes place when customers buying at the lower price in one sub-market resell in another sub-market at a price that undercuts the oligopolist's own selling price in that market. In the European car market, car manufacturers have often charged higher prices for vehicles in the UK market than in mainland Europe. Seepage has occurred when specialist car importers have bought cars on the continent to resell in the UK market, thereby undercutting the manufacturers' recommended prices in the UK.

Why do firms price discriminate?

To understand why firms undertake price discrimination, we must first understand the concept of **consumer surplus**. As Chapter 5 explains, consumer surplus is a measure of the economic welfare enjoyed by consumers. It is the difference between the *maximum price* consumers are prepared to pay and the *actual price* they need to pay. The greater the quantity of consumer surplus enjoyed by consumers, the greater their 'happiness' or economic welfare. A rightward shift of the supply curve, which reduces the price of a good, increases consumer surplus. Conversely a leftward shift, which increases the good's price, reduces consumer surplus.

As Figures 6.4 and 6.5 illustrate, price discrimination allows firms to increase profit by taking consumer surplus away from consumers and converting it into extra above-normal profit. Figures 6.4(a) and (b) are basically the same diagram as Figure 6.3, but Figure 6.4(c) has been added to show the combined market: that is,

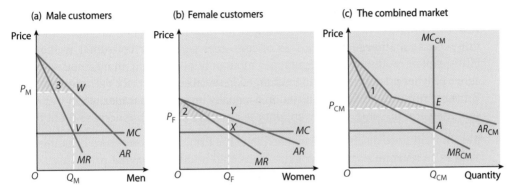

Figure 6.4 Price discrimination and the transfer of consumer surplus

male and female *AR* and *MR* curves added together. Note that for the combined market (but *not* the male and female sub-markets considered separately), the marginal cost curve is vertical as soon as the nightclub reaches full capacity.

In the absence of price discrimination, all consumers pay the same price, namely P_{CM} shown in Figure 6.4(c). Without price discrimination, consumer surplus is shown by the shaded area (labelled 1) above P_{CM} in Figure 6.4(c). But with price discrimination, when male customers are charged price P_M and female customers P_F, consumer surplus falls to equal the shaded areas 3 and 2 in Figures 6.4(a) and (b). The firm's profit has increased by transferring consumer surplus from consumers to the producer. **Producer welfare** (or producer surplus) has increased at the expense of **consumer welfare** (or consumer surplus).

Figure 6.5 illustrates a situation in which *all* the consumer surplus is transferred into producer surplus or producer welfare. Every customer is charged the maximum price that he or she is prepared to pay. Figure 6.5 is basically the same diagram used in the previous chapter to show monopoly equilibrium. In the absence of price discrimination, the firm produces the level of output Q_1 where $MR = MC$ and all customers are charged the price P_1. Supernormal profit is shown by the rectangle C_1P_1AB, and consumer surplus by the triangular area P_1ZA.

Now consider what happens when the firm charges each customer the maximum price that he or she is prepared to pay.

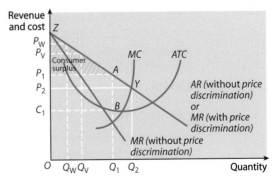

Figure 6.5 Price discrimination: the limiting case, when each consumer is charged the maximum price he or she is prepared to pay

Customer Q_V depicted in the diagram is charged price P_V, customer Q_W is charged P_W, and so on. In this situation, there may be as many prices as there are customers. Because each customer is paying the maximum price that he or she is prepared to pay, all the consumer surplus is transferred away from consumers to the firm, thereby boosting monopoly or oligopoly profit.

Can consumers benefit from price discrimination?

Price discrimination leads to a loss of consumer surplus or consumer welfare. Firms exploit producer sovereignty and monopoly power, and charge *most* consumers higher prices than would be charged in the absence of price discrimination. For these reasons, price discrimination is usually regarded as undesirable.

Nevertheless, *some* consumers (who may also be the poorest consumers) can benefit from price discrimination. Each time the firm sells to one more consumer, total sales revenue rises by the extra units sold multiplied by the price that the customer pays. Because consumers are charged different prices, the prices paid by other consumers are not affected. In the absence of price discrimination, the demand curve is the firm's *AR* curve, with the *MR* curve located below the demand curve. But when each customer is charged the maximum price he or she is prepared to pay, the demand curve becomes the firm's *MR* curve. The profit-maximising level of output, where $MR = MC$, shifts to Q_2, located at point Y in Figure 6.5. Customers who would not have bought the good at price P_1 buy the extra output. As a result, *most* consumers end up paying a price that is higher than P_1 (the equilibrium price in the absence of price discrimination), but *some* consumers pay a lower price. The lowest of all the prices charged is P_2, which is the price charged to the marginal, and perhaps the poorest, customer.

Consider also a situation in which a firm cannot make enough profit to stay in business unless some consumer surplus is taken from consumers and transferred to the producer. Market provision of healthcare by a doctor in an isolated village or very small town is an example. When charging the same price to all her patients, a doctor cannot earn enough income to continue to provide the service. Without an increase in income, the doctor will move to a larger city and local medical care will no longer be available in the village. But with price discrimination, the rich pay a higher price than the poor. Everybody gets some benefit and a needed service is provided.

> **examiner's voice**
> You must learn to explain how some consumers, as well as producers, can benefit from price discrimination.

Prices involving cross-subsidy

Many students confuse *price discrimination* with *cross-subsidy*, but the two concepts are completely different. In price discrimination, the marginal cost incurred by the firm is usually assumed to be the same for all customers, but the firm charges different prices based on customers' different willingness to pay. By contrast, when **cross-subsidy** takes place, all customers pay the same price, but the marginal cost of supplying the good varies between different customers.

For example, the Royal Mail charges the same price for all first-class letters of standard weight, whether posted locally or to distant parts of the UK. For local letters the marginal cost incurred by the Royal Mail delivering an extra letter is less than the price charged, but for letters delivered over a long distance, *MC* exceeds *P*. Customers posting local letters (for which *P* > *MC*) cross-subsidise letters mailed over greater distances (for which *P* < *MC*). The Post Office uses profits made on the former group to subsidise losses borne on letters posted over longer distances.

As price does not equal marginal cost, cross-subsidy results in allocative inefficiency. For firms, cross-subsidy is administratively convenient and it can maximise consumer goodwill, even though it fails to maximise profits. From the public interest point of view, cross-subsidy is sometimes justified for social or regional policy reasons — for example, when the better-off cross-subsidise the poor, or when customers in the more prosperous parts of the UK cross-subsidise those living in depressed regions. The provision of a universal service in which the same price is charged to people wherever they live in the UK also involves cross-subsidy.

> ### examiner's voice
> Firms often cross-subsidise because they want to charge administratively simple prices. You must not confuse cross-subsidy with price discrimination, but you can use cross-subsidy to provide an example of allocative inefficiency.

Marginal cost pricing and off-peak pricing

It is often argued that, to avoid cross-subsidy and to improve allocative efficiency, firms should charge customers different prices that reflect the marginal cost of providing the good or service consumed. This is called **marginal cost pricing**. In perfectly competitive markets, where firms would be passive 'price-takers', the market mechanism would automatically ensure that *P* = *MC*. But market pressures do not operate in this way in imperfectly competitive markets, where *P* > *MC*.

Nevertheless, when demand varies on a daily, weekly or seasonal basis, firms operating in imperfect markets may charge off-peak prices, which are a special case of marginal cost pricing. Transport, energy and tourist industries provide good examples. Consider the demand for electricity, which is higher in winter than in summer. Suppose demand for electricity increases in winter months. To meet this demand, power station companies must invest in new fixed capacity. This is a long-run marginal cost. By contrast, the marginal cost involved when meeting a surge in off-peak demand in the summer months is much lower. It is the short-run marginal cost of additional raw materials and labour. In summer, the electricity industry meets an increase in seasonal demand by using existing fixed capacity, which would otherwise lie idle in the off-peak months.

Electricity companies need extra capacity in winter months

Low off-peak prices and high peak prices are justified on the basis of differences in long-run and short-run marginal costs when providing a good or service at different times of day or year. By encouraging consumers to shift demand from the peak period of demand, off-peak pricing can achieve a better or more productively efficient utilisation of fixed capital throughout the day or year.

Transfer prices

Recent years have seen the proliferation of large business corporations, including multinational corporations operating subsidiary factories in many parts of the world. Many goods and services are transferred within the corporations, being 'sold' by one part of an enterprise to another part of the same business. These 'sales' are coordinated through the firm's administrative framework rather than through the market.

The setting of internal transfer prices between the subsidiaries owned by multi-national corporations has attracted attention because of the potential effects upon the economies of the countries in which the multinationals operate. A multi-national may set transfer prices to minimise the corporation's overall tax burden. Suppose, for example, that a multinational car company operates plants in the UK and Germany, which exchange engines and other car components with each other. If company taxation in the UK is significantly higher than in Germany, top management might order the UK subsidiary to sell below cost the components supplied to the German branch of the business. Conversely, the German plant might be instructed to set a high price for its 'exports' to the UK subsidiary. By manipulating transfer prices in this way, the parent company can declare profits in Germany so as to avoid company taxation in the UK.

In extreme cases, multinationals may set up subsidiary plants or offices in 'off-shore' tax havens: that is, countries with extremely liberal or relaxed tax regimes, which are often combined with a legal system allowing a high degree of business secrecy. Transactions undertaken between the multinational's productive subsidiaries are then diverted through the intermediary of the tax haven. Transfer prices are fixed to maximise the profits taken 'off-shore' and to minimise the taxes paid in the countries where the company actually produces. As a further spin-off, the multinational might use the resulting 'low profitability' of its UK subsidiary to justify low wage increases. It could argue that poor profitability results from the 'low value' of the goods produced by its UK labour force, rather than from the artificially set transfer prices.

Non-price competition in oligopoly

As we have noted, the theory of the kinked demand curve provides a possible explanation of stable prices in oligopolistic markets. However, there is a much simpler explanation for the absence of price competition. Realising that a price war will be self-defeating for all the firms involved, firms may tacitly agree not to indulge in aggressive price competition as a means of gaining extra profits or

market share at the expense of each other. In the absence of keen price competition, oligopolistic firms are therefore likely to undertake various forms of **non-price competition**. These include:

- **marketing competition**, including obtaining exclusive outlets such as tied public houses and petrol stations, through which breweries and oil companies sell their products
- the use of **persuasive advertising**, **product differentiation**, **brand imaging**, packaging, fashion, style and design
- **quality competition**, including the provision of point-of-sale service and after-sales service

> **examiner's voice**
> Exam questions might ask you to explain why firms use various forms of non-price competition, and to describe and explain some of these forms, such as persuasive advertising.

Barriers to entry

Monopolies and firms in oligopolistic markets use entry barriers to protect the firm's position in the market. There are two main types of entry barrier: natural barriers and artificial or man-made barriers.

Natural barriers

Natural barriers, which are also known as **innocent barriers**, include economies of scale and indivisibilities, which have not been created by firms already in the market to deter new firms from entering. **Economies of scale** mean that established large firms produce at a lower long-run average cost, and are more productively efficient, than smaller new entrants, which become stranded on high-cost short-run average cost curves. **Indivisibilities** prevent certain goods and services being produced in plants below a certain size. They occur in metal smelting and oil-refining industries.

Artificial barriers

Artificial or man-made entry barriers, which are also known as **strategic barriers**, are the result of deliberate action by incumbent firms to prevent new firms from entering the market. Strategic entry barriers include:

- **Patents.** Incumbent firms acquire patents for all the variants of a product that they develop.
- **Limit pricing and predatory pricing.** As already explained, large firms often set limit prices to deter entry by new firms. Some firms also use predatory pricing to kill off small firms that have already entered the market. Predatory pricing is generally illegal, but a large firm may feel it can get away with it, as it is difficult to prove that predatory pricing has taken place.
- **Deliberately building excess capacity.** Firms considering entering a market may be put off by excess capacity owned by firms already in the market. Excess capacity allows incumbent firms to step up production in order to drive down the price to a level at which new entrants cannot compete.
- **Benefiting from the learning curve.** Incumbent firms enjoy the benefits of past experience, having learnt from past mistakes, whereas a new firm enters at the beginning of its learning curve.

- **The ability to hide profits.** Highly profitable activities undertaken by incumbent firms may be camouflaged by accounting practices and by the use of profits to cross-subsidise loss-making business activities.

examiner's voice

Exam questions may ask how entry barriers protect oligopolists and monopolists, and influence the behaviour of firms in protected markets.

Barriers restricting demand

Most barriers that prevent entry by a new firm restrict the firm's ability to *supply* the good. But some entry barriers operate by restricting *demand* for the product:

- **Saturation advertising** by established or incumbent firms may have this effect. Retailers are reluctant to stock new product lines, preferring to devote scarce shelf space to the brands of large firms already in the market, which heavily advertise their products.
- **Network externalities** and **first mover advantage** also lead to entry barriers resulting from the way they affect demand. Network externalities arise when the value to a consumer of a product used by many other consumers is greater than that of an alternative product used by few consumers. For example, Microsoft's Windows operating system for personal computers attracts consumers because it makes their computers compatible with most other PCs throughout the world, and because of the wide range of software developed to run on the Windows system. Microsoft achieved this advantage over 20 years ago, as a first mover in the market, when personal computers were first developed. **Switching costs** now help to protect Microsoft's market dominance. Because of the costs involved in switching to a rival product, consumers are effectively locked in to the Windows operating system.

Cost advantages, product differentiation and capital requirements

In 1956, Joseph Bain identified absolute cost advantages, product differentiation advantages and capital requirements, as well as advantages created by economies of scale, as a way of classifying entry barriers.

- **Absolute cost advantages** result from ownership of a scarce resource (a form of natural monopoly), or ownership of a patent or a form of intellectual copyright.
- Consumer loyalty built up over time, and the creation of a reputation for style, fashion or design, provide examples of **product differentiation advantages**. In recent years, the cult of designer labels has increased the importance of product differentiation advantage.
- Finally, large amounts of **capital** may be needed for a new firm to enter a market. Capital requirements function as a barrier to entry when a potential entrant finds it difficult or impossible to raise the capital necessary to finance a period of loss making before the firm can break even.

Height barriers

The height of entry barriers provides another method of classification. Height determines whether limit pricing can be used, and whether it is profitable. Four types of entry barrier are classified on the basis of height:

- **Easy entry.** When firms already established in the market lack cost or other advantages over new entrants, then, in the long run, competitive pressure

reduces prices to the level of the firms' average costs. Supernormal profits are not earned in the long run.

- **Ineffectively impeded entry.** Limit pricing is possible, but incumbent firms can gain more from charging the short-run profit-maximising price than from using limit pricing as a barrier to entry.
- **Effectively impeded entry.** Higher entry barriers allow firms already in the market to charge limit prices that yield larger long-run profits than would occur if short-run profit-maximising prices were set.
- **Blockaded entry.** New firms do not or cannot enter the market even when prices are set to maximise short-term profits. Established firms do not, therefore, need to charge limit prices.

Collusive oligopoly

Collusive oligopoly occurs when the small number of firms in the market cooperate with each other. Collusion or cooperation is often a reaction to the uncertainty faced by competitive oligopolists.

Cartel agreements

The uncertainty facing competitive oligopolists can be reduced and perhaps eliminated by the rival firms forming a **cartel agreement** or **price ring**. In Figure 6.6, five firms jointly agree to charge a price to keep firm E, which is the least efficient firm, in the market. In a competitive market, firm E would have to reduce costs or go out of business. Cartel agreements enable inefficient firms to stay in business, while other more efficient members of the price ring enjoy super-normal profit. By protecting the inefficient and enabling firms to enjoy an easy life without the threat of competition, cartels display the disadvantages of monopoly (high prices and restriction of choice). However, this is without the benefits that monopoly can sometimes bring, namely economies of scale and improvements in dynamic efficiency.

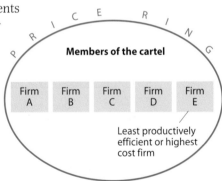

Figure 6.6 *A cartel or price ring*

Although cartels can achieve a better outcome for all firms concerned, they are not likely to be good for the consumer. For this reason, cartel agreements are usually illegal and judged by governments as contrary to the public interest. Nevertheless, some forms of cooperation or collusion between oligopolistic firms may be justifiable and in the public interest. These include joint product developments (such as the Galaxy and Sharan people carrier cars developed jointly by Ford and VW), and co-operation to improve health and safety within industries, or to ensure that product and labour standards are maintained.

examiner's voice

Collusive or cooperative behaviour enables firms to reduce uncertainty at the expense of the consumer. However, some forms of collusion — for example, on joint product development or ensuring industry safety standards — are in the public interest.

Joint profit maximisation

Joint profit maximisation, which is illustrated in Figure 6.7, occurs when a number of firms decide to act as a single monopolist, yet keeping their separate identities. The monopoly MC curve depicted on the right of the diagram is the sum of the identical MC curves of the three firms (one of which is shown on the left of the diagram). The three firms share an output of 750 units, determined on the right of the diagram where the industry MR and MC curves intersect. Each firm charges a price of £10, which, as the diagram shows, is the maximum price that consumers are prepared to pay for 750 units of the good. The monopoly output of 750 units is well below 1,000 units, which would be the output if the industry were perfectly competitive. The shaded area on the right shows the efficiency or welfare loss caused by the cartel raising the price to £10 and restricting output to 750 units. In this example, the members of the cartel split the 750 units equally, each firm producing 250 units. The shaded area on the left shows the supernormal profit made by each firm.

examiner's voice

Joint profit maximisation illustrates how firms can make more profit by colluding and restricting competition than by acting independently.

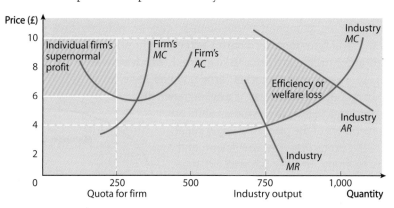

Figure 6.7
Joint profit maximisation by members of a cartel

The theory of joint profit maximisation can be used to show how each member of the cartel has an incentive to cheat on the agreement. The marginal cost of producing the 250th unit of the good is only £4, yet for the firm (but not the whole industry) the marginal revenue received from selling 1 more unit is £10 (that is, the price set by the cartel). One member of the cartel can increase its profit at the expense of the other firms by secretly selling an output over and above its quota of 250 units at a price less than £10, but greater than the marginal cost incurred (£4). This is an example of a divergence between individual and collective interest. The firms' collective interest is to maintain the cartel so as to keep total sales down and the price up. But each firm can benefit by cheating on the agreement — providing all the others don't cheat.

Game theory and oligopoly

Game theory provides the most interesting and fruitful method of modelling the competitive behaviour of firms in oligopolistic markets. Most examples of game

theory are mathematically complicated and beyond the requirements of an A-level economics course. However, there is one example of game theory, known as the **prisoners' dilemma** game, which provides a useful insight into both the *interdependence* of competitive oligopolists and the *incentive to collude* or cooperate. Consider the following situation in the international arms market, in which there are just two firms, a duopoly.

George W. Fixit IV is president of United States Arms Suppliers Inc. By paying bribes of $100 million to government ministers in the Middle East, he can be sure that they will purchase some of his weapons worth $600 million for their armed forces. However, his total sales to these governments depend on the actions of Sir Jasper Underhand, chairman of Exploitation Holdings plc, a UK producer of similar weapons who is Mr Fixit's only serious rival.

If Sir Jasper Underhand also bribes the ministers responsible for the arms purchases, the deal will be shared between the two suppliers. George W. Fixit's profits will then be much less than if he alone pays bribes and gets all the business for his company. Mr Fixit thinks it a pity to pay out $100 million, but if he did not and Sir Jasper did, the UK company would get all the business and he would make zero profit.

In the absence of collusion, two strategies are available to each firm:

1 One firm pays the bribe, while the other firm does not. Outcome:
  ▪ for the firm paying the bribe: $500 million
  ▪ for the firm refusing to bribe: nothing

2 Both firms pay the bribe. Outcome:
  ▪ the sale is shared: each firm gets $200 million

By paying the bribe, United States Arms Suppliers Inc. earns $200m if Exploitation Holdings plc also bribes. If the US company bribes but Sir Jasper refuses to bribe, the US company's earnings rise to $500m, but Exploitation Holdings plc makes no profit at all. The same options face the UK company. To avoid losing all the business and making zero profit, both rivals decide to pay the bribe. In this scenario, paying the bribe is each firm's **dominant strategy**: that is, the strategy to be pursued whatever rival firms do. Paying the bribe makes George W. Fixit better off, whatever Sir Jasper does, and vice versa.

However, the dominant strategy in a competitive market does not deliver the best possible outcome for both firms considered together. The best outcome is illustrated in the bottom right-hand panel of the pay-off matrix in Figure 6.8, which shows all the possible outcomes facing the duopolists. If both firms refuse to bribe, each receives $300 million,

Sir Jasper Underhand ╲ George W. Fixit	Pay bribe	Don't pay bribe
Pay bribe	$200m / $200m	0 / $500m
Don't pay bribe	$500m / 0	$300m / $300m

Figure 6.8 Payoff matrix for the prisoners' dilemma game

assuming the business is shared and that the Middle East government still wants to buy the arms. This outcome is unlikely in a competitive market because each firm fears bribery by its rival. The best way to overcome this fear is to agree not to pay the bribe: that is, to collude or cooperate. There is always the possibility, however, that one of the firms will not honour the agreement and secretly bribe the government ministers. A collusive agreement can never completely get rid of uncertainty. If the firms really wanted to get rid of uncertainty, they would have to merge or be involved in a takeover.

> **examiner's voice**
> You should try to learn a relatively simple example of game theory, based, for example, on the prisoners' dilemma game.

You might be wondering how the prisoners' dilemma model obtained its name. In the original prisoners' dilemma, two prisoners are jointly charged with a serious crime such as armed robbery and are held in isolation from each other. The prosecutor, hoping to have his task simplified, knows that a confession from one will convict the other, but he also knows that the available evidence is insufficient to ensure a conviction. If both prisoners plead not guilty, they are likely to go free. Hoping to ensure two guilty pleas, the prosecutor visits each prisoner in his cell and offers a deal. The prosecutor informs each prisoner that he will receive one of two possible punishments, depending on how he pleads:

1 If both prisoners plead guilty, each will go to prison for 1 year.

2 If one prisoner pleads guilty and the other not guilty, the prisoner pleading guilty is freed and receives a reward (if he gives evidence to convict the other prisoner), while the other prisoner gets a 5-year jail sentence.

We shall leave it to you to work out what each prisoner should do. Would your answer be different if both prisoners were placed in the same cell and could cooperate? Or does the offer of a reward mean that both prisoners will be tempted to cheat on any deal they agree between them, thereby ensuring that the prosecutor obtains his two convictions?

Summary

Oligopoly is a market structure more typical of the real economy in which we live than the models of perfect competition and monopoly examined in Chapter 5. Oligopoly markets are highly concentrated, comprising relatively few firms. However, *competitive* oligopoly is better defined by market *behaviour* rather than by market *structure*. When deciding its best market strategy, a competitive oligopolist must guess how its rivals will react. There are many ways in which the reactions of rival oligopolistic firms may be modelled. Therefore, modern oligopoly theory is more concerned with particular aspects of firms' pricing and output behaviour than with developing a general or universal theory of oligopoly. Among the examples of oligopoly pricing behaviour surveyed in this chapter are cost-plus pricing, price leadership, limit pricing, predatory pricing and discriminatory pricing. However, there are theories that provide

useful insights into aspects of oligopolists' behaviour. Despite being an incomplete theory with significant weaknesses, the kinked demand curve theory illustrates the uncertainty and interdependence of competitive oligopoly.

Game theories, such as those based on the 'prisoners' dilemma', provide a fruitful way of modelling both competitive and collusive oligopoly. Game theories show that oligopolists can produce a better outcome for themselves by colluding or cooperating than by competing for profit or market share. Collusion may take the form of a cartel or price ring. Such collusion allows oligopolists to reduce uncertainty and to undertake joint profit maximisation. Unless, however, the members of the cartel merge and form a monopoly, uncertainty can never be eliminated completely. There is always an incentive for a cartel member to cheat on the agreement. As cartels exploit consumers and allow member firms to remain productively inefficient, governments usually make such restrictive and anti-competitive agreements illegal.

Self-testing questions

1 Define an oligopoly.

2 Why is there no general theory of oligopoly?

3 Distinguish between perfect and imperfect oligopoly.

4 Why may oligopolists collude and what forms might the collusion take?

5 What forms of competition are likely in an oligopoly?

6 What does the kinked demand curve theory of oligopoly predict?

7 What is cost-plus pricing?

8 Explain price parallelism.

9 Distinguish between limit pricing and predatory pricing?

10 What are the requirements for successful price discrimination?

11 Explain the effect of price discrimination upon consumer surplus and producer surplus.

12 Why is cross-subsidy considered inefficient and marginal cost pricing efficient?

Chapter 7
Further aspects of the growth of firms

Specification focus

This chapter provides a descriptive account of the growth of firms, covering how and why firms grow and problems resulting from the growth of firms.

AS **Module 1 Markets and Market Failure**
Production and Efficiency

A2 **Module 5 Business Economics and the Distribution of Income**
Theory of the Firm; Concentrated Markets

A2 **Synoptic coverage**
The study of objectives of firms, economies of scale and productive efficiency at A2 should draw on material already learnt in the AS course. Most other chapter topics are examined solely at A2, but two of the topics on types of business enterprise and the capital market and stock exchange provide useful background information rather than examinable information.

Introduction

As the previous three chapters have shown, firms are extremely important in the economy. However, the previous chapters focused more on what economists often call 'the theory of the firm' than on describing how firms are actually constructed and how they behave in the real economy. In attempting to redress the balance, this chapter introduces economics students to a more industrial economics approach to the study of firms.

What is a firm?

A **firm** is a business enterprise that either *produces* or *deals in and exchanges* goods or services. Unlike non-business organisations — for example, a central government department — firms are commercial, earning revenue to cover the production costs they incur.

Firms operate in both the **private sector** and the **public sector** of the economy. Public sector business enterprises include **nationalised industries**, such as the Royal Mail, and certain **municipally owned trading enterprises**. The dividing line between private and public sector business enterprise is not always clear cut. In the past, some businesses were **joint ventures**, owned partly by the private sector and partly by the state, while others were **state-majority shareholdings**, in which the state owned a controlling interest in a nominally private sector company. Since around 1980, these and other nationalised industries have mostly been privatised. **Privatisation** occurs when industries or firms are transferred from the public sector to the private sector.

The main forms of business enterprise in the UK economy are shown in Figure 7.1. However, it must be stressed that some of these, such as **mutually owned societies** (in the private sector) and the various forms of public sector business enterprise, have become much less important in recent years.

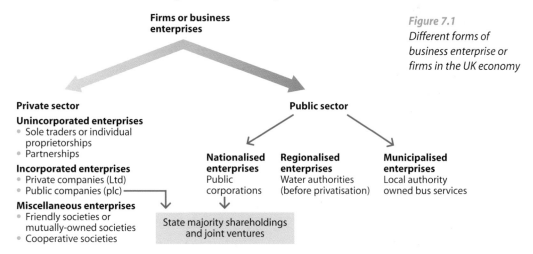

Figure 7.1
Different forms of business enterprise or firms in the UK economy

Types of private firm

In terms of *legal status*, firms in the private sector of the UK economy include sole traders (or individual proprietors), partnerships and companies.

Sole traders and partnerships

In the private sector, there are more than a million small businesses, many of which are **sole traders** or individual proprietorships. Sole traders are common in the

labour-intensive provision of personal services, where not much capital is needed. Along with other forms of small business, such as partnerships and smaller private companies, sole traders often occupy specialised market niches, sometimes providing services to much larger companies in the same or related markets. But although there are many of them, their small size means that individual proprietorships produce only a small proportion of national output.

A **partnership** is formed whenever two or more people agree to undertake a business or trading activity together, instead of operating separately as sole traders. There are in fact two rather different kinds of partnership. On the one hand,

Window cleaners often work as sole traders

there are many thousands of small informal partnerships, usually with just two or three partners functioning much as if they were sole traders. The second type of partnership is more formal and often much larger. Formal partnerships dominate the supply of professional services, such as architects, accountants and solicitors. Some partnerships in the accountancy and legal professions are very large, with scores of partners providing funds for the business. In these and other professions, professional ethic, which requires a member of the profession to be fully liable to clients for the service provided, prevents members of the profession from forming companies. Along with sole traders, partners generally have **unlimited liability**, which means they are personally liable for any loss incurred by the firm.

Companies

Outside the professions, the owners of growing and successful small businesses usually prefer to run their businesses as companies rather than as sole traders or partnerships. Companies are owned by shareholders, who benefit from **limited liability**. This limits the shareholder's financial risk to the amount invested in the company. Without limited liability, only the safest and most risk-free business ventures could attract the large-scale supply of funds or savings required to finance large-scale capital investment.

There are two main types of company: **private companies** and **public companies**. A private company has the word 'Limited' (often shortened to 'Ltd') in its business name, whereas a public company can be recognised by the letters 'plc' in its business name. Members of the general public can buy shares issued by public companies. By contrast, shares issued by private companies are not on general sale and can only be bought through private negotiation with the company's board of directors. The word 'public' in public company does *not* refer to the 'public sector'. Most private companies are small or medium-sized, though a few are quite large. Some private companies are wholly-owned subsidiaries of public companies. For example, Lever Brothers Ltd is owned by Unilever plc, which is an Anglo-Dutch public company. Household-name public companies such as Tesco plc and Marks & Spencer plc are usually much larger than private companies. Due to their large size, public companies are the most important form of business organisation in the UK, despite the fact that there are considerably fewer public companies than private companies.

Plant and firms

In microeconomic theory, it is often assumed that a typical firm operates a single manufacturing plant to produce a specific product within a well-defined industry. Although single plant/single product firms certainly exist, particularly among small businesses, large firms tend to be much more diverse.

> **examiner's voice**
> Large firms have usually invested in a large number of plant sites such as factories, office buildings and retail outlets.

A **plant** or establishment is an individual productive unit within the firm or enterprise, such as a factory, office or shop. Many big firms operate a large number of plant sites, producing a range of products. Such multi-plant and multi-product firms, often organised as **holding companies** owning subsidiary companies in each of the industries in which they operate, are much more typical among big business than the single product/single plant firm.

The largest business corporations are multinational companies owning subsidiary enterprises throughout the world. Some multinationals, such as BP and GlaxoSmithKline (GSK) are UK owned, with their headquarters and most of their shareholders located in the UK. However, many of the multinational corporations operating subsidiary companies and branch factories in the UK are overseas owned. The Nissan Corporation, which produces cars in the northeast of England, and the Sony Corporation, producing television sets in South Wales, are Japanese-owned multinationals that have built factories in the UK in recent years. Ford, General Motors and IBM are examples of US multinationals that have operated subsidiaries in the UK for many years.

Economies of scale

Microeconomic theory generally assumes that a firm seeks to grow in order to enable more profit to be made. Profit depends on both demand conditions and supply conditions, with the latter depending, in the long run, on whether average costs of production fall or rise as the firm's scale of operations increases. Chapter 4 explained economies and diseconomies of scale in terms of a firm's long-run average cost curve. This chapter examines the causes of the different types of economy of scale.

Internal and external economies

Economies of scale are of two types: internal and external. Internal economies of scale occur when a firm's long-run average costs or unit costs fall as a result of an increase in the size of the firm itself, or of an increase in the size of a plant or various sites operated by the firm. By contrast, a firm benefits from external economies of

scale when unit production costs fall because of the growth of the scale of the whole industry or market, rather than from the growth of the firm itself.

Internal economies of scale

Sometimes firms grow larger but the plant sites they operate do not generally grow significantly in size. For this reason, it is useful to distinguish between those internal economies of scale that occur at the level of a single plant or establishment owned by a firm and those occurring at the level of the whole firm. In recent years, continued opportunities for further firm-level economies of scale have contributed to the growth of larger firms, but expansion of plant size has been less significant.

examiner's voice
Avoid drifting into a descriptive account of different types of economy of scale when an examination question asks for explanation of the effect of economies of scale on a firm's cost of production and competitiveness in the market.

Plant-level economies of scale

Economies of scale that occur at the level of a single plant or factory operated by a firm are largely technical economies of scale, though some management economies are also possible at plant level.

Technical economies of scale. Chapter 4 explains how some economies of scale are simply the translation of increasing returns to scale into money costs of production. Increasing returns to scale mean that as plant size increases, a firm can combine its inputs in a technically more efficient way. The resulting economies are called technical economies of scale. Increasing returns to scale therefore 'explain' technical economies of scale. Technical economies affect the size of the typical plant or establishment, rather than the overall size of the firm, which may own and control several different plant sites. Where technical economies of scale are great, the typical plant or establishment is also large in size. However, in industries where size provides few technical advantages and where the methods of large plant sites can be adopted by smaller establishments, the typical plant will usually be smaller.

The main types of technical economy of scale are as follows:

- **Indivisibilities.** Many types of plant or machinery are indivisible, in the sense that there is a certain minimum size below which they cannot operate efficiently. A firm requiring only a small level of output must therefore choose between installing plant or machinery that it will be unable to use continuously, or using a different but less efficient method to produce the smaller level of output required. It also has a third option of buying from an outside supplier.
- **The spreading of research and development costs.** Research and development (R & D) costs associated with new products also tend to be indivisible and independent of the size of output to be produced. With large plants, R & D costs can be spread over a much longer production run, reducing unit costs in the long run.
- **Volume economies.** These are also known as **economies of increased dimensions**. With many types of capital equipment (for example, metal smelters, transport containers, storage tanks and warehouses), costs increase

less rapidly than capacity. When a storage tank or boiler is doubled in dimension, its storage capacity actually increases eightfold. Since heat loss depends on the area of the container's walls (which will only have increased fourfold) and not upon volume, a large smelter or boiler is technically more efficient than a small one. Volume economies are thus very important in industries such as transport, storage and warehousing, as well as in metal and chemical industries, where an increase in the scale of plant provides scope for the conservation of heat and energy.

- **Economies of massed resources.** The operation of a number of identical machines in a large plant means that proportionately fewer spare parts need be kept than when fewer machines are involved. This is an application of the **law of large numbers**, since we can assume that not all the machines will develop a fault at the same time. (The massing of resources also allows for firm-level economies of scale. A multi-product, multi-plant firm may benefit from the cross-fertilisation of experience and ideas between its various subsidiaries.)

- **Economies of vertically linked processes.** Much manufacturing activity involves a large number of vertically related tasks and processes, from the initial purchase of raw materials, components and energy, through to the completion and sale of the finished product. Within a single firm, these processes may be integrated through the links between the various plants owned by the firm. The output of one plant will provide an input or source of component-supply for another plant further along the route to the finished product. Alternatively, the tasks or processes may be integrated within the workshops of a single large plant, enabling the plant to benefit from substantial economies of scale. The linking of processes in a single plant can lead to a saving in time, transport costs and energy, and the close physical proximity of specialist workshops within a plant may allow a subsequent stage in the production process to be sure of obtaining exactly the supplies it needs in the right quantity and technical specification and at the right time.

Managerial economies of scale. Managerial economies of scale can be achieved both by increasing the size of an individual plant or, at the level of the firm, by grouping a large number of establishments under one management. Both methods of expansion allow for increased managerial specialisation and the division of labour. This involves the delegation of detail to junior managers and supervisors and a 'functional division of labour', namely the employment of specialist managers (for example, in the fields of production, personnel and sales).

Multi-plant economies of scale

Multi-plant economies of scale occur when long-run average costs fall as a result of operating more than one plant. When two or more plant sites are operated, a firm may be able to grow larger without exhausting plant-level economies of scale. Not only may plant sites be duplicated, but also the firm can benefit from plant specialisation and from the switching of production between plant sites – for example, to meet seasonal or peak-load demand.

Firm-level economies of scale

It is obviously in a firm's interest to benefit as much as possible from plant-level economies of scale. Firms will also try to take advantage of any scale economies associated with the growth of the enterprise that are largely independent of plant size. Economies of scale at the firm level arise from the firm itself being large rather than from operating a single big plant or a number of large sites. As well as covering some of the R & D economies, massed resources economies and managerial economies already described, firm-level economies of scale also include marketing, financial and risk-bearing economies.

- **Marketing economies.** These are of two types: bulk buying and bulk marketing economies. Large firms may be able to use their market power both to buy supplies at lower prices and also to market their products on better terms negotiated with wholesalers and retailers. It is worth noting that such bargaining advantages make a large firm more profitable, but they do not necessarily make it more efficient in a strictly economic sense. Essentially, the firm gains an advantage at the expense of other firms (its suppliers or market outlets), but we can conclude that true economies have resulted only if production costs fall for *all* the firms considered together. It follows, therefore, that if a big firm becomes a monopoly and increases its selling price, there are no economies of scale involved — only the exploitation of a monopoly position. Nevertheless, monopolies can often benefit from scale economies that are unobtainable by smaller, more competitive firms, and the possibility of achieving economies of scale can be an important justification of monopoly.

- **Financial or capital-raising economies of scale.** These are similar to the bulk-buying economies just described, except that they relate to the 'bulk buying' or the bulk borrowing of funds required to finance the business's expansion. Large firms can often borrow from banks and other financial institutions at a lower rate of interest and on better terms than those available to small firms.

- **Risk-bearing economies of scale.** Large firms are usually less exposed to risk than small firms because risks can be grouped and spread. The grouping of risks is another application of the law of large numbers and the massing of resources to which we have already referred. It is usually possible to predict what will happen on average over a large number of similar events with a reasonable degree of certainty, but individual events may be impossible to predict. Thus a bank can predict with some confidence the number of customers who will turn out to be bad debtors, but it is unlikely to know in advance which customers they will be. But because it knows that for each bad debt there will be many other solvent customers whose business is profitable for the bank, risks are spread and uncertainty is reduced. Thus large firms can spread risks by diversifying their output, their markets, their sources of supply and finance, and the processes by which they manufacture their output. Such economies of diversification or risk-bearing can make the firm less vulnerable to sudden changes in demand or conditions of supply that might severely harm a smaller, less-diversified business.

Learning effects

When a firm increases the scale of its plant, it is quite likely that a new technology or new methods of working an old technology will be adopted. But if the firm's workers and managers are initially unfamiliar with the new methods, production is likely to be inefficient. A learning effect occurs when managers and workers learn from experience how to operate particular technologies and methods of production more effectively. Learning effects are usually associated with a change in the scale of a firm's operations, but they can also occur as a result of the reorganisation of existing capacity.

External economies of scale

As noted earlier, external economies of scale are shared by a number of firms (or indeed by a number of industries) when the scale of production of the whole industry (or group of industries) increases. External economies are conferred on a firm, not as a result of its own growth, but because other firms have grown larger (although, of course, the firm's own growth may also contribute to other firms benefiting from external economies). Indeed, if the firms were to merge, external economies enjoyed by previously independent firms would become internal economies within the plants and subsidiaries of the combined enterprise. Thus takeovers and mergers internalise external economies (and diseconomies) of scale.

examiner's voice
Avoid confusing external economies and diseconomies of scale with positive and negative externalities.

As with internal scale economies, it is possible to identify a number of different types of external economy of scale.

- **Economies of concentration.** When a number of firms in the same or related industries locate close together, they are able to gain mutual advantages through better transport facilities, the training of a pool of skilled labour and supplying each other with sources of components and market outlets. This is called a 'cluster effect'.
- **Economies of information.** In a large industry, it is worthwhile for specialist firms and for public bodies such as universities to undertake research and to provide information (for example, through technical and trade journals), from which all firms can benefit.
- **Economies of disintegration.** Although firms can often benefit from internal economies that result from linking processes internally, there may be circumstances when vertically linked production processes can be provided more efficiently by independent specialist firms. An obvious example occurs in the case of indivisibilities. If a firm is too small to use continuously plant or machinery that cannot be built on a smaller scale, it makes sense to buy supplies from an independent firm that can use the plant efficiently because it supplies a number of firms within the industry.

Internal and external growth of firms

We have seen how, as a business grows, it may decide to change its legal status: for example, from sole trader to private company, or from private to public company. Businesses may also grow internally or externally. **Internal growth**

(which is also known as **organic growth**) occurs when a business expands by investing in new capacity (for example, a new factory, office block or retail store) which it builds from scratch. By contrast, **external growth** involves takeover of, merger with or acquisition of another, previously independent firm. Whichever 'growth path' a business follows — internal, external or a mix of the two — its growth may be vertical, horizontal or lateral, or again a mix of all three.

*e*xaminer's voice

Questions may be set in the Unit 5 examination on why and how firms grow. The 'why' relates to business objectives such as profit maximisation, but the 'how' relates to internal and external growth, and to vertical, horizontal and lateral growth.

The vertical growth of firms

Vertical growth occurs when a firm grows backward along its supply chain, or forward along its distribution chain. The vertical line drawn above and below firm X in Figure 7.2 illustrates both processes. Backward vertical growth (illustrated by arrow 1) takes place when firm X (a car assembly firm) decides to produce for itself the engines, gear boxes and other components needed to make a car. Without such vertical growth, firm X would have to buy components from independent contractors. Arrow 2 illustrates forward growth, namely firm X owning the distribution chain through which the company sells the cars that it manufactures.

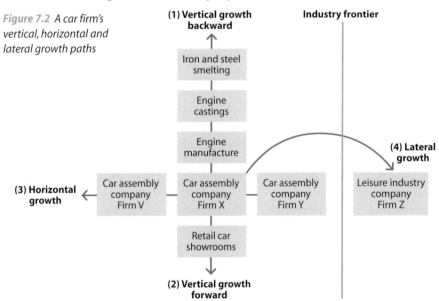

Figure 7.2 A car firm's vertical, horizontal and lateral growth paths

In theory, vertical growth enables a firm to exercise greater control over its supply chain and/or its distribution chain: for example, in controlling the quality of components and the timing of their delivery. Often, however, it may be better to outsource component supply to independent contractors, and to sell through independent retailers. Such a strategy can enhance competition, which in turn improves quality and drives down costs. These days, many large firms outsource a varied range of activities previously undertaken 'in-house'. For example,

ICT-provided customer service and other 'back office' activities are increasingly being outsourced to countries with cheap labour, such as India.

In some circumstances, vertical growth creates monopoly power. A firm may deny competitors access to the supply of raw materials it has acquired. Likewise, by investing in market outlets, such as public houses and petrol stations, breweries and oil companies can prevent competitors selling through these outlets.

All the forms of growth illustrated in Figure 7.2 can be internal or external. For example, vertical internal growth could be illustrated by the car manufacturer investing from scratch in its own engine factory. By contrast, acquiring a previously independent engine manufacturer through takeover or merger illustrates vertical external growth.

Horizontal growth

Besides growing vertically, a firm can grow horizontally and laterally. **Horizontal growth** takes place when a firm expands by building or acquiring more plants at the same stage of production in the same industry. The possibility of achieving multi-plant economies of scale is an obvious motive for horizontal growth. A less benign motive might be to eliminate competitors so as to build up and exploit a monopoly position. Firm X acquiring firms V and Y in Figure 7.2 illustrates horizontal external growth. In the motor industry, Volkswagen's acquisition of Audi and the alliance between Peugeot and Citroën have both been successful. The newly merged companies have been able to rationalise their production plant and product lines, and to exploit scale economies more fully. By contrast, BMW's takeover of the Rover Group was less successful, leading to eventual demerger of the German company's UK acquisition.

Lateral growth

Lateral growth occurs when a firm diversifies into completely different industries. Figure 7.2 provides an example of lateral external growth, or conglomeration, when firm X acquires firm Z, a leisure industry firm operating cinemas and theme parks. Firms diversify in order to gain the scale economies of massed resources and risk spreading described earlier in this chapter. Lateral external growth may also allow the firm to benefit from financial and managerial economies. Lateral mergers, such as those undertaken by tobacco companies, can involve diversifying out of a declining market into what the firm believes to be markets with growth potential. However, managerial and organisational *diseconomies* may also result from the fact that the diversifying company lacks expertise in the fields into which it is expanding.

Small firms

Most small businesses are sole traders, partnerships and private companies, whereas the overwhelming majority of large businesses are public companies. Nevertheless, the concepts of small and large businesses are less easy to define, since they do not refer to a precise legal status. In the early 1970s, the UK

government defined a **small firm** as one with not more than 200 employees. But, because this definition is unsuitable for most industries, the definition of a small firm was extended to one that:

- has a relatively small share of its market
- is managed by its owners or part-owners in a personalised way
- is independent (thus subsidiary firms are excluded from the definition of a small firm)

In 1979 the Wilson Committee on the Financing of Small Firms revised the way of defining a small firm. However, because prices have often more than tripled over the decades since 1979, some of the criteria suggested by the Wilson Committee are now out of date. The Wilson Committee suggested that for various industries, small firms should be defined in the following way:

Manufacturing	200 employees or fewer
Retailing	annual turnover of £185,000 or less
Wholesale trades	annual turnover of £730,000 or less
Construction	25 employees or fewer
Mining and quarrying	25 employees or fewer
Motor trades	annual turnover of £365,000 or less
Road transport	5 vehicles or fewer
Catering	all firms except multiples and brewery-managed public houses

For most of the years after 1945, the number of small firms and their relative importance in the UK economy decreased. In the last 25 years, there has been some recovery, partly because the growth of the small firm sector has been encouraged by successive governments. In the next chapter we describe various financial incentives that governments have introduced to assist the growth of small firms. Conservative governments, in particular, have believed in the virtues of 'popular capitalism' and the 'enterprise economy'. There has also been much disenchantment with the performance of large firms, particularly in the manufacturing sector. Small firms may be more effective than large firms in job creation, since they tend to be more labour intensive. It has also been argued that small firms are a major source of technical innovation, and that they are more cost-effective than large firms in their research and development. Many new technologies appear to suit small-scale enterprise, since they are less dependent than older technologies upon economies of large-scale production and long production runs.

Indeed, some new products in the field of information technology have been developed initially, not by established giants such as IBM, but by completely new **start-up** businesses. These are often founded by university research workers or by employees of the established large companies who decide to leave and set up on their own. In the USA, the Hewlett-Packard (HP) electronic instruments company provides a classic example of a start-up firm that has grown into a large business with worldwide operations. However, many small start-up firms are very different.

Workers laid off through the closure or **downsizing** of large businesses enter self-employment in 'low-tech' activities such as mini-cab driving, window cleaning, and painting and decorating.

Small and medium-sized firms have also been created by the setting up of franchises, and by management and worker buyouts. **Franchising** is common in retailing and catering, where an individual operates his or her own business, but trades under the franchiser's name and sells the franchiser's products or services. The McDonald's and Kentucky Fried Chicken (KFC) chains provide examples. The franchisee pays the franchiser an annual royalty payment in return for trading under the franchiser's brand name and for receiving the benefits of national advertising and other supporting services.

Many conglomerates established when lateral growth of firms was fashionable have now **demerged**. Because of the disappointing results often achieved by diversified businesses, the recent fashion has been for large firms to concentrate on core business activities and to sell off or divest peripheral or 'non-core' activities. Sometimes large companies have demerged or broken into smaller units as a defensive measure against unwelcome and potentially asset-stripping takeover bids. A demerger may result in a **worker or management buyout**. Confident that their expertise allows them to manage an activity better, the firm's managers and workers may offer to buy a part of the company being sold off, in order to run it themselves.

The capital market and the growth of firms

All firms require finance to enable them to grow and to undertake production. Short-term finance is used to pay for the purchase of raw materials (circulating or working capital) and to pay wages. Long-term sources of funds are used to finance the internal or external growth of the firm via direct investment in new fixed plant, or through a process of takeover and merger. For all types of business enterprise, self-finance or the ploughing back in of profits (**internal finance**) is by far the most important source of finance, although the ability to engage successfully in self-finance depends upon profitability.

The main sources of **external finance** divide into borrowing (or debt) and the raising of capital by share issue. For public companies, this involves the capital market. Because private companies cannot generally raise funds on the capital market, the most important reason for private companies 'going public' (that is, becoming public companies) is to raise funds by selling new issues of shares and corporate bonds to whoever wishes to buy them. The government also raises funds on the capital market to finance its budget deficit and its borrowing requirement. The government does this by selling new issues of government bonds (called **gilt-edged securities** or **gilts**) to the general public.

Many students confuse the capital market with the stock exchange. The stock exchange is indeed an important part of the capital market, but it is only a part, and the capital market and stock exchange are not interchangeable terms. The **capital**

market can be understood as comprising two elements: a new issues market or primary market; and a secondary market on which previously issued shares and bonds can be sold second-hand. The **stock exchange** is the most important part of the secondary or 'second-hand' market.

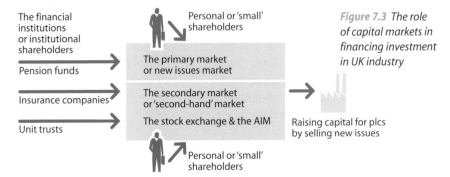

Figure 7.3 *The role of capital markets in financing investment in UK industry*

The relationship between the primary and the secondary parts of the main capital market is illustrated in Figure 7.3. The actual raising of new capital or long-term finance takes place in the primary market when public companies (in the private sector of the economy) or the government (in the public sector) decide to issue and sell new marketable securities. Companies can borrow long-term by selling **corporate bonds**, or they may sell an ownership stake in the company by issuing **shares** or **equity**. When selling corporate bonds, the company extends its debt, and the purchaser of the bond becomes a creditor of the company.

By contrast, new issues of shares are sold when a company 'goes public' for the first time, or when an existing public company decides to raise extra capital with a new equity issue. In the latter case, the new share issue is most often a **rights issue**, in which the company's existing shareholders are given the right to buy the new issue of shares at a discount.

New issues of shares are seldom sold directly on the stock exchange. Instead, the direct sale of new issues to the general public takes place in the primary market, usually being arranged by specialised banks called **investment banks** via newspaper advertisements and the post. Nevertheless, by providing **liquidity** to the capital market, the stock exchange has an important role. Shares in private companies are illiquid and difficult to exchange for cash. By contrast, shares in listed public companies can be sold second-hand on the stock exchange. The stock exchange enables shares to be converted quickly into cash. Without the

The London Stock Exchange

stock exchange, the general public would be reluctant to buy shares that could not easily be resold. An important source of funds necessary to finance the growth of a firm would be denied to public companies.

The growth of venture capital or private equity finance

Until quite recently, it was not usually possible for a private company to finance expansion by extending significantly its share capital or equity, while still remaining a private company. When an ambitious private company wanted to raise a large capital sum, there was normally only two options. The company could either borrow and increase its debt or extend its share capital by 'going public' with a flotation on the stock exchange. However, the 1980 Companies Act introduced a significant change in the financing of private companies which has led to the growth of the modern venture capital industry. The Act allows private companies to take on new shareholders who invest considerable stakes in the business without the necessity of converting to a plc.

Venture capital is finance provided, usually to 'young' private companies and unquoted public companies, through the sale of shares or an equity ownership stake to specialist private equity finance institutions. In the boom years and 'enterprise culture' of the 1980s, banks and other financial institutions such as insurance companies set up specialist venture capital subsidiaries. Typically, a venture capital firm invests a large sum of money in a private company, in return for an equity stake that is highly illiquid as long as the company remains private.

Part of the deal might be that the company — having successfully grown as a result of the capital injection provided by the venture capital firm — eventually 'goes public', either on the junior stock market known as the alternative investment market (AIM), or on the main stock exchange. 'Going public' provides an exit route for the venture capital firm. The private equity finance provider could then sell its stake in the client company and take its profit. The funds released may be used by the venture capital firm to invest in another start-up private company needing long-term funding.

The trade-off facing public companies

Except in a few special circumstances such as insolvency and boardroom disputes, the directors of an independent private company generally have complete control of the business. The directors own all the shares issued by the company. Complete control means, however, that no capital has been raised by selling shares on the capital market. Figure 7.4 illustrates what may happen when the directors decide to 'go public' by converting the company into a plc.

The left-hand box (labelled A) in Figure 7.4 is the private company's share capital, all of which is owned by the directors. When the company 'goes public', new shares (shown by boxes B and C in Figure 7.4) are sold on the capital market. The people buying these shares comprise two very different groups of shareholders, namely

small shareholders (or personal shareholders) and institutional shareholders. Small shareholders (shown by box B in Figure 7.4) are generally in the minority, particularly after selling the new issue 'second hand' to the institutions on the stock exchange. As a result of these sales, insurance companies, pension funds and other financial institutions end up owning most of the shares of plcs listed on the stock exchange. Institutional shareholdings are shown in box C in Figure 7.4.

Controlling most of the shares in public companies, the fund managers employed by pension funds and insurance companies can decide who runs these companies. The financial institutions are best regarded as sleeping owners of the companies in which they hold shares. Lacking specialised management expertise, fund managers prefer not to take an active entrepreneurial role in running the companies that their institutions effectively own. When a company's board does a good job, the financial institutions generally support the directors. But if the board makes bad management decisions which reduce the company's profit and share price, fund managers may lose confidence in the directors. In these circumstances, fund managers can quickly switch allegiance and support a hostile takeover bid for the company.

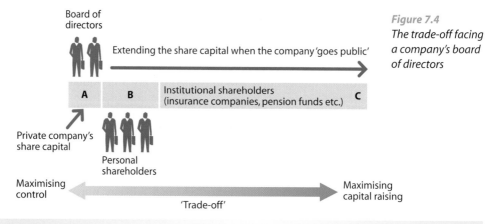

Figure 7.4
The trade-off facing a company's board of directors

examiner's voice
Growing public companies may become vulnerable to hostile takeover bids. It is useful to know how takeovers and mergers can affect resource allocation in the economy.

Entrepreneurs and the divorce between ownership and control

An **entrepreneur** is a decision maker and financial risk taker, providing answers to such standard economic questions as *what*, *how*, *how much*, *where* and *when* to produce. In many small firms, the owner of the business is the entrepreneur, so ownership and control lie in the same person. But this is not true for public companies, where ownership and control are almost always split. Medium-sized and large public companies are owned by thousands of shareholders, although as Figure 7.4 shows, the majority of shares are usually owned by a relatively small number of pension funds and insurance companies. However, management decisions are made by executive directors, who are members of the company's corporate board, and by the salaried managers or executives whom the board employ.

In theory, the directors of a public company who exercise the entrepreneurial function are answerable to the shareholders, which means that, in the event of bad performance, the directors can be voted out of office. In practice, this seldom happens, although as we saw in the last section, institutional shareholders sometimes back hostile takeover bids, which, if successful, remove the incumbent board of directors.

Perhaps the most important problem resulting from the **divorce between ownership and control** is the possibility that directors and managers will pursue an agenda of their own, which is not in the interests of the shareholders as a body. This is the **principal/agent problem**. A principal is a person owning a company, namely a shareholder, whereas an executive employed by the principals to make decisions is the agent. The principal/agent problem results from the fact that due to their lack of knowledge, the principals cannot ensure that the agents they employ act in their best interest.

> **examiner's voice**
> It is important to understand both the *causes* and the *effects* of the divorce between ownership and control in large firms.

Alternative theories of the firm

In earlier chapters, we assumed that a firm has only one business objective: to produce and sell at the level of output at which profit is maximised. In real life, however, the people who run firms may have other business objectives. There are two alternative theories of the firm: managerial theories and organisational or behavioural theories. Both claim to be more realistic in their assumptions and hence better at explaining the actual behaviour of firms in the real economy than the traditional profit-maximising theory of the firm.

> **examiner's voice**
> Knowledge of the objectives of firms other than profit maximisation may be tested in the Unit 5 examination.

Managerial theories

Managerial theories of the firm also assume a maximising objective, but they focus on a managerial objective rather than shareholders' profit. Managerial theories take as their starting point the principal/agent problem involving the split between shareholders as owners, and managers as decision-makers. As explained in the previous section, shareholders own companies, but they employ salaried managers or executives to make business decisions. It is argued that managers, who possess a monopoly of technical knowledge about the actual running of the company, concentrate on managerial objectives such as sales, growth and managerial career prospects.

Organisational/behavioural theories

Organisationalists or behaviouralists see the firm as an organisation comprising coalitions of different groups within the firm. These include production managers, financial managers, production workers and research scientists, each possessing

different group objectives. These days, such coalitions are also regarded as company **stakeholders**: that is, groups of people with a vested interest in how the business performs.

Different stakeholders have different views on what the company should be doing. Managers form one coalition or stakeholder group, seeking prestige, power and high salaries. Other coalitions include production workers wanting higher wages and improved job security and working conditions, and shareholders desiring higher profits. Differing goals or aspirations can result in group conflict. Because of this, management may try to resolve conflict between the different interest groups within the organisation. But attempting to satisfy the aspirations of as many groups within the organisation as possible means compromise and the possible setting of minimum rather than maximum targets.

For this reason, organisationalists introduce the concept of **satisficing** to replace the assumption of a maximising objective. Satisficing, or achieving a satisfactory outcome rather than the best possible outcome, is particularly likely for monopolies and firms in imperfectly competitive markets protected by entry barriers. In these circumstances, in seeking an 'easy life', a firm's managers may content themselves with satisfactory profit, combined with a degree of X-inefficiency (or unnecessary costs).

Satisficing also helps to resolve the conflict between managers' and shareholders' objectives. While trying to maximise executive creature-comforts such as managerial status, salaries, fringe benefits and career structures, a company's board of directors must keep shareholders happy. According to this theory, managers maximise their own objectives, subject to the constraint of delivering a satisfactory level of profit for shareholders.

The theory of economic natural selection

The theory of economic natural selection supports the traditional profit-maximising theory. Natural selection theory operates in two ways: through the economy's goods or product markets; and through the capital market.

In the product market version of the theory, firms are assumed to sell their output in highly competitive goods markets. If managers make price and output decisions for reasons other than profit maximisation, they inevitably incur unnecessary production costs. But if goods markets are sufficiently competitive (perhaps approx-imating to perfect competition), the firms that stray from the profit-maximising path must mend their ways by reducing costs or go out of business. Whatever the conscious or deliberate aim of decision-makers, the 'hidden hand' of the market means that only profit-maximising firms survive. To put it another way, decision-makers who behave 'as if' they are profit-maximisers survive; the rest fail to make normal profit and leave the market.

However, in many real-world goods markets, the forces of competition are not strong enough to allow this selection process to operate. Barriers to entry permit inefficient high-cost firms to survive. For large firms in imperfectly competitive goods markets, the second version of the theory of economic natural selection may be more significant. According to this theory, non-profit-maximising behaviour by firms is disciplined by competition in the capital market rather than by competition in the goods or product market. As we have seen earlier in the chapter, the capital market is the financial market in which a modern large business corporation raises funds to finance investment by selling shares or ownership in the business. When a firm's managers make decisions that are inconsistent with profit maximisation, the resulting low level of profit causes the company's share price to fall. This makes the company vulnerable to takeover on the stock exchange by a new owner (or corporate raider) who believes the company's assets can be managed better and more profitably. In financial jargon, the company comes 'into play'. Even if the company is not taken over, fear of a possible takeover may prevent the corporate board and its managers from straying too far from the profit-maximising path.

Summary

The chapter started by looking at the nature of firms in the UK economy. Firms can be classified in a number of different ways: on the basis of legal status, size, or according to the industrial sector of the economy that they occupy. While there are many thousands of unincorporated sole traders or individual proprietors, in terms of their contribution to national output they are less important than the much smaller number of public companies. Most large businesses in the UK are public companies, or private companies wholly owned by overseas-owned multinational corporations. All sole traders and most private companies are small businesses. However, most public companies are large businesses. The concepts of small and large businesses are vague and imprecise. Nevertheless, there has been general recognition in the UK in recent years that small businesses have a useful role to play in making the economy more adaptable and responsive to change.

Large firms dominate markets and industries where there are economies of large-scale production. Scale economies can be classified into external and internal economies of scale,

with internal economies being further subdivided into plant-level and firm-level economies. Technical economies of scale are the most important type of plant-level economy, with marketing, financial and risk-bearing economies being significant at the firm level. But the fact that plant size has remained remarkably stable over a long period, while the overall size of the largest firm has grown, suggests that firm-level economies of scale are now more important than those occurring at the level of a single plant or establishment.

Firms can grow either by a process of internal growth, involving investment in new productive capacity, or by the external growth process of takeover and merger. Both forms of growth can be classified according to whether the expansion is vertical, horizontal or lateral, with diversification or lateral growth being an important reason for takeovers and other forms of external growth.

Successful growth requires finance. For public companies, the capital market is an important source of long-term externally provided finance. Companies borrow funds on the capital market by selling corporate bonds, and they also raise money from the general public by selling new issues of ordinary shares or equity. In general, for a firm to gain access to the capital market (in which the stock exchange is the main secondary market), the firm must be a public company. These days, however, entrepreneurial private companies can raise funds from venture capital firms, without needing to go public (at least for several years).

The theories of the firm examined in Chapters 5 and 6 assume that firms wish to maximise profit. These theories are part of the 'traditional' theory of the firm. This chapter has surveyed a number of alternative theories of the firm, known as managerial and behavioural (or organisational) theories. By questioning the profit-maximising assumption of the traditional theory of the firm, these theories claim to be more realistic. Managerial theories assume that firms aim to maximise objectives such as sales, growth and managerial career ambitions. By contrast, behavioural theories argue that firms are satisficers rather than maximisers. However, the differences between alternative and traditional theories of the firm may be more apparent than real. Alternative theories can be made consistent with the traditional theory by way of the theory of economic natural selection.

Self-testing questions

1 Distinguish between a firm and a plant.

2 Outline the main forms of business organisation in the private sector of the UK economy.

3 Explain the difference between internal and external economies of scale.

4 Explain three examples of internal economy of scale.

5 Distinguish between the internal and the external growth of a firm.

6 Explain the differences between the vertical, horizontal and lateral growth of firms.

7 Define a small firm.

8 Describe how the capital market and the stock exchange may assist the growth of firms.

9 What is private equity finance, and how do venture capital firms provide finance for private companies?

10 Explain how the divorce between ownership and control may affect a firm.

11 Why may the 'traditional' theory of the firm be unrealistic?

12 Name two managerial theories of the firm.

13 Distinguish between maximising and satisficing.

14 What is meant by economic natural selection?

Part 3

Government and markets

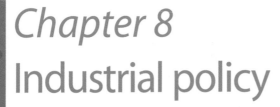

Chapter 8
Industrial policy

Specification focus

This chapter centres solely on the A2 Module 5 specification, covering the main areas of government microeconomic intervention in industries.

A2 **Module 5 Business Economics and the Distribution of Income**
  Government Intervention in the Market

A2 **Synoptic coverage**
  Specific synoptic knowledge is not required to answer questions on the topics covered in this chapter.

Introduction

This chapter examines the meaning of industrial policy and assesses the effectiveness of the industrial policy implemented by UK governments in recent years. The chapter investigates three important elements of industrial policy: competition policy; private versus public ownership of industry; and the regulation and deregulation of the UK economy.

A short history of UK industrial policy

Industrial policy is part of the government's microeconomic policy. It aims to improve the economic performance of individual economic agents, firms and industries on the supply side of the economy. Since the 1930s, when industrial policy first began as a response to the Great Depression, all UK governments have had some sort of industrial policy. However, significant changes have occurred in the nature of the policy, and also in the importance attached by different governments to industrial policy in comparison to other aspects of economic policy. Far-reaching changes occurred in UK industrial policy when, from the late 1970s until quite recently at least, free-market **supply-side economics** replaced **Keynesianism** as the prevailing economic orthodoxy.

Before this, for much of the period from 1945 until 1979, successive UK governments pursued an **interventionist** industrial policy. This reflected the Keynesian view that economic problems result from a failure of market forces, and that the problems can be cured (or at least reduced) by appropriate government intervention. During the Keynesian era, industrial policy in particular (and Keynesian economic policy in general) extended the roles of government and state planning in the economy. By contrast, the industrial policy pursued by governments since 1979 has essentially been **anti-interventionist** and based on the belief that the correct role of government is not to reduce the role of market forces, but to create the conditions in which market forces can work effectively and efficiently.

But although recent governments have generally replaced interventionist industrial policy with a more free-market policy, the importance attached to industrial policy in the overall economic strategy has increased in one important way. During the Keynesian era, industrial policy and microeconomic policy were subordinate and subservient to macroeconomic policy. Keynesian macroeconomic policy was aimed overwhelmingly at the demand side of the economy, attempting to influence and control output and employment by managing the level of aggregate demand in the economy. But free-market economists believe that Keynesian demand management policies led to inflation rather than to full employment and economic growth. They also believe that the almost exclusive Keynesian concern with demand management served to divert attention away from the supply side of the economy, where the real problems that stand in the way of increased output and employment must be tackled. In recent years, therefore, industrial policy has been used to try to increase economic efficiency, productivity and competitiveness in the goods markets and labour markets that make up the supply side of the UK economy.

Competition policy

For over 50 years, since its inception in 1948, competition policy has formed an important part of the UK government's wider

> ***examiner's voice***
> The Module 5 specification states that knowledge of the general features of UK and EU competition policy is required. Detailed knowledge of EU competition policy is not required, and if the topic formed a part of a Unit 4W case study question, plenty of information about EU policy would be provided in the case study.

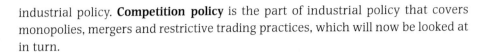

industrial policy. **Competition policy** is the part of industrial policy that covers monopolies, mergers and restrictive trading practices, which will now be looked at in turn.

Monopoly policy

The USA was the first industrialised country to introduce a monopoly policy — or anti-trust policy, as it was called — with the 1890 Sherman Anti-Trust Act. (In the USA, monopolies are known as *trusts*.) Several decades then passed before a UK government decided that the problem of monopoly deserved special policy attention. Nevertheless, of the three main elements of competition policy examined in this chapter, monopoly policy is the one with the longest history, dating back over half a century to the establishment of the Monopolies Commission in 1948. The role of the **Competition Commission** (CC), as the commission is now called, is not restricted solely to the investigation of *pure* monopoly. The commission investigates mergers that might create a new monopoly as well as established monopolies. But more generally, it investigates monopoly power in oligopolistic industries that are dominated by a few large firms.

Statutory monopoly

The UK government currently identifies two types of monopoly, known as **scale monopoly** and **complex monopoly**, which taken together are sometimes known as **statutory monopoly** (that is, monopoly as defined in law). A statutory monopoly exists in law if:

- one firm has at least 25% of the market for the supply or acquisition of particular goods or services (scale monopoly)
- a number of firms that together have a 25% share conduct their affairs so as to restrict competition (complex monopoly)

> *e*xaminer's voice
>
> Don't confuse the definitions of a scale monopoly and a complex monopoly with the definition of a pure monopoly. Pure monopoly means that one firm produces 100% of the market output and *not* 25% or more.

The theoretical background to monopoly policy

At this stage you should refer back to Chapter 5 and read through the sections that compare perfect competition and monopoly. The main points to note are:

- In the absence of economies of scale, perfect competition is more productively and allocatively efficient than monopoly, and it is also likely to be more X-efficient.
- In perfect competition, the 'consumer is king' and consumer sovereignty rules, whereas monopoly leads to the manipulation of consumers and the exploitation of producer sovereignty. By restricting output and raising prices, monopoly results in a net welfare loss as well as a transfer of consumer surplus into producer surplus and monopoly profit.
- While the model of perfect competition provides the theoretical justification for UK competition policy, there are two main circumstances in which monopoly may be preferable to small firms producing in a competitive market. First, when the size of the market is limited but economies of scale are possible, monopolies

can produce at a lower average cost than smaller, more competitive firms. Second, under certain circumstances, firms with monopoly power may be more innovative than firms that are not protected by entry barriers. When this is the case, monopoly may be more dynamically efficient than a more competitive market.

Cartels versus fully integrated monopolies

Whether a monopoly promotes or reduces dynamic efficiency, and generally 'behaves itself', depends to a large extent upon the type of monopoly and upon the circumstances in which the monopoly power was created. With this in mind, it is useful to distinguish between two very different types of monopoly: cartels and fully integrated monopolies.

- **Cartels.** As Chapter 6 explained, a cartel is usually regarded as the worst form of monopoly from the public interest point of view, since it is likely to exhibit most of the disadvantages of monopoly with few, if any, of the benefits. A cartel is a price ring formed when independent firms make a collective restrictive agreement to charge the same price, and possibly to limit output. A cartel acts as a monopoly in the marketing of goods, but the benefits of economies of scale are unlikely to occur because the physical or technical integration of the productive capacity of the members of the cartel does not take place. Consumer choice is restricted, and cartels tend to keep inefficient firms in business while the more efficient members of the cartel make monopoly profits. In these circumstances, it is probable that the incentive to innovate by developing new products and methods of production will be lacking. Cartels are thus likely to be dynamically inefficient.

- **Fully integrated monopoly.** A fully integrated monopoly (or fully unified monopoly) may result from accident rather than design. A dynamic firm grows and benefits from economies of scale, becoming a monopoly as the reward for successful competition. Monopoly is the end result of the firm's success in innovating, reducing costs and introducing new products — which are all factors indicating that the firm is dynamically efficient. A fully integrated monopoly may be the unintended spin-off of essentially benign motives for the firm's growth. Once established as a monopoly, the firm may continue to behave virtuously, retaining its innovating habits and using monopoly profit to finance new developments, though government regulation may be necessary to ensure continued good behaviour.

A cost–benefit approach to monopoly policy

Because it is recognised that monopoly can be either good or bad depending upon circumstances, UK policy has always been based on the view that each case must be judged on its merits. If the likely costs resulting from the reduction of competition exceed the benefits, monopoly should be prevented, but if the likely benefits exceed the costs, monopoly should be permitted. Ongoing regulation is needed to make sure the monopoly continues to act in the public interest.

The Competition Commission and the Office of Fair Trading

UK monopoly policy is implemented by two governmental agencies, the **Office of Fair Trading** (OFT) and the **Competition Commission**, which are responsible to a government ministry, the **Department of Trade and Industry** (DTI). The OFT uses market structure, conduct and performance indicators to scan or screen the UK economy on a systematic basis for evidence of monopoly abuse. **Concentration ratios** provide evidence of monopolistic market structures. **Market conduct indicators** allow the OFT to monitor anti-competitive business behaviour. Conduct indicators include:

- consumer and trade complaints
- evidence of parallel pricing, price discrimination and price leadership
- evidence of merger activity
- the ratio of advertising expenditure to sales

The four main **performance indicators** used to measure a firm's efficiency have been:

- price movements
- changes in profit margins
- the ratio of capital employed to turnover
- the return on capital employed

examiner's voice

Evidence provided by market structure, conduct and performance indicators can be used to analyse and evaluate the costs and benefits of monopoly.

When the OFT discovers evidence of statutory monopoly that it believes is likely to be against the public interest, it refers the firms involved to the Competition Commission for further investigation. Until recently, the OFT asked the Competition Commission to decide the relatively narrow issue of whether particular trading practices undertaken by the investigated firm(s) were in the **public interest**. The public interest was fairly vaguely defined. The 2002 Enterprise Act changed this, introducing **competition-based tests** to replace the public interest test. The tests centre on whether any features of the market (which include structural features and conduct by firms or customers in the market) prevent, restrict or distort competition.

Before the Enterprise Act was implemented, the Competition Commission lacked direct power to implement or enforce its recommendations. It was criticised for lacking teeth. This has changed and the commission's role is now *determinative* rather than just *advisory*. It can order firms to cease particular trading practices. Indeed, virtually all the decisions on markets or firms to be investigated and on policy enforcement are now taken by the Competition Commission and the OFT. In practice, recommendations don't need to be forced through very often. The Competition Commission and the OFT will talk with the firms involved, to persuade them to alter business behaviour voluntarily. Typically, firms will be asked to drop undesirable trading practices and to give undertakings about future conduct.

Since 2002, competition policy has largely been independent of government ministers. In the majority of cases, the government cannot override decisions made by the Competition Commission and the OFT. The role of these agencies is similar to the status of the Monetary Policy Committee (MPC) in implementing monetary policy. Nevertheless, there is still some scope for the government to create **exceptional public interest gateways** (EPIs), which allow the government to intervene. Existing EPIs relate only to national security and public interest considerations with regard to newspapers, namely the accurate presentation of news, freedom of expression and plurality of views.

Alternative approaches to the problem of monopoly

Ever since the initial establishment of the Monopolies Commission, the UK has adopted a regulatory and investigatory approach to the problem of monopoly. Relatively few firms and takeover bids are actually investigated. The policy rationale is that the possibility of a Competition Commission investigation creates sufficient incentive for most large firms to behave well and to resist the temptation to exploit monopoly power.

But although the Competition Commission has adopted a 'watchdog investigatory/ regulatory' role, a number of other strategic approaches could, in principle, be used to deal with the problem of monopoly. These include:

- **Compulsory breaking up of all monopolies ('monopoly busting').** Many free-market economists believe that the advantages of a free market economy, namely economic efficiency and consumer sovereignty, can be achieved only when the economy is as close as possible to perfect competition. In itself, monopoly is bad and impossible to justify. The government should adopt an automatic policy rule to break up monopolies wherever they are found to exist. UK policy-makers have never adopted a monopoly-busting approach, although, as we have seen, powers do exist that allow the government to order the break-up of an established monopoly. By contrast, US anti-trust policy does require the break-up of firms with a very large share of the US market. However, the huge size of the US market has meant that most US firms can grow to a very large size by UK standards, without dominating the domestic market and running the risk of being broken up by the courts.
- **Use of price controls to restrict monopoly abuse.** Although price controls have been used by UK governments at various times to restrict the freedom of UK firms to set their own prices, this has been part of an interventionist policy to control inflation, rather than a policy to control monopoly abuse. Under the influence of free-market economic theory, price controls have generally been abandoned in the UK in recent years. Nevertheless, as explained later in this chapter, regulatory agencies have required privatised monopolies such as British Telecom (BT) to keep price rises below the rate of inflation.
- **Taxing monopoly profits.** As well as controlling prices directly, the government can tax monopoly profit to punish monopolistic firms for making excess profit. Monopoly taxes have not generally been used in the UK, except on a few occasions — for example, on the 'windfall' gain that landlords receive when the land they own is made available for property development. Similarly, windfall profits received by banks from high interest rates have been subject to a special tax. Also, in the late 1990s, the incoming Labour government imposed a windfall profit tax on the privatised utilities.

- **Rate of return regulation.** In the USA, the regulators have imposed maximum rates of return on the capital that the utility companies employ. In principle, these act as a price cap, as the utilities are fined if they set prices too high and earn excessive rates of return. However, in practice, instead of increasing productive efficiency, rate of return regulation often has the opposite effect. This type of intervention has the *unintended consequence* of encouraging utility companies to raise costs (knowing they are protected by entry barriers), rather than to cut prices to comply with the rate of return regulation.

- **The public ownership of monopoly.** In the past, UK Labour governments have sometimes regarded the problem of monopoly as resulting solely from private ownership and the pursuit of private profit. At its most simplistic, this view leads to the conclusion that the problem of monopoly disappears when the firms are nationalised or taken into public ownership. Once in public ownership, the monopolies are assumed to act solely in the public interest.

- **Privatising monopolies.** In contrast to the public ownership theory, Conservative governments have argued that state ownership produces particular forms of abuse that would not be experienced if the industries were privately owned. These include a general inefficiency and resistance to change, which stem from the belief by workers and management in the state-run monopolies that they will always be baled out by government in the event of a loss. According to the Conservative view, monopoly abuse occurs in nationalised industries, not from the pursuit of private profit, but because the industries are run in the interest of a feather-bedded workforce that is protected from any form of market discipline. The Conservatives believe that the privatisation of state-owned monopolies should improve efficiency and commercial performance, because privatisation exposes the industry to the threat of takeover and the discipline of the capital market.

- **Deregulation and the removal of barriers to entry.** Most economists believe that privatisation alone cannot eliminate the problem of monopoly abuse; it merely changes the nature of the problem to private monopoly and the commercial exploitation of a monopoly position. The privatisation of the telecommunication and gas monopolies was accompanied by the setting up of regulatory bodies (originally known as OFTEL and OFGAS). This source of regulation, additional to that available from the Competition Commission and the OFT, was a recognition of this problem. One method of exposing monopolies — including the privatised utility industries — to increased competition is to use deregulatory policies to remove artificial barriers to entry. Deregulation is explained in greater detail later in the chapter.

BT has been exposed to market competition

Contestable market theory

In recent years, much of the debate about the best way of dealing with monopoly
abuse and regulating monopoly has centred upon the need to deregulate and
remove barriers to market entry. This debate reflects the growing influence of
contestable market theory. Before the free-market revival (of which the theory of
contestable markets is a part), industrial policy involved an ever-increasing
extension of regulation by government into the activities of private sector firms.
Increased intervention was justified by the belief that regulatory powers must be
strong enough, first, to countervail the growing power of large business organisations and, second, to make monopolies behave in a more competitive fashion.

At this time, monopoly was normally defined by the number of firms in the market
and by the share of the leading firms, measured by a concentration ratio. The basic
dilemma facing the policy-makers centred on how to reconcile the potential gains
in large-scale productive efficiency, with the fact that lack of competitive pressure
can lead to monopoly abuse and consumer exploitation. But in contestable market
theory, monopoly is defined not by the number of firms in the market or by concentration ratios, but rather by the potential ease or difficulty with which new firms
may enter the market. Industrial concentration is not a problem, providing that an
absence of barriers to entry and exit creates the potential for new firms to enter and
contest the market. *Actual* competition in a market is not essential; the threat of
entry by new firms (or *potential* competition) is quite enough, according to
contestable market theory, to ensure efficient and non-exploitative behaviour by
existing firms within the market.

For a market to be perfectly contestable, there must be no barriers to entry and no
sunk costs. **Sunk costs** are costs incurred when entering a market that are irrecov-
erable should the firm decide to leave the market. *Sunk costs* must not be confused
with *fixed costs*, although some sunk costs are also fixed costs. Suppose a firm
invests in new machinery when it enters the market. This is a fixed cost, but if the
machinery can be sold at a good price to another firm, it is not a sunk cost. In this
situation, the cost can be recovered if the firm decides to leave the market. By
contrast, if the machinery has no alternative use and a cost of disposal rather than
a second-hand value, investment in the fixed capital is also a sunk cost. Another
sunk cost might be expenditure on advertising to establish the firm in the market.
If market entry is unsuccessful and the firm decides to leave, the expenditure
cannot be recovered.

In recent years, contestable market theory has had a major impact upon UK
monopoly policy. The theory implies that, providing there is adequate *potential* for
competition, a conventional regulatory policy is superfluous. Instead of interfering

with firms' pricing and output policies, the government should restrict the role of monopoly policy to discovering which industries and markets are potentially contestable. Deregulatory policies should be used to develop conditions in which there are no barriers to entry and exit, to ensure that reasonable contestability is possible. Appropriate policies suggested by the theory of contestable markets include:

- the removal of licensing regimes for public transport and television and radio transmissions
- the removal of controls over ownership, such as exclusive public ownership
- the removal of pricing controls that act as a barrier to entry, such as those practised in the aviation industry

> **ℯxaminer's voice**
>
> Good answers to exam questions on competition policy should use the theory of contestable markets and the concept of sunk costs.

Merger policy

Whereas a government's monopoly policy deals with *established* monopoly, or markets already dominated by large firms, **merger policy** is concerned with take-overs and mergers that might create a *new* monopoly. Strictly, a **merger** involves the *voluntary* coming together of two or more firms, whereas a **takeover** is usually *involuntary*, at least for the victim being acquired through a hostile takeover. However, the term *merger policy* is used to cover all types of acquisition of firms, friendly or hostile, willing or unwilling.

> **ℯxaminer's voice**
>
> Mergers and takeovers, which occur when firms grow *externally*, can be analysed in terms of the vertical, horizontal and lateral growth of firms.

Until recently, the government rather than the OFT decided merger references. This laid government open to the criticism that, when deciding against a merger reference, it was bending to the lobbying power of big business and engaging in political opportunism. However, recent competition policy legislation gives the OFT power to make virtually all merger references. The Office keeps itself informed of all merger situations that might be eligible for investigation on public interest grounds by the Competition Commission. Currently, a takeover or merger is eligible for reference to the Competition Commission if it is expected to lead to a **substantial lessening of competition** (SLC).

In the 1990s, barely 100 mergers (out of a total of over 3,000) were in fact referred to the Competition Commission for investigation. Of these, only a minority were found to be against the public interest and banned. These figures give some support to the argument that UK governments were not serious in their attitude to mergers and the problem of growing industrial concentration. Governments tended to assume that all mergers were beneficial unless it could clearly be shown that the effects were likely to be adverse.

But, as with monopoly policy, UK merger policy has begun to reflect the influence of contestable market theory. Since the 2002 Enterprise Act changed the law, a higher proportion of mergers have been referred by the OFT to the Competition

Commission for investigation. Because firms can never be sure whether a takeover bid will be referred for investigation, the mere possibility of referral might be quite sufficient to deter takeover activity. However, this effect has now been reduced because the Enterprise Act requires merger investigations to be completed in a matter of weeks.

One effect of current legislation is that horizontal mergers are far more likely to be investigated than lateral mergers. This is unfortunate because lateral mergers often produce managerial diseconomies of scale. By contrast, horizontal mergers, which tend to fall foul of current merger policy, may be **synergetic**. (In this context, synergy means that when two firms merge, the sum is greater than the two parts. By contrast, lateral mergers may have the opposite effect, with the sum being less than the two parts.)

European Union merger policy

The **European Commission**, which is the executive body of the European Union (EU), has long had powers to prevent and control mergers in member countries of the EU, but before 1990, the commission did not apply these powers systematically. However, in 1990 a new EU merger policy came into operation to control the growing number of mergers involving companies active in more than one member country. The EU policy is based on the principle of **subsidiarity**, which delegates policy as much as possible to national governments. Member countries will continue to use national policy to deal with smaller mergers, but the European Commission will adjudicate on larger mergers with a community dimension. As with UK merger policy, nearly all the commission's criteria for assessing whether a merger is justified are competition related, showing again the influence of contestable market theory.

The European Commission justifies its policy as providing a one-stop regulatory system for mergers, in which the borderline between national and EU jurisdiction is clear-cut. However, many commentators believe that the opposite is the case. They criticise EU merger policy as an unclear, time-consuming lawyers' paradise, involving growing firms in increased costs and bureaucracy. UK firms contemplating a merger or takeover bid have to register their plans with both UK and EU authorities to minimise the chance of falling foul of either.

Restrictive trading practice policy

Restrictive trading practices undertaken by firms in imperfect product markets can be divided into two broad kinds: those undertaken independently by a single firm, and collective restrictive practices that involve either a written or an implied agreement among two or more firms.

examiner's voice
Avoid confusing *trading* restrictive practices with *labour* restrictive practices, which are mentioned in Chapter 11.

Independent restrictive trading practices

Cases of independent restrictive practices are initially considered by the OFT, which decides whether or not to refer firms to the Competition Commission for further

investigation. Having investigated the evidence of anti-competitive conduct, the Competition Commission may then recommend that the firm drops the restrictive trading practices, on the ground that they are against the public interest. Independently undertaken restrictive practices include:

- decisions to charge discriminatory prices
- the refusal to supply a particular resale outlet
- full-line forcing, whereby a supplier forces a distributor that wishes to sell one of its products to stock its full range of products

Collective restrictive trading practices

Collective restrictive agreements and practices can be referred by the OFT to a court of law, the **Restrictive Practice Court** (RPC). Arguably, policy towards collective restrictive practices is more effective than other aspects of competition policy because the policy is enforced by a court. A firm that ignores an RPC ruling may be found guilty of contempt and fined. Nevertheless, the punishments that the RPC can hand out are quite weak — usually a fine of just a few thousand pounds. Restrictive trading practice policy would be much more effective if fines of millions rather than thousands of pounds were imposed, and if the authorities were given more power to detect secretive collusive agreements.

However, most agreements registered with the RPC are voluntarily dropped by the firms concerned because the firms realise that the legality of the agreements will not be upheld by the court. A collective agreement, such as a cartel agreement, is illegal unless the firms involved persuade the court that it is in the public interest — for example, to protect the public from injury. Collective agreements usually declared illegal by the RPC include:

- limiting the supply of goods or services
- standardising contractual terms of sale
- fixing a standard selling price
- purchasing raw materials at an agreed price in a common pool
- reciprocal trading, whereby two firms agree to purchase each other's products exclusively
- long-term contracts tying a distributor exclusively to a supplier's product for several years

Private versus public ownership of industry

Nationalised industries

A **nationalised industry** or business is one that is owned by the state. The history of nationalisation in the UK extends back to the middle of the nineteenth century, when the Post Office was established as a civil service department. Several nationalisations occurred in the 1920s when the Central Electricity Board, the London Passenger Transport Board and the BBC were established as public corporations (usually during Conservative governments) by Acts of Parliament. Most of the early public corporations represented what has been called 'gas and water' socialism.

This describes the regulation through public ownership of an essential utility or service regarded as too important to be left to the vagaries of private ownership and market forces.

However, the main periods of nationalisation and extension of public ownership in the UK occurred during two periods after the Second World War when Labour governments were in office. Back in 1929, the UK Labour Party had adopted the commitment to 'common ownership of the means of production, distribution and exchange'. Certainly before the advent of New Labour in the mid-1990s, Labour governments argued that increased public ownership was necessary to give the government proper control of the key industries. These 'commanding heights' of the economy were deemed vital to socialist planning. The Labour Party believed that nationalisation would lead to improved industrial relations and to a more equitable or fair distribution of income and wealth among the population.

In summary, industries were nationalised in the UK for two main reasons: as an instrument of socialist planning and control of the economy; and as a method of regulating the problem of monopoly — in particular, the problem of natural monopoly in the utility industries.

Significant nationalisations took place in the 1940s, when industries such as coal mining, the railways and steel were taken into public ownership. The next 30 years until 1979 saw relatively little additional nationalisation. Many of the acts of nationalisation undertaken by Labour governments in this period merely reorganised assets already in the public sector. But equally, when Conservative governments were in office, there was relatively little privatisation (or denationalisation).

The 1950s to the 1970s were the decades of the **mixed economy**, when the major political parties agreed that the mix of public and private enterprise worked and was 'right' for the UK. But with the election of a radical free-market-orientated administration under Margaret Thatcher in 1979, this consensus broke down. The Conservative governments of the 1980s and 1990s set about the task of breaking up the mixed economy and moving the UK economy closer to a pure market economy.

examiner's voice
Examination questions are unlikely to be set on nationalised industries, but they may be set on privatisation, which changes a firm or industry from being owned by the state to private ownership.

Privatisation

Privatisation involves the transfer of publicly owned assets to the private sector. In the UK this has usually involved the sale to private ownership of nationalised industries and businesses that were previously owned by the state and accountable to central government. British Aerospace was the first large nationalised industry to be privatised in 1981. This and the other main privatisations are shown in Table 8.1. Although the main privatisations have involved the sale of nationalised industries, other state-owned assets such as land and council houses have also been privatised.

Table 8.1 *The main privatisations in the UK*

British Aerospace	1981
National Freight Corporation	1982
British Leyland (Rover)	1984
British Telecom (BT)	1984
British Shipbuilders	1985
National Bus Company	1985
British Gas	1986
British Airports Authority	1987
British Airways	1987
British Steel	1989
Water authorities	1989
Electricity distribution (regional electricity boards — RECs)	1990
Electricity generation (PowerGen and National Power duopoly)	1991
British Coal	1994–95
British Rail	1995–96

Privatisation of a nationalised industry has usually started with a change in the organisation's legal status, from public corporation to public limited company or plc. At this stage, the state owns all the shares in the newly created plc. Sometimes, as in the privatisation of the railways, the public corporation was split into more than one plc. A controlling stake (at least 51% of the shares) was then sold by the state to private owners.

With some privatisations, the government has sold 100% of the share capital. In other cases, notably BT and latterly the electricity-generating duopoly Powergen and National Power, the government sold at least 51% of the shares, but held back a block of shares for sale to the public at a later date. When two or more companies were created, not all the companies were necessarily sold off. Thus the nuclear power element of electricity generation remained in the public sector when Powergen and National Power were privatised.

Before privatisation some state-owned industries, such as electricity, gas and the railways, were vertically integrated. When selling these industries to the private sector, their privatisation involved significant vertical disintegration. The industries were split into horizontal layers, with different companies in each layer buying or selling from companies above or below them in the supply or distribution chain. However, the gas industry was initially privatised in fully, vertically integrated form, with British Gas owning all the stages of production from purchasing natural gas to selling through regional marketing boards to the customer. The industry was split into separate layers a few years after the initial privatisation. As explained later in this chapter, the industries were split into horizontal layers in order to weaken natural monopoly and promote competition.

For gas and electricity, this strategy has generally been successful. Consumers now choose between competing electricity and gas marketing companies, and the prices of electricity and gas have fallen in real terms, at least for a number of years. However, the vertical disintegration of the railway industry, initially into Railtrack, which owned the track, and train-operating companies, such as Virgin, has been much less successful. Railtrack under-invested in maintaining the quality of the track and the company eventually became insolvent. Network Rail, the company that replaced Railtrack, and which now owns the railway lines, is effectively state-owned. Meanwhile, the train-operating companies possess monopoly power over particular routes and provide a highly variable service for passengers. Passengers face difficulties when planning routes involving more than one train-operating company, and most passengers agree that selling the railways was 'a privatisation too far'.

examiner's voice
Several years ago, exam questions were set on the reasons for privatisation, and on the advantages and disadvantages of privatisation. While such questions are still possible, modern questions are more likely to ask for an evaluation of the success or failure of privatisation — for example, of the railway industry.

Privatisation and the free-market revival

The general case for privatisation can only be properly understood when seen as part of the revolution (or counter-revolution) in economic thinking known as the **free-market revival**. In the past, socialists often regarded nationalisation as an end in itself, apparently believing that by taking an industry into public ownership, efficiency and equity would automatically improve and the public interest be served. In much the same way, supporters of the free-market revival at the opposite end of the political and economic spectrum believe that private ownership and capitalism are always superior to public ownership. Whatever the circumstances, they believe that the privatisation of state-run industries must inevitably improve economic performance.

examiner's voice
Avoid confusing privatisation with other policies that have reduced the role of the state in the economy, such as marketisation and deregulation. These are considered later in this chapter.

The advantages of privatisation

Specific arguments used to justify privatisation include:

- **Revenue raising.** Privatisation, or the sale of state-owned assets, provides the government with a short-term source of revenue, which at the height of privatisation was at least £3–4 billion a year. But obviously an asset cannot be sold twice.
- **Reducing public spending and the government's borrowing requirement.** After 1979, Conservative governments aimed to reduce public spending and government borrowing. By classifying the moneys received from asset sales as *negative expenditure* rather than as *revenue*, governments were able, from an accounting point of view, to reduce the level of public spending as well as government borrowing. In addition, when the state successfully sold loss-making industries such as the Rover Group, public spending on subsidies sometimes fell. Government borrowing can also fall if private ownership returns the industries to profitability, since corporation tax revenue is boosted and the state earns dividend income from any shares that it retains in the privatised company.
- **The promotion of competition.** Privatisation has been justified on the ground that it promotes competition through the break-up of monopoly. As state

monopolies, many of the nationalised industries were legally protected from competition. But the industries were also natural monopolies, which were difficult to split into competitive smaller companies without a significant loss of economies of scale and productive efficiency. There was also a practical conflict between the aims of promoting competition and raising revenue. To maximise revenue from the sale of a nationalised industry such as BT or British Gas, the government chose to sell the industry whole, merely switching the industry from a public to a private monopoly. A few years later, however, once the industry was in the private sector, governments had few qualms about introducing new legislation to split the industry into separate firms or to encourage the entry of new firms. (The regulatory agencies such as OFGEM, set up at the time of privatisation, have also tried to remove barriers to entry.)

■ **The promotion of efficiency.** For free-market economists, this is perhaps the most important justification of privatisation. Supporters of privatisation believe that public ownership gives rise to special forms of inefficiency which disappear once an industry moves into the private sector — even if the industry remains a monopoly. The 'culture' of public ownership makes nationalised industries resistant to change. As noted earlier in this chapter, state-owned industries tend to be protected from market discipline. Managers and workers in state-owned industries may believe they will always be baled out by government in the event of making a loss. Taken together, it is argued that these factors lead to dynamic inefficiency and X-inefficiency. Through exposure to the threat of takeover and the discipline of the capital market, the privatisation of a state-owned monopoly should improve the business's efficiency and commercial performance.

■ **Popular capitalism.** The promotion of an **enterprise culture** was an important reason for privatisation in the UK. Privatisation extended share ownership to employees and other individuals who had not previously owned shares, and thus added to the incentive for the electorate to support the private enterprise economy. Privatisation has generally proved popular with voters, so Conservative governments and the New Labour government saw no point in abandoning a winning programme.

The disadvantages of privatisation

Privatisation has the following disadvantages:

■ **Monopoly abuse.** Opponents of privatisation have argued that, far from promoting competition and efficiency, privatisation increases monopoly abuse by transferring socially owned and accountable public monopolies into weakly regulated and less accountable private monopolies.

■ **Short-termism versus long-termism.** Many of the investments that need to be undertaken by the previously nationalised industries can only be profitable in the long term. There is a danger that under private ownership, such investments will not be made because company boards concentrate on the short-termism of delivering dividends to keep shareholders and financial institutions happy. Under-investment in maintaining the rail track and in technically advanced trains by the privatised railway companies provides an example. However, there

is a counter-argument: that under public ownership, the government starved the nationalised industries of investment funds in order to keep government borrowing down.

- **Selling the 'family silver'.** Opponents of privatisation also argue that if a private sector business were to sell its capital assets simply in order to raise revenue to pay for current expenditure, it would rightly incur the wrath of its shareholders. The same should be true of the government and the sale of state-owned assets. Taxpayers should not sanction the sale of capital assets owned on their behalf by the UK government to raise revenue to finance current spending on items such as wages and salaries. In reply, supporters of the privatisation programme argue that, far from selling the family silver, privatisation merely returns the family's assets to the family: that is, from the custody of the state to direct ownership by private individuals.
- **The 'free lunch' syndrome.** Opponents of privatisation also claim that state-owned assets have been sold too cheaply, encouraging the belief among first-time share buyers that there is such a thing as a free lunch. This is because the offer-price of shares in newly privatised industries has normally been pitched at a level which has guaranteed a risk-free capital gain or one-way bet at the taxpayer's expense. This encourages the very opposite of an enterprise economy.

Economic liberalisation

Privatisation is one of the policies of economic liberalisation pursued by UK governments since 1979. Other main elements of economic liberalisation include:

- contractualisation
- marketisation
- public–private partnerships and the private finance initiative
- deregulation

Contractualisation

Contractualisation or **'contracting out'** takes place when services such as road cleaning and refuse collection are put to private sector tender, although the taxpayer still ultimately pays for the service. To try to get value for money for the taxpayer, services that were previously provided *in house* by public sector workers are provided *out of house* through **competitive tendering**.

Marketisation

Whereas privatisation (narrowly defined) involves transferring assets from the public sector to the private sector, **marketisation** (or **commercialisation**) shifts the provision of services from the non-market sector into the market sector. A price is charged for a service that consumers previously enjoyed 'free'. Governments have also experimented in creating **internal markets**, whereby one part of a state-owned enterprise charges a price to another part of the same enterprise for the service it provides within the organisation. This is a form of **transfer pricing** (see Chapter 6).

Public–private partnerships and the private finance initiative

Since 1997, the Labour government has been against full-scale privatisation of services. It argues that it does not matter who provides public services (it could be the public, private or voluntary sector) so long as it is efficient, responsive and of good quality. Labour's 2001 election manifesto stated:

> Where the quality [of public services] is not improving quickly enough, alternative providers should be brought in. Where private sector providers can support public endeavour, we should use them.

As the name implies, **public–private partnerships (PPPs)** are partnerships between the private and public sectors to provide public services. They include the contractualisation of services that we have already described, but also cover activities such as the transfer of council homes to housing associations using private loans. PPP has been particularly important in the provision of health services, but private sector providers are running prisons, local authority revenue and benefit services, the majority of residential homes for the elderly, and schools.

Public–private partnerships provide many residential homes for the elderly

The **private finance initiative (PFI)**, which was introduced by the Conservative government in 1993 and enthusiastically taken up by the subsequent Labour government, is closely related to PPP. Before PFI, the government was involved in all stages of planning, building and then running a public investment project such as a new school. Under PFI, the government's role is restricted to deciding the service it requires and then seeking tenders from the private sector for designing, building, financing and running the project. The government becomes an *enabler* rather than a *provider*.

Governments like PFI because public sector services can be provided, but government borrowing does not increase, at least in the short run. The capital costs of the project are paid for by the private sector provider, but the taxpayer pays if a subsidy is required if the project is not self-financing. Taxpayers also contribute towards the profit made by the private provider. The government hopes, however, that efficiency gains resulting from private sector provision will more than offset the payment of taxpayers' funds into private sector profits. Public service trade unions oppose PPPs, and especially the PFI, because they see them as the creeping privatisation of public services. By contrast, the government believes that PPPs can provide the public sector with the cultural values of the private sector, injecting a fresh, innovative and entrepreneurial 'can-do' approach. Otherwise public services may have a tendency to be entrenched, reactive and conservative.

Deregulation

The nature of economic regulation

Economic regulation involves the imposition of rules, controls and constraints, which restrict freedom of economic action in the marketplace. There are two types of regulation: external regulation and self-regulation.

- **External regulation**, as the name suggests, involves an external agency laying down and enforcing rules and restraints. The external agency may be a government department such as the DTI, or a special regulatory body or agency set up by government, for example the Competition Commission or the OFT.
- By contrast, **self-regulation** or **voluntary regulation** involves a group of individuals or firms regulating themselves, for example through a professional association such as the Law Society or the British Medical Association.

Regulation and market failure

Competition can sometimes bring about a situation in which social costs and benefits are not the same as the private costs and benefits incurred and received by the people actually undertaking the market activity. As Chapter 10 explains, the over-production of externalities such as environmental pollution, and the under-consumption of education, healthcare and other merit goods, provide familiar examples of divergence between private and social costs and benefits. Governments use regulation to try to correct such market failures and to achieve a socially optimal level of production and consumption. Monopoly is also a form of market failure, and regulation is used to limit and deter monopoly exploitation of consumers.

Other examples of government regulation aimed largely at reducing the social costs of market activity include health and safety at work, anti-discrimination and safeguards of workers' rights, and consumer protection legislation. Much of this regulation is concerned with the adequate provision of information for customers and workers, and the setting of quality standards for the production of goods. Such regulation may affect advertising standards, consumers' rights of redress when purchasing faulty goods, and workers' rights in the event of discrimination or unfair dismissal.

*e*xaminer's voice

Examination questions may require a justification for removing or keeping government regulation of markets and businesses. While there is a strong case for removing regulations that protect incumbent firms or which raise businesses' costs unnecessarily, many regulations can be justified on the ground that they protect people from exploitation of monopoly power and from harmful externalities.

Deregulation

Deregulation involves the removal of any previously imposed regulations that have adversely restricted competition and freedom of market activity. For about 25 years, significant deregulation has taken place in the UK and the USA. Systems of regulation built up during the Keynesian era have on occasion been completely abandoned, while in other cases they have been watered down or modified. The UK government

has removed the protected legal monopoly status enjoyed, for example, by bus companies, airlines and commercial television and radio companies. Access to BT's distribution network of land lines has been given to competitors in the telecommunication industry, and private power companies have been allowed to rent the services of the national electricity and gas distribution grids.

There are two main justifications of deregulation:

- the promotion of **competition** and **market contestability** through the removal of artificial barriers to market entry
- the removal of **'red tape'** and **bureaucracy** which imposes unnecessary costs on economic agents, particularly businesses

Deregulation and the free-market revival

The switch away from the imposition of ever more stringent rules and regulations upon private sector economic activity, and towards the opposite policy of deregulation, reflects the decline of Keynesianism and the resurgence of free-market economics. Deregulation should be regarded as a part of an overall policy of economic liberalisation, which, as already explained, has also involved the policies of privatisation, contractualisation and marketisation (or commercialisation). In recent years, governments in most industrialised countries, including most recently those in the formerly centrally planned economies of eastern Europe, have begun this process of economic liberalisation and 'rolling back' the economic functions of the state.

Deregulation and the theory of contestable markets

Much of the justification for the policies of deregulation and economic liberalisation that have been pursued in recent years has been provided by the **theory of contestable markets**, which was explained earlier in the chapter. Contestable market theory argues that the most effective way to promote competitive behaviour within markets is not to impose ever more regulation upon firms and industries, but to carry out the opposite process of deregulation.

According to this view, the main function of deregulation is to remove **barriers to entry**, thereby creating incentives both for new firms to enter and contest the market and for established firms to behave in a more competitive way so as to deter new market entrants. Under the influence of the theory of contestable markets, governments have sought to remove or loosen all regulations whose main effect has been to reduce competition and to promote unnecessary barriers to market entry.

The theory of regulatory capture

Another theory that has had some influence upon the trend towards deregulation is the **theory of regulatory capture**. This theory argues that regulatory agencies created by government can be 'captured' by the industries or firms they are intended to oversee and regulate. Following 'capture', the regulatory agencies begin to operate in the industry's interest rather than on behalf of the consumers whom they are supposed to protect.

Even if regulatory capture does not take place, the supporters of deregulation argue that much regulatory activity is unnecessary and ultimately burdensome upon industry and consumers. Once established, the regulators have an incentive to extend their role by introducing ever more rules and regulations, since in this way they justify their pay and their jobs. Regulation acts both as an informal tax upon the regulated, raising production costs and consumer prices, and also as an extra barrier to market entry, restricting competition within the regulated industry.

The regulation of the privatised utility industries

As noted above, deregulatory policies have been implemented alongside privatisation in the liberalisation of the UK economy. In the 1980s and 1990s, UK governments realised that once industries such as telecommunications, gas, water and electricity were privatised, there was a danger they might abuse their monopoly position and exploit the consumer. For this reason, special regulatory bodies such as OFGEM, which now regulates the gas and electricity industries, were set up at the time of privatisation to act as 'watchdogs' over the performance of the utilities in the private sector. At the time of privatisation, industry-specific regulatory bodies were created. Some of these agencies have recently been merged and now cover more than one industry. For example, in the energy industry, OFGEM has replaced OFGAS and OFFER, which used to regulate the gas and electricity industries respectively.

The paradox of deregulation

The establishment of regulatory agencies such as OFGEM at a time when governments have actively been pursuing a policy of deregulation and economic liberalisation has created a rather strange paradox and a source of possible conflict. On the one hand, by setting markets free, deregulation reduces the role of the state; on the other hand, new 'watchdog' bodies such as OFGEM have extended the regulatory role of government and its agencies.

However, successive governments have argued that there need be no conflict between regulation and deregulation. This is because the regulatory bodies are themselves actively involved in deregulating the industries they oversee — for example, by enforcing the removal of barriers that prevent the entry of new firms. Recent technical progress has made it increasingly possible for new firms to enter the utility industries, particularly in the telecommunications industry. By 'contesting' the market away from established companies such as BT and British Gas, new market entrants have eroded the natural monopoly position previously enjoyed by the privatised utilities.

Supporters of the liberalisation programme hope that the new 'watchdog' agencies will prove so successful that eventually the new regulatory bodies can 'wither on the vine', when the markets they oversee have become sufficiently competitive. However, this is likely to be a long process. Although new firms are beginning to compete in the markets previously completely dominated by state-owned utilities, established companies like British Gas are still dominant. Their continuing market power means that, certainly for the next few years, the

regulatory bodies set up at the time of privatisation must continue as a surrogate for competition. Some commentators argue that, far from withering away, the new regulatory agencies may gradually extend their powers and functions. Free-market critics of economic regulation believe that the UK regulatory system provides a classic example of a bureaucracy growing. It needs to justify its own existence and also to provide a career structure for the regulators themselves.

The role of the regulatory agencies

The regulation of all the privatised utilities has displayed the following main features:

- Each privatised utility has been created by Act of Parliament or 'statute', which has also established the general regulatory framework.
- The privatisation statute lists the duties and responsibilities of the regulatory agency. Formally all the new regulatory bodies are non-ministerial government departments headed by a Director General appointed by government. Along with the OFT and the Competition Commission, regulatory agencies such as OFGEM are quasi-autonomous governmental organisations (**quagos**).
- The real power of the regulator lies in the fact that the privatisation statute requires that a utility must meet the terms of its operating licence. The details of each industry's licence were initially laid down by the government at the time of privatisation, but after privatisation it is the regulator who reviews and renews or changes the terms of the utility's licence.
- The licence sets out the duties of both the privatised utility and the regulator. There is some diversity in the regulators' responsibilities, but in all the utility industries, the regulators have a duty to promote effective competition by liberalising entry to the market. This means that they must ensure a 'level playing field' to enable both established firms and new entrants to compete fairly. The director-generals of the regulatory agencies must also protect customers and ensure that both quality standards and the social aspects of a utility's operations are maintained — for example, by providing a universal service of guaranteed standard to all parts of the UK.
- The most significant feature of the licensing system has been the pricing formula set out in each industry's licence, which limits the privatised utility's freedom to choose its own prices. It is this pricing formula, known as **RPI minus X**, and the regulator's power to change the formula, which lies at the heart of the current system for regulating the utility industries in the UK. The prices charged by a privatised utility are effectively capped because the utility must limit average price increases to X percentage points below the rate of inflation as measured by the retail price index. For example, a price cap of '*RPI* minus 5', set when the rate of inflation is 4%, means that the industry would actually have to reduce its average prices by 1%.
- The regulatory agencies act in conjunction with older established agencies such as the Office of Fair Trading and the Competition Commission. The OFT systematically scans all of UK industry for evidence of monopoly abuse. If it discovers evidence of anti-competitive behaviour by one of the privatised industries, it

may decide to investigate the industry in more depth. The OFT can also refer the industry to the Competition Commission for further investigation, and any restrictive agreements could be referred to the Restrictive Practices Court.

- The Competition Commission also has a role in the review of the licence terms and pricing formulas, which are the joint responsibility of the director-generals of the regulatory agencies and the Competition Commission. Formally, the Commission acts as an 'appeal court' for licence revision and the price formulas if industry and regulator fail to agree. But in practice, the Competition Commission is seldom directly involved because all the negotiation and bargaining is undertaken by the regulatory agencies. The threat of possible referral to the Commission is usually sufficient to ensure that the utility agrees to its regulator's demands.

A closer look at the RPI minus X price formula

According to Professor Stephen Littlechild, who devised the *RPI* minus *X* price cap formula and later became the regulator of the electricity industry, the key feature of the pricing formula is that:

> for a pre-specified period of four to five years, the company can make any changes it wishes to prices, provided that the average price of a specified basket of its goods and services does not increase faster than *RPI* minus *X*, where '*X*' is initially set by the government. At the end of the period, the level of '*X*' is reset by the regulator, and the process is repeated.

examiner's voice
Examination questions may ask for an evaluation of price controls imposed on firms.

The *X* factor reflects the improvements in productive efficiency that the regulator believes the utility can make and share with its consumers each year. The price cap formula is designed to put pressure on the utility to improve productivity and to cut costs. With factor *X* set for a known period of 5 years, the utility has the incentive to reduce costs by more than *X*%. In this situation, both the utility and its consumers will benefit from any improvements in productive efficiency. Consumers benefit because real prices — and sometimes also actual prices — fall, and because they know with reasonable certainty the prices they will have to pay. By improving efficiency by more than the factor *X* set by the regulator, the utility can also benefit from increased profits. The *RPI* minus *X* pricing formula thus creates an incentive for UK utilities actually to reduce the amount of capital they employ, and to use the subsequently smaller capital stock more efficiently.

Two significant problems have emerged with the *RPI* minus *X* pricing formula since the price cap was first imposed on BT around 1984.

- Initially, the utilities believed that, as a part of a **regulatory bargain**, they would be left alone for 5 years after factor *X* was set, to get on with the task of running their businesses. They also believed that, if they achieved an efficiency gain during that 5-year period over and above the factor *X* set by the regulator, they would not be punished when the regulator reset factor *X* at the end of 5 years. In practice, however, the regulators have intervened throughout the

5-year licence period, and have generally raised X every time they have reviewed it. Critics of the way *RPI* minus X has been implemented believe that this has reduced a utility's incentive to improve efficiency and reduce costs. This is because the regulator claws back the utility's share of any productivity gain by increasing factor X, on the grounds that the utility is making excess profits.

■ The *RPI* minus X pricing formula can work properly only if the regulator has a good idea of how efficient the privatised utility is, and of how efficient it might become. In order to set the X factor for 5 years ahead, the regulators must possess considerable technical information about the industries they oversee. A regulator that fails to foresee the direction that technical progress is likely to take over the next 5 years may have to reset X before the 5 years are up, thus triggering the disadvantages already mentioned. A regulator is most likely to set X accurately when the technology in the industry is fairly mature and not subject to sudden change. In these circumstances, the rate at which the regulator can learn about the industry is faster than the rate at which technology changes.

Technology-driven competition

Regulatory agencies have been able to lower and sometimes to remove barriers to market entry by promoting **technology-driven competition**. This type of competition occurs when technical progress enables new firms to enter markets that were previously natural monopolies. In the telecommunications industry, developments such as mobile telephony, satellite technology and the falling real cost of laying fibre-optic land lines have meant that new market entrants such as Vodafone and the cable television companies can invest in their own distribution networks. BT's distribution network is no longer a natural monopoly.

In the gas, water and electricity industries, it is less feasible for firms to enter the market by building their own distribution networks. In these industries, and also to some extent in the telecommunications industry, technology-driven competition centres largely on the introduction of sophisticated computerised metering and payments systems. This allows new firms to enter the market by renting the services of the existing distribution network or grid. New electronic information and recording systems allow customers living, for example, in Manchester to buy electricity from a distribution company located in another region. These developments make it possible for customers to shop around and find the distributor that offers the most attractive price.

Technology-driven competition can be thwarted if the distribution network through which the service is delivered into people's homes is owned by an established utility company, which is a major producer of the good or service transported through the system. In this situation, there is an obvious danger that the vertically integrated company owning the network might prevent new market entrants from using the distribution grid. For example, a vertically integrated British Gas Corporation could charge new gas suppliers artificially high prices for using its distribution grid, to prevent the new firms gaining market share.

This explains why government and the regulators have forced previously vertically integrated utility companies to disintegrate. Separate companies now own different layers of the gas and electricity industries. This means that the distribution layer (owned by the National Grid Company in electricity and Transco in the gas industry) is free to carry the electricity or gas of as many suppliers as it wishes, and not just the energy supplied by Powergen or British Gas.

Yardstick competition

The telecommunications industry offers the greatest scope for technology-driven competition, with new market entrants able to bypass BT's distribution network or pay fair rents for its use. However, at the other end of the spectrum, the water industry possesses the least scope for technology-driven competition to remove barriers to entry and break up the natural monopoly.

For this reason, the Office of Water Services (OFWAT) uses **yardstick competition** as the main regulatory device to promote efficient and competitive behaviour by the water companies. After comparing the performance and costs of all the water companies, OFWAT sets prices so that all the water companies have to match the standards achieved by the best in the industry. If and when the other utility 'watchdogs' run up against the realistic limits to technology-driven competition in the industries they regulate, they may turn to yardstick competition to assess the efficiency of the companies they oversee.

*e*xaminer's voice

Technology-driven competition and yardstick competition provide examples of methods of competition that firms can use in addition to, or in place of, price competition.

Summary

In this chapter we have examined competition policy, privatisation and the benefits of regulation and deregulation — three elements in recent UK government industrial policy. From the 1940s to the 1970s, the industrial policy or microeconomic policy implemented by successive governments, Labour and Conservative, extended the role of the state in the market economy, yet at the same time microeconomic policy was generally less important than macroeconomic policy. This was the heyday of the mixed economy, when it was widely agreed that, by active intervention, governments could correct market failures such as the problem of monopoly abuse. There was also a considerable measure of agreement that the mix of public and private ownership was 'about right for the UK'.

But with the free-market revival, this consensus fell into disarray, particularly in the 'Thatcher years' of the 1980s. In this decade, interventionist industrial policy gave way to a laissez-faire approach that favoured a pro free market industrial policy. The thrust of industrial policy from about 1980 onwards has been to 'roll back' direct intervention by the state in economic activity, and to create conditions that enable markets and economic agents to function competitively and efficiently. The policies of privatisation, marketisation and deregulation have been central to this strategy. At the same time, competition policy (which includes monopoly, merger and trading restrictive practice policy) has been strongly influenced by the theory of contestable markets. This theory suggests that it is less necessary for the state to break up a monopoly than to remove barriers to entry that would deny the potential for a market to be contested.

Recent governments have tried to deregulate rather than to regulate the UK economy. Nonetheless, regulation has been extended to limit the ability of privatised industries such as the utility industries and railway companies to exploit monopoly power. To some extent this has created a 'paradox of deregulation', in the sense that regulatory agencies such as OFGEM have tried to remove barriers to entry and to open the industries under their remit of greater competition. If successful, the regulatory agencies may 'wither on the vine'. Technology-driven competition and yardstick competition are two of the methods used to improve efficiency in the privatised industries.

Self-testing questions

1 Define industrial policy.

2 What are the three main elements of competition policy?

3 Distinguish between a scale monopoly and a complex monopoly.

4 What is a 'natural' monopoly?

5 Distinguish between a cartel and a fully integrated monopoly.

6 Briefly explain the possible costs and benefits of monopoly.

7 What are the roles of the Competition Commission and the Office of Fair Trading?

8 Outline possible approaches to the problem of monopoly.

9 What is the theory of contestable markets?

10 How does UK merger policy operate?

11 What is meant by privatisation?

12 State three arguments in favour of privatisation.

13 What are the disadvantages of privatisation?

14 Explain the difference between regulation and deregulation.

15 What is regulatory capture?

16 Explain the 'RPI minus X' pricing rule for privatised industries.

17 Distinguish between technology-driven competition and yardstick competition.

Chapter 9
Market failure

Specification focus

This chapter covers the market failure content of the Module 1 specification Markets and Market Failures and of the Module 5 specification Business Economics and the Distribution of Income.

AS **Module 1 Markets and Market Failure**
Market Failure

A2 **Module 5 Business Economics and the Distribution of Income**
Government Intervention in the Market

A2 **Synoptic coverage**
When studying Module 5 candidates are expected to extend and develop the models of market failure first studied at AS.

Introduction

Market failure occurs whenever the market mechanism or price mechanism performs unsatisfactorily. There are two main ways in which markets fail. Markets can function inequitably or they can function inefficiently. It is also useful to distinguish between complete market failure, when the market simply does not exist, and partial market failure, when the market functions but produces the wrong quantity of a good or service. In the former case, there is a missing market. In the latter case, the good or service may be provided too cheaply, in which case it is over-produced and over-consumed. Alternatively, as in monopoly, the good may be too expensive, in which case under-production and under-consumption result.

Equity and efficiency in markets

Markets functioning inequitably

For the purposes of this chapter, **equity** means fairness or justice (though in other contexts, such as the housing market, equity has the very different meaning of *wealth*). As soon as considerations of equity are introduced into economic analysis, **normative** or **value judgements** are being made about, for example, 'socially fair' distributions of income and wealth. (The AS specification requires you to understand the difference between a positive statement and a normative statement. A positive statement is a statement of fact, or a statement that can be tested to see if it is true or untrue. By contrast, normative statements are simply opinions involving value judgements. By their nature they cannot be shown to be true or false. Normative statements often contain words such as 'should' or 'ought'.)

As the experience of many poor countries shows, unregulated market forces tend to produce highly unequal distributions of income and wealth. Some economists, usually of a free-market persuasion, dispute whether this is a market failure. Some argue that people who end up being rich deserve to be rich, and that people who end up being poor deserve to be poor. According to this view, the market has not failed — it merely creates incentives that, if followed, cause people to generate more income and wealth.

However, most economists reject as too extreme the view that the market contains its own morality with regard to the distributions of income and wealth. They argue that the market is 'value-neutral' as to the social and ethical desirability or undesirability of the wealth and income distributions that result from the way it functions. Few economists now believe that markets should be replaced by the command mechanism. There is, however, much more agreement that, instead of replacing the market, governments should modify the market so that it operates in a more equitable way than would be the case without government intervention. Taxing the better-off and redistributing tax revenues as transfers to the less well-off is the obvious way of correcting market failure to ensure an equitable distribution of income and wealth. (However, as the next chapter explains, redistributive policies can promote new types of inefficiency and distortion within the economy.)

> **examiner's voice**
>
> The Module 1 specification states that an unequal distribution of income and wealth may result in an unsatisfactory allocation of resources. The distribution of income and wealth and the problem of poverty are also in the Module 5 specification.

Markets functioning inefficiently

Monopoly and other forms of imperfect competition provide examples of market failure resulting from markets performing inefficiently. The wrong quantity is produced in monopoly, particularly when there are no economies of scale, and the wrong price is charged.

> **examiner's voice**
>
> Allocative efficiency is the most relevant efficiency concept for analysing and evaluating market failure.

Too little is produced and is sold at too high a price, and the market outcome is both allocatively and productively inefficient.

The rest of this chapter covers three types of market failure in which markets produce an allocatively inefficient outcome. These are:

- public goods and their opposite, public 'bads'
- externalities
- merit goods and demerit goods

Public goods and public 'bads'

Public and private goods

Public goods provide an example of market failure resulting from **missing markets**. In a market economy, markets may fail to provide any quantity at all of a pure public good such as national defence.

To understand this, a public good can be compared to a **private good**. Most goods are private goods, possessing two important characteristics. The owners can exercise private property rights, preventing other people from using the good or consuming its benefits. This is called **excludability**. The second characteristic possessed by a private good is **diminishability**. When one person consumes a private good, less of its benefits are available for other people. (Private goods also have a third characteristic: **rejectability**. People can opt out and refuse to purchase private goods.)

In contrast, pure public goods exhibit the opposite characteristics of **non-excludability**, **non-diminishability** and **non-rejectability**. It is particularly the first two of these which lead to market failure.

> *e**xaminer's voice**
>
> Public goods are *not* defined as goods provided by the state, and they must not be confused with merit goods.

Non-excludability and public goods

Consider a situation in which the state does not provide national defence. Instead the government lets individual citizens purchase the defence or protection they want. But markets only provide defence when entrepreneurs can successfully charge prices for the services they supply. Suppose an aspiring citizen, who believes that a fortune can be made in the defence industry, sets up a company, Nuclear Defence Services Ltd, with the aim of persuading the country's residents to purchase the services of nuclear missiles, strategically located around the country. After estimating the money value of the defence received by each individual, Nuclear Defence Services bills each household accordingly and waits for the payments to flow in...

But the payments may never arrive. As long as the service is provided, every household can benefit without paying. Nuclear Defence Services Ltd cannot provide nuclear defence to the country's inhabitants who are prepared to pay, while excluding the benefits from those who are not prepared to pay. Withdrawing the benefits from one means withdrawing them from all. But all individuals face the temptation to consume without paying, or to **free-ride**. If enough people choose to

free-ride, Nation Defence Services Ltd makes a loss. The incentive to provide the service through the market thus disappears. Assuming, of course, that the majority of the country's inhabitants believe nuclear defence to be necessary (that is, a 'good' rather than a 'bad'), the market fails because it fails to provide a service for which there is a need.

Non-pure public goods or quasi-public goods

Most public goods are **non-pure public goods** or **quasi-public goods** rather than pure public goods. This is because various methods can be used to exclude free-riders. Non-pure public goods include roads, television and radio broadcasts, street lighting and lighthouses. In principle, roads can be converted into private goods, provided for profit through the market, by limiting points of access, by constructing toll gates or by introducing a scheme of electronic road pricing. But even though non-pure public goods such as roads can be provided through the market, the second characteristic of a public good, non-diminishability, creates a strong case for non-market provision. Such provision will normally be made by the state (or command mechanism), at zero price to the consumer, being financed collectively out of general taxation.

Non-diminishability and public goods

Non-diminishability (which is also known as **non-rivalry** and **non-exhaustibility**) means that when an extra person benefits from a public good, the benefits available to other people are not reduced. In turn, this means that the marginal cost incurred by the provider of the public good when an extra person benefits from the good is zero ($MC = 0$). For example, when a person switches on a television set, the availability and benefits of the broadcast programme are not diminished for people viewing the programme on other television sets. Equally, the broadcasting company incurs no extra cost.

Public goods and allocative efficiency

The allocatively efficient or 'correct' quantity of any good produced and consumed is the quantity that people choose to consume when $P = MC$. But as just noted, assuming a public good is already being provided, the MC of providing the good to an extra consumer is zero. Allocative efficiency therefore occurs when $P = 0$ and the good is *free* for consumers. But private entrepreneurs only willingly provide goods if profits can be made, and for this to happen, the price must be above zero ($P > 0$). In the case of public goods, this means that markets can only provide the goods (assuming free-riders have been excluded) if the price is set above the marginal cost of supply ($P > MC$). This reduces consumption of the public good to below the allocatively efficient level. Market provision thus results in under-production and under-consumption of the good.

Public goods and government goods

Because markets either fail to provide or under-provide public goods, there is a strong case for the state providing the goods at zero price. Charities such as Trinity House, which is responsible for lighthouses in the UK, can also provide public goods.

In theory, free provision achieves the allocatively efficient level of consumption of the public good: that is, the quantity that people wish to consume when the good is free.

Students often wrongly define a public good as a good that is provided by the government. This is confusing *cause* with *effect*. The word *public* in public good refers to the fact that members of the general public cannot be excluded from enjoying the good's benefits. It is this that *causes* market failure. To correct the market failure, governments provide public goods. This is the *effect*. Government goods include public goods such as defence, police and roads, but they also include merit goods such as education and healthcare, which are explained later in this chapter.

Public 'bads'

A *bad* is the opposite of a good, yielding disutility, dissatisfaction or displeasure. Consumption of a bad reduces rather than increases economic welfare. People are generally prepared to pay a market price to gain the benefit of a consumer good or service, although, as we have seen, public goods suffer from the free-rider problem. The free-rider problem also affects public bads, such as rubbish, but in a different way to public goods. People are generally prepared to pay for the removal of a bad or nuisance good, to avoid the unpleasantness otherwise experienced. But in the case of rubbish, payment can be avoided by dumping the bad in a public place, or on someone else's property.

In the UK, local authorities generally empty dustbins without charging for each bin emptied. Suppose this service is not provided, and private contractors remove rubbish and charge households £1 for each dustbin emptied. To avoid paying £1, some households decide to dump their waste in the road or in neighbours' dustbins. (Builders' skips provide a good example of this practice. A household hiring a skip is well advised to fill the skip as quickly as possible, before the rest of the street takes advantage of the facility!) If too many households free-ride, it is impossible for the private contractor to make a profit, and a service for which there is a need is no longer provided — hence the case for 'free' local authority provision, financed through taxation.

Local authority waste disposal avoids the free-rider problem

Externalities

An **externality** is a special type of public good or public bad, which is dumped by those who produce it on other people who receive or consume it, whether or not they choose to. (These people are known as **third parties**, and the externality is sometimes called a **spin-off effect**.) Because externalities are generated and received outside the market, they provide examples of **missing markets**.

examiner's voice
Externalities are perhaps the main cause of market failure. Understanding cost–benefit analysis (which is explained in the next chapter) also requires an understanding of externalities.

Externalities also exhibit the **free-rider problem**. The provider of an external benefit such as a beautiful view cannot charge a market price to any willing free-riders who enjoy it. Conversely, the unwilling free-riders who receive or consume external costs such as pollution and noise cannot charge a price to the polluter for the bad that they reluctantly consume.

Externalities are classified in two main ways: first, into **external costs** and **external benefits** (also known as **negative externalities** and **positive externalities**); and second, into **pure production externalities**, **pure consumption externalities** and **externalities involving a mix of production and consumption**.

Table 9.1 provides examples of all these externalities, while Figure 9.1 shows a number of the production and mixed external costs and benefits that might be produced by a coal-burning power station. The right-hand side of the diagram shows the external costs. These include acid rain pollution and visual or 'eyesore' pollution, caused by the unsightly nature of the power station and by the transmission lines carrying electricity to customers.

Table 9.1 Examples of the different types of externality

Types of externality	External costs	External benefits
Pure production externalities (*generated and received in production*)	Acid rain pollution discharged by a power station which harms a nearby commercially run forest	A farmer benefiting from drainage undertaken by a neighbouring farmer
Mixed production externalities (*generated in production but received in consumption*)	Dust pollution discharged by a brickworks, breathed by asthmatic children living nearby	Commercially owned bees pollinating fruit trees in neighbouring gardens
Pure consumption externalities (*generated and received in consumption*)	Noisy music at a party disturbing neighbouring households	Households benefiting from the beauty of neighbouring gardens
Mixed consumption externalities (*generated in consumption but received in production*)	Congestion caused by private motorists increasing firms' transport and delivery costs	Commercial bee keepers benefiting from the private gardens of nearby houses

By contrast, the left-hand part of Figure 9.1 shows external benefits that might result from burning fossil fuel. We have assumed that hot water, used to rotate turbines so as to produce electricity, warms the temperature of the lake adjoining the power station. Warmer temperatures increase fish stocks, and commercial fishing boats and private anglers then benefit. (However, disruption of a local ecosystem might also cause *negative* externalities, such as algae pollution.)

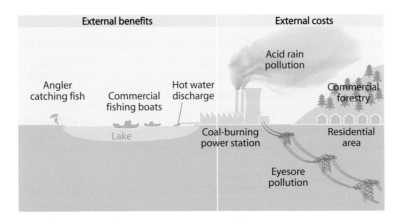

Figure 9.1
Some of the externalities that a fossil-fuel-burning power station might produce

Divergence between private and social cost and benefit

At the heart of microeconomic theory lies the assumption that, in a market situation, an economic agent considers only the private costs and benefits resulting from its market actions, ignoring any costs and benefits imposed on others. For the agent, **private benefit maximisation** occurs when:

marginal private benefit = marginal private cost

or:

$MPB = MPC$

However, **social benefit maximisation**, which maximises the public interest or the welfare of the whole community, occurs when:

marginal social benefit = marginal social cost

or:

$MSB = MSC$

The important point is that households and firms seek to maximise private benefit or private self-interest, and not the wider social interest of the whole community. They ignore the effects of their actions on other people. However, when externalities are generated, costs and benefits are inevitably imposed on others, so private benefit maximisation no longer coincides with social benefit maximisation.

Social benefit is defined as private benefit plus external benefit. As a result:

$$\text{marginal social benefit} = \text{marginal private benefit} + \text{marginal external benefit}$$

or:

$MSB = MPB + MEB$

Likewise, social cost is defined as private cost plus external cost, which means that:

$$\text{marginal social cost} = \text{marginal private cost} + \text{marginal external cost}$$

or:

$MSC = MPC + MEC$

examiner's voice
Examination questions require confident understanding of marginalist conditions, which determine the point at which the optimal level of an activity takes place.

Negative externalities

Negative externalities provide examples of divergence between private and social costs. Figure 9.2 shows the costs and benefits occurring when a power station producing electricity for sale in the market generates negative production externalities such as acid rain pollution. Unlike Figure 9.1, Figure 9.2 assumes that no positive externalities result when fossil fuels are burned. As a result, the marginal private benefit accruing to the power station from the production of electricity, and the marginal social benefit received by the whole community, are the same. But because pollution is discharged in the course of production, the marginal social cost of electricity production exceeds the marginal private cost that is incurred by the power station.

> @*xaminer's voice*
> This type of diagram is required for the Unit 5 exam at A2, but is not needed for Unit 1 at AS.

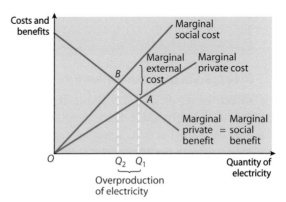

Figure 9.2 *A fossil-fuel-burning power station discharging pollution*

The power station maximises private benefit by producing output Q_1, where $MPB = MPC$. This is shown at point A in Figure 9.2.

However, the socially optimal level of output is Q_2, where $MSB = MSC$. This is at point B in the diagram. The *privately optimal* level of output is thus above the *socially optimal* level of production. To put it another way, market forces overproduce electricity by the amount $Q_1 - Q_2$. The market fails because it produces the 'wrong' quantity of electricity: that is, too much electricity.

Negative externalities and allocative inefficiency

Chapter 5 explained how a perfectly competitive economy can achieve a state of **allocative efficiency** when $P = MC$ in all markets, provided:

- there are competitive markets for all goods and services, including future markets
- there are no economies of scale
- all markets are simultaneously in equilibrium

We can now add a fourth requirement for allocative efficiency: there must be no externalities, negative or positive. Long-run equilibrium occurs in a perfect market at the price at which $P = MPC$, which, in the absence of externalities, means also that $P = MSC$. But if negative production externalities are present, $P < MSC$ when $P = MPC$. To achieve allocative efficiency, price must equal the *true* marginal cost of production: that is, the marginal social cost and not just the marginal private cost. But in a market situation, firms can only take account of private costs and benefits, so when externalities exist, the market mechanism does not result in an allocatively efficient equilibrium.

Firms evade part of the true or real cost of production by dumping the externality on third parties. The price that the consumer pays for the good reflects only the private cost of production, and not the true cost, which includes the external cost. In a market situation, the firm's output is thus under-priced, encouraging too much consumption at Q_1 in Figure 9.2 rather than Q_2. Because the 'wrong' price is charged, a misallocation of resources occurs. Too much consumption, and hence too much production, means that too many scarce resources are being used by the industry that is producing the negative externalities.

Government policy and negative externalities

There are two main ways in which governments can intervene to try to correct the market failure caused by negative externalities. It can use quantity controls (or regulation) or it can use taxation. Regulation directly influences the quantity of the externality that a firm or household can generate. By contrast, taxation adjusts the market price at which a good is sold and creates an incentive for less of the negative externality to be generated.

Regulation or quantity controls

In its most extreme form, regulation can be used to ban completely, or criminalise, the generation of negative externalities such as pollution and noise. It may be impossible to produce a good or service such as electricity in a coal-burning power station without generating at least some of a negative externality. In this situation, banning the externality has the perverse effect of preventing production of a *good* (for example, electricity) as well as the *bad* (pollution). Because of this, quantity controls that fall short of a complete ban may be more appropriate. These include maximum emission limits, and restrictions on the time of day or year during which the negative externality can legally be emitted.

Taxation

Completely banning a negative externality such as pollution is a form of market *replacement* rather than market *adjustment*. By contrast, because taxes placed on goods affect incentives that consumers and firms face, they provide a market-orientated solution to the problem of externalities. Taxation compensates for the fact that there is a missing market in the externality. In the case of pollution, the government calculates the money value of the negative externality and imposes this on the firm as a pollution tax. This is known as the **polluter must pay** principle.

The pollution tax creates an incentive, which was previously lacking, for less of the bad to be dumped on others. By so doing, the tax **internalises the externality**. The polluting firm must now cover all the costs of production, including the cost of negative externalities, and include these in the price charged to customers. By setting the tax so that the price the consumer pays equals the marginal social cost of production ($P = MSC$), an allocatively efficient level of production and consumption could in theory be achieved.

But note that we can only be certain that the firm or industry is allocatively efficient if every other market in the economy is simultaneously setting price equal

to *MSC*. This is an impossible requirement. We should also note that the pollution tax, like any tax, will itself introduce new inefficiencies and distortions into the market, associated with the costs of collecting the tax and with incentives created to evade the tax illegally. For example, firms may try dumping waste at night or fly-tipping to escape detection.

Until recently, governments have been much more likely to use regulation rather than taxation to reduce negative externalities such as pollution and congestion. Indeed, in the past, it has been difficult to find examples of pollution taxes outside the pages of economics textbooks, possibly because politicians have feared that pollution taxes would be too unpopular. But in recent years, governments have become more prepared to use pollution and congestion taxes. This reflects growing concern, among governments and the public alike, of environmental issues such as global warming and the problems posed by fossil fuel emissions and other pollutants. It may also reflect the growing influence of green or environmental pressure groups such as Friends of the Earth and a growing preference to tackle environmental problems with market solutions rather than through regulation.

Pollution permits

Until recently, the main choice of policy for dealing with the problem of pollution was between regulation and taxation. As we have explained, the former is an inter-ventionist solution, whereas taxation, based on the principle that the polluter must pay, has been seen as a more market-orientated solution. But nevertheless it is a solution which requires the government to levy and collect the pollution tax.

In the 1990s, another market-orientated solution started in the USA, based on a trading market in **permits** or **licences to pollute**. This still involves regulation, namely imposing maximum limits on the amount of pollution that coal-burning power stations are allowed to emit, followed by a steady reduction in each subsequent year (say, by 5%) of the maximum amount. But once this regulatory framework has been established, a market in traded pollution permits takes over, creating market-orientated incentives for the power station companies to reduce pollution because they can make money out of it.

A tradable market in permits to pollute works in the following way. Energy companies able to reduce pollution by more than the law requires sell their 'spare' permits to other power stations, which, for technical or other reasons, decide not to, or cannot, reduce pollution below the maximum limit. The latter still comply with the law, even when exceeding the maximum emission limit, because they buy the 'spare' permits sold by the former group of power stations. But in the long run, even power stations that find it difficult to comply with the law have an incentive to reduce pollution. By doing so, they avoid the extra costs that otherwise result from the requirement to buy pollution permits.

Establishing markets for trading private property rights

In 1960, Professor Ronald Coase argued that if markets can be created for private property rights, government intervention to correct market failures may not be

good. By contrast, a **consumer subsidy**, which is paid directly to consumers for spending on a particular good, shifts the demand curve for the good rightward. For example, a government can use both types of subsidy to encourage use of public transport. It can give money to railway or bus companies, or it can provide subsidised travel passes for passengers.

Merit goods and demerit goods

Merit goods and demerit goods provide further examples of the divergence between private and social cost and benefit, and of the generation of externalities. Students often confuse *merit goods* with *public goods*. Like public goods, merit goods such as education are often provided by the state, but, as explained below, the reason for doing so is different. Students also confuse demerit goods with 'bads' or nuisance goods. As explained earlier in the chapter, a bad such as rubbish yields only disutility (nastiness or displeasure) to any unlucky individual 'consuming' it. By contrast, a demerit good such as tobacco certainly fulfils a need and provides satisfaction (in the short run at least) to an addicted smoker.

Merit goods

Merit goods (and demerit goods) can be defined in two rather different ways: first, in terms of externalities; and second, in terms of informational problems facing the consumer.

Merit goods and externalities

Consumption of merit goods such as education or healthcare produces positive externalities that benefit the whole community. As a result, the social benefit of consumption exceeds the private benefit enjoyed by the consumer. The community benefits from an educated (and civilised) population, and a healthy population means that there are fewer people from whom to catch diseases.

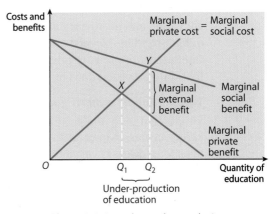

Figure 9.6 *A market under-producing a merit good*

Markets do produce merit goods, as the existence of private fee-paying schools and hospitals demonstrate, but they produce too little. As Figure 9.6 shows, when education is available only through the market, at prices unadjusted by subsidy, many people (especially the poor) end up consuming too little education. In the absence of regulation or subsidy, the quantity of education consumed is Q_1, which is below the socially optimal level of Q_2. (Note that Figure 9.6, showing under-consumption of a merit good, is very similar to Figure 9.5. This is not surprising; both diagrams show divergence between social and private benefit maximisation when positive externalities are generated.)

Merit goods and the informational problem

For a merit good, the long-term private benefit of consumption exceeds the short-term private benefit of consumption. When deciding how much to consume, individuals take account of short-term costs and benefits, but ignore or undervalue the long-term private cost and benefit. Preventative dentistry provides a good example. Many people ignore the long-term benefit of dental check-ups and decide, because of the short-term unpleasantness and the cost of the experience, not to consume the service. Unfortunately, these people can end up later in life with rotten teeth or gum disease.

Government policy and merit goods

As with other examples of positive externalities, governments can use regulation, subsidy or both to enforce or encourage consumption of merit goods. For merit goods such as car seat belts and motorcycle crash helmets, which are infrequently purchased by road users, the UK government uses regulation but not subsidy. Consumption is compulsory, but road users must pay a market price for the merit good. In these cases, the government has decided that, as spending on a seat belt or crash helmet forms only a small part of total consumer spending, road users can afford to pay. By contrast, other merit goods, such as vaccination against contagious diseases, are completely subsidised and provided free, but in the UK consumption is not compulsory.

In the UK, education is both compulsory and completely subsidised, at least for children between the ages of 5 and 16. Low-income families would be in an impossible situation if required to pay to send their children to school. In the UK, education and healthcare are provided by the state and form an important part of public spending. Nevertheless, private sector provision also exists, and is growing. One reason for growing private sector provision of merit goods lies in the fact that free state provision does not necessarily mean good-quality provision.

Vaccination as a merit good

Vaccination is a merit good that illustrates the free-rider problem, explained earlier in this chapter in the context of public goods. Suppose that, for a serious infectious disease, vaccination is 100% effective in preventing people catching the disease. The vaccination has no adverse side-effects, but the market price of vaccination is £50. The disease is contagious and will spread rapidly through the country if a significant number of people in the population choose to remain unvaccinated. Given this information, we might conclude that everybody chooses to purchase vaccination for themselves and for their children, believing that complete immunisation is well worth the price.

Vaccination is under-consumed at market prices

However, people may choose to remain unvaccinated. This is because for each individual, the best possible solution is to remain unvaccinated — provided everyone else chooses vaccination. In this way, the person saves £50 and free-rides on the rest of the community. If everyone else is vaccinated, there is nobody from whom to catch the disease! However, other people will make their choices in exactly the same way, and if too many people choose to free-ride, the 'best solution' for the individual breaks down. Vaccination becomes under-consumed at market prices and an epidemic occurs. Therefore it makes sense to subsidise the provision of vaccination and possibly to make it compulsory, to ensure that everyone benefits from the merit good.

Merit goods and uncertainty, moral hazard and adverse selection

Uncertainty about future long-term benefits and costs contributes to under-consumption of merit goods. For example, a person does not know in advance when, if ever, the services of a specialist surgeon might be needed. Sudden illness may lead to a situation in which a person cannot afford to pay for costly surgery, if provided solely through a conventional market. One market-orientated solution is for private medical insurance to pay for the cost of treatment at the time when it is needed. However, private medical insurance often fails to pay for treatment for the chronically ill or for the poor. Private insurance may also fail to provide medical care for risk-takers in society who decide not to buy insurance, as distinct from risk-averters, who are always the most ready customers for insurance.

Like all private insurance schemes, healthcare insurance suffers from two further problems, both of which lead to market failure. These are the problems of moral hazard and adverse selection. **Moral hazard** is demonstrated by the tendency of people covered by health insurance to be less careful about their health because they know that, in the event of accident or illness, the insurance company will pick up the bill. **Adverse selection** relates to the fact that people whose health risks are greatest are also the people most likely to try to buy insurance policies. Insurance companies react by refusing to sell health policies to those who most need private health insurance. For those to whom they do sell policies, premium levels are set sufficiently high to enable the companies to remain profitable when settling the claims of customers facing moral hazard or who have been adversely selected.

Public collective provision, perhaps organised by private sector companies but guaranteed by the state and funded by compulsory insurance, may be a better solution. Both private and public collective-provision schemes are a response to the fact that the demand or need for medical care is much more predictable for a large group of people than for an individual.

Demerit goods

As their name suggests, **demerit goods** are the opposite of merit goods. Moreover, as noted earlier in the context of merit goods, demerit goods can be defined in two different ways, relating to externalities and to informational problems.

Demerit goods and externalities

The social costs to the whole community resulting from the consumption of a demerit good such as tobacco or alcohol exceed the private costs incurred by the consumer. The private cost can be measured by the money cost of purchasing the good, together with any health damage suffered by the person consuming the good. However, the social costs of consumption include the costs of damage and injury inflicted on other people, resulting, for example, from passive smoking and road accidents caused by drunk drivers. The social costs also include the costs imposed on other people through taxation to pay for the care of victims of tobacco- and alcohol-related diseases.

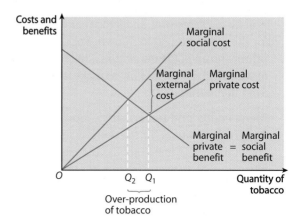

Figure 9.7 How a free market over-provides tobacco

In the same way as the consumption of merit goods generates positive externalities that benefit the wider community, the consumption of demerit goods leads to negative externalities being dumped on others. As Figure 9.7 shows, too much of a demerit good is consumed when bought at market prices. At least in the short term, the privately optimal level of consumption is Q_1, where $MPB = MPC$. This is greater than the socially optimal level of consumption, Q_2, located where $MSB = MSC$. Free-market provision of demerit goods therefore leads to over-consumption, and hence over-production. In a free market, too many scarce resources are used to produce demerit goods.

Figure 9.7 indicates that some smoking is socially optimal. There may, of course, be more extreme situations in which the social costs resulting from the consumption of demerit goods are so severe that the good should be banned. But because of the addictive or habit-forming nature of the consumption of demerit goods such as heroin and cocaine, attempts to ban their use are often counterproductive. Consumption is not abolished; the market is simply driven underground.

examiner's voice

Banning consumption of a demerit good leads to secondary or underground markets. The Unit 1 exam tests knowledge of different forms of underground market (which are sometimes called black markets).

The social costs of consumption in an illegal and completely unregulated market may well exceed the social costs occurring when consumption is legal but closely regulated. Because of this, governments often prefer to discourage or limit consumption of demerit goods by taxation and regulations. Examples include spatial limits on where the demerit good can legally be consumed: for example, no-smoking areas and licensed premises for the sale of alcohol, restrictions on young people consuming the good, and limits on the times of day when alcohol can be consumed in a public place. The latter constraint has recently been relaxed in the United Kingdom.

The effectiveness of a tax in discouraging consumption of a demerit good such as alcohol depends on the size of the tax and on the price elasticity of demand for the good. Because of their addictive nature, demand for demerit goods is often inelastic. This limits the effectiveness of the tax in discouraging consumption.

Demerit goods and the informational problem

As we saw in the context of merit goods, when deciding how much of a good to consume, individuals take account of short-term costs and benefits, but ignore or undervalue the long-term private costs and benefits. But in the case of demerit goods, it is the long-run private costs rather than the long-run private benefits that are significant. For a demerit good, the long-term private cost of consumption exceeds the short-term private cost of consumption. A person who started smoking at a young age may regret the decision later in life when affected by a smoking-related illness. But when a person starts to smoke and gradually becomes addicted to tobacco, private costs that will only emerge many years into the future are often ignored. This means that even in the short run, the good is over-consumed.

Value judgements and merit and demerit goods

Many people believe that an external authority, such as the state or a religious body, is a better judge than individuals of what is good for them. State and/or religion should therefore encourage the consumption of merit goods and discourage and sometimes completely ban the consumption of demerit goods.

Whether one agrees with this rather paternalistic view depends, of course, on one's own personal value judgement. Indeed, whether a good is regarded in the first place as a merit good or as a demerit good depends upon similar personal value judgements. Goods regarded by some people as merit goods are regarded by others as demerit goods. Examples include birth control, sterilisation and abortion, which, depending on ethical or religious standpoints, are regarded by some people as good for society, but by others as bad. The question of deciding whether, and to what extent, a good is a merit or a demerit good, or indeed neither, depends on value judgements that are likely to vary greatly from individual to individual, and between societies.

Summary

This chapter has examined three main types of market failure: public goods, externalities, and merit and demerit goods. We have also briefly surveyed other examples of market failure. Some of these occur in imperfectly competitive markets and monopoly, where producers can use their market power and producer sovereignty to reduce consumer welfare.

Often, such markets are characterised by imperfect market information and conditions of uncertainty. The chapter has also noted that market forces cannot ensure a socially fair or equitable distribution of income and wealth.

Markets fail for two main reasons: inefficiency and inequity. Some examples of market failure exhibit aspects of both problems. For instance, the provision of merit goods and demerit goods through markets, at prices unadjusted by taxation or subsidy, leads to inefficient levels of production and consumption because of divergences between private and social costs and benefits. At the same time, market provision of these goods is inequitable when it denies poor people access to merit goods such as education and healthcare, and creates too much access to a demerit good such as tobacco which can eventually harm consumers.

It is also useful to distinguish between missing markets, when a market fails to provide any quantity at all of a good, and a situation in which some of a good is provided, but not the correct (allocatively efficient) quantity. Pure public goods such as national defence illustrate the former, whereas merit and demerit goods are examples of goods provided through the market, but in the wrong quantities. Externalities exhibit characteristics of both situations: they provide examples of missing markets as there are no markets in the externalities themselves, but at the same time, externalities are usually generated as a 'spin-off' of market behaviour, in either production or consumption.

Governments intervene to try to promote correct levels of production and consumption of public goods, merit goods and demerit goods, and goods which, when produced or consumed, generate externalities. The correct or allocatively efficient level of consumption occurs when $MSB = MSC$. Provided the price correctly reflects the marginal social benefit enjoyed by the whole community, the economically efficient level of production and consumption occurs where $P = MSC$.

In the case of public goods, the missing market problem means that direct state provision is usual. The state provides public goods such as roads and national defence 'free' at the point of consumption, and finances the provision collectively from general taxation.

Governments often provide merit goods such as healthcare and education in this way, although merit goods can also be provided by markets. But because markets under-provide merit goods, governments use subsidies and/or regulations to encourage higher levels of production and consumption. Making consumption compulsory is the most extreme form of regulation.

Because markets over-provide demerit goods such as tobacco and alcohol, regulations are used to discourage their consumption. In this case, outright prohibition is the most extreme form of regulation. Taxes (which are the opposite of subsidies) are also used to discourage consumption.

For merit and demerit goods, the subsidy or tax tries to close the divergence between private and social costs and benefits, so as to create the incentive, lacking at market prices, for the correct or economically efficient quantity of the good to be produced and consumed.

The policy framework of regulation or quantity control on the one hand, and taxation and subsidy on the other hand, is used to regulate the production and consumption of external costs and benefits. Markets in tradable 'permits to pollute' are now also used to create market-orientated incentives to reduce polluting emissions.

Self-testing questions

1 In what sense is monopoly a market failure?

2 Distinguish between market failures resulting from inefficiency and those resulting from inequity.

3 Provide an example of a missing market.

4 Define a public good and explain the 'free-rider' problem.

5 With examples, explain the difference between a pure and a non-pure public good.

6 Distinguish between a public good and a government good.

7 Define an externality.

8 Why do externalities create allocative inefficiency?

9 How can a government reduce negative externalities?

10 How does a market in tradable 'pollution permits' function?

11 With examples, explain the difference between a merit good and a public good.

12 Distinguish between a demerit good and a bad.

13 Explain how subsidies and taxes may be used to promote the allocatively efficient level of consumption of merit goods and demerit goods.

Chapter 10
Cost–benefit analysis and government failure

Specification focus

This chapter covers the topics of cost–benefit analysis, which is examined solely at A2, and government failure, which is both an AS and an A2 topic.

AS Module 1 **Markets and Market Failure**
Government Intervention in the Market

A2 Module 5 **Business Economics and the Distribution of Income**
Government Intervention in the Market

A2 **Synoptic coverage**
Cost–benefit analysis requires understanding of positive and negative externalities first learnt in the AS specification. Government failure at A2 extends and develops AS coverage of the topic.

Introduction

In Chapter 9, we explained how, when negative or positive externalities are discharged, divergences between private and social costs and benefits occur. In such a situation, the government or an organisation with a vested interest, such as a pressure group, may undertake a cost–benefit analysis (CBA). Cost–benefit analysis is a method of decision making that takes account of external as well as private costs and benefits. CBA assesses whether a particular decision — for example, an investment project — is socially optimal and in the public interest, and not just privately optimal and in the interest of the economic agent undertaking the activity.

Cost–benefit analysis can, of course, lead to government intervention in the economy to try to correct a perceived market failure. On the one hand, the government may decide to invest in a project rejected by the private sector as too risky or unprofitable. On the other hand, the government might prevent the private sector building a project that, according to the CBA, is against the public interest. Examples include out-of-town shopping malls, which generate traffic congestion and contribute to the decline of inner-city shopping areas. But government intervention in the market economy is not always successful. Government failure occurs whenever government activity in the economy leads to unsatisfactory consequences.

Why cost–benefit analysis is needed

Suppose the economy in which we live displayed the following conditions:
- perfect competition in all economic activities
- all effects relevant to the welfare of individuals are priced through the market
- no economies of scale and no externalities

Over 200 years ago, using the **invisible hand** metaphor, the great classical economist Adam Smith described such an economy. If this economy actually existed, cost–benefit analysis (CBA) would not be needed. Individuals pursuing private greed to maximise self-interest would at the same time ensure that the social benefit of the whole community was achieved.

But, for good or for bad, real-world economies are not like this. As we have seen in previous chapters, market imperfections, economies of scale, missing markets and externalities do exist. This means that instead of maximising the social welfare of the whole community, the price mechanism misallocates resources and produces unjustifiable inequality in the distributions of income and wealth. Cost–benefit analysis is a technique for evaluating all the costs and benefits of any economic action or decision: that is, the *social* costs and benefits to the whole community and not just the *private* costs and benefits accruing to the economic agent undertaking the action.

The use of cost–benefit analysis

In the past, CBA has most often been used by governments to help decide whether to invest in a major public project such as a motorway, an airport or a major investment by a nationalised industry. However, there is no reason in principle why a private sector investment such as the Channel Tunnel, or indeed any action by a private economic agent or by the government (for example, a tax change), cannot be examined by CBA.

For example, a cost–benefit analysis of the proposed decision to extend Stansted Airport would take into account costs such as building and maintenance costs of the extension; improved road and train links; compensation paid to local landowners and house-holds; and environmental damage caused by the extension and by additional flights that will use the airport. Benefits would include any time saved by travellers; possible reductions in congestion near other airports; and the additional jobs created by the expansion.

> **examiner's voice**
> Cost–benefit analysis is usually associated with investigations, commissioned by government, into large and expensive infrastructure investment projects. However, in recent years such examples of CBA have been thin on the ground. Governments appear to have decided that the costs of CBA are greater than any likely benefits!

Cost–benefit analysis is really an extension of methods that are used by private sector businesses to decide whether particular investment projects are worthwhile. So, before explaining the extra problems involved in CBA, we shall first describe how a private sector business might decide whether particular investment projects are worthwhile. This is called **investment appraisal**.

examiner's voice

Examination questions will not be set on the techniques of private sector investment appraisal, but knowledge of investment appraisal helps to build up an understanding of CBA.

Private sector investment appraisal

Investment in fixed capital projects, such as building a new factory, involves calculating all the *future costs* that the project will incur and all the *future benefits* it will yield. A business has to put a monetary value on the project's expected **net future income stream** (that is, future benefits minus future costs). Private sector investment appraisal places a monetary value on an expected net future income stream which is restricted to *private* costs and benefits.

The central problem is guessing and putting money values to an unknown and uncertain future. If a firm is to maximise profit after investing in a capital project, the following condition must be met:

$$\begin{matrix} \text{rate of return per year} \\ \text{expected over the life of} \\ \text{an investment} \end{matrix} \quad > \quad \begin{matrix} \text{expected rate of interest per} \\ \text{year which must be paid on} \\ \text{borrowed funds to finance} \\ \text{the investment} \end{matrix}$$

This requires the firm to estimate the initial fixed cost of the investment, together with details of its expected future income stream. The firm may be reasonably sure of the initial fixed cost of an investment. It also knows the current rate of interest or cost of borrowing, which has to be paid to raise the funds to finance the investment. However, some of the most important features of an investment are not known, and these have to be estimated or guessed. The firm must estimate the expected life of the investment, together with the size and shape of the income stream that the investment is expected to yield over the years of its life.

Figure 10.1 illustrates some of the problems facing a business when deciding whether or not to invest in particular fixed capital projects. The diagram assumes that, because of a shortage of investment funds, the business is choosing between two investment projects. These are a fleet of trucks to transport the firm's goods to customers, and a computer system for organising business activities such as customer orders, payments to suppliers and the company's wage bill.

Estimating the size and shape of the expected income stream (future revenues minus future costs) is fraught with uncertainty. The investment's physical output must be calculated for each year of the asset's expected economic life. In addition the prices at which the output is sold and the running costs of the investment need to be calculated, including future borrowing costs and future prices of other inputs such as labour and raw materials.

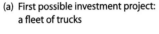
(a) First possible investment project:
   a fleet of trucks

(b) Second possible investment project:
   a computer system

Trucks' expected income stream

Computer system's expected income stream

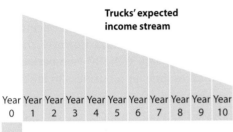

| Year 0 | Year 1 | Year 2 | Year 3 | Year 4 | Year 5 | Year 6 | Year 7 | Year 8 | Year 9 | Year 10 |

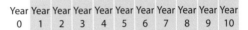

| Year 0 | Year 1 | Year 2 | Year 3 | Year 4 | Year 5 | Year 6 | Year 7 | Year 8 | Year 9 | Year 10 |

Cost of the fixed investment £1,000,000

Cost of the fixed investment £1,000,000

Figure 10.1 Two investment projects available to a business

For the sake of simplicity, Figure 10.1 assumes both investment projects are identical in all respects except one. Each investment costs £1 million and takes a year to complete (year 0 in the diagram), before the investment can be used by the firm. Each investment has an expected economic life of 10 years (years 1 to 10 in the diagram), and the business expects each investment to deliver exactly the same total income stream over the 10-year period. Expected income is shown by the wedge-shaped area drawn for each investment project. Finally, at the end of 10 years, neither investment has a second-hand or scrap value, but equally, no disposal costs are incurred.

BRAND X PICTURES/ALAMY

Trucks provide an early income

Although both investment projects are expected to earn exactly the same *total income*, the key difference between the two projects lies in the *shape* of the expected income streams, which are mirror images of each other. The business expects the trucks to suffer breakdown and mechanical problems as they get older. This means that the trucks earn most of their income early in the 10-year period. However, the computer system is expected to yield most of its income late in the 10-year period. A possible reason for this lies in the fact that it takes time for a business to make full use of an ICT system.

Given all the information about the two competing projects, which project should be chosen by a profit-maximising business? The answer is the fleet of trucks. Two reasons justify this decision. First, the future is always uncertain, and the further we go into the future, the greater the uncertainty. Businesses must face the possibility that an investment's *economic life* (or *business life*) will be much shorter than its *technical life*. The development of new technologies, or changes in the price of labour or energy, may render an investment productively inefficient long before it actually wears out or permanently breaks down. This is particularly true in the case of computer systems. The firm may have to write off the computer system long before the 10 years are up and replace it with a new system that was not around at the time of the initial investment.

Second, and even more importantly, income received early in a project's life can be reinvested, either in another project or to earn the rate of interest when deposited in a bank. This is true for all projects, but projects that earn most of their income early in life have more potential for earning income in this way than projects earning income mostly late in life.

Discounting the future

The example just described illustrates an important feature of investment appraisal. Costs and benefits occurring many years ahead have lower monetary values placed on them than similar costs and benefits occurring in the near future. Firms use a mathematical technique known as **discounting the future** to place appropriate monetary values on costs and benefits expected in the future. Discounting the future enables firms to calculate the monetary value now of costs and benefits expected in the future. The further we go into the future, the lower is the current value of expected future costs and benefits.

examiner's voice
The marginal efficiency of capital (MEC) theory (a *macroeconomic* theory explaining the aggregate level of investment in the economy) is based on the assumption that individual businesses discount the future when making investment decisions. The MEC theory is explained in Chapter 14.

The differences between private sector investment appraisal and CBA

As noted earlier, *social* cost–benefit analysis is really just an extension of private sector investment appraisal to assess *all* the costs and benefits, for society as a

whole, of making particular economic decisions. CBA of major investment projects involves exactly the same problems already explained for private sector investment appraisal. These include estimating the initial cost of the investment; the size, shape and length of its future income stream; and the appropriate rate of discount to use when placing monetary values on future costs and benefits.

But because CBA calculates expected future *external* costs and benefits, it is more difficult than private sector investment appraisal. Many of the social costs and benefits resulting in the future from an action undertaken now take the form of externalities that are difficult to quantify. How does one put a monetary value on the saving of a human life resulting from fewer accidents on a proposed motorway? What is the social cost of the destruction of a beautiful view? It is extremely difficult to decide on all the likely costs and benefits and to know where to draw the line on which to include and exclude. On top of that, it is difficult to put monetary values on all the chosen costs and benefits accruing immediately, and on those which will only be received in the distant future.

Because of market failures, the market prices of goods and services do not always reflect the true social marginal cost of resources in alternative uses. For this reason, cost–benefit analysis often uses prices that are different from market prices. The artificial set of prices used in CBA are known as **shadow prices**. Shadow prices are imputed prices designed to reflect the true social costs and benefits of a particular course of action. For example, the extra journey time spent by people travelling from central London to Stansted rather than Heathrow might be valued at an appropriate hourly wage rate, as would the time saved by travellers living closer to Stansted.

Some difficulties involved in CBA

We have already mentioned some of the problems involved when undertaking a cost–benefit analysis. These include the problem of placing a monetary value on externalities, which by their nature are delivered and received outside the market; the problem of choosing an appropriate rate at which to discount the future; and the problem of setting shadow prices accurately. In addition to these problems, CBA suffers from the difficulties and limitations discussed below.

Forecasting

It is hard to forecast all the costs and benefits that might occur in the future. Supply and demand patterns must be predicted, together with the development of completely new technologies that at the time of the CBA can only be guessed. Population distributions may change, and different rates of inflation can have different impacts on future costs and benefits.

Objectives

Cost-benefit analysis is most appropriate for analysing the best way to achieve a particular objective, for example the site of a new airport. CBA is less relevant for choosing between completely different projects, for example whether to invest solely in transport, healthcare or education. With completely different projects, the political objectives of each project are likely to be different. This means that political criteria should override the strictly economic considerations included in a CBA.

Social welfare

The value of CBA is limited by the definition of an increase in **social welfare**, which it includes. In CBA, an increase in social welfare is defined according to the Hicks–Kaldor test, devised around 50 years ago by two eminent UK economists, Sir John Hicks and Lord Kaldor. In this test, social welfare improves if the welfare *gain* enjoyed by the 'winners' from a policy measure is greater than the welfare *loss* suffered by the 'losers'. To put it another way, if part of the welfare gain is paid by the 'winners' to compensate the 'losers', there is still a net welfare gain, even though in practice such compensation is seldom paid. CBA has often justified a particular project on the ground that, when all costs and benefits have been evaluated, there is a net welfare gain using the Hicks–Kaldor test. However, CBA can reach this conclusion by effectively bypassing the distributional consequences of the project. In the case of some projects, most of the 'winners' are the already better-off and most of the 'losers' are the already disadvantaged.

Value judgements

Critics argue that cost–benefit analysis is 'pseudo-scientific'. By this, they mean that CBA appears to be a scientific technique of evaluating projects, undertaken by impartial 'experts'. In practice, however, it is loaded with value judgments and arbitrary decisions disguised as objectivity. For example, different decisions on how to value an hour of a business executive's time, or for that matter a tourist's time, when travelling from London to Stansted might lead to different results in an analysis of the proposed airport extension. At best, CBA may be simply a costly waste of time and money or, to put it another way, a job-creation scheme for economists and planners. At worst, CBA may reach the 'wrong' decisions. Some critics also argue that CBA is a cynical method used by politicians to distance themselves from, and induce delay in, unpopular decisions. They can therefore deflect the wrath of local communities away from themselves and on to the 'impartial experts' undertaking the CBA.

Supporters of CBA reject these arguments and counter that, for all its defects, it remains the best method of appraising public investment decisions because all the likely costs and benefits are exposed to public discussion. Whatever one's view, in recent years UK governments have largely abandoned officially undertaken CBAs, tending instead to evaluate public investment projects largely on commercial or private profit criteria.

*e*xaminer's voice

Unit 5 examination questions may ask for an explanation and evaluation of the problems encountered when undertaking a cost–benefit analysis.

Government failure

We assumed in Chapter 9 that market failure can be reduced or completely eliminated through appropriate government intervention, for example by imposing taxes, controls and regulation. But there is another possibility. When the government intervenes to try to deal with a problem, far from curing or ameliorating it, intervention actually makes matters worse. When this happens, the problem of **government failure** replaces the problem of market failure. Indeed, from a free-market economist's point of view, a cost–benefit analysis undertaken on behalf of the government is *likely* to lead to government failure.

The law of unintended consequences

The **law of unintended consequences** predicts that, whenever the government intervenes in the market economy, effects will be unleashed which the policy-makers had not foreseen or intended. Sometimes, of course, the unintended effects may be advantageous to the economy, while in other instances they may be harmful but relatively innocuous. In either of these circumstances, government intervention can be justified on the grounds that the social benefits of intervention exceed the social costs and therefore contribute to a net gain in economic welfare. But if government activity — however well intentioned — triggers harmful consequences which are greater than the benefits that the government intervention is supposed to promote, then government failure results.

Public interest theory

The view that the role of government in the economy is to correct market failure wherever it is found to exist, is part of the **public interest theory** of government behaviour. Public interest theory argues that governments intervene in a benevolent fashion in the economy in order to eliminate waste and to achieve an efficient and socially desirable resource allocation.

Public interest theory, applied at the *microeconomic* level in the economy to correct market failure, is matched at the *macroeconomic* level by Keynesian economic management of the economy. As we shall learn in Chapter 12, Keynesians believe that government intervention at the macro level can anticipate and counter the destabilising forces existent in the market economy, thereby achieving a better outcome than could be achieved in an economy subject to unregulated market forces. Keynesians justify discretionary government intervention in the economy on the ground that, provided the intervention is *smart* and sensible, government activity stabilises an otherwise inherently unstable market economy.

Public choice theory

Public interest theory was dominant in the Keynesian era, which lasted from the 1940s to the 1970s. However, Keynesianism gave way to a revival of free-market economics in the late 1970s. To some extent, in recent years, there has been a synthesis between free-market and Keynesian economics, but free-market theory is probably still a little more dominant. Free-market theory is strongly influenced by the **public choice theory** of government behaviour, which is very different from public *interest* theory in its view of the role of government intervention in the economy.

According to public choice theory, not only can market failure arise in the situations described in Chapter 9, but there is also the possibility — perhaps even the likelihood — of government failure occurring whenever the state attempts to improve on the working of the market. In contrast to Keynesians, free-market economists regard a market economy as a calm and orderly place. The price mechanism, working through the incentives signalled by price changes in competitive markets, achieves a more optimal and efficient outcome than could result from a policy of government intervention. Free-market economists believe that risk-taking business people or entrepreneurs, who lose or gain through the correctness of their decisions in the marketplace, know better what to produce than civil servants and planners employed by the government on risk-free salaries with secured pensions. Providing only that markets are sufficiently competitive, what is produced is ultimately determined by **consumer sovereignty**, with consumers knowing better than governments what is good for them.

According to this philosophy, the correct function of government is to reduce to a minimum its economic activities and interference with private economic agents. Thus government should be restricted to a 'night-watchman' role, maintaining law and order, providing public goods and offering other minor corrections when markets fail. In other words, the 'correct' role of government is to ensure a suitable environment in which wealth-creating entrepreneurship can function in competitive markets subject to minimum regulation. This philosophy of the correct role of markets and of government leads free-market economists to reject intervention in the economy by the government as a means of achieving goals such as reduced unemployment. They believe that, at best, such intervention will be ineffective; at worst, it will be damaging, destabilising and inefficient.

Government failure and theories of political behaviour

Government failure may also result from the fact that, in democracies such as the UK and the USA, elected politicians must face the ballot box every 4 or 5 years in the electoral voting cycle. Public choice theory assumes that both politicians and bureaucrats (the officials or civil servants employed in government departments) behave so as to maximise their self-interest — that is 'vote maximisation' and re-election in the case of politicians, and, for bureaucrats, the maximisation of their departments' budgets and spending plans.

For politicians, the electoral pressure to find favour with voters can lead to very short 'time horizons' in the government's decision-making process. This causes government ministers to favour public spending programmes with an immediate payoff, while rejecting those with an initially high investment cost, but with benefits several years ahead. Thus governments may be tempted to duck expenditure on research, training, and conservation and environmental protection, in favour of a spending programme that boosts voters' short-term consumption prospects, particularly in the run-up to general elections.

Government failure and theories of bureaucracy

The role of bureaucracy in the machinery of government may also contribute to government failure. To some extent, the role of bureaucrats in the implementation of public policy works in the opposite direction to that of the 4- or 5-year electoral cycle, causing governments to do too much for too long.

In the model of bureaucracy developed by William Niskanen in 1971, it is assumed that government officials aim to maximise the budget of the department in which they work. The bigger the budget, the greater are the department's prestige and the opportunities for promotion for departmental officials. Thus, since all the civil servants employed within a particular department have a vested interest in increasing the department's budget and spending plans, bureaucrats or officials think up arguments to justify extra spending. If all government departments behave in this way, the net effect is to exert upward pressure on government spending. Furthermore, unlike private business, many government spending programmes do not face the discipline of a profit and loss statement, through which their economic value can be calculated. This provides another reason for governments to over-expand their activities and for spending projects, once started, to develop their own momentum and be difficult to stop or rein back.

Summary

In economics, we assume that consumers, workers and firms act in a self-interested way, trying at all times to maximise private benefit. For any economic activity, private benefit maximisation occurs when the marginal private benefit received equals the marginal private cost incurred ($MPB = MPC$). But in the course of maximising private benefit, external costs and benefits are generated which affect other people's welfare. External costs (or negative externalities) reduce total welfare, whereas external benefits (or positive externalities) have the opposite effect.

For the social benefit (or the public interest of the whole community) to be maximised, economic activity must occur up to the point at which marginal social benefit equals marginal social cost (MSB = MSC). Social cost–benefit analysis (CBA) is a technique that governments sometimes use to try to ensure this happens. CBA tries to estimate all the costs and benefits, now and in the future, that are likely to result from a decision undertaken now. In the past, CBA has been used by UK governments when choosing whether to invest in big public sector infrastructure projects, such as new motorways and airports. In recent years, governments have made much less use of CBA, largely on the grounds of the cost and length of time involved when undertaking a large-scale cost–benefit analysis. However, from a government's point of view, the time taken to complete a CBA can sometimes be an advantage. Commissioning a cost–benefit analysis enables a government to delay a potentially unpopular decision and to deflect the unpopularity towards the 'impartial experts' undertaking the CBA.

Supporters of cost–benefit analysis argue that it is a scientific way of choosing between competing public sector investment decisions. But while CBA is appropriate for choosing between *similar* projects, for example alternative routes for a motorway, it is less appropriate for choosing between completely different projects, for example hospitals versus schools. Critics counter that CBA is ultimately unscientific because it is riddled with value judgements. Which costs and which benefits should be included in the CBA? How far into the future should estimates be made? How should external costs and benefits be quantified, and how should the present value of costs and benefits occurring in the future be calculated? Different answers to these and other questions may lead to completely different conclusions as to whether a particular investment project should go ahead.

Cost–benefit analysis can, of course, lead to government failure. Just as market failure occurs when markets perform unsatisfactorily, so government failure occurs when government intervention in markets leads to undesirable results. Free-market economists argue that, more often than not, government intervention to try to correct market failure succeeds only in creating government failure. In their view, a government should resist the temptation to intervene and should restrict its role to trying to make markets more competitive and flexible. Perhaps not surprisingly, Keynesian economists tend to reach the opposite conclusion, namely that smart government intervention can reduce market failure and make markets work better.

Self-testing questions

1 Distinguish between private and social costs and benefits.

2 Explain the difference between investment appraisal and social cost–benefit analysis.

3 What sort of prospective policy decisions might a government subject to cost–benefit analysis?

4 Explain how problems of quantification affect cost–benefit analysis.

5 Outline problems that may arise when identifying and evaluating future costs and benefits.

6 What is meant by 'discounting the future'?

7 Why is shadow pricing important in cost–benefit analysis?

8 Is cost–benefit analysis scientific or pseudo-scientific?

9 Distinguish between government failure and market failure.

10 What is the law of unintended consequences?

11 In the light of the possibility of government failure, should governments intervene in markets to try to correct market failures?

Part **4**

Labour markets

part 4

Chapter 11
Labour markets

Specification focus

This chapter explains how the market mechanism operates in an economy's labour markets. Though not a part of the AS specification, except to the extent that candidates must know that labour is a factor of production, labour markets are an important part of the A2 Module 5 specification.

A2 **Module 5 Business Economics and the Distribution of Income**
   The Labour Market

A2 **Synoptic coverage**
   At A2 candidates are expected to apply knowledge of supply and demand and the price mechanism learnt at AS to the labour market.

Introduction

Earlier chapters of this book explained and analysed the behaviour of households and firms in the economy's product markets. When explaining the price of a good, we assumed that the prices of inputs or factor services necessary for production to take place are generally given. This chapter reverses this assumption. When studying how wage rates and levels of employment are determined in the economy's labour markets, we generally assume that the prices of the goods that labour produces are given.

Price theory and the labour market

Much of the theory explained in this chapter is really just the price theory already studied in the goods market of an economy, operating in the labour market. As Figure 11.1 shows, households and firms function simultaneously in both sets of markets, but their roles are reversed. Whereas firms are the source of supply in the goods market, in the factor market firms exercise demand for factor services supplied by households. The incomes received by households from the sale and supply of factor services contribute, of course, in large measure to the households' ability to demand the output supplied by the firms in the goods market.

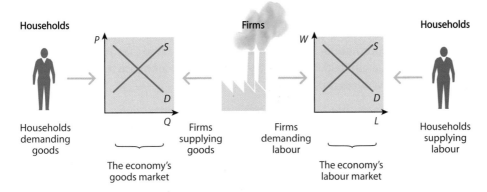

Figure 11.1 *The goods market and the factor market*

Indeed, the relationship between households and firms in the two markets is essentially circular. In the goods market, output or finished goods flow from firms to households in return for money revenues. In the factor market, the money revenues received enable the firms to purchase factor services supplied by the households. The circle is complete when households spend this income on the goods produced by the firms.

As we have noted, this chapter uses **price theory** to explain how wage rates and levels of employment are determined. There is, however, an alternative theory, which was developed by Karl Marx, one of the great nineteenth-century classical economists. **Marxist (or Marxian) theory** argues that a class struggle between capitalists and workers determines the level of wages. By treating labour as a commodity and forcing their workers' wages down, capitalists extract **surplus value** from them. This chapter provides no further explanation of Marxist theory, but it does explain how, in imperfectly competitive labour markets without trade unions or minimum wage legislation, monopsonistic employers can use market power to exploit the labour force.

First we shall explain the theory of a perfectly competitive labour market. As with a perfectly competitive goods market, it does not exist in real life. Perfect competition is always a theoretical abstraction, which can be criticised for its departure from real life. Critics argue that in reality imperfectly competitive labour markets are the norm, and perfect competition should be treated as an unrealistic limiting case.

Real-world labour markets do range in their competitiveness from the highly competitive, to those at the other extreme that resemble monopoly. However, in labour market theory, we use the term **monopsony** rather than monopoly. Whereas monopoly means a single seller, monopsony is a single buyer. A monopsony labour market is one in which the workers face a single employer.

Perfectly competitive labour markets

As in a perfectly competitive *goods* market, a perfectly competitive *labour* market contains a large number of buyers and sellers, each unable to influence the ruling market price (in this case the ruling market *wage*), and operating in conditions of perfect market information. Employers and workers are free to enter the market in the long run, but an individual employer or firm cannot influence the ruling market wage through its independent action.

In Chapter 5 we saw that a firm in a perfectly competitive goods market can sell as much as it wants at the ruling market price, which is also the perfectly elastic demand curve facing the firm and the firm's average and marginal revenue curve. Each firm is a passive price-taker at the ruling price determined in the market as a whole, choosing the quantity to sell but not the price.

A very similar situation exists when a firm takes on workers in a perfectly competitive labour market, except that now the firm can buy as much labour as it wants at the ruling market wage. To state this another way, each employer faces a perfectly elastic supply of labour in a perfectly competitive labour market. Figure 11.2 illustrates why.

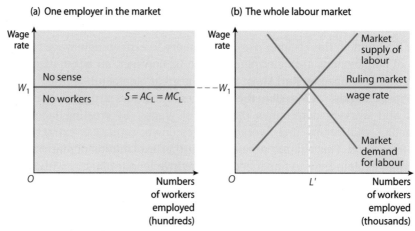

Figure 11.2 *The supply curve of labour facing each firm in a perfectly competitive labour market*

examiner's voice

Economic theory is easier to understand when you see how the same reasoning and way of thinking applies in different contexts. Compare Figure 11.2 with Figure 5.2 on p. 66. The diagrams show perfect competition in the labour market and in the goods market. In Figure 11.2, the wage rate lies along the perfectly elastic *supply* curve of labour facing each employer. By contrast, in Figure 5.2 the price that each firm charges lies along the perfectly elastic *demand* curve for the firm's output.

The right-hand panel of Figure 11.2 shows demand and supply conditions in the whole of the labour market. The ruling market wage facing all employers and workers is W_1. Each firm (depicted in the left-hand panel of the diagram) could pay a wage higher than W_1, but there is no need to, since as many workers as the firm plans to employ are available at the ruling wage. In any case, such a course of action means that the firm incurs unnecessary production costs, leading to X-inefficiency and a failure to maximise profits — hence the label 'no sense' positioned *above* W_1 in Figure 11.2. Conversely, any firm offering a wage *below* W_1 would lose all its workers. In a perfectly competitive labour market, workers regard all employers as perfect substitutes for each other. Why work for a firm paying below the market wage when work is available from employers offering the market wage?

In a perfectly competitive labour market, each employer is just one among many in the market, able to hire whatever number of workers it wishes, providing only that the ruling market wage is offered to all employees taken on. This also means that W_1 (the ruling market wage rate) is each firm's average cost of labour curve (AC_L) and its marginal cost of labour curve (MC_L). Average costs of labour are calculated by dividing total wage costs by the number of workers employed. Likewise, marginal costs of labour are measured by the growth of the total wage bill whenever an extra worker is hired.

The market supply of labour

The market supply curve of labour in the right-hand panel of Figure 11.2 is obtained by adding the individual supply curves of labour of all the workers in the labour market. To make sense of the market supply curve of labour, we must first derive an individual worker's supply curve of labour. This curve shows how many hours of labour the worker plans to supply at different hourly wage rates. The starting point is the assumption that a worker supplies more labour to increase personal economic welfare: that is, to maximise private benefit.

The welfare that a worker derives from the supply of labour divides into two parts, which taken together are sometimes called **net advantage**. Net advantage includes:

- welfare derived from the wage (or strictly from the goods and services bought with the money wage)
- **welfare derived from work** (popularly known as **job satisfaction**, or if negative, **job dissatisfaction**).

Monotonous work can lead to job dissatisfaction

Different types of work yield different amounts of positive or negative welfare (job satisfaction and dissatisfaction). When a worker enjoys the job, the net advantage of work is greater than the welfare of the wage. In this situation, the worker is willing to work for a money wage lower than the wage that would be acceptable if there were no satisfaction from the work itself. But for some workers, work such as routine assembly-line work in factories and heavy manual labour is unpleasant, yielding job dissatisfaction. The supply of labour for this type of employment reflects the fact that the hourly wage rate must be high enough to compensate for the unpleasantness (or sometimes the danger) of the job.

The upward-sloping supply curve of labour

As a simplification, we shall now assume that work yields neither job satisfaction nor dissatisfaction, and that a worker's net advantage derives solely from the wage. The worker must choose whether to supply an extra hour of labour time in order to earn money or whether to enjoy an extra hour of leisure time. The choice is illustrated in Figure 11.3.

There is an **opportunity cost** whenever a person decides to work. The opportunity cost of supplying one more hour of labour time (in order to earn money) is the hour of leisure time sacrificed. Because of the time constraint (there are only 24 hours in a day), a decision to supply one more hour of labour time means that the worker chooses one hour less of leisure time. Labour time and leisure time are substitutes for each other, and working longer hours eats into leisure time.

Figure 11.3 The choice between supplying labour and enjoying leisure time

But both the money wage and leisure time yield less and less extra welfare, the greater the quantity a person has. As more labour time is supplied at a particular hourly wage rate, the extra income yields less and less extra satisfaction. But the decision to supply more labour simultaneously means the decision to enjoy less leisure time. In this situation, each extra hour of leisure sacrificed is accompanied by an *increasing* loss of economic welfare. At the margin, to maximise personal welfare, a worker must supply labour up to the point at which:

$$\frac{\text{welfare from the last unit}}{\text{of money earned}} = \frac{\text{welfare from the last unit of}}{\text{leisure time sacrificed}}$$

In this situation, the marginal private benefit received by a worker from supplying labour equals the marginal private cost incurred from giving up leisure time. Providing personal preferences remain stable, there is no incentive for the worker to supply more labour at the going hourly wage rate.

However, a higher hourly wage disturbs this equilibrium. With a higher wage rate, at the margin, the welfare derived from the wage becomes greater than the welfare derived from the last unit of leisure time enjoyed. To maximise personal welfare at the higher wage rate, the worker must supply more labour and enjoy less leisure time. The result is the upward-sloping individual's supply curve of labour shown in Figure 11.4. An increase in the hourly wage rate from W_1 to W_2 means that the worker increases the hours of labour time supplied from L_1 to L_2.

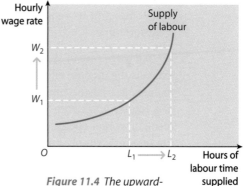

Figure 11.4 The upward-sloping supply curve of labour

The backward-bending supply curve of labour

Under some circumstances, however, a worker's labour supply curve may be backward bending, regressive or 'perverse', showing that as the wage rises, less labour is supplied. This is illustrated in Figure 11.5. When the wage rate rises from W_1 to W_2, the worker responds by working longer. The supply of labour increases from L_1 to L_2. But in Figure 11.5, the supply curve is upward sloping for only part of the curve. At hourly wage rates higher than W_2, the supply curve bends back towards the vertical axis of the graph, and the curve's slope is negative rather than positive. Following an increase in the hourly wage rate from W_2 to W_3, a worker reduces the number of hours of labour supplied from L_2 to L_3.

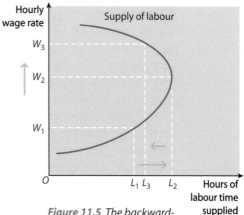

Figure 11.5 The backward-bending supply curve of labour

To explain the possibility of a backward-bending supply curve of labour, we must introduce two new concepts: the **substitution effect** of a change in the hourly wage rate; and the **income effect** of such a change.

- **The substitution effect of an increase in the hourly wage rate.** To understand the idea of a substitution effect, think of the hourly wage rate as the price of an hour of leisure time. For example, at an hourly wage rate of £10, the price of an hour of leisure time is also £10, rising to £11 if the wage rate is increased by a pound. As the wage rate rises, an hour of leisure time becomes more expensive compared to the goods that the money wage can buy. Acting rationally, a worker responds to the rise in the hourly wage rate (and the price of leisure time) by substituting more labour time in place of leisure time.

- **The income effect of an increase in the hourly wage rate.** If the substitution effect is the only effect operating, a worker's supply curve slopes upwards, showing labour time being substituted for leisure time as the hourly wage rate increases. However, matters can be complicated by the existence of an income effect resulting from the price change. The income effect of a wage rate increase results from the fact that, for most people, leisure time is a normal good and not an inferior good. A rise in the hourly wage rate increases the worker's real income, and as real income rises, so does the demand for the normal good, leisure time.

Up to a wage rate of W_2 in Figure 11.5, the substitution effect of any wage increase exceeds the income effect. As a result, a worker chooses to work longer hours and to enjoy less leisure time. But when the wage rate rises above W_2, the income effect of a higher wage rate becomes more powerful than the substitution effect. As a result, a worker chooses to work fewer hours so as to enjoy more leisure time — and the worker's supply curve of labour slopes backwards. Total money income may not fall. Given freedom of choice, a worker may, for example, decide to work 40 hours a week when the wage rate is £10 an hour, for a weekly income of £400. When the wage rate rises to £11, the worker may respond by working for only 38 hours, with a weekly income of £418.

A possibly simpler approach to the backward-bending supply curve is to assume that a worker aspires to a target standard of living measured in the goods and services that the money wage can buy. When the money wage rate rises, a worker can meet the target and fulfil aspirations by working fewer hours, choosing more leisure time rather than more material goods and services. Workers are especially likely to behave in this way when the work itself is highly unpleasant or dangerous, yielding negative job satisfaction.

*e**xaminer's voice***

It is important to understand what upward-sloping and backward-bending supply curves of labour *show*. However, AQA examination questions will seldom ask for theoretical explanations of the shape and slope of supply curves of labour.

The shape of the supply curve of labour and government policy

Whether an individual's supply curve of labour is upward sloping as in Figure 11.4, or backward bending as depicted in Figure 11.5, is very important for a

government's tax and fiscal policies (and also for supply-side policy). An increase in the rate of income tax is equivalent to a fall in the hourly wage rate. With an upward-sloping supply curve of labour, a rise in income tax is a disincentive to work and the supply of labour. When, however, the supply curve bends backwards, a rise in income tax increases the supply of labour. The tax increase has an incentive effect — a worker must now work longer to maintain a target material standard of living.

In real life, a tax increase may create an even greater need for laws to deal with tax avoidance and illegal tax evasion. People may decide to supply their labour untaxed in the informal, underground economy, rather than formally, but subject to taxation, in the 'overground' economy.

Whatever the shape of an *individual's* supply curve of labour, the *market* supply curve of labour will probably slope upwards. The explanation lies in the fact that more workers enter the labour market in response to a wage rise, attracted both from other labour markets and from unemployment.

The demand curve for labour

Just as the market supply curve of labour in a perfectly competitive labour market is the sum of the supply curves of all the individual workers in the labour market, so the market demand curve for labour is obtained by adding together each firm's demand curve for labour at different wage rates. We must therefore derive a perfectly competitive firm's demand curve for labour in order to understand the market demand curve for labour.

A firm demands labour only if profits can be increased by employing more workers. But this assumes that households in goods markets demand the goods and services that workers are employed to produce. This means that a firm's demand for labour is a **derived demand** — derived from the demand for goods. Assuming a profit-maximising objective on the part of firms, there can be no demand for labour in the long run unless the firms employing labour sell the outputs produced for at least a normal profit in the goods market. We shall now show that, in a perfectly competitive labour market, a firm's demand curve for labour is the marginal revenue product of labour (*MRP*) curve.

When deciding whether it is worthwhile employing one more worker, a firm needs to know the answers to three questions:

- How far will total *output* rise?
- How far will total *sales revenue* rise when the extra output is sold in the goods market?
- How far will total *costs of production* rise as a result of paying the worker a wage?

In a perfectly competitive labour market, a firm's demand curve for labour is derived from the answers to the first two of these questions. The answer to the third question is provided by the horizontal ruling market wage explained earlier in the chapter, which is illustrated in Figure 11.2.

The marginal physical product of labour

When answering the first of the three questions posed above, a firm has to calculate the value of the **marginal physical product of labour** (MPP). The marginal physical product or MPP of labour is (rather confusingly) just another name for the **marginal returns** (or **marginal product**) of labour, which is explained in Chapter 4. MPP measures the amount by which a firm's total output rises in the short run (holding capital fixed), as a result of employing one more worker. Chapter 4 explains how the **law of diminishing returns** or **diminishing marginal productivity** operates as a firm employs more labour when capital is held fixed. In the context of labour market theory, it is usual to assume that the law of diminishing returns begins to operate as soon as a second worker is added to the labour force. (This means that the possibility of increasing marginal returns at low levels of employment is ignored.)

Given this simplifying assumption, the impact of the law of diminishing returns is illustrated in Figure 11.6(a), which shows the marginal product of labour falling as additional workers are hired by the firm.

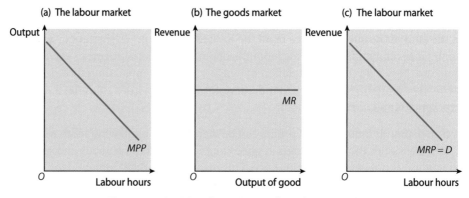

Figure 11.6 Deriving the MRP curve from the MPP curve

The marginal revenue product of labour

The falling *MPP* curve provides the answer to the first of the three questions posed, showing how much total output will rise when an additional worker is employed. But as its name indicates, the *MPP* curve only shows the physical output produced by an extra worker — measured, for example, in automobiles or loaves of bread, or whatever goods the firm produces. To convert the marginal *physical* product of labour into a money value, the *MPP* of labour has to be multiplied by the addition to the firm's total sales revenue resulting from the sale in the goods market of the extra output produced by labour. We therefore multiply *MPP* by marginal revenue (*MR*) to answer the second of the three questions. When the economy's goods market is perfectly competitive, *MR* is identical to the good's price or average revenue, and is shown by the horizontal *MR* curve in Figure 11.6(b).

Figure 11.6(c), which shows the marginal revenue product curve of labour (*MRP*), can be explained with the use of the following equation:

marginal physical product × marginal revenue = marginal revenue product

or:

$$MPP \times MR = MRP$$

As the equation shows, the marginal revenue product of labour is calculated by multiplying the MPP of labour in Figure 11.6(a) by the horizontal MR curve in Figure 11.6(b). When a firm sells its output in a perfectly competitive goods market, the falling diminishing marginal revenue productivity of labour is explained solely by the diminishing marginal physical product: that is, by the law of diminishing returns. (But if output is sold in an imperfectly competitive goods market, marginal revenue product of labour declines faster than in a perfectly competitive goods market. This is because in imperfectly competitive goods markets, the marginal revenue earned from selling an extra worker's output also falls as output increases. In this situation, there are two reasons for the MRP curve to fall as employment increases.)

The equilibrium wage rate and level of employment in a perfectly competitive labour market

We are now in a position to show the determination of the equilibrium wage rate and level of employment, both for a single employer in a perfectly competitive labour market and for the whole labour market. These are shown respectively in Figure 11.7(a) and (b). Figure 11.7 is identical to Figure 11.2, except that an *MRP* curve has been added in Figure 11.7(a).

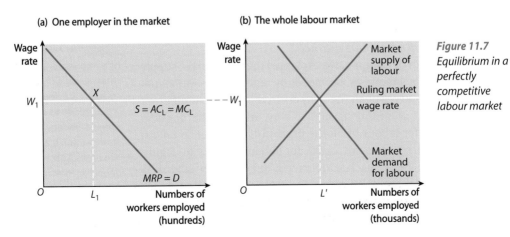

(a) One employer in the market

(b) The whole labour market

Figure 11.7
Equilibrium in a perfectly competitive labour market

A perfectly competitive firm's demand curve for labour

As we saw earlier in the chapter, each employer is a price-taker at the ruling wage in the labour market. The ruling wage, determined in Figure 11.7(b), is also the perfectly elastic supply curve of labour facing the firm and the AC_L and MC_L curve. Each firm can hire as many workers as it wishes at the ruling market wage, but cannot influence the ruling wage by its own actions. To maximise profit when selling the output produced by labour, the firm must choose the level of employment at which:

> the addition to sales revenue resulting from the employment of an extra worker = the addition to production costs resulting from hiring the services of an extra worker

or:

$$MRP = MC_L$$

The marginal revenue product of labour or *MRP* is the **marginal private benefit** accruing to the employer when hiring an extra worker. Likewise, the **marginal cost of labour** or MC_L is the marginal private cost incurred by the firm. Since, in a perfectly competitive labour market, the marginal cost of labour always equals the wage paid to the workers, the perfectly competitive firm's level of employment is where:

$$MRP = W$$

Point X in Figure 11.7(a) shows the number of workers that a firm is willing to employ at the ruling wage of W_1. Consider what happens if the firm employs a labour force larger than L_1. Additional workers add more to total cost than to total revenue, and profit falls. Conversely, with a workforce below L_1, the *MRP* of the last worker is greater than the wage, and the profits that a larger labour force would generate are not made.

Summarising:

- If $MRP > W$, more workers should be hired.
- If $MRP < W$, fewer workers should be employed.
- If MRP = W, the firm is employing the number of workers consistent with profit maximisation.

The market demand for labour in a perfectly competitive labour market

Earlier in the chapter, we explained that the market supply curve of labour is obtained by adding the individual supply curves of all the workers in the market at different possible wages. In a similar way, we add the demand curves for labour of all the firms in the market to obtain the market demand curve for labour shown in Figure 11.7(b). Since each employer's demand for labour is shown by the *MRP* curve, the market demand curve for labour is the horizontal sum of the *MRP* curves.

> **examiner's voice**
>
> It is important to realise that *all* real world labour markets are imperfectly competitive to some degree. Perfect competition is as much a theoretical abstraction in labour markets as it is in goods markets.

Monopsony labour markets

As we noted earlier, **monopsony** means a single buyer, just as **monopoly** means a single seller. In a monopsony labour market, workers cannot choose between alternative employers, since there is only one firm or employer available to hire them.

Although in some ways a monopsony labour market resembles a monopoly goods market, there are also significant differences. In much the same way that the *market demand curve* facing a monopoly supplier of a good is the monopolist's *average revenue curve*, so in a monopsony labour market, the *market supply curve of labour* is the firm's *average cost of labour curve* (AC_L). The AC_L curve shows the different wage rates that the monopsonist must pay to attract labour forces of different sizes. For example, Figure 11.8 shows a monopsony employer hiring 5 workers at an hourly wage rate or AC_L of £10. As the diagram shows, the hourly wage per week must rise to £11 to attract a sixth worker into the firm's labour force.

The supply or AC_L curve facing the monopsonist shows the wage that has to be paid to all workers at each size of the labour force, to persuade the workers to supply their services. However, in a monopsony labour market, the AC_L curve is *not* the marginal cost of labour curve (MC_L). As explained in the previous paragraph, to attract an extra worker, the monopsonist must raise the hourly wage rate and pay the higher wage to all the workers. In this situation, the marginal cost of labour incurred by employing an extra worker includes the *total* amount by which the wage bill rises, and not just the wage rate paid to the additional worker hired. The MC_L curve of labour illustrated in Figure 11.8 is positioned *above* the AC_L or supply curve (just as, in the goods market, a monopolist's *MR* curve is *below* its *AR* curve). In Figure 11.8, the MC_L incurred per hour by employing the sixth worker is £16, made up of the £11 wage rate paid to the sixth worker, plus the £1 extra paid to each of the 5 workers already employed before the sixth worker joined the labour force.

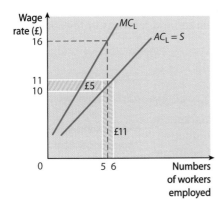

Figure 11.8 In a monopsony labour market, the MC_L curve lies above the AC_L or supply of labour curve

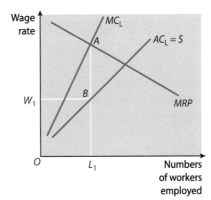

Figure 11.9 Equilibrium in a monopsony labour market

The equilibrium wage rate and level of employment

Figure 11.9 shows how the equilibrium wage and the equilibrium level of employment are determined in a monopsony labour market. As in the case of a perfectly competitive employer in the labour market, the monopsonist's level of employment is determined by the point where $MRP = MC_L$. This occurs at point A in Figure 11.9, producing L_1 number of workers.

However, in a monopsony labour market, the equilibrium wage rate is determined at point B, which lies below A, in Figure 11.9. The wage rate paid by the monopsonist (W_1 in Figure 11.9) is *less* than the value of the marginal revenue product of labour. Point B is positioned on the supply curve of labour facing the monopsonist. The supply curve shows that L_1 workers are willing to work for an hourly wage rate of W_1. Although the wage rate determined at A and equal to the MRP of labour *could* be paid without the firm incurring a loss on the last worker employed, the monopsonist has no need to pay such a high wage rate. Why pay more, when W_1 attracts all the workers the monopsonist requires? Indeed, if the monopsonist were to pay a wage higher than W_1, it would inevitably incur unnecessary production costs and end up being X-inefficient. It would fail to maximise profits when selling its output in the goods market. Profit maximisation requires that a wage no higher than W_1 is paid.

Wage equalisation in a perfectly competitive market economy

If all labour markets in the economy were perfectly competitive, there would be no barriers preventing workers moving between labour markets. In this situation, the forces of competition would reduce many of the differences in wages between different occupations. Some differences would probably remain because different types of work have different skill requirements, and innate abilities and skills would still vary between workers. Nevertheless, higher wages in one occupation would attract workers from other labour markets, causing the supply curve of labour to shift rightward in the high-wage labour market and leftward in the low-wage market.

At the same time, wage differentials would create incentives for firms in the high-wage market to reduce their demand for labour by substituting capital for labour, and for firms in the low-wage labour markets to adopt more labour-intensive methods of production. Demand and supply curves and wages would continue to adjust until there was no further incentive for firms to change their method of production or for workers to shift between labour markets. Wage differentials would diminish throughout the economy, but would not completely disappear.

examiner's voice

Exam questions may ask for explanations of why some workers, say brain surgeons, are paid more than other workers, such as supermarket cashiers. You must use theory to answer this type of question, and not just 'common sense'.

Explanations of different wage levels

Wage differences in competitive labour markets

Even in highly competitive labour markets, wage differences exist, largely because labour demand and supply curves are in different positions in different labour markets, reflecting factors such as different labour productivities, abilities and required skills. We might also expect wage differentials to exist in highly competitive labour markets for two further reasons:

- **Different jobs have different non-monetary characteristics.** We have already explained how the net advantage of any type of work includes job satisfaction or dissatisfaction as well as economic welfare gained from the wage. Other things being equal, a firm must pay a worker a higher wage to compensate for any relative unpleasantness in the job. An **equalising wage differential** is the payment that must be made to compensate a worker for the different non-monetary characteristics of jobs. Following such a payment, there is no incentive for a worker to switch between jobs or labour markets.
- **Disequilibrium trading.** Economies are subject to constant change, such as the development of new goods and services and improved methods of production or technical progress. Patterns of demand also change. Because market conditions are always changing, labour markets — like other markets — are usually in disequilibrium rather than in equilibrium. Although market forces *tend* to equalise wages in competitive labour markets, at any point in time disparities exist, reflecting the disequilibrium conditions existent at the time.

Wage differences in imperfectly competitive labour markets

In imperfectly competitive labour markets, including monopsony labour markets, there are a number of other reasons why differences in wages occur. These include: immobility of labour; different elasticities of demand for, and supply of, labour; wage discrimination; differences in pay between women and men; the effect of trade unions; and the effect of different methods of pay determination, such as collective bargaining.

Immobility of labour

There are two main types of labour immobility: occupational immobility and geographical immobility.

- **Occupational immobility of labour.** This occurs when workers are prevented by either *natural* or *artificial* barriers from moving between different types of job. Workers are obviously not homogeneous or uniform, so differences in natural ability may prevent or restrict movement between jobs. Some types of work require an innate ability, such as physical strength or perfect eyesight, which prevents a worker immediately switching between labour markets. Examples of artificial barriers include membership qualifications imposed by professional bodies such as accountancy associations; and trade union restrictive practices such as pre-entry closed shops, which restrict employment to those already

House prices in the southeast of England have soared

belonging to the union. Various forms of racial, religious and gender discrimination are also artificial causes of occupational immobility of labour.

- **Geographical immobility of labour.** This occurs when factors, such as ignorance of job opportunities, family and cultural ties, and the financial costs of moving or travel, prevent a worker from filling a job vacancy located at a distance from his or her present place of residence. Perhaps the most significant cause of geographical immobility in the UK in recent years has been the state of the housing market, which itself reflects imperfections in other factor markets. During house price booms, low-paid and unemployed workers in the northern half of the UK have found it difficult or impossible to move south to fill job vacancies in the more prosperous southeast of England. The prices of owner-occupied housing have soared and there has been very little housing available at affordable rents in either the private or the public sectors. At the same time, workers living in their own houses in the southeast may be reluctant to apply for jobs elsewhere in the country, for fear that they will never be able to afford to move back to southern England.

Different elasticities of demand for and supply of labour

Both the mobility of labour and wage rates in different labour markets are affected by the elasticities of the supply of, and the demand for, labour. We shall now look briefly at factors affecting labour market elasticities.

Determinants of the wage elasticity of labour demand. If the wage rate increases, but nothing else that might affect the demand for labour changes, by how much will employment fall? The answer is affected by firms' elasticity of demand for labour. The demand for a particular type of labour is likely to be relatively inelastic:

- if the relevant wage cost forms only a small part of total production costs (this has been called 'the importance of being unimportant')
- if the demand for the good or service being produced by the labour is inelastic
- if it is difficult to substitute other factors of production, or other types of labour, for the labour currently employed
- in the short run, rather than the long run, since it often takes time for employers to adjust their production process

Determinants of the wage elasticity of labour supply. The supply of unskilled labour is usually more elastic than the supply of a particular type of skilled labour. The training period of unskilled labour is usually very short, and any innate abilities required are unlikely to be restricted to a small proportion of the total population. All the factors reducing the occupational and geographical mobility of labour tend to reduce the elasticity of labour supply. The supply of labour is also likely to be more elastic in the long run than in the short run. Finally, the availability of a pool of unemployed labour increases the elasticity of supply of labour, while full employment has the opposite effect.

> **examiner's voice**
>
> Unit 5 exam questions are likely to require synoptic application of elasticity theory, learnt in the context of the goods market in Module 1, to the demand for and supply of labour.

Wage discrimination

In imperfectly competitive labour markets, employers often possess sufficient market power to reduce the total wage bill through **wage discrimination**.

Figure 11.10 illustrates the effect of wage discrimination introduced into a previously competitive labour market (though, in real life, discrimination is more likely in imperfectly competitive labour markets). In the absence of wage discrimination, all workers are paid the same wage, W_1, determined by supply and demand. Employers' total wage costs are shown by the rectangle OW_1AL_1.

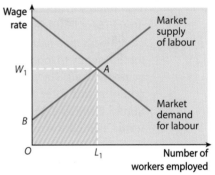

Figure 11.10 Wage discrimination

But if, instead of paying W_1 to all workers, employers pay each worker the minimum he or she is prepared to work for, the total wage bill falls to equal the shaded 'wedge' area $OBAL_1$. Employers thus gain at the expense of workers, which is why firms pay, and trade unions resist, discriminatory wages whenever possible.

Differences in earnings between men and women

In recent years, although women have accounted for an increasing share of total employment in the UK, women's pay often continues to be lower than men's pay, despite the fact that equal pay legislation has been in place since 1972.

According to a poll undertaken by the Equal Opportunities Commission (EOC) in 2004, 88% of women expect to earn the same as a man with the same qualifications, rising to 94% among women under 25. According to the EOC report, however, these women are 'heading for disappointment' because the latest data showed that the difference in average pay between men and women working full time is just over £6,700 a year — about 18%. The poll also found that 29% of women did not know what their colleagues earned, compared with 20% of men. As a result, women were more likely than men to be unaware of pay discrimination. More people in professional and managerial positions than in clerical and manual jobs knew what most of their colleagues earned. The EOC concluded, rather depressingly, that 'discrimination flourishes in this culture of secrecy when people cannot be sure they are rewarded fairly'.

There are two main reasons why women earn less than men:

- Women work predominantly in low-paid industries and occupations.
- Within many occupational groups, women are paid less than men. This is often because women are under-represented in the higher-paid posts within an occupation, rather than because women are paid less for doing the same job.

Discrimination against women in labour markets may contribute to both these sets of circumstances. In addition, women are disproportionately represented in industries where the average size of firm and plant is small. These industries tend to pay lower wages and offer fewer promotional prospects than large firms and large industries. Such industries are also seldom unionised. Indeed, within all industries, women workers are less unionised than men.

This relates to another reason why women earn less than men: on average, their attachment to the labour force is weaker. Each year of work experience raises the pay of both men and women by an average 3%. Yet when women leave the labour force, usually to look after young children, their potential pay falls by 3% for each year involved. For example, a man and woman enter employment with equal potential and after 8 years the woman leaves the work force in order to raise a family. If she re-enters the labour force 8 years later she would be 16 years, in pay terms, behind the man.

The higher labour turnover of women also imposes costs on the employer – for example, the costs of training replacement workers. This may reduce the incentive for employers to train female workers. Similarly, women may have less incentive to spend time and money on their own education and training if they expect the benefits that they will eventually receive to be less than the costs initially incurred.

> ### examiner's voice
> Examination questions may be set on the impact of gender, ethnic and other forms of discrimination on wages, levels and types of employment. Questions will not be set on the theory of wage discrimination, though the theory can be used as part of an explanation of why workers are paid different wage rates.

The effect of introducing a trade union into a perfectly competitive market

A **trade union** is an association of workers formed to protect and promote the interests of its members. A major function of a union is to bargain with employers to improve wages and other conditions of work. As we shall explain at the end of the chapter, many UK employers are now reluctant to recognise and bargain with the unions to which their employees belong. However, for the purposes of our analysis, we shall regard a trade union as a monopoly supplier of labour, which is able to keep non-members out of the labour market and also to prevent its members from supplying labour at below the union wage rate. Of course, in real life a union may not necessarily have the objectives specified above, and even if it does, it may not be able to achieve them. We shall make one other increasingly unrealistic assumption, namely that a union can fix any wage rate it chooses, and that employment is then determined by the amount of labour that employers will hire at this wage.

Given these assumptions, Figure 11.11 shows the possible effects resulting from workers organising a trade union in a labour market that had previously been perfectly competitive. Without a trade union, the competitive wage rate is W_1.

The workers join a trade union, which raises the minimum wage rate acceptable to union members to W_2. Without the union, the market supply of labour curve is the upward-sloping line labelled $S = AC_L$. With the union, the market supply of labour curve is the kinked line W_2XS. For all sizes of labour force to the left of, or below, L_3, the supply curve of labour is horizontal or perfectly elastic, lying along the wage W_2 set by the trade union. If employers wish to hire a labour force larger than L_3 (and to the right of point X), a wage higher than W_2 has to be offered. Beyond L_3, the supply curve of labour slopes upwards because higher wage rates are needed to attract more workers.

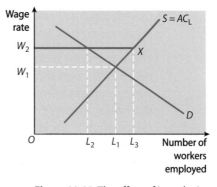

Figure 11.11 *The effect of introducing a trade union into a previously perfectly competitive labour market*

At the wage level set by the union, employers only wish to hire L_2 workers. However, L_3 workers are willing to work at this wage rate. This means there is excess supply of labour and unemployment in the labour market. More workers wish to work than there are jobs available. The resulting unemployment, called **classical unemployment**, is shown by the distance $L_3 - L_2$.

examiner's voice
Note that the effect described above can also be used to explain the effect of imposing a national minimum wage rate above the free-market equilibrium wage rate.

The effect described above is sometimes used to justify the argument that any attempt by a union to raise wages must inevitably be at the expense of jobs, and that if unions are really interested in reducing unemployment, they should accept wage cuts. However, many economists — especially those of a Keynesian and left-of-centre persuasion — dispute this conclusion. They argue, first, that it is unrealistic to assume that conditions of demand for labour are unchanged. By agreeing to accept technical progress, by working with new capital equipment and new methods of organising work and by improving the skills of their members a union can ensure (with the co-operation of management) that the *MRP* curve of labour shifts rightward. In these circumstances, increased productivity creates scope for both increased wages and increased employment.

Second, both wages and employment can rise when a union negotiates for higher wages to be paid by firms producing in an expanding goods market. In these conditions, increased demand for output creates increased demand for labour to produce the output. Indeed, rising real wages throughout the economy are likely to increase the aggregate demand for the output of all firms producing consumer goods because wages are the most important source of consumption expenditure in the economy.

So far, we have assumed that trade unions try to increase pay by preventing union members supplying labour at wage rates below the rate set by the union. Figure 11.12 illustrates a second way in which much the same result can be achieved. In this case, the trade union establishes a **closed shop**, which keeps non-union workers out of the labour market. The union-controlled entry barrier shifts the supply curve of labour leftward, and increases the inelasticity of the curve. Employment falls from L_1 to L_2, and the wage rate is hiked up to W_2.

The word 'shop' in the term *closed shop* refers to the workshop or the shop floor, where manufacturing firms undertake the tasks involved in production. A closed shop is an example of a labour **restrictive practice**. There are two types of closed shop, both of which have been made illegal in the UK. Figure 11.12 illustrates the effect of a *pre-entry* closed shop, which requires workers to join the union before starting employment. By imposing a quota or ceiling on the number of union members, a union uses a pre-entry closed shop to shift the supply curve of labour leftward. By contrast, a *post-entry* closed shop permits non-members to get jobs, but all workers have to join the union to *keep* their jobs. Post-entry closed shops have little effect on entry barriers, but they are a means of dealing with the free-

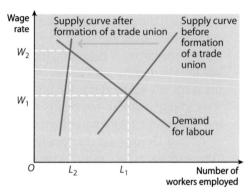

Figure 11.12 A trade union shifting the market supply curve of labour

examiner's voice

Avoid confusing *labour market* restrictive practices with *trading* restrictive practices used by firms in imperfectly competitive goods markets.

rider problem in labour markets. Free-riding occurs when workers decline to join a union while accepting pay rises that the union negotiates. Free-riders benefit from the union 'mark-up' — that is, the generally higher pay in unionised rather than non-unionised places of work — but save themselves the cost of paying union membership fees.

How a trade union can increase both the wage rate and employment in a monopsonistic labour market

The assertion that unions raise wages at the expense of jobs is heavily dependent on the assumption that, before the union was formed, the labour market was perfectly competitive. In the case of a monopsony labour market, it is possible for a union to raise *both* the wage rate and employment, even without the MRP curve shifting rightward. This is illustrated in Figure 11.13. As in Figure 11.11, if the labour market is non-unionised, the equilibrium wage rate is W_1 and the level of employment is L_1.

The introduction of a trade union into a monopsony labour market has the same effect on the labour supply curve as in perfect competition. In Figure 11.13, the kinked line W_2XS is the labour supply curve and the average cost of labour curve (AC_L) when the union sets the wage rate at W_2. But in monopsony, W_2XS is *not* the marginal cost of labour curve (MC_L). The MC_L curve is the 'double-kinked' line W_2XZV. The 'double kink' is explained in the following way. Providing the monopsonist employs a labour force *smaller* than or equal to L_2, the MC_L of employing an extra worker equals both the AC_L and the union-determined wage of W_2. But

beyond L_2 and point X, the monopsonist must offer a higher wage in order to persuade additional workers to supply labour. In this situation, with all the workers now being paid the higher wage, the MC_L curve lies above the supply curve or AC_L curve. The upward-sloping line ZV drawn in Figure 11.13 shows the MC_L of increasing employment above L_2.

This means there is a vertical gap between the horizontal section of the MC_L curve (for levels of employment at or *below* L_2 and point X) and the upward-sloping section of the curve (ZV). In the absence of a union, the level of employment is L_1, determined at point A (with point B determining the wage rate W_1). But when the union sets the wage rate at W_2, employment rises to L_2, which is the level of employment at which the MRP curve intersects the vertical section of the MC_L curve at point C, between X and Z. The union has managed to increase both the wage rate and the level of employment.

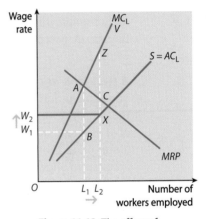

Figure 11.13 *The effect of introducing a trade union into a monopsony labour market*

Indeed, the analysis can be taken a stage further. As Figure 11.14 shows, providing the union possesses the necessary bargaining power, the wage rate can be raised above W_2 and still more employment can result.

Suppose, for example, the trade union sets the wage rate at W_3 in Figure 11.14. At W_3, the double-kinked line W_3CZV is the MC_L curve. The level of employment (L_3) is determined at point C, where the MC_L and MRP curves intersect. In fact, point C and the wage rate W_3 locate the maximum level of employment that the union can achieve. Although employment is maximised at point C, it may still be possible for the union to increase the wage

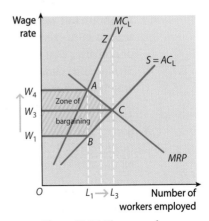

Figure 11.14 *The zone of bargaining*

rate above W_3. However, if this were to happen, some of the extra employment would be lost. Indeed, if the union sets the wage rate at W_4, employment falls back to its initial level before the union intervened in the labour market, namely L_1. Finally, any attempt to increase the wage rate above W_4 causes employment to fall to a level below L_1.

This analysis leads to a very important conclusion. It shows that, providing a trade union has sufficient market power, both the wage rate and the level of employment can be increased towards those of a perfectly competitive labour market (W_3 and L_3, shown at point C in Figure 11.14).

In Figure 11.14, the shaded wedge between the wages of W_1 and W_4 is called the **zone of bargaining**. The zone of bargaining indicates that, in an imperfect labour market, a union may be able to achieve higher wage rates and/or higher employment levels, without in this case having to accept a reduction in employment below L_1.

examiner's voice

Exam questions may ask if trade unions (or a national minimum wage) can raise the level of employment as well as the wage rate. The answer depends on the competitiveness of the labour market.

A first look at the national minimum wage

The explanation in the previous section, of how a trade union can increase both the wage rate and the level of employment, can also be used to analyse the effect of a national minimum wage set by the government. Under the unrealistic assumption that labour markets are perfectly competitive, Figure 11.11 can be adapted to show how a national minimum wage set above the market-clearing wage rate leads to a loss of jobs and unemployment. But if, more realistically, labour markets are imperfectly competitive, Figures 11.13 and 11.14 should be used. These can be adapted to show how a national minimum wage can increase *both* the wage rate and the level of employment.

Some further aspects of trade union activity

So far, we have assumed that trade unions can set wage rates or restrict the supply of labour, but we have not explained how unions might exercise this power. Trade unions may exercise power by threatening, or actually undertaking, strike action or activities that stop short of an actual strike, such as a work-to-rule or a go slow. Strikes and related activities disrupt the continuous-flow production processes on which much economic activity depends.

The threat of such disruption may persuade employers to sacrifice profit maximisation for the sake of securing at least some profit from uninterrupted production. When this happens, both the wage and the level of employment are determined at a point off the *MRP* curve. For example, a union may force firms to incur otherwise avoidable costs by employing more workers than are strictly necessary; hence firms sacrifice potential profit at the wage fixed by the union in order to secure industrial peace.

But in this situation, are firms really sacrificing profit? The answer depends on whether we are considering short-run or long-run profit. By conceding to the

union's demands and sacrificing short-term profit, firms may ensure long-run profit maximisation in conditions of industrial peace. (This is an example of **constrained profit maximisation**.) However, this conclusion depends on the assumption that the employers are unable to break the power of the union, which means that they have had to learn to live with the union. This is not always the case. In an extreme scenario, employers may decide to sacrifice short-term profits to an even greater extent, in an all-out industrial dispute. They may hope to destroy the union or its power, and to create conditions in which, in the long run, profit maximisation can occur in a union-free labour market. With the backing of a Conservative government the nationalised industry, British Coal, took this course of action in 1984–85 to break the power of the National Union of Mineworkers during a prolonged strike.

Payment methods

So far, this chapter has focused on the economic theory of labour markets, with only cursory mentions of institutional arrangements within labour markets. The next sections describe methods of wage determination operational within the UK economy and the changes that have taken place in these methods.

Methods of pay determination in the UK

Up to now, we have assumed that pay is determined either by supply and demand and market forces or by a trade union (or a government-imposed minimum wage). There are, however, several other institutional aspects of wage and pay determination in the UK.

*e*xaminer's voice

Exam questions may be set on different methods of pay determination and on reasons for the decline of *collective bargaining* as a method of pay determination.

Collective bargaining

Traditionally, the main function of trade unions has been to undertake **collective bargaining**: that is, to bargain collectively with employers on behalf of the union's members. This is to determine rates of pay and other conditions of employment, ranging from pensions, holidays and disputes procedures to conditions of work within a particular workplace.

There are many different forms of collective bargaining, which reflect the varied structure of industries and labour markets, and also the haphazard way in which both unions and employers' associations have developed their present-day structure. In one industry there may be a single trade union representing all the employed workers, which bargains either with a single employer or perhaps with all the firms in the industry, organised as an employer's association. In other industries, separate unions representing specific groups of skilled and unskilled workers may jointly bargain with the employer or employers, or they may bargain separately and perhaps in competition with each other.

We can also distinguish between national collective bargaining and various forms of local collective bargaining, for example at regional, plant and shop-floor level. *National* bargaining may determine basic or minimum agreed wage rates in an industry, while *local* bargaining determines any payments, such as bonuses, paid over and above the nationally agreed minimum and piece-work rates.

At various times in the past, when free collective bargaining was restricted and distorted by the government's incomes policy, there was a tendency for more and more of total earnings to be negotiated locally, so that the basic wage formed a declining proportion of total earnings. This process is known as **wage drift**. When a government imposes an incomes policy or period of wage restraint aimed at keeping down the rate of pay increases, unions find it easiest to evade the impact of the policy by bargaining informally with local employers. During such periods of imposed pay restraint, it has proved difficult to prevent locally negotiated pay deals, which are specific to a particular piece of work passing through a factory, and which raise pay by more than the incomes policy officially permits.

Individual negotiation

This generally takes place in the non-unionised parts of the economy. Two very different types of worker usually determine their pay by individual negotiation. At the one extreme are highly paid executives, managers and consultants offering specialist professional services. At the other extreme, unorganised low-paid workers, especially those who are casually employed in industries such as tourism and agriculture, negotiate individually with a prospective employer. In the latter circumstances, however, when the weight of bargaining power often lies with employers who offer wages on a 'take it or leave it' basis, the method of pay deter-mination may more accurately represent employer determination, rather than individual negotiation. (It is also worth noting that when pay is negotiated indi-vidually, the employer is most likely to undertake the wage discrimination described earlier in the chapter.)

State determination

In economic activities where the state or a public authority is the employer, trade unions have long been recognised and wages have been determined by collective bargaining. There have always been some exceptions, such as the armed forces and the police, where pay is fixed by state determination rather than by collective bargaining. In recent years, however, as a part of their policy of reducing the power of trade unions, UK governments have significantly reduced the role of the trade unions in the public sector. At one point, the government forced civil servants working in jobs related to national security to leave their unions. It has also unilat-erally abandoned collective bargaining in the case of teachers, whose pay is now determined in part by the state and in part by headteachers. Where the state determines pay, it has usually done so with the aid of an independent review body that advises the government on pay awards, on the basis of comparability with other groups of workers in either the private or public sector. However, on occasions, governments have been quite prepared to override these arrangements to set a crude limit on public sector pay.

The national minimum wage and income policies

Before the first of Margaret Thatcher's three Conservative governments came into office in 1979, successive UK governments had believed in the need to use the powers of the state to protect low-paid workers in industries such as catering and agriculture, where trade unions are ineffective and difficult to organise. Wages councils had been established in these industries to determine minimum rates of pay. In many European countries, a minimum legal wage has been in existence for decades, covering all industries. But from 1979 until 1997, UK Conservative governments opposed the introduction of a minimum legal wage, believing that its main effect would be to increase unemployment. Indeed, the powers of wages councils were restricted in the 1980s and the Conservative government finally abolished them in 1993.

By contrast, the Labour Party and the trade union movement were both committed to the introduction of a national minimum wage, arguing that evidence from other European countries suggests that the benefits in terms of social fairness exceed any costs involved. The national minimum wage (NMW) introduced in April 1999 was set at a level of £3.60 per hour throughout the UK, or 45% of median earnings. But young workers below the age of 18 were excluded from its protection.

The government decides the level of the national minimum wage, taking advice from the Low Pay Commission. The government does *not* guarantee to increase the NMW each year, although in recent years the NMW has been raised annually. The main details of the NMW proposed for October 2005 are shown in Table 11.1.

Table 11.1 UK national minimum wage rates

	Rate from October 2005
The full NMW rate All workers aged 22 and over, who qualify for the NMW and who are not 'accredited trainees'.	£5.05 per hour (increasing to £5.35 in October 2006)
The development rate (for workers aged 18–21) This rate is also paid to workers aged 22 and above during their first 6 months in a new job with a new employer when receiving accredited training.	£4.25 per hour (increasing to £4.45 in October 2006)
16 and 17 year olds' rate (Apprentices exempt)	£3.00 per hour

The national minimum wage imposes a lower limit or floor below which bargaining cannot legally take place. By contrast, an incomes policy usually means imposing an upper limit or ceiling constraining bargaining. For obvious reasons, trade unions have often been suspicious of incomes policies, believing that they undermine the central bargaining function of a union. In the past, the main purpose of incomes policies has been to attack the causes of cost-push inflation, which are closely related to the nature of wage bargaining in the UK. Governments also justified incomes policies as a method of ensuring a fairer distribution of income than that achieved by market forces and collective bargaining.

Arbitration and conciliation

Another function of the state in processes of pay and wage determination relates to arbitration and conciliation, although again the state's role in this respect has diminished in recent years. When bargaining collectively, a trade union may demand a pay rise greater than the increase an employer is at first prepared to pay. In theory, bargaining then takes over. **Bargaining** is a process in which each party modifies its offer or claim, perhaps to the accompaniment of threats, until agreement is reached. For example, a union may threaten a strike or other forms of industrial action, such as a work-to-rule, whereas an employer's threats can include redundancy and 'lock-outs'.

It must be stressed that the vast majority of pay agreements that are eventually signed are reached without a breakdown in the bargaining process and without an industrial dispute. Nevertheless, on occasion agreement cannot be reached; bargaining breaks down and a dispute occurs or is threatened. Many collective agreements contain negotiating procedures that both unions and employers agree to follow when breakdown occurs, to speed the process to eventual agreement without a harmful dispute. The procedural arrangements commonly specify the stage in the breakdown of bargaining at which outside conciliators or arbitrators should be brought in to assist both sides to reach agreement. Since 1975, an official government-sponsored conciliation service has existed, the **Advisory Conciliation and Arbitration Service** (ACAS), which, if both sides agree, is available to try and settle a dispute.

The decline of trade unions in the UK

In 2004 in the UK, there were 6.7 million members of the 71 trade unions affiliated to the Trades Union Congress (TUC). This contrasts with 1979, the peak year for union membership, when over 12 million members belonged to 109 TUC-affiliated unions. Total union membership is normally larger than the TUC figures suggest, as there are a number of trade unions outside the TUC. In 1979 total membership outside and inside the TUC had been over 13.3 million, or over half the labour force, and there were 453 unions in total.

As the figures indicate, trade union influence and membership was at its greatest in the 1970s. During this decade, the trade union movement expanded membership into previously non-unionised 'white-collar' office and professional workers. Its traditional base of support has been skilled, semi-skilled and unskilled 'blue-collar' manual workers in the transport, mining and manufacturing industries. Because most large and medium-sized employers recognised trade unions, collective bargaining became the most significant form of pay determination in the UK.

At the same time, the trade union movement enjoyed an increasing influence on government policy, both directly through its hold on the Labour Party when the party was in government and also through a growing trend towards **corporatism** in government decision making. Corporatism is a situation in which government decision making largely bypasses the formal democratic process. Thus important economic decisions – for example, on pay policy – were made not in Parliament, but at informal meetings at 10 Downing Street attended by government ministers (the political executive), the Confederation of British Industry (CBI) representing 'big business', and the TUC representing organised labour.

By the late 1970s, many people – especially on the political right – believed that the unions had gained far too much economic power and political influence. A majority of people seemed to accept the view that the performance of the UK economy was being adversely affected by the power of the trade union movement – for example, through uncompetitive labour markets and the unions' resistance to economic change. Following a series of strikes and other forms of trade union militancy, which culminated in a 'winter of discontent' in 1978–79, Margaret Thatcher's Conservative government was elected in 1979 with a mandate to 'cut the unions down to size' and to reverse the trend towards corporatism.

Over the years since 1979, a number of Employment Acts and related legislation have had just these effects. Indeed, government policy was so successful in reducing the power and influence of trade unions that, by 1997, many people believed that the pendulum had swung too far the other way. The law provided workers with too few rights and insufficient protection from exploitation by 'rogue' employers. Much of the debate over this issue centred on whether or not the UK should sign the European Union's **Social Chapter**. Under the Social Chapter provisions of the Maastricht Treaty, signed by leaders of 11 EU countries (but not

The majority of UK union members are now 'white-collar' workers

the UK) in 1991, the EU co-ordinated a number of aspects of social and labour market policy. The EU countries that signed the Social Chapter agreed to observe EU criteria for minimum pay, the length of the working week and holiday entitlement.

At the time of the Maastricht Treaty, the Conservative government refused to sign and observe the Social Chapter, regarding it as a form of 'back-door socialism' which, if observed, would adversely affect employment prospects. The government believed that, in a globalised economic environment, the Social Chapter would cause the UK and the wider EU to lose out to competition from the **newly industrialised countries** (NICs) in Asia and the 'Pacific rim'.

Privatisation and, in particular, deindustrialisation have also contributed to the decline of trade unionism in the UK. Almost all the privatised industries such as British Gas and BT continue to recognise and bargain with trade unions. However, the deregulation that has accompanied privatisation has allowed new gas supply and telecommunications companies to gain market share. These market entrants are much less likely to recognise trade unions. By destroying or decimating industries such as the coal industry, deindustrialisation has had perhaps the most devastating effect upon trade union membership, with major unions losing over half their members.

Unions have responded to the fall in membership and the decline in employers recognising unions by amalgamating and forming **'super unions'**. There are now three large 'super unions': UNISON catering for 'blue-collar' and 'white-collar' public sector workers; the merged TGWU/GWB union representing semi-skilled and unskilled manual workers, mostly in the private sector; and an expanded AEEU. This group was itself the product of an earlier merger between the old engineering workers' and electricians' unions, which has merged with the technical union MSF to form a third bloc with about 1.4 million skilled members.

The growth of female union membership has partially offset the fall in male membership. The growth of female membership reflects the growing importance of women workers in the labour force, but may also be a response to the fact that women workers are much more likely than men to suffer low-pay and labour market exploitation. Overall, the highest membership densities are in professional 'white-collar' work, where over half of employees are union members compared to lower percentages for craft workers and low-grade 'white-collar' clerical staff.

Summary

This chapter has examined price theory from the perspective of the labour market rather than the market for consumer goods and services. As was the case in the goods or product market, we have assumed that wage rates are determined by supply and demand, as are equilibrium levels of employment. However, roles are reversed in the labour market, where households supply labour to firms, which demand the services of labour. Because labour is demanded not for itself, but for its contribution to entrepreneurial profit via the sale of the goods and services it produces, the demand for labour is a derived demand. Likewise, workers supply labour, not so much for money, but for the utility gained from the goods and services that the money wage can buy.

In a perfectly competitive labour market, equilibrium wage rates and levels of employment are determined by the price mechanism in the market as a whole. In such a market, each firm or employer is a passive 'price-taker' at the ruling market wage, choosing how much labour to employ but having no influence on its own over the wage.

Equilibrium in a perfectly competitive labour market requires workers to be employed up to the point at which the marginal revenue product (MRP) of labour equals the market-determined wage rate. The marginal productivity theory of wages is sometimes used to support the view that wage rises must inevitably be at the expense of jobs, and that the 'market contains its own morality'. According to this view, the well paid deserve their relatively high reward because they are productive, while conversely, the lowly paid deserve their station in life because of their lack of productivity. However, arguments and conclusions like these should be treated with caution, since they depend on assumptions of perfect markets, equilibrium trading and unchanged conditions of supply and demand (the ceteris paribus assumption).

Normative judgments should not be built on the supposed virtue of the market mechanism; market forces are 'value neutral' with regard to the social fairness and equity of the outcome they achieve.

Indeed, it is possible that in conditions of expanding demand in the goods market or increasing labour productivity, both wages and employment can be increased. Additionally, there may be scope for increasing both wages and employment in monopsony labour markets where a single firm is the only employer of labour. Equilibrium in a monopsony labour market is achieved at the level of employment at which the marginal revenue product of labour equals the marginal cost of hiring labour ($MRP = MC_L$). However, in a monopsony labour market, the wage is less than the MRP of labour.

In any case, marginal productivity theory alone cannot explain wage rates; conditions affecting the supply of labour must also be taken into account. But while supply and demand theory must inevitably be a part of the explanation of wage rates and levels of employment, it does not provide a complete or sufficient explanation of either. For a fuller explanation, we must take account of institutional arrangements such as systems of collective bargaining through which the wages of a significant, though falling, proportion of the working population are determined. In the UK, the national minimum wage has also affected wage rates and levels of employment.

Self-testing questions

1 Distinguish between the average cost of labour (AC_L) and the marginal cost of labour (MC_L).

2 When may a worker's net advantage be less than the utility of the worker's wage?

3 Why may a worker's supply curve of labour bend backwards?

4 Explain three factors significant in determining a firm's demand for labour.

5 What is meant by marginal revenue product (MRP)?

6 In what sense is a firm a passive price-taker in a perfectly competitive labour market?

7 Explain two reasons for differences in wage rates.

8 How is the equilibrium wage rate determined in a monopsony labour market?

9 How may a trade union affect the equilibrium level of employment and the wage rate in a perfectly competitive labour market and in a monopsony labour market?

10 State two determinants of the elasticity of supply of labour with respect to the wage rate.

11 Distinguish between occupational and geographical immobility of labour.

12 State two determinants of the elasticity of demand for labour with respect to the wage rate.

13 Describe two of the social determinants of wages.

14 Why are women often paid less than men?

15 What is collective bargaining?

16 Why have trade unions declined in importance in the UK?

17 Use a supply and demand diagram to analyse the national minimum wage as a price floor.

Macroeconomic
theory

Chapter 12
The growth of modern macroeconomics

Specification focus

This chapter provides a historical overview of macroeconomics, suitable for both AS and A2 study, preparing candidates for more detailed coverage of macroeconomic issues, problems and policies in later chapters.

AS **Module 2 The National Economy**
  Performance of the UK Economy and Government Policy Objectives

A2 **Module 6 Government Policy, the National and International Economy**
  Inflation and Unemployment; Managing the National Economy

A2 **Synoptic coverage**
  Module 2 and Module 6 cover similar macroeconomic topics, but greater depth and breadth is required by Module 6 at A2. Candidates are expected to know about events in the UK and world economies extending back 10 years before the examination. Knowledge of earlier events is useful but not essential.

Introduction

When we investigate questions such as 'What determines the price of bread?' and 'How many workers might an employer wish to hire?' we are dealing with the subject of microeconomics. Microeconomics is the part of economics concerned with economic behaviour in the individual markets that make up the economy. In this chapter, we switch attention away from the 'little bits' of the economy towards such questions as 'What determines the average price level?' and 'How do we explain the overall levels of employment and unemployment in the economy?' These are the concern of macro-economics, the part of economics that attempts to explain how the whole economy works. Macroeconomics examines the aggregates rather than the 'little bits': the aggregate levels of output, income, prices, employment and unemployment, and the trade flows that make up the balance of payments.

This chapter explains how modern macroeconomics has its origins in the Keynesian revolution of the 1920s and 1930s, and how it developed during the Keynesian era, which lasted from the Second World War until the monetarist or 'free-market' counter-revolution of the 1970s and 1980s. We shall conclude by taking an introductory look at the conflicts and controversies that separate Keynesians and 'free-market' economists today, which dominate current macroeconomic discussion.

Keynesian macroeconomics

John Maynard Keynes, 1945

The term **macroeconomics** is a fairly recent addition to economic vocabulary. Before the 1970s, macroeconomics was associated largely with the work of John Maynard Keynes, arguably the greatest twentieth-century economist, who lived from 1883 to 1946. In the 1920s and 1930s, Keynes changed the nature of economic science by creating modern macroeconomics. Indeed, until the advent of monetarism in the late 1960s and the 1970s, macroeconomics and Keynesian economics were much the same thing, growing out of Keynes's great and influential book, *The General Theory of Employment, Interest and Money*, published in 1936. Before Keynes, most economists belonged to a school of thought now known as the 'neo-classical school', referred to by Keynes somewhat confusingly as 'the classicals'.

*e***xaminer's voice**
Although the AQA economics specification makes no reference to economists such as Keynes and Milton Friedman, good examination answers often display knowledge of eminent economists and their contributions to economic theory, debate and policy.

Full employment and unemployment

Neo-classical or pre-Keynesian economists were concerned largely with micro-economics and the functioning of individual markets within the economy. At the macroeconomic level, the pre-Keynesians believed that market forces, operating in competitive markets, would provide a self-adjusting mechanism that, in the long run, would automatically ensure full employment and economic growth.

In the 1920s, large-scale persistent unemployment occurred in the UK, preceding the spread of worldwide unemployment in the Great Depression of the 1930s. Much of UK unemployment in the 1920s probably resulted from the lack of competi-tiveness and decline of nineteenth-century staple industries such as shipbuilding and textiles. This problem was made worse by an over-valued exchange rate.

The pre-Keynesians blamed a substantial part of the unemployment on excessively high wages. But if the labour market worked properly, this unemployment should only have been temporary. Wage rates should have fallen and the market mechanism should have priced the unemployed into jobs again. When this did not happen, pre-Keynesian economists blamed trade unions and other causes of labour market imperfection. Responsibility for unemployment lay with the workers in work and their trade unions, who by refusing to accept lower wages, prevented the unemployed from pricing themselves into jobs.

The theory we have just described is called the **classical** or **real-wage theory of unemployment**. This theory will be explained in greater depth in Chapter 16.

Keynes and the classical theory of unemployment

Keynes did not completely reject the classical theory; he accepted that high wages could cause unemployment and that, under certain circumstances, cuts in wages would create employment. But whereas the economists of his day blamed the real world rather than free-market theory for persistent large-scale unemployment, Keynes started from the opposite premise. If a theory inadequately explains the real world, do not blame the real world, instead improve or replace the theory.

Hence, in 1936 in his *General Theory*, Keynes set out what he clearly thought was a 'better and more general' theory to explain the determination of output and employment in the economy than that offered by the 'classical' theory. From Keynes's *General Theory*, modern macroeconomics developed.

The money wage and the real wage

So far, the 'wage level' and 'wage cuts' have been discussed without distinguishing between the money wage (or nominal wage) and the real wage. **Money** or **nominal wages** are simply the money income that workers are paid — for example, £500 per week. By contrast, workers' **real wages** are the purchasing power of their money wages, or their command over goods and services. The relationship between the money wage and the real wage is:

$$\text{real wage} = \frac{\text{money wage} \times 100}{\text{price index}}$$

Note that the demand curve for labour is specified in terms of the real wage rather than the money wage, showing that firms are only willing to employ more workers if the real wage falls. But in a monetary economy in which firms pay their workers in money rather than in goods or services, the only wage that a firm can cut is the money wage. For real wages to fall following a cut in money wages, prices must either remain unchanged, increase, or fall by a smaller percentage than money wages. Keynes doubted whether this happens. He argued that if the labour market is sufficiently competitive for employers to be able to cut money wages, the goods market will be sufficiently competitive for prices also to fall. A fall in money wages will induce an equal proportionate fall in prices, leaving the real wage and hence the level of unemployment unchanged. In Keynesian theory, therefore, cuts in money wages are insufficient to price the unemployed into jobs.

> **examiner's voice**
>
> It is important to understand the difference between the *money* (or *nominal*) value of an economic variable, and its *real* value. Examples include money and real wages, interest rates and exchange rates, and also the difference between the nominal money supply and the real money supply.

The fallacy of composition

Keynes went on to argue that even if real wages fall, the neo-classical theory of unemployment suffers from a fundamental defect known as a fallacy of composition. A **fallacy of composition** occurs when what is true at the individual or micro

AQA Advanced Economics

economic level becomes untrue at the aggregate or macroeconomic level. If an individual employer or, indeed, all employers cut wages in a particular labour market, more workers will be hired. This is because, at the microeconomic level, we can invoke the ceteris paribus assumption of holding constant all other influences upon the demand for labour. In particular, we can assume that the cut in wages has no effect upon the state of aggregate demand in the economy because the firm or industry is only a tiny part of the whole economy.

But this assumption, which is reasonable when studying a single labour market, becomes unreasonable when examining the effects of a cut in real wages in *all* the economy's labour markets. At the aggregate or macroeconomic level, the ceteris paribus assumption can no longer be invoked. In addition, at the macro level, wages must be viewed as the most important component of aggregate demand in the economy. It follows that, if real wages are cut and employment does not rise throughout the economy, aggregate demand falls and firms are unable to sell all their output. Thus, far from reducing unemployment, wage cuts may increase the number of jobs lost in the economy.

Wage cuts also redistribute income in favour of profit. But people who receive profit as their main source of income are usually better off and save a bigger fraction of income than people who rely on wages. This means that a cut in real wages and the resulting increase in profit reduces the level of consumption spending in the economy. Too much saving and too little spending creates **deficient aggregate demand** in the economy.

Demand-deficient unemployment and Say's Law

Keynes believed that deficient aggregate demand caused unemployment in the UK economy in the 1920s and 1930s. By contrast, the neo-classical or pre-Keynesian economists refused to believe that deficient demand existed in the economy, except for temporary periods in the business cycle. They argued that such cyclical unemployment would quickly be eliminated by the self-regulating nature of market forces.

To explain this, we must introduce **Say's Law**, named after an early-nineteenth-century French economist, Jean-Baptiste Say. In popular form, Say's Law states that 'supply creates its own demand'. Whenever an output or 'supply' is produced, factor incomes such as wages and profits are generated which are just sufficient, if spent, to purchase the output at the existing price level, thereby creating a demand for the output produced. As stated, there is nothing controversial about Say's Law; it is really an identity that is true by definition.

The controversial and critical issue concerns whether the *potential* demand or incomes generated are actually spent on the output produced. The pre-Keynesians believed that the incomes are spent and that Say's Law holds; Keynes argued that under some circumstances, incomes are saved and not spent, Say's Law breaks down and the resulting deficient demand causes unemployment.

The pre-Keynesians and Say's Law

To explain the differences between Keynes and his predecessors over Say's Law and deficient demand, it is useful to introduce the two principal functions of money in a monetary economy: the **medium of exchange** and the **store of value** functions.

The pre-Keynesians believed that money functions mainly as a medium of exchange – that people hold money in order to finance transactions or the purchase of goods and services. This is called the **transactions motive** for holding money. According to this view, which has been revived by modern monetarists, because money earns little or no interest, it is irrational for people to hold money as an idle store of value. Thus, in a monetary economy, workers, who are paid in money and not in kind, quickly spend their money incomes or, if they save, lend part of their income in return for interest to enable others to spend. Under these circumstances, all money incomes are quickly spent, Say's Law holds, and aggregate demand is just sufficient to purchase the output produced.

Keynes, Say's Law and the paradox of thrift

Unlike his predecessors, Keynes considered the store of value function of money to be important. Keynes believed that in monetary economies people hold part of money income as an idle store of value, despite the fact that no interest is earned. Unlike other wealth assets such as shares and government bonds, money cannot lose its value, except in the sense that inflation erodes money's value. When share prices, or the prices of other non-money assets, are expected to fall, it becomes rational to hold money as a store of value.

If money incomes are saved without being lent to other households or firms to spend, aggregate demand becomes insufficient to purchase the output that the economy produces. Herein, according to Keynes, lies the explanation of how deficient demand can initially occur in the economy. Saving, regarded as a virtue at the individual level, can become a vice at the aggregate level if people save too much of their income and spend too little. This is the **paradox of thrift**. If real wages are cut in the mistaken belief that too high real wages and not deficient demand is the true underlying cause of most unemployment, then, according to Keynes, unemployment might become worse rather than better.

The Keynesian revolution

Following the publication of Keynes's *General Theory* in 1936, his theory of aggregate demand gradually became the new orthodoxy in economics, replacing the domination of neo-classical and free-market thinking for the next generation. However, for the first few years after 1936, the *General Theory*'s influence was restricted to converting many of Keynes's fellow academic economists to his way of thinking. Before the Second World War, governments and government policy were not significantly influenced by Keynesian economics. Policies of public spending adopted in the early 1930s in the US New Deal and by the Nazi regime in Germany were certainly Keynesian in their effect, although hardly inspired by

Keynes's writing. In the UK, Keynes's theories had minimal influence upon government policy during the 1930s and it is wrong to link Keynes with the rather slow but 'natural' recovery from the Great Depression.

But during the Second World War, Keynesian policies were adopted by the war-time coalition government in the UK, first, to prevent excess demand from causing inflation, and then towards the end of the war in the preparation for peace. In 1944, a famous White Paper on Employment Policy, inspired by Keynes but largely written by Lord Beveridge, effectively committed the next generation of postwar governments to the management of aggregate demand, and to achieving full employment. For the first time, **full employment** — defined by Beverage as occurring when unemployment falls to 3% of the labour force — became an objective of government economic policy. For the next 30 years Keynesianism became the new orthodoxy. However, Keynes, who died in 1946, did not live to experience the era in which his followers implemented demand management policies based on the theory that he had developed in the 1930s.

*e*xaminer's voice
The AQA specification states that, while candidates are expected to have a good knowledge of events in the 10 years before the examination, they can also benefit from a general awareness of earlier events that help to put the last decade into a meaningful context.

Keynesian deficit financing

If, as Keynes believed, unemployment is caused by excessive saving and by deficient demand, it follows that the correct policy solution is to inject just enough demand back into the economy to counter the leakage of demand through saving. To understand this further, it is useful to divide the economy into the four large sectors of demand:

- households (sometimes slightly inaccurately called the *personal sector*)
- firms (also slightly inaccurately called the *corporate sector*)
- the government sector (or *public sector*)
- the overseas sector

Each sector can be a source of either **injections** or **leakages** of demand. The household sector is the source of consumption demand (C), but any household saving (S) represents a leakage of demand. Investment spending (I) by firms is an injection of demand. The government sector and the overseas sector are sources both of injections, in the form of government spending (G) and export demand (X), and of leakages: taxation (T) and import demand (M).

Suppose now that within the private sector (that is, households and firms), household saving exceeds firms' investment: $S > I$. Keynes argued that in these circumstances an attempt by the government in its fiscal policy to balance the budget (to set $G = T$) would result in deficient demand in the economy unless, of course, the excess savings of households were matched by an excess of export demand over imports in the overseas sector.

Keynes's predecessors, the neo-classical economists, believed that governments had a moral duty to indulge in the 'financial orthodoxy' or 'sound finance' of a

balanced budget. By contrast, Keynes believed that when saving by households exceeds the investment spending of firms, the government should deliberately deficit finance, and run a budget deficit ($G > T$) exactly equal to the excess of saving over investment. Via public sector borrowing, the government borrows the excess savings of the private sector, which it then spends, in order to inject demand back into the economy and prevent the emergence of deficient demand.

The objectives of macroeconomic policy

Since the advent of the Keynesian era, it has been usual to identify five principal objectives of government macroeconomic policy. These are:

- full employment (or low unemployment)
- economic growth (and higher living standards and levels of economic welfare)
- a fair or equitable distribution of income and wealth
- control of inflation (or a stable price level)
- an external objective (a satisfactory balance of payments or supporting a particular exchange rate)

The order in which these objectives of macroeconomic policy are listed is not accidental. It represents a Keynesian ordering of priority. During the Keynesian era, UK governments implemented Keynesian macroeconomic policies aimed at achieving full employment, economic growth and an equitable distribution of income and wealth, namely the objectives we have placed at the head of the list. The Keynesians regarded these as the primary objectives of macro-policy. In the Keynesian management of the economy, control of inflation and a satisfactory balance of payments were better regarded as constraints rather than as prime policy objectives in themselves. On several occasions during the Keynesian era, a poor performance in controlling inflation or a deteriorating balance of payments constrained the government's ability to expand the economy and achieve full employment and growth. This demonstrates the problem of policy conflicts faced by governments in managing the economy.

Policy conflicts and trade-offs

If all the five macroeconomic policy objectives we have listed could be achieved simultaneously, the 'economic problem' would largely disappear. But as the previous paragraph has indicated, it may be difficult, if not impossible, to 'hit' all five objectives at the same time. Because they cannot achieve the impossible, policy-makers generally accept some trade-off between policy objectives. A **trade-off** exists when two or more desirable objectives are mutually exclusive. Success in achieving a particular objective or set of objectives is at the expense of a poor and deteriorating performance with regard to other policy objectives.

examiner's voice
Understanding of possible policy conflicts, and of trade-offs between conflicting objectives, may be tested in the Unit 2 or the Unit 5 examination.

Over the years, UK macroeconomic policy has been influenced and constrained by four significant conflicts between policy objectives. Governments have often tried to resolve these conflicts by trading-off between policy objectives.

The conflict between internal and external policy objectives

The *internal* objectives of full employment and growth may be sacrificed to the *external* balance of payments or exchange rate objective, or vice versa.

Full employment and economic growth ⟷ Satisfactory balance of payments or exchange rate

Policy conflict and trade-off

The conflict between achieving full employment and controlling inflation

This is often called the **Phillips curve trade-off**, which is explained in more detail in Chapter 16.

Full employment and economic growth ⟷ Control of inflation

Policy conflict and trade-off

The conflict between increasing the rate of economic growth and achieving an equitable distribution of income and wealth

During the Keynesian era, progressive taxation and transfers to the poor were used (as part of fiscal policy) to reduce inequalities between rich and poor. In recent years, free-market supply-side economists have argued that such policies reduce entrepreneurial and personal incentives in the labour market, which make the economy less competitive and the growth rate slower. In the free-market view, greater inequalities are necessary to promote the conditions in which rapid and sustainable economic growth can take place.

Economic growth ⟷ Greater income equality

Policy conflict and trade-off

The conflict between higher living standards now and higher living standards in the future

In the short term, the easiest way to increase living standards is to boost consumption. However, this 'live now, pay later' approach means sacrificing saving and investment, which reduces economic growth.

Current living standards ⟷ Future living standards

Policy conflict and trade-off

Keynesian demand management in practice

The Keynesian era fully began after the end of the Second World War, when governments started to use demand management policies to achieve the objective of full

employment. The era ended in the 1970s with the advent of monetarism and the 'free-market' or 'neo-classical revival'. In the intervening 30 years, governments in many industrial countries, including the UK, used fiscal policy and monetary policy to manage demand.

During the Keynesian era, macroeconomic policy was used primarily to manage the level of aggregate demand. In order to achieve full employment and economic growth, the government reflated the economy by injecting demand into the economy. Monetary policy and fiscal policy (which are explained in Chapters 17 and 18) were used for this purpose. With monetary policy, the government would reduce interest rates, while fiscal policy would be used to cut taxes and to increase public sector spending. Overall, this became known as **fine-tuning** the level of aggregate demand.

The government tried to manage aggregate demand so as to achieve relatively full employment and economic growth, without excessive inflation or an unsustainable deterioration in the balance of payments. However, as the economy approached full employment (that is, with 3% of the labour force or around 600,000 people unemployed), the expansion of demand drew too many imports into the economy or led to a significant increase in inflation. On a number of occasions, the resulting balance of payments or inflationary crisis forced the government to reverse policy and reduce the level of aggregate demand in the economy. Deflationary policies such as increased interest rates (monetary policy), public spending cuts and increased taxes (fiscal policy) were used to reduce inflationary pressures or to improve the balance of payments. For a time at least, the policy objectives of full employment and economic growth would have to be sacrificed. The name **stop–go** was given to the successive periods of deflation and reflation characteristic of the Keynesian years.

The decline of Keynesianism

In 1944 Beveridge defined full employment as being consistent with 3% of the working population unemployed. In light of the history of the Great Depression, Beveridge doubted whether governments would be able to reduce unemployment to 3%. Nevertheless, in the event, the Keynesian governments of the 1950s and 1960s succeeded in performing better, reducing unemployment to an average of about 2% of the working population, about 500,000. Indeed, for some periods during the Keynesian era, unemployment actually fell to as low as 1%.

The Keynesian economic policy of demand and management without excessive inflation appeared to be working, even though, as we have noted, a continuing expansion of demand was constrained by recurrent balance of payments crises. This was a period of continuous economic growth — literally a 'postwar boom'. Although the annual growth rate of about 2% was low by the standards of economic 'miracle' countries such as Japan and West Germany, at the time it was the longest ever sustained period of growth in UK history.

But as the postwar boom proceeded, the periods of 'stop' lengthened and the periods of 'go' shortened, resulting in a decline in the economy's average growth rate. At the same time, the rate of inflation, which averaged well under 5% a year in the early part of the Keynesian era, began to creep up, rising towards 10% during the late 1960s and accelerating above 20% in the early 1970s. As a result of these unfortunate trends, opponents of Keynesianism became more confident in their criticism of Keynesian theories and policies. It appeared that Keynesian demand management could achieve full employment only through injecting greater and greater doses of inflation into the economy.

Moreover, once achieved, full employment was becoming less and less sustainable. Any expansion of demand seemed to bring about an acceleration of inflation or a balance of payments crisis much more quickly than previously. A reduction of demand was required almost before the reflation had got off the ground.

The crisis in Keynesian economics

We used to think that you could spend your way out of a recession and increase employment by cutting taxes and boosting government spending. I tell you in all candour that that option no longer exists and that in so far as it ever did exist it worked by injecting bigger doses of inflation into the economy followed by higher levels of unemployment as the next step . . . that is the history of the past 20 years.

Extract from a speech made by Prime Minister James Callaghan
at the Labour Party Conference, 28 September 1976

By the mid-1970s Keynesianism was in disarray. Keynesian economic management had been relatively invulnerable to serious attack as long as it performed reasonably well when measured against the five principal objectives of economic policy listed earlier in this chapter.

Keynesianism had become the prevailing orthodoxy when neo-classical economics appeared to fail to deal satisfactorily with the interwar problem of unemployment. A generation later Keynesianism itself became vulnerable to attack when there was a simultaneous failure to achieve any of the primary policy objectives in the mid-1970s. At this time the economy went through a period of **stagflation** or **'slumpflation'** involving stagnant or declining output, growing unemployment and accelerating inflation. This situation, together with social conflict over the distribution of income and a deteriorating balance of payments, signalled the end of the Keynesian era.

The monetarist and free-market counter-revolution

We are all monetarists now

From time to time a revolution in political ideas takes place. The trouble is that the process is so slow and so subtle that hardly anybody notices until it has happened.

But if you can spot the thing immediately it is worth noting and discussing. In the end the country, indeed the world, is governed by ideas and hardly anything else. In the management of the UK economy for the last 20 years or so the prevailing idea has been a doctrine called 'Keynesianism'. Now most of us get a bit impatient when people start going on about various 'isms'. But this particular 'ism' matters to you. If you have the misfortune to be out of work, if you are a housewife appalled by the constantly rising cost of living, if you are angry when you look at your wage-packet or salary cheque and see how much has gone in tax, then you ought to know that all this is a product not of chance or of the stars but of an idea.

The big-spending high-taxing governments we have had have largely created the inflation, unemployment and falling living standards that you now suffer. They did what they did because they thought Keynes was the Great Economist and this was what he advised. What has happened is that, through unpleasant experience, Keynesianism has been discredited. Callaghan and Healey are now talking a quite different language. It is the old language of controlling the money supply, trying to hold back public spending, balancing the budget.

If you think this is just common sense, then you are right. The *Daily Express* has been calling for it for years. We are not always wrong. And of course this is excellent news for Britain.

Daily Express editorial, 19 August 1977

*e*xaminer's voice

Students often regard monetarism and free-market economics as interchangeable terms. This is only partially true. Narrowly interpreted, monetarism refers solely to the belief that inflation is caused by a prior increase in the money supply. Its key theory is the quantity theory of money. More broadly, however, most monetarists believe in the virtues of an unregulated market economy and they distrust government intervention in markets.

The 1970s witnessed the decline of Keynesianism and the ascendancy of **monetarism**. It is useful to distinguish between a 'narrow' and a 'wider' meaning of monetarism, a term first introduced in the USA by Professor Karl Brunner in 1968. In a strictly narrow sense, a monetarist is a person who believes that the immediate cause of all inflation lies in a prior increase, permitted by governments, of the money supply. But in a wider sense, monetarism has become a label attached to the revival in a 'New Classical' body of theory of the 'old neo-classical' or 'classical' theories that predated Keynes. In this looser meaning, monetarism is essentially the economics of a self-adjusting or self-regulating private enterprise market economy, subject to minimal government intervention and regulation. The monetarist counter-revolution represents a return to the economics that Keynes opposed in the 1920s and 1930s.

The revival of old theories

The beginning of the monetarist counter-revolution can be dated to 1956 when Professor Milton Friedman of the University of Chicago revived the pre-Keynesian theory of inflation, the **quantity theory of money**. Broadly, the quantity theory argues that the quantity of money in the economy determines the price level and therefore the rate of inflation. If the government allows the money supply to expand at a rate faster than the growth of output, the price level will rise when people spend the excess money balances that they hold. The revival of the quantity theory underpinned the later growth of monetarism, and Milton Friedman went on to become the leading theoretician of the monetarist counter-revolution and the most forceful advocate of monetarist economic policy.

Early monetarism

Although for a time monetarism failed to displace Keynesianism as the dominant influence upon the UK and US governments, many bankers and especially the International Monetary Fund (IMF) became converts. The conversion of the IMF to monetarism was particularly significant. When in 1976 the UK faced a very serious balance of

Milton Friedman, 1980

payments and sterling crisis, the IMF forced the Labour government to sign a Declaration of Intent which effectively committed the UK to adopting monetarist economic policies as the condition for securing a loan.

However, the Labour government remained then — as 'old' Labour still is today — predominantly Keynesian. The Labour government did not really believe in the monetarist policies of announcing target rates of growth for the money supply and for government borrowing. Essentially, this early period of monetarism from 1976 to 1979 in the UK was a period of superficial or cosmetic monetarism imposed on the government from outside. Indeed, because the Labour government had not really been converted to monetarist theories and ways of thinking, this was a period of 'monetarily constrained Keynesianism' rather than monetarism proper.

The short-lived monetarist experiment

The more full-blooded implementation of monetarist policies in the UK had to wait until the election in 1979 of a Conservative government under the premiership of Margaret Thatcher. Between 1979 and 1983, Margaret Thatcher's first government was firmly committed to monetarist theories and policies. In the USA, the election of President Ronald Reagan in 1980 marked a similar transition from Keynesianism to monetarism. In the political arena, Thatcherism and Reaganomics were terms associated with the monetarist counter-revolution (and later with the advent of supply-side economics).

In the early 1980s, the UK Conservative government completely abandoned the discretionary demand management policies of the Keynesian era — a process already begun in the period of 'cosmetic' monetarism — and adopted a policy based on automatic policy rules. The government's monetary policy rule involved the publication of a target rate of growth of the money supply for a medium-term period of about 3 years. This was accompanied by an announcement that it would implement monetary policy so as to hit the money supply target.

The Conservatives also decided to subordinate all other aspects of macro policy — including the full employment objective — to the monetary policy aim of controlling monetary growth so as to bring down the rate of inflation. With this aim in mind, the government adopted a fiscal policy rule based on reducing the size of public sector spending and public sector borrowing as proportions of national output. In this way, fiscal policy was subordinated to the needs of monetary policy. The government believed it was necessary to create fiscal conditions that would allow its monetary policy to be successful.

At the beginning of the 1980s, the Thatcher government was optimistic that its policy of monetary control would be successful, but at that time monetarism — unlike Keynesianism — lacked a track record. Monetarist policies could not be judged by results because they had not as yet been implemented on a sufficient scale. Over the next few years, the Conservative government claimed that its policies were successful because the rate of inflation did fall during the early and mid-1980s. For the government, the proof of the pudding was apparently in the eating!

The 'death' of monetarism

The Conservative government's success in reducing inflation during the 'monetarist experiment' of the early and mid-1980s masked the fact that, in most years, the growth in the money supply had consistently outstripped the growth in prices. This unfortunate fact cast great doubt upon the central tenet of narrow monetarism, namely that an increase in the money supply will inevitably cause inflation. Perhaps because of their reduced faith in narrow monetarism, many economists of a free-market persuasion became rather less keen on referring to themselves as 'monetarists'. Instead, they chose to be known by other self-styled labels, such as 'supply-side economists' or 'economic liberals' — terms which embrace the free-market rather than the purely monetarist aspects of the 'neo-classical revival'.

At the same time, and as a direct result of its failure to hit the pre-announced monetary targets, the Conservative government more or less abandoned the pure monetarist policies for which it had had such high hopes at the beginning of the 1980s. When, in 1985, money supply targets were relaxed to such an extent that they became virtually meaningless, *The Times* published the headline: 'Monetarism, It's Dead — Official!'

Supply-side economics

Although the strictly 'monetarist' aspects of macroeconomic policy were quietly dropped by Mrs Thatcher's and John Major's Conservative governments after the mid-1980s, the Conservatives remained committed to the 'wider' free-market aspects of economic policy. Much of the economic policy implemented since the 'death of monetarism' is now known as **supply-side economic policy**. Supply-side economics and supply-side economic policy are explained in some depth in Chapter 19, while Chapter 18 contrasts the 'supply-side' fiscal policy implemented by recent and current UK governments with the 'demand-side' fiscal policy of earlier Keynesian UK governments.

Whereas demand management policies are essentially short-term, supply-side policies try to improve the economy's ability to produce in the medium and long-term, perhaps many years in the future. Supply-side policies, which are generally microeconomic rather than macroeconomic, aim to increase the efficiency and competitiveness of *all* the markets in the economy: goods markets (or product markets), the labour market, and financial markets. The expression *first the pain, and then the gain* captures a key element of supply-side policy. By making it easier for firms to hire and fire workers, and by removing state support for industry, supply-side policies initially increase personal risk and insecurity. However, by creating incentives to be entrepreneurial, to supply labour, to save and to invest, supply-side policies may eventually improve long-run economic performance. Supply-side economists argue that tax cuts encourage businesses to take greater risks and entrepreneurs and workers respond by working harder. Note that in supply-side fiscal policy, taxes are cut, not to increase aggregate demand, Keynesian-style, but to encourage all economic agents to work harder, workers as well as businessmen and women.

e*xaminer's voice
Most economists now agree that supply-side economic policy is just as important as demand-side policy for successful management of economic performance. However, they should be regarded as complementary policies rather than as substitutes for each other. Deep recessions at the beginning of the 1980s and the 1990s have shown that aggregate demand must be sufficient to absorb the increase in output that supply-side policies can bring about.

Monetary policy in recent years

As we have explained, 'pure' or 'technical' monetarism rather went out of fashion in the second half of the 1980s. In the UK, the Conservative government continued to use monetary policy to try to control inflation, but it switched to using the exchange rate as the key instrument of policy rather than the strictly 'monetarist' instrument of controlling the domestic money supply. The strategy involved fixing the pound at a high exchange rate against other currencies. This policy was formalised for a short period between 1990 and 1992 when the pound was in the **exchange rate mechanism (ERM)** of the European monetary system (EMS), fixed at a high exchange rate or parity.

There are a number of channels through which a high exchange rate can reduce inflation. By bringing down the prices of imported raw materials, foodstuffs and consumer goods, a high exchange rate has a direct effect on the domestic inflation rate. It may also act as a source of 'discipline' against domestically induced inflationary pressures. Thus, if UK workers and firms strongly believe that the government has not only fixed the exchange rate at a high level, but also means to keep it there, they may act more 'responsibly' and in a less inflationary way. In theory, the high exchange rate will deter UK workers from pushing for wage increases, and UK firms from increasing prices, lest they price themselves out of world markets and into unemployment or bankruptcy.

There is general agreement that ERM membership at a high exchange rate did contribute to the UK government's success in controlling inflation in the early 1990s. However, the costs were too high. The loss of competitiveness brought about by the high exchange rate, and the high interest rates needed to maintain the ERM parity, both contributed significantly to the length and depth of the very severe recession of the early 1990s. ERM entry and the high exchange rate boxed the government in and eventually led to an ignominious forced exit from the system in September 1992. Because monetary policy had been 'assigned' to supporting the exchange rate within the ERM, the government had not been able to reduce interest rates and relax monetary policy sufficiently to bring the economy out of the recession.

During the period of ERM membership, a number of economists who were generally sympathetic to the Conservative government recommended leaving the system and returning instead to strict 'monetarism'. Economists such as Professor Sir Alan Walters, who had been economic adviser to Margaret Thatcher in the 1980s, argued that the government should abandon the policy of trying to control inflation via an exchange rate fixed at a high parity, and should return instead to a floating exchange rate. This would give the government the freedom to follow the monetarist policy of controlling the rate of growth of the money supply within the domestic economy.

From a different perspective, some commentators have also claimed that the Conservative government not only abandoned monetarism in the late 1980s, but began in the early 1990s to pursue policies of a distinctly *Keynesian* nature. As we have noted, in the period of more or less strict 'monetarism' in the early 1980s, the government had clearly rejected Keynesian demand management policies. Instead of relaxing fiscal policy and increasing the budget deficit, as Keynes had recommended, to 'spend the economy out of recession', the government introduced quite swingeing cuts in public expenditure in an attempt to reduce the budget deficit and free resources for private sector use.

But by the late 1980s, many economists who were generally sympathetic to the government's commitment to controlling inflation had swung round to the view that the 'monetarist' public spending cuts of the early 1980s had unnecessarily reduced output and increased unemployment. By the onset of the next recession in 1990, this view was having some influence on the Conservative government. The government was now prepared to allow public finances to move into deficit in the recession so as to inject some demand back into the economy. However, the Conservative governments of the early and mid-1990s denied the charge that they had reverted to a form of 'back-door' Keynesianism.

This charge has also been levelled at the New Labour government which replaced John Major's Conservative administration in 1997. Monetary policy, which since 1997 has been implemented by an operationally independent Bank of England, has been used for managing demand, primarily to control inflation, but also to influence growth, output and employment levels. Modern monetary policy is now quite different from the monetarist policy implemented in the early 1980s, although control of inflation continues to be its primary objective. Instead of attempting to hit a money supply target, the policy operates through interest rates, which are raised or lowered to manage the level of aggregate demand.

We shall explain the main features of present-day monetary policy and fiscal policy in Chapters 17 and 18. Although monetary policy is used to manage aggregate demand, fiscal policy is not now generally used for this purpose (however, Chapter 18 explains how automatic stabilisers affect aggregate demand). As already noted, fiscal policy is now used primarily as a supply-side policy. Supply-side economics and policy are explained in some depth in Chapter 19.

Summary

This chapter has traced a brief history of macroeconomic theory and policy from its origins in the Keynesian revolution of the 1930s through to the return to dominance of the older neo-classical or classical orthodoxy in its guise as monetarism, and then in the current post-monetarist era.

Until the monetarist counter-revolution of the 1970s, macroeconomics and Keynesianism were largely interchange-able terms. Macroeconomic theory was predominantly a theory of the demand side of the economy, and Keynesian economic policy was dominated by the macroeconomic and essentially short-term management of demand.

Under monetarism and the free-market revival, short-term discretionary demand management was abandoned in favour of a more medium-term policy aimed at improving the supply side of the economy. Monetarism also reversed the trend evident under Keynesianism of extending the economic role of the state and of government. In the mid-1980s strict 'monetarism' was abandoned when the Thatcher government switched to targeting the exchange rate rather than the money supply in order to control inflation. However, this policy was also short-lived, ending in 1992 when the pound was forced out of the European Union's fixed exchange rate system.

Since 1992, first under John Major's Conservative government and then under New Labour, macroeconomic policy has generally been pragmatic, following the dictum: if it seems to be working, don't try to change it. Though they abandoned monetarism, recent governments have continued to accept the monetarist argument that control of inflation is a prerequisite for achieving other macro-economic objectives, such as growth and full employment. As a result, control of inflation arguably continues to be the most important macroeconomic objective. Monetary policy is still used to manage demand, but these days fiscal policy is used primarily to influence the supply side rather than the demand side of the economy.

Self-testing questions

1 Distinguish between macroeconomics and microeconomics.

2 What is meant by neo-classical economics?

3 What is the difference between pre-Keynesian and Keynesian approaches to real-wage unemployment?

4 Distinguish between the money wage rate and the real wage rate.

5 What is a fallacy of composition?

6 Explain Say's Law.

7 Relate Say's Law to demand-deficient unemployment.

8 What is deficit financing?

9 Briefly explain Keynesian demand management.

10 What are the objectives of macroeconomic policy?

11 State the main conflicts affecting macroeconomic policy.

12 What is a policy trade-off?

13 What is monetarism?

14 Relate monetarism to supply-side economics.

15 In what sense has UK economic policy been Keynesian in recent years?

Chapter 13
National income, standards of living and economic growth

Specification focus

This chapter covers the basic knowledge of national income required by the AS specification, together with the A2 requirement to use national income data to compare living standards in different countries. Likewise, the basic coverage of economic growth required at AS is followed by the deeper coverage needed at A2, which includes the distinction between economic cycles and the long-term or trend rate of growth.

AS Module 2 **The National Economy**
Performance of the UK Economy and Government Policy Objectives

A2 Module 6 **Government Policy, the National and International Economy**
Growth of the Economy and Cyclical Instability

A2 Synoptic coverage
National income and economic growth may figure in questions in both the Unit 2 and the Unit 6 examinations. The AS specification concentrates on definitions and the use of production possibility frontier diagrams to illustrate economic growth. The Unit 6 exam will expect candidates to build on this knowledge when answering questions on the use and limitations of national income as a measure of welfare, or on the causes of short-term or long-term economic growth.

Introduction

This chapter begins by explaining the meaning of national income, and of related concepts such as national wealth and the national capital stock. It then discusses whether measures of economic development such as the Human Development Index and the Index of Sustainable Economic Welfare provide better indicators than gross domestic product (GDP) of standards of living and people's quality of life. The chapter continues by distinguishing between short-term and long-term economic growth. Short-term growth is examined in the context of the business cycle. Having surveyed the roles of investment and technical progress in causing long-term growth, together with the distinction between neoclassical growth theory and new growth theory, the chapter concludes with a discussion of the benefits and costs of growth and the issue of growth sustainability.

Measuring national income

National income, wealth and capital

Figure 13.1 illustrates the concepts of national income, national wealth and the national capital stock. National wealth and national capital are examples of economic *stocks*, but national income is an economic *flow*.

> ### *e*xaminer's voice
> Make sure you understand the difference between stocks and flows. You will come across other examples in later chapters, such as the distinction between the national debt (a stock) and the government's budget deficit (a flow).

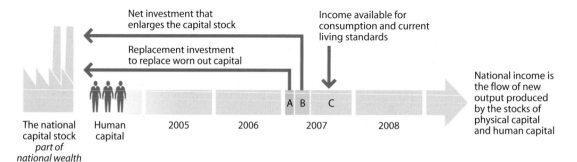

Figure 13.1 The flow of national income

- **National wealth** comprises all physical assets owned by the nation's residents that have value.
- The **national capital stock**, which is the part of national wealth capable of producing more wealth, includes all the capital goods and raw materials owned by the country's residents, as well as social capital such as roads, hospitals and schools which are owned by the state. However, the national capital stock excludes consumer goods, which are a part of national *wealth* but not of national *capital*. All capital is wealth, but not all wealth is capital.
- **National income** is the flow of new output or wealth produced by using the national capital stock (and also the stock of human capital in the economy). As part of a continuing flow, national income is measured per time period: monthly, quarterly or, more usually, yearly.

National product, national income and national expenditure

The flow of new national output can be measured in three ways:
- **The product method.** All the goods and services produced in the economy are added. The total is called national product or national output, represented by the symbol Q.
- **The income method.** All the incomes received by the factors of production to produce national output are added. The total is national income, represented by Y.

AQA Advanced Economics

■ **The expenditure method**. All expenditure upon output is added. The total is national expenditure, shown by the symbol *E*.

Since these are three methods of measuring the same *flow of new wealth or output*, national income, national product and national expenditure are identical. You must always remember that:

$$\frac{\text{national}}{\text{product}} = \frac{\text{national}}{\text{income}} = \frac{\text{national}}{\text{expenditure}}$$

or:

$$Q = Y = E$$

Gross national product and gross domestic product

Two of the most commonly used measures of national income or output are **gross national product** (GNP) and **gross domestic product** (GDP). Gross national product measures the total value of national output, including the part that is produced in other countries. UK residents and UK-based multinational companies (MNCs) receive profit and interest payments from capital assets located overseas. Likewise, overseas-based MNCs such as IBM and Nissan receive profit from assets that they own in the UK. The difference between inward and outward profit flows is called **net investment income**. Net investment income, or net income from abroad, is included in GNP, but excluded from GDP.

As it measures all the income available to spend in the UK, GNP is a better measure of the standard of living currently enjoyed by UK residents. However, GDP is a better measure of the productivity of industries actually located *within* the UK. For the UK and other rich developed countries, net investment income is usually positive, reflecting the fact that, over the years, richer countries have invested and accumulated assets in other countries. As a result, UK GNP is generally larger than UK GDP. In 2004, UK GDP was £1,160 billion, while net investment income was £23 billion, which meant that UK GNP was £1,183 billion. Unfortunately, for most poor developing countries GDP usually exceeds GNP. Profit outflows and interest payments to MNCs and banks in developed countries explain why this is the case.

Gross national product and net national product

When added together, the three rectangles labelled *A*, *B* and *C* in Figure 13.1 show total national income or GNP for 2007. However, in the course of producing 2007's national income, part of the national capital stock wears out. To make good the worn-out capital or depreciation of the national capital stock, replacement investment must take place. **Net national product** (NNP) measures the flow of new output *after* replacement investment is subtracted from GNP. In Figure 13.1, net national product in 2007 is shown by *B + C*.

Nominal national income and real national income

In 1948, UK GDP was nearly £12 billion. By 2004, GDP had increased to over £1,160 billion. At face value, this appears to show that average UK living standards, measured by the goods and services included in GDP, had increased by nearly 1,000% over the 55-year period. However, the real increase in GDP (and in living standards) was much smaller, at about 300%.

To explain this, it is necessary to understand the difference between *nominal* national income (which is also known as *money* national income) and *real* national income. We shall follow the convention of using upper-case or capital letters for nominal variables, and lower-case letters for real variables. We have already used the symbol *Y* for measuring nominal national income. We use the symbol *y* to measure real national income, or the physical output of new goods and services produced in the economy in a year. The relationship between nominal and real national income (*Y* and *y*) is shown by the following equations:

$$\text{real national income} = \frac{\text{nominal national income}}{\text{average price level}} \qquad (1)$$

or:

$$y = \frac{Y}{P}$$

where *P* is the price level, and:

$$\text{nominal national income} = \text{the average price level} \times \text{real national income} \qquad (2)$$

or:

$$Y = Py$$

Equation (1) shows that real national income, measured in terms of GDP, can be calculated by dividing nominal GDP by a measure of the average price level; this measure is known as the **GDP deflator**. However, in the UK, a more statistically complicated method is now used. This method (called the **chained volume method**) takes account of improvements in the quality of goods that occur over time.

Equation (2) shows that nominal national income (or GDP) can grow for one or both of two possible reasons: real output rises; or inflation occurs and the price level rises.

Measuring economic welfare and standards of living

Using national income statistics to measure welfare

Because GNP, GDP and other national income statistics are the main source of data on what has happened and what is happening in the economy, they are often used as indicators of economic growth, economic and social welfare, and changing living standards, and for comparison with other countries.

To see how living standards change over time, we must look at real per capita GNP figures (real GNP divided by the number of people living in the country). Rising real GNP per capita gives a general indication that living standards are rising, but it may, of course, conceal great and sometimes growing disparities in income *distribution*. This is especially significant in developing countries, where the income distribution is typically extremely unequal and where only a small fraction of the population may benefit materially from economic growth.

Besides the problem of income distribution, a number of other problems surface when using national income statistics to measure living standards.

- **The non-monetised economy.** National income statistics underestimate the true level of economic activity because the non-monetised economy is under-represented. In the UK, housework and 'do-it-yourself' home improvement take place without money incomes being generated. When measuring national income, a decision has to be made on whether to estimate or to ignore the value of this production. The UK accounts can be criticised for estimating the value of some but not all of the non-monetised economy. 'Imputed rents' are estimated for the 'housing services' delivered to owner-occupiers by the houses they live in, based on an estimate of the rent that would be paid if the house-owners were tenants of the same properties. But house-keeping allowances paid within households are not estimated, implying that housework — most of which is undertaken by women — is unproductive. Judgments such as these lead to the anomaly that national income appears to fall when a man marries his housekeeper or paints his own house, having previously employed a decorator.

- **The hidden economy.** Economic activity undertaken illegally in the hidden economy may be omitted. The hidden economy (which is also known as the **informal economy**, the **underground economy** and the **black economy**) refers to all the economic transactions conducted in cash which are not recorded in the national income figures because of tax evasion. It is impossible to make a completely accurate estimate of the size of the hidden economy, but it can be approximated by the gap between the GNP total obtained by the income and expenditure methods of measurement. The hidden economy probably equals about 10% of the UK's measured GNP, while countries such as Greece, Spain and Portugal have hidden economies equal to 20–30% of GNP.

- **Quality of goods and services.** Over time, the quality of goods changes for better or worse, presenting a particularly difficult problem in the construction and interpretation of national income figures. This is also true of services. When services such as public transport and healthcare deteriorate, GNP may rise even though welfare and real living standards decline.

- **Negative externalities.** National income statistics *over-estimate* living standards because of the effects of negative externalities such as pollution and congestion, and of activities such as crime. What is, in effect, a welfare loss may be shown as an increase in national output, falsely indicating an apparent welfare gain. For example, the stresses and strains of producing an ever-higher national output lead to a loss of leisure time; and people become ill more often. Loss of leisure and poorer health cause welfare to fall. But in the national accounts, these show up as extra production and as extra consumption of healthcare, both of which imply a welfare gain. Traffic congestion increases the cost of motoring, and hence the value of national income. Motorists would prefer uncongested roads and less spending on petrol and vehicle wear and tear. Likewise, installing 'regrettables' such as burglar alarms raises national income, but most people would prefer a crime-free environment and no burglar alarms. Along with the effects of divorce and other elements of social breakdown, national income statistics treat the effect of crime on economic activity as a welfare gain.

*e*xaminer's voice
The use and limitations of national income as an indicator of changing living standards is a very important topic in the Unit 6 specification. As well as understanding how measures of national income, such as GDP, provide a reasonably good measure of consumption of material goods, A2 candidates need to be able to explain at least three problems incurred when using national income to measure economic welfare.

Comparing national income between countries

Comparisons of national income per head between countries are misleading if the relative importance of the non-monetised economy differs significantly. There are also differences in the degree of statistical sophistication in data collection, particularly between developed and developing countries, and a lack of international uniformity in methods of classifying and categorising the national accounts. There are further problems in making comparisons when different commodities are consumed. Expenditure on fuel, clothing and building materials for cold winters is usually greater in developed countries than in much warmer developing economies. However, greater expenditure on these goods may not indicate higher real incomes and living standards.

It is possible to compare GNP per capita in different countries by converting GNP figures for each country into a common currency such as the US dollar. However, such calculations suffer from the assumption that the exchange rates between local currencies and the dollar are correctly valued, in the sense that a dollar's worth of output in one country becomes immediately and accurately comparable with a dollar's worth of output in any other country. This can never be so. Exchange rates can only correctly reflect the values of internationally traded goods such as automobiles, foodstuffs and raw materials. The purchasing power of a currency over domestically produced goods and services, which do not enter into international trade or compete domestically with imports, may be completely different from the currency's purchasing power over imported goods. Exchange rate changes only reflect the price changes of internationally traded goods. In so far as there is a much wider gap in developing countries than in developed countries between the price changes of internationally traded and non-traded goods, GNP figures measured in US dollars tend to underestimate real levels of income and output in developing economies.

The solution to this problem is to establish **purchasing power parity** (PPP) exchange rates. PPP exchange rates are based on the idea that, in the long run,

exchange rates should move towards rates that equalise the prices of an identical basket of goods and services in any two countries. Stated simply, a dollar, or any other unit of currency such as the euro, should buy the same everywhere.

Standards of living and the quality of life

We have mentioned the term **standard of living** on several occasions in this chapter, but no explanation has been provided of the term's meaning. In a strictly narrow sense, the standard of living can be defined as the per capita rate of consumption of purchased goods and services. However, because it concentrates solely on material goods and services, this definition is not very satisfactory. More widely defined, the term includes the quality of life and general economic welfare, as well as narrow GNP-related consumption. A wider definition of living standards might include the three elements shown in the following equation:

$$
\begin{array}{l}
\text{standard} \\
\text{of living}
\end{array} =
\begin{array}{l}
\text{economic welfare} \\
\text{derived from} \\
\text{goods and} \\
\text{services} \\
\text{purchased in the} \\
\text{market economy}
\end{array} +
\begin{array}{l}
\text{economic welfare} \\
\text{derived from} \\
\text{public goods and} \\
\text{merit goods} \\
\text{collectively} \\
\text{provided by the} \\
\text{state}
\end{array} +
\begin{array}{l}
\text{economic welfare} \\
\text{derived from quality} \\
\text{of life factors,} \\
\text{including external} \\
\text{benefits and} \\
\text{intangibles minus} \\
\text{external costs and} \\
\text{intangibles}
\end{array}
$$

If used carefully, national income figures can provide a reasonable estimate of economic welfare derived from the first two of these three elements, both of which relate to the direct consumption of material goods and services. However, as the chapter has already explained, national income fails to estimate how externalities and other quality of life factors affect economic welfare and living standards. In addition, national income fails to reflect the effect of resource depletion and environmental degradation resulting from producing *current* income on humankind's ability to produce *future* income. This means that national income and GDP do not address the issue of sustainability.

*e*xaminer's voice

Living standards, but not the quality of life, is mentioned in the A2 Unit 6 specification. Neither term figures in the AS Unit 2 specification, although economic welfare is briefly mentioned. It is a good idea for A2 candidates to be familiar with all three concepts.

Alternatives to national income as measures of economic welfare

The gross national product includes air pollution and advertising for cigarettes, and ambulances to clear our highways of carnage. It counts special locks for our doors, and jails for the people who break them. GNP includes the destruction of the redwoods and the death of Lake Superior. It grows with the production of napalm and missiles and nuclear warheads...And if GNP includes all this, there is much that it does not comprehend. It does not allow for the health of our families, the quality of their education, or the joy of their play. It is indifferent to the decency of our factories and the safety of our streets alike. It does not include the beauty of our poetry or the strength of our marriages, or the intelligence of our public debate or the integrity of our public officials... GNP measures neither our wit nor our courage, neither our wisdom nor our learning, neither our compassion nor our devotion to our country. It measures everything, in short, except that which makes life worthwhile; and it can tell us everything about America — except whether we are proud to be Americans.

US Senator Robert Kennedy, 1967

The environmental pressure group Friends of the Earth argues that measures of national income such as GDP were never intended to be indicators of progress or welfare. Indeed, over 70 years ago, Simon Kuznets, the inventor of the GDP concept, argued that 'The welfare of a nation can scarcely be inferred from a measurement of national income.' Not surprisingly, therefore, other measures that are less dependent on 'raw' GNP or GDP are increasingly used to place a value on economic and social progress. One of the earliest of these was the Measure of Economic Welfare (MEW), developed by Nordhaus and Tobin in 1972. The MEW showed that welfare in the USA grew, but at a slower rate than GDP, between 1950 and 1965. More recent attempts to adjust conventional national income figures include the United Nations Human Development Index (HDI), the Index of Sustainable Economic Welfare (ISEW) and the Misery Index.

examiner's voice

The AQA specification makes no mention of the United Nations Human Development Index or of any other measure of welfare, apart from national income. However, the Unit 6 specification requires A2 candidates to be able to interpret and discuss the limitations of different types of economic data and to use the data to compare the living standards of residents of different countries. With this in mind, it would certainly be useful to familiarise yourself with at least one alternative measure to national income.

The United Nations Human Development Index

The HDI is the average of three indicators:

- standard of living, measured by real GNP per capita, valued at US dollars purchasing power parity
- life expectancy at birth, in years
- educational attainment, measured by a weighted average of adult literacy and enrolment ratio in schools and colleges

The poverty in Ethiopia is typical of much of sub-Saharan Africa

The maximum value of the HDI is 1 (or unity). The closer a country's HDI is to 1, the greater its human development, measured in terms of the three indicators specified in the index. Table 13.1 shows the 15 highest-ranked countries in the Human Development Index for 2004, and also the 15 lowest-ranked countries.

Table 13.1 The 'top 15' and the 'bottom 15' countries in the Human Development Index, 2004

Country	Life expectancy index	Education index	GDP index	Human development index
TOP 15				
1 Norway	0.90	0.99	0.99	0.956
2 Sweden	0.92	0.99	0.93	0.946
3 Australia	0.90	0.98	0.94	0.946
4 Canada	0.90	0.98	0.95	0.943
5 Netherlands	0.89	0.99	0.95	0.942
6 Belgium	0.90	0.99	0.94	0.942
7 Iceland	0.91	0.96	0.95	0.941
8 USA	0.87	0.97	0.98	0.939
9 Japan	0.94	0.94	0.93	0.938
10 Ireland	0.86	0.96	0.98	0.936
11 Switzerland	0.90	0.95	0.95	0.936
12 UK	0.88	0.99	0.93	0.936
13 Finland	0.88	0.99	0.93	0.935
14 Austria	0.89	0.96	0.95	0.934
15 Luxembourg	0.89	0.91	1.00	0.933
BOTTOM 15				
163 Ivory Coast	0.27	0.47	0.45	0.399
164 Zambia	0.13	0.68	0.36	0.389
165 Malawi	0.21	0.66	0.29	0.388
166 Angola	0.25	0.38	0.51	0.381
167 Chad	0.33	0.42	0.39	0.379
168 Democratic Republic of Congo	0.27	0.51	0.31	0.365
169 Central African Republic	0.25	0.43	0.41	0.361
170 Ethiopia	0.34	0.39	0.34	0.359
171 Mozambique	0.22	0.45	0.39	0.354
172 Guinea-Bissau	0.34	0.39	0.33	0.350
173 Burundi	0.26	0.46	0.31	0.339
174 Mali	0.39	0.21	0.37	0.326
175 Burkina Faso	0.35	0.16	0.40	0.302
176 Niger	0.35	0.18	0.35	0.292
177 Sierra Leone	0.16	0.39	0.28	0.273

In 2004, Scandinavian counties led the way in the 'top 15', with the USA and the UK respectively in eighth and twelfth positions. At the other end of the spectrum, all the countries in the 'bottom 15' were located in sub-Saharan Africa. The HDI is by no means a perfect index of human development, since it ignores the distribution of income and expenditure on healthcare. For example, although Ireland was in tenth position in the HDI for 2004, the country's healthcare expenditure per capita was significantly less than any of the other 'top 10'. However, its human poverty index value (which increases, the more unequal the income distribution) was much higher than in all but the USA.

The Index of Sustainable Economic Welfare

The ISEW attempts to capture the effects of externalities and other intangibles upon human welfare. According to Friends of the Earth, the Index of Sustainable Economic Welfare is significantly better than GDP for looking at how sustainable welfare changes over time. Although starting from the method of measuring consumer expenditure used in the construction of GDP, the ISEW adjusts GDP figures to account for a number of aspects of economic life that GDP ignores. These include pollution, noise, commuting costs, capital growth, healthcare and education spending, urbanisation and the loss of natural resources.

In summary, the key differences between ISEW, as a measure of sustainable economic welfare, and GDP, as a measure of production, are that the ISEW:

- takes out spending that merely offsets social and environmental costs
- accounts for longer-term environmental damage and the depreciation of natural capital
- includes the net formation of man-made capital (that is, investment)
- includes changes in the distribution of income, reflecting the fact that an additional pound in the pocket means more to the poor than to the rich
- includes a value for household labour

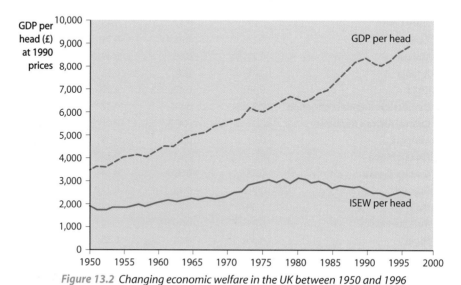

Figure 13.2 Changing economic welfare in the UK between 1950 and 1996 measured by GDP and the Index of Sustainable Economic Welfare

Figure 13.2 shows that UK GDP (per head) was 2.5 times greater in real terms in 1996 than in 1950, with an average year-on-year growth rate of 2%. In contrast, the trend in the ISEW over the same period has fluctuated, with the index falling by about 22% between 1980 and 1996. The key factors causing the decline were environmental degradation and the depletion of non-renewable resources, involving long-term environmental damage and income inequality. Over the same period, the decline would have been greater had it not been for positive factors in the ISEW, such as services derived from household labour.

Since publication of early results, such as those shown in Figure 13.2, the methodology used in constructing the ISEW has been criticised. In response to these criticisms, a revised version of ISEW has been constructed. In the original index, the adjustment for income inequality was essentially ad hoc. The revised method includes an input to reflect society's aversion or otherwise to income inequality. The original ISEW method of accounting was also criticised for the way it measured the long-term environmental costs resulting from fossil and nuclear fuel consumption. A simple tax of 50 cents (in 1972 dollars) was levied for every barrel of oil, with an equivalent tax for nuclear power. The revised UK ISEW now makes use of cost estimates for long-term damage from global warming, related directly to carbon emissions. The main effect of these and other revisions has been to reduce somewhat the difference between welfare measured by GDP and by the ISEW.

The Misery Index

Another indicator of economic welfare is glumly known as the Misery Index. The Misery Index is constructed by adding the unemployment rate to the inflation rate, although a later version also adds the short-term interest rate. Robert Barro, who invented the index in the 1970s, assumed that a combination of higher unemployment and higher inflation means a higher level of economic and social costs for a country.

The Misery Index shows that in recent UK history, misery or unhappiness peaked in 1975, before dropping consistently through the 1990s and early 2000s. Earlier in the chapter, we distinguished between a narrow and a broad definition of standards of living. The *Guardian*'s Larry Elliot goes one stage further by distinguishing between *living standards* and *standards of life*. Elliot argues that when thinking of 'living standards', people focus primarily on the material comforts of life, which are captured reasonably accurately by national income figures and the Misery Index. But the concept of 'standards of life' centres on quality of life, which alternatives to national income such as the ISEW are much better at measuring.

Economic growth

Short-run and long-run economic growth

Economic growth is usually measured by the percentage annual change in real GNP or real GDP. However, the *measurement* of economic growth must not be confused with the *definition* of economic growth. Chapter 1 defined economic growth as an increase in the *potential* level of real output that the economy can produce. Strictly, this is *long-run economic growth*, which is not the same as *short-run economic growth* or economic recovery.

Long-run and short-run economic growth are both illustrated in Figure 13.3. Short-run growth is shown by the movement from point *C* inside the economy's production possibility frontier (PPF) to point *A* on the frontier. Long-run growth is depicted by the shift from point *A* (on PPF$_1$) to point *B* (on PPF$_2$). Short-run growth or economic recovery makes use of spare capacity and takes up slack in the economy, whereas long-run growth increases total productive capacity.

At this point, it is useful to refer back to Figure **13.1**. Economic growth generally requires investment to take place, over and above the *replacement investment* shown by rectangle **A** in *Figure 13.1*. The extra investment, which is called **net investment**, is shown by rectangle *B*. *Gross investment* (shown by *A* + *B*) is the sum of replacement investment and net investment. Only net investment enlarges the capital stock, thus enabling long-run economic growth to take place.

Rectangle *C* in Figure 13.1 shows the fraction of national income available for consumption in 2007, assuming that replacement and net investment take place. As Chapter 1 explains, a decision to sacrifice *current* consumption in favour of a higher level of *future* consumption means that more of society's scarce resources go into investment or the production of capital goods, enabling the national capital stock to increase in size. However, in the short run, the easiest way to increase living standards is to boost current consumption. This 'live now, pay later' approach sacrifices saving and investment, which ultimately reduces long-run economic growth. The policy conflict and trade-off diagram first introduced in Chapter 12 illustrates this choice between current and future consumption.

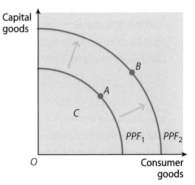

Figure 13.3 Long-run and short-run economic growth

examiner's voice

The AQA AS specification states that candidates should be able to use a production possibility diagram to illustrate economic growth. Make sure you practise drawing PPF diagrams to illustrate both short-run and long-run economic growth.

Current living standards ⟷ Future living standards

Policy conflict and trade-off

Fluctuations in economic activity and the business cycle

Fluctuations in economic activity occur in two main ways: through seasonal fluctuations and through cyclical fluctuations taking place over a number of years.

Seasonal fluctuations are largely caused by changes in climate and weather. Examples include the effect of very cold winters closing down the building trade and seasonal employment in travel and tourism.

Rather longer **cyclical fluctuations** divide into the short **business cycle**, which lasts for just a few years, and **long cycles** (or **long waves**), which may extend over about

60 years. In a business cycle (which is also known as a **trade cycle** or **economic cycle**), the economy's growth rate fluctuates considerably from year to year. Figure 13.4 shows two complete business cycles, together with a line showing the economy's **trend growth rate** or **long-run growth rate. Actual growth,** which is measured by the percentage change in real GDP over a 12-month period, varies in the different phases of the business cycle. In the cycle's upswing, growth is positive, but as Figure 13.4 shows, 'growth' becomes negative if and when a recession occurs in the cyclical downturn. A **recession** is defined as negative economic growth (or falling real GDP) for 6 months or more.

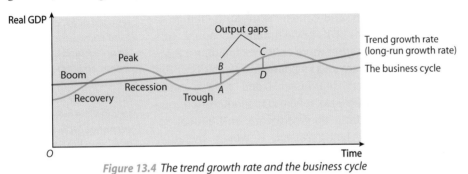

Figure 13.4 *The trend growth rate and the business cycle*

There have been two recessions in the UK during the last 30 years. The first recession occurred between 1979 and 1981. The country suffered the second recession a decade later between 1990 and 1992. Both recessions (which raised unemployment to around 3 million) were followed by longer periods of recovery and boom in the rest of the 1980s and 1990s. However, economic cycles can still be identified even when there are no recessions. In this situation, the annual growth rate falls in the cycle's downswing, but remains positive.

Although there has not been a recession since 1992, the length of a cycle depends on the dates at which actual output meets the trend rate of growth line. The most recent cycle began in 1999 and is expected to end in 2005. The choice of dates is significant because the government's ability to meet its fiscal policy rules (explained in Chapter 18) depends to some extent on when the cycle begins and ends. Slightly changing the dates at which economic cycles start and finish can affect whether fiscal rules are met or broken.

The economy's trend (or potential) growth rate is the rate at which output can grow, on a sustained basis, without putting upward or downward pressure on inflation. The trend growth rate is measured over a period covering more than one (and preferably several) economic cycles. Until quite recently, the UK's trend growth rate was judged to be about 2.25% a year. At first sight, this growth rate appears low, especially when compared to higher trend growth rates in newly industrialising countries. Nevertheless, the UK's trend growth rate is similar to the long-run growth rates of other developed economies in western Europe and North America. The absolute increase in real output delivered by a 2.25% growth rate may also exceed that delivered by a 10% growth rate in a much poorer country.

Moreover, because of the compound interest effect, a 2.25% growth rate means that average UK living standards double every generation or so. The compound interest effect also explains why the trend growth rate line in Figure 13.4 becomes steeper from year to year, moving along the line. For example, 2.25% of £1,000 billion is a larger absolute annual increase in GDP than 2.25% of £800 billion.

In 2002, the Office for National Statistics estimated that the trend growth rate in the UK had increased from 2.25% to about 2.75%. This could be explained by new technologies such as ICT and the internet improving labour productivity and causing structural change in the economy. The UK government accepted this estimate, but was rather more cautious, building a 2.5% projected growth rate into its financial calculations. The government hoped that faster trend growth could deliver sufficient extra tax revenue to finance increased government spending on healthcare and education, without tax *rates* being raised. However, by 2005 estimates of future growth were more pessimistic, and tax revenues were also less than had been expected. Lower trend growth means that tax rates will have to rise to pay for increases in public spending already announced.

> **e*xaminer's voice**
> Detailed knowledge of business cycles (or economic cycles) is not required at AS, although candidates are expected to understand the terms 'boom' and 'recession'. Nevertheless, it is probably a good idea for AS candidates to know the meaning of an economic cycle. By contrast, at A2 the Unit 6 specification does require knowledge of the nature and causes of cyclical instability in the economy.

Output gaps

If the economy's actual growth rate were always to equal the trend growth rate, there would be no output gaps. (In this situation, there would also be no business cycles.) An **output gap** measures the difference between the actual level of GDP and the level it would be were the economy to grow continuously at the trend rate of growth at which inflation is stable.

As **Figure 13.4** shows, output gaps can be negative or positive. **Negative output gaps** occur when the business cycle curve lies *below* the line showing the economy's trend growth rate. The vertical line drawn from point *A* to point *B* illustrates the negative output gap occurring at a particular point in time. By contrast, **positive output gaps** occur when the business cycle curve lies *above* the trend growth rate line. The vertical line drawn from point *C* to point *D* depicts a positive output gap.

Production possibility frontier diagrams can also be used to illustrate output gaps. A negative output gap is illustrated by a point *inside* the production possibility frontier (such as point *C* in Figure 13.3). A positive output gap can be shown by the economy *temporarily* producing at a point outside its current production

> **e*xaminer's voice**
> The AS Unit 2 specification states that candidates should understand the concept of an output gap. This reinforces the advice given earlier that candidates at both AS and A2 should possess at least some knowledge of economic cycles.

possibility frontier. As it represents overuse of capacity, such a point cannot be sustained for very long, although long-run economic growth should, of course, eventually shift the frontier outward.

The recovery and boom phases of the business cycle

The upswing of a business cycle divides into a **recovery** phase and a **boom** phase. Real output or GDP grows in both phases, but the two phases differ according to whether real output is below or above the trend growth rate line drawn in Figure 13.4. The recovery phase accompanies a negative output gap. But when real output rises above the trend growth line, recovery gives way to boom and a positive output gap.

Explanations of the business cycle

In the 1930s, John Maynard Keynes argued that economic recessions are caused by fluctuations in aggregate demand. Chapter 14 explains how, in Keynes's theory, investment and aggregate demand rise and fall as business confidence gives way to pessimism, and vice versa. However, it is now recognised that supply-side factors can also trigger business cycles. Edward Prescott and Finn Kydland, the 2004 Nobel Laureates in economics, have recently developed a theory of 'real business cycles', which argues that changes in technology on the supply side of the economy might be as important as changes in aggregate demand in explaining economic cycles. (Later sections of this chapter explain the role of technical progress in causing long cycles and long-term economic growth.)

Several factors may cause or contribute to business cycles.

Climatic factors

The nineteenth-century neoclassical economist, Stanley Jevons, was one of the first economists to recognise the business cycle. Perhaps taking note of the bible's reference to 'seven years of plenty' followed by 'seven years of famine', Jevons believed that a connection exists between the timing of economic crises and the solar cycle. Variations in sunspots affect the power of the sun's rays, influencing the quality of harvests and thus the price of grain, which, in turn, affects business confidence and gives rise to trade cycles.

Although Jevons's sunspot theory was never widely accepted, there is no doubt that climate changes do affect economic activity. The El Niño effect has renewed interest in Jevons's theory. El Niño is a severe atmospheric and oceanic disturbance in the Pacific Ocean occurring every 7–14 years. The disturbance leads to a fall in the number of plankton, upsetting the entire ocean food chain which badly damages the fishing industry. The effect leads to a complete reversal of trade winds, bringing torrential rain, flooding and mudslides to the otherwise dry Pacific coastal areas of central South America. By contrast, droughts occur in much of Asia and in areas of Africa and central North America.

The role of speculative bubbles

Rapid economic growth leads to a rapid rise and speculative bubble in asset prices. When people realise that house prices or share prices have risen far above the

assets' real values, asset selling replaces asset buying. This causes the speculative bubble to burst, which in turn destroys consumer and business confidence. People stop spending and the economy may fall into recession.

Changes in inventories

Besides investing in fixed capital, firms invest in stocks of raw materials and in stocks of finished goods waiting to be sold. This type of investment is called **inventory investment** or **stock building**. Although stock building accounts for less than 1% of GDP in a typical year, swings in inventories are often the single most important determinant of recessions. Firms hold stocks of raw materials and finished goods in order to smooth production and cope with swings in demand. But paradoxically, changes in stocks tend to trigger and exacerbate business cycles. Stocks of unsold finished goods build up when firms over-anticipate demand for finished goods. Firms are then forced to cut production by more than the original fall in demand. The resultant de-stocking turns a slowdown into a recession. Swings in inventory investment account for about half of the reductions in GDP in the USA's past nine recessions. De-stocking has also made UK recessions worse.

Political business cycle theory

In democratic countries, general elections usually have to take place every 4 or 5 years. As an election approaches, the political party in power may 'buy votes' by engineering a pre-election boom. After the election, the party in power will normally then deflate aggregate demand to prevent the economy from overheating. But when the next general election approaches, demand is once again expanded.

'Outside shocks' affecting the economy

These divide into 'demand shocks', which affect aggregate demand, and 'supply shocks', which impact on aggregate supply. In some cases, an outside shock hitting the economy may affect both aggregate demand and aggregate supply. Thus the outbreak of a Middle East war may affect demand by causing a sudden collapse in consumer and business confidence, and also aggregate supply through its effects on the supply of crude oil.

Marxist theory

Marxist economists explain business cycles as part of a restructuring process that increases the rate of profit in capitalist economies. Under normal production conditions, a fall in the rate of profit caused by competitive pressure threatens to bankrupt weaker capitalist firms. Marxists believe that recessions create conditions in which stronger firms either take over weaker competitors, or buy at rock-bottom prices the assets of rivals forced out of business. Either way, restructuring by takeover or bankruptcy means that the 'fittest' capitalist firms survive. (Note how this process is similar to the theory of economic natural selection explained in Chapter 7.) In Marxist analysis, business cycles are deemed necessary for the regeneration and survival of capitalism.

Marxists also argue that, in the upswing of a cycle, high employment generates wage inflation. Labour's share of output increases, but at the expense of capitalists' profits and future investment and output. The reduction in output in turn reduces demand for labour and employment, leading to lower wage inflation or wage deflation, which reduces labour's share of output. As the workers' wage share declines, profits and investment increase. This increases the demand for labour, which improves workers' bargaining power. Wages once again rise at the expense of profit, and the cycle repeats itself.

Multiplier/accelerator interaction

Keynesian economists have argued that business cycles may be caused by the interaction of two dynamic processes: the multiplier and the accelerator (multiplier and accelerator interaction are explained in Chapter 14). Via an increase in investment, the multiplier process leads to an increase in national income. The change in income then leads, via the accelerator, to a further change in investment, and the process then repeats itself.

examiner's voice
The A2 Unit 6 specification states that candidates should understand the various phases of the economic cycle and some of the causes of cyclical instability — for example, supply-side and demand-side shocks. Exam questions may refer to the 'causes of fluctuations in economic activity', without explicit mention of economic cycles in the wording of the question. Nonetheless, good answers are likely to focus on at least two possible causes of business cycles, possibly backed by briefer mention of seasonal fluctuations and/or the long cycle.

Stabilising the business cycle

As Chapter 12 explains, from the early 1950s to the 1970s, Keynesian-inspired governments managed the level of aggregate demand in the UK in order to stabilise the business cycle. In the downswing, fiscal policy and monetary policy were used to increase or reflate aggregate demand. Conversely, in the upswing, governments contracted or deflated aggregate demand, before the economy overheated in the cycle's boom phase.

However, stable and milder business cycles may result more from the role of automatic stabilisers (which are explained in Chapter 18) than from demand-management policies. Demand management led to the 'stop–go' problem. In successive business cycles, periods of slow growth (or 'stop') became longer, while periods of 'go' were quickly brought to a halt by the economy running into higher rates of inflation, or a balance of payments crisis.

Some economists argue that in the Keynesian era, government intervention actually destabilised business cycles, widening rather than reducing cyclical fluctuations and possibly reducing the economy's trend growth rate. There are several reasons why Keynesian demand-management policies may have done this. In the first place, the success of demand management depends on correct timing. By responding to changes in unemployment rather than to changes in output or GDP, governments may have got their timing wrong. (Changes in employment and unemployment often occur several months after changes in output.) Instead of expanding demand when the growth of output slowed, governments intervened too late, *after* output had already begun to recover. Likewise, governments contracted demand *after* the peak of the business cycle, thus worsening the downturn.

Second, the timing of intervention may have resulted from the government's need to win votes rather than to manage the economy properly. (See the theory of the political business cycle in the previous section.) Third, by causing the public sector to grow in size, expansionary fiscal policies may have crowded out the private sector, thereby reducing the economy's trend growth rate. (The crowding-out theory is explained in Chapter 18.)

In the monetarist era in the early 1980s, stabilising the business cycle through the use of demand management policies went out of fashion. But since the early 1990s, managing aggregate demand has been back in fashion — although almost solely through raising or lowering interest rates in monetary policy. Fiscal policy is no longer generally used to manage demand, except through the automatic stabilisers we mentioned briefly earlier in this section.

e*xaminer's voice

At AS and especially at A2, knowledge learnt in the context of stabilising the business cycle could also be included in the answer to a question on the objectives of monetary policy or fiscal policy, or on the effects of such policies. Note, however, that in the UK, only monetary policy is currently used to manage aggregate demand. Apart from its automatic stabiliser effect, fiscal policy is now used primarily as a supply-side policy.

Long cycles

Earlier sections of this chapter have explained how fluctuations in economic activity are explained by seasonal factors, and by the possible causes of the business cycle. A business cycle, which is usually between 4 and 6 years long, is sometimes called a **short cycle**. This is to distinguish business cycles from much longer cycles that may last as long as 60 or 70 years. **Long cycles** are also called **Kondratieff cycles**, after the Russian economist who first identified them in the 1930s.

The famous Austrian/American economist, Joseph Schumpeter, provided a theory to explain long cycles. Schumpeter argued that long cycles are caused by sudden bursts of technical progress, occurring on the supply side of the economy. Each burst stems from a major innovation or set of innovations, which changes the means of production in a significant part of the economy. A major innovation or set of innovations is often linked to a new general purpose technology (GPT). GPTs that may have triggered the start of a long cycle include those that relate to the development of railways, chemical industries and electric power in the nineteenth century, and the automobile and ICT in the twentieth century. Innovations and new GPTs significantly increase the rate of investment, in order to equip the economy with the capital goods needed to implement the new technology. The subsequent investment boom greatly increases aggregate demand. But eventually, the 'new' technology becomes an old technology. A form of diminishing returns sets in and the economy's growth rate slows, until the next significant bout of technical progress ushers in a new long cycle.

Economic growth in the long run

While business cycles are important in explaining *short-run* economic growth, they are less relevant for explaining the long-run causes of growth. Long-run economic

growth is explained almost exclusively by **supply-side factors**. However, sufficient aggregate demand has to be generated to absorb the extra output produced by the growth process. The immediate supply-side cause of long-run growth is increased labour productivity, which itself results from investment in, and accumulation of, capital goods and human capital, and from technical progress.

There are two main theories of long-term economic growth. Both theories link to some extent with Joseph Schumpeter's theory of long cycles outlined above.

Neoclassical growth theory

The older theory, known as **neoclassical growth theory**, argues that a sustained increase in investment increases the economy's growth rate, but only temporarily. The ratio of capital to labour goes up, the marginal product of capital declines and the economy moves back to a long-term path, which is determined by output growing at the same rate as the workforce, plus a factor to reflect improving labour productivity. In neoclassical growth theory, the rate at which labour productivity improves is determined by technical progress. But the theory does not explain why technical progress occurs. This is the theory's weakness. The determinants of the ultimate engine of economic growth, namely technical progress, are exogenous to the theory. (**Exogenous** means outside.) Neoclassical growth theory fails to provide a complete explanation of economic growth because changes in technical progress are not explained *within* the model.

*e***xaminer's voice**
The AS Unit 2 specification states that candidates should understand the main factors that influence the rate of economic growth. The A2 Unit 6 specification develops this requirement by stating that candidates should understand that supply-side factors, such as investment, education and training and technological change, are likely to determine the underlying trend rate of economic growth. A basic knowledge, such as that provided in this chapter, of the difference between neoclassical growth theory and new growth theory might be useful at A2. However, the Unit 6 specification does not require this knowledge, and it is certainly not needed at AS. Neoclassical growth theory and new growth theory are difficult theories; you may decide to ignore them.

New growth theory

In recent years, neoclassical growth theory has been replaced to a significant extent by **new growth theory**. New growth theory is also called **endogenous** growth theory, reflecting the fact that, unlike in neoclassical growth theory, the determinants of technical progress are brought *inside* the theory. The three main sources of technical progress explained by new growth theory are profit-seeking research, openness to foreign ideas and accumulation of human capital:

- **Profit-seeking research.** The rate at which technical progress occurs depends on the *stock* of ideas. The *flow* of new ideas thought up by current researchers adds to the 'capital stock' of existing ideas. How many new ideas there are depends on the number of researchers, but the extent to which new ideas improve technical progress depends on whether or not 'over-fishing' occurs. 'Over-fishing' means that the discovery of new ideas makes it harder to find further

new ideas. But conversely, the opposite may be true, as accumulating ideas may make researchers more productive rather than less productive. This is the so-called 'standing on the shoulders' effect. Paul Romer, one of the most influential developers of new growth theory, assumes that the 'standing on the shoulders' effect is dominant, which means that countries with more researchers can have higher growth rates.

- **Openness to foreign ideas.** Economic growth can derive either from domestic innovation or from technological transfer from other countries. In 1999, Cameron, Proudman and Redding argued that the rate at which technical progress occurs in a country depends on three factors: the domestic rate of growth of technology in the absence of technology transfer; the rate at which technology can be adopted from abroad; and the proportion of foreign technologies that can be adopted. This means that for a technology *follower*, technology grows at its own domestic rate of technology growth, plus some extra 'catch-up' generated by technology-leading countries.

- **Accumulation of human capital.** Human capital accumulates through educating and training a skilled workforce from among a country's indigenous population, and through migration from other countries. Migration adds to human capital providing migrants possess appropriate education and skills, or are willing and able to attain appropriate education and skills. A high level of human capital is best regarded as a *necessary* condition, but not as a *sufficient* condition, for successful economic growth. This is because technological change requires workers to possess the skills and aptitudes required for adapting to new technologies, rather than those that used to be necessary for old, declining technologies.

New growth theory suggests that appropriate government intervention can create the supply-side conditions which favour growth. These include:

- conditions that encourage profit-seeking research and appropriate accumulation of human capital
- externalities or external economies provided by the state which benefit private sector businesses
- patent legislation and a judicial system that enforces the law of contract and intellectual property rights, which create the incentive for firms to innovate

Productivity and technical progress

To the layman, the term **productivity** usually means labour productivity. As Chapter 4 explains, labour productivity can be measured in terms of the average product of labour, or output per worker, and the marginal product of labour, which measures the addition to total output brought about by employing an extra worker.

These definitions are *short-run* definitions that assume capital is fixed and technical progress remains unchanged. In much the same way, the productivity of capital can be measured by adding capital to a fixed labour force, once again with a given state of technical progress. In either case, by adding labour to fixed capital, or by adding capital to fixed labour, the **law of diminishing returns** sets in, eventually reducing the average productivity of the input being changed.

To escape the impact of diminishing returns to labour or capital, labour and capital must be changed together. In this situation, when returns to scale operate, the key concept is **total factor productivity** (TFP). A change in TFP measures the change in total output when *all* the factors of production are changed in the economic *long run.*

The rate of growth of technology is simply the rate of growth of total factor productivity. It measures how much more productive capital, labour and other factors of production have become in total. There is general agreement among economists that the growth of TFP (or technical progress) is the main cause of economic growth. But as the previous section indicates, economists disagree on the actual *causes* of technical progress.

examiner's voice

Productivity is a key concept in both the AS Module 1 and Module 2 specifications, which means that an understanding of the term is also expected for all the A2 unit examinations. Questions usually centre on labour productivity, although candidates should be aware of other meanings of the term. Questions may also mention the UK's productivity gap, which is the difference in productivity levels between the UK and competitor countries. Don't confuse a productivity gap with an output gap (which was explained earlier in this chapter).

The benefits and costs of economic growth

This book has repeated on several occasions that the ultimate purpose of economic activity is to improve economic welfare and people's standards of living. Economic growth can help to achieve this, but only if growth is compatible with economic development. (Refer back to Chapter 1, pp. 5–6, which explains the distinction between economic growth and economic development.)

Economic growth can have a number of costs that reduce economic welfare. The United Nations Human Development Programme has identified 'five damaging forms of growth' that are neither sustainable nor worth sustaining. These are:

- **jobless growth**, which does not translate into jobs
- **voiceless growth**, which is not matched by the spread of democracy
- **rootless growth**, which destroys separate cultural identity
- **futureless growth**, which despoils the environment
- **ruthless growth**, where most of the benefits are seized by the rich

examiner's voice

The costs and benefits of growth are an important topic at A2. The Unit 6 specification states that candidates should be able to discuss whether or not economic growth is sustainable and to evaluate the impact of growth on individuals and the environment.

Is economic growth sustainable?

Environmentalists, ecologists and some economists predict that the pursuit of ever-growing GNP is unsustainable, arguing that growth will eventually lead to the depletion of non-renewable resources. However, many, although certainly not all, economists believe this is too simplistic. They question the environmentalists' assumptions of an ever-faster rate of resource usage accompanied by an ever-faster rate of decline of resource reserves.

As Chapter 2 explains, prices perform three main functions in a market economy: signalling, creating incentives or allocating scarce resources between competing uses. Other things being equal, an increase in the rate of resource usage causes resource prices to rise. In their turn, rising resource prices create incentives for consumers and producers to alter economic behaviour — literally, to economise. Consumers buy less of goods and services whose relative prices are rising. Producers, meanwhile, respond to the changing relative prices of their inputs or factors of production: first, by altering methods of production; and, second, by exploring the earth's crust for new supplies of minerals and fossil fuels, which would be uneconomic to search for and extract at a lower resource price.

Nevertheless, most economists have taken on board the environmentalists' belief that governments should aim for sustainable economic growth and development. R. K. Turner has defined an optimal sustainable growth policy as one that maintains 'an "acceptable" rate of growth in per capita incomes without depleting the national capital asset stock or the natural environment asset stock'. Environmental economists such as David Pearce certainly believe it is possible to achieve sustainable economic growth. Pearce argues that running out of materials and energy is unlikely to be a real limit to growth, as there are many resources that humankind has not begun to develop and there are almost limitless energy sources from the sun. Pearce believes the limits to growth lie more in the problem of resource degradation than in the problem of resource depletion, with used-up resources reappearing elsewhere as waste.

While rejecting environmentalists' calls for an end to economic growth as a policy aim, Pearce has little time for 'cornucopists' who believe that economic growth is more important than environmental loss, which they regard simply as the inevitable price of growth. Pearce believes we must have growth to meet human desires and aspirations, and to lift the world's poor out of poverty. But we must also have environmental quality because it is essential to human well-being. The trick is getting both at the same time. Environmental concerns must be properly integrated

Wind farms are one source of renewable energy, but can they provide enough power for sustainable economic growth?

into economic policy from the highest (macroeconomic) level to the most detailed (microeconomic) level. The environment must be seen as a valuable, frequently essential input to human well-being. Sustainable development means a change in consumption patterns towards environmentally more benign products, and a change in investment patterns towards augmenting environmental capital.

Summary

This chapter has surveyed and identified some of the links between three important macro-economic topic areas: the meaning of national income; comparing GDP and other methods of measuring changes in living standards; and defining and explaining possible causes of economic growth. At both AS and A2, it is not necessary to know about the national income accounts in any depth. But since Unit 2 and 6 examination papers may include data presented in the form of GNP or GDP figures, students should be familiar with the main measures of national income, particularly GDP. For both AS and A2, it is also necessary to know the difference between nominal national income and real national income.

Examination questions sometimes ask for discussion and evaluation of whether the growth of national income (or GDP) provides an adequate measure of improvements in economic welfare or living standards. GDP is a reasonable indicator of improvements in material standards of living. Nevertheless, GDP understates the role of the non-monetised and hidden economy, while overstating other ways in which production and consumption of goods and services improve economic welfare. But perhaps the main drawback in using GDP to measure changes in economic welfare stems from the fact that the impact of externalities and other factors affecting quality of life are not included in the measure.

The chapter surveyed three alternatives to national income and GDP for measuring standards of living, quality of life and economic welfare. The most widely known is the Human Development Index, calculated and published by the United Nations. Each year the UN uses life expectancy, education and GDP indices to construct the weighted Human Development Index, and publishes tables that rank the world's countries in terms of HDI performance. However, the HDI ignores the effect of income inequalities within countries, and lacks the breadth of the Index of Sustainable Economic Welfare in measuring quality of life factors. The ISEW tries to capture the effects of externalities and other intangibles upon human welfare. It measures economic performance against around 20 indicators, including pollution and the loss of natural resources. The Misery Index, which was the last of the three welfare indicators considered in the chapter, is the most basic, measuring quality of life very narrowly in terms of the assumed effect on welfare of unemployment, inflation and interest rates.

The sections of the chapter on economic growth began by distinguishing between the measurement of economic growth and the definition of economic growth. The causes of short-term growth and long-term growth were discussed, and business cycles and seasonal fluctuations were explained in the context of short-term growth. The nature of technical progress and investment in physical and human capital were highlighted as factors causing long-term growth. After surveying the main difference between neoclassical growth theory and new growth theory (or endogenous growth theory), the chapter concluded with a discussion of the benefits and costs and the sustainability of economic growth.

Self-testing questions

1 Distinguish between income, wealth and capital.

2 What are the three methods of measuring national income?

3 Explain the difference between NNP and GDP.

4 Distinguish between nominal national income and real national income.

5 Outline two problems that occur when using national income or GDP to measure living standards.

6 Distinguish between narrow and broad definitions of 'standards of living'.

7 How is the United Nation's Human Development Index (HDI) constructed?

8 What are the differences between the Index of Sustainable Economic Welfare (ISEW) and GDP as measures of economic welfare?

9 Outline two weaknesses of the ISEW.

10 What is the Misery Index?

11 Illustrate short-term and long-term economic growth on a PPF diagram.

12 State three ways in which economic activity fluctuates.

13 Briefly explain three possible causes of business cycles.

14 What is a recession?

15 Distinguish between a positive and a negative output gap.

16 Outline the determinants of long-term economic growth.

17 State two benefits and two costs of economic growth.

18 What is meant by sustainable economic growth?

Chapter 14
Aggregate demand

Specification focus

This chapter provides a detailed coverage of aggregate demand. Make sure you read the *Examiner's voice* advice on how much knowledge is required by AS and A2 exam questions on this topic.

AS **Module 2 The National Economy**
How the Macroeconomy Works

A2 **Module 6 Government Policy, the National and International Economy**
Managing the National Economy

A2 **Synoptic coverage**
In the AQA specification, aggregate demand is primarily an AS topic. The coverage of aggregate demand in this chapter goes beyond the requirements of the Module 2 specification, covering consumption and investment theories and the multiplier in greater depth, to enable A2 candidates to answer synoptic questions at a more sophisticated level.

Introduction

This chapter begins by explaining the importance of aggregate demand in the economy and the nature of the circular flow of income. The chapter then investigates in more detail the determinants of two of the components of aggregate demand: consumption and investment. The other components of aggregate demand — namely government spending, exports and imports — are mentioned briefly, but are covered in greater depth in later chapters. The relationships between consumption and saving, and between saving and investment, are explained, as are the implications of the personal saving ratio. The chapter concludes by examining the multiplier and the accelerator, and possible links between the two processes.

e*xaminer's voice*

This chapter focuses on the components of aggregate demand. At AS, Unit 2 exam questions may ask for an explanation of the factors determining consumption or investment. The chapter does not explain the aggregate demand/aggregate supply (*AD/AS*) macroeconomic model, which is analysed in Chapter 15.

Aggregate demand

The meaning of aggregate demand

Aggregate demand must not be confused with national expenditure, which we explained in Chapter 13. **Aggregate demand** is defined as total *planned* spending on the goods and services produced *within* the economy. By contrast, **national expenditure**, which figures in the country's national income accounts, measures the realised or actual spending that has already taken place.

The components of aggregate demand

Four sources of spending are included in aggregate demand, each originating in a different sector of the economy: households, firms, the government sector and the overseas sector. The sources of spending, or **components of aggregate demand**, are shown in the following equation:

$$\text{aggregate demand} = \text{consumption} + \text{investment} + \text{government spending} + \text{exports (net of imports)}$$

or:

$$AD = C + I + G + (X - M)$$

where C, I, G, X and M are the symbols used respectively for planned consumption, investment, government spending, exports and imports.

Aggregate demand and the circular flow of income

One way of understanding the role of aggregate demand in the economy is to explain it in the context of the **circular flow of income**. A simplified circular flow diagram is shown in Figure 14.1. Later diagrams will drop the simplifying assumptions and explore the circular flow in more realistic detail.

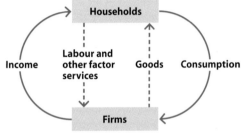

Figure 14.1 A circular flow diagram for a two-sector economy

Figure 14.1 shows an economy containing just households and firms. This simplified economy has no government and there is no foreign trade. We call this a **two-sector economy** or a **closed economy** with no government sector. The dashed flow lines in Figure 14.1 show the **real flows** of factor services and goods between households and firms. Households supply labour and other factor services in exchange for goods and services produced by the firms. But the real flows generate **money flows** of income and expenditure shown by the solid flow lines. (Money flows are also called **nominal flows**.) Aggregate demand in this simplified economy is represented by the equation:

$$AD = C + I$$

In Figure 14.1, there is no saving, but also no investment by firms. All the income received by households (shown in the left-hand curve of the diagram) is spent on consumption (shown in the right-hand curve of the diagram). This means there is no excess demand or deficient demand in the economy. At the current price level, spending is just sufficient to purchase the real output produced.

Figure 14.2 is more realistic than Figure 14.1, since it shows that households save as well as consume, and that firms invest in capital goods. When house-holds save part of their income, less is available for consumption. Saving, which is an example of a **leakage** or **withdrawal** from the circular flow of income, is depicted by the upper of the two horizontal arrows in Figure 14.2. The lower of the two horizontal arrows shows investment, or spending by firms on raw materials, machinery and other capital goods, which is an **injection** of demand into the economy.

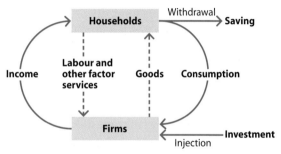

Figure 14.2 Introducing saving and investment into the circular flow of income

Now, if planned saving (or the *planned* withdrawal of spending) equals planned investment (or the *planned* injection of spending into the flow), national income is in equilibrium. However, there is no particular reason why households' saving plans should exactly equal firms' planned investment because the decisions are made for different reasons.

Consider a situation in which households plan to save more than firms wish to borrow to finance the purchase of capital goods. In this situation, when with-drawals of demand from the circular flow exceed injections, the resulting net leakage of spending from the circular flow causes output and income to fall. Likewise, a net injection of demand, which occurs when planned investment exceeds planned saving, causes national income to rise. In these situations, national income is in **disequilibrium**.

Figure 14.3 introduces a possible reason why households' planned saving quickly moves to equal firms' planned investment, without the need for a change in the level of national income. The box drawn on the right-hand side of Figure 14.3 illus-trates what pre-Keynesian economists called the **market for loanable funds**. For

households, loanable funds are the savings lent for others to spend. By contrast, firms borrow loanable funds to finance investment or the purchase of capital goods. The rate of interest, which is the price of loanable funds, is shown on the vertical axis of the graph in the box.

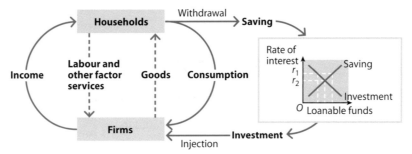

Figure 14.3 A fall in the rate of interest to equate planned saving and investment

When households wish to save more than firms wish to borrow to finance investment decisions, the market for loanable funds fails to clear. According to the loanable funds theory, the rate of interest (r_1) is too high, encouraging too much saving and too little investment. The solution is that the rate of interest must fall to r_2 to eliminate the excess supply of saving.

Pre-Keynesian economists believed that an economy never suffers from deficient aggregate demand, except as a *temporary* phenomenon. Whenever households' saving plans exceed firms' planned investment decisions, the rate of interest quickly falls to restore equality between saving and investment intentions.

But as Chapter 12 stated, John Maynard Keynes disputed this view. Keynes believed that interest rates are determined by money market conditions, which differs from the loanable funds explanation just described. Moreover, even if rates of interest fall to bring planned saving and investment decisions into line, Keynes believed the process to be very slow. In the *very* long run it might work, but in Keynes's memorable phrase, 'in the long run we are all dead'.

Keynesian economics differs from the free-market view we have just described by arguing that when planned leakages of demand from the circular flow of income exceed planned injections of demand, the **level of income or output** falls to restore equilibrium. In the Keynesian view, this causes recessions.

We shall now use Figure 14.4 to extend the Keynesian analysis a stage further. Figure 14.4 illustrates the **four-sector model** of the economy depicted by the aggregate demand equation that we introduced at the beginning of the chapter:

$$AD = C + I + G + (X - M)$$

examiner's voice

The difference between the loanable funds theory of how planned saving is equated with planned investment, and Keynes's theory, illustrates how different economic schools of thought explain economic problems.

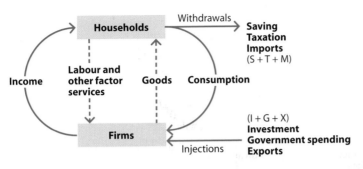

Figure 14.4 The components of aggregate demand and the circular flow of income in an open economy with a government sector

We are now examining an **open economy** with a government sector. We have added government and overseas sectors to the households and firms of our earlier circular flow model.

In the two-sector circular flow model, national income is in equilibrium when:

planned saving = planned investment

or:

$S = I$

Having extended the circular flow model, national income is in equilibrium, tending neither to rise nor to fall, when:

planned saving + taxation + imports = planned investment + government spending + imports

or:

$S + T + M = I + G + X$

But whenever:

$S + T + M > I + G + X$

a net leakage of demand *out of* the circular flow occurs, which in Keynesian analysis causes the equilibrium level of national income to fall.

Conversely, if:

$S + T + M < I + G + X$

a net injection of demand *into* the circular flow occurs, which for Keynesians causes the equilibrium level of national income to rise.

Consumption and saving

The rest of this chapter examines consumption, saving and investment in greater depth. In this section we will look at consumption and saving.

*e*xaminer's voice

Equilibrium is a state of balance or state of rest, in which all the economic agents being modelled fulfil their market plans. By contrast, in disequilibrium, one or more of the set of agents fails to fulfil its plans. Chapter 2 explained that a market (within the economy) is in equilibrium when *planned* demand equals *planned* supply. At the macroeconomic level, national income is in equilibrium when *planned* leakages or withdrawals from the circular flow of income equal *planned* injections of spending into the circular flow. (You should note that Chapter 15 states macroeconomic equilibrium in a slightly different way, in terms of aggregate demand equalling aggregate supply.)

The meaning of consumption and saving

Consumption is the spending by all the households in the economy upon consumer goods and services. Many consumer goods are, of course, imported, so imports have to be deducted from aggregate consumption spending to measure spending on domestically produced consumer goods and services.

Saving is household income that is not consumed. Economists make a clear separation between saving and *investment*, even though in everyday language the two terms are often used interchangeably. Private investment comprises spending by firms on capital goods, while similar spending by the government (for example, on roads and hospitals) builds up the country's stock of social capital.

The January sales are a busy time for UK consumers

Savings can be hoarded, or the funds being saved may be lent for others to spend. **Hoarding**, which takes place, for example, when keeping money hidden in a tin box beneath the floorboards, means that a fraction of income ends up not being spent. However, as we have seen, savings can also be **lent** — for example, to financial intermediaries such as banks. The financial institutions then lend the savings to firms and to other consumers to spend.

The propensities to consume and save

The propensity to consume and the propensity to save are used to measure *planned* or *intended* consumption and saving as a ratio of income. At any level of income (Y), the **average propensity to consume** (*APC*) measures total planned consumption as a ratio of the level of income. Likewise, the **average propensity to save** (*APS*) measures total planned saving as a ratio of income. Since it is very easy to confuse the *average* propensity to consume with the *marginal* propensity to consume, make sure that you learn how the two concepts differ. The **marginal propensity to consume** (*MPC*) measures a *change* in planned consumption as a ratio of a *change* in the level of income. In a similar way, the **marginal propensity to save** (*MPS*) measures the *change* in planned saving as a ratio of a *change* in income.

Using the symbols C and S for *planned* consumption and saving, the *average* propensities to consume and save can be shown by the equations:

$$APC = \frac{C}{Y}$$

$$APS = \frac{S}{Y}$$

The *marginal* propensities to consume and save can be shown by the equations:

$$MPC = \frac{\Delta C}{\Delta Y}$$

$$MPS = \frac{\Delta S}{\Delta Y}$$

The symbol Δ is used to show a change in planned consumption, planned saving and in income.

The following numerical example illustrates the difference between the various propensities to consume and save. Suppose, when disposable income is £10, a woman plans to spend £8 on consumption and to save £2. Her *APC* is 0.8 and her *APS* is 0.2. (The *APC* and the *APS* *always* sum to 1 or unity, although people may wish to spend part of planned consumption on imports.) When the woman's disposable income increases to £11, she decides to consume 60p of the additional income and to save 40p. For the extra pound, her *MPC* is 0.6 and her *MPS* is 0.4. Again the *MPC* and *MPS* sum to unity. At the new higher level of income (£11 rather than £10), her *APC* is slightly lower than before: that is, smaller than 0.8. Can you work out why?

*e*xaminer's voice

The AQA specifications do not require knowledge of the propensities to consume and save, but this knowledge is extremely useful.

The personal saving ratio and the household saving ratio

The propensities to consume and save indicate how much people *wish* or *plan* to consume and to save at different levels of income, rather than how much they *actually end up* consuming and saving. Because it is difficult to measure people's *plans* accurately, the **personal saving ratio** is generally used as an indicator of the average propensity to save under the assumption that people actually succeed in fulfilling their market plans. The personal saving ratio measures the actual or realised savings of the personal sector as a ratio of total personal sector disposal income:

$$\text{personal saving ratio} = \frac{\text{realised or actual personal saving}}{\text{personal disposable income}}$$

The **household saving ratio** is used in a similar way. As the name indicates, the household saving ratio measures households' realised saving as a ratio of households' income. However, the personal saving ratio and the household saving ratio are not the same. The personal sector comprises more than just households, including unincorporated businesses such as partnerships, and charitable organisations such as universities and independent schools.

The determinants of consumption and saving

If we ignore taxation, household income can be either consumed or saved:

$$Y = C + S$$

*e*xaminer's voice

The AS Module 2 specification states: 'candidates should be able to explain and analyse the determinants of consumption, investment and the other components of aggregate demand'. Examination questions will not be set on specific theories, such as the Keynesian theory of consumption, but very good answers could display such knowledge.

Rewritten as $C = Y - S$, or as $S = Y - C$, the equation means that a theory of consumption behaviour also involves a theory of saving, and vice versa. As explained earlier in the chapter, pre-Keynesian economists approached the matter through the loanable funds theory of saving and investment. In the loanable funds theory, a rise in the rate of interest encourages more saving by households. This in turn means that, at any level of income, households spend less on consumption as the rate of interest rises.

The Keynesian theory of consumption

John Maynard Keynes agreed that the rate of interest influences consumption and saving, but in his view the rate of interest is less significant than the level of disposable income. In the *General Theory*, Keynes explained his theory of aggregate consumption in the following way:

> The fundamental psychological law, upon which we are entitled to depend with great confidence...is that men are disposed, as a rule and on average, to increase their consumption as their income increases, but not by as much as the increase in their income.

More specifically, Keynes believed that although aggregate planned consumption (C) rises as income rises, it rises at a *slower* rate than income, so that at high levels of income, planned consumption is less than income and planned saving is positive. Keynes's theory of consumption can be shown by the following equation:

$$C = a + cY$$

The Keynesian consumption line (or Keynesian **consumption function**) is illustrated in the two parts of Figure 14.5. The diagrams show planned consumption comprising two elements: **autonomous consumption** and **income-induced consumption**.

Autonomous consumption (represented by the symbol *a*) is constant at *all* levels of income. It is determined by influences upon consumption *other than* the level of income. The factors determining autonomous consumption (and the value of *a*) include the rate of interest (which we have already covered), wealth, consumer confidence and the availability of credit.

As its name indicates, the second Keynesian component of consumption, income-induced consumption, depends on the level of income. When people have no income, income-induced consumption is zero — in which case, *planned* consumption is restricted to the autonomous component already described. Autonomous consumption is shown by the vertical distance labelled a in Figure 14.5(b). But at the level of income Y_1 in the diagram, consumption equals a plus the distance cY_1 shown above the horizontal dashed line in the diagram. The distance cY_1 measures income-induced consumption at this particular level of income.

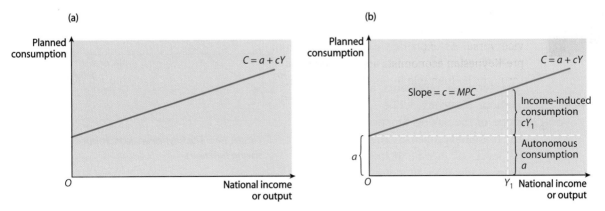

Figure 14.5 *The Keynesian consumption function*

Autonomous consumption determines the *position* of the consumption function (that is, the point at which the consumption line intersects the vertical axis in the diagrams in Figure 14.5). When, for example, wealth increases or people become more confident about the future, the value of a increases and the consumption function shifts upwards to a new position.

By contrast, income-induced consumption is determined by the *slope* of the consumption line as well as by the level of income. The symbol c, which measures the slope of the consumption function, is also the marginal propensity to consume (*MPC*), which we explained earlier. A larger value for *MPC* (at all levels of income) leads to a *steeper* consumption function and a higher level of income-induced consumption at each size of income. Nevertheless, the *position* of the consumption function remains unchanged, unless of course autonomous consumption also changes.

Because the consumption function in Figure 14.5 is a straight line (we call this a **linear** consumption function), the value of *MPC* is constant at all levels of income. But this is not so for *APC*. The diagram shows that planned consumption exceeds income at low levels of income. When this is the case, *APC* > 1. As income rises, consumption eventually falls below the level of income, which means that the average propensity to consume falls to less than unity (*APC* < 1).

Deriving the Keynesian saving function

For households to spend more than their income at low levels of income, they must **dissave**. People can dissave (or indulge in negative saving) in two ways. First, they may borrow, and second, they may run down previously accumulated stocks of wealth. This leads us to the shape of the Keynesian saving function.

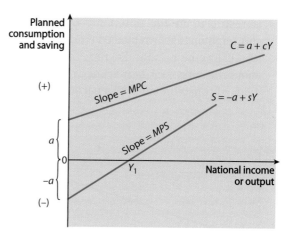

Figure 14.6 shows how a saving function can be derived from a Keynesian consumption function by subtracting planned consumption from income at every level of income. The equation of the saving function illustrated in Figure 14.6 is:

$$S = -a + sY$$

The term $-a$ represents autonomous dissaving, while s, the slope of the saving function, is the marginal propensity to save. At levels of income below Y_1, households plan to dissave —

Figure 14.6 The Keynesian consumption and saving functions

either by borrowing or by running down previously accumulated stocks of saving — in order to finance consumption plans that are in excess of the level of income. Y_1 is the level of income at which planned consumption equals income and planned saving is zero.

The average propensity to save (*APS*) thus rises as income rises, becoming positive as saving replaces dissaving. In the diagram, the marginal propensity to save (*MPS*), or the slope of the savings function, remains constant.

The significance of the Keynesian theory of consumption and saving

The Keynesian theory of aggregate consumption and the related theory of saving, which we have just described, are very significant in macroeconomic theory. Keynes's consumption function carries the message that, at the high levels of income typical of advanced industrial economies, households will on average wish to consume less than all their income. As Chapter 12 states, Keynes located the underlying cause of deficient demand in this tendency for households to save part of their income. But the tendency for savings to increase at a faster rate than income is not in itself a sufficient explanation for deficient demand. For deficient demand to occur in the economy, not only must households save, but also the saving must remain idle. There must be a failure on the part of firms to invest, or on the part of government to spend, the income saved but not spent by households.

The life-cycle theory of consumption

The Keynesian theory just described assumes that *current* income is the main determinant of *current* consumption and saving decisions. It is generally agreed that by ignoring the importance of **expected future income**, as well income earned now, upon consumption and saving decisions, the theory does not go far enough. Expected future income, extending over the whole of a person's **expected life cycle**, is regarded as an important determinant of current consumption and saving. The **life-cycle theory**, which is illustrated in Figure 14.7, is based on the assumption that rational consumers aim to maximise utility over an expected lifetime by allocating a stream of lifetime earnings to an optimal lifetime pattern of consumption and saving.

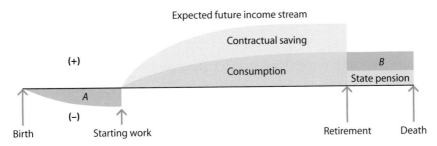

Figure 14.7 Consumption and contractual saving over the life cycle

In order to understand the life-cycle theory developed by the Italian/American economist Franco Modigliani, it is useful to distinguish between two different types of saving: contractual saving (or non-discretionary saving) and non-contractual saving (or discretionary saving).

Non-contractual or **discretionary saving** takes place when a person saves, for example, to buy Christmas presents. This type of saving is usually short term. Income saved in September may be spent in December, so over the course of a year, net discretionary saving is likely to be close to zero.

By contrast, people plan **contractual saving** on the basis of a long-term view of expected lifetime (or **permanent**) income, and of likely spending and borrowing plans over the remainder of their expected life cycle. Temporary fluctuations in yearly income often have little effect on how much people contribute to pension schemes or to life insurance policies. Many people sign savings contracts, especially early in their working lives, to finance a house purchase, and then continue to save to finance retirement or to protect dependants against the financial problems that otherwise result from the saver's early death. Thus, with contractual saving, saving takes place at regular intervals over a number of years, to be followed in later years by dissaving when a house is purchased or upon retirement.

We can use Figure 14.7 to explain how consumption and contractual saving may vary at different levels of income and at different stages in a worker's life cycle. The worker whose real income is shown in Figure 14.7 is a professional worker (for example, a lawyer) rather than a manual worker. Professional workers usually earn their highest incomes relatively late in working life, whereas the peak earnings of manual workers generally occur earlier. Between birth and leaving full-time education, we assume no income at all. Thus area *A* shows the 'worker', not yet in employment, living off her parents' income. We then assume that, as soon as she starts a job, the worker starts to save in order to finance future expenditures and, eventually, retirement. (The diagram shows saving to finance retirement, but not contractual savings for other purposes, such as financing house purchase.)

Most professional workers expect to benefit from two forms of retirement income. First, there is the state pension, for which workers pay national insurance contributions, a form of *compulsory* contractual saving. But for most workers, the state pension is smaller than income received in work, and is not enough to live on. The second source of retirement income 'tops up' the state pension. This is a private pension financed by *voluntary* contributions to pension funds and life insurance schemes.

In Figure 14.7 the professional worker aims to achieve the same level of real consumption before and after retirement. The worker hopes that contractual savings, voluntarily undertaken *before* retirement, will yield a private pension totalling to area B *after* retirement. Of course, because the future is always uncertain, our worker may get things wrong. For example, her pension fund may collapse or fail to deliver sufficient income. In this case, to achieve desired retirement income, the worker will have to run down stocks of wealth built up or inherited during her working life, unless of course she can rely on the charity of relatives. At the other extreme, some wealthy 'greys' enjoy a retirement income sufficiently high to allow them to continue to save and to accumulate wealth. On death, the wealth is usually passed on to the next generation.

examiner's voice

The famous monetarist economist, Milton Friedman, developed a theory of consumption very similar to the life-cycle theory. Friedman's theory, which is called the **permanent income consumption theory**, argues that people decide to consume and save on the basis of the permanent (or relatively reliable) income they expect to receive in future years, rather than on the basis of unexpected and temporary windfall gains or losses of income in particular years.

Other influences on consumption and saving

Apart from the rate of interest and current and future disposable income, the following influences on consumption and saving can be identified:

- **The distribution of income.** When we explained the Keynesian theory of consumption and saving, we assumed that the marginal propensities to consume and save (though not the average propensities) are constant at all levels of income. However, this is unrealistic. The rich generally have a lower *MPC* than the poor, saving a larger fraction of any increase in income. (Indeed, the poor may not be able to save at all.) An important implication of this is that, at any overall level of aggregate income, a redistribution of income from rich to poor is likely to increase consumption and to reduce saving.

- **Wealth.** The *stock* of personal wealth, as well as the *flow* of income, influences consumption and saving decisions. In the Keynesian consumption function, wealth is one of the determinants of autonomous consumption and of the position of the consumption function. An increase in wealth shifts the consumption function upward, increasing consumption at all levels of income, while a decrease in wealth reduces consumption.

- **Expectations of future inflation.** Uncertainty caused by rising inflation can increase precautionary saving and reduce consumption. But sometimes the opposite effect can occur. Households may decide to bring forward consumption decisions by spending now on consumer durables such as cars or television sets, thereby avoiding expected future price increases. As can be seen in the context of house price inflation, there may be even more reason to borrow to finance the purchase of goods such as houses and flats if their value is expected to rise at a faster rate than general inflation. In this situation, and particularly if the real rate of interest paid on financial assets is low or negative, people are likely to buy land, property and other physical assets such as fine art and antiques as a 'hedge' against inflation. In inflationary times, physical assets that hold their real values are preferable to financial assets whose real values are expected to fall.

Collecting antiques may be a good way of holding wealth during times of inflation

■ **The availability of credit.** Besides the rate of interest, other aspects of monetary policy, such as controls on bank lending and hire purchase, affect autonomous consumption and the position of the Keynesian consumption function. If credit is easily and cheaply available, consumption is likely to increase at all levels of income because people can supplement current income by borrowing on credit created by the banking system. Conversely, a tight monetary policy shifts the consumption function downward.

Explaining changes in the personal saving ratio and the household saving ratio

At various times in the recent past, households have saved over 10% of disposable income. At other times, the personal and household saving ratios have dropped as low as 2%. There are various explanations for this.

When the economy booms and house prices rise faster than general inflation, some people decide there is no need to save. Why save now, when incomes are expected to rise in the future, and when wealth created by rapid house price inflation will look after you in old age?

Secondly, in a time of rapid inflation, the price level might rise faster than money or *nominal* interest rates. When this happens, *real* interest rates are negative. Common sense suggests that saving should fall when real interest rates are low or negative. However, the opposite may occur. To their dismay, households may discover that inflation has eroded the real value of savings accumulated over earlier years of working life. In these circumstances, it becomes rational for households to take out new contractual savings in order to 'top up' or restore the real value of accumulated saving. Only in this way — by saving — can people hope to finance retirement in the manner they had previously planned. But, on the other hand, if they distrust the recent track record of savings institutions such as Equitable Life and Standard Life, people may choose the opposite course of action, ending their saving contracts and refusing to lend any more to risky financial institutions.

Investment

The meaning of investment

Investment is the second of the components of aggregate demand covered in this chapter. In everyday speech, investment is often used to describe a situation in which a person 'invests' in stocks or shares, paintings or antiques. However, in economic theory the term **investment** has narrower and more specific meanings. The purchase of financial assets such as shares and bonds issued by firms is called **financial investment**. In this chapter, however, we are looking at **physical investment** by firms in the capital goods they need in order to produce other goods and services.

Physical investment can be of two types:

- investment in **fixed capital**, such as new factories or plant, and **social capital**, such as roads or publicly owned hospitals
- investment in **stocks of raw materials** or **variable capital**

It is important to remember that, as Chapter 13 explains, capital is a stock concept, but investment is a flow. We can measure the national capital *stock* at any particular point in time. It represents the total of all the nation's capital goods, which are still in existence and capable of production. By contrast, we measure the *flow* of investment over a period, usually a year. A country's **gross investment** includes two parts:

- **replacement investment** (to make good depreciation or capital consumption), which simply maintains the size of the existing capital stock by replacing worn-out capital
- **net investment**, which adds to the capital stock, thereby increasing productive potential

Net investment is one of the engines of economic growth that are briefly explained in Chapter 13.

Microeconomics and the macroeconomic theory of investment

As with other areas of macroeconomics, it is important always to realise that *macroeconomic* theories must be based firmly in sound *microeconomics*. Thus, the macroeconomic theory of investment derives ultimately from the theory of how a profit-maximising firm decides how much capital and other factors of production, such as labour, to employ.

*e***xaminer's voice**

Remember that a good macroeconomic theory should always be underpinned by sound microeconomic theory. Thus the macroeconomic theory of aggregate investment spending derives from the microeconomic theory of how individual firms make investment decisions.

To understand the microeconomic theory of investment in fixed capital, go to Chapter 10 and read the explanation of how firms choose between competing investment projects. As a firm adds more and more capital to labour, the law of diminishing marginal returns sets in, causing the marginal product of capital to fall.

However, the returns on a new investment are *future* returns, produced over the expected useful economic life of the investment. For a firm, an investment in fixed capital is worthwhile only if the *current* value (also called the **present value** or **discounted value**) of the future returns expected to flow from the investment exceeds the cost of financing the investment (that is, the rate of interest).

The marginal efficiency of capital

The main theory of investment explained in this chapter is the **marginal efficiency of capital** (MEC) theory. (This theory is also known as the **marginal efficiency of investment** (MEI) theory.) This is the theory developed by Keynes from the microeconomic theory of investment that we have just summarised. The MEC theory is illustrated in Figure 14.8.

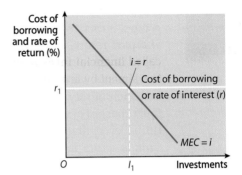

Figure 14.8 The marginal efficiency of capital theory

At any point in time, there are thousands, if not millions, of potential investment projects not yet undertaken in the economy. Each potential project has its own expected rate of return, depicted by the symbol i in Figure 14.8. If the expected future return were to be calculated for each and every possible capital project available to all the business enterprises in the economy, we could, in principle, rank the investments in descending order of expected future yields. Plotted on a graph, the resulting function is known as the **marginal efficiency of capital (*MEC*) curve**.

Taking the rate of interest as given at r_1, the equilibrium level of aggregate investment is determined in Figure 14.8 at the point where the marginal efficiency of capital equals the cost of borrowing: that is, where $i = r$. The investment labelled I_1 in the diagram is the marginal investment. This investment is expected to be only just worthwhile, since the value of its future returns is expected to match exactly the cost of borrowing the funds to finance the investment. All investments to the left of I_1 on the diagram are supra-marginal or worthwhile. For them, $i > r$. Conversely, investments to the right of I_1 are sub-marginal and should not be undertaken. Future returns are expected to be less than the interest payments needed to finance the investments.

The stability of the *MEC* curve

The *position* of the *MEC* curve (as distinct from its *slope*) is determined by firms' expectations of an unknown and uncertain future. In the 1930s, Keynes stated in colourful language that, in his view, businessmen's 'animal spirits' are perhaps the key determinant of the level of aggregate investment in the economy. When 'animal spirits' are high, business confidence improves and entrepreneurs immediately revise upward their expectations of future profits and income streams to be yielded

by the investments they are considering. The expected future productivity of most potential investment projects increases, which causes the *MEC* curve to shift outward.

In Figure 14.9, the aggregate level of investment increases from I_1 to I_2, following a rightward shift of the *MEC* curve from MEC_1 to MEC_2. But when a collapse of business confidence or 'animal spirits' occurs, firms revise downward the expected return of each project and the *MEC* curve shifts inward to MEC_3. In Keynes's view, businessmen are extremely jittery creatures, prone to rapid changes of mood and confidence. He believed that sudden changes in 'animal spirits' are responsible for the erratic shifts of the *MEC* curve, which cause the volatile nature of aggregate investment.

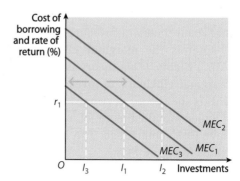

Figure 14.9 Shifts of the MEC *curve*

Other determinants of investment

Other determinants of investment besides expected future productivity and the rate of interest include the relative prices of capital and labour; the nature of technical progress; the adequacy of financial institutions in the supply of investment funds; and the impact of government policies and activities upon investment by the private sector.

When the price of capital increases (for example, when the prices of capital goods increase), in the *long run* firms adopt more labour-intensive methods of production, substituting labour for capital. A decrease in the relative prices of capital goods has the opposite effect.

To understand the importance of technical progress, we shall return to the distinction between an investment's technical life and its economic or business life, which we briefly mentioned in Chapter 10. Technical progress makes machinery obsolete or out of date. This means that a machine's business life is usually shorter than its technical life (that is, the number of years before the machine wears out). A sudden burst of technical progress may cause firms to replace capital goods early, long before the end of the equipment's technical life.

The multiplier

The national income or Keynesian multiplier

A **multiplier** exists whenever a change in one variable induces or causes multiple and successive stages of change in a second variable. Each succeeding stage of change is usually smaller than the previous one, so that the process effectively comes to an end when later stages of change approach zero. We can calculate the value of a multiplier by dividing the total change induced in the second variable by the size of the initial change in the first variable. For example, a multiplier of 8 tells us that an increase in the first variable will cause successive stages of change in the second variable which are eight times greater in total than the initial 'triggering' change.

In macroeconomic theory, the two main multipliers are the **national income multiplier** and the **money multiplier**, both of which are significant for economic policy. Chapter 17 provides a brief coverage of the money multiplier, which measures the relationship between a change in cash and reserve assets owned by the banking system and the resulting change in total bank deposits in the economy. The size of the money multiplier is significant for monetary policy. This chapter focuses on the national income multiplier, which measures the relationship between a change in aggregate demand in the economy and the resulting change in the equilibrium level of national income. The size of the national income multiplier is significant for fiscal policy.

*e**xaminer's voice***
AQA examination questions do not require the use of multiplier formulae or calculations. However, candidates must understand that an initial change in expenditure may lead to a larger impact on local or national income.

The national income multiplier first came into prominence as a key part of Keynesian economic theory. The multiplier concept was stated first in 1931 by R. F. Kahn, a colleague and former pupil of John Maynard Keynes at Cambridge. In its early days, the multiplier theory centred on an employment multiplier, which showed how a change in public sector investment (for example, in road building) might trigger subsequent multiple growth in employment. Keynes made use of Kahn's employment multiplier for the first time in 1933 when discussing the effects of an increase in government spending of £500, a sum which he assumed to be just sufficient to employ one man for one year in road construction. Keynes wrote:

> If the new expenditure is additional and not merely in substitution for other expenditure, the increase of employment does not stop there. The additional wages and other incomes paid out are spent on additional purchases, which in turn lead to further employment...the newly employed who supply the increased purchases of those employed on the new capital works will, in their turn, spend more, thus adding to the employment of others and so on.

By 1936, when Keynes's *General Theory* was published, the multiplier had become part of Keynes's explanation of how unemployment might be caused by deficient aggregate demand. In his *General Theory*, Keynes explained the investment multiplier, suggesting how a collapse in investment and business confidence might cause a multiple contraction in output, leading in turn to large-scale unemployment. Keynes then went on to argue that, with an active fiscal policy, the government spending multiplier might reverse this process.

A change in one of the components of aggregate demand can induce multiple stages of change in the level of money national income or output. The national

income multiplier is really a generic term, covering multiplier effects arising from a change in *any* of the components of aggregate demand. The national income multipliers include the autonomous consumption multiplier, the investment multiplier, the government spending multiplier and various tax and foreign trade multipliers. The **government spending multiplier** and the **investment multiplier** are the most frequently encountered national income multipliers.

The multiplier as a dynamic process

The multiplier process is essentially dynamic, taking place over time. The multiplier resembles ripples spreading over a pond after a stone has been thrown in the water. However, the ripples in a pond last only a few seconds, whereas the ripples spread-ing through the economy following a change in aggregate demand can last for months and even years. Figure 14.10 shows the ripple effect. The diagram, which illus-trates the government spending multiplier, can easily be adapted to illustrate the investment multiplier or indeed any other national income multiplier.

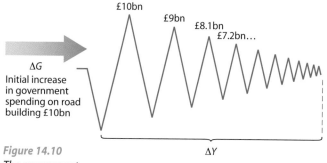

Figure 14.10
The government spending multiplier

In order to explain the govern-ment spending multiplier, we shall assume that there is demand-deficient unemploy-ment in the economy, and that the levels of taxation and imports do not change when aggregate demand increases. To reduce demand-deficient unemployment, the government decides to spend an extra £10 billion on road building.

■ In the first stage of the multiplier process, £10 billion is received as income by building workers, who, like everybody in the economy, spend 90p of every pound of income on consumption. (We are assuming that the marginal propensity to consume (*MPC*) is 0.9 throughout the economy.)

■ At the second stage of the multiplier process, £9 billion of the £10 billion income is spent on consumer goods and services, with the remaining £1 billion leaking into unspent savings.

■ At the third stage, the consumer goods sector employees spend £8.1 billion, or 0.9 of the £9 billion received at the second stage of income generation.

■ Further stages of income generation then occur, with each successive stage being 0.9 of the previous stage. Each stage is smaller than the preceding stage to the extent that part of income leaks into savings.

Assuming that nothing else changes in the time taken for the process to work through the economy, the eventual increase in income (ΔY) resulting from the initial injection of government spending is the sum of all the stages of income generation. ΔY is larger than ΔG, which triggered the initial growth in national income.

Providing consumption is the only income-related component of aggregate demand (with saving thus being the only income-induced leakage of demand from the circular flow of income), the value of the multiplier depends on the values of the marginal propensities to consume and save. In this example, the formula for the multiplier (k) is:

$$k = \frac{1}{1 - c}$$

where c is the marginal propensity to consume (*MPC*), or:

$$k = \frac{1}{s}$$

where s is the marginal propensity to save (*MPS*).

The formula reflects the fact that at each succeeding stage of the dynamic multiplier process, a fraction of income, determined by the *MPS*, leaks into saving and is not available for consumption at the next stage of income generation. The larger the *MPC* (and the smaller the *MPS*), the larger is the value of the multiplier.

In the example we have used, the size of the multiplier is:

$$k = \frac{1}{1 - 0.9} = 10$$

Using the equation:

$$\Delta Y = k\,(\Delta G)$$

where k is the symbol for the multiplier, we arrive at:

$$\Delta Y = 10 \times \text{£10bn}$$

which tells us that the increase in government spending causes equilibrium national income to increase by £100 bn.

The multiplier and Keynesian demand management

During the Keynesian era, governments in many industrialised mixed economies, including the UK, based macroeconomic policy on the **management of aggregate demand**. This became known as **discretionary fiscal policy**.

To achieve full employment, governments deliberately ran **budget deficits** (setting $G > T$). This expanded aggregate demand, but sometimes too much demand 'overheated' the economy. Excess demand raised the price level through **demand-pull inflation**, or pulled imports into the country and caused a balance of payments crisis. In these circumstances, governments were forced to reverse the thrust of fiscal policy, cutting public spending or raising taxes to reduce the level of demand in the economy.

The Keynesians used fiscal policy in a discrete way, supplemented at times by monetary policy, to **fine-tune** the level of aggregate demand. The aim was to

stabilise the fluctuations in the business cycle, and to try to achieve the macro-economic objectives of full employment and economic growth, without excessive inflation or an unsustainable deterioration in the balance of payments.

When using discretionary fiscal policy in this way, the size of the government spending multiplier is significant. The larger the government spending multiplier, the smaller the increase in public spending needed to bring about a required increase in national income. Similarly, the greater the size of the tax multiplier, the smaller is the required tax cut. It follows that if the government spending and tax multi-pliers are large, and if the multiplier affects real output more than the price level, fiscal policy used as a demand management instrument can be an effective way of con-trolling the economy.

e*xaminer's voice*

See Chapter 18 for further explanation of Keynesian fiscal policy and demand management.

The multiplier in the UK economy

In reality, particularly in the case of the UK economy, neither assumption may hold. Free-market economists believe that an increase in government spending stimulates *prices* rather than *real output*, and that government spending **crowds out** private sector investment. (Crowding out is explained in Chapter 18.) But even without accepting the free-market argument, the size of the multiplier is likely to be small. The UK economy is an economy open to imports, with a relatively high income tax rate when national insurance contributions are included.

The earlier formula for the multiplier treated saving as the only income-induced leakage or withdrawal from the circular flow of income. But this is unrealistic. Taxation and imports also change as income changes. A more realistic formula for the multiplier is:

$$\frac{1}{s + t + m}$$

where t is the marginal tax rate and m is the marginal propensity to import.

The marginal tax rate (t) and the marginal propensity to import (m) respectively measure what proportion of a change in income is paid in tax and the proportion that people wish to spend on imports. Once the marginal propensity to import and the marginal tax rate are included in the multiplier formula, the size of the multiplier falls significantly. In the United Kingdom, the marginal tax rate is around 0.4 and the economy is open to trade. This means that the marginal propensity to import is also quite high. Given a marginal propensity to save (s) of 0.15, and setting the marginal tax rate (t) at 0.4 and the marginal propensity to import (m) at 0.35, the value of the multiplier becomes:

$$\frac{1}{0.9}$$

or 1.1. The value of the government spending multiplier in the UK economy is therefore quite small. This means that we must modify the conclusion reached in the preceding section about the effectiveness of fiscal policy for managing demand. This is because a significant fraction of the income received from an increase in government spending leaks into taxation and imports, as well as into savings. The main effect of an expansionary fiscal policy may be to pull imports into the economy – even when there is substantial unemployment – with relatively little increase in domestic output and employment.

The accelerator

The accelerator principle stems from a rather simple and mechanical assumption that firms wish to keep a relatively fixed ratio, known as the **capital–output ratio**, between the output they are currently producing and their existing stock of fixed capital assets. If output grows by a constant amount each year, firms invest in exactly the same amount of new capital each year to enlarge their capital stock and maintain the desired capital–output ratio. From year to year, the level of investment is therefore constant. But when the rate of growth of output speeds up or *accelerates*, investment also increases as firms take action to enlarge the stock of capital to a level sufficient to maintain the desired capital–output ratio. Conversely, when the rate of growth of output slows down or *decelerates*, investment declines.

To illustrate the accelerator principle, we shall assume the economy's capital–output ratio is 4:1, or simply 4. This means that 4 units of capital are required to produce 1 unit of output. We also assume that the level of *current* net investment in fixed capital depends on the change in income or output in the *previous* year:

$$I = v(\Delta Y)$$

or:

$$I_t = v(Y_t - Y_{t-1})$$

where I_t is net investment this year, Y_t is current national income, Y_{t-1} is national income last year and v is the capital–output ratio. The capital–output ratio (v) is also known as the **accelerator coefficient**, or simply as the **accelerator**. To illustrate the accelerator principle, we shall assume no replacement investment is needed, and that the average capital–output ratio in the economy stays at 4. Given these assumptions, consider the numerical example of the accelerator principle shown in Table 14.1.

Table 14.1

Year	Net investment		Current income		Last year's income
t = 2005	£40bn	=	4 × (£100bn	–	£90bn)
t = 2006	£40bn	=	4 × (£110bn	–	£100bn)
t = 2007	£80bn	=	4 × (£130bn	–	£110bn)
t = 2008	£40bn	=	4 × (£140bn	–	£130bn)

In each of the years from 2004 to 2008 national income grows. Between 2004 and 2005, income grows by £10 billion (row 1). Via the capital–output ratio, the £10 billion income growth induces net investment of £40 billion in 2005. The size of the capital stock increases by £40 billion, which enables the desired capital–output ratio to be maintained at the now higher level of income.

In row 2, income continues to grow by £10 billion, so investment in 2006 remains at £40 billion.

However, the next year is different. In 2007, shown in row 3, the growth of income speeds up or accelerates, doubling from £10 billion to £20 billion. Investment also doubles from £40 billion to £80 billion to maintain the value of the capital–output ratio. Thus, a £10 billion increase in income induces a £40 billion increase in investment.

But in row 4, the growth of income falls back to £10 billion in 2008. Although income is still growing, net investment also falls back to £40 billion.

This example shows how the accelerator derives its name. The figures show the rate of growth of income and output determining whether investment grows, falls or remains at a constant level. In summary:

- if income grows by the *same amount* each year, net investment is *constant*
- if income growth speeds up or *accelerates*, net investment *increases*
- if income growth slows down or *decelerates*, net investment *declines*

Thus, as firms adjust the stock of capital to the desired level, relatively slight changes in the rate of growth of income or output cause quite large absolute rises and falls in investment. The acceleration principle therefore provides a second explanation (the *MEC* theory provides the first explanation) of why investment in capital goods is a more volatile or unstable component of aggregate demand than consumption.

Limitations of the accelerator principle

The accelerator is subject to the following limitations:

- **The accelerator theory is too mechanical.** It assumes that all firms react to increased demand for their output in the same way. Some firms may wait to see if the higher level of demand is maintained, while others may order more plant and machinery than is immediately required.
- **The acceleration principle assumes that there is no spare capacity or unused capital.** If, when demand for output increases, firms possess excess capacity left over from a previous boom in demand, they can increase output by using spare capacity, without needing to invest in additional fixed capital.
- **Demand may increase at a time when the capital goods industries are themselves at full capacity and unable to meet a higher level of investment demand.** In this situation, the price of capital goods rises. This creates incentives for firms to economise in the use of capital and to switch to more labour-intensive methods of production. The value of the capital–output ratio falls, and firms increase output to meet the new levels of demand without having to invest in more capital.

The multiplier/accelerator theory of business cycles

Chapter 13 surveyed a number of possible theories which explain the fluctuations in economic activity known as the business cycle. One theory briefly mentioned was the multiplier/accelerator theory. We shall now explain this theory in a little more depth.

Writing the investment multiplier relationship as:

$$\Delta Y = k\,(\Delta I)$$

and the accelerator relationship as:

$$I = v\,(\Delta Y)$$

where *k* is the investment multiplier and *v* is the accelerator, we can bring the two together in a multiplier/accelerator model of dynamic change in the economy. In essence:

initial increase in investment $\;\rightarrow\; \underset{k}{\Delta I} \;\rightarrow\; \underset{v}{\Delta Y} \;\rightarrow\; \underset{k}{\Delta I} \;\rightarrow\; \underset{v}{\Delta Y} \;\rightarrow\; \Delta I \;\rightarrow\;$ and so on...

multiplier   accelerator   multiplier   accelerator

An initial multiplier effect, triggered by an increase in investment, causes income to rise, which then in turn induces, via the accelerator, a 'feedback' to investment, leading to a further multiplier effect, and so on.

Summary

The chapter began by explaining the relationship between aggregate demand and the circular flow of income. After comparing free-market and Keynesian theories of the adjustment process occurring when households' saving plans exceed firms' investment plans, various theories that explain the determination of the aggregate levels of consumption and investment in the economy were examined.

When explaining consumption, the principal distinction to be made is between the free-market view that saving and hence consumption decisions are determined primarily by the rate of interest, and the Keynesian view that the level of income is the dominant influence. The former theory supports the view that the market mechanism, working through the rate of interest, automatically rids the economy of any deficient demand that has temporarily come into existence. Conversely, the Keynesian consumption function is an extremely important element in the wider Keynesian argument that deficient demand can

be permanent, and that the economy, left to itself, may settle into an under-fully employed equilibrium. We briefly surveyed other influences upon consumption, namely expected *future* income, wealth, consumer confidence, expected inflation and the availability of credit.

When deciding to invest in new fixed capital, a firm considers the future productivity or yield of the investment over the life of the capital asset, rather than just the current productivity. In the marginal efficiency of capital (MEC) theory, the expected return on investment — itself heavily dependent on the state of business confidence — and the rate of interest are the main determinants of investment. The acceleration principle, which stems from the assumption that firms wish to maintain a fixed capital–output ratio, provides another explanation of investment. The MEC theory and the accelerator both suggest that firms' demand for new capital goods is more volatile or unstable than the demand for consumer goods and output in general.

There are, of course, other factors influencing investment, such as the role of the relative prices of capital and labour, the nature of technical progress, the influence of government and the adequacy or otherwise of a country's financial institutions in the supply of investment funds.

A change in the level of investment triggers a multiplier process. The investment multiplier is one of the national income multipliers, another being the government spending multiplier. National income multipliers measure the relationship between a change in aggregate demand in the economy and the resulting change in the equilibrium level of national income.

The larger the size of the multiplier in terms of real output, the more powerful and effective is fiscal policy as a method of controlling the economy through the management of aggregate demand. The size of the multiplier depends not only on whether real output is stimulated rather than prices, but also on leakages of demand at each stage of the multiplier process. In the UK, which is open to trade and in which effective tax rates are quite high, the multiplier is small, probably not significantly greater than 1. The multiplier and the accelerator can together provide an explanation of the business cycle additional to the other explanations covered in Chapter 13.

Self-testing questions

1 What is aggregate demand?
2 What is the circular flow of income?
3 Distinguish between consumption, saving and investment.
4 How does saving affect the circular flow of income?
5 Distinguish between the average and marginal propensities to consume and save.
6 What is the personal saving ratio?
7 How may the rate of interest affect consumption and saving?
8 Distinguish between autonomous consumption and income-induced consumption.
9 Briefly describe the life-cycle theory of consumption.
10 List other influences upon consumption.
11 What is the relationship between capital and investment?
12 What is the marginal efficiency of capital (MEC)?
13 How is the level of investment determined in the MEC theory?
14 Define a multiplier.
15 Explain the stages of the multiplier process.
16 Why has the multiplier concept been important for Keynesian economic policy?
17 Why is the value of the multiplier small in the UK economy?
18 How may the multiplier interact with the accelerator?

Chapter 15

The aggregate demand and aggregate supply macroeconomic model

Specification focus

This chapter provides detailed coverage of the aggregate demand/aggregate supply (*AD/AS*) macroeconomic model. The *AD/AS* model provides the theoretical framework candidates are expected to use at both AS in the Unit 2 examination and A2 in the Unit 6 examination.

AS **Module 2 The National Economy**

How the Macroeconomy Works; The Main Instruments of Government Macroeconomic Policy

AS **Module 6 Government Policy, the National and International Economy**

Inflation and Unemployment; Managing the National Economy

A2 **Synoptic coverage**

The Unit 6 examination at A2 expects candidates to develop and apply the knowledge and understanding of the *AD/AS* macroeconomic model first learnt at AS. At both levels, written examination questions seldom explicitly mention the *AD/AS* model, but the model should be used to answer questions on economic problems such as unemployment and inflation, and on how economic policy may be used to reduce or solve such problems. Basic knowledge and understanding of the derivation of the *AD* and *AS* curves is useful at A2, but not required at AS.

Introduction

Chapter 14 introduced the concept of aggregate demand. This chapter introduces aggregate supply and then examines the interaction of aggregate demand and supply in the AD/AS macroeconomic model of the economy. In recent years, the AD/AS model has become the preferred theoretical framework that economists use to investigate macroeconomic issues, problems and policies. The model is particularly useful for analysing the effect of an increase in aggregate demand upon the economy. This addresses a key issue: will expansionary fiscal policy and/or monetary policy increase real output and jobs (i.e. will it be reflationary), or will the price level increase instead (i.e. will it be inflationary)? As this chapter explains, the answer to this key macroeconomic question depends on the position and shape of the aggregate supply (AS) curve, both in the short and long run.

This chapter explains in some detail the economic theory lying behind the *AD* and *AS* curves in the aggregate demand/aggregate supply macroeconomic model. However, *applying* the model to analyse and evaluate economic problems, issues and policies provides the main way in which A-level students should use the model. Detailed understanding of the model is certainly useful at A2, but it is not essential. It definitely is not needed at AS.

The *AD/AS* model: two cautionary notes

Before explaining the *AD/AS* macroeconomic model, it is useful to introduce two aspects of the model that can trouble students.

- Different textbooks and different teachers explain the *AD/AS* model in different ways. This is particularly the case with the shape and slope of the *AS* curve, both in the short and long run. As a result, the explanations provided in this chapter may differ somewhat from those encountered elsewhere. This leads to the second problem.

- As you read the following sections of the chapter, you will see that the explanations of the shapes and slopes of *AD* and *AS* curves are based on quite difficult economic theory. However, examination questions usually require explanation of the *effect* of a shift of the *AD* curve upon the economy. Questions seldom require detailed theoretical explanation (which this chapter provides) of *causes* of the shape and slope of the two curves. For the most part, such knowledge is useful background information, but not essential knowledge. Detailed explanation of shape and slope is seldom required at A2, and is not required at all at AS.

Macroeconomic equilibrium

Before explaining the shapes and slopes of *AD* and *AS* curves, it is first useful to understand the concept of **macroeconomic equilibrium**. Macroeconomic equilibrium occurs in an economy's aggregate goods market when the aggregate demand for real output equals the aggregate supply of real output: that is, where

$$AD = AS$$

In Figure 15.1 macroeconomic equilibrium initially occurs at point X, where the curve AD_1 intersects the *AS* curve. The equilibrium level of real output is y_1, and the equilibrium price level is P_1. When the aggregate demand curve shifts to AD_2, a new macroeconomic equilibrium is established at point Z. The new equilibrium level of real output is y_2, and the price level has risen to P_2. In a similar way, a leftward shift of aggregate demand and rightward and leftward shifts of the *AS* curve would also disturb the initial equilibrium and bring about a new macroeconomic equilibrium.

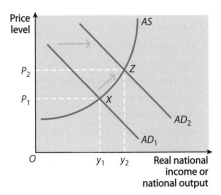

Figure 15.1 *Macroeconomic equilibrium*

The aggregate demand curve

The aggregate demand or *AD* curve illustrated in Figure 15.1 shows the total quantities of *real* output that all economic agents within the economy (households, firms, the government and the overseas sector) plan to purchase at different price levels, when all the factors influencing aggregate demand *other* than the price level are held constant.

If any of the determinants of aggregate demand (apart from the price level) change, the *AD* curve shifts rightward or leftward, depending on whether there has been an increase or a decrease in aggregate demand. For example, an increase in consumer or business confidence shifts the *AD* curve rightward, via its effect on consumption or investment. Expansionary monetary policy and expansionary fiscal policy also shift the *AD* curve rightward. By contrast, contractionary monetary or fiscal policy, or a collapse in consumer or business confidence, shifts the *AD* curve leftward.

> ***e**xaminer's voice*
>
> Make sure you understand the difference between a movement *along* an *AD* or *AS* curve and the factors causing a *shift* of one of the curves.

Explaining the shape and slope of the *AD* curve

You must not confuse the *position* of the *AD* curve with the *shape* and *slope* of the curve. The curve slopes downward to the right, showing that as the price level falls, aggregate demand expands. Three factors explain this.

- **The wealth effect or real balance effect.** Assuming a given *nominal* stock of money (or money supply) in the economy, a decrease in the price level increases people's *real* money balances: in other words, the same amount of money buys more goods and services. Because money is a part of people's wealth, an increase in real money balances makes people feel wealthier. As Chapter 14 explained, when wealth increases, consumption also increases, which in turn means that the demand for real output increases following a fall in the price level.

An increase in the supply of real money reduces interest rates

- **Changes in real interest rates.** The increase in *real* money balances just described means that the *real money supply* has increased, relative to people's desire to hold real money balances. Basic supply and demand analysis tells us that when the supply of *any* commodity increases relative to the demand for the commodity, its price tends to fall. Now, the rate of interest is the price of money. The increase in the supply of real money balances relative to demand reduces real interest rates, which in turn leads to higher levels of consumption and investment.

- **The effect on the demand for exports and imports.** When the domestic price level falls (and assuming the exchange rate remains unchanged), demand increases for the country's exports. Within the country, demand also increases for domestically produced goods, which are now cheaper compared to imports.

Aggregate supply

Just as the *AD* curve shows the total quantities of real output that economic agents plan to purchase at different domestic price levels, the *AS* curve shows the quantities of real output that businesses plan to produce and sell at these different price levels.

There are in fact two very different aggregate supply curves: the *short-run* aggregate supply (*SRAS*) curve and the *long-run* aggregate supply (*LRAS*) curve. (The *SRAS* curve usually slopes upwards, whereas the *LRAS* curve is a vertical line. This means that the curve labelled *AS* in Figure 15.1 should be interpreted as a short-run curve.) Before we explain the shape of the vertical *LRAS* curve, we shall first examine a number of possible *SRAS* curves.

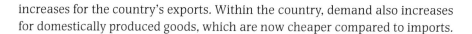

examiner's voice

Short-run *AS* curves generally slope upwards, but the long-run *AS* curve is generally assumed to be vertical. Note also that *SRAS* curves show the levels of real output that firms *plan* to produce and sell at different price levels, whereas the *LRAS* curve shows the economy's capacity constraint at a particular point in time.

Explaining the shape and slope of the short-run *AS* curve

Whereas the *AD* curve is almost always downward sloping, different assumptions about the nature of aggregate supply lead to different shapes and slopes of the *SRAS* curve. It is important to understand how these different *SRAS* curves carry different implications for macroeconomic policy.

The Keynesian inverted L-shaped SRAS curve

We start by introducing the inverted L-shaped *SRAS* curve, based on the Keynesian theory of how the economy works, which was prevalent through much of the Keynesian era in the 1950s, 1960s and early 1970s. The shape of the inverted L-shaped *SRAS* curve illustrated in Figure 15.2 depends on assumptions about the economy's spare capacity. The *SRAS* curve is horizontal as long as the economy produces inside its production possibility frontier, in which case there is spare capacity and unemployed labour. But as soon as full employment is reached at output y_{FE}, the slope of the *SRAS* curve becomes vertical.

Taking the explanation a stage further, the horizontal section of this *SRAS* curve results from two simplifying assumptions made by the Keynesians about the nature of aggregate supply. First, when there was spare capacity, Keynesians assumed that workers are willing to supply more labour without the money wage rate having to rise. Second, the Keynesians assumed that the marginal product of labour is constant. This means that when a firm takes

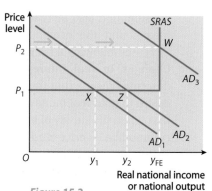

Figure 15.2

The Keynesian inverted L-shaped SRAS *curve*

on an extra worker, the extra output produced by the worker is the same as that produced by all the workers already hired.

Taken together, these two assumptions mean that marginal cost of production remains constant as output increases — until full employment is reached. Given these assumptions, firms are prepared to respond to increased demand by increasing output, without requiring an increase in the price level to induce the supply of more output.

Now let's examine how the shape of the Keynesian *SRAS* curve affects economic policy. In Figure 15.2, with the aggregate demand curve in position AD_1, macroeconomic equilibrium is initially at point X. The price level is P_1 and real national output is y_1, which is below the full capacity or full employment level of real income y_{FE}. Suppose the government is unhappy with this situation and decides to use fiscal policy or monetary policy to increase aggregate demand. Figure 15.2 tells us that as long as the increase in aggregate demand is restricted to the horizontal section of the *SRAS* curve — for example, from AD_1 to AD_2 with a new macroeconomic equilibrium at point Z — the effect is solely *reflationary* and not *inflationary*. Real output and hence employment both increase, but there is no reason for the price level to rise.

However, once full employment is reached at the level of real income y_{FE}, any further increase in aggregate demand (for example, to AD_3) causes prices, but *not* output, to rise. In the new macroeconomic equilibrium (at point W), real output is constrained at y_{FE}, but excess demand pulls up the price level to P_2. **Demand-pull inflation** occurs. There is no spare capacity, so output cannot increase in the short run to meet the increase in demand.

The upward-sloping SRAS curve

Most economists (including present-day Keynesians) now agree that the two assumptions underlying the inverted L-shaped *SRAS* curve are unrealistic. In particular, the second assumption requires that the law of diminishing returns does not operate. Economists now believe that the *SRAS* curve slopes upward, as depicted in Figure 15.3.

The shape of the upward-sloping *SRAS* curve is explained by two assumptions of the microeconomic theory of the firm described in Chapters 4 and 5:

■ all firms aim to maximise profit
■ the law of diminishing returns (or diminishing marginal productivity)

examiner's voice

Some textbooks argue that Keynesians believe that the long-run aggregate supply curve has an inverted L-shape. However, in this book, the inverted L-shaped curve is treated as a short-run aggregate supply curve. The AQA specification states that the *LRAS* curve should be assumed to be vertical. Make sure you also remember that when the *AD* curve shifts rightward or leftward, in the short run, the effect on the supply of real output and prices depends on the shape and slope of the *SRAS* curve.

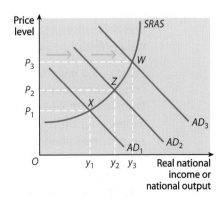

Figure 15.3 An upward-sloping SRAS curve

Following an expansion of aggregate demand from AD_1 to AD_2 in Figure 15.3, which disturbs an initial macroeconomic equilibrium at point X, the price level rises to P_2. At the new price, profit-maximising firms are happy to supply more output. If the prices that firms could charge were not to rise, it would be unprofitable to increase supply. The explanation for this is as follows. First, we assume that firms are already producing the profit-maximising level of output, which occurs when $MR = MC$. If firms increase output beyond this point, marginal costs rise, which leads to falling profit. This is because the marginal product of the workers needed to produce the extra output falls, which increases marginal costs. For profit-maximising firms to produce more output in the face of rising marginal costs, marginal revenues must also rise. This requires higher prices. Without a higher price level, profit-maximising firms will not voluntarily increase the supply of output.

There is a second way of explaining the upward-sloping *SRAS* curve. The *real* wage rate paid by firms must fall (to match the declining marginal product of labour) to make it profitable to employ the workers needed to increase the supply of output. Given a constant money wage rate (which is assumed for all *SRAS* curves), a rise in the price level (for example, to P_2) reduces the real wage rate, thereby making it attractive to employ more labour and supply more output. Hence the *SRAS* curve is upward sloping, showing that a rise in the price level is necessary to persuade firms to supply more output.

It is important to emphasise that because, as we have just noted, each *SRAS* curve is drawn under the assumption that the money wage rate remains unchanged, there will be a *different SRAS* curve for *each* money wage rate. When the money wage rate rises, production costs increase and firms reduce the quantity of output they are willing to supply at the current price level. As a result, the *SRAS* curve shifts leftward to a new position. Conversely, a fall in the money wage rate reduces money costs of production and shifts the *AS* curve rightward.

Other factors beside the money wage rate and other costs of production, which fix the *position* of the *SRAS* curve, include business taxation, technology, productivity, attitudes, enterprise, factor mobility, economic incentives facing workers and firms, and the institutional structure of the economy. As with the *AD* curve, if any of the factors fixing the curve's position change, the *SRAS* curve shifts to a new position.

Figure 15.3 tells us that, with an upward-sloping *SRAS* curve, expansionary fiscal policy simultaneously *reflates* real output and creates jobs, and *inflates* the price level. The extent to which demand expansion is reflationary or inflationary depends on the steepness of the *SRAS* curve to the right of the initial macroeconomic equilibrium.

Initially, macroeconomic equilibrium in Figure 15.3 occurs at point X, with the aggregate demand curve in position AD_1. In this situation, which depicts a *recessionary* economy suffering significant demand deficiency, an increase in aggregate demand is largely reflationary rather than inflationary, at least to start with. When aggregate demand increases to AD_2, real output and the price level both increase, respectively to y_2 and P_2, to bring about a new macroeconomic equilibrium at point Z. However, any further increase in aggregate demand — for example, to AD_3 — increases the inflationary impact of the demand expansion at the expense of the effect on output and jobs. The reflationary effect becomes smaller and the inflationary effect greater as the AS curve becomes steeper.

The three-section SRAC curve

Figure 15.4 shows another possible *SRAS* curve. This is a variant of the *SRAS* curve shown in Figure 15.3, but in this version the curve also includes horizontal and vertical sections. Drawn in this way, the *SRAS* curve gives extra emphasis to the points made in the previous paragraph. At an initially low and recessionary level of real national income such as y_1, an increase in aggregate demand from AD_1 to AD_2 increases real output but has no effect on the price level, which remains at P_1. Conversely, in an already fully employed economy, an increase in aggregate demand from AD_5 to AD_6 has the opposite effect. The economy possesses no spare capacity, so prices, but *not* output, rise when demand is increased.

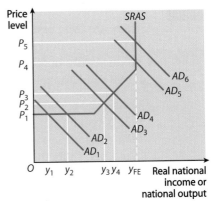

Figure 15.4 A three-section SRAS curve

These two situations are the same as those illustrated by the inverted L-shaped *AS* curve drawn in Figure 15.2. However, Figure 15.4 differs from Figure 15.2 because an upward-sloping section lies between the horizontal and vertical parts of the *SRAS* curve. When, for example, aggregate demand increases from AD_3 to AD_4 along the upward-sloping section of the *SRAS* curve, the effect is both reflationary and inflationary, with reflation giving way to inflation when full employment is reached at y_{FE}.

The vertical LRAS curve

As we have explained, the *SRAS* curve shows the supply of real output in a time period when costs of production such as money wage rates remain unchanged. We now extend the analysis to explain the economy's *LRAS* curve. The *LRAS* curve is vertical because it shows the *potential* level of real output that the economy is capable of producing. Potential output is not affected by the price level. Hence the *LRAS* curve is vertical.

The fact that the *LRAS* curve is vertical means that, in the long run, a rightward shift of aggregate demand increases the price level, but not real output. We shall use Figure 15.5 to explain this.

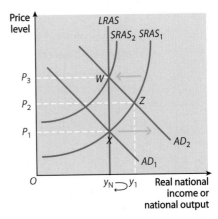

Figure 15.5 The LRAS curve and the economy's natural level of real output

In Figure 15.5 we assume that the economy starts off in macroeconomic equilibrium at point X, where AD_1 equals *short-run* aggregate supply (depicted by the curve $SRAS_1$). Suppose that the government decides to increase aggregate demand (to AD_2) in order to increase output and employment. As already explained, for aggregate supply to increase *in the short run*, following an increase in aggregate demand, the price level must rise to make the extra output profitable. But when prices rise, real wage rates fall, unless of course money wages also rise. What happens next depends upon how workers respond to this cut in real wage rates.

There are two possibilities. First, if money wage rates remain unchanged, the fall in real wage rates results in workers refusing to supply the extra labour needed to produce extra output. This in turn results in income or output falling back to the initial equilibrium level prevailing before the rightward shift of the AD curve.

The second possibility is that workers respond to the higher price level by success-fully bargaining for higher money wage rates in order to restore real wage rates to their previous levels. This increases firms' money costs of production, which, as explained, shifts the short-run AS curve leftward from $SRAS_1$ to $SRAS_2$. The net effect is that the new AD and $SRAS$ curves (AD_2 and $SRAS_2$) once again intersect at the original equilibrium level of output y_N, but at a higher equilibrium price level, P_3. The new macroeconomic equilibrium is at point W rather than at point X.

The economy's natural level of output

For free-market, monetarist and supply-side economists, y_N is the economy's natural level of output, towards which market forces and a flexible price mechanism eventually adjust. The natural level of *output* is the long-run equilibrium level of *potential* output associated with the natural levels of *employment* and *unemployment* in the economy's labour market. (We explain the natural levels of employment and unemployment in Chapter 16.)

> *e***xaminer's voice**
>
> The economy's natural level of *output*, explained in this chapter, is closely related to the natural levels (and rates) of *employment* and *unemployment*, which are explained in Chapter 16. At A2, you must understand all three concepts and the links between them. This knowledge is not required at AS.

In the free-market view, the vertical line drawn in Figure 15.5 between the intersections of each pair of AD and $SRAS$ curves at the natural level of output is the economy's long-run aggregate supply curve. The $LRAS$ curve shows the *potential* output the economy can produce, or the output at full capacity and full employment. The next section explains what happens when output *temporarily* rises above its natural level.

Milton Friedman and money illusion

Economists who believe in the virtues of free markets divide into a number of camps. Among these are the Friedmanite school (named after the monetarist economist Milton Friedman) and the new classical school. Chapter 16 explains the different views of both schools regarding the role of **expectations** in causing inflation. This chapter considers their views on **money illusion**.

Money illusion occurs when people confuse the *money* values (or *nominal* values) of variables with their *real* values. Suppose, for example, the nominal or money interest rate is 10% at a time when the rate of inflation is 6%. In this situation, the real rate of interest (which is the nominal rate minus the rate of inflation) is only 4%. Any saver or lender who ignores this truth and wrongly believes the real rate of interest to be 10% suffers money illusion. Likewise, when the rate of inflation is above zero, a worker who wrongly believes a 10% money wage rate increase to be a 10% real wage increase suffers money illusion.

Milton Friedman has argued that economic agents suffer money illusion, but only in the short run. An increase in aggregate demand *temporarily* increases output above its natural level to y_1 in Figure 15.5, provided workers suffer money illusion and remain happy with existing money wage rates. But as soon as workers realise that higher prices mean lower *real* wage rates, money illusion disappears. When this happens, as we saw earlier, one of two processes may operate. On the one hand, with unchanged money wage rates, workers refuse to supply the labour required for output to remain above y_N. Alternatively, money wage rates rise and the short-run aggregate supply curve shifts leftward to $SRAS_2$. The price level then rises to P_3. Either way, output falls back to its natural level y_N. In Friedman's theory, an increase in aggregate demand causes real output to rise temporarily *above* its natural level in the short run, but *not* in the long run.

New classical theory

In contrast to Milton Friedman, new classical economists reject the concept of money illusion. Acting rationally, workers immediately realise that real wage rates fall whenever prices rise more than money wages. In the new classical view, the *SRAS* curve and the *LRAS* curve might *both* be vertical, meaning that it is impossible to increase real output above its natural level by increasing aggregate demand.

In fact, many new classical economists accept that the short-run aggregate supply curve slopes upward, but for a reason rather different from Milton Friedman's explanation, which depends on workers suffering money illusion. New classical economists assume that market prices are highly flexible, instantly adjusting to balance supply and demand. As noted, if markets continuously clear and are always effectively in equilibrium, it should not be possible to distinguish between short-run and long-run aggregate supply. Both short-run and long-run conditions should be represented by the same vertical curve. Nevertheless, following Professor Robert Lucas, new classical economists do distinguish between an upward-sloping *SRAS* curve and the vertical *LRAS* curve.

Professor Lucas, who is perhaps the most eminent new classical economist, explains the new classical *SRAS* curve in the following way. Although markets and prices are highly flexible, individual firms have imperfect information about the general price level. When the price of its own product rises, a firm does not know

whether this is a *relative* price rise of its product alone, or whether the higher price is a part of a *general* price rise of all goods and services. Only a *relative* price rise justifies an expansion of output.

Suppose the general price level rises unexpectedly. New classical economists call this a **price surprise**. Initially, a producer believes this to be a rise solely in its own product's relative price. In the short run, therefore, each firm increases production and the aggregate supply of output increases. But when firms realise that general prices, rather than their own relative prices, have risen, the short-run *AS* curve shifts leftward and aggregate output falls back to its natural level.

Keynesian *LRAS* curves

As we have explained, free-market economists of both Friedmanite and new classical schools disagree about how money illusion affects the *SRAS* curve, but they agree that the *LRAS* curve is vertical (as indeed it must be because the *LRAS* curve is located at the *potential* level of output that the economy is capable of producing, irrespective of the price level). However, modern Keynesians (known as *New Keynesians* or *neo-Keynesians*) explain the relationship between the *SRAS* and the *LRAS* curves in a way that differs from the explanations put forward by the free-market schools.

To understand the New Keynesian vertical *LRAS* curve, we must first understand the New Keynesian theory of wage determination. New Keynesian economists stress that wage rates are usually negotiated and set for a **contract period**, customarily for the year ahead. This is so, whether wages are set through collective bargaining or through individual negotiation. As a result of the system of wage setting, wage rates adjust only sluggishly to new conditions. They are characterised by what Keynesians call **wage stickiness**. When the price level rises, money wages lag behind, not catching up until the current contract period runs out.

During this period, real wages fall and the aggregate supply of output increases. However, **contract renewal** gives workers the opportunity to negotiate an increase in the money wage sufficient to restore the real wage to its previous level. This raises production costs and reduces profits, causing firms to reduce the output they are prepared to supply: in other words, the short-run *AS* curve shifts leftward. In summary, in New Keynesian analysis, *SRAS* curves relate to the period during which wages are in effect pre-set, while the *LRAS* curve relates to the longer period in which all wage contracts are revised to take account of price changes. When prices rise while money wages are fixed, employment and output rise.

*e*xaminer's voice

At AS, the Module 2 specification requires candidates to know that the *LRAS* curve is vertical, but it does not require an explanation of why this is so. By contrast, knowledge of why the *LRAS* curve is vertical is useful, though a full explanation is not needed at A2. At both levels, candidates should understand that the *LRAS* curve shows the economy's potential output.

Over the longer period, money wages adjust to higher prices and the *LRAS* curve is vertical.

The vertical long-run aggregate supply curve and economic policy

Whichever theoretical explanation of the vertical *LRAS* curve you prefer, the curve is located at the natural or equilibrium level of real output, which is the level of output consistent with the natural rate of unemployment in the labour market. (Chapter 16 qualifies this statement by distinguishing between the **natural rate of unemployment** (NRU) favoured by free-market economists and the **non-accelerating inflation rate of unemployment** (NAIRU), which is a New Keynesian concept.) Providing output and employment are initially at their natural or equilibrium levels, any expansion of aggregate demand — for example, from AD_1 to AD_2 in Figure 15.5 — causes the price level to rise, with no long-term increase in the levels of real output and employment.

In this situation, free-market and supply-side economists conclude that it is irresponsible for governments to use expansionary fiscal or monetary policies to try to increase national output and employment above their natural rates and levels. While such policies *may* succeed in the short run, although at the expense of inflation, they are doomed eventually to fail. In the long run, output and employment fall back to their equilibrium or natural rates and levels, which are determined by the economy's production potential or ability to supply.

Instead of increasing aggregate demand to reduce unemployment *below* its natural rate, free-market economists believe that governments should use micro-economic supply-side policies to *reduce the natural rate itself.* Market-orientated supply-side policies (which are explained in Chapter 19) are meant to improve incentives and the performance of individual economic agents and markets. Successful supply-side policies improve the economy's production potential by shifting the *LRAS* curve rightward and increasing the natural rates and levels of output and employment.

In the extreme new classical supply-side or free-market view, there is little or no case for demand management, and macroeconomic policy in general should be subordinated to the needs of a supply-side microeconomic policy. However, some free-market economists (those who are *not* new classical economists) do accept that government policy can sometimes be used to increase aggregate demand. In the more moderate free-market view, aggregate demand can be increased — by interest rate cuts (monetary policy) rather than by fiscal policy — if the economy is initially in recession. In a recession, output and employment are below their natural rates and levels, and unemployment is above its natural rate or level. In this situation, there is a case for increasing aggregate demand so as to close the economy's **output gap**, and to provide the required demand to absorb the economy's ability to produce and supply extra output.

The *AD/AS* model and economic policy: some fundamentals

examiner's voice

If you have found much of this chapter difficult, focus on this last section. This summarises the really essential features of the *AD/AS* macroeconomic model that you need to know. Also read the chapter's summary.

Because much of the theory covered in the preceding sections is quite complicated, the chapter shall conclude by returning to some basic coverage of how the *AD/AS* model can be used to illustrate economic problems and policy.

Figure 15.6(a) illustrates **demand-pull inflation**. (The theories of inflation are explained in more detail in Chapter 16.) An increase in aggregate demand from AD_1 to AD_2 *reflates* real output from y_1 to y_{FE}, but also *inflates* the price level, which rises from P_1 to P_2. The diagram suggests that, to reduce demand-pull inflation, the government (or its central bank) must contract or *deflate* aggregate demand.

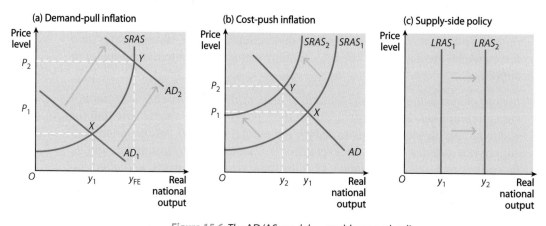

Figure 15.6 The AD/AS model — problems and policy

Figure 15.6(a) can also be used to illustrate **recession** in the economy. Macroeconomic equilibrium in the economy is initially at point *X*. The recessionary level of real output y_1 is below the full employment level of output y_{FE}.

By contrast, Figure 15.6(b) illustrates the other main theory of inflation: **cost-push inflation**. Rising costs of production shift the *SRAS* curve leftward from $SRAS_1$ to $SRAS_2$. The price level rises from P_1 to P_2, but in the new macroeconomic equilibrium at point *Y*, real income has now fallen from y_1 to y_2.

Figure 15.6(c) illustrates the impact of supply-side policies on the economy. Successful supply-side policies shift the vertical *LRAS* curve rightward, thereby increasing the *potential* output that the economy can produce.

Summary

The aggregate demand and aggregate supply (*AD/AS*) macroeconomic model provides the framework in which economists analyse the effects of changes taking place in the economy and the effects of government economic policy. Aggregate demand is the *planned* total spending on real national output exercised by households, firms, the government and overseas sectors. Likewise, short-run aggregate supply is the *planned* level of real output that economic agents in the economy, including the government, wish to produce. Long-run aggregate supply is the *potential* output that the economy is capable of producing. Since this does not depend on the price level, the *LRAS* curve is vertical with respect to the price level.

Aggregate demand and aggregate supply curves model planned spending and production as functions of the average price level in the economy. *AD* curves slope downward to the right, showing that aggregate demand increases the lower the price level. Short-run *AS* curves are generally assumed to slope upward, showing that a higher price level is necessary for firms to produce more output. Macroeconomic equilibrium occurs at the level of output at which *AD = AS*.

Increases in consumption, investment and exports shift the *AD* curve rightward, as do expansionary fiscal policy and monetary policy. A rightward shift of the *AD* curve is called an increase in aggregate demand. Likewise an increase in aggregate supply, caused perhaps by a fall in money costs of production or by increased productivity and more efficient production, shifts the short-run *AS* curve rightward. The shape and slope of the *SRAS* curve indicate whether expansionary demand-side government policies are *reflationary* or *inflationary*.

Short-run aggregate supply is the supply of real output produced in the time period when costs of production such as money wage rates remain unchanged. Long-run aggregate supply is the supply of real output when the price level and costs of production have adjusted with respect to changes in aggregate demand in the economy. The *LRAS* curve shows the *potential* output that the economy can produce.

Many, though not all, economists, especially those of a free-market persuasion, believe that the *LRAS* curve is vertical. A vertical *LRAS* curve means that an increase in aggregate demand, intended to take the level of output above its natural level, raises prices but not real output. Friedmanite economists believe there may be a *short-run* increase in output beyond the natural level as long as economic agents suffer money illusion. New classical economists suggest a different reason for such a short-run increase in output. All schools of free-market economists reject the use of demand-side policies to increase output and employment *above* their natural levels, and support the use of supply-side policies to shift short-run and long-run *AS* curves rightward. However, many argue that the government and central bank should increase aggregate demand (via monetary policy) when output is initially *below* its natural level, and also to make sure there is enough demand to absorb the increase in output.

Self-testing questions

1 What is macroeconomic equilibrium?

2 Define aggregate demand.

3 Define aggregate supply.

4 Explain the shape of the aggregate demand curve.

5 Explain the shape and slope of a short-run aggregate supply curve.

6 Considering only the *SRAS* curve and not the *LRAS* curve, explain how an increase in aggregate demand may affect output and the price level.

7 Distinguish between short-run and long-run aggregate supply.

8 Why is the *LRAS* curve vertical?

9 What is the economy's natural level of output?

10 What is money illusion?

11 How may money illusion affect short-run aggregate supply?

12 Explain the difference between the new classical and the New Keynesian explanations of the relationship between the *SRAS* and the *LRAS* curves.

13 What are the implications of a vertical *LRAS* curve for demand management policies?

Chapter 16
Unemployment and inflation

Specification focus

This chapter covers the topics of employment, unemployment and inflation, all of which figure significantly in both the AS Module 2 specification and the A2 Module 6 specification.

AS **Module 2 The National Economy**
Performance of the UK Economy and Government Policy Objectives; Main Instruments of Government Macroeconomic Policy

A2 **Module 6 Government Policy, the National and International Economy**
Inflation and Unemployment; Managing the National Economy

A2 **Synoptic coverage**
At A2 candidates are expected to develop in greater depth and sophistication their knowledge and understanding of the causes and consequences of unemployment and inflation.

Introduction

Until quite recently, large-scale unemployment and inflation were two of the most serious economic problems facing UK governments. Before the 1970s, unemployment and the rate of inflation generally moved in opposite directions, with the movements closely linked to the phases of the business cycle. In the recovery and boom phases of the economic cycle, unemployment fell but the rate of inflation increased. Conversely, in the recessionary phase, unemployment grew but the rate of inflation slowed down. However, the 1970s were different, witnessing stagflation or slumpflation, in which unemployment and the rate of inflation both grew together. Although the rate of inflation fell considerably during the early 1980s, inflation climbed again in the UK in the mid-1980s, before subsiding again from the early 1990s onwards. From 1992, at least until 2005, the UK has benefited from the opposite situation to the 1970s. Following the end of the last severe recession in 1992, economic growth has been continuous, unemployment has fallen and the rate of inflation has also fallen (at least until 2004).

In this chapter we shall examine the causes of unemployment and inflation, and the impact of government policies to reduce these two evils. Although the chapter concentrates on government policy, it is worth noting that a number of other factors have been suggested to explain how unemployment has continued to fall without the economy running into inflation. These include the impact of ICT and other new technologies in the 'New Economy', and the benefits of globalisation, both of which have tended to reduce inflationary pressure as the economy has continued to grow.

Unemployment

Measuring unemployment

Until quite recently the main measure of unemployment officially used in the UK was the monthly **claimant count**. This is a by-product of the administrative system for paying out unemployment-related benefits – the main benefit currently being the jobseeker's allowance. Many economists believe that the claimant count provides an inaccurate measure of true unemployment. Free-market economists argue that the claimant count overstates true unemployment because many claimants are either not genuinely looking for work or not genuinely unemployed because they already have undeclared jobs in the informal economy.

But in other ways, the claimant count understates true unemployment. The toughening up of eligibility requirements in the 1980s and early 1990s reduced the claimant count without actually reducing unemployment. In addition, various groups of unemployed, such as young workers on government training schemes and unemployed workers approaching retirement (who were reclassified as 'early retired'), have been removed from the register even though they would like full-time jobs.

The government now recognises a second measure of unemployment based on the **Labour Force Survey** (LFS) of households, which uses internationally recognised definitions recommended by the International Labour Organisation (ILO). The LFS is a quarterly survey of 60,000 households, which counts people as unemployed if they are actively seeking work (that is, if they have been looking for a job in the last 4 weeks) and have not had a job in the week in question.

Those people actively seeking work are unlikely to represent the total number of people out of work

On the basis of the LFS, as Table 16.1 shows, in 2004 there were more than half a million people unemployed in the UK over and above those measured in the claimant count.

Table 16.1 Employment and unemployment in the UK, 1990–2004

	Employment: LFS count (millions)	Unemployment: claimant count (millions)	Unemployment: LFS count (millions)
1990	26.78	1.65	2.02
1991	26.21	2.27	2.46
1992	25.63	2.74	2.80
1993	25.28	2.88	2.95
1994	25.45	2.60	2.75
1995	25.73	2.29	2.47
1996	26.00	2.09	2.34
1997	26.45	1.58	2.04
1998	26.71	1.35	1.78
1999	27.05	1.25	1.75
2000	27.43	1.09	1.64
2001	27.69	0.97	1.43
2002	27.86	0.95	1.54
2003	28.16	0.93	1.49
2004	28.38	0.85	1.44

Source: www.statistics.gov.uk, accessed 8 May 2005.

Both the claimant count and the LFS measure may understate true unemployment because they ignore discouraged workers – people who have given up hope of finding a job even though they would take one if it were offered – and roughly half a million people who are classified as economically inactive.

*e**xaminer's voice**

It is important to know the difference between the two methods of measuring unemployment used in the UK. Examination questions, at both AS and A2, may contain data using either or both of the two methods.

Interpreting the data

The data in Table 16.1 show a more or less continuous fall in unemployment (and rise in employment) over the 11-year period from 1993 to 2004. By 2001, unemployment had fallen below the psychologically important level of 1 million, at least when measured by the claimant count. As we have noted, the fall in unemployment is explained by the performance of the UK economy over most of the 1990s and early 2000s. Indeed, some economists say the economy has experienced a second 'golden era' (the first one having been in the 'golden age' of Keynesian economics in the 1950s and 1960s). By the early 2000s, many communities in the UK, particularly in southeast England, were fully employed. However, other regions in the north and west of the UK have not been so fortunate, and there are also pockets of unemployment in parts of London such as Hackney.

It is worth noting that much of the increase in employment in recent years results from the growth of the public sector. Private sector growth has been weak and has not created many jobs. However, it is possible that public sector growth is now weakening, since job cuts have been announced, for example in the civil service. The figures may mask a more deep-seated and perhaps intractable feature of UK society: the gap between households in which every adult works, apart from those in education or those who have retired, and those in which nobody works, surviving on welfare benefits.

The meaning of full employment

Figure 16.1 shows the aggregate demand for labour and the aggregate supply of labour in an economy's aggregate labour market. The aggregate demand for labour curve (AD_L) is the sum of the demand curves of all the firms in the labour market. The AD_L curve slopes downward to the right, showing that the demand for labour increases as the real cost of hiring labour falls. There are two main reasons for this:

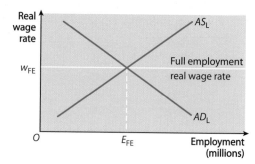

Figure 16.1 Full employment in an economy

- In the short run, labour's diminishing marginal product means that it is unprofitable for firms to take on more workers unless the cost of hiring labour falls.
- When the real wage falls relative to the cost of capital, firms substitute labour for capital and adopt more labour-intensive methods of production.

The aggregate supply curve of labour (AS_L) slopes upward, showing that more people are prepared to work at a higher real wage rate. Again, there are two principal reasons:

- As the real wage rate rises, workers with jobs are prepared to work longer hours.
- People unwilling to join the economically active labour force at lower real wage rates, such as family members with children, decide to supply labour at a higher real wage rate.

Full employment does not necessarily mean that every single member of the working population is in work. Rather it means a situation in which the number of people wishing to work at the going market real wage rate equals the number of workers that employers wish to hire at this real wage rate. In Figure 16.1, full employment occurs at the level of employment E_{FE}, where the aggregate demand for labour equals the aggregate supply of labour at real wage rate w_{FE}.

examiner's voice

Chapter 12 noted how in the 1940s, Lord Beveridge defined full employment as occurring when 3% of the labour force are unemployed. In this chapter, we have defined full employment in terms of the demand for, and supply of, labour. This is generally a better definition.

Equilibrium unemployment

In a dynamic economy, change constantly takes place in the economy, with some industries declining and others growing. Workers moving between jobs may decide to take a break between the two employments. This is called **frictional unemployment**. Moreover, as new products are developed and demand and cost conditions change, firms demand more of some labour skills while the demand for other types of labour declines. This leads to **structural unemployment**. Frictional and structural unemployment make up what is called **equilibrium unemployment**. Equilibrium unemployment exists even when the real wage rate is at its market-clearing level.

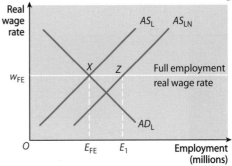

Figure 16.2 *Equilibrium unemployment*

In Figure 16.2, equilibrium unemployment is equal to the distance between Z and X, or $E_1 - E_{FE}$. The curve labelled AS_{LN} includes all the workers willing to work at different real wage rates, plus the equilibrium unemployment at each real wage rate.

Frictional unemployment

Frictional unemployment, which is also known as **transitional unemployment**, is 'between jobs' unemployment. As its name suggests, this type of unemployment results from frictions in the labour market which create a delay or time-lag during which a worker is unemployed when moving from one job to another. Note that the definition of frictional unemployment assumes that a job vacancy exists, and that frictions in the job market prevent unemployed workers from filling vacancies. It follows that the number of unfilled job vacancies is a measure of the level of frictional unemployment in the economy.

Among the causes of frictional unemployment are geographical and occupational immobilities of labour, which prevent laid-off workers from filling job vacancies immediately. Family ties, ignorance about vacancies in other parts of the country and, above all, the cost of moving and difficulties of obtaining housing are responsible for the *geographical* immobility of labour. The need for training and the effects of restrictive practices and discrimination in labour markets are among the causes of *occupational* immobility.

The **search theory of unemployment** provides a further explanation of frictional unemployment. Consider the situation illustrated in Figure 16.3, in which a worker earning £1,000 a week in a skilled professional occupation loses his job. While there appear to be no vacancies in his current line of work, there are vacancies for low-skilled office workers earning around £300 a week. Suppose now that the newly unemployed worker sets his aspirational wage at £1,000. This means that he will choose to remain unemployed, at least to start with, rather than to fill the lower-paid vacancy. The lower weekly wage on offer, and perhaps also poorer conditions of work and status associated with the lower-paid job, render the vacancy unattractive. He also lacks accurate information about the state of the job market. All this means that the newly unemployed worker needs to search the labour market to find out whether better-paid and higher-status vacancies exist.

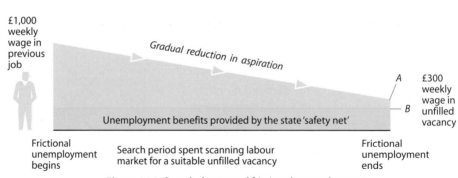

Figure 16.3 *Search theory and frictional unemployment*

Under this interpretation, frictional unemployment is a *voluntary* search period in which newly unemployed workers scan the labour market, searching for vacancies that are likely to meet their aspirations. There are a number of ways in which this voluntary search period can end. First, the newly unemployed worker eventually learns of a vacancy, which meets his initial aspiration and for which he is qualified. Indeed, the vacancy may have been there all the time but, until he searched the job market, the worker did not know about it. Second, the vacancy may have arisen during his search period, perhaps resulting from a general improvement in the labour market. Third, he may end his voluntary unemployment as soon as he realises that his initial aspirations were unrealistically high, meaning he decides to settle for a lower-paid, less attractive job.

Long search periods, which increase the amount of frictional unemployment in the economy, can be caused by the welfare benefit system. Without welfare benefits, search periods must be financed by running down stocks of saving, or through the charity of family and friends. In this situation, the threat of poverty creates incentives to search the job market more vigorously and to reduce aspirational wage levels. However, the availability of a state safety net of unemployment and other income-related welfare benefits, together in some cases with redundancy payments, permits unemployed workers to finance longer voluntary search periods. Because of this, free-market economists support a reduction in the real value of unemployment benefits, together with restricting the benefits to those who can prove they are genuinely looking for work. They believe that these policies create incentives for the unemployed to reduce aspirations quickly, which in turn shortens search periods.

The replacement ratio

For a relatively low-paid worker losing a job, the **replacement ratio** is a factor influencing the length of time searching for work while unemployed. It is given by the following formula:

$$\text{replacement ratio} = \frac{\text{disposable income out of work}}{\text{disposable income in work}}$$

The size of the replacement ratio is determined largely by the level of welfare benefits claimable when unemployed, relative to income after taxation and receipt of benefits when in work. A replacement ratio of 100% means that a worker is no better off in work than out of work, 'living off the state'.

Even for low-paid workers, replacement ratios are seldom as high as 100%. Nonetheless, high replacement ratios approaching 100% destroy the incentive to work, at least in the formal economy. For people whose job prospects are poor, a high replacement ratio leads to the **unemployment trap**, which is explained in Chapter 18. For the worker shown in Figure 16.3, the replacement ratio equals B/A. Point B shows the level of welfare benefit claimable out of work, while point A shows disposable income in work.

Casual and seasonal unemployment

Casual unemployment is a special case of frictional unemployment, occurring when workers are laid off on a short-term basis in trades such as tourism, agriculture, catering and building. **Seasonal unemployment** is casual unemployment resulting from seasonal fluctuations in demand — for example, fruit pickers or deck chair attendants laid off at the end of summer.

Structural unemployment

Structural unemployment results from the structural decline of industries, unable to compete or adapt in the face of either changing demand and new products or the emergence of more efficient competitors in other countries. Structural unemployment is also caused by changing skill requirements as industries change ways of producing their products.

Technological unemployment is a special case of structural unemployment, resulting from the successful growth of new industries using labour-saving technology. In contrast to **mechanisation** (workers operating machines), which has usually increased the overall demand for labour, **automation** (machines operating other machines) reduces the demand for labour. Whereas the growth of mechanised industry increases employment, automation of production can lead to the shedding of labour, even when industry output is expanding.

The growth of international competition is an important cause of structural unemployment. During the Keynesian era from the 1950s to the 1970s, structural unemployment in the UK was concentrated in regions where nineteenth-century staple industries such as textiles and shipbuilding were suffering structural decline. Regional unemployment caused by the decline of **sunset industries** was more than offset by the

Structural unemployment as a result of the decline of the manufacturing industry has been offset by the growth in employment opportunities in sunrise industries such as electronics

growth of employment elsewhere in the UK in the **sunrise industries** that replaced them. However, in the severe recessions of the early 1980s and the early 1990s, structural unemployment affected almost all regions in the UK, as **deindustrialisation** spread across the manufacturing base.

*e*xaminer's voice

Some unemployment in the UK is regional, but much of this is really a special case of structural unemployment.

At the time of writing in 2005, the UK economy has experienced continuous economic growth since the end of the last recession in 1992. It is difficult to say whether structural unemployment has grown or fallen in this period, as it is not easy to separate changes in structural unemployment from other causes of falling unemployment, particularly the increase in aggregate demand. In many years, manufacturing output has grown, but manufacturing employment has fallen. There is a danger of exaggerating the growth of unemployment in manufacturing industries because many activities, ranging from cleaning to information technology (IT) maintenance, previously undertaken 'in house' by manufacturing firms, have been out-sourced to external service sector providers.

Structural unemployment has also occurred within the service sector, partly due to the increasing use of information and communication technology (ICT) and automated services. Call centre employment has grown significantly in the service sector in recent years. However, a decline has been forecast, partly due to call centres moving overseas, but also because companies employ automated communication software rather than humans to provide customer services.

Disequilibrium unemployment

As explained, equilibrium unemployment, which is illustrated in Figure 16.2, comprises the frictional and structural unemployment occurring when the labour market is in equilibrium. By contrast, as the name indicates, **disequilibrium unemployment** results from the labour market being out of equilibrium. It occurs when:

*e*xaminer's voice

At A2, but not at AS, it is important to understand the difference between equilibrium and disequilibrium unemployment.

- the aggregate supply of labour exceeds the aggregate demand for labour
- market imperfections prevent the real wage rate falling to restore labour market equilibrium (**wage stickiness**)

There are two main types of disequilibrium unemployment. These are:

- classical or real-wage unemployment
- cyclical, Keynesian or demand-deficient unemployment

Classical unemployment or real-wage unemployment

Before the Keynesian era, economists believed that a large part of unemployment in the 1920s and 1930s was caused by excessively high real wages in labour markets, which were insufficiently competitive for market forces to eliminate unemployment. In recent years, the view that a large part of unemployment in the UK, especially youth unemployment, has been caused by too high a level of real wages has been revived by free-market economists.

In Figure 16.4, full employment is determined where the aggregate demand for labour equals the aggregate supply of labour, at the real wage rate w_{FE}. But suppose wages are fixed at a higher real rate, at w_1 rather than w_{FE}. At this real wage rate, employers wish to hire E_1 workers, but E_2 workers wish to supply their labour. There is **excess supply** of labour in the labour market.

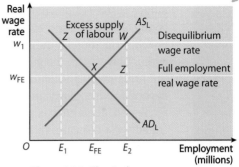

Figure 16.4 Classical or real-wage unemployment

The pre-Keynesians believed that, as long as the labour market remained competitive, the resulting classical or real-wage unemployment would be temporary. Competitive forces in the labour market would cure the problem, bidding down the real wage rate to w_{FE}, thereby eliminating the excess supply of labour. Full employment would quickly be restored when the number of workers willing to work equalled the number that firms wished to hire.

But suppose labour market rigidity, perhaps caused by trade unions, prevents the real wage rate falling below w_1. In this situation, the market mechanism fails to work properly, the excess supply of labour persists, and real-wage or classical unemployment occurs.

Cyclical, Keynesian or demand-deficient unemployment

Chapter 12 introduces the possibility of demand-deficient unemployment. The chapter explains how Keynes believed that deficient aggregate demand was a major cause of persistent mass unemployment in the 1920s and 1930s. Now, free-market economists generally agree that *temporary* unemployment (called **cyclical unemployment**) may be caused by a lack of demand in the downswing of the business cycle. However, Keynes went further, arguing that the economy could settle into an under-full employment equilibrium, caused by a continuing lack of effective aggregate demand. The reasons for this are explained in the sections of Chapter 12 covering the **fallacy of composition** and the **paradox of thrift**, and in Chapter 14's coverage of the **Keynesian theories of consumption and saving**.

> ⓔ**xaminer's voice**
> Make sure you understand the differences between frictional unemployment, structural unemployment, real-wage (or classical) unemployment and demand-deficient (or cyclical) unemployment.

Other causes of unemployment

Three other causes of unemployment relate to hysteresis, the insider/outsider theory of unemployment, and queuing unemployment.

Hysteresis

Hysteresis is the name given to a cause of unemployment which emerged in the recessions of the early 1980s and 1990s. Previous to these downturns, in earlier,

milder post-1945 downswings, firms reacted to decreases in aggregate demand by laying off workers and by 'mothballing' productive capacity. When the downswing ended, firms quickly rehired workers and brought idle capacity into production again. However, in the more recent recessions, many factories were bulldozed and the firms owning them disappeared completely. As a result, productive capacity declined, particularly in manufacturing and coal mining. When the economy recovered, demand was met by imports. In an *AD/AS* diagram, hysteresis is illustrated by a leftward shift of the *AD* curve (showing the start of the recession), followed by a leftward shift of both the short-run and the long-run *AS* curves, as capacity is destroyed.

The emergence of long-term unemployment also contributes to hysteresis. By eroding job skills and work habits, long-term unemployment makes workers unemployable. Employers who might otherwise hire and retrain workers who have been unemployed for several years perceive that workers with more recent job experience present fewer risks.

The insider/outsider theory of unemployment

Trade union members are, according to this theory, **insiders** in the labour market, while unemployed workers, especially those who allowed their union membership to lapse on losing their jobs, are **outsiders**. The theory is based on the assumption that unionised workers enjoy higher wages than non-unionised workers, but that this **union mark-up** is achieved at the expense of fewer jobs. Although trade union pay negotiators claim to be concerned about job losses and the diminishing prospects of former members who are now unemployed, they don't really care. Instead, unions care only about the employment prospects of insiders (their members who are currently employed). The insider/outsider theory suggests that unions are prepared to push for higher real wages even when unemployment is high, because unemployment among 'outsiders' is not their concern.

Queuing unemployment

According to New Keynesian economists, **collective bargaining** in imperfectly competitive labour markets results in higher wage rates than there would be in the absence of unions. The union mark-up is the difference between a union-negotiated wage rate and the wage rate offered for similar non-unionised employment. The higher wage established through collective bargaining creates an incentive to wait for unionised jobs. Queuing unemployment occurs when workers reject lower-paid jobs in the non-unionised sector of the economy, in the hope that a better-paid unionised job will turn up.

Continuous turnover in the labour market also contributes to queuing. Every week some employees retire or leave the labour force, others switch jobs, while simultaneously new jobs are created. Waiting for a suitable vacancy may be a sensible strategy. In this second interpretation, queuing unemployment is closely related to the search theory of voluntary frictional unemployment, explained earlier.

The costs and consequences of unemployment

Unemployment is a waste of human capital. By definition, when unemployment occurs, the economy produces inside its production possibility frontier. Nevertheless, free-market economists believe that a certain amount of unemployment is necessary to make the economy function better. They believe that, by providing downward pressure on wage rates, unemployment reduces inflationary pressures. But unemployment widens income differentials and increases absolute and relative poverty. Higher unemployment also means greater spending on unemployment and poverty-related benefits, the opportunity cost of which is less spending on the provision of hospitals, schools and other useful resources.

Governments generally implement policies to try to reduce unemployment, but the appropriate policy obviously depends on identifying correctly the underlying cause of unemployment. For example, if unemployment is diagnosed incorrectly in terms of demand deficiency, when the true cause is structural, a policy of fiscal or monetary expansion to stimulate aggregate demand will be ineffective and inappropriate. Indeed, in such circumstances reflation of demand would create excess demand, which raises the price level through demand-pull inflation, with no lasting beneficial effects upon employment.

It is now widely agreed, by Keynesians as well as by free-market economists, that the cause of most modern unemployment in countries such as the UK lies on the supply side of the economy rather than on the demand side. However, there is disagreement on the appropriate policies to improve supply-side performance. Free-market economists argue that poor supply-side performance is the legacy of the three decades of Keynesian interventionism from the 1950s to 1970s. In the free-market view, the economic role of the state must be reduced to cut frictional, structural and real-wage unemployment. By setting markets free, encouraging competition and fostering private enterprise and the entrepreneurial spirit, an enterprise culture can be created in which the price mechanism, and not the government, delivers economic growth and reduces unemployment. Free-market economists believe that the correct role of government is to create the conditions in which the market mechanism and private enterprise function properly — through controlling inflation, promoting competitive markets and maintaining the rule of law and social order. Keynesian economists disagree, believing that unemployment results from a massive market failure that can be cured only by interventionist policies to modify markets and make them function better.

> *e*xaminer's voice
> Don't confuse the *consequences* of unemployment with the *causes* of unemployment. Examination candidates often muddle the two.

Inflation

Inflation is best defined as a persistent or continuous rise in the price level, or as a continuing fall in the value of money. **Deflation** is the opposite, namely a persistent tendency for the price level to fall or for the value of money to rise. However, the *overall* price level has seldom fallen in western industrialised countries since the 1930s. The term deflation is therefore usually applied in a rather looser way to describe a reduction in aggregate demand and levels of economic activity, output and employment. A **deflationary policy** (also known as a **disinflationary policy**) uses fiscal or monetary policy to reduce aggregate demand. Likewise, **reflation** refers to an increase in economic activity and output, and a **reflationary policy** stimulates aggregate demand. Very often, inflation is 'reflation gone wrong', stimulating the price level rather than real output and employment.

*e*xaminer's voice

Avoid confusing a rise in the *average price level* with a *relative price change*, occurring when the price of one good rises or falls.

Measuring inflation

Until 2003, the UK government measured changes in the rate of inflation through changes in the **retail price index (RPI)**. The RPI measures the *headline* rate of inflation, whereas another measure, the RPIX, measures the *underlying* rate of inflation: that is, the headline rate minus mortgage interest rates. The government still uses RPIX for deciding the level at which welfare benefits such as the state pension and the jobseeker's allowance should be set.

However, when setting a target inflation rate for the Bank of England to meet through monetary policy, the consumer prices index (CPI) has replaced the RPIX. Currently, the Bank of England aims to hit a CPI target rate of 2%, rather than the old RPIX target rate of 2.5%. The CPI, which is based on the method of measuring the price level used in the European Union, is likely eventually to replace the RPI and RPIX completely.

*e*xaminer's voice

You must learn how to interpret index numbers. The specification states that candidates must also understand how index numbers are calculated and used to measure inflation.

Table 16.2 shows how the rate of inflation changed in the UK between 1990 and 2004, when measured by the RPI, RPIX and the CPI. A price index such as the RPIX or the CPI attempts to measure the cost of living of a representative family in the economy. (Other price indices, such as an input price index or a wholesale price index, can be used for other purposes.) The rate of inflation is calculated by comparing the RPI or CPI for 2 successive years.

Table 16.2 UK inflation rate shown by changes in the RPI, RPIX and the CPI, 1990–2004

	RPI (%)	RPIX (%)	CPI (%)		RPI (%)	RPIX (%)	CPI (%)
1990	9.5	8.1	7.0	1998	3.4	2.6	1.6
1991	5.9	6.7	7.5	1999	1.5	2.3	1.3
1992	3.7	4.7	4.2	2000	3.0	2.1	0.8
1993	1.6	3.0	2.5	2001	1.8	2.1	1.2
1994	2.4	2.3	2.0	2002	1.7	2.2	1.3
1995	3.5	2.9	2.6	2003	2.9	2.8	1.4
1996	2.4	3.0	2.5	2004	3.0	2.2	1.3
1997	3.1	2.8	1.8				

Source: www.statistics.gov.uk, accessed 8 May 2005.

The average price level of all goods is affected by the prices of millions (or perhaps billions) of goods and services in the economy. Because it is impossible to measure all prices, a price index measures the prices of a **representative sample** of goods and services. The representative sample (or **national shopping basket**) used for calculating the RPI contains about 650 items. For an index to measure the cost of living and inflation accurately, the sample has to change regularly to reflect new products and changing tastes, and each item in the sample has to be given a **weight** that reflects its relative importance in spending patterns. For example, brown ale was removed from the RPI sample in 2003, to be replaced by a cup of café latte, and a year later a bottle of mineral water replaced a bottle of gin.

Even with such changes and the use of accurate weights, a price index can never be completely accurate. There are a number of reasons for this. First, different income groups buy different goods and services and therefore some will experience higher inflation rates than others. Second, because it is difficult to accommodate improvements in the quality of goods in a price index, price indices may tend to overstate slightly the true rate of inflation. But in the case of RPIX and the CPI, this effect may be more than countered by excluding from the index 'big ticket', high-inflation items such as mortgage costs and the council tax.

Table 16.2 shows the underlying annual rate of inflation, measured by RPIX, falling in the UK from 8.1% in 1990 to 2.2% at the end of 2004. The table also shows that while the RPIX inflation rate has generally been lower than the headline rate measured by RPI, the RPIX rate has been higher than the inflation rate measured by the CPI. The reason for these differences lies largely in the way the price of housing is treated in the three measures of inflation. The mortgage interest rate and the council tax are both included in the RPI, but only the council tax is included in RPIX. Both are excluded from the CPI.

None of the three methods of measuring inflation takes account of changes in house prices directly. Given that house price inflation was significantly higher than the rate of general inflation through much of the 1990s and early 2000s, all *three* measures may understate the true rate of inflation. However, this factor may be more than balanced by the fact that in other ways the three price indices overstate the rate of inflation. Perhaps the most important reason for a price index over-stating the true inflation rate lies in the fact that for many goods, for example cars, computers and cameras, the quality of the goods has improved while the prices have changed.

Reducing the rate of inflation to a rate of around 2% must not, of course, be confused with achieving absolute **price stability**: that is, 0% inflation every year. Inflation at 2% may not seem a very high figure, but it is important to realise the compound effect that occurs over several years whenever the inflation rate is above zero. Even with annual inflation at 2% a year, the price level doubles within about a generation. Annual rates as high as 4% or 5% a year produce a much faster doubling of prices.

The benefits and costs of inflation

Everybody agrees that inflation can have serious adverse effects or costs. However, the seriousness of the adverse effects depends on whether inflation is *anticipated* or *unanticipated*. If inflation could be anticipated with complete certainty, it would pose few problems. Households and firms would simply build the expected rate of inflation into their economic decisions, which would not be distorted by wrong guesses.

When inflation is relatively low, with little variation from year to year, it is relatively easy to anticipate more or less fully next year's inflation rate. Indeed, **creeping inflation**, which is associated with growing markets, healthy profits and a general climate of business optimism, *greases the wheels* of the economy. Viewed in this way, a low rate of inflation — and not absolute price stability — may be a necessary side-effect or cost of expansionary policies to reduce unemployment.

A low but stable inflation rate may also be necessary to make labour markets function efficiently. Even if average real wage rates are rising, there will be *some* labour markets in which real wages must fall in order to maintain a low rate of unemployment. To save jobs, workers may be willing to accept falling real wages caused by *nominal* wage rates rising at a slower rate than inflation. However, workers are much less willing to accept absolute cuts in nominal wage rates. Thus, with zero inflation, the changes required in *real* wage rates to make labour markets function efficiently fail to take place. Labour markets function best when inflation is low but also stable. By contrast, absolute price stability produces real wage stickiness, which then results in unnecessarily high unemployment.

However, the adverse effects of inflation begin to exceed the benefits as soon as inflation becomes difficult to anticipate. It is very difficult for people fully to anticipate strato-inflation in which the actual inflation rate varies substantially from year to year. Inflation that is both high and difficult to anticipate creates distortions which increasingly destabilise normal economic activity. Free-market economists generally argue that when inflation creeps upward, all too soon it acts as *sand thrown in the wheels* of the economy, making markets less efficient and competitive. When the *sand in the wheels* effect becomes stronger than the *greasing the wheels* effect, the costs of inflation exceed the benefits. (Don't confuse a **strato-inflation**, in which the inflation rate varies between about 10% and 30%, with a **hyper-inflation**, which may accelerate into an inflation rate of well over 100%. Both a strato-inflation and a hyper-inflation are difficult to anticipate, but the latter may eventually destroy economic activity.)

Particular costs of inflation are:

- **Distributional effects.** Weaker social groups in society, such as pensioners on fixed incomes, lose; while others, in strong bargaining positions, gain. Moreover, in times of rapid inflation, real rates of interest are often negative. In this situation, lenders are really paying borrowers for the doubtful privilege of lending to them, and inflation acts as a hidden tax, redistributing wealth from creditors to debtors.

■ **Distortion of normal economic behaviour.** Inflation actually distorts consumer behaviour by causing households to bring forward purchases and hoard if they expect the rate of inflation to accelerate. Similarly, firms may divert funds out of productive investment in fixed investment projects into unproductive commodity hoarding and speculation. People are affected by **inflationary noise**. This occurs when changes in *relative* prices are confused with a change in the *general* price level.

■ **Breakdown in the functions of money.** In a time of severe inflation, money becomes less useful and efficient as a medium of exchange and store of value. Rapidly changing prices erode money's functions as a unit of account and standard of deferred payment. In a hyper-inflation, in which the inflation rate may accelerate to several hundred per cent a year or even higher, less efficient barter replaces money and imposes extra costs on most transactions.

Hyper-inflation in Germany in the early 1920s meant that banknotes were virtually worthless

■ **International uncompetitiveness.** When the inflation rate is higher than in competitor countries, exports increase in price, making them uncompetitive. This puts pressure on a fixed exchange rate. With a floating exchange rate, the rate falls to restore competitiveness, but rising import prices may fuel a further bout of inflation.

■ **Shoe leather and menu costs.** With rapid inflation, consumers incur **shoe leather costs**, spending time and effort shopping around to check which prices have or have not risen. By contrast, **menu costs** are incurred by firms having to adjust price lists and vending machines more often.

> ***e*xaminer's voice**
> An A2 Unit 6 exam question may ask for a discussion of the circumstances, if any, in which inflation can be justified. By contrast, an AS Unit 2 exam question might ask for an explanation of the benefits and costs of inflation.

Theories of inflation

Table 16.3 provides a summary of how theories of inflation have developed over the years. The following sections explain in some detail the main theories of the causes of inflation.

Table 16.3 A brief history of the main theories of inflation

Eighteenth century to the 1930s: the old **quantity theory of money**.

1930s: Keynes's *General Theory* explains deflation in terms of **deficient aggregate demand**.

1940s: Keynes develops his *General Theory* to explain how, in conditions of full employment, excess demand can pull up the price level through **demand-pull inflation**.

1950s/1960s: many Keynesians switch to the **cost-push** or **structuralist theory** of inflation.

1950s/1960s: Keynesian demand-pull versus cost-push debate conducted with the aid of the **Phillips curve**.

1950s: the foundation of **early monetarist theory** of inflation; Milton Friedman's revival of the quantity theory of money (the **modern quantity theory**).

1968: the incorporation of the role of **expectations** in the inflationary process into the monetarist theory of inflation; development of **adaptive expectations** in Milton Friedman's theory of the **expectations-augmented Phillips curve**.

1970s: the **breakdown of the Phillips relationship**.

1970s/1980s: the incorporation of the role of **rational expectations** into the inflationary process; the **new classical school**.

1980s onwards: the **current controversy**; cost-push or structural explanations of inflation (e.g. New Keynesian explanations) versus monetarist and new classical explanations.

The 'old' quantity theory of money

The quantity theory of money is the oldest theory of inflation, dating back at least to the eighteenth century. For two centuries until the 1930s, when it went out of fashion with the Keynesian revolution, the quantity theory was *the* theory of inflation. However, Milton Friedman's revival of the quantity theory in modern form in the 1950s is usually regarded as marking the beginning of the monetarist counter-revolution. In recent years, the quantity theory has once again occupied a central place in debate and controversy about the causes of inflation.

All versions of the quantity theory, old and new, are based on a special case of demand inflation, in which rising prices are caused by excess demand. In the quantity theory, the source of excess demand is located in monetary rather than real forces, in an **excess supply of money** created or condoned by the government. At its simplest, the quantity theory is sometimes stated as *too much money chasing*

too few goods. The starting point for developing the theory is the **Fisher equation of exchange**, devised by an American economist, Irving Fisher, early in the twentieth century:

money supply (stock of money) × velocity of circulation of money = price level × total transactions

or:

$$MV = PT$$

In the Fisher equation, for a particular time period, say a year, the stock of money in the economy (or money supply) shown by the symbol (M) multiplied by the number of times money changes hands (V) equals the price level (P) multiplied by the total number of transactions (T). A transaction occurs when a good or service is bought. T measures all the purchases of goods and services in the economy.

To convert the equation of exchange ($MV = PT$) — which is true by definition — into a *theory* of inflation, it is necessary to make three assumptions. The first two are:
■ The velocity of circulation (or speed at which money is spent) and total transactions (which are determined by the level of real national output in the economy) are both fixed, or at least stable.
■ In the quantity theory, money is a medium of exchange but not a store of value, which means that people quickly spend any money they receive.

Suppose the government allows the money supply to expand faster than the rate at which real national output increases. As a result, households and firms possess money balances (or stocks of money) that are greater than those they wish to hold. According to the quantity theory, these excess money balances will quickly be spent. This brings us to the third assumption in the quantity theory: changes in the money supply are assumed to bring about changes in the price level (rather than vice versa).

> *e*xaminer's voice
> The A2 Unit 6 exam may test a basic knowledge of the quantity theory of money.

Keynesian theories of inflation

The Keynesian demand-pull theory of inflation

The quantity theory of money and the Keynesian **demand-pull theory** are both *demand* theories of inflation, which locate the cause of inflation in excess demand for goods and services. After 1945, Keynesian economists accepted the argument that inflation results from excess demand pulling up the price level, but they rejected the 'quantity theory' view that the source of the excess demand lies solely in excess monetary growth. Instead the Keynesians located the 'engine of inflation' firmly in the real economy, in behavioural factors that cause the planned expenditure of economic agents (households, firms, the government and the overseas sectors) to exceed the quantity of output that the economy was capable of producing. In Keynesian theory, inflation is explained by the *real* forces determining how people behave, and not by money.

In the Keynesian era, governments were committed to achieving full employment. Arguably, this caused people to behave in an inflationary way, both as workers and as voters. Workers and their unions bargained for money wage increases in excess of any productivity increase without fear of unemployment. At the same time in the political arena, the electorate added to the pressure of demand by voting for increased public spending and budget deficits.

Nonetheless, the Keynesian demand-pull theory and the quantity theory of inflation may not really be very different. In both theories, the *ultimate* cause of inflation may lie with the government. In the quantity theory of money (as explained in Chapters 17 and 18), the government's budget deficit and borrowing requirement cause monetary expansion, which first triggers, and then sustains, demand-pull inflation. In the Keynesian demand-pull theory, a budget deficit is also responsible for excess demand.

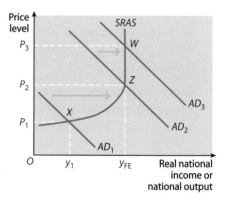

Figure 16.5 uses a short-run AD/AS diagram to illustrate demand-pull inflation. Suppose the aggregate demand and supply curves are initially in positions AD_1 and $SRAS$, with macroeconomic equilibrium at point X. Real national output is y_1 and the price level is P_1. There is spare capacity in the economy, which means that demand-deficient unemployment (explained earlier in the chapter) is also present.

Figure 16.5 Demand-pull inflation and an inflationary gap, illustrated on an AD/AS *diagram*

If the government increases aggregate demand to AD_2, real output and the price level both increase, respectively to y_{FE} and P_2. The government eliminates demand-deficient unemployment and creates full employment, at the expense of some inflation.

But once full employment arrives, real output cannot increase any more, at least in the short run. As a result, the $SRAS$ curve is vertical above point Z. A further rightward shift of the aggregate demand curve — for example, to AD_3 — creates excess demand, which pulls up the price level to P_3.

With the aggregate demand curve in position AD_3 in Figure 16.5, the vertical distance between points W and Z illustrates an **inflationary gap**. An inflationary gap measures the extent to which excess demand exists at the full employment level of real income or output. Likewise, a **deflationary gap** measures the extent to which there is deficient aggregate demand in the economy.

Keynesian cost-push or structuralist theories of inflation
During the Keynesian era, creeping inflation continued even when there was no evidence of excess demand in the economy. Towards the end of the 1950s and during the 1960s and 1970s, this caused many Keynesians to switch away from the

demand-pull theory of inflation to a new theory: the **cost-push** or **structuralist theory** of inflation. Cost theories of inflation locate the cause of inflation in structural and institutional conditions on the supply side of the economy, particularly in the labour market and the wage bargaining process. Most cost-push theories are essentially wage-push theories, although other variants include profits-push and import cost-push theories.

Cost-push theories generally argue that the growth of monopoly power in both the labour market and the goods market is responsible for inflation. They usually assume that wages are determined in the labour market through the process of collective bargaining, while in the goods market, prices are formed by a cost-plus pricing rule in which imperfectly competitive firms add a standard profit margin to average cost when setting prices. In labour markets, growing trade union strength in the Keynesian era enabled trade unions to bargain for money wage increases in excess of any rise in labour productivity. Monopoly firms were prepared to pay these wage increases, partly because of the costs of disrupting production, and partly because they believed that they could pass cost increases on to consumers through higher prices when output was sold.

The question then arises as to why trade union militancy and power grew in the Keynesian era. The guarantee of full employment by the state and the provision of a safety net of labour protection legislation and welfare benefits may have sustained the inflationary process. In the cost-push theory this created the conditions in which trade unions could successfully be more militant.

Cost-push inflation is illustrated on an aggregate demand and supply diagram in Figure 16.6. Initially, macroeconomic equilibrium is at point X, with real output and the price level respectively at y_1 and P_1. Firms' money costs of production rise — for example, because money wages or the price of imported raw materials increase — which causes the $SRAS$ curve to shift leftward and upward from $SRAS_1$ to $SRAS_2$. The cost-push inflationary process increases the price level to P_2, but higher production costs have reduced the equilibrium level of output that firms are willing to produce to y_2. The new macroeconomic equilibrium is at point Z.

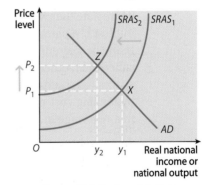

Figure 16.6 *Cost-push inflation illustrated on an AD/AS diagram*

A model of cost-push inflation

We shall now construct a model of cost-push inflation to illustrate the roles of pay relativities and different rates of productivity growth in the inflationary process. We begin by assuming two productivity sectors in the economy, one with a high rate of growth of labour productivity, such as 6% a year, and the other with a zero rate. We shall assume that firms are prepared to grant money wage increases in line with productivity growth, which means a wage rise of 6% in the high productivity growth sector but a zero increase in the second sector.

Providing wage increases in the high productivity growth sector do not exceed 6%, cost-push inflation is not initially generated in this sector of the economy. But we now assume that workers in the second sector use a different tactic to increase money wage rates. By arguing the case for 'equal pay for equal work', the unions bargain to maintain comparability with workers of similar skills in the first sector and to restore differentials, which have been eroded, relative to less skilled workers employed in the high productivity growth sector. Unions in the zero productivity growth sector therefore try to achieve the same percentage wage increase as that granted to workers in the high productivity growth sector. But if a 6% wage increase is granted to workers in both sectors, cost inflation results when firms in the zero productivity sector raise prices in line with increased wage costs.

Once started, a **wage–price spiral** and **leapfrogging** may continue the cost-push inflationary process. The wage–price spiral occurs when workers in both sectors realise that their real wage increase has been eroded by price inflation, and attempt to restore the real wage increase through further wage claims. Leapfrogging refers to the fact that when one group of workers improves its relative position in the pay league table, other groups lodge retaliatory wage claims in order to restore their relative position, or to improve upon it.

In contrast to free-market economists, who often treat the labour market as one large aggregated and relatively competitive market, Keynesians generally view the labour market as a collection of non-competitive and separated markets for different skills and trades. Although workers generally realise that, if all wage rises are limited to matching productivity increases, inflation need not occur, they also appreciate that what is in the *collective* interest of workers is not necessarily in the interest of a *particular* group of workers. If one union accepts a wage increase lower than the current rate of inflation in order to bring inflation down, its members suffer when other unions do not behave in a similar fashion. Thus each trade union strives to preserve its relative position in the pay league table, even knowing that, by fuelling cost-push inflation, a *money* wage increase may not eventually result in a *real* wage increase.

The rise of the Phillips curve

About 50 years ago, Keynesians could be divided into demand-pull and cost-push schools in terms of the views held by members of each school on the causes of inflation. After 1958, the debate between demand-pull and cost-push Keynesians was conducted with the aid of a statistical relationship, the **Phillips curve**, which is illustrated in Figure 16.7.

A. W. Phillips, the Keynesian economist who researched the relationship, argued that a stable inverse statistical relationship

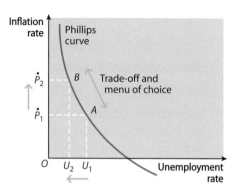

Figure 16.7 The original Phillips curve, now known as a short-run Phillips curve

AQA Advanced Economics

existed between the rate of change of wages (the rate of *wage* inflation) and the percentage of the labour force unemployed. Later versions of the Phillips curve, such as the one illustrated in Figure 16.7, measure the inverse relationship between unemployment and the rate of *price* inflation.

The Phillips curve is *not* a theory of inflation, but it does give support to both the main Keynesian theories of inflation. In the demand-pull theory, falling unemployment is associated with excess demand, which pulls up money wages in the labour market. In the cost-push theory, falling unemployment means that trade union power increases, enabling unions to use their monopoly power to push for higher wages.

Although the Phillips curve illustrates the conflict between full employment and control of inflation as policy objectives, it also suggests how the conflict can be dealt with. Suppose unemployment initially is U_1 and the rate of inflation is $\dot{P}_1$, with the economy at point A on the Phillips curve. (Note, we are using the symbol $\dot{P}$ to show the rate of price inflation.) By expanding aggregate demand, the government can move the economy to point B. Unemployment falls to U_2, but at the cost of a higher rate of inflation at $\dot{P}_2$. By using demand management policies, it appears possible for governments to trade off between increasing the number of jobs in the economy and reducing inflation. Points such as A and B on the Phillips curve represent a menu of choice for governments when deciding an acceptable combination of unemployment and inflation.

> **examiner's voice**
> Knowledge and understanding of the Phillips curve is required at A2 but not at AS. You must understand that the short-run Phillips curve slopes downward, but the long-run Phillips curve is vertical (see below). Don't confuse a Phillips curve diagram with an *AD/AS* diagram, but try to learn the links between the two diagrams.

The monetarist theory of inflation

To understand the monetarist theory of inflation, it is useful to divide its development into three stages:

- the revival in 1956 by Milton Friedman of the **quantity theory of money**
- the development, also by Milton Friedman, of the theory of the **expectations-augmented Phillips curve**, which gave rise to gradualist monetarism
- the incorporation of the theory of **rational expectations** into the explanation of the inflationary process, which became known as new classical monetarism

In order to understand how the monetarist theory of inflation has developed through these three stages, we need first to take a look at the modern quantity theory of money and at the breakdown of the Phillips curve relationship that occurred in the 1970s.

The modern quantity theory of money

In 1956 Milton Friedman revived the quantity theory of money, which in effect gave birth to monetarism. The modern quantity theory, which is really a theory of the demand for money, in relation to the range of alternative physical and financial assets that people can hold, is quite technical and is not explained in this book.

The main point to note is that both 'old' and 'new' versions of the quantity theory predict that a growth of the money supply causes inflation. The reasoning is more complicated in the modern theory, which accepts that an increase in the money supply can increase real national income in the short run. However, in the long term (defined by Friedman as about 2 years), *only* the price level is affected. Real income returns to its equilibrium value, which is determined by real forces in the economy.

The breakdown of the Phillips relationship

In the 1970s, the Phillips relationship broke down when accelerating inflation and growing unemployment occurred together. The nicknames **stagflation** and **slumpflation** were given to the combination of these two evils. Out of stagflation and the breakdown of the Phillips relationship developed the second and third stages in the monetarist explanation of inflation, in which theories on the role of expectations in the inflationary process were tacked on to the quantity theory of money. First, in 1968 Milton Friedman developed the theory of the expectations-augmented Phillips curve, and in the 1970s and 1980s the new classical school of monetarists explained inflation in terms of the theory of rational expectations.

The theory of the expectations-augmented Phillips curve

The word 'augment' means to 'add'. The rather clumsy term 'expectations-augmented Phillips curve' reflects the fact that expectations of *future* inflation are now viewed as a determinant of *current* inflation.

Economists now generally recognise that the Phillips curve in Figure 16.7 is a short-run Phillips curve (*SRPC*), representing the *short-run* relationship between inflation and unemployment. In Figure 16.8, a vertical long-run Phillips curve (*LRPC*) has been added to the diagram, intersecting the short-run Phillips curve where the rate of inflation is zero. The rate of unemployment at this point is called the **natural rate of unemployment** (NRU), depicted by the symbol U_N. (When expressed as the number of workers unemployed, it is called the natural *level* of unemployment.)

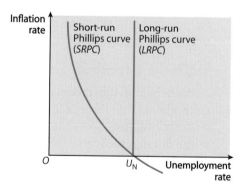

Figure 16.8 The long-run Phillips curve and the natural rate of unemployment

Free-market economists argue that it is impossible to reduce unemployment below the NRU, except at the cost of suffering an ever-accelerating unanticipated inflation. This is likely to accelerate into a hyper-inflation, which in any case eventually destroys the economy. The explanation for this lies in the fact that the original Keynesian explanation of the (short-run) Phillips curve wrongly took into account only the *current* rate of inflation and ignored the important influence of the *expected* rate of inflation.

The theory of the expectations-augmented Phillips curve brings together two important theories supported by modern free-market economists:

- the free-market theory of the labour market
- a theory of the role of expectations in the inflationary process

The free-market theory of the labour market assumes that the natural levels of employment and unemployment are determined at the equilibrium real wage, at which workers voluntarily supply exactly the amount of labour that firms voluntarily employ. Because monetarists, and free-market economists in general, do not recognise demand-deficient unemployment except as a temporary phenomenon, and believe that an efficient market mechanism prevents the emergence of structural unemployment, it follows that the natural rate of unemployment comprises just frictional unemployment.

We now introduce the role of expectations into the inflationary process (see Figure 16.9). As a simplification, we shall assume that the rate of growth of labour productivity is zero and that the rate of increase of prices (*price* inflation) equals the rate of increase of wages (*wage* inflation). The economy is initially at point A, with unemployment at the natural rate U_N. At point A, the rate of inflation is zero, as is the rate of increase of money wages. We shall also assume that people form expectations of *future* inflation in the next time period solely on the basis of the *current* rate of inflation. Thus at point A, current inflation is zero, so workers expect the future rate of inflation also to be zero.

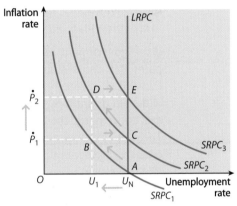

Figure 16.9 *The role of expectations in the inflationary process*

Suppose the government expands demand, to trade off along Phillips curve $SRPC_1$ to a point such as B, where unemployment at U_1 is below the natural rate, U_N. Inflation initially rises to $\dot{P}_1$, or 5%. But a point such as B is unsustainable. For workers to supply more labour, the real wage must rise, yet a rising real wage causes employers to demand less labour. In the short run, more workers may indeed enter the labour market in the false belief that a 5% increase in *money* wages is also a *real* wage increase. (As explained in Chapter 15, this false belief is an example of **money illusion**.) Similarly, firms may be willing to employ more labour if they also suffer money illusion, falsely believing that rising prices mean that sales revenues are rising faster than labour costs.

This means that, to sustain an increase in employment *above* the natural rate (and to reduce unemployment *below* the NRU), workers and employers must suffer money illusion in equal but opposite directions, thereby keeping expectations of inflation, formed in the previous time period, consistently below the actual rate to which inflation has risen. But as workers continuously adjust their expectations of future inflation to the rising actual rate and bargain for ever-higher money wages to restore the real wage to the level necessary to reduce unemployment below U_N,

the short-run Phillips curve shifts outward from $SRPC_1$ to $SRPC_2$ and so on. There is indeed a separate short-run Phillips curve for each expected rate of inflation. *Further out* short-run Phillips curves such as $SRPC_2$ and $SRPC_3$ are associated with higher expected rates of future inflation. Conversely, the short-run Phillips curve shifts inward when the expected rate of inflation falls.

Free-market economists argue that, in the long run, the only way to keep unemployment *below* the NRU is to permit the money supply to expand and finance an ever-accelerating inflation. *Actual* inflation always has to be above the *expected* rate for workers and firms to be willing respectively to supply and to demand more labour. But, as noted earlier, accelerating inflation will eventually create a hyperinflation, which, in the resulting breakdown of economic activity, is likely to increase the NRU. Any attempt to reduce unemployment below the NRU is therefore foolhardy and irresponsible. In the short run it accelerates inflation, while in the long run it perversely increases the NRU to an unnecessarily high level.

If the government realises it made a mistake when expanding the economy to point *B*, it can stabilise the rate of inflation at 5%. Workers and employers 'see through' their money illusion and realise that they have confused money quantities with real quantities. As soon as this happens, they refuse respectively to supply and to demand the labour necessary to keep unemployment below the NRU. The economy now moves to point *C*. Once point *C* is reached, any further expansion of aggregate demand moves the economy to point *D* and an inflation rate of $\dot{P}_2$ — and to a repeat of the process just described, but starting from a higher initial rate of inflation.

Rational expectations

The theory just described is based on the **theory of adaptive expectations**, in which workers and firms form expectations of what will happen in the *future* only on the basis of what is happening *currently* and upon what has happened in the *recent past*. However, new classical economists favour an alternative theory of how expectations are formed, called the **theory of rational expectations**. According to this theory, it is unrealistic to assume that workers and firms, acting rationally in their self-interest, form expectations of future inflation *solely* on the basis of current or recent inflation.

To understand the difference between the theories of adaptive and rational expectations, consider the situation of a gambler deciding whether to place a bet on a particular horse winning a race. Three races ago, the horse ended the race in fourth position, improving to third place two races ago, and to second place recently. Forming his expectations adaptively, the gambler decides to bet on the horse, expecting it now to win. But gambling on the basis of recent form alone could be less successful than a strategy that makes use of all the information available, including, of course, past form. Information about the quality of the jockey, and about other matters such as the qualities of the other horses and their jockeys, the length of the race, the state of the track, and perhaps 'inside information' provided by a stable lad, might lead to a more rational gambling decision.

This story does not mean that a gambler, forming expectations rationally, *always* wins his bets. He may win or lose, just as bets made on decisions formed adaptively, or by picking a name out of a hat, may be right or wrong. However, over a long sequence of races, it is likely that gambling decisions formed on the basis of rational expectations produce better outcomes than decisions formed adaptively or randomly. The more 'perfect' the information on which rational expectations are formed, the more likely it is that the expectations prove correct. It is less sensible to gamble on the basis of limited information when more up-to-date and relevant information is available.

Returning to the causes of inflation, new classical economists argue that it is unrealistic to assume that a rational economic agent, acting on self-interest, forms expectations of future inflation *solely* on the basis of past or experienced inflation. Self-interest requires quick modification of economic behaviour in line with expect-ations formed on the basis of the most up-to-date information available. This means that it is in people's interests not to suffer money illusion.

As a result, new classical economists reject the idea that economic agents suffer money illusion for quite long periods. If expectations are formed *rationall*y rather than *adaptively*, any attempt by a government to reduce unemployment below its natural rate fails, and leads solely to accelerating inflation. The correct way to reduce unemployment is to reduce the natural rate itself, rather than to increase demand to try to reduce unemployment *below* the NRU. To do this, the government should use appropriate free-market supply-side policies.

The incorporation of the theory of rational expectations into the explanation of the inflationary process represents the third stage in the development of monetarist and free-market theories of inflation. New classical economists continue to accept the Friedmanite concept of the natural rate of unemployment. But whereas Milton Friedman believed that, in the short run at least, governments can trade off along a short-run Phillips curve and reduce unemployment below the natural rate, the theory of rational expectations rejects this possibility.

In new classical thinking, it is in workers' and employers' interests to realise instantly any mistakes made when forming expectations, and to 'see through' any attempt by an 'irresponsible' government to reflate the economy beyond the full employment level. New classical economists believe that in this situation, attempts by government to expand demand to stimulate output and employment are anticipated fully by private economic agents. Workers and firms modify their behaviour to offset or neutralise the effects intended by the government, so the expansion of demand has no effect upon real activity and employment. In extreme new classical economics, this is the case in both the short run and the long run because output and employment are *always* assumed to be at their natural or equilibrium levels.

An important difference separating the adaptive and rational expectations versions of free-market economics is the length of time unemployment must remain above its natural rate as the cost or penalty of an attempt to reduce unemployment below the natural rate. In Friedmanite theory, the economy experiences a lengthy period of deflation, with unemployment above its natural rate, to 'bleed' the system of inflationary expectations built up during the period of fiscal or monetary expansion.

In contrast to this *gradualist* theory, new classical theory assumes that economic agents *immediately* reduce expectations of future inflation, providing they believe in the *credibility* of a tough free-market government's commitment to reducing inflation. Believing that the government means business in pursuing tight fiscal and monetary policies to control inflation, workers and firms immediately build a lower expected rate of inflation into their wage-bargaining and price-setting behaviour. Inflation falls quickly and painlessly, without the need for a lengthy period of unemployment above its natural level. In effect, a firmly free-market government reduces inflation by 'talking down' inflation. But if credibility in government policy were to disappear, its ability to control inflation would also be lost. People would now expect higher prices, and would alter behaviour accordingly. Expectations of higher prices would become self-fulfilling.

Free-market and New Keynesian theories of unemployment and inflation

NAIRU and NRU

Economists often treat the **non-accelerating inflation rate of unemployment** (NAIRU) and the **natural rate of unemployment** (NRU) as interchangeable terms. However, there is a difference between the two measures of the equilibrium rate of unemployment (although candidates are not penalised for treating the two as the same in examination answers).

Both the NRU and the NAIRU measure the economy's *sustainable* rate of unemployment. The NRU is a concept developed by free-market economists, who define the natural rate of unemployment in terms of voluntary frictional unemployment. Of course, there are other types of unemployment (such as real-wage unemployment and structural unemployment), but in the free-market view, these only occur when market imperfections prevent labour market equilibrium being achieved. For free-market economists, the labour market (and indeed any market) is a calm and orderly place in which the price mechanism quickly and efficiently eliminates disequilibrium and achieves a market-clearing outcome.

By contrast, the NAIRU derives from New Keynesian theory. Keynesians argue it is misleading to view labour markets in terms of one large aggregated and competitive market. Rather, the economy comprises a large number of labour markets of varying competitiveness, which are separated by barriers to entry. Keynesians stress the imperfect nature of these labour markets, characterised by monopsony and monopoly power, uncertainty and the lack of correct market information. In these labour markets, wages may be determined by collective bargaining.

Equilibrium in the market-clearing sense favoured by free-market economists is not a part of the Keynesian explanation of the functioning of labour markets. For New Keynesians, equilibrium in the economy's labour markets requires consistency between wages and prices for both employers and workers. This involves mutual accommodation on the part of employers and workers to each other's require-ments, within an economy in which the wage rates of a significant part of the employed labour force are determined by collective bargaining. For employers, the prices set for their products must give an adequate mark-up or profit margin over the wages they pay. For workers, wages received must be satisfactory, given the prices they must pay for goods.

In New Keynesian parlance, the NAIRU is the overall rate of unemployment at which mutual consistency is achieved between the aspirations of employers and workers in all the economy's labour markets, with the price level constant. At higher rates of unemployment, bargaining power favours employers, so mutual consistency of aspirations is not achieved. Wage rates are forced down, causing the rate of inflation to fall. The opposite occurs at rates of unemployment lower than the NAIRU: the balance of bargaining power favours workers, and wages (and hence the rate of inflation) are forced up. As the name 'non-accelerating inflation rate of unemployment' indicates, mutual consistency between the aspirations of employers and workers means that the balance of bargaining power between employers and workers ensures that the inflation rate is constant.

> **examiner's voice**
>
> At A2 but not at AS, candidates must under-stand the meaning of the natural rate of unemployment (NRU). However, it is not necessary to understand the difference between the NRU and the non-accelerating inflation rate of unemployment (NAIRU). The two terms can be treated interchangeably.

How large are the NRU and the NAIRU?

As we have noted, free-market economists assume that the economy functions as if it is perfectly competitive. By contrast, Keynesians assume that the economy is imperfectly competitive. This explains why the NAIRU (the equilibrium rate of unemployment in New Keynesian theory) is higher than the NRU (the equilibrium rate in the free-market theory). The NAIRU also exceeds the NRU for a second reason. The NRU comprises frictional unemployment only, but the NAIRU also includes structural unemployment.

There is general agreement that the long-run equilibrium rate of unemployment rose in the UK from the 1960s to the early 1980s, whether measured as the NRU or as the NAIRU. However, at any particular point in time, actual measured unem-ployment might be above the NRU or the NAIRU. In the depths of the last recession in 1992, registered unemployment in the UK was just over 3 million and above 10% of the labour force. Output began to recover from recession towards the end of 1992, followed by unemployment falling from early 1993 onwards. Since then, unemployment has fallen almost continuously to its present level of under 1 million (and under 4%) measured in the claimant count. Two questions arise: has unem-ployment fallen back to either the NRU or the NAIRU; and have the NRU and the NAIRU themselves fallen?

Richard Layard has estimated the NAIRU from within a model of imperfectly competitive labour markets, where firms are price-makers. His figure for the NAIRU during the years 1980–83 was 10.47%. Layard detected a slight upward trend until 1986, when the NAIRU was 11.7%. By contrast, using the market-clearing model, Patrick Minford estimated that the natural level of unemployment rose from 2.1 million to 3.7 million in 1981, before falling to 1.6 million by 1986.

Around 1997 free-market economists were divided about the size of the NRU. Professor Patrick Minford, who had been an adviser to the departing Conservative government, argued that the government's supply-side reforms of the 1980s and early 1990s had successfully created a competitive, flexible labour market. Supply-side policies had caused the natural rate of unemployment to fall to about 800,000, or around 3% of the labour force. Given that the continuing fall in unemployment since 1997 has not caused the UK economy to run into the 'wall of inflation', Minford's argument is persuasive.

Inflation psychology

It is now widely agreed, by Keynesians as well as by free-market economists, that a factor that, until quite recently, made inflation particularly difficult to control in the UK was the existence, built up over decades, of an **inflation psychology**. Over the years, many

> *e**xaminer's voice***
> Governments and central banks now realise that when people *expect* the rate of inflation to be low, they start to behave in a less inflationary way. If the authorities can establish the *credibility* of their anti-inflationary policies, their eventual success in controlling inflation stems in large part from *talking down* the rate of inflation.

groups in UK society, including house owners and wage earners in strong bargaining positions, did extremely well out of inflation. For example, house owners with large mortgages have a vested interest in allowing inflation to continue, in order to reduce the real value of their personal debt. Indeed, house owners do even better when house price inflation exceeds the general rate of inflation. In this situation, the real value of houses increases while the real value of mortgages falls.

In recent years, UK governments have managed to erode much of this inflation psychology, and most people now expect inflation (except house price inflation) to be relatively low. Because of this benign effect on people's behaviour, it has recently been much easier to control inflation. However, some economists believe that circumstances can quickly change for the worse again, and that inflation is dormant rather than dead.

The possible problem of price deflation

In the late 1990s and early 2000s, when the UK inflation rate fell toward 1%, some economists argued that inflation would soon be replaced with deflation (i.e. a continuously falling price level). As yet, this has not happened. Consumer durable prices have fallen (e.g. the prices of television sets and computers), but this has been more than matched by the price of services rising at a rate close to 10% in some instances. If price deflation does eventually occur, it will bring its own problems. As explained earlier, hoping for even lower prices, people may postpone 'big ticket' consumption decisions. This may erode business confidence and trigger recession. This happened

in Japan in the 1990s. However, at the time of writing in 2005, the rising prices of crude oil and of commodities such as steel, which have been partly caused by China's booming demand for energy and industrial raw materials, are making it much less likely that a general price deflation will occur.

Summary

In this chapter we have examined the two significant economic problems of unemployment and inflation. After describing possible causes and types of unemployment, including frictional, structural, real-wage and demand-deficient unemployment, the chapter explained various theories of inflation, themed in a historical perspective. From 1958 onwards, Keynesians used the Phillips curve to explain the policy conflict between reducing unemployment and controlling inflation. The Phillips curve illustrated an apparently stable statistical relationship between the two variables, but it was not, in itself, a theory of inflation. Nonetheless, the Phillips curve appeared to be consistent with both the demand-pull and the cost-push theories of inflation.

In later years, the debate between demand-pull and cost-push inflation was overtaken first by the growth of monetarism and then by theories of the role of expectations in the inflationary process. By introducing the idea of a 'natural' rate of unemployment, the monetarists have revived the old pre-Keynesian belief that the economy naturally tends towards equilibrium levels of output and employment.

Early monetarist inflation theory was based on the revival of the oldest theory of inflation, the quantity theory of money. The quantity theory explains inflation purely as a monetary phenomenon, unrelated to the 'real economy'. However, later developments in the monetarist theory of inflation centred on the role of expectations in the inflationary process. This involved two rather different theories of expectation formation — the theories of adaptive and rational expectations. Milton Friedman, who had revived the quantity theory of money in 1956, included adaptive expectations in his theory of the expectations-augmented Phillips curve. This theory was published in the late 1960s. In later years, the theory of rational expectations became more significant and forms an important part of new classical economics.

Much of the economic debate about unemployment and inflation is now conducted between new classical and New Keynesian economists. Both schools accept the idea, first introduced by Milton Friedman, of a vertical long-run Phillips curve. Both Friedmanite and new classical theories locate the long-run Phillips curve immediately above the economy's natural rate of unemployment or NRU. Friedmanite, but not new classical, theory accepts the idea of a downward-sloping *short-run* Phillips curve. Milton Friedman argued that expansionary policies are able to reduce unemployment below the NRU in the short run, but not in the long run. The new classical economists, who believe that the Phillips curve is vertical in the short run as well as in the long run, reject this possibility.

The NRU, which is derived from free-market theory, is defined in terms of the frictional unemployment existing when the economy's aggregate labour market is in equilibrium. By contrast, New Keynesian theory locates the long-run Phillips curve immediately above the non-accelerating inflation rate of unemployment (NAIRU), which includes structural as well as frictional unemployment. In both free-market and New Keynesian theory, the NRU and the NAIRU are the equilibrium unemployment levels at which inflation is stable.

Self-testing questions

1 Define full employment.

2 What is equilibrium unemployment?

3 Define frictional unemployment.

4 Relate frictional unemployment to search theory.

5 Explain the difference between frictional and structural unemployment.

6 Relate real-wage unemployment to 'sticky' wage rates.

7 Explain demand-deficient unemployment.

8 Why is it important to identify correctly the cause of unemployment?

9 Define inflation.

10 List four costs of inflation.

11 What is the quantity theory of money?

12 What are the similarities of, and the differences between, the quantity theory of money and the Keynesian demand-pull theory of inflation?

13 Explain the Phillips curve relationship.

14 Distinguish between short-run and long-run Phillips curves.

15 Distinguish between the theories of adaptive expectations and rational expectations.

16 What is the natural rate of unemployment (NRU)?

17 What may be the effect of reducing unemployment below its natural rate?

18 How may the natural rate of unemployment be reduced?

Part 6

Macroeconomic policy

part **6**

Chapter 17
Money, banking and monetary policy

Specification focus

This chapter provides introductory background coverage of money and the banking system in order to explain the nature of the monetary policy implemented in the UK. Monetary policy is an important part of both the AS Module 2 specification and the A2 Module 6 specification.

AS **Module 2 The National Economy**
  Main Instruments of Government Macroeconomic Policy

A2 **Module 6 Government Policy, the National and International Economy**
  Managing the National Economy

A2 **Synoptic coverage**
  The Unit 6 examination expects candidates to apply their knowledge of interest rates, first learnt at AS, to analysing the role of the Monetary Policy Committee of the Bank of England. A more detailed knowledge of monetary policy instruments is required in the Unit 6 examination.

Introduction

Besides being a mixed economy, the economy we live in is a monetary economy, in which most of the goods and services produced are traded or exchanged via the inter-mediary of money. This chapter starts by examining the nature and functions of money in a modern economy, before explaining how bank deposits, which are created by the private enterprise and commercial banking system, form the largest part of modern money. The second half of the chapter surveys the changes that have taken place in monetary policy in the UK, showing how the main features of current monetary policy developed out of the monetary policies implemented by UK governments and the Bank of England over the last 20–30 years.

What is money?

For most people, money is both so desirable and so central to everyday life that what actually constitutes money hardly merits a second thought. For people living in the UK, money comprises coins and Bank of England notes, and any funds on deposit in banks such as HSBC and Barclays. These days, some building society deposits are also regarded as money, although until quite recently this was not the case. But where do we draw the line on what is money? Is a credit card money? Or a foreign currency such as the American dollar or the Indian rupee, given the fact that we may not be able to spend or even always to exchange a foreign banknote or coin in the UK? Do we include financial assets such as National Savings securities which possess some, but not all, of the characteristics of money?

Consider also the social relationship that takes place whenever modern banknotes are spent on goods or services. Why, for example, are shopkeepers prepared to hand over to complete strangers, brand new valuable goods, in exchange for rather grubby and unhygienic pieces of paper with no apparent intrinsic value? The answer lies in a single word: *confidence*. In a modern economy, people are prepared to accept such tokens in settlement of a contract or debt because they are confident that these notes and coins will also be accepted when they, in turn, decide to spend them.

*e**xaminer's voice*

The AS and the A2 specifications for Modules 2 and 6 require that candidates know about the money supply. Detailed knowledge of the assets functioning as money is not required, but such knowledge makes it easier to understand monetary policy.

The functions of money

Economists cut through these issues by defining money in terms of the two principal functions that it performs in an economy. These are:

- **A medium of exchange.** The economy we live in is a monetary economy in which most of the goods and services produced are traded or exchanged via the intermediary of money, rather than through barter. Whenever money is used to pay for goods or services, or for the purpose of settling transactions and the payment of debts, it functions as a medium of exchange or means of payment.
- **A store of value (or store of wealth).** Instead of being spent, money may be stored as a **wealth asset** in preference to property or *financial* assets, such as stocks and shares. When stored rather than spent, money's purchasing power is transferred to the future, although inflation may erode money's future purchasing power.

Money also has two other functions besides its roles as a medium of exchange and a store of value. These functions are:

- **A unit of account.** Money is the unit in which the prices of goods are quoted and in which accounts are kept. The 'unit of account' function of money allows us to compare the relative values of goods even when we have no intention of actually spending money and buying goods — for example, when we 'window-shop'.

■ **A standard of deferred payment.** Money's function as a standard of deferred payment allows people to delay paying for goods or settling a debt, even though goods or services are being provided immediately. Money acts as a standard of deferred payment whenever firms sell goods on credit or draw up contracts specifying a monetary payment due at a later date.

The development of modern money

Barter

Before the development of money, exchange and trade took place in simple and primitive village economies, based on **barter** — the swapping of goods and services. However, barter is inefficient and impractical in a more complex economic system. Successful barter requires a **double coincidence of wants**, which means that a person wishing to trade a television set for a refrigerator must not only establish contact with someone with equal but opposite wants (that is, an individual possessing a refrigerator who wishes to exchange it for a television set); they must also agree that the television set and refrigerator are of equal value.

Barter is inefficient because the time and energy spent searching the market to establish the double coincidence of wants results in unnecessary search costs, shoe-leather costs and transaction costs. These, in turn, promote a much greater inefficiency: namely, preventing the development of specialisation, division of labour and large-scale production. All of these contribute to the productive efficiency and range of consumer choice available in modern and sophisticated monetary economies.

*e*xaminer's voice

A market economy *can* function without money, using barter as the means of exchange. However, all national economies are monetary economies, using money as the main medium of exchange.

Commodity money

Figure 17.1 shows the three main forms of money that have developed since money replaced barter.

The earliest form of money was **commodity money**. Commodities that functioned as money had an intrinsic value of their own — they yielded utility and consumer services to their owners. Beads, shells, sharks' teeth and other commodities could be used for decorative purposes while being stored as wealth, and some commodities used as money, such as cattle, could be slaughtered and eaten.

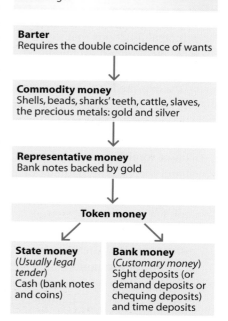

Barter
Requires the double coincidence of wants

↓

Commodity money
Shells, beads, sharks' teeth, cattle, slaves, the precious metals: gold and silver

↓

Representative money
Bank notes backed by gold

↓

Token money

↓   ↓

State money
(*Usually legal tender*)
Cash (bank notes and coins)

Bank money
(*Customary money*)
Sight deposits (or demand deposits or chequing deposits) and time deposits

Figure 17.1 Barter and the different forms of money

Representative money

As money evolved, gold and silver gradually replaced other forms of commodity money because they possessed, to a greater degree, the desirable characteristics necessary for a commodity to function as money: relative scarcity, uniformity, durability, portability and divisibility. All of these help to create confidence in money, which is necessary for its acceptability. Nevertheless, gold and silver are vulnerable to theft and are difficult to store safely. Eventually, wealthy individuals deposited the precious metals they owned with goldsmiths for safekeeping.

At the next stage, the goldsmiths developed into banks, and the receipts they issued in return for deposits of gold became the first banknotes or paper money. These notes were **representative money**, representing ownership of gold. Early banknotes were acceptable as a means of payment because they could be exchanged for gold on demand. They were issued by privately owned banks rather than by the state, although the state continued to issue gold and silver coinage. Although worthless in themselves, banknotes functioned as money because people were willing to accept them — as long as there was confidence that notes could be changed into gold, which does, of course, have an intrinsic value.

Token money

Modern money is almost all **token money** with no intrinsic value of its own. It takes two main forms: **cash** and **bank deposits**.

In the UK, the state, or rather its agent, the Bank of England, has a monopoly over the issue of cash (although, for a reason explained in the next section, Scottish and Northern Ireland banks also have a limited ability to issue banknotes). However, for reasons we shall also explain, cash is literally the 'small change' of the monetary system; bank deposits form by far the largest part of modern money.

Bank deposits are created by private enterprise commercial banks such as Lloyds TSB and the NatWest. This fact has a very important implication for monetary policy. For the Bank of England (the country's **central bank**) to control or influence the growth of the stock of money in the economy (the **money supply**), it has to control or influence the ability of the private enterprise banks to create bank deposits.

Banks and bank deposits

A bank is an institution that:
- accepts deposits from the general public that can be transferred by cheque
- creates deposits owned by the general public when it makes advances or bank loans (these can be either **overdrafts** or **term loans**)

Almost all banks in the UK are commercial companies. Most banks aim to make a profit for their owners; the Bank of England is an exception, since its aims are primarily to oversee the financial system and to implement the country's monetary policy. Commercial banks divide into **retail banks** such as the Halifax and the Bank

of Scotland, whose main business is with the general public, and **wholesale banks**, which deal with each other and with other financial institutions largely located in the City of London. Wholesale banks are often called **investment banks**, although until very recently they were generally known as merchant banks.

To understand how a bank operates, it is useful to divide the bank's customers into two different groups: those in credit and those in debit. Members of the former group deposit cash in the bank, while members of the latter group borrow from the bank. The bank makes a profit by charging borrowers a higher interest rate than it pays to attract deposits.

Before the middle of the nineteenth century, banks printed their own banknotes. Some of these were given to customers depositing gold in the

The Halifax has retail branches all over the country

banks, but the rest were lent to customers borrowing from the banks. By printing and lending notes in this way, the banks' note issue grew to exceed the gold deposits held by the banks. Prudent banking requires a bank to keep sufficient **reserve assets** (in this case, gold) to meet all likely calls by customers on the bank's liabilities. However, greedy or imprudent banks were often tempted, in pursuit of profit, to over-extend their note issue by printing and lending banknotes greatly in excess of the gold they owned. In these circumstances, the banks' holdings of gold might prove insufficient to meet the demand by customers to convert banknotes (the banks' liabilities) into gold. Imprudent over-extension of the note issue thus led to bank crashes, which occurred periodically when banks ran out of gold. The large number of bank crashes which occurred in the early nineteenth century led to the 1844 Bank Charter Act, which largely removed the right of British banks to issue their own notes.

However, the 1844 Bank Charter Act encouraged a new monetary development, namely the creation of **deposit money**, which is now the main form of modern money. Apart from Scottish and Northern Irish banks (which have to deposit an equivalent amount of gold at the Bank of England), banks can no longer print and issue their own notes. But banks get round this inconvenience simply by crediting a deposit to the account of a customer to whom a loan is given. Whenever loans are made, bank deposits are created. **Sight deposits** or **demand deposits** (which in the UK are known as **current account deposits**), upon which cheques can be drawn, are money because they are both a store of value and a medium of exchange. (Note that the *deposit*, and not the *cheque*, is money. The cheque is just an instruction to make a cash withdrawal or to shift ownership of a bank deposit from one person to another. However, the fact that cheques are **customarily acceptable** as a means of payment turns bank deposits into money.)

Cash became mere token money, rather than representative money, when the state withdrew the promise to convert its notes and coins into gold on demand: that is, when the currency came off the **gold standard**. Cash is also usually **legal tender** — 'fiat money' made legal by government decree — which must be accepted as a medium of exchange and in settlement of debts. Like cash, bank deposits created by the private enterprise banking system — or **bank money** — are token money, but they are also **customary money** rather than legal tender. This means that bank deposits are generally accepted because of people's confidence in the banks and in the monetary system. However, people can refuse to accept payment by cheque, demanding instead payment in legal tender. In the UK, the use of cheque guarantee cards adds to the acceptability of bank deposits as a medium of exchange, since banks guarantee in advance to honour a payment by cheque up to a certain value, usually between £100 and £500 per transaction.

Bank deposits make up by far the largest part of modern money, between about two-thirds and 90% depending on how money is defined. These days, cash or state money is just the 'small change' of the monetary system. But cash is the platform or **monetary base** upon which the private enterprise banking system creates bank money.

examiner's voice

Bank deposits are by far the largest part of modern money. Monetary policy tries to control or influence the total size of bank deposits and the willingness of the general public to spend these deposits.

Money, money substitutes and near money

As already explained, to function as money, an asset must be both a medium of exchange and a store of value or wealth. Bank demand deposits (sight deposits) are money because they possess both of these functions. Bank time deposits are not quite as liquid as demand deposits. Customers may have to wait several days to convert a time deposit into cash, and a chequing facility is not usually available. However, a bank may allow a time deposit to be converted into cash almost immediately, but with the loss of a few days interest.

To understand the nature of money, it is useful to compare money with **substitutes for money** and **near money**. These are all shown in Table 17.1. Credit cards (but *not* debit cards, which are similar to cheques) are substitutes for money. By contrast, a National Savings security is near money rather than a money substitute.

Table 17.1 Money, substitutes for money and near money

Money substitutes	Money	Near money
Medium of exchange, but not a store of value (e.g. credit cards and charge cards)	Medium of exchange and store of value (e.g. cash, bank and building society deposits)	Store or value, but insufficiently liquid to be a medium of exchange (e.g. National Savings certificates)

Over the last 30 years, credit cards, mostly operating in the Visa and MasterCard networks, have increasingly replaced cash and the use of cheques as a means of

payment. But although it is a medium of exchange, a credit card is not a store of wealth. Indeed, the use of a credit card builds up a personal liability in the form of a debt with the credit card company, which must eventually be settled with a cash or cheque transaction. Because a credit card transfers rather than settles a debt, it is a substitute for money rather than money itself.

Whereas a money substitute such as a credit card is a medium of exchange but *not* a store of value, the reverse is true for near money. A financial asset such as a National Savings security provides an example, being too illiquid to be a means of payment. In the past, building society deposits were near moneys rather than money. However, most building society deposits can now be converted into cash and withdrawn on demand and without penalty, and some building societies issue cheque books and allow cheques to be drawn on deposits. Thus, building society deposits have developed into money, since they have become a medium of exchange as well as a store of value.

*e**xaminer's voice***

The financial assets functioning as money often change. Over the years, financial assets previously functioning as *near money* took on the functions of money, particularly when monetary policy was trying to control the growth of the money supply.

The problem of defining the money supply

Before the advent of monetarism, few economists gave much attention to the precise definition of the money supply or stock of money in the economy. This reflected the Keynesian view that money did not matter in the macroeconomic management of the economy. But when monetarism replaced Keynesianism as the new prevailing orthodoxy in the 1970s, money did begin to matter — particularly in the years before monetarism itself drifted from favour around 1985. For a few years from the mid-1970s to the mid-1980s, during the 'monetarist era', control of the money supply became an important part of monetarist economic management in general and monetary policy in particular. During this period, monetarist economists devoted considerable attention to the problem of precisely which assets to include and exclude when defining the money supply.

A significant problem that faced the monetarists as they set about trying first to define and then to control the growth of the money supply stems from what has become known as **Goodhart's Law**. This is named after Charles Goodhart, formerly a professor at the London School of Economics and a Bank of England official. Goodhart argued that, as soon as a government tries to control the growth of a particular measure of the money supply, any previously stable relationship between the targeted measure of money and the economy breaks down. The more successful the Bank of England appears to be in controlling the rate of growth of the financial assets defined as the money supply, the more likely it is that other financial assets, regarded previously as near money outside the existing definition and system of control, will take on the function of a medium of exchange and become money.

In this way, attempting to control the money supply is rather like a man trying to catch his own shadow. As soon as he moves, his shadow also moves. Although what is defined as money may be controlled, this ends up as irrelevant. This is because other financial assets become money, rendering control of what was previously defined as money, cosmetic and ineffective.

Over the years, the Bank of England has used more than one definition of the money supply. These divide into measures of narrow money and broad money. **Narrow money**, which restricts the measure of money to cash and bank and building society sight deposits, reflects the medium of exchange function of money, namely money functioning as a means of payment. **Broad money** also measures time deposits, which are a store of value rather than a medium of exchange.

examiner's voice

The Bank of England uses a number of measures of the money supply, such as M0, M2 and M4. Knowledge of these will not be tested in AQA examinations, but it is useful to know that M0 measures cash or the *monetary base*, M2 is the main measure of 'narrow money', while M4 measures 'broad money'. These days, the Bank of England uses measures of the money supply as *indicators* of the tightness or looseness of monetary policy.

Why bank deposits are the most important form of money

Bank deposits rather than cash form the largest part of the stock of money, whichever way the money supply is measured (apart from M0, the monetary base). In contrast to cash, which is tangible and can be seen and touched, bank deposits are intangible. Customers only 'see' a bank deposit when reading the statement of a bank account, or when viewing the electronic display in a cash-dispensing machine.

Bank deposits are the main form of money because banks possess the ability to create new deposits, almost out of thin air, where none previously existed. As already noted, a bank makes a profit by charging borrowers a higher rate of interest for the loans granted to customers than the bank has to pay to attract deposits of cash. But when creating a new loan for a customer, a bank also creates a deposit owned by the customer. Bank loans simultaneously expand the total volume of bank deposits, which end up being much greater in total than the sum of cash deposited with the banks.

But there is a limit to the extent to which banks can create loans (or credit). This limit depends on two factors:

- the amount of cash deposited with the banks, which forms a 'platform' for the launch of bank loans
- the size of the money multiplier

The **money multiplier** measures the maximum expansion of bank deposits (**low-powered money**) which is possible following a given increase in cash (**high-powered money**) deposited in the banking system. Cash and bank deposits are respectively called 'high-powered' and 'low-powered' money because only the former has the power to launch the credit- and deposit-creating process. If the banking system decides to keep cash and other liquid assets equal to 20% of total bank deposits, the size of the money multiplier is 5. Total lending and bank deposits can expand to a

total of £50,000 for every £10,000 increase in the banking system's cash and liquid assets. The credit and deposit creation just described explains why bank deposits rather than cash form the largest part of modern money.

Banks holds cash and other reserve assets, even though they yield little or no profit, to maintain liquidity and confidence, and to meet any likely demand by customers for cash. To increase profit, a greedy or imprudent bank might be tempted to reduce cash and other liquid assets to a smaller ratio of total bank deposits. In this situation, the bank chooses to operate a larger money multiplier, say 20 rather than 5. But this means the bank runs the risk of illiquidity and a loss of confidence among customers about the bank's ability to meet its liabilities. A 'run' on the bank could then occur, leading to a 'crash'. But at the other extreme, keeping too much cash and liquid assets in relation to deposits means that the bank sacrifices potential profit. Prudent banking means ploughing a middle way between these two extremes. This means trading off profitability against liquidity. The trade-off limits the new deposits that banks can create when cash and reserve assets increase.

Portfolio balance decisions

On several occasions in this chapter, the terms **assets** and **liabilities** have been used. An asset is something which is owned, and which has a value, whereas a liability is something which is owed. Everyone, except the destitute, makes decisions on the form of asset in which to keep their wealth. In the first instance, people choose between holding physical assets, such as houses (which provide a good hedge against inflation), and holding financial assets.

When choosing the form of financial asset to hold, people make **portfolio balance decisions**. A portfolio balance decision is illustrated in Figure 17.2, which, besides making the distinction between physical and financial assets, arranges financial assets according to **liquidity** and **profitability**. Liquidity measures the ease with which an asset can be converted into cash, and the certainty of what it will be worth when converted. Providing it is acceptable and can be used as a means of payment, cash is the most liquid of all assets. For the most part, bank deposits are not quite as liquid as cash, but as we have seen, bank deposits are sufficiently liquid to be treated as money. The other financial assets shown in Figure 17.2 are examples of non-money financial assets. Shares and government bonds (gilt-edged securities, or gilts) are marketable (they can be sold second hand on the stock exchange), but they are less liquid than money. In contrast to money, which earns little or no interest, shares and gilts generally provide a profit for their owners.

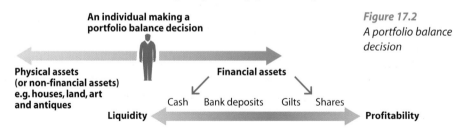

Figure 17.2
A portfolio balance decision

It is important to realise that pieces of paper and coins which function as financial assets are also financial liabilities. A share, which is an asset to the shareholder, is a liability for the company that initially sold the share. The company's profit is owned by the shareholders and the company is accountable to its shareholders for the way in which it spends and distributes the profit. Likewise, a bank deposit is simultaneously an asset and a liability. It is an asset for the customer owning the deposit, but a liability for the bank itself. The bank must honour cash withdrawals and cheques drawn on the deposit, which transfer ownership of part of the deposit to other people.

The Bank of England and monetary policy

As we have noted, most banks are commercial banks, whose main aim is to make a profit for their owners. Although it makes a considerable profit, the most significant exception is the Bank of England, which is the UK's central bank. For most of the period since its formation in 1694, the Bank of England was a private enterprise company. The Bank is now a nationalised industry, and its surplus profit goes to the state. The Bank of England's principal function (besides overseeing and trying to maintain confidence in the whole of the financial system) is to implement monetary policy on behalf of the UK government.

Monetary policy is the part of economic policy that attempts to achieve the government's macroeconomic objectives using **monetary instruments**, such as controls over bank lending and the rate of interest. Before 1997, monetary policy was implemented more or less jointly by central government and the Bank of England, which were known as the 'monetary authorities'. But the Treasury abandoned its hands-on role in implementing monetary policy in 1997 when making the Bank of England operationally independent. Unless it is leaned on by the Treasury, there is now only one monetary authority: the Bank of England.

examiner's voice

Examination questions expect candidates to know that the Bank of England, which is the UK's central bank, implements monetary policy to try to meet targets set by the government, and that the Treasury, which is the government's finance ministry, implements fiscal policy.

Objectives and instruments of monetary policy

To understand monetary policy, it is useful to distinguish between policy *objectives* and policy *instruments*. A **policy objective** is the target or goal that the Bank of England aims to hit. By contrast, a **policy instrument** is the tool or technique of control used to try to achieve the objective.

Monetary policy objectives and instruments can be classified in different ways. Policy objectives can be divided into *ultimate* and *intermediate* objectives. Policy instruments separate into those that affect the supply of new deposits that the commercial banks can create and those that affect the demand for loans or credit.

examiner's voice

As noted, the money supply is one of the indicators the Bank of England uses when implementing monetary policy. These days, the inflation rate target set by the government is the main policy objective, while the Bank's lending rate is the principal policy instrument.

Monetary policy objectives

For over 25 years, *control of inflation* has been the main objective of UK monetary policy. The government needs to control inflation in order to create conditions in which the ultimate policy objective of *improved economic welfare* can be attained. However, before 1992, the Bank of England tried to control inflation by first meeting an intermediate monetary policy objective. There have been two intermediate monetary policy objectives. First, from the mid-1970s until 1985, under the influence of monetarist economic theory, the *money supply* was the intermediate target of monetary policy. Second, from 1985 until 1992, the *exchange rate* replaced the money supply as the intermediate policy objective. Intermediate policy objectives were finally abandoned in 1992 when the pound was forced out of the exchange rate mechanism (ERM) of the European monetary system (EMS). Since 1992, monetary policy has targeted the control of inflation directly, without the use of any intermediate policy objectives.

Monetarism and monetary policy

Monetarists believe that inflation is caused by a prior increase in the quantity of money in the economy. The key theory in monetarism is the **quantity theory of money**. The quantity theory, which is explained in Chapter 16, predicts that if the quantity of money increases and people end up holding money balances larger than those they wish to hold, the excess money holdings will be spent. This creates excess demand for real goods and services in the economy, which in turn pulls up the price level in a **demand-pull inflation**.

From the late 1970s until the mid-1980s, monetarist monetary policy was based on announcing, first, a target rate of growth of the money supply, and second, that policy would then be implemented to achieve the announced target. Suppose, for example, growth of real GDP is 2% and that the government aims for a maximum inflation rate of 3%. Under these conditions, the target rate of growth of the money supply should be set at a maximum rate of 5%, to enable goods and services to be purchased at prices up to 3% higher than last year's prices.

The 'monetarist' period in UK monetary policy ended in 1985 when Mrs Thatcher's Conservative government abandoned setting formal money supply targets. There were two main reasons for the 'death of monetarism', both suggested by Goodhart's Law. First, the growth of the money supply proved difficult if not impossible to control. Second, the relationship between the growth of the money supply and the rate of inflation, which had seemed stable *before* monetarist policies were implemented, broke down *after* the attempt was made to control the growth of the money supply.

The exchange rate and monetary policy

From 1985 to 1992, the exchange rate replaced the money supply as the intermediate target or monetary policy objective. Monetary policy was implemented, first to achieve a high exchange rate, and then to maintain the exchange rate at a high level. The monetary authorities believed that a high exchange rate, which they would not allow to float downward, creates a source of external discipline against inflationary pressure in the UK economy. A high exchange rate reduces inflation in three ways:

- Most directly, the high exchange rate reduces the prices of imported food and consumer goods.
- The cost of imported oil and raw materials falls, which dampens cost-push inflationary pressure.
- Less directly, a high exchange rate may reduce inflation through its effect on trade unions' and employers' behaviour. When the exchange rate is free to float downward, workers and firms know that inflationary pay deals and price rises won't lead to punishment through job losses and loss of profit. Instead, the exchange rate simply floats downward to restore competitiveness for the country's goods with imports. In effect, the exchange rate takes the strain. But with a high (and relatively fixed) exchange rate, workers and firms fear that cost-push inflationary pressure will indeed be disciplined by job losses and bankruptcy. This fear stiffens the resolve of unions and employers to behave in a less inflationary way.

> **examiner's voice**
>
> The A2 Module 6 specification requires candidates to know how monetary policy affects aggregate demand via its effect on the exchange rate. It is also important to know at A2 how a fixed exchange rate constrains the Bank of England's ability to use monetary policy to influence the domestic economy. This knowledge is not required at AS. The Module 2 specification states simply that candidates must understand how the Bank of England uses interest rates to influence the economy.

Monetary policy instruments

As mentioned earlier, policy instruments are the tools used to achieve policy objectives. There are two categories of monetary policy instrument: those that affect the retail banks' ability to *supply* credit and to create bank deposits; and those that affect the general public's *demand* for bank loans.

Controlling the supply of credit

In the Keynesian era, the Bank of England limited the ability of commercial banks to *supply* more credit and bank deposits in two main ways. The first method was to impose **required reserve ratios** on the banks, which then had to reduce total lending and bank deposits when the Bank of England reduced the supply of reserve assets available for the banks to hold.

With the second method, the Bank of England imposed **direct controls on bank lending**. Two types were used: **quantitative** and **qualitative controls**. Quantitative controls impose maximum limits or ceilings on the amount that banks can lend, or on the rate at which banks can expand total deposits. By contrast, qualitative controls are 'directional' controls that instruct or persuade banks to lend only to certain types of customer. For example, business customers requiring credit to finance investment or exports might be given a high priority, with consumer credit being relegated to a much lower position in the queue for advances.

In the 1980s, the Bank of England abandoned these policies. Two main factors explain why. First, Mrs Thatcher's Conservative government believed that free markets are far more effective than interventionist policies in achieving efficient and competitive resource allocation. Second, abolition of foreign exchange controls in 1979 meant that UK-based banks, which were subject to restrictive controls, could no longer compete profitably for banking business with overseas competitors. The controls meant that UK banks competed internationally on an un-level playing field. Because the controls encouraged banking business to move offshore, the government decided to abolish them to attract the business back to the UK.

Using interest rates to influence the demand for credit

Whereas the direct controls on bank lending described above ration the supply of credit available, modern monetary policy operates almost solely through interest rate policy. To influence the quantity of bank deposits being created (and also the level of aggregate demand in the economy), the Bank of England rations demand for credit by raising or lowering its official rate of interest.

(**Technical note:** the Bank of England's official interest rate or lending rate is also called the **repo rate**. When implementing monetary policy, the Bank of England deliberately keeps the commercial banks short of cash. However, the Bank is always ready to supply the cash needed by commercial banks — at a price the Bank of England chooses. This price is set by the Bank of England's lending rate, or repo rate. The word 'repo' is short for sale and repurchase agreement. The Bank of England supplies cash to commercial banks by purchasing some of the banks' reserve assets, such as bills and gilt-edged securities. In return, the commercial banks agree to repurchase the bills and gilts about two weeks later, but at a higher price. The repo rate determines the difference between the two prices. The higher the repo rate, the more expensive it is for the commercial banks to obtain cash from the Bank of England.)

An increase in the Bank of England's lending rate or repo rate means that commercial banks have to raise the interest rates they charge to their own customers. Bank loans immediately become more expensive. This in turn causes households and firms to reduce their demand for credit, and to repay existing loans wherever possible. This reduces total bank deposits, and hence the money supply in the economy.

> ### examiner's voice
>
> The AS Module 2 and A2 Module 6 specifications require candidates to understand that the Bank of England's interest rate or lending rate is the main monetary policy instrument. Technical knowledge of the Bank's lending rate, such as the repo rate, is not required, but at A2 candidates should understand how the demand for and supply of funds in different financial markets affect interest rates. Detailed knowledge of financial markets is not required.

Current and recent monetary policy in the UK

The monetary policy currently implemented in the UK developed out of monetarism, and still shares some features of the monetarism practised in the early 1980s. Then, the monetarists had abandoned direct controls on bank lending in

favour of a free-market approach to money. This is still the approach of modern monetary policy.

But modern monetary policy differs from monetarism in quite significant ways, even though control of inflation remains the policy objective. The monetarists attempted to control bank lending, primarily by controlling the *supply* of cash and reserve assets possessed by the commercial banks. The monetarists believed that, via the money multiplier, banks would have to reduce the credit and deposits they could create, if their cash and reserve assets holdings were squeezed. But interest rates, rather than the control of the banks' cash and liquid asset ratios, are now the principal instrument of monetary policy, and changes in interest rates affect the *demand* for bank loans or credit rather than the supply of bank deposits.

Since 1992, UK monetary policy has been directed explicitly at a published inflation rate target. This has been called 'pre-emptive' monetary policy because the authorities have announced that they are prepared to raise interest rates even when there is no immediate sign of accelerating inflation, to anticipate and pre-empt a rise in the inflation rate that would otherwise occur many months ahead. The policy-makers at the Bank of England estimate what the inflation rate is likely to be 18 months to 2 years ahead (the medium term), if policy (that is, interest rates) remain unchanged. If the forecast rate of inflation is different from the target rate set by the government, the Bank will change interest rates to prevent the forecast inflation rate becoming a reality at some point in the future. The Bank will also raise or lower interest rates to pre-empt or head off any likely adverse effects upon the inflation rate of an 'outside shock' hitting the economy.

The 'Ken and Eddie show'

We shall now look at modern monetary policy before and after 1997, when the incoming New Labour government made the Bank of England operationally independent. Between 1992 and 1997, monetary policy was nicknamed the 'Ken and Eddie show', after the chancellor of the exchequer (Kenneth Clarke) and the governor of the Bank of England (Eddie George).

Before May 1997, pre-emptive monetary policy was implemented more or less jointly by the Treasury and the Bank of England. The 'Ken and Eddie show' had a deflationary bias in the sense that the policy was asymmetrical. The further actual inflation fell below the target rate of 2.5%, the more successful the policy was judged to be, even if output and employment in the real economy were suffering. However, this deflationary bias was offset to some extent by an inflationary bias brought about by the fact that the chancellor, a politician, might persuade the governor, an official, to reduce interest rates in order to expand the economy, especially before a general election.

Monetary policy since 1997

After 1997, the general nature of pre-emptive monetary policy first established in 1992 was retained, including the inflation rate target set by the government. However, important changes were introduced by the incoming New Labour

government. The most significant of the changes were the granting of operational independence to the Bank of England, and the creation of the Monetary Policy Committee (MPC) within the Bank to implement monetary policy. Other features of the Monetary Policy Framework introduced in 1997 were as follows:

- *Transparency* and *accountability* became central to the framework.
- The roles of those concerned and what they are responsible for were made clear. The role of the Bank of England's Monetary Policy Committee is to set interest rates and to meet the government's published inflation rate target. In discharging this responsibility, the MPC is subject to parliamentary scrutiny.
- The inflation rate target was made *symmetrical*. This means that the Bank of England must stimulate aggregate demand, which will generally *raise* the rate of inflation, whenever actual inflation is *below* the target rate, just as the Bank must try to *reduce* the rate of inflation whenever actual inflation is *above* the target rate.
- The MPC was made accountable for any deviations from the target rate of inflation, which applies at all times. If inflation is more than 1 percentage point higher or lower than the target, the 'open letter' system requires the governor of the Bank of England to write to the chancellor, explaining why the divergence has occurred. Any such letter must be published to facilitate public scrutiny.

Monetary policy is decided by the Bank of England

Especially significant is the fact that the inflation rate target is now symmetrical. As explained earlier, under the 'Ken and Eddie show', monetary policy centred on getting the inflation rate on or below the target 2.5% RPI rate. This meant that the policy had an in-built deflationary bias. After 1997, this was no longer the case. In the early 2000s, after the terrorist outbreak in the USA, a collapse of confidence meant that the UK economy was threatened with recession, but it did not occur. The MPC was prepared to reduce interest rates to stimulate output and employment because it believed that, on unchanged policies, an inflation rate below 2.5% would be accompanied by an undesirable fall in output and employment. The government stated that although the primary objective of monetary policy is price stability, the Bank of England must also support the government's economic policy objectives, including those for growth and employment.

Some commentators believe that modern monetary policy represents a return, for good or for bad, to a policy of Keynesian discretionary demand management, albeit undertaken by an independent Bank of England that is unlikely, unless leaned on by the government, to engineer an inflationary pre-election boom. But there are two reasons for believing that this has not really been the case, although monetary

policy does now involve a degree of discretion in the pursuit of a pre-stated policy rule of achieving the inflation rate target. The two reasons are:

- The Fiscal Policy Framework that accompanies the Monetary Policy Framework (and which is described in Chapter 18) is definitely non-discretionary.
- The New Keynesian economists who influence the New Labour government accept the free-market economic argument that the long-run aggregate supply curve of output is vertical. This limits the role of demand expansion, using either monetary policy or fiscal policy, for increasing levels of output and employment.

However, the **'one-club golfer'** argument has been used to criticise the operation of UK macroeconomic policy, with its emphasis on the role of monetary policy. This argument was first used by the Conservative ex-prime minister Edward Heath to criticise the economic policies of the next Conservative prime minister, Margaret Thatcher. Heath argued that, just as a golfer, however great his talents, cannot hope to win a major championship playing all his shots with a single golf club, so the chancellor can't hope to manage the economy successfully with just a single policy instrument, namely interest rates.

According to its critics, by relying too much on monetary policy and interest rates, the New Labour government has behaved just like a 'one-club golfer'. They believe the chancellor should be prepared to use fiscal policy in a more active way to manage demand. But as Chapter 18 explains, the UK government does not currently wish to use fiscal policy for this purpose. These days, fiscal policy is used primarily to create supply-side conditions in which the economy can grow. Only monetary policy is used actively to manage aggregate demand.

> **examiner's voice**
>
> The AS Module 2 specification does not require detailed knowledge of the current institutional framework through which monetary policy is implemented. However, a broad knowledge of the Bank of England's role is required. By contrast, the A2 Module 6 specification requires candidates to understand the role of the Monetary Policy Committee of the Bank of England.

The transmission mechanism of monetary policy

The Bank of England believes that monetary policy affects aggregate demand and inflation through a number of channels, which form the **transmission mechanism of monetary policy**. The flow chart in Figure 17.3 shows the routes through which changes in the Bank's official interest rate (the instrument of monetary policy), shown at point **1** in the diagram, eventually affect inflation (the objective of monetary policy), shown at point **11**.

Official interest rate decisions (point **1** in Figure 17.3) affect **market interest rates** (point **2**), such as mortgage rates and bank deposit rates set by commercial banks and financial institutions. At the same time, policy actions and announcements affect **expectations** about the future course of the economy and the **confidence** with which these expectations are held (point **4**). They also affect **asset prices** (point **3**) and the **exchange rate** (point **5**).

These changes in turn affect **aggregate demand** in the economy (point **8**). This comprises **domestically generated demand** (point **6**) and **net external demand** (point **7**), which is determined by export and import demand. Domestic demand results from the spending, saving and investment behaviour of individuals and firms within the economy. Lower market interest rates increase domestic demand by encouraging consumption rather than saving by households, and investment spending by firms. Conversely, higher market interest rates depress domestic spending. When the official interest rate falls, asset prices rise and people feel wealthier and generally more confident about the future. As a result, consumption increases. A lower official interest rate causes financial capital to flow out of the pound and into other currencies, which in turn causes the exchange rate to fall. A falling exchange rate reduces UK export prices, while raising the price of imports. Demand for UK-produced goods increases.

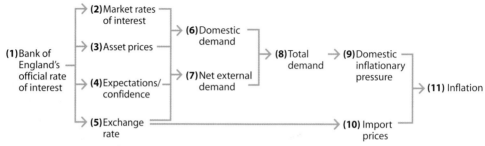

Figure 17.3 The transmission mechanism of monetary policy

Changes in aggregate demand (relative to the economy's ability to supply output) affect **domestic inflationary pressures** in the economy (point **9**). Changes in aggregate demand affect demand-pull inflationary pressures. However, there are also cost-push pressures from the effects of changes in aggregate demand on domestic wage rates. Changes in **import prices** (point **10**), brought about by changes in the exchange rate, affect inflation in two ways. Changes in the prices of imported food and consumer goods affect inflation directly, while changes in the prices of imported raw materials affect cost-push inflationary pressures.

The Bank of England estimates a time lag of up to 2 years between an initial change in the Bank's official rate of interest (point **1**) and the resulting change in the rate of inflation (point **11**). Output is affected within 1 year, but the fullest effect on inflation occurs after a lag of 2 years. In terms of the size of the effect, the Bank believes a 1% change in its official interest rate affects output by about 0.2–0.35% after about a year, and inflation by around 0.2–0.4% per year after 2 years.

Neutral, expansionary and contractionary monetary policy

A **neutral monetary policy** is one in which interest rates neither boost nor hold back aggregate demand. Neutral monetary policy is broadly consistent with the economy growing at its sustainable trend rate over the medium term: that is, without positive or negative output gaps. A negative output gap occurs when output is below the level that would have been achieved had the economy grown continuously at its trend rate. A positive output gap, which occurs in the boom phase of the business cycle, is the opposite. Actual output is above the trend rate of growth level. Growth must either fall back or become negative to restore sustainability.

The pre-emptive nature of monetary policy, and the fact that the Bank of England does not wish to influence financial markets and credibility adversely, mean that the Bank is unwilling to state the official rate of interest that it deems to be neutral. However, a member of the MPC has stated that, in his view, monetary policy is expansionary when the official interest rate is 4% and that the neutral interest rate 'is in the range of 5% to 5.5%, although it could be a bit lower'. Thus, according to this view, monetary policy is contractionary when the Bank's lending rate is above 5.5%.

examiner's voice

It is important to understand, particularly at A2, that UK monetary policy is *pre-emptive*. To understand this, think of the MPC looking into its crystal ball to forecast the inflation rate in 18 months' time, assuming that over the 18-month period, the Bank's interest rate remains unchanged. If the crystal ball shows inflation rising above the government-set target, the MPC raises interest rates, arguing that a bit of nasty medicine *now* is preferable to a much bigger dose in the future, to stop inflation rising out of control.

Summary

The chapter started by examining the nature of money, before explaining how, through the credit- and deposit-creating process, banks create the larger part of modern money, namely bank deposits. The rest of the chapter explained how monetary policy in the UK has changed over the last 30 or so years, and how it is implemented today.

We defined monetary policy as the part of the government's overall economic policy that attempts to achieve the government's objectives using monetary instruments. A range of techniques of control are available to the Bank of England, which divide into the instruments which try to control the supply of money and those that affect the general public's demand for money. Recent and current monetary policy has relied almost exclusively on the latter, attempting to influence the demand for money, and thence aggregate demand for output. This is done by raising or lowering the Bank of England's official rate of interest (which is also known as the Bank's lending rate and repo rate).

Since 1992, UK monetary policy has been based on a pre-emptive strategy of targeting the inflation rate directly, without the use of intermediate policy objectives such as the money supply or the exchange rate. An operationally independent Bank of England now implements monetary policy, aiming to meet an inflation rate target (currently 2.0% measured by the CPI) set by the government. According to the Bank of England, changes in the repo rate affect inflation by operating through a fairly complicated transmission mechanism. The process, which comprises several channels, involves a time lag of about 2 years, extending from an initial change in the repo rate to the eventual resulting change in the rate of inflation.

Since 1997, monetary policy has taken account of levels of output and employment in the real economy as well as the rate of inflation, and has been made symmetrical. The Bank must now cut interest rates to expand the economy if a negative output gap is anticipated, as well as raising interest rates above the neutral level when a positive output gap is expected.

Self-testing questions

1 List the four functions of money.

2 What is token money?

3 Distinguish between money, near money and money substitutes.

4 What is Goodhart's Law?

5 What is the money multiplier?

6 Define monetary policy.

7 Distinguish between an intermediate and the ultimate objective of monetary policy.

8 Why are direct controls no longer imposed by the Bank of England on commercial banks?

9 How do changes in the Bank of England's official interest rate affect bank lending and the economy?

10 What is meant by pre-emptive monetary policy?

11 Explain the 'one-club golfer' criticism of UK macroeconomic and monetary policy.

12 What is meant by neutral monetary policy?

part **6**

Chapter 18
Taxation, government spending and fiscal policy

Specification focus

This chapter covers the topics of taxation and public expenditure, which are part of the Module 6 specification, together with fiscal policy, which is part of both the Module 2 specification at AS and the Module 6 specification at A2.

AS Module 2 The National Economy
   Main Instruments of Government Macroeconomic Policy

A2 Module 5 Business Economics and the Distribution of Income
   Government Intervention in the Market

   Module 6 Government Policy, the National and International Economy
   Managing the National Economy

A2 Synoptic coverage
   Knowledge of particular forms of taxation and public expenditure is required for A2, developing the AS requirement that candidates understand that government expenditure and taxation affect the pattern of economic activity. The Module 6 specification also builds on the Module 2 introduction to fiscal policy. Module 5 coverage of poverty and the distribution of income draws on Module 6 coverage of taxation, public expenditure and fiscal policy.

Introduction

The subject of this chapter is public finance. In the UK, central government, local government and government agencies usually spend over 40% of national income, although at times the proportion falls below 40%. Most public sector spending is financed by taxation. The chapter first examines the main types of taxes and forms of public spending, and then explains the differences between Keynesian (or demand-side) and free-market (or supply-side) fiscal policy. During the Keynesian era, fiscal policy was used primarily to manage the level of aggregate demand in the economy. The government's budgetary position was crucial for this. When revenue equals expenditure, the government balances its budget, but at other times a budget deficit or a budget surplus occurs. Keynesian fiscal policy centred on the use of deficit financing to inject demand into the economy. Budget deficits also mean that the government has a positive borrowing requirement. The government has to borrow to finance expenditure which is not covered by revenue. The chapter explains how a borrowing requirement affects monetary policy.

With the exception of the use of automatic stabilisers, fiscal policy is no longer generally used to manage aggregate demand. These days, fiscal policy is an important part of the supply-side economic policy used to improve personal incentives to save, invest, supply labour and be entrepreneurial. The chapter concludes by examining the current fiscal policy framework, and by explaining how fiscal policy affects the distribution of income and the problem of poverty.

Taxation and other sources of government revenue

Taxation is the principal source of government revenue for most economies. In the financial year 2005/06, central and local government in the UK expected to collect total taxation receipts of £404 billion, out of total government revenue of £487 billion. There are sources of government revenue other than taxation, resulting, for example, from rents payable to the government, and the sale of government services and assets (that is, privatisation proceeds). Although, in strict legal terms, national insurance contributions (NICs) are *not a tax*, from an economic point of view they function as a tax. NICs, which were expected to raise £83 billion in 2005/06, are a compulsory levy on employers, employees and the self-employed to pay for unemployment and other welfare benefits or social security provided by the state.

> **e**xaminer's voice
> The A2 Module 6 specification requires candidates to evaluate the relative merits of different taxes. Knowledge of particular taxes is not required at AS, but candidates must know how different indirect taxes affect supply curves. The Module 2 specification also requires understanding of the fact that government expenditure and taxation can affect the pattern of economic activity.

Methods of classifying taxes

A **tax**, which is a compulsory levy charged by government or by a public authority to pay for its expenditure, can be classified in a number of ways.

Who levies the tax?

In the UK about 89% of total taxation is levied by central government, with local government taxation — currently the council tax and business rates — accounting for the remaining 11% of taxation levied by government.

What is taxed?

Figure 18.1 illustrates the relative importance in the UK in 2005/06 of the main categories of taxation as a proportion of all sources of government revenue. Taxes on *income* were expected to raise 37.4% of total revenue, with this figure rising to 54.4% if national insurance contributions are included. There are two main income taxes in the UK, personal **income tax** and **corporation tax**, which is a tax on company income or profit. Taxes on *expenditure* were expected to raise a further 24% of government revenue, but *capital* taxes (**inheritance tax** and **capital gains tax**) are insignificant, raising less than 1% of revenue in the UK.

Expenditure taxes, or taxes on spending, divide into ad valorem or percentage taxes such as **value added tax** (VAT), and specific taxes or unit taxes, which include the

excise duties levied on alcohol, tobacco and motor vehicle fuels such as petrol. In 2005/06, the government expected to collect 15.6% of its total revenue from VAT, and 8.4% of revenue from excise duties. Some taxes, such as motor vehicle tax and the television licence fee, are user taxes because the person driving the car or watching the television set has legal responsibility for making sure the tax has been paid.

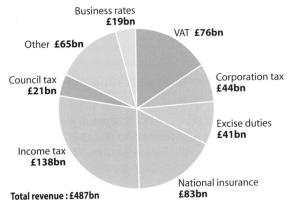

Business rates **£19bn**

VAT **£76bn**

Other **£65bn**

Council tax **£21bn**

Corporation tax **£44bn**

Excise duties **£41bn**

Income tax **£138bn**

National insurance **£83bn**

Total revenue : **£487bn**

Figure 18.1 Expected UK general government revenues by source, 2005/06

Source: Budget statement, March 2005.

Note: Other revenues include capital taxes, stamp duties, vehicle excise taxes and some other tax and non-tax revenues, for example interest and dividends.

In 1990 the local rate, which was a tax on property classified as an expenditure tax, was replaced by a community charge or poll tax, although the local rate was kept in Northern Ireland and a business rate continued to be levied on commercial property. Centuries earlier, in the Middle Ages, the introduction of a poll tax had caused social unrest and a peasants' revolt which led to its hasty withdrawal. Much the same occurred in the UK in the early 1990s. In 1993, the **council tax**, which is a property tax not too dissimilar to the old local rate, replaced the poll tax. However, because the amount paid in council tax to local authorities has risen at a faster rate than taxation in general, the council tax is nearly as unpopular as the poll tax. The unpopularity results from the fact that successive governments have reduced the transfer of central government funds to finance local authorities, while at the same time requiring the authorities to provide a greater number of local services.

PAUL BIGLAND/PHOTOFUSION

***e**xaminer's voice*

At both AS and A2, it is useful to know the difference between income tax and expenditure taxes. At A2, Unit 5 exam questions require understanding of how taxes and benefits can be used to reduce poverty.

Fuel lobby demonstration, Hyde Park, 2000

Direct or indirect?

The concepts of direct and indirect taxes are often used interchangeably with taxes on income and expenditure, although it is not strictly true that a tax on spending *must* be an indirect tax. Income tax is a direct tax because the person who receives and benefits from the income is liable to pay the tax. By contrast, *most* taxes on spending are indirect taxes, since the seller of the good, and not the purchaser who benefits from its consumption, is liable to pay the tax. Nevertheless, the purchaser *indirectly* pays some or all of the tax when the seller passes on the **incidence of the tax** through a price rise.

Progressive, proportionate and regressive taxation

In a **progressive tax system**, the proportion of a person's income paid in tax *increases* as income rises, while in a **regressive tax system**, the proportion paid in tax *falls* as income increases. A tax is **proportionate** (a **flat tax**) if exactly the same proportion of income is paid in tax at all levels of income. Progressivity can be defined for a single tax or for the tax system as a whole.

The word 'progressive' is value-neutral, implying nothing about how the revenue raised by the government is spent. Nevertheless, progressive taxation has been used by governments, particularly during the Keynesian era, to achieve the social aim of a 'fairer' distribution of income. But progressive taxation cannot by itself redistribute income — a policy of transfers in the government's public expenditure programme is required for this. Progressive taxation used on its own merely reduces post-tax income differentials compared to pre-tax differentials.

> **e*xaminer's voice**
>
> It is important at A2, and to a lesser extent at AS, to understand the difference between progressive and regressive taxation. Progressive and regressive taxes affect supply-side incentives, the distribution of income, poverty and automatic stabilisers.

Average and marginal rates of income tax

For single taxes such as income tax or inheritance tax, we can identify whether the tax is progressive, regressive or proportionate by examining the relationship between the average rate at which the tax is levied and the marginal rate. For income tax to be progressive, the marginal rate at which the tax is levied must be higher than the average rate, although the average rate, which measures the proportion of income paid in tax, rises as income increases. Conversely, with a regressive income tax, the marginal rate of tax is less than the average rate, while the two are equal in the case of a proportionate tax.

For income tax, the average tax rate is calculated as total tax paid divided by total income. By contrast, the marginal tax rate is calculated as the *change* in total tax paid divided by the *change* in total income.

$$\text{average tax rate} = \frac{\text{total tax paid}}{\text{total income}}$$

$$\text{marginal tax rate} = \frac{\text{change in total tax paid}}{\text{change in total income}}$$

As a general rule, the *average* tax rate indicates the overall burden of the tax upon the taxpayer, but the *marginal* rate may significantly affect economic choice and decision making. In the case of an income tax, it influences the choice between work and leisure when deciding how much labour to supply. The marginal rate of income tax also influences decisions on whether to spend income on consumption or to save.

*e*xaminer's voice

Make sure you revise the relationship between the average and the marginal values of an economic variable. This is explained in Chapter 4. Average and marginal tax rates provide an example of this relationship.

Is the UK tax system progressive?

It is often assumed that the UK tax system is highly progressive, being used by governments to reduce inequalities in income and wealth. In fact, apart from capital gains tax and inheritance tax, which is quite easily avoidable, wealth (and capital) is not taxed in the UK. This means that inequalities in the distribution of *wealth* have not really been reduced by the tax system.

UK income taxes are progressive, but not nearly as progressive as people sometimes think. As Table 18.1 shows, personal income tax is only slightly progressive for most income groups, becoming rather more progressive for the richest fifth of households. The progressivity of income tax was significantly reduced by the abolition of all the higher marginal rates of income tax in 1988, with the exception of the 40% rate, which is now the highest marginal tax rate in the UK.

Table 18.1 *Selected taxes in the UK: percentage of gross household income paid in taxation, 2001/02*

	Bottom	Quintile groups 2nd	3rd	4th	Top	All households
Income tax	3.2	6.3	10.3	13.5	18.3	13.7
National insurance contributions paid by workers	1.2	2.4	4.0	4.8	3.8	3.8
Council tax (and local tax in Northern Ireland)	7.1	4.8	3.7	2.9	1.8	3.0
Value added tax	11.3	7.5	7.0	6.2	4.6	6.1
Duty on alcohol	1.6	1.0	1.0	0.9	0.6	0.8
Duty on tobacco	3.1	1.8	1.5	0.9	0.3	1.0
Duty on oil and vehicle excise duty	3.3	2.4	2.4	2.1	1.3	1.9
Source: Office for National Statistics, 2003.						

Table 18.1 also shows that national insurance contributions reduce the progressivity of the direct tax system for the top 20% of households. NICs are *regressive* on higher incomes because no further contributions are paid once a worker's income rises above a given ceiling. Additionally, as the table shows, the council tax and indirect taxes — mostly expenditure taxes — are regressive, taking a declining proportion of the income of rich households. Therefore, overall the UK tax system is at best only slightly progressive, and it may even be regressive.

The principles of taxation

Taxpayers commonly view all taxes as 'bad', in the sense that they do not enjoy paying them, although most realise that taxation is necessary in order to provide for the useful goods and services paid for by the government. A starting point for analysing and evaluating whether a tax is 'good' or 'bad' is Adam Smith's four **principles or canons of taxation**. Adam Smith suggested that taxation should be equitable, economical, convenient and certain, and to these we may add the canons of efficiency and flexibility. A 'good' tax meets as many of these canons as possible, although because of conflicts and trade-offs, it is usually impossible for a tax to meet them all at the same time. A 'bad' tax meets few if any of the guiding principles of taxation.

- **Equity.** A tax system should be fair, although, of course, there may be different and possibly conflicting interpretations of what is fair or equitable. Specifically, a particular tax should be based on the taxpayer's **ability to pay**. This principle is one of the justifications of progressive taxation, since the rich have a greater ability to pay than the poor.
- **Economy.** A tax should be easy to administer and cheap to collect, so that the yield is maximised relative to the cost of collection.
- **Convenience.** The method of payment should be convenient to the taxpayer.
- **Certainty.** The taxpayer should know what, when, where and how to pay, in such a manner that tax evasion is difficult. **Tax evasion** is the illegal failure to pay a lawful tax, whereas **tax avoidance** involves the arrangement of personal or business affairs within the law to minimise tax liability.
- **Efficiency.** A tax should achieve its intended aim or aims with minimum undesired distortion or side-effects. If, for example, the cut in the top marginal rate of taxation in the UK to 40%, which was designed to increase incentives and in the long run to increase total tax revenue, instead causes the rich to spend more time on leisure activities, the tax change could be viewed as inefficient. Since it is almost always impossible to avoid all the undesirable side-effects and distortions resulting from taxation, the tax system should aim to minimise these distortions.
- **Flexibility.** If the tax system is used as a means of economic management, then, in order to meet new circumstances, the tax structure and the rates at which individual taxes are levied must be capable of easy alteration.

> ***e*xaminer's voice**
>
> The A2 Module 6 specification requires that candidates are aware of the ability to pay and the benefit principle of taxation. The benefit principle means that the amount people pay in tax should be related to the benefit they derive from public spending. The benefit principle can lead to hypothecated taxes, such as spending revenue raised from motor vehicle taxes solely on roads. UK taxes are generally not hypothecated, and the policy of redistributing taxes paid by high income earners to people on low income goes against the benefit principle.

Public expenditure

The UK public sector can be divided into three parts: central government, local government and nationalised industries. The measurement of **public expenditure** is mostly restricted to spending by central and local government. Spending on net investment in new capital by nationalised industries is also included in the definition of public expenditure, but most spending by nationalised industries is excluded on the grounds that it is financed by revenue raised from the sale of the industries' output and is not dependent on finance from the taxpayer. In any case, privatisation of most of the former nationalised industries means that spending by the few enterprises that remain in the state sector is very small.

Spending by central and local government taken together is known as **general government expenditure**. Figure 18.2 shows the government's plans for the main categories of public spending in 2005/06.

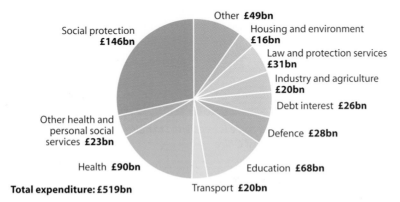

Social protection £146bn

Other health and personal social services **£23bn**

Health **£90bn**

Total expenditure: £519bn

Other **£49bn**

Housing and environment **£16bn**

Law and protection services **£31bn**

Industry and agriculture **£20bn**

Debt interest **£26bn**

Defence **£28bn**

Education **£68bn**

Transport **£20bn**

Figure 18.2 Expected UK general government spending by function, 2005/06

Source: Budget statement, March 2005.

Note: Other expenditure includes spending on general public services, recreation, culture and religion, international cooperation and development and public service provisions. Social protection includes tax credit payments to individuals. Figures do not sum to total due to rounding.

Perhaps more significant than the absolute totals of public expenditure is the **ratio of public expenditure to national income or GDP,** which indicates the share of the nation's resources taken by the government. Apart from the periods 1914–18 and 1939–45 which saw very rapid, but temporary, increases in government spending to pay for the First and Second World Wars, the twentieth century witnessed a steady but relatively slow increase in government expenditure from around 10% to over 40% of GDP, reaching 46.75% in 1982/83. The ratio continued to rise in the early 1980s, but fell in the late 1980s, before rising and falling again in the 1990s. By 2005/06, the ratio had increased again to over 42%.

A major explanation for these changes lies in changes taking place in employment and unemployment, which in turn relate to the business cycle. As Figure 18.2 shows, spending on social security (under the heading 'social protection'), which includes unemployment-related benefits, is by far the largest single category of public spending. The main unemployment benefit, the **jobseeker's allowance,** only amounts to about 5% of total welfare benefits. The income-support benefit claimed by poor families and the state pension are much more important — except when unemployment grows in a recession. When the economy booms, unemployment falls, so spending on social security also falls. The reverse is true in a recession. This issue shall be considered later in the chapter when explaining the

cyclical and structural components of the government's budget deficit and borrowing requirement, and the role of automatic stabilisers in the economy.

The ratio of public spending to GDP is an accurate measure of the share of the nation's total financial resources under the command of the government. However, because a large part of government expenditure is on **transfers**, such as the unemployment-related benefits just described, it is a misleading indicator of the share of national output produced by government itself. Transfers do not involve a claim by the government on national output, or a diversion of resources by the government away from the private sector. Rather, spending on transfers merely redistributes income and spending power from one part of the private sector to another — from taxpayers to recipients of state benefits and pensions.

Income is transferred to many pensioners via the Post Office

When transfers are excluded, government spending falls from around 40% of GDP to between only 20 and 30%. This figure is a more accurate measure of the share of national output directly commanded by the state (and thus unavailable for use in the private sector) to produce the hospitals, roads and other goods and services which government collectively provides and finances mostly out of taxation.

Figure 18.2 also shows the interest paid by the government to people who have lent to the government (that is, to holders of the **national debt**). In 2005/06, interest payments on the national debt were expected to be £26 billion, or 5% of public spending. For an obvious reason, this item of public spending increases when interest rates rise. However, *total* interest payments are also affected by the government's budgetary position. A budget deficit generally increases interest payments because it increases the total *stock* of government debt. Conversely, a budget surplus allows the government to reduce the national debt by paying back past borrowing. As a result total interest payments fall. In the early 2000s, low interest rates and a budget surplus both reduced debt repayments as a proportion of public spending and of GDP. By 2005, however, a budget deficit was once again increasing debt repayments, although to some extent this was offset by interest rates remaining low.

The aims of taxation and public spending

An obvious aim of taxation is to raise the revenue required to finance government spending. In addition, as Chapters 3 and 9 explain, taxes and subsidies can be used to alter the relative prices of goods and services in order to change consumption patterns.

Ultimately, the aims of both taxation and public spending depend on the underlying philosophy and ideology of the government in power. They differ significantly, for example, between Keynesian and free-market or supply-side inspired governments. We may divide the aims or objectives of public spending and taxation into three main categories: allocation, distribution and economic management.

Allocation

As just noted, taxes are used to alter relative prices and patterns of consumption. Demerit goods, such as alcohol and tobacco, are taxed in order to discourage consumption, while merit goods, such as museums, are untaxed and subsidised. Taxes are also used to finance the provision of public goods, such as defence, police and roads, and merit good services such as healthcare and education. Under the 'polluter must pay' principle, taxes are used to discourage and reduce the production and consumption of negative externalities, such as pollution and congestion. Subsidies are also used to encourage the production or provision of external benefits or positive externalities. Taxation can be used to deter monopoly by taxing monopoly profit through removing the windfall gain accruing to a monopolist as a result of barriers to entry and inelastic supply.

Distribution

The price mechanism is value-neutral with regard to the equity or social fairness of the distributions of income and wealth resulting from market forces in the economy. If the government decides that the distributions of income and wealth produced by free market forces are undesirable, taxation and transfers in its public spending programme can be used to modify these distributions and reduce the market failure resulting from inequity.

Before 1979, UK governments of all political complexions used progressive taxation and a policy of transfers of income to the less well-off, in a deliberate attempt — albeit with limited success — to reduce inequalities in the distribution of income. Governments also extended the provision of merit goods such as free state education and healthcare, in order to improve the **social wage** of lower-income groups. The social wage is the part of a worker's standard of living received as goods and services provided at zero price or as 'income in kind' by the state, being financed collectively out of taxation.

Between 1979 and 1997, Conservative governments changed the structure of both taxation and public spending to *widen* rather than *reduce* inequalities in the distributions of income and wealth. The reason for this change relates to the conflict between two of the canons of taxation: equity and efficiency. The Conservatives believed that greater incentives for work and enterprise were necessary in order to increase the UK's growth rate. For the Conservatives, progressive taxation and transfers to the poor meant that people had less incentive to work harder and to engage in entrepreneurial risk. Moreover, the ease with which the poor could claim welfare benefits and the level at which they are available created a situation in which the poor rationally chose unemployment and state benefits in preference to

wages and work. In this so-called **dependency culture**, the unwaged were effectively 'married to the state', but some of the poor, obviously not enjoying this marriage, drifted into antisocial behaviour, attacking bus shelters and other public property as well as privately owned property.

The Conservatives argued that income tax rates and benefit rates should *both* be reduced. They believed that tax and benefit cuts would alter the labour/leisure choice in favour of supplying labour, particularly for benefit claimants who lack the skills necessary for high-paid jobs. They also believed that to make everyone *eventually* better-off, the poor must first be made worse off. Increased inequality was necessary to facilitate economic growth from which all would eventually benefit. Through a 'trickle down' effect, the poor would end up better off in *absolute* terms, but because inequalities had widened, they would still be *relatively* worse off compared to the rich.

Since 1997, policy has again been reversed. Using initiatives such as the New Deal, New Labour governments have tried to reduce income inequalities. But although the real incomes of most of the poor have increased, income inequalities have continued to grow, largely because high incomes have grown at a much faster rate than low incomes.

> *e*xaminer's voice
>
> The aims of taxation and public spending are relevant for *all* the AS and A2 specifications. For Modules 1 and 5, taxation and public spending are relevant for correcting market failure and the causes of government failure. In addition, Module 5 requires understanding of how taxation and government spending affect poverty and the distribution of income. The use of taxation and public spending in macroeconomic fiscal policy is an important part of Modules 2 and 6.

Economic management

Taxation, public spending and the budget deficit or surplus provide the government with a range of policy instruments — known collectively as **fiscal policy instruments** — which the government can use in the overall management of the economy, in pursuit of its economic objectives. The next part of this chapter explains how fiscal policy has operated in the UK, changing from the Keynesian fiscal policy of the 1950s, 1960s and 1970s to the more supply-side-orientated fiscal policy implemented in recent years.

Fiscal policy

Fiscal policy is used to achieve the government's economic objectives through the use of the fiscal instruments of taxation, public spending and the budgetary position. As an economic term, fiscal policy is often associated with Keynesian economic theory and policy. In the 1950s and 1960s, Keynesian governments abandoned the fiscal neutrality of sound finance and balanced budgets, preferring an active fiscal policy based on managing the level of aggregate demand.

However, it is misleading to associate fiscal policy exclusively with Keynesianism. These days, the Keynesian fiscal policy implemented in the UK in the three decades before 1979 has been replaced by a very different, supply-side fiscal policy.

But before we explain the instruments and the objectives of this more free-market fiscal policy, we shall first explain the main features of the demand-side fiscal policy pursued by Keynesian governments in the years before 1979.

Keynesian fiscal policy

During the Keynesian era, fiscal policy took on a meaning more narrow and specific than the rather general definition given at the beginning of the previous section. In the Keynesian era, fiscal policy came to mean the use of the overall levels of public spending, taxation and the budget deficit to manage the level of aggregate demand in the economy. The aim was to achieve full employment and to stabilise the business cycle, without at the same time creating excessive inflationary pressures. Keynesian fiscal policy was implemented with varying degrees of success in the decades before 1979. The key elements of the theory behind fiscal policy are explained below.

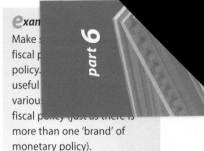

examiner's voice

Make
fiscal
policy.
useful
variou
fiscal p
more than one 'brand' of
monetary policy).

- It was believed that, left to itself, an unregulated market economy results in unnecessarily low economic growth, high unemployment and volatile business cycles.
- A lack of aggregate money demand, caused by a tendency for the private sector to save too much and invest too little, can mean that the economy settles into an under-full employment equilibrium characterised by demand-deficient unemployment.
- By deliberate deficit financing, the government can, using fiscal policy as a demand management instrument, inject demand and spending power into the economy to eliminate deficient demand and achieve full employment.
- Having achieved full employment, the government can then use fiscal policy in a discretionary way (that is, changing tax rates and levels of public spending to meet new circumstances) to fine-tune the level of aggregate demand. For much of the Keynesian era, governments believed that fiscal policy could achieve full employment and stabilise the business cycle, while avoiding an unacceptable increase in the rate of inflation.
- The overall 'stance' of fiscal policy — and, indeed, of economic policy in general — was orientated towards the demand side of the economy. The more micro-economic elements of fiscal policy, such as transfers to industry, were aimed at improving economic performance on the supply side. But on the whole, supply-side fiscal policy was treated as sub-ordinate to the macroeconomic management of aggregate demand and to the assumption that output would respond to demand stimulation. In any case, the microeconomic elements of Keynesian fiscal policy were generally inter-ventionist rather than non-interventionist, extending rather than reducing the state's role in the mixed economy.

examiner's voice

At AS, the Unit 2 exam may ask you to use *AD/AS* analysis to explain how fiscal policy can be used to manage aggregate demand. At A2, you are more likely to be expected to understand that fiscal policy is currently used in the UK in a supply-side way to create personal incentives.

Supply-side fiscal policy

As we have seen in earlier chapters, in the Keynesian era, fiscal policy played a central role in the creation of a mixed economy based on the political consensus that the UK economy should contain a mix of market and non-market economic activity, and of public and private ownership. The more supply-side and free-market fiscal policy pursued since 1979 has been very different. Along with policies such as privatisation and deregulation, fiscal policy has been used to change the mixed economy by increasing the role of markets and private sector economic activity, and by reducing the economic role of the state.

The main elements of the fiscal policy implemented first by Conservative governments and then by New Labour governments in the UK since 1979 are as follows:

- The government has ceased using taxation and public spending as discretionary instruments of demand management. Under supply-side influence, recent governments have argued that a policy of using fiscal policy to stimulate or reflate aggregate demand to achieve growth and full employment is, in the long run, at best ineffective and at worst damaging. They have argued that any growth of output and employment resulting from an expansionary fiscal policy is short-lived and that in the long term the main effect of such a policy is inflation, which quickly destroys the conditions necessary for satisfactory market performance and wealth creation.
- A medium-term policy 'rule' has been recommended (in place of short-term discretionary fiscal changes) to reduce public spending, taxation and government borrowing as proportions of national output. Besides wishing to reduce what they see as the inflationary effects of 'big government spending', many supply-side economists believe that the high levels of government spending, taxation and borrowing of the Keynesian era led to the 'crowding out' of the private sector. (Crowding out is explained later in the chapter.)
- Microeconomic fiscal policy has become more important than macroeconomic fiscal policy. Governments have subordinated the more macroeconomic elements of fiscal policy, which were dominant during the Keynesian era, to a much more microeconomic fiscal policy, intended to combine an overall reduction in the levels of taxation and public spending with the creation of incentives aimed at improving economic performance on the supply side of the economy.
- As well as being subordinated to a more microeconomic supply-side orientated fiscal policy, the macroeconomic elements of fiscal policy have become subservient to the needs of *monetary* policy. Control over public spending and borrowing is now regarded as a precondition for successful control of the monetary conditions needed to control inflation. This is explained in more detail later in the chapter.

The government's budgetary position

Using the symbols G for government spending and T for taxation and other sources of revenue, the three possible budgetary positions of the government (and of the whole of the public sector) are:

$G \ = \ T$ (balanced budget)

$G \ > \ T$ (budget deficit)

$G \ < \ T$ (budget surplus)

A **budget deficit** occurs when public sector expenditure exceeds revenue. A budget deficit can be eliminated by cutting public spending or raising taxation, both of which can balance the budget or move the budget into surplus. But assuming that a deficit persists, the extent to which spending exceeds revenue must be financed by public sector borrowing. The Treasury uses various official terms for public sector borrowing, including the **public sector's net cash requirement** and **net public sector borrowing**. However, because the Treasury frequently changes its official terminology, the most important thing to learn is that public sector borrowing is 'the other side of the coin' to the budget deficit. Whenever there is a budget deficit there is a *positive* borrowing requirement. Conversely, a budget surplus means that the government can use the tax revenues that it is not spending to repay previous borrowing. In this case, the borrowing requirement is *negative*.

Automatic stabilisers

The previous sections have tended to assume that the fiscal policy choice facing a government lies between Keynesian-style discretionary demand management and balancing the budget as advocated by many supply-side economists. But in reality, there is an alternative approach that lies between these extremes, in which a government bases fiscal policy on the operation of **automatic stabilisers**. These dampen or reduce the multiplier effects resulting from any change in aggregate demand within the economy.

Suppose, for example, that a collapse of confidence or export orders causes aggregate demand to fall. National income then also begins to fall, declining by the initial fall in demand × the multiplier. But as national income falls and unemployment rises, *demand-led* public spending on unemployment pay and welfare benefits also rises. If the income tax system is progressive, the government's tax revenues fall faster than national income. In this way, increased public spending on transfers and declining tax revenues inject demand back into the economy, thereby stabilising and dampening the deflationary impact of the initial fall in aggregate demand, and reducing the overall size of the contractionary multiplier effect.

Automatic stabilisers also operate in the opposite direction to dampen the expansionary effect of an increase in aggregate demand. As incomes and employment rise, the take-up of means-tested welfare benefits and unemployment-related benefits automatically falls, while at the same time tax revenues rise faster than income. By taking demand out of the economy and reducing the size of the expansionary multiplier, automatic stabilisers reduce **over-heating** in the boom phase of the business cycle.

It is now widely agreed that automatic stabilisers such as progressive taxation and income-related transfers have contributed to milder business cycles. Before 1939, business cycles — or trade cycles, as they were then known — were much more volatile, displaying greater fluctuations between boom and slump than in the years between the Second World War and 1979. Keynesians have claimed that the relatively mild modern business cycle is evidence of the success of Keynesian demand management policies in stabilising cyclical fluctuations. But the business cycle was relatively mild both in the UK and in countries such as Germany, which did not use fiscal policy to manage aggregate demand in a discretionary way. This suggests that the automatic stabilisers of progressive taxation and the 'safety net' provided by welfare benefits for the poor — both of which were introduced widely in western industrialised economies after 1945 — were more significant than discretionary fiscal policy in reducing fluctuations in the business cycle.

The two most severe recessions of the last 60 years occurred in the early 1980s and a decade later in the early 1990s. The first of these recessions occurred just after Margaret Thatcher's first Conservative government took office. The Thatcher government abandoned Keynesian 'counter-cyclical' demand management policies, replacing them with severely deflationary monetary and fiscal policies which destabilised rather than stabilised the business cycle. As a result, the recession of the 1980s cut deeper than the recessions affecting other developed countries. However, by the time the next recession hit the UK economy in 1990, the Conservative government appreciated the need to use automatic stabilisers.

As the next section explains, UK governments now aim to balance the *cyclical* element of the budget over the *whole* of the economic cycle, rather than for a particular year *within* the cycle. Economists generally agree that a deficit should grow in the downswing of the business cycle, provided the deficit is matched by a surplus in the subsequent upswing.

*e*xaminer's voice

Although fiscal policy is now used in a supply-side way, it is recognised that the government's budget deficit or surplus should still be used to stabilise the business cycle.

The cyclical and the structural budget deficit and borrowing requirement

To understand fully the links between the government's budgetary position and the wider economy, it is useful to distinguish between the cyclical and the structural components of the budget deficit and borrowing requirement. As the previous paragraphs indicate, the **cyclical budget deficit** is the part of the overall budget deficit which rises and falls with the downswings and upswings of the business cycle as automatic stabilisers kick in. In the recessionary or downswing of the business cycle, tax revenues fall but public spending on unemployment and poverty-related welfare benefits increases. As a result, the government's finances deteriorate. Conversely, in the recovery and boom periods, tax revenues rise and spending on benefits falls.

If all the growth of the budget deficit and the related borrowing requirement were cyclical, the problem of a growing budget deficit would disappear when economic growth occurred — providing growth was sufficiently buoyant and sustained. But this does not happen if the cyclical changes are overridden by more powerful structural changes operating in the reverse direction. As the name suggests, growth in the *structural* component of the budget deficit and borrowing require-ment relates to the changing structure of the UK economy. In recent years, a number of factors and trends, ranging from deindustrialisation eroding the tax base, through to an ageing population and the growth of single-parent families dependent on welfare benefits, have contributed to the growth of the **structural budget deficit**.

The growing structural deficit carries the rather dispiriting message that a government that seriously wishes to improve public sector finances will need to introduce significant tax increases or public spending cuts, or possibly both. From 1997 to 2001, the first New Labour government decided to stick to the spending plans inherited from the previous Conservative administration. During this period, little change occurred in the structural deficit, which in any case was more than offset by the cyclical surplus resulting from the boom phase of the business cycle.

However, after 2001, the government's finances deteriorated and moved into overall deficit. The reasons were partly cyclical and partly structural. Growth still occurred, but at a weaker rate, at least to start with, so the cyclical surplus diminished in size. But the main effect was structural. Labour promised that in its second term of office, capital spending on hospitals, schools and transport would improve significantly. To an extent the government was relying on an increase in the economy's trend rate of growth (from about 2.25% to 2.75%) to deliver the extra tax revenue needed to finance the increase in capital spending. But actual growth was rather lower, and at the same time, for structural reasons, tax revenues were disappointing. This is explained by falling company profits and tax avoidance by multinational companies, both partly caused by **globalisation**, together with the fact that a growing army of self-employed workers also had scope for tax avoidance. Meanwhile, the government had promised not to raise income tax rates. So, even though hidden or **'stealth' taxes** were increased, disappointing tax revenues and the structural increase in public spending caused the budget deficit to grow, despite the fact that the economy also grew.

*e*xaminer's voice

It is important to understand the difference between the cyclical and structural elements of the government's budget deficit and its borrowing requirement.

Crowding out

As previously noted, many supply-side economists believe that government spending and taxation crowds out private sector spending and output. There are two forms of crowding out: resource crowding out and financial crowding out.

Resource crowding out is associated with two very basic economic concepts: scarcity and opportunity cost. Because it is impossible to employ real resources simultaneously in both the private and public sectors, the opportunity cost of employing more capital and labour in the public sector inevitably involves sacrificing the opportunity to use the same resources in private employment.

Financial crowding out results from the method of financing an increase in public spending. As we have explained, public spending can be financed by taxation or borrowing. Taxation obviously reduces the spending power of the private individuals and firms paying the taxes. Note, however, that if extra tax revenues paid by high income earners with a relatively low marginal propensity to consume are transferred as welfare benefits to poorer people with higher marginal propensities to consume, higher taxation may *increase* private sector spending, although at the probable cost of reduced personal incentives.

However, suppose, for example, that the government increases public spending by £40 billion, financing the resulting budget deficit with a sale of new gilt-edged securities or 'gilts' on the capital market. In order to persuade insurance companies, pension funds and the other financial institutions in the market for gilts to buy the extra debt, the guaranteed annual interest rate offered on new gilt issues must increase. But the resulting general rise in interest rates makes it more expensive for firms to borrow and to raise capital. Private sector investment thus falls.

Crowding out versus crowding in

The resource crowding out argument assumes full employment of all resources. But when spare capacity and unemployed labour exist in the economy, increased public spending does not necessarily reduce the private sector's use of resources. Instead, by using previously idle resources, increased government spending merely takes up the slack in the economy. Indeed, with unemployed resources, increased public spending financed by a budget deficit may, via the multiplier process, stimulate or *crowd in* the private sector. For example, increased spending on a public works road-building programme creates orders or contracts for private sector construction firms which, through their own spending in the subsequent stages of the multiplier process, generates further business for the private sector.

Resource crowding out and crowding in are illustrated in Figure 18.3. The production possibility frontier drawn in the diagram shows maximum levels of output that can be produced with various combinations of public sector and private sector spending and output. There is full employment at all points on the frontier. Assuming the economy is initially at point A, an increase in public sector spending from Pu_1 to Pu_2 crowds out or displaces private sector spending, which falls from Pr_1 to Pr_2, shown at point B. The size of the multiplier with respect to real output is therefore zero. Indeed, extreme free-market economists go further, arguing that the multiplier may be negative because an increase in public sector spending causes the production possibility frontier to shift inward.

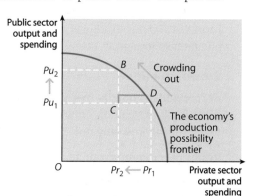

Figure 18.3 Crowding out and crowding in illustrated on a production possibility diagram

According to this extreme neo-classical view, real output falls because unproductive or 'wealth-consuming' public sector spending displaces 'wealth-creating' private sector spending. (In the extreme, this argument is rather silly, since it implies that *all* private sector spending, such as gambling, is 'wealth-producing', while *all* public sector spending, for example on roads or hospitals, is 'wealth-consuming' or unproductive.)

Keynesians agree that crowding out occurs if the economy is initially fully employed with no spare capacity. But suppose the economy is initially producing *inside* the frontier, at a point such as *C* in Figure 18.3. In this situation, *crowding in* rather than *crowding out* may occur. An increase in public sector spending that is sufficient, via the multiplier process, to increase output to point *D* on the frontier, brings idle capacity into production. The stimulus is shown by the thick kinked line running from *C* to *D*. The line contains a vertical section and a horizontal section. The vertical section shows the initial increase in public spending, which triggers the multiplier process. By contrast, the horizontal section shows the resulting increase in private sector spending and output following on from the initial increase in public spending.

Whether an increase in public sector spending crowds out or crowds in the private sector should depend on whether the economy is initially on its production possibility frontier — at a position such as *A* — or inside the frontier, such as at *C*. Keynesians argue that the size of unemployment indicates whether or not the economy is 'on' or 'inside' the production possibility frontier, and that, in periods of recession, the economy is definitely inside its frontier. Free-market economists respond by arguing that unemployment figures provide a misleading indicator of whether the economy is on its production possibility frontier — the correct indicator is the existence of spare and *competitive* capacity capable of producing goods and services of a quality that people actually want. According to this view, increased public spending can crowd out the private sector even when unemployment is high. If the required supply-side production capacity is not in place to respond to the stimulus of extra government spending, the economy behaves as if it is fully employed.

> **e*xaminer's voice**
>
> It is useful to understand that many free-market economists believe that an increase in public spending crowds out the private sector, whereas Keynesian economists argue that, provided there is unemployment, public spending can stimulate or crowd in private sector spending.

The subordination of fiscal policy to the needs of monetary policy

Governments (and the Bank of England) now realise that, because monetary and fiscal policy are *interdependent* rather than *independent* of each other, the success of *monetary policy* depends on the *fiscal policy* implemented by the Treasury. As we have seen, whenever it runs a budget deficit, the government has to borrow to finance the difference between spending and revenue. Conversely, a budget surplus enables repayment of past borrowing and a fall in the national debt. The government borrows in two main ways — by selling short-dated debt or Treasury bills and by borrowing long term by selling government bonds or gilts. The government sells Treasury bills to the banks, which create new bank deposits

when they buy the bills. Because bank deposits are a form of money, this type of government borrowing increases the money supply and makes it difficult to control monetary growth.

By contrast, new issues of gilts are largely sold to non-bank financial institutions such as pension funds and insurance companies. To persuade these institutions to finance a growing budget deficit, the government may have to raise the rate of interest offered on new gilt issues. But higher interest rates discourage investment in capital goods by private sector firms. This is the *financial crowding out* process referred to earlier.

Either way, government spending financed by borrowing produces an arguably undesirable result. Either the borrowing increases the money supply (which may be inflationary) or it raises interest rates (which may crowd out private sector investment). The undesirable monetary consequences resulting from budget deficits and government borrowing explain why UK governments now try to make fiscal policy *consistent with*, and *subordinate to*, the needs of monetary policy.

The UK government's fiscal rules

The realisation that fiscal policy has a significant effect on monetary conditions helps to explain how fiscal policy is used in the UK today. Monetary policy rather than fiscal policy is now primarily used to manage the level of aggregate demand. By creating conditions in which competitive markets function efficiently, fiscal policy aims to achieve macroeconomic stability. The government believes that households and firms should not be hit by unexpected tax increases that adversely affect consumer and business confidence, and distort economic decision making.

Having a year earlier set out the **Monetary Policy Framework** to inform people of the way monetary policy is implemented, in 1998 the New Labour government published the **Fiscal Policy Framework**. The government announced four fiscal policy objectives; two short term and two medium term.

The short-term objectives of fiscal policy, which are concerned with demand management, are:
- to allow automatic stabilisers to smooth the path of the economy
- to take other necessary action so that fiscal policy supports the role of monetary policy

By contrast, fiscal policy's medium-term objectives are:
- to fulfil the government's tax and spending commitments, while avoiding a damaging and unsustainable increase in the burden of public sector debt
- to make sure that the generations who benefit from public spending, as far as possible, pay the tax revenues needed to finance the spending

Seeking to ensure the credibility of fiscal policy (that is, to maintain the general public's belief in the government's ability to achieve these objectives), the Fiscal Policy Framework includes a **Code for Fiscal Stability**. The code commits the UK government to the five principles of transparency, stability, responsibility, fairness and efficiency. To perform in accordance with these principles, the code requires the government to publish each year a number of reports and information on fiscal policy and the state of the public finances. These include the **Pre-Budget Report**, published in the late autumn, and the **Financial Statement and Budget Report** (nicknamed the 'Red Book'), which, as the name indicates, is published on Budget Day, usually in March.

Central to the code are two fiscal rules:

- **The golden rule.** Over the economic cycle, net government borrowing should only be to fund new social capital such as roads and schools, and not to fund current spending, such as welfare benefits.
- **The sustainable investment rule.** Over the economic cycle, public sector debt (mostly central government debt: that is, the national debt) is held at a 'stable and prudent' level of less than 40% of GDP.

The difference between current and capital spending explains the golden rule. **Current spending** (for example, on public sector wages and salaries) does not create assets for future generations to use. If long-term debt is used to finance current spending, future generations have to pay taxes to pay back past borrowing, without receiving any benefit in the form of useful goods and services. It is very much a case of 'live now, pay later'.

This is not the case with **capital spending** on assets such as roads, hospitals and schools. Providing social capital is properly maintained, future generations benefit from public sector investment undertaken now. Future generations should therefore pay part of the cost of capital spending.

For these reasons, the government has decided that, over a single economic cycle, the public sector's budget should balance with regard to current public spending, but run a deficit with regard to capital spending on assets that future generations will use.

The general public tends to notice cuts in current spending more than it notices cuts in capital spending. This is because cuts in current spending affect the general public immediately, whereas the effect of cuts in capital spending will mainly be noticed in the future. In the past, therefore, governments have generally cut infrastructure projects when faced with the need to rein in public expenditure. The golden rule is meant to prevent politicians succumbing to this temptation. It should protect necessary investment in social capital from public spending cuts.

The golden rule also allows fiscal policy to be used in support of monetary policy to manage aggregate demand, although not in a discretionary way. Because the rule allows deficits and surpluses to occur on current spending, within the

constraint that the current spending budget must balance over the economic cycle, automatic stabilisers can operate and dampen fluctuations during the cycle. The fact that the government makes the decision on when a cycle begins and ends also adds to flexibility, although at the cost of possibly destroying credibility in the golden rule. According to the government, the cycle affecting the UK economy in the early 2000s began in 1999, and not in 1992 when the last recession ended.

As the government has fudged the distinction between current and capital spending, the credibility of the golden rule has been reduced. To some extent, however, this credibility loss has been offset by greater credibility in the government's ability to meet the sustainable investment rule. Keeping public sector debt within 40% of GDP increases the confidence of financial markets in the government's handling of the public finances.

The publication of the Code for Fiscal Stability meant that the government officially recognised that, for the most part, fiscal policy should not be used in a discretionary way to manage aggregate demand. However, two qualifications must be made. First, the growth of the structural budget deficit has caused the government to introduce new 'stealth' taxes that it hopes people won't notice. Having, for electoral reasons, announced its unwillingness to increase income tax to reduce the budget deficit, the government had to find other ways of raising revenue.

Second, when in 2003 *nominal* interest rates fell toward zero (which meant that when inflation is taken into account, *real* interest rates might actually be negative), monetary policy became less and less effective for stimulating aggregate demand. Some economists then argued that fiscal policy should once again be used primarily as a demand-side policy. This argument was further boosted by the possibility of euro entry. Euro entry would prevent the government implementing a national monetary policy designed for the needs of the UK economy. Without an independent monetary policy at its disposal, the government might decide to use fiscal policy to manage aggregate demand.

Fiscal policy and income distribution

The problem of poverty

Poverty is caused both by low output in relation to a country's total population size and by inequalities in the distributions of income and wealth. The former leads to *absolute* poverty for most of a country's inhabitants, whereas the latter causes *relative* poverty. **Absolute poverty** occurs when income is below a particular specified level. By contrast, a household suffers **relative poverty** if its income is below a specified proportion of average income for all households (for example, less than a third of average income). When *all* incomes grow, *absolute* poverty falls; but *relative* poverty only falls if low incomes grow at a faster rate than average incomes. For the most part, the

> ### examiner's voice
> The problem of poverty is a Module 5 topic, but candidates may be expected to apply knowledge learned when studying Modules 2 and 6 to explain how fiscal policy can be used to reduce poverty problems.

problem of poverty in the UK is one of relative poverty. Because the UK is a high-income, developed economy in which welfare benefits provide a minimum income and 'safety net' for the poor, very few people suffer from absolute poverty.

Four of the main causes of poverty in the UK are old age, unemployment, the effects of the tax and benefits systems on those in work, and low wages for those in work.

Poverty and old age

Old age causes poverty largely because many old people rely on the state pension and lack a private pension. Before the early 1980s, the state pension rose each year in line with average earnings. This meant that pensioners, albeit from a lower base, shared in the increase in national prosperity delivered by economic growth and higher real earnings. However, since the early 1980s, the state pension has risen in line with the retail price index (RPI) rather than with average earnings. This has kept the real value or purchasing power of the state pension at its early-1980s level, while the real earnings of those in work have continued to rise. Pensioners reliant solely on the state for a source of income have become *relatively* worse off, even though the real value of the state pension has not fallen. The state pension is now regarded very much as a 'poverty income'.

Poverty in the UK is relative and relates to such circumstances as poor housing conditions

Poverty and unemployment

Unemployment benefits are also now linked to the RPI and, for similar reasons as the state pension, have fallen behind average earnings. An increase in unemployment therefore increases poverty. It follows that absolute poverty (and potentially relative poverty) can best be reduced by fast and sustained economic growth and by creating jobs. Economic growth can also create the wherewithal, if the electorate and state are so minded, to increase the real value of the state pension.

Poverty and the tax and benefits system

Relative poverty can be reduced by using progressive taxation and welfare benefits to reduce inequalities in the distribution of income. However, if in the drive to reduce inequality, these changes worsen labour market incentives, competitiveness and economic growth, they can cause average incomes to rise at a slower rate, even though *relative* poverty is successfully reduced.

The tax system has affected poverty partly through a process known as **fiscal drag**. Fiscal drag occurs in a progressive income tax system when the government fails to raise tax thresholds (or personal tax allowances) to keep pace with inflation. Figure 18.4(a) shows an income pyramid (with the rich at the top of the pyramid

and the poor at the bottom), with the tax threshold fixed at an income of £3,000. In this example, a person with an income of £2,900 is just below the threshold and pays no income tax.

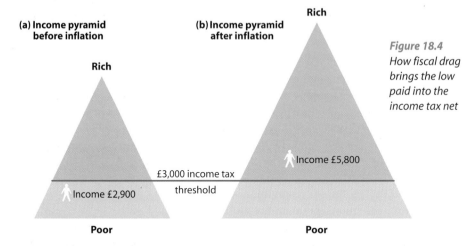

(a) Income pyramid before inflation

(b) Income pyramid after inflation

Rich

Rich

Income £5,800

£3,000 income tax threshold

Income £2,900

Poor

Poor

*Figure 18.4
How fiscal drag brings the low paid into the income tax net*

Suppose that both prices and all money incomes exactly double. If there are no taxes, real incomes will remain unchanged, with households no better off or worse off. But if there are taxes, and the government fails to increase personal tax allowances in line with inflation (that is, to raise the tax threshold to £6,000), a doubling of money income to £5,800 means that £2,800 of income is now taxable. The individual concerned is now worse off in real terms.

The new situation is shown in Figure 18.4(b). Inflation has dragged the low-paid worker across the basic tax threshold and into the tax net. In a similar way, higher-paid workers are dragged deeper into the tax net if the higher 40% marginal tax rate remains unadjusted for inflation.

When fiscal drag occurs, the government's total revenue from income tax rises faster than the rate of inflation, even though tax rates and the basic structure of taxation have not changed. This is because more people are dragged into the income tax net, paying a growing proportion of their income in tax. But a second process, known as **fiscal boost**, has an opposite effect. In inflationary times, the real value of specific taxes such as excise duties on tobacco, alcohol and petrol falls (but *not* ad valorem taxes such as VAT), unless duties are raised each year in line with inflation. When both fiscal drag and fiscal boost occur at the same time, the structure of taxation shifts away from expenditure taxes and towards income taxation.

Governments can reduce relative poverty among the low paid by raising income tax thresholds by more than the rate of inflation. This takes the low paid out of the income tax net and 'claws back' the fiscal drag that has taken place in previous years. However, unless the government simultaneously reduces public spending (which generally benefits the low paid more than the high paid), taxes have to be raised elsewhere in the economy, which may also adversely affect the poor.

The meaning of supply-side economics

> Supply-side economics provides a framework of analysis which relies on personal and private incentives. When incentives change, people's behaviour changes in response. People are attracted towards positive incentives and repelled by the negative. The role of government in such a framework is carried out by the ability of government to alter incentives and thereby affect society's behaviour.

> Professor Arthur Laffer, University of Southern California, 1983

The term **supply-side economics** was first used in 1976 by Professor Herbert Stein of the University of Virginia in the USA. The term came to prominence in 1980 to describe the economic policies promised by Ronald Reagan in his successful campaign for the US presidency. Supply-side economics then became associated with 'Reaganomics', the nickname given to the Republican president's economic programme in the early 1980s. The ideology and policies of other free-market-orientated governments were also strongly influenced by supply-side theories in the 1980s, particularly the Conservative administrations of Margaret Thatcher in the United Kingdom from 1979 to 1990, from which the term 'Thatcherism' was coined.

Supply-side economics is associated with the free-market revival, which accompanied and partially caused the decline of Keynesianism. As Chapter 12 explains, a number of schools of economic and political theory have been part of the free-market or neo-classical revival. Supply-side economics is closely associated with the free-market schools of the radical right or New Right. Although there is some disagreement over points of both emphasis and detail, all members of the radical right believe in the virtues of capitalism and free-market forces, a belief that is matched by a distrust and dislike of big government and the role of state intervention in the economy. In the late 1980s, many monetarist economists rebranded themselves as supply-side economists. In part, this was a response to the failure of monetarist policies to control inflation by controlling the growth of the money supply. Monetarism became less influential after 1985 when governments generally stopped using monetarist policies.

Ronald Reagan and Margaret Thatcher, November 1988

examiner's voice

The AS Module 2 specification states that candidates should understand the role of supply-side policies in influencing the underlying trend rate of economic growth and the potential output of the economy. In addition candidates should understand their contribution in reducing unemployment, inflation and improving the balance of payments. The A2 Module 6 specification is less specific about supply-side economics and supply-side policy, but requires understanding and application of supply-side theory.

Supply-side economic policy

The original meaning of supply-side economic policy

As developed by the radical right, supply-side economics described a particular way of looking at the effects of a government's fiscal policy upon the economy. During the Keynesian era, most economists regarded fiscal policy — and especially taxation — as a *macroeconomic* policy that affects the economy through demand management techniques. In Keynesian economics, the government's budget deficit was at the centre of fiscal policy. However, the Keynesians largely ignored the impact of public spending and tax changes upon the economy at the *microeconomic* level.

By contrast, supply-side economics initially grew out of the concern expressed by free-market economists in the 1970s about the microeconomic effects of demand-side Keynesian fiscal policy. Indeed, in many respects, supply-side economics is just a revival of the old classical public finance theory that largely disappeared from view during the Keynesian era. The central idea of supply-side economics is that a tax cut should be used, not to stimulate aggregate demand Keynesian-style, but to create incentives by altering relative prices. This is particularly to affect the choice between labour and leisure in favour of supplying labour rather than enjoying leisure time and voluntary unemployment, but also to favour saving and investment.

The wider meaning of supply-side economic policy

Supply-side economic policy now encompasses more than just fiscal policy. In a rather broader interpretation, supply-side economic policy can be defined as the set of government initiatives that aim to change the underlying structure of the economy and improve the economic performance of markets and industries, and of individual firms and workers within markets. For the most part, supply-side policies are also microeconomic rather than simply macroeconomic, since they act on the motivation and efficiency of individual economic agents within the economy to improve general economic performance.

Supply-siders, along with other members of the free-market revival, believe that the economy is usually close to its natural levels of output and employment. However, due to distortions and inefficiencies resulting from Keynesian neglect of the supply side, towards the end of the Keynesian era these natural levels became unnecessarily low. To increase the natural levels of output and employment, and to reduce the natural rate of unemployment (NRU), supply-side economists recommend the use of appropriate microeconomic policies to remove distortions, improve incentives and generally make markets more competitive.

During the Keynesian era of the 1960s and 1970s, government microeconomic policy in the UK was generally interventionist, extending the roles of the state and of the planning mechanism. The policy became known as **industrial policy**. Aspects of industrial policy, such as regional policy, competition policy and industrial relations policy, generally increased the role of the state and limited the role of markets. By contrast, supply-side micro-economic policy is anti-interventionist, attempting to roll back government interference in the activities of markets and of private economic agents, and to change the economic function of government from provider to enabler. Key elements of supply-side economic policy include: tax cuts to create incentives to work, save and invest; cuts in welfare benefits to reduce the incentive to choose unemployment rather than a low-paid work alternative; and policies of privatisation, marketisation (commercialisation) and deregulation, which are described in earlier chapters.

In essence, the supply-siders, together with the other free-market economists, wish to create an **enterprise economy**. In this broad interpretation, supply-side policies aim to promote entrepreneurship and popular capitalism and to replace the dependency culture and statism. Indeed, for free-market economists in general, the Keynesian *mixed economy* could perhaps best be described as a *mixed-up economy*.

*e*xaminer's voice

Supply-side economists are generally very pro-free market. They wish to reduce government intervention in the economy, and indeed the size of government itself. The term 'supply-side economics' can also be used to encompass inter-ventionist government policies of the type advocated by Keynesian economists. Nevertheless, for most examination questions, candidates should stick to the pro-free-market nature of supply-side economics.

The Laffer curve

Supply-side economists believe that high rates of income tax and the overall burden upon taxpayers create disincentives which, by reducing national income as taxation increases, also reduce the government's total tax revenue. This effect is illustrated by the Laffer curve in Figure 19.1.

The **Laffer curve**, which is named after the leading supply-side economist Arthur Laffer, who was quoted at the beginning of this chapter, shows how the government's total tax revenue changes as the average tax rate increases from 0% to 100%. Tax revenue must, of course, be zero when the average tax rate is 0%, but the diagram also shows that total tax revenue is again zero when the tax rate is 100%. With the average tax rate set at 100%, all income must be paid as tax to the government. In this situation, there is no incentive to produce output other than for subsistence, so with no output produced, the government ends up collecting no tax revenue.

Between the limiting tax rates of 0% and 100%, the Laffer curve shows tax revenue first rising and then falling as the average rate of taxation increases. Tax revenue is maximised at the highest point on the Laffer curve, which in Figure 19.1 occurs at an average

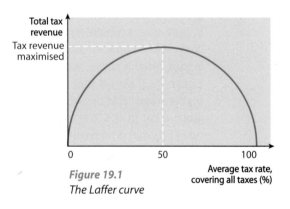

Figure 19.1
The Laffer curve

*e*xaminer's voice

Remember the definition of the average tax rate provided in Chapter 18. The average tax rate measures total tax paid as a ratio of income, whereas the marginal tax rate measures the *change* in total tax paid as a ratio of a *change* in income.

tax rate (for all taxes) of 50%. Beyond this point, any further increase in the average tax rate becomes counter-productive, causing total tax revenue to fall.

Supply-side economists argue that the increase in the tax burden in the Keynesian era, needed to finance the growing size of the government and public sectors, raised the average tax rate towards or beyond the critical point on the Laffer curve at which tax revenue is maximised. As noted, in this situation any further tax increase has the perverse effect of reducing the government's total tax revenue. This means that if the government wishes to increase total tax revenue, it must cut tax rates rather than increase them. A reduction in tax rates creates the incentives needed to stimulate economic growth. Faster growth means that *total tax revenue* increases despite the fact that *tax rates* are lower. Arguably, the effect is reinforced by a decline in tax evasion and avoidance, as the incentive to engage in these activities reduces at lower marginal tax rates.

Supply-side microeconomic theory and the supply of labour

The supply-side theory of the effects of taxation on labour market incentives, which lies at the heart of free-market supply-side economics, depends significantly on the assumed shape of the supply curve of labour. Supply-side economists usually assume a conventional upward-sloping supply curve of labour. Such a curve, which is illustrated in Figure 19.2, shows that workers respond to higher wage rates by supplying more labour. Since a cut in the rate at which income tax rates is levied is equivalent to an increase in the wage rate, the upward-sloping supply curve implies that workers respond to cuts in the marginal rate of income tax by working harder. If this is the case, a reduction in income tax rates creates the incentive for workers to supply more labour (and for entrepreneurs to become more enterprising), while an increase in income tax rates has a disincentive effect on effort and the supply of labour.

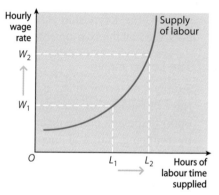

Figure 19.2 An upward-sloping supply curve of labour

But as Chapter 11 explains, the supply curve of labour need not slope upward throughout its length. The backward-bending labour supply curve drawn in Figure 19.3 is another possibility. Figure 19.3 shows that, above the hourly wage rate W_1, any further wage rate

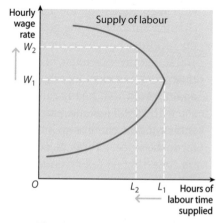

Figure 19.3 A backward-bending supply curve of labour

increase (or income tax decrease) causes workers to supply *less* rather than *more* labour. In this situation, workers prefer to enjoy extra leisure time rather than to work. Following an increase in the hourly wage rate from W_1 to W_2, the hours of labour time supplied fall from L_1 to L_2.

Whether the supply curve of labour slopes upward or eventually bends backward depends on the relative strength of the **substitution effect** and the **income effect** resulting from any wage rate change. The two effects are explained in Chapter 11. In the substitution effect, higher wage rates cause workers to substitute leisure time for labour. But higher wage rates also increase workers' real income and their demand for normal goods. For most people, leisure time is a normal good. The income effect of a wage rate increase causes workers to choose more leisure time, which reduces the hours of labour time they are prepared to supply. In summary, if the substitution effect of the wage rate increase (or income tax cut) is stronger than the income effect, the supply curve of labour slopes upward. But if the size of the income effect outweighs that of the substitution effect, a backward-bending labour supply curve results.

It is important to note that, if supply curves of labour bend backwards, the supply-side argument, that tax reductions increase national output and efficiency through their effect on labour market incentives, becomes much weaker. Far from encouraging people to work harder, a wage rise or income tax cut might have the opposite effect, causing people to work fewer hours and to enjoy more leisure time instead.

Given the assumption that the labour supply curve slopes backwards, it is sometimes argued that, far from acting as a *disincentive* and discouraging the supply of labour, higher income tax rates make people work harder. Faced with tax increases that cut real income and spending power, people decide to work longer hours simply to maintain living standards. This argument suggests that governments should raise rather than cut income tax rates to create appropriate labour market incentives.

However, this argument is very naive. Tax increases aimed at making people work harder would drive economic activity underground into a hidden or informal economy, where tax evasion reduces government revenue. Workers would end up supplying untaxed labour in the underground economy in preference to supplying taxed labour formally in the official economy. Normal economic activity would give way to a 'car boot sale' economy.

Supply-side macroeconomic theory

So far this chapter has explained supply-side microeconomic theory, which developed out of the dissatisfaction felt by free-market economists with the way the

e_xaminer's voice_

It is worth repeating the advice given in Chapter 11 that, while it is useful to understand what upward-sloping and backward-bending supply curves of labour *show*, AQA examination questions do not usually ask for theoretical explanations of the shape and slope of supply curves of labour.

Keynesians focused on the role of aggregate demand and ignored supply consid-erations at the microeconomic level. However, it is wrong to see supply-side economics solely in terms of microeconomics. Supply-side economists also have strong views on how the economy functions at the macro level and on the type of macroeconomic policy the government should adopt.

To explain supply-side macroeconomics, we shall use the aggregate demand/ aggregate supply (*AD/AS*) macroeconomic model. Chapter 15 has already explained the *AD/AS* model in some depth. The two panels of Figure 19.4 illustrate downward-sloping aggregate demand curves, which show the aggregate demand for real output increasing as the price level falls. However, the *AS* curves shown in the two diagrams depend on different sets of assumptions about how the economy works, and they carry different implications for government economic policy. The *SRAS* curve in Figure 19.4(a) is a short-run 'inverted L-shaped' Keynesian aggregate supply curve, whereas Figure 19.4(b) shows a vertical long-run aggregate supply curve.

(a) **The short-run, 'inverted L-shaped' aggregate supply curve**

(b) **The long-run aggregate supply curve**

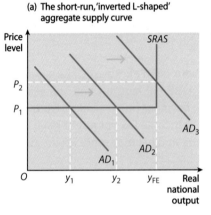

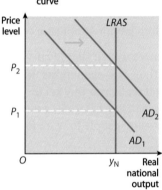

Figure 19.4
Analysing the effect of an increase in aggregate demand given different assumptions about the shape of the AS curve

Figure 19.4(a) illustrates the view held by Keynesian economists during the Keynesian era, 30 and more years ago, that expansionary fiscal or monetary policy *reflates* real output rather than *inflates* prices, providing initially there is unem-ployment and spare capacity in the economy. Following an increase in aggregate demand, which shifts the aggregate demand function from AD_1 to AD_2, real output increases from y_1 to y_2 but the price level does not change. Firms respond to increased demand by increasing output, without requiring an increase in the price level to induce increased supply. But once full employment is reached at the level of real output y_{FE}, any further increase in aggregate demand (for example, to AD_3) causes prices but not output to increase.

These days, however, there is general agreement, shared by New Keynesian as well as by supply-side economists, that in the *long run*, the *AS* curve is vertical. Figure 19.4(b) illustrates a vertical *LRAS* curve. Supply-side economists argue that the position of the *LRAS* curve is fixed by the economy's natural or equilibrium level of real output. This is the level of output consistent with the natural rate of unemployment in the labour market. Because output and employment are assumed to be at their natural or equilibrium levels, any expansion of aggregate demand — for example, from AD_1 to AD_2 — causes the price level to rise with no effect at all upon the levels of real output and employment, at least not in the long run. Although in the *short run* an increase in aggregate demand may increase output and employment above their natural levels (and reduce unemployment below its natural level), this cannot be sustained. In the long run, output and employment fall back to their natural levels, excess demand is created, and inflation results.

examiner's voice

The *AD/AS* model explained in Chapter 15 provides the theoretical framework that candidates are expected to use at both AS and A2 to explain macroeconomic problems and policy. Make sure you understand that successful supply-side policies shift the *LRAS* curve rightward (see below).

Bringing together the main elements of supply-side macroeconomic theory

The three panels of Figure 19.5 bring together three of the main elements of supply-side macroeconomics. Figure 19.5(a) depicts the economy's aggregate labour market, while Figure 19.5(b) and (c) respectively show Phillips curve and long-run aggregate supply diagrams.

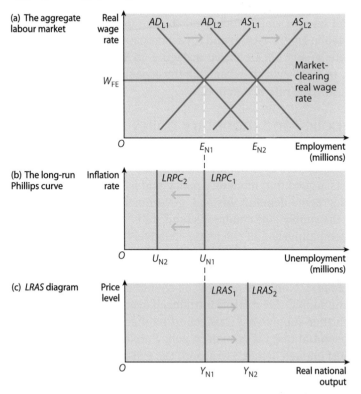

Figure 19.5 *Bringing together the natural level of employment, the natural rate of unemployment and the* LRAS *model in supply-side analysis*

examiner's voice

A good understanding of macroeconomics is underpinned by a sound knowledge of micro-economics. It is also reinforced by the skill of seeing links between different aspects of macroeconomic theory, in this case the aggregate labour market, the Phillips curve relationship and the *LRAS* curve.

Figure 19.5(a) and (c) respectively show equilibrium in the economy's labour market and product market. As Figure 19.5(a) shows, the natural or equilibrium

level of employment E_{N1} is determined in the economy's aggregate labour market at real wage rate w_{FE}. When the labour market is in equilibrium, the number of workers willing to work equals the number of workers whom firms wish to hire.

Figure 19.5(b) shows the natural *level* of unemployment (or natural *rate* if stated as a percentage of the labour force) immediately below E_{N1} in Figure 19.5(a). Likewise, the natural level of real output (y_{N1}) is depicted in Figure 19.5(c) immediately below E_{N1} and U_{N1} in Figures 19.5(a) and (b).

We shall now use Figure 19.5 to show how supply-side tax cuts affect employment, unemployment and the equilibrium level of real output in the economy. Suppose the government cuts *employers'* national insurance contributions. Employment costs fall and it becomes more attractive for firms to employ labour. As a result, in Figure 19.5(a), the aggregate demand for labour curve shifts rightward from AD_{L1} to AD_{L2}. Likewise, income tax cuts, which increase workers' disposable income, shift the aggregate supply curve of labour rightward from AS_{L1} to AS_{L2}. Both these changes increase the economy's natural level of *employment*, which rises from E_{N1} to E_{N2}.

In Figure 19.5(b), the long-run Phillips curve shifts leftward from $LRPC_1$ to $LRPC_2$, and the economy's natural level of *unemployment* falls from U_{N1} to U_{N2}. Finally, the *increase* in the natural level of employment and the *fall* in the natural level of unemployment depicted in Figure 19.5(a) and (b) accompany a rightward shift of the long-run aggregate supply (*LRAS*) curve in Figure 19.5(c). The curve shifts rightward from $LRAS_1$ to $LRAS_2$, which means that the economy can produce more output without increasing the rate of inflation.

The roles of fiscal policy and monetary policy in supply-side macroeconomics

When supply-side policies were first implemented in the early 1980s, extreme supply-side economists argued that monetary policy and fiscal policy should *not* be used to manage aggregate demand. Instead, government activity should be restricted to creating the supply-side conditions (and stable prices) which enable markets to function competitively and efficiently. Relatively few economists now support this extreme view. As described in Chapters 17 and 18, the new consensus is that monetary policy, but not fiscal policy (except in a supporting role), should be used to manage demand. Monetary policy itself should be supportive, both of the supply-side reforms introduced over the years and of any further supply-side changes to be made in the future. The essential tasks of monetary policy are to make sure there is just enough demand to absorb the extra output produced on the supply side of the economy and to maintain the general public's belief that the inflation rate will remain stable.

examiner's voice

As Chapter 18 explains, much supply-side economic policy centres on the use of fiscal policy to reduce the size of 'big government' (at the macro level) and to increase personal incentives (at the micro level).

With regard to fiscal policy, few economists or politicians now call for large budget deficits as the way to achieve growth and

full employment, and there is general agreement that the tax structure should be used in a supply-side way to create incentives for work, entrepreneurship, saving and investment.

Supply-side economics, New Keynesianism and New Labour

> We can safely abandon the basic doctrine of the 1980s: namely that the rich were not working because they had too little money, the poor because they had too much.
>
> Keynesian economist J. K. Galbraith, quoted in 1991

Since 1990 and the end of Margaret Thatcher's third and final government, Keynesian theories have once again had some influence on UK economic policy. However, Keynesianism has not really replaced free-market theory and supply-side economics. Rather, a synthesis has occurred between the two traditions.

The 'Old' Labour governments that pre-dated Thatcher's first government in 1979 believed that, in many spheres of economic activity, increased government spending and the growth of the public sector should replace market provision of goods and services. By contrast, Thatcher's New Right governments rolled back the frontiers of the state in favour of capitalism and free markets.

In 1997, Tony Blair achieved power by promising a **'Third Way'** lying somewhere between the 'Old' Labour and New Right extremes. Attempting to define the exact nature of the Third Way is difficult because both the literature supporting the venture and the New Labour government's policies have been ambiguous, populist and pragmatic. Critics have attacked the Third Way (and the term 'progressive politics' that has tended to replace it) for lacking any logical coherence.

However, three features of the Third Way's economic philosophy can be identified. First, in terms of macroeconomics, the Third Way accepted the basic principles of supply-side economics and the virtues of the free market. New Labour has continued to use 'appropriate' supply-side policies and has accepted that relying solely on demand-side policies neglects underlying problems which limit the economy's ability to produce goods and services that consumers actually want.

Second, New Labour claims that when it intervenes in markets, its policies are 'smart', in the sense they make the market economy function better. In the New Labour view, 'smart' interventionist policies oil the wheels of the economy rather than throw sand in its wheels.

Third, it is possible to identify a redistributive feature of the Third Way that seeks to prevent the development of social exclusion by encouraging people previously living on welfare to enter the labour market. New Labour governments have used three main policies to raise low incomes: the **national minimum wage**; the **working families tax credit**; and the **New Deal**, which aims to offer training and work opportunities to unemployed people between the ages of 18 and 24.

However, under New Labour, an important area of supply-side economics has largely fallen into disrepute. This is the central idea, illustrated by the Laffer curve,

which started the supply-side revolution in the late 1970s. According to this view, substantial income tax cuts increase the government's total tax revenue because the rich, who mainly benefit from tax cuts, work harder and earn more money. But statistical evidence, collected over the years in which supply-side policies have been implemented, gives little support to the supply-side argument that tax reductions increase total tax revenue. Paul Krugman, an acerbic critic of supply-side economics, comments:

> Any ideology whose main policy prescription is lower taxes on the rich is likely to have extra staying power. Those who preach [supply-side economics] are not going to have trouble putting bread on the table. [Despite the evidence,] the supply-siders will be with us for a long time to come. Failure may have brought out the silly side in some supply-siders, but they have not suddenly become cranks. They always were.

examiner's voice

Don't confuse New Labour's 'New Deal', introduced in the UK in the late 1990s, with the 'New Deal' introduced in the USA in the 1930s. The US New Deal, introduced by President Franklin Roosevelt, centred on using public works to try to end the Great Depression in the USA. By contrast, the Labour government's much more recent New Deal focused on labour market and welfare benefit reform.

Examples of supply-side economic policies

> There can be no doubt that the transformation of Britain's economic performance in the 1980s...is above all due to the supply-side policies we have introduced to allow markets of all kinds to work better.
>
> Nigel Lawson, Conservative chancellor of the exchequer, July 1988

We shall conclude the chapter with a brief survey of supply-side policies and an assessment of the extent to which supply-side policies have influenced recent New Labour governments. Most of the policies listed below have been implemented in the UK over the last 20 or so years. However, some policies, such as creating internal markets in the provision of state healthcare and education, have been partially implemented and then largely withdrawn. The supply-side policies are listed under three headings: industrial policy measures; labour market measures; and financial and capital market measures.

examiner's voice

While examination candidates are not expected to know every possible supply-side policy, it is a good idea to learn and understand at least two examples of the three main categories of supply-side policy listed in this section. Remember too that a question on labour markets requires knowledge of labour market supply-side policies, whereas an understanding of privatisation and commercialisation is much more relevant for explaining how supply-side policies may change the structure of goods markets.

Industrial policy measures

- **Privatisation.** This involves the sale or transfer of assets such as nationalised industries from the public sector to the private sector.
- **Contractualisation.** The state 'contracts out' to the private sector the provision of services that it previously produced itself, although taxation still pays for the services. Competitive tendering is usually employed in the contracting out process.

- **Marketisation (or commercialisation).** This involves shifting economic activity from non-market provision (financed by taxation) to commercial or market provision, for which the customer pays.
- **Deregulation.** This is the removal of previously imposed regulations in order to promote competition. Deregulation removes barriers to market entry to make markets contestable, and gets rid of unnecessary 'red tape' or bureaucracy, which increase firms' costs of production.
- **Internal markets**. In the National Health Service and education, where the state continues to be a major producer and provider of services, internal markets can be introduced to provide a form of commercial discipline and to improve efficiency. In an internal market, which is a substitute for privatisation, the taxpayer continues to finance hospitals and schools, but hospitals and schools 'earn' the money according to how many patients and pupils they attract.

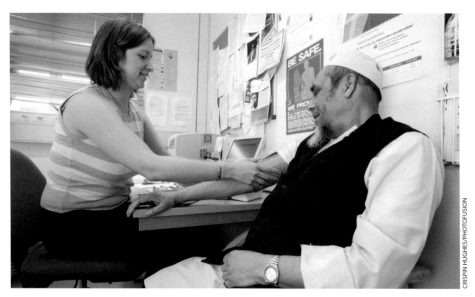

Although the NHS is paid for by the state, it is under various commercial pressures

- **Reducing and bypassing local government.** Governments can set up agencies accountable to central government to deliver local services, and establish an 'enterprise culture' in such agencies to instil private sector 'commercial disciplines'. Schools and further education authorities can be removed from local government control.
- **Quangofication.** In contrast to a **non-governmental organisation (NGO)**, which is completely independent of government, quangos and quagos are linked with, and paid for by, the state. The term **quango** is an acronym for 'quasi-autonomous *non-governmental* organisation': that is, an agency accountable to government, but not strictly a part of government, publicly funded, but with considerable freedom of executive action. Quangos undertake services for which the government is ultimately responsible. A **quago** (quasi-autonomous *governmental*

organisation) is similar to a quango, but staffed by civil servants employed by central government and more directly under the control of central government. The Competition Commission, Ofsted and regulatory agencies such as OFCOM and OFGEM are examples of quagos.

Labour market measures

- **Lower rates of income tax.** Marginal rates of income tax may be reduced to create labour market incentives, and tax thresholds or personal tax allowances may be raised to remove the low-paid from the tax net. There may soon be pressure for the UK to adopt a flat-rate income tax, i.e. a proportionate income tax, as flat taxes (which are more regressive) have been successfully introduced in some of the central European countries that joined the EU in 2004.
- **Reducing state welfare benefits relative to average earnings.** Lower benefit levels create incentives to choose low-paid employment in preference to claiming unemployment-related benefits. In addition, welfare benefits can be made more difficult to claim, and available only to claimants genuinely looking for work. Making benefits less attractive may also reduce the unemployment trap.
- **Changing employment law to reduce the power of trade unions.** This may involve removing trade unions' legal protection; encouraging employers not to recognise and negotiate with unions; replacing collective bargaining with individual wage negotiation and employer determination of pay; and restricting the right to strike and to undertake other industrial action.
- **Introducing short-term contracts.** This involves replacing 'jobs for life' with short-term labour contracts, and introducing profit-related and performance-related pay. Critics of these policies believe that they lead to even greater poverty and inequality for ordinary workers in an increasingly casualised and exploited part-time labour force.
- **Repealing legislation which limits employers' freedom to employ.** This makes it easier for employers to 'hire and fire' workers.
- **More flexible pension arrangements.** Governments may encourage workers to 'opt out' of state pensions and to arrange private pension plans so as to reduce the burden on taxpayers. Workers may also be allowed to transfer private sector pensions between employers when changing jobs.
- **Improving the efficiency of UK housing markets.** Much of the stock of socially provided housing (council houses) has been privatised, though it is debatable whether this has improved the geographical mobility of labour between different parts of the country. Governments have encouraged the private sector and housing associations to build more affordable housing, but the number of new houses built each year remains relatively small by historical standards.
- **Improving the training of labour.** Training agencies and City Technology Colleges have been established to develop vocational technical education. However, UK governments have rejected the proposal to impose a 'training tax' on all employers to prevent 'free-riding' by firms with no training schemes which 'poach' trained workers from firms that do train their workers.

Financial and capital market measures

- **Deregulating financial markets.** The cost of borrowing for UK firms can be reduced by creating greater competition among banks and building societies, and opening up the UK financial markets to overseas banks and financial institutions. Financial deregulation and the removal of foreign exchange controls also encourage 'inward' investment or FDI, by overseas firms such as Toyota and Nissan.
- **Encouraging saving.** Governments have created special tax privileges for saving. They also encouraged saving by giving individual shareholders first preference in the market for the shares issued when former nationalised industries, such as British Gas, were privatised. However, most individual shareholders quickly sold their shares to institutional shareholders. This negated one of the main reasons for privatisation.
- **Promoting entrepreneurship.** Governments have encouraged the growth of 'popular capitalism' and an 'enterprise culture'. Company taxation has been reduced and markets deregulated to encourage risk taking. However, critics of the New Labour governments believe that many of the regulations introduced since 1997 have had the opposite effect: discouraging rather than encouraging entrepreneurship.
- **Reducing public spending and public sector borrowing.** This has been done to free resources for private sector use and avoid crowding out, although again the policy has been reversed in recent years.

Summary

This chapter has brought together a number of themes introduced in earlier chapters. Chapter 8 explained the *industrial policy* aspects of supply-side economics, covering privatisation and deregulation, while Chapters 11 and 18 introduced supply-side theories of the working of labour markets and the role of supply-side fiscal policy. This chapter has stressed that supply-side theories and policies primarily affect incentives and disincentives at the microeconomic level, although the more macroeconomic aspects of supply-side economics are also significant.

To understand a school of thought and its ideology, it is necessary to appreciate its historical origin, and the way it has developed over the years. This chapter has covered the historical development of supply-side economics, from the growth of the New Right in the 1970s and 1980s, originating out of dissatisfaction with Keynesian demand management policies, to its recent significance in the Third Way policies of New Labour. The association of supply-side economics with Reaganomics and Thatcherism was also mentioned.

Although, at present, supply-side theory and policy continue to be very important, the idea that started the supply-side revolution has fallen into disrepute. There is little evidence that income tax cuts, from which the rich benefit the most, increase tax revenue, though the supporters of flat taxes dispute this.

Self-testing questions

1 What is supply-side economics?

2 Distinguish between the 'narrow' and the 'wider' meaning of supply-side economics.

3 Distinguish between a government's role as provider and enabler.

4 What does the Laffer curve show?

5 What is the significance of an upward-sloping supply curve of labour for supply-side economics?

6 Distinguish between tax avoidance and tax evasion.

7 Explain the case for and against a flat-rate income tax.

8 List the main supply-side policies.

9 What is (or was) New Labour's 'Third Way'?

10 Relate the New Deal and the national minimum wage to supply-side economics.

11 Briefly describe an example of an industrial supply-side policy, a labour market supply-side policy, and a financial or capital market supply-side policy.

12 Assess the success of supply-side policies in the UK.

Part **7**

International economics

Chapter 20
International trade and globalisation

Specification focus

This chapter covers the Module 1 topics of specialisation, division of labour and exchange, before focusing on the various international trade topics included in the Module 6 specification.

AS **Module 1 Markets and Market Failure**
Production and Efficiency

A2 **Module 6 Government Policy, the National and International Economy**
The International Economy

A2 **Synoptic coverage**
The A2 Unit 6 examination expects candidates to extend the Module 1 coverage of the benefits of specialisation. Candidates should also know why specialisation necessitates an efficient means of exchanging goods and services, and be able to provide an explanation of the benefits of internationalisation and free trade.

Introduction

This is the first of three chapters devoted to international economics. The chapter begins by explaining the case for international specialisation and trade. Having explained the benefits of the international division of labour and the principle of comparative advantage, the chapter then considers counter-arguments to justify import controls or protectionism. This section of the chapter is followed by an analysis of the welfare gains resulting from free trade and of the welfare losses caused by tariffs.

The chapter goes on to explain changes in the patterns of world trade and UK trade. The main changes have been a switch from a 'North/South' pattern to a 'North/North' pattern of trade, and the growth of exports of manufactured goods produced in newly industrialising countries (NICs), particularly China. The chapter concludes with a brief survey of the meaning of globalisation and of the role of the World Trade Organisation (WTO).

The case for international trade

Widening choice

Imagine a small country such as Iceland in a world without international trade. As a closed economy, Iceland's production possibilities are limited to the goods and services that its narrow resource base can produce. This means that its average costs of production are likely to be high because its small population and the absence of export markets mean that economies of scale and long production runs cannot be achieved. At the same time, the consumption possibilities of Iceland's inhabitants are restricted to the goods that it can produce.

Compare this with Iceland's position in a world completely open to international trade. In an open economy, imports of raw materials and energy greatly boost Iceland's production possi-

International trade can bring higher living standards

bilities. In theory at least, Iceland can now produce a much wider range of goods. In practice, however, Iceland produces the relatively few goods and services that it is good at producing, and imports all the rest. By gaining access to the much larger world market, Iceland's industries benefit from economies of scale and long production runs. Likewise imports of food and other consumer goods present Iceland's inhabitants with a vast array of choice and the possibility of a much higher living standard and level of economic welfare than are possible in a world without trade.

Specialisation and the division of labour

To explain these benefits further, we must understand two very important economic principles: the division of labour and the principle of comparative advantage.

Over 200 years ago, the great classical economist, Adam Smith, first explained how, within a single production unit or firm (he took the example of a pin factory), output can increase if workers specialise in different tasks in a manufacturing process. Smith established one of the most fundamental of all economic principles: the benefits of **specialisation** and the **division of labour**. According to Adam Smith, there are three main reasons why specialisation increases total output:

- Workers don't need to switch between tasks, so time is saved.
- More and better machinery or capital is employed. Increasing capital at the same rate at which the labour force is increasing

@xaminer's voice
The AS Module 1 specification requires candidates to understand the benefits of the division of labour and specialisation. The A2 Module 6 specification extends this knowledge to cover trade theory, requiring candidates to understand the model of comparative advantage and to evaluate its importance and limitations. A knowledge of trade theory is not needed for AS.

is called **capital widening**. Increasing the amount of capital per worker is called **capital deepening**.

■ Practice makes workers more efficient and productive when performing specialised tasks (although because of 'deskilling', boredom and the creation of alienation towards employers, this can easily become a disadvantage).

The principle of the division of labour not only explains specialisation between workers within a factory: it can also be extended to explain the specialisation between productive units, plants or factories within a firm; specialisation between separate firms; and lastly, geographical or 'spatial' specialisation both internally within a country and externally between countries. *International* specialisation is the subject of this chapter.

*e*xaminer's voice

Chapter 4 explains how specialisation and the division of labour cause the marginal product of labour to increase. However, when the benefits of specialisation are exhausted, the law of diminishing marginal productivity (or diminishing returns) sets in, assuming of course that capital employed is fixed in quantity.

Absolute advantage

The benefits of the division of labour suggest that if each of the world's countries, with its own endowment of natural resources such as soil, climate and minerals, and of 'man-made resources' such as capital, know-how and labour skills, specialises in what it does best, total world output or production can increase compared to the outcome without specialisation. Being 'better at' producing a good or service means that a country can produce the good at the lowest cost in terms of resources used. Using microeconomic terminology, the country is technically and productively efficient in producing the good. We can also say that a country that is absolutely 'best at', or most technically efficient at, producing a good or service, possesses an **absolute advantage** in the good's production. Conversely, if it is not the best, the country suffers an absolute disadvantage compared to other more technically efficient producers.

*e*xaminer's voice

The A2 Module 6 specification requires candidates to be aware of the distinction between absolute advantage and comparative advantage.

To explain absolute advantage, we shall assume that there are two countries, Atlantis and Pacifica, each with just 2 units of resource. Only two goods can be produced: guns and butter. Each unit of resource, or indeed a fraction of each unit (because we shall assume that resources or inputs are divisible), can be switched from one industry to another if so desired in each country. In each country the production possibilities are such that 1 unit of resource can produce:

in Atlantis: 4 guns   or   2 tonnes of butter

in Pacifica: 1 gun   or   6 tonnes of butter

Quite clearly, in terms of technical efficiency, Atlantis is 'best at' — or has an absolute advantage in — producing guns. It is four times more technically efficient in gun production than Pacifica. However, this is not the case for butter production. Pacifica is three times more technically efficient in butter production and so possesses an absolute advantage in this good.

Suppose that both countries devote half their total resources to each activity (that is, 1 unit of resource out of the 2 units available for each country). Atlantis produces 4 guns, Pacifica produces 1 gun, which means that 5 guns are produced in total. Likewise, total butter production is 8 tonnes. Atlantis produces 2 tonnes and Pacifica produces 6 tonnes.

Now let's see what happens when each country produces only the good in which it has an absolute advantage. Atlantis devotes both its resource units to guns, producing 8 guns. Likewise, Pacifica completely specialises, producing 12 tonnes of butter with its 2 units of resource.

- Without specialisation, outputs are 5 guns and 8 tonnes of butter.
- With specialisation, outputs become 8 guns and 12 tonnes of butter.

In this example, specialisation produces a net output gain of 3 guns and 4 tonnes of butter.

But for output gains to translate into 'gains from trade', two further factors have to be taken into account. First, administration and transport costs occur whenever trade takes place. As a result, the output gains from trade are:

(3 guns + 4 tonnes of butter) – transport and administration costs

Clearly, specialisation and trade are not worthwhile if transport and administration costs exceed the output gains resulting from specialisation.

Second, assuming that only two countries trade with each other, for output gains to transfer into *welfare* gains for the inhabitants of both countries, the goods being traded must be in demand in the importing country. Assuming that both goods are demanded in both countries, each country exports its surplus to the other country once it has satisfied its own inhabitants' demand for the good in which it specialises. (This **double coincidence of wants** is not necessary when more than two countries trade together.)

But suppose Atlantis's inhabitants are vegans who refuse to eat animal products, while Pacifica's inhabitants are pacifists who hate guns. For Atlantis's inhabitants, butter is a *bad* rather than a *good*. Likewise, guns are a bad for Pacifica's residents. (A **good** yields **utility** or **economic welfare** to consumers, but a **bad** yields **disutility** or **negative welfare**.) Atlantis refuses to import butter, and Pacifica refuses to buy guns. Specialisation and trade do not take place. Without suitable demand conditions, the case for specialisation and trade disappears.

Comparative advantage

Absolute advantage must not be confused with the rather more subtle concept of **comparative advantage**. To introduce and illustrate this very important economic principle, we shall change the production possibilities of both countries so that

Atlantis possesses the absolute advantage for *both* guns and butter (which, of course, means that Pacifica has an absolute disadvantage in both goods).

One unit of resource now produces:

in Atlantis: 4 guns   or   2 tonnes of butter

in Pacifica: 1 gun   or   1 tonne of butter

Although Atlantis is 'best at' — or has an absolute advantage in — producing both guns and butter, the country possesses a comparative advantage only in gun production. This is because comparative advantage is measured in terms of **opportunity cost**, or what a country gives up when it increases the output of an industry by 1 unit. The country that gives up *least* of the other commodity when increasing output of a particular commodity by 1 unit possesses the comparative advantage in that good. Ask yourself how many guns Atlantis has to give up in order to increase its butter output by 1 tonne. The answer is 2 guns. But Pacifica only has to give up 1 gun to produce an extra tonne of butter. Thus Pacifica possesses a *comparative* advantage in butter production even though it has an *absolute* disadvantage in both products.

When one country possesses an absolute advantage in both industries, as in the example above, its comparative advantage always lies in producing the good in which its absolute advantage is greatest. Similarly, the country that is absolutely worst at both activities possesses a comparative advantage in the industry in which its absolute disadvantage is least.

examiner's voice

An absolute advantage model of two economies can also be used to illustrate comparative advantage. In the absolute advantage model, in which each country has an absolute advantage in a different activity, each country has a comparative advantage in the activity in which it has an absolute advantage.

In this example, *complete* specialisation results in *more* guns but *less* butter being produced, compared to a situation in which each country devotes half its total resources to each activity. Without specialisation, the combined output of both countries is 5 guns and 3 tonnes of butter. With complete specialisation, this changes to 8 guns and 2 tonnes of butter. While production of guns has increased, production of butter has fallen.

When one country has an absolute advantage in both goods, *complete* specialisation in accordance with the principle of comparative advantage does not result in a net output gain. The output of one good rises, but the output of the other good falls. However, *partial* specialisation can produce a net output gain. For example, suppose Pacifica (which suffers an *absolute* disadvantage in *both* goods) completely specialises and produces 2 tonnes of butter. By contrast, Atlantis (which has the absolute advantage in both goods) devotes just enough resource (half a unit) to 'top up' world production of butter to 3 tonnes. This means that Atlantis can still produce 6 guns using 1.5 units of resource. Total production in both countries is therefore 6 guns and 3 tonnes of butter. At least as much butter and more guns are now produced compared to the earlier 'self-sufficient' outcome. This example

shows that specialisation can produce a net output gain, even though one country is absolutely better at both activities.

Comparative advantage and the occupational division of labour

The division of labour explains why different people have different jobs, as well as why different countries produce different goods and services. Comparative advantage provides one of the explanations of the occupational division of labour.

Consider a situation in which a solicitor who advises clients employs a secretary to type her letters. If she wished to, the solicitor could perform the secretary's job. Likewise, having watched his boss at work, the secretary could advise the solicitor's clients. Assuming that both individuals can do both jobs, 1 hour of labour time produces for each worker:

for the solicitor: advising 4 clients   or   writing 2 letters

for the legal assistant: advising 1 client   or   writing 1 letter

These production possibilities show that the solicitor is not only a better lawyer than the person she employs, she is also better at typing letters. So why doesn't the solicitor do her secretary's work herself? Comparative advantage provides *part* of the answer. Although possessing an *absolute* advantage in both activities, the solicitor's *comparative* advantage is in being a lawyer. Time is limited and if the solicitor writes her own letters, she forgoes the opportunity to advise 2 clients in the time taken to write a letter. By contrast, her secretary sacrifices the opportunity to advise just 1 client for each letter he writes. (There are, of course, other factors influencing the occupational division of labour, not least the fact that restrictive practices and entry barriers prevent many workers switching between jobs.)

> **examiner's voice**
>
> The division of labour is an AS topic in Module 1. However, it could be tested synoptically by an A2 examination question. Comparative advantage could be used as part of an explanation of the division of labour.

The assumptions underlying the principle of comparative advantage

When arguing that definite benefits result from specialisation and trade in accordance with the principle of comparative advantage, we made a number of rather strong but not necessarily realistic assumptions. Indeed, the case for trade — and hence the case *against* import controls and other forms of protectionism — is heavily dependent upon these assumptions. Likewise, some of the arguments in favour of import controls and against free trade, which shall be explained shortly, depend on showing that the assumptions necessary for the benefits of specialisation and trade to occur are simply not met in real life. These assumptions are as follows:

- Each country's endowment of factors of production, including capital and labour, is fixed and immobile between countries, although factors can be switched between industries within a country. In the course of international trade, finished goods rather than factors of production or inputs are assumed to be mobile between countries.

- The principle of comparative advantage assumes constant returns to scale. In our example, 1 unit of resource is assumed to produce 4 guns or 2 tonnes of butter in Atlantis, whether it is the first unit of resource employed or the millionth unit. But in the real world, increasing or decreasing returns to scale are both possible and indeed likely. In a world of increasing returns, the more a country specialises in a particular industry, the more efficient it becomes, thereby increasing its comparative advantage. But if decreasing returns to scale occur, specialisation erodes efficiency and destroys the initial comparative advantage. A good example occurs in agriculture, where over-specialisation can result in monoculture or the growing of a single cash crop for export. Monoculture often leads to soil erosion, vulnerability to pests and falling future agricultural yields.
- The principle of comparative advantage implicitly assumes relatively stable demand and cost conditions. Over-specialisation can cause a country to become particularly vulnerable to sudden changes in demand or to changes in the cost and availability of imported raw materials or energy. Changes in costs, and new inventions and technical progress, can quickly eliminate a country's earlier comparative advantage. The greater the uncertainty about the future, the weaker the case for complete specialisation. Indeed, if a country is self-sufficient in all important respects, it is neutralised against the danger of importing recession and unemployment from the rest of the world when international demand collapses.

Comparative advantage and competitive advantage

A country may possess a comparative advantage, even though it is absolutely worse than other countries at producing the good. For this reason, *comparative* advantage must not be confused with *competitive* advantage. A country, or a firm within a country, enjoys a **competitive advantage** when it produces better-quality goods at lower costs and better prices than its rivals. Competitive advantage is indeed more similar to *absolute* advantage than to comparative advantage.

Dynamic factors such as those we came across in the context of endogenous growth theory in Chapter 13 can create competitive advantage. Successful investment undertaken over many years equips a country with modern, 'state-of-the-art' production capacity, capable of producing high-quality goods that people want to buy. Properly funded and organised research and development (R & D) contributes in a similar way, while the stock of human capital resulting from investment in education and training adds to competitive advantage.

Factors that create competitive advantage can trigger a **virtuous spiral** of larger profits, higher investment, better products and greater sales, which in turn leads to even higher profits, and so on. Conversely, countries and firms that are not competitive may enter a **vicious spiral** of decline. Inability to compete causes profits to fall, which in turn reduces investment.

*e*xaminer's voice

Competitive advantage is not the same as comparative advantage. Make sure you understand the difference between the two concepts.

The quality of goods declines and sales are lost to more competitive countries or firms. Profits again fall (maybe disappearing altogether), and a further round in the vicious circle of decline is unleashed.

The case for import controls and protectionism

Import controls can be divided into quantity controls such as **import quotas**, which put a maximum limit on imports, and **tariffs or import duties** (and their opposite, **export subsidies**), which raise the price of imports (or reduce the price of exports).

Supporters of free trade believe that import controls prevent countries from specialising in activities in which they have a comparative advantage and trading their surpluses. As a result, production takes place inefficiently, and the growth of economic welfare is reduced. But as we have already noted, the case for free trade depends to a large extent upon some of the assumptions underlying the principle of comparative advantage. Destroy these assumptions, and the case for free trade is weakened.

> **e*xaminer's voice**
>
> The case *for* import controls and protectionism is really the same as the case *against* free trade. Likewise, the case *against* import controls is really the same as the case *for* free trade or trade liberalisation.

The following arguments can be made in support of import controls:

- **Infant industries.** As we have already explained, many economic activities benefit from increasing returns to scale, which mean that the more a country specialises in a particular industry, the more efficient it becomes. This increases its competitive advantage. Developing countries justify the use of import controls to protect infant industries from established rivals in advanced economies. Protectionism is needed while newly established industries develop full economies of scale.
- **Strategic trade theory.** The infant industry argument is closely related to strategic trade theory, a relatively new theory that has grown in influence in recent years. Strategic trade theory argues that comparative and competitive advantage is often not 'natural'. Rather, governments try to create competitive advantage by nurturing strategically selected industries or economic sectors. This justifies protecting the industries while competitive advantage is being built up. The skills that are gained will then spill over to help other sectors in the economy. Strategic trade theory also argues that protectionism can prevent exploitation by a foreign-based monopoly.
- **Agricultural efficiency.** As we noted earlier in the context of agriculture, mono-culture erodes efficiency and destroys comparative advantage that existed before specialisation took place. Decreasing returns to scale weaken the case for complete specialisation.
- **Changes in demand or cost conditions.** As we have seen, over-specialisation may cause a country to become particularly vulnerable to sudden changes in demand or to changes in the cost and availability of imported raw materials or energy.

- **Sunset industries.** A rather similar case to the infant industry argument is sometimes made in advanced industrial economies such as the UK to protect older industries from the competition of infant industries in developing countries. Keynesian economists have sometimes advocated the selective use of import controls as a potentially effective supply-side policy instrument to prevent unnecessary deindustrialisation and to allow orderly rather than disruptive structural change in the manufacturing base of the economy. According to this view, import controls are justified, at least on a temporary basis, to minimise the social and economic cost of the painful adjustment process, as the structure of an economy alters in response either to changing demand or to changing technology and comparative advantage.

- **Dumping.** When a country produces too much of a good for its own domestic market, the surplus is then sold at a price below cost in overseas markets. Import controls are sometimes justified as a means to prevent 'unfair' competition.

- **Demerit goods.** In the case of demerit goods such as narcotic drugs and weapons, an *output* gain does not necessarily lead to a *welfare* gain. Governments argue they have a moral duty to ban imports of heroin, cocaine and handguns to protect the welfare of their citizens.

- **Self-sufficiency.** Politically, it is often argued that protection is necessary for military and strategic reasons to ensure that a country is relatively self-sufficient in vital foodstuffs, energy and raw materials in a time of war.

- **Employment.** Trade unions argue that import controls are necessary to prevent multinational firms shifting capital to low-wage developing countries and exporting their output back to the countries from which the capital was moved. They further argue the case for employing labour, however inefficiently, in protected industries rather than allowing labour to suffer the greatest inefficiency of all: mass unemployment. This is an example of **second-best theory**. The 'second-best' argument stems from the fact that the 'first best' (free trade in a world of fully employed economies and perfect markets) is unattainable. Therefore, a country can settle legitimately for the 'second best'. Employing resources inefficiently, protected by tariffs, is better than not employing resources at all.

Three different views of world trade

The American economist, Paul Krugman, has identified three different views of international trade. Krugman calls these the *classical*, *strategic* and *mercantilist* views. The **classical view**, which supports completely free trade, is the view set out in the early sections of this chapter: that all countries can benefit from higher output and economic welfare, providing they specialise in accordance with the principle of comparative advantage.

The **strategic trade theory** argument leads to the opposite conclusion: that import controls can sometimes be justified. However, Krugman believes that many governments justify import controls for **mercantilist** rather than strategic reasons, using strategic arguments to disguise the true reason why they wish to impose import

controls. Adopting the view that 'exports are good and imports are bad', mercan-tilists believe that a government should use all possible means to maximise its trade surpluses at the expense of other countries. If free trade can achieve this 'beggar my neighbour' aim, the country pressures other countries to drop import controls. But if its own industries become uncompetitive and go into decline, the government switches tack and uses all available arguments ('unfair' competition, dumping and strategic trade theory) to justify the introduction of import controls.

According to Krugman, rich developed countries benefited from protectionism while they established their national wealth. However, they now put pressure on poor countries to abandon import controls and to allow overseas-based multinational corporations unlimited access to their economies. Opponents of globalisation argue that free trade theory is used to justify first world economic imperialism.

International trade and welfare

Welfare gains and transfers resulting from free trade and welfare losses resulting from tariffs

Figure 20.1 shows how economic welfare is affected by free trade. In the absence of trade, domestic demand for a good within a country can only be met by domestic supply (that is, by firms producing *within* the country).

If trade is solely domestic, market equilibrium occurs at point X in Figure 20.1. Consumers pay price P_1 for the good, and the quantity bought and sold is Q_1. Consumer welfare (or consumer surplus) is area A, a triangle with points XZP_1. Likewise, producer welfare (or producer surplus) is areas $B + D$, a triangle with points XP_1U.

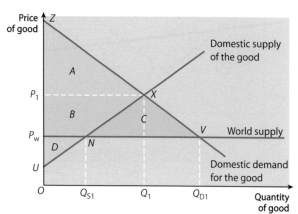

Figure 20.1 *The welfare gain and loss resulting from free trade*

But consider what happens in a world of completely free trade, in which domesti-cally produced goods have to compete with cheaper imports. Imports are priced at the ruling world price of P_W, which is lower than P_1. In this situation, equilibrium now occurs in the domestic market at point V. Although domestic demand has increased to Q_{D1}, domestic supply (located where the domestic supply curve cuts the horizontal price line at P_W) falls to Q_{S1}. Imports (equal to $Q_{D1} - Q_{S1}$) fill the gap between domestic demand and supply.

To know how imports affect economic welfare within the country, it is important to understand how consumer surplus and producer surplus change. Consumer surplus increases by the wedge-shaped area $B + C$, bounded by the points $P_W VXP_1$. But producer surplus falls by the wedge-shaped area B, bounded by $P_W NXP_1$.

Area *B* shows a welfare *transfer* from producers to consumers, occurring because imports have reduced the good's price. Because the consumer surplus gain exceeds the size of this transfer (or the loss of producer surplus), a **net welfare gain** results, equal to the area *C*. Although domestic firms have lost the producer surplus shown by area *B*, they still receive *some* producer surplus, but this is restricted to area *D*.

How a tariff affects economic welfare

Domestic firms may pressure the government to introduce a tariff to protect the home market. Of course, if the tariff equals the distance between P_1 and P_W (in Figure 20.1), equilibrium returns to the original position before imports entered the country. But suppose the government imposes a smaller tariff, which is just sufficient to raise the price of imports (and also of domestically produced goods) to $P_W + t$ in Figure 20.2. At price $P_W + t$, domestic demand falls to Q_{D2}, while domestic supply rises to Q_{S2}. Imports fall to $Q_{D2} - Q_{S2}$.

> **examiner's voice**
>
> How a tariff affects economic welfare is highly relevant for analysing the effect of the common external tariff and the levy on agricultural imports imposed by the European Union.

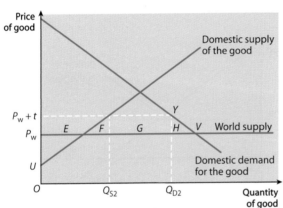

Figure 20.2 *The welfare loss resulting from a tariff*

At the higher price brought about by the tariff, consumer surplus *falls* by the wedge-shaped area $P_W V Y P_W + t$ (which equals the area $E + F + G + H$). The higher price increases the producer surplus of domestic firms by the area E, and the government gains tariff revenue shown by the area G. The areas E and G are *transfers* of welfare away from consumers, respectively to domestic producers and to the government. Taking account of these transfers, the **net welfare loss** resulting from the tariff is $(E + F + G + H) - (E + G)$, which equals $F + H$.

Optimal tariff theory

According to optimal tariff theory, which is illustrated in Figure 20.3, a country (though not *all* countries) can benefit or gain a 'beggar my neighbour' advantage by setting an **optimal tariff**. An optimal tariff creates a net welfare gain for the importing country, which is gained at the expense of countries exporting the good. This is because the tariff reduces demand for the good to such an extent that the world price of the good falls to P_{W2}. Providing the tariff is set at a level that maintains the price of the good within the country at $P_W + t$, the net welfare gain enjoyed by the importing country is shown by the area $(G + J) - (F + H)$. Area $G + J$ measures the revenue that the government gains from the tariff. Once again, area G measures the transfer of welfare from consumer surplus to the government. However, area J measures the 'beggar my neighbour' transfer of welfare from overseas producers to the government, brought about by the fall in the world price of the good. Because area *J* is larger than area *F* + *H*, the country as a whole achieves a net welfare gain.

Arguably, rich countries in the European Union and the USA possess sufficient economic power to benefit from optimal tariffs. But poor developing countries lack such power. The high import duty imposed by the EU on sugar imports from the developing world is an optimal tariff, although hardly so for the millions of poor sugar cane producers who find themselves barred from the lucrative EU

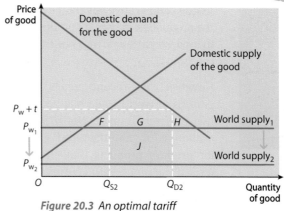

Figure 20.3 An optimal tariff

market. As a result of the tariff, in 2004 high-cost European sugar beet producers enjoyed EU guaranteed prices of € 716 a tonne, while producers in developing countries such as Brazil and Cuba had to sell at the world price of € 157. EU producers and the EU budget benefit. However, EU sugar consumers do not benefit (at least not directly), and sugar cane producers in the rest of the world suffer a welfare loss and do not benefit at all.

The changing pattern of world and UK trade

Comparative advantage and the pattern of world trade

When, over two centuries ago, Adam Smith first explained the advantages of the division of labour, and a few years later in the early nineteenth century another distinguished classical economist, David Ricardo, developed Adam Smith's ideas into the principle of comparative advantage, they were not just interested in abstract theory. Instead, like most great economists, they

examiner's voice

The A2 Module 6 specification requires candidates to understand the reasons for changes in the pattern of trade between the UK and the rest of the world.

wished to change society for the better by influencing the politicians of their day. Smith and Ricardo believed in the virtues of a competitive market economy and industrial capitalism. Ricardo, in particular, believed that a single country such as the UK and, indeed, the whole world economy could only reach their full productive potential, maximising output, welfare and living standards, if the market economy was truly international. He argued that each country should specialise in what it did best and trade the output that was surplus to its needs in a world free of tariffs and other forms of protectionism.

To many people living in industrial countries during the nineteenth century and the first half of the twentieth century, it must have seemed almost 'natural' that the earliest countries to industrialise, such as the UK, had done so because they possessed a competitive and comparative advantage in manufacturing. It probably seemed equally 'natural' that a pattern of world trade should have developed in which industrialised countries in what is now called the 'North' exported manufactured goods in exchange for foodstuffs and raw materials produced by countries

whose comparative advantage lay in the production of primary products — in modern parlance, the countries of the 'South'.

However, in recent years, the pattern of world trade has become quite different from the North/South exchange of manufactured goods for primary products that charac-terised the nineteenth century. In a North/North pattern of trade, the developed industrial economies now exchange goods and services mostly

Countries of the 'South' have traditionally exported raw materials and foodstuffs such as sugar cane

with each other. Only a relatively small proportion of their trade is with the non-oil-producing developing world. Indeed, a growing proportion of UK trade takes place with other European countries, and especially with other members of the EU. (Nonetheless, countries in the South increasingly sell more manufactured goods to the North than to each other — an indication of the growth within the developing world of newly industrialising countries (NICs), such as South Korea and China.)

The Heckscher–Ohlin theory of international trade

In the 1930s two Swedish economists, Heckscher and Ohlin, explained the North/South exchange of manufactured goods for primary products in terms of factor endowments. The **Heckscher–Ohlin theory**, which is really an extension of the principle of comparative advantage, argues that a capital-rich country is likely to industrialise and export capital-intensive manufactured goods, but if capital is scarce relative to labour, the country specialises in and exports labour-intensive primary products.

More recently, the theory has been attacked by supporters of the **dependency theory** of trade and development. Opponents of globalisation argue that developing countries possess little capital because the system of world trade and payments has been organised by developed industrial economies to their own advantage. The **terms of trade** — the ratio of a country's export prices to its import prices — have as a general rule moved in favour of industrialised countries and against primary producers. This means that, by exporting the same amount of manufactured goods to the developing world, a developed economy can import a greater quantity of raw materials or foodstuffs in exchange. By the same token, the developing country must export more in order to buy the same quantity of capital goods or energy vital for development. Globally, the movement of the terms of trade in favour of developed nations has raised levels of income and standards of living in the richer countries at the expense of poorer developing countries. However, there have been some exceptions, namely NICs and the oil-producing non-industrial countries, which have benefited from substantial increases in the price of oil.

Economists of the dependency school argue that the transfer of wealth and resources to the richer countries is further promoted by profit flows and interest payments. On an international scale, dividends and profits flow to multinational corporations with headquarters in North America, western Europe and Japan, from their subsidiaries in the developing world. Similarly, there is a flow of interest payments to western banks from loans originally made to finance development in Third World countries. In most years, flows of dividends and interest payments from South to North exceed aid flows in the opposite direction.

Explaining the pattern of world trade

How, then, can we explain the modern pattern of international trade, dominated as it is by the exchange of manufactured goods and increasingly services between the industrialised market economies of the North? We shall offer four possible explanations:

- a modified Heckscher–Ohlin theory
- the technology gap theory
- the product life cycle theory
- the role of consumption patterns in determining world trade

A modified Heckscher–Ohlin theory

By extending the concept of capital to include labour skills in the form of human capital, in slightly modified form the Heckscher–Ohlin theory explains why developed economies export apparently labour-intensive manufactured goods, which in fact incorporate a considerable amount of investment in training and labour skills.

The technology gap theory

This theory explains the growth and the pattern of world trade in terms of the nature of technical progress. Technical changes are always occurring, but at different rates in different countries, and the advanced industrial economies are usually the leaders. This gives these countries an advantage in developing and exporting products based on the new technologies. This initial advantage is often reinforced by economies of scale, leading to long production runs, which the monopoly position of the innovating country creates.

But when the new technology 'matures' and becomes widely available to other countries, competitive and comparative advantage may shift to less sophisticated economies. Indeed, apparently less-developed economies may take the lead in developing later generations of the new technology, while the initial innovator experiences the disadvantage of factories fitted with what becomes out-of-date equipment. Often, foreign subsidiaries of multinational firms, and independent firms operating under licence, will produce the good and export it back to the original pioneering country, which may have gone on to develop other products and technologies. Thus a technological gap between the western industrial market economies and others, including the NICs, explains much of the pattern of world trade in manufactured goods.

The product life-cycle theory

Like the technology gap theory, the product life-cycle theory explains the pattern of world production, specialisation and trade in manufactured goods in terms of the nature of technical progress. Early in its life cycle and immediately following its successful innovation, a product is likely to be strongly differentiated from competing products. Product differentiation creates monopoly power and high profits for the innovative firm, which in turn provide an important motive for further technical development. At this early stage of the product's life cycle, manufacture is usually located in the country of origin of the innovative company, where the company's research and development facilities are concentrated.

At the next stage, the company that developed the product loses its monopoly over existing technology. By this time, the product has become more standardised and subject to agreed international specifications. Mass production, economies of scale and the use of relatively unskilled and cheap labour for routine jobs allow production to move to NICs.

At a late stage in the product life cycle, the firms that innovated the product attempt to maintain their lead by introducing further technical progress and product development. At the same time, they produce older versions of the product in NICs, either under licence to local firms or in their own branch factories and subsidiary companies. Many of the goods produced in NICs are then exported back to the developed world.

The changing location pattern of personal computer manufacture, since the launch of the IBM personal computer or PC in 1981, provides a good illustration of the product life-cycle theory. Personal computer manufacturing is still dominated by US companies such as Dell and HP, which maintain their headquarters and undertake their pioneering research and development in locations such as California's 'silicon valley'. However, to maintain their profit and industry leadership, US computer companies currently source much of the manufacture of computer components to independent companies or to their own branch factories in countries such as Malaysia and China.

In 2004, the company that had launched the PC went one stage further. IBM sold a controlling stake in its personal computer business to Lenovo, China's biggest PC manufacturer. The sale shows that China is no longer content to be just the world's low-cost workshop. Following the lead by Korean companies such as Samsung, China's emerging multinational corporations are acquiring global brands to sell in world markets.

The role of consumption in determining the pattern of world trade

The theories discussed so far explain a country's comparative advantage and the patterns of world trade solely in terms of supply conditions in different countries. We have said little about the role of demand, except to assume that for a country to specialise and trade, demand for its exports must exist in other countries.

An alternative approach is to examine patterns of income, tastes and consumption, or **demand conditions**, in the world's most important trading countries, to explain why so much of international trade involves the exchange of essentially rather similar manufactured goods between already industrialised economies. It can be argued that a country's comparative and competitive advantage often lies in producing goods related to its inhabitants' domestic tastes. Close contact with the needs of the domestic market makes a country's firms efficient at meeting domestic demand, and very often the inhabitants of other industrial countries with similar incomes possess similar demand. Trade therefore takes place between countries with similar tastes and incomes.

At the same time, high-income consumers value choice and product differentiation. A pattern of trade thus develops between industrialised countries (encompassing the NICs) in which a very wide range of differentiated manufactured consumer goods, such as cars and television sets, is made available to all. A single country could seldom provide its consumers with the desired variety, so international trade extends the range of choice.

The UK's international trade

Table 20.1 shows that over the 48-year period from 1955 to 2003, the UK's international trade changed from a North/South to a North/North pattern. The UK now trades mainly with other developed countries in the North, and especially with other EU countries. In 1955, only 15% of UK exports and 12.6% of UK imports were with countries that eventually formed the EU. By contrast, 26.2% of UK exports and 23.4% of UK imports were with developing

examiner's voice

To develop your understanding of the pattern of UK trade with the rest of the world, see Tables 21.2 and 21.3 in Chapter 21.

countries. By 2003, this situation was reversed: respectively 57.2% and 57.6% of UK exports and imports were with EU countries, while exports to non-oil exporting developing countries had fallen to 11.9% for exports, though imports had recovered somewhat to 18%, from their lower percentage in 1992.

Table 20.1 *The changing pattern of the UK's international trade*

	1955		1992		2003	
	Exports (%)	Imports (%)	Exports (%)	Imports(%)	Exports (%)	Imports (%)
European Union	15.0	12.6	56.4	52.5	57.2	57.6
Other western Europe	13.9	13.1	7.9	11.6	5.5	5.6
North America	12.0	19.5	13.0	12.6	17.3	11.7
Other developed countries	21.1	14.2	3.6	7.1	4.1	5.4
Oil-exporting developing countries	5.1	9.2	5.6	2.5	4.0	1.7
Rest of the world	32.9	31.4	13.5	13.7	11.9	18.0

Source: *Annual Abstract of Statistics*, various, ONS.

Globalisation

Globalisation is the name given to the processes that integrates all or most of the world's economies, making countries increasingly dependent upon each other.

History of globalisation

Some economists argue that globalisation has occurred over centuries, going back at least as far as the creation of a system of relatively free worldwide trade in the nineteenth century, and perhaps extending even further back to the Spanish and Portuguese occupation of much of South America. In the late nineteenth century and the period before 1914, communication and transport networks expanded throughout much of the world and international trade grew significantly. At the same time, older industrial countries, and particularly the UK, began to invest their surplus savings in capital projects located overseas rather than in their domestic economies.

*e*xaminer's voice

The A2 Module 6 specification requires candidates to be aware of the globalisation of the world economy and to have an understanding of the consequences of globalisation for the developing world and for advanced countries such as the UK. Knowledge and understanding of globalisation are also useful for assessing the impact of the world economy on the UK economy: for example, globalisation's contribution to deindustrialisation and to the low rate of inflation experienced in recent years by the UK.

However, these changes are better described as aspects of **internationalisation** rather than globalisation. Globalisation, which has come to mean rather more than mere internationalisation of economic relationships, began to feature in the economics literature of the mid-1980s. The use of the term has increased dramatically ever since. Recent globalisation has been made possible by improvements in information and communication technology (ICT), as well as by developments in more traditional forms of technology.

Examples of globalisation include service industries in the UK dealing with customers through call centres in India, and fashion companies designing their products in Europe, making them in southeast Asia and finally selling most of them in North America.

The debate about globalisation

Free-market economists generally support globalisation and regard its growth as inevitable. They argue that the benefits of further global economic integration, which include the extension of political freedom and democracy as well as the economic benefits of more production and higher living standards, significantly exceed the disadvantages, such as the destruction of local cultures. But opponents argue that globalisation is a respectable name for the growing exploitation of the poor, mostly in developing countries, by international capitalism and US economic and cultural imperialism.

For its critics, low-paid workers in sweatshops, farmers in the developing world being forced to grow genetically modified crops, the privatisation of state-owned industry to qualify for IMF and World Bank loans, and the growing dominance of US corporate culture and multinational companies symbolise what is wrong with globalisation. According to this view, globalisation has led to a 'McDonaldisation' or 'Coca-Colonisation' of significant parts of the world's economy, which involves the destruction of local and national products, identities and cultures by US 'world

brands'. What is needed is a counter-process of 'glocalisation', or local action that prevents or offsets the damage done by globalisation to vulnerable local cultures. However, this view is not taken seriously by supporters of globalisation, who believe that people in the rest of the world demand US products because they consider them superior to traditional local produce.

Even in Vietnam it is hard to escape Coca-Cola's global presence

Features of globalisation

Some of the main features of globalisation are:

- the growth of international trade and the reduction of trade barriers — a process encouraged by the World Trade Organisation (WTO)
- greater international mobility of capital and to some extent of labour
- a significant increase in the power of international capitalism and multinational corporations (MNCs)
- the deindustrialisation of older industrial regions and countries, and the movement of manufacturing industries to newly industrialised countries (NICs)
- more recently, the movement of internationally mobile service industries, such as call centres and accounts offices, to NICs
- a decrease in governmental power to influence decisions made by MNCs to shift economic activity between countries

Employment practices

Closely related to the 'world brand' process has been the alleged treatment of local labour by multinational corporations. This works in two ways. First, companies such as Nike are accused of selling trainers and footballs in developed countries such as the UK at prices far above the cost of raw materials and the low wages paid to Third World labour making the goods. In response, the multinationals argue that the 'low wages' they pay far exceed the local wages paid by firms indigenous to the countries in which they manufacture. They believe this encourages local

wages to rise. MNCs also claim to improve health and safety and other labour market conditions in the poor countries in which they operate.

Second, by threatening to close down factories and to move production to poor countries, it is argued that MNCs reduce wages and living standards in First World countries. Whether this is true depends, of course, on the type of jobs that emerge in developed countries to replace those lost through deindustrialisation and globalisation. Are the new jobs created in the highly skilled service sector, or are they menial, low-paid, unskilled 'McJobs'?

Globalisation in the service sector

Until recently, it was said that manufacturing was much more internationally mobile than service sector employment. This is no longer completely true. Call centres became one of the fastest-growing sources of employment in the UK in the 1980s and 1990s. At that time, UK-based companies favoured locating call centres in regions of high unemployment (and relatively low wages) *within* the UK. To some extent this has now changed. Call centres and 'back office' activities of firms in industries such as financial services are being moved to the Indian subcontinent. This results from the 'death of distance', which is a part of the globalisation process. The rapid development of electronic methods of communication means that many service activities can now be located anywhere in the world, with little or no effect on a company's ability to provide the service efficiently to its customers.

Four factors encouraging the overseas location of call centres are:
- relatively low wages
- highly reliable and cheap telecommunications
- 24-hour shift employment to overcome the problem of time zones
- workers fluent in the English language

However, for call centres, a fifth factor is often lacking: many overseas workers are insufficiently familiar with UK culture and habits, which for call centres leads to a communication problem. This disadvantage is much less significant for 'back office' employment: for example, employing people in India to administer a UK company's accounts.

Labour and capital mobility

As the previous paragraphs indicate, globalisation involves moving capital to lower-cost labour much more than it involves allowing low-paid workers born in poor countries to enter rich countries in North America and Europe. However, since the late nineteenth century there has been a much greater movement of poor people into rich countries than ever before. To some extent, immigration controls introduced by countries such as the USA and Australia, which replaced an earlier completely free movement of labour, have slowed this process. But this has been offset by illegal immigration and by the fact that rich countries informally encourage migration to fill the relatively low-paid jobs that their own citizens do not wish to do.

Enlargement of the EU is increasing both labour and capital mobility on a regional basis. As we have noted, western European firms have been moving eastward, but

this is balanced by workers from countries such as Poland and Hungary migrating westward. Nonetheless, it is still much easier in a globalised world for a brain surgeon or a highly-paid business executive to move between countries than it is for a Chinese or Indian peasant.

Globalisation and economic policy

In recent decades, globalisation has considerably reduced the power of national governments to control multinational firms operating within their boundaries. National governments have also lost much of the freedom to undertake the economic policies of their choice with respect to managing domestic economies. Governments enjoy less freedom to introduce tariffs and other import controls. At the same time, capital flows into and out of currencies severely constrain a government's ability to implement an independent monetary policy, even when the country's exchange rate is freely floating.

The role of international trade in the globalisation process has to some extent been explained earlier in this chapter, in the context of trade theory and the North/North pattern of world trade. The final section of this chapter explains in greater detail how the General Agreement on Tariffs and Trade and latterly the World Trade Organisation have contributed to globalisation through a process of trade liberalisation.

examiner's voice

Detailed knowledge of international economic institutions such as the WTO and (in the context of the balance of payments) the IMF is not required, although it is useful to be aware of the broad functions of these institutions.

GATT and the World Trade Organization

Supporters of globalisation claim there has been *too little* rather than *too much* international integration of countries' economies. In their view, if countries get rid of *all* protectionist measures, the 'invisible hand' of the market will promote international trade, which benefits poor countries as well rich ones. This view explains the creation of the **General Agreement on Tariffs and Trade** (GATT) and the **World Trade Organization** (WTO), the two worldwide organisations established to remove trade barriers and liberalise world trade.

To understand GATT and the WTO, it is necessary to go back to events occurring in the 1930s and 1940s. In the 1940s, during the Second World War, it was widely believed (especially in the UK and the USA) that the worldwide depression and mass unemployment of the 1930s had been made worse, and possibly caused, by a collapse of international trade. 'Beggar my neighbour' protectionist policies introduced by countries desperately trying to save local jobs were blamed. By 1945 the USA and the UK had decided to try to create a postwar world of free trade. Because this required international agreement, GATT was established as a multilateral organisation of member countries whose aim was trade liberalisation. To begin with, GATT was supposed to be a temporary organisation, to be replaced with a WTO as soon as member countries could agree. However, because member countries were unable to agree, the 'temporary' organisation lasted much longer than intended, from the 1940s until the mid-1990s when the WTO at last replaced GATT.

GATT and later the WTO have organised 'rounds' of talks among member countries to reduce import controls. The rounds, which have taken place at about 5-year intervals, have often been named after the city or country in which the talks were initiated: for example, the Tokyo round, the Uruguay round and, more recently, the Doha round. Out of respect, the Kennedy round in the 1960s was named after the recently assassinated American president. Each round of talks ends with an agreement to reduce import controls. GATT, and latterly the WTO, then tries to get member countries to implement the tariff cuts they have agreed.

GATT and WTO agreements have been very successful in reducing import controls on manufactured goods. There has been much less success in securing agreement to reduce tariffs and quotas on trade in services and agricultural goods. Currently, the WTO is trying to get the developed countries of the EU and the USA to open their markets to cheap food imports from the developing world. However, the most recent rounds of talks organised by the WTO at Doha (in Africa) and Cancún (in Mexico) have not been successful. Economists and politicians in many developing countries claim that this lack of success provides further evidence of globalisation and international organisations serving the interests of rich countries at the expense of the poor.

Summary

As we have stated on several occasions in this book, the purpose of economic activity is to increase human welfare. This is the main justification for international specialisation and trade, as it is for trade or exchange within a country. Indeed, the main arguments supporting international trade are really just an extension of the 'invisible hand' principle, justifying market-based activity within a country, to relationships between countries.

The gains from specialisation and trade result from a number of factors. Trade not only widens a nation's production possibilities, but also broadens the consumption possibilities of its people. The international division of labour and specialisation in accordance with the principle of comparative advantage enable the world's production possibility frontier to shift outward, thereby increasing the quantity of goods and services available for consumption. But trade produces losers as well as winners — hence the case for import controls. When trade takes place on an un-level playing field, some countries gain at the expense of others. Countries that have already built up a competitive advantage praise the joys of free trade, but are often the first to squeal and advocate protectionism against cheap imports 'unfairly' produced in low-income developing countries.

The pattern of world trade has changed significantly over the last half-century. North/South trade, in which rich countries trade manufactured goods for primary products, has largely given way to a North/North pattern in which rich countries trade with each other. Exceptions to this pattern include energy exports from oil-producing developing countries and the shift of manufacturing production to the NICs.

The growth of international trade, itself partly caused by programmes of tariff reduction initiated by GATT and the WTO, has been a major part of the globalisation process. However, globalisation extends beyond trade liberalisation to include changes in the world economy brought about by multinational companies and the increased mobility of factors of production, particularly capital and to a lesser extent labour.

AQA Advanced Economics

Self-testing questions

1 Explain how international trade widens choice.

2 What are the benefits of the division of labour?

3 Why is a 'double coincidence of wants' unnecessary when more than two countries trade together?

4 Distinguish between absolute advantage and comparative advantage.

5 Distinguish between comparative advantage and competitive advantage.

6 Outline two arguments used to support import controls.

7 How has the pattern of world trade changed?

8 Explain one reason for the changing pattern of world trade.

9 How important is the EU for UK trade?

10 What is meant by globalisation?

11 Outline the main features of globalisation.

12 How have multinational corporations promoted globalisation?

13 Why is capital generally more internationally mobile than labour?

14 Explain the role of the WTO in the world economy.

Chapter 21
The balance of payments

Specification focus

This chapter covers the Module 2 topic of the balance of payments on the current account and the Module 6 topic of the whole of the balance of payments, including the difference between the current account and capital flows.

AS **Module 2 The National Economy**
Performance of the UK Economy and Government Policy Objectives

A2 **Module 6 Government Policy, the National and International Economy**
The International Economy

A2 **Synoptic coverage**
The Unit 6 examination at A2 expects candidates to extend the Module 2 coverage of the current account of the balance of payments and to understand the interrelationship between net income flows in the current account and investment overseas by UK-based firms.

Introduction

Whenever international trade takes place between countries, payment must eventually be made in a currency, or by another means, which is acceptable to the person or business selling the goods or services. The balance of payments is the part of the national accounts which attempts to measure all the currency flows into and out of the economy within a particular time period, such as a month, quarter or year. However, activities such as smuggling and money laundering, together with errors and delays in data collection and reporting, mean that the published balance of payments tables are never completely accurate.

The structure of the balance of payments in the UK

Since the balance of payments is an official record collected by a government, the presentation of the currency flows depends on how the government decides to group and classify all the different items of payment. Until quite recently, the UK government divided the balance of payments into two main categories:

- the current account
- the capital account

But to fit in with the method of classification used by the International Monetary Fund (IMF), the format of the UK's balance of payments has been changed. Unfortunately, the new method of presentation, which is shown in slightly simplified form in Table 21.1, is confusing. Capital flows, which used to form the *capital account*, are now listed in the *financial account* of the balance of payments. Misleadingly, the capital account now comprises various transfers of income that were previously part of the current account before the new method of classification was adopted.

For this reason, this chapter presents a general survey of the current account and capital flows and tries to avoid unnecessary detail. The examination boards, including AQA, no longer require knowledge of official methods of presentation of balance of payments accounts.

*e***xaminer's voice**

The AQA specifications state that detailed knowledge of the balance of payments accounts is not required at either AS or A2.

The current account (*mostly trade flows*)	
Balance of trade in goods	−57,944
Balance of trade in services	+19,118
Net income flows	+24,004
Net current transfers	−10,860
Balance of payments on the current account	**−25,682**
The capital account	
(transfers, which used to be in the current account)	**+2,073**
The financial account	
(*capital flows, which used to be in the capital account*)	
Net direct investment	+7,105
Net portfolio investment	−55,709
Other capital flows (*mostly short-term 'hot money' flows*)	+75,825
Drawings on reserves	−193
Financial account balance	**+27,028**
The balance (*errors and omissions*)	**−3,419**
Source: National Statistics website (**www.statistics.gov.uk**), accessed 26 April 2005.	

Table 21.1 Selected items from the UK balance of payments, 2004 (£m)

The current account of the balance of payments

For the most part, the balance of payments on the current account measures the *flow* of expenditure on goods and services, broadly indicating the country's income

gained and lost from trade. The **current account** is usually regarded as the most important part of the balance of payments because it reflects the economy's international competitiveness and the extent to which the country may or may not be living within its means.

The current balance is obtained by adding together the **balance of trade in goods** and the **balance of trade in services**. (The balance of trade in goods can also be called the **balance of visible trade**, while the balance of trade in services comprises **invisible trade** items.) If receipts from exports of goods and services are less than payments for imports of goods and services, there is generally a **current account deficit**. Conversely, a **current account surplus** occurs when receipts from trade exceed payments for trade. However, because there are other items in the current account besides trade flows, this is not always true. The other items are net income flows and net current transfers.

> *e**xaminer's voice***
>
> At AS, candidates must understand the difference between the three main items in the current account: trade in goods, trade in services and net income flows.

The balance of trade in goods

The **balance of trade in goods** measures the value of goods exported minus the value of goods imported, expressed in the country's own currency. In Table 21.1, the value of goods exports exceeds the value of goods imports by nearly £5.8 billion, but the table does not indicate the absolute level of exports and imports in 2004. However, like other parts of the balance of payments, the balance of trade in goods can be **disaggregated** into exports of goods and imports of goods. Alternatively, the balance of trade in goods can be disaggregated into different forms or categories of trade, such as the balances of trade in manufactured goods and non-manufactured goods. Some of the different ways of disaggregating the balance of trade in goods on this basis are shown in Table 21.2.

Balance of trade in food, drinks and tobacco	−11,517
Balance of trade in raw materials	−2,614
Balance of trade in oil	+1,954
Balance of trade in manufactured goods	−40,614
Balance of trade in all goods	−57,944

Source: National Statistics website (**www.statistics.gov.uk**), accessed 26 April 2005.

Table 21.2 Selected items from the UK balance of trade in goods, 2004 (£m)

Table 21.2 shows that the UK is a net importer of primary products (food and raw materials), but has recently been a net exporter of oil. The balance of trade surplus in oil results from the development of the North Sea oil and gas fields in the 1970s and 1980s. However, North Sea oil and gas fields are being depleted, so the UK will once again become a net importer of oil and gas. Between 2003 and 2004, the UK's balance of trade surplus in oil fell from £4,443 million to £1,954 million. Most of the coal used in the UK is also now imported.

The balance of payments deficit in manufactured goods is significant. From the beginning of the Industrial Revolution in the eighteenth century until the 1980s, in peacetime the UK was a net exporter of manufactured goods. In the early nineteenth century, Britain became the 'workshop of the world'. Things are now very different. In the early 1980s, the UK switched to becoming a net importer of manufactured goods. The manufactured goods deficit is now huge, reflecting a loss of competitiveness, the resulting deindustrialisation of the UK, and the fact that most manufactured goods are now produced in the newly industrialised countries (NICs) of Asia, particularly in China. Arguably, the UK now has a **post-industrial economy**.

The balance of trade in services

The post-industrial nature of the UK's economy is reflected in the fact that services are now much more important than manufacturing. Indeed, as Table 21.3 shows, the UK's comparative advantage in the financial, insurance and ICT services has led overall to a balance of trade surplus in services.

Balance of trade in transport	–3,199
Balance of trade in travel and tourism	–15,638
Balance of trade in communications	+261
Balance of trade in insurance	+5,186
Balance of trade in financial services	+11,738
Balance of trade in computer and information services	+3,334
Balance of trade in all services	+19,118

Source: National Statistics website (**www.statistics.gov.uk**), accessed 26 April 2005.

Table 21.3 Selected items from the UK balance of trade in services, 2004 (£m)

However, trade in services differs in a significant respect from trade in manufactured goods. Whereas most manufactured goods are *internationally tradable*, this is not true of services such as restaurant meals, haircuts and car servicing. These services are generally produced and consumed in the *non-internationally traded* economy, or sheltered economy.

Although the UK exports more services than it imports, a growing number of services that were previously produced within the UK are now being imported. To a large extent, this reflects the globalisation process described in Chapter 20. UK companies that used to produce services 'in-house' now outsource or buy-in the services from outside suppliers, often located in cheap-labour countries. Increasingly, UK-based companies locate 'back-office' service activities overseas. Examples include many financial and ICT-related services. Call centres providing customer services and direct marketing services have relocated to India.

*e*xaminer's voice

You are not expected to possess detailed knowledge of the different items in the balance of trade in goods and the balance of trade in services. However, this information may be presented in a data-response question, which then asks for explanation of an issue, such as why trade in manufactured goods is in deficit, or why trade in financial services is in surplus. Such topics are relevant for both the AS Unit 2 exam and the A2 Unit 6 exam.

Table 21.3 also shows that the UK has a significant deficit in travel and tourism. Britons now spend much more in other countries than foreign tourists spend in the UK.

Heathrow Airport: Britain's trade balance in tourism is in deficit

Net income flows

The next section explains how UK-based multinational companies (MNCs) invest in capital assets located in other countries. The profit income generated when the investment is complete and the capital assets are up and running flows in the opposite direction, back to the parent company and its UK shareholders. The investment itself is an outward capital flow, but the income it generates is *current* income, figuring in the current account of the balance of payments.

Profits also flow out of the country to the overseas owners of assets located in the UK — for example, to Japanese or US multinational companies owning subsidiary companies in the UK. In Table 21.1, the item **net income flows** shows the difference between these inward and outward profit flows resulting from capital investment undertaken in the past. The fact that the UK's net income flows were +£24,004 million in 2004 seems to indicate that UK companies own more profitable assets in the rest of the world than overseas-based MNCs own in the UK. However, not all income flows are profit payments by multinational companies. Interest payments on loans within the international banking system, which form part of the overseas earnings of the City of London, contribute significantly to net income flows.

Capital flows

As the previous paragraph indicates, it is important to avoid confusing *capital* flows with *investment income.* As explained, *outward* capital flows generate *inward* investment income flows in subsequent years. The capital outflow enlarges the *stock* of capital assets located in other countries, owned by MNCs based in the country exporting the capital. **Net capital flows** are the difference between inward and outward capital movements. Positive net outward capital flows, over a period of years, mean that the country acquires capital assets located in other countries that are greater in value than the country's own assets bought by overseas companies.

As Table 21.1 shows, net investment income flows into the UK were over £24 billion in 2004. A positive net investment *flow* (in the *current account* of the balance of payments) suggests that, in previous years, UK residents and MNCs invested in a larger and more profitable *stock* of capital assets in the rest of the world than that acquired by overseas residents and MNCs in the UK. Following the UK's abolition of virtually all foreign exchange controls in 1979, the UK became a very large net exporter of capital, presumably because UK MNCs believed that investment abroad would be more profitable than investment within the UK. During the 1980s, the positive net capital outflow meant that the UK became a very large owner of overseas capital assets. By contrast, the USA became a 'debtor' nation in the 1980s: that is, assets owned in the USA by other countries grew to exceed those owned by the USA in the rest of the world. This position remains largely true today.

> *e***xaminer's voice**
>
> AS questions do not test knowledge of capital flows, although it is useful to have some understanding of what they are. Knowledge, but not detailed knowledge, is definitely required at A2.

Long-term capital flows

In order to understand properly the importance of capital flows in the balance of payments, it is useful to distinguish between long-term and short-term capital flows. Long-term capital flows are dividable into direct investment and portfolio investment flows:

- **Direct investment** involves acquisition of real productive assets, such as factories, oil refineries, offices and shopping malls, located in other countries. On the one hand, a UK-based MNC may decide to establish a new subsidiary company — for example, in the USA. On the other hand, direct investment can also involve acquisition, through merger or takeover, of an overseas-based company. The UK company ICI investing in a chemical factory in a developing country provides an example of outward direct investment. Conversely, the decisions by the Japanese vehicle manufacturers, Nissan, Toyota and Honda, to invest in automobile factories in the UK led to inward direct investment, or **foreign direct investment** (FDI).
- **Portfolio investment** involves the purchase of financial assets (that is, pieces of paper) rather than physical or directly productive assets. Typically, portfolio investment occurs when fund managers employed by financial institutions such as insurance companies and pension funds purchase shares issued by overseas companies, or securities issued by foreign governments. The globalisation of

world security markets or capital markets and the abolition of exchange controls between virtually all developed countries have made it easy for UK residents to purchase shares or bonds that are listed on overseas capital markets. This has led to a massive increase in portfolio investment. UK residents can now buy shares and corporate bonds, either directly or through financial intermediaries, which were previously only available on the capital market of the company's country of origin. Securities issued by foreign governments, such as US Treasury bonds, can also be bought.

Short-term capital flows

Long-term capital flows can partly be explained by comparative and competitive advantage. The flows are a response to people's decisions to invest in economic activities and industries located in countries that have a competitive advantage. Comparative advantage (which, as Chapter 20 explains, must not be confused with competitive advantage) may also rest in the same country. But since changes in competitive and/or comparative advantage usually take place quite slowly, long-term capital flows tend to be relatively stable and predictable.

This is not true of short-term capital flows. Short-term capital movements, which are also called **'hot money'** flows, are largely speculative. The flows occur because the owners of funds, which include companies and banks as well as wealthy private individuals, believe that a quick speculative profit can be made by moving funds between currencies. Speculating that a currency's exchange rate is about to rise, owners of funds move money into that currency and out of other currencies whose exchange rates are expected to fall. 'Hot money' movements are triggered too by differences in interest rates. Funds flow into currencies with high interest rates and out of currencies with lower interest rates. International crises, such as the outbreak of a Middle East war, also cause funds to move into the currency of a 'safe haven' country, regarded as politically stable.

If the pool of 'hot money' shifting between currencies were small, few problems would result. However, as the next section explains, short-term capital flows have grown significantly over the last 50 years. A large-scale movement of funds from one currency to another creates an excess supply in the former currency and an excess demand for the second currency. To eliminate excess supply and demand, the exchange rates of the two currencies respectively fall and rise. As a result, the movement of funds between currencies produces the changes in exchange rates that speculators were expecting. More importantly, a large-scale 'hot money' flow of funds between currencies destabilises exchange rates, the current accounts of balance of payments and, indeed, domestic economies.

Speculative flows between currencies such as the dollar, the pound and the euro, which occupy a central place in the finance of international trade, can destabilise the international monetary system. In the late 1990s and the early 2000s, 'hot money' flowed into the dollar. Arguably, this overvalued the dollar and under-valued the euro and to a lesser extent the pound, thus artificially increasing the price competitiveness of European goods in the US market.

Because of the threat to US jobs, in 2003 the US central bank reduced interest rates to encourage a downward float of the dollar. By late 2004, low US interest rates and a US government policy of 'benign neglect', in which the US administration seemed to 'encourage' the dollar's fall, resulted in an undervalued dollar and an overvalued euro. This increased the USA's trade competitiveness against the rest of the world, and especially the eurozone. Europe and to some extent the USA also suffered from the fact that some Asian currencies, particularly the Chinese renminbi (rnb), were fixed against the dollar. This meant that against the euro and the pound, the rnb also fell, making Chinese goods especially competitive in Europe.

Eurodollars

Perhaps the most important single cause of the growth of short-term capital or 'hot money' flows lies in the growth after 1957 of the eurodollar market. A **eurodollar** is a US dollar owned or deposited in a bank outside the USA. Over the last 50 years, the pool of eurodollars has grown dramatically. The US balance of payments deficit has caused much of this growth.

For most countries, a balance of payments deficit creates excess supply of the country's currency on foreign exchange markets. When this happens, excess holdings of the currency are sold, which in turn causes the exchange rate to fall. However, the dollar is different. The US dollar is the world's **reserve currency**: that is, the currency that governments and central banks outside the USA wish to hold. This means that, unlike other countries, the USA has been able to finance a large balance of payments deficit on the current account by paying for imports in its own currency. Because of the **superpower** and **hegemonic** roles of the US economy and the dollar in the world economy, other countries have been happy to accept, and then to retain, dollars earned from exports to the USA. This has led to a massive growth of dollars held outside the USA.

The growth of the eurodollar pool has also been fuelled by US companies investing overseas and by the growth of bank deposits owned by US residents outside the USA. Indeed, much of the early growth of the eurodollar market was caused by restrictions imposed by the US monetary authorities on the domestic US banking system. US residents evaded domestic monetary restrictions by depositing dollars in overseas bank accounts (often subsidiaries of US-owned banks) rather than in deposits held in the USA. Overseas banks then re-lent the eurodollars to whoever wished to borrow dollars to finance trade, investment or speculation.

From its origins in the late 1950s and early 1960s, the eurodollar market grew rapidly in the 1970s and 1980s, greatly aided at this time by the growth of **petrodollars** after the oil crises of the 1970s. A petrodollar is a dollar received by an oil-producing country as payment for oil exports, which are priced in dollars. Following massive increases in the price of crude oil in the 1970s, OPEC countries accumulated large current account surpluses, which were matched by growing deficits in oil-consuming industrial countries. The OPEC countries deposited a large proportion of the dollars they earned in the European banking system, thus adding to the pool of footloose money, able to switch quickly and with little or no cost between currencies.

The eurocurrency market

Today, the eurodollar market is perhaps better called the *eurocurrency* market, reflecting the fact that, while the dollar is still the most important currency deposited in the European banking system, other currencies, such as the euro, sterling and the yen, are to a lesser extent also involved. Nevertheless, the dollar continues to be the dominant eurocurrency, partly because of its reserve currency role, and partly because the USA's huge payments deficits have transmitted the dollar into overseas ownership. The prefix 'euro' in the eurocurrency market refers not to the role of the euro, but to the fact that most of the market takes place in European financial centres, and particularly in London. International banks, operating from European financial centres, make large profits from a growing and thriving business in the short-term borrowing and lending of eurocurrencies, outside any exchange controls existent in the currency's country of origin.

examiner's voice

It is useful but not essential to know about eurodollars and eurocurrencies. 'Hot' money flows in the eurocurrency market have contributed significantly to exchange rate instability in recent years.

Equilibrium and disequilibrium in the 'balance' of payments

Balance of payments equilibrium

It is important to avoid confusing balance of payments *equilibrium* with the last item in Table 21.1, which ensures that the balance of payments *balances*. **Balance of payments equilibrium** (or **external equilibrium**) occurs when trade and capital flows into and out of the country are more or less equal over a number of years. Sometimes, balance of payments equilibrium is more narrowly defined, referring only to the current account. In this narrow sense, the balance of payments is in equilibrium when the current account more or less balances over a period of years. Defined in this way, balance of payments equilibrium is perfectly compatible with the occurrence of a short-term current account deficit or surplus. However, fundamental disequilibrium exists when there is a persistent tendency for payments for imports to be greater or less than payments for exports over a period of years.

The balance of payments is a balance sheet and, like all balance sheets, must balance in the sense that all items must sum to zero. In the UK balance of payments, this means that all items in the current account, the capital account and the financial account must sum to zero. In practice, this never happens because items are inaccurately measured and recorded – hence, the need for a **balancing item** to make the balance of payments sum to zero. The balancing item is a *mistakes* item equalling the number required to make the balance of payments sum to zero.

Government statisticians who construct the UK balance of payments use a **continuous revision** method of measurement. When the balance of payments statistics for a

examiner's voice

Because the balance of payments is a balance sheet, it must always balance. Make sure you don't confuse the 'balance' with 'balance of payments equilibrium'.

particular year are first published, soon after the end of the year in question, the balancing item may be quite large. In this situation, too much trust should not be placed in the figures. In subsequent months and years, the balancing item gradually decreases. In the light of new and previously unavailable information, the statisticians whittle away the balancing item, allocating elements of the item to one or more of the flows in real trade, investment income or capital.

Does a current account deficit pose a problem?

While a *short-run* deficit or surplus on the current account does not pose a problem, a persistent or *long-run* imbalance indicates a fundamental disequilibrium. However, the nature of any resulting problem depends upon the size and cause of the deficit or surplus, and also upon the nature of the exchange rate regime. The larger the deficit, the greater the problem is likely to be. The problem is also likely to be serious if the deficit is caused by the uncompetitiveness of the country's industries. In the short run, a deficit allows a country's residents to enjoy living standards boosted by imports, higher than would be possible from consumption of the country's output alone. But in the long run, the decline of the country's industries in the face of international competition may lower living standards.

A balance of payments deficit poses more problems when the exchange rate is fixed than when it floats freely. In both cases, the immediate cause of a deficit usually lies in the fact that exports are too expensive in overseas markets, while imports are too cheap at home. Obviously, there can be more deep-seated causes of over-priced exports and under-priced imports, relating, for example, to domestic wage costs being higher than in other countries. However, in a floating exchange rate regime, the external price of the currency — the exchange rate — simply responds to market forces and falls, thereby restoring export competitiveness and curing or reducing balance of payments disequilibrium. This is explained in Chapter 22.

By contrast, in a fixed exchange rate system, currencies may remain more or less permanently over- or undervalued. An overvalued fixed exchange rate leads to a large current account deficit, which then puts downward pressure on the exchange rate. However, in a fixed exchange rate system, the country's central bank takes action to prevent the exchange rate falling. In a process known as **exchange equalisation**, the central bank uses reserves of gold and hard currencies to purchase its own currency on the foreign exchange market. (A hard currency is one which other countries wish to hold and for which demand tends to exceed supply. By contrast, a soft currency has the opposite characteristics.) Official reserves are, of course, limited, so a country cannot go on propping up a fixed exchange rate and financing a deficit for ever. In a fixed exchange rate system, eventually a country must take action to try to reduce or eliminate a persistent payments deficit.

*e*xaminer's voice

In recent years, the UK's balance of payments deficit on the current account has been huge, yet there has been little talk of a 'sterling crisis'. As this section explains, currency crises usually occur when a government and its central bank try to prop up or support a clearly overvalued fixed or semi-fixed exchange rate, and not when the currency is floating freely.

Policies to cure or reduce a balance of payments deficit

A government (or its central bank) can use three different policies to try to cure a persistent deficit caused by an overvalued exchange rate. These are the '3 Ds' of **deflation**, **direct controls**, and **devaluation** or currency **depreciation**, which are shown in Figure 21.1.

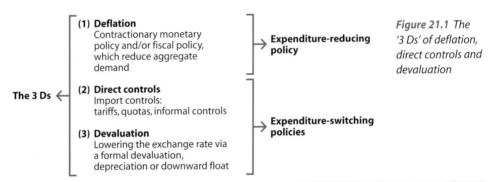

The 3 Ds

(1) Deflation
Contractionary monetary policy and/or fiscal policy, which reduce aggregate demand
→ **Expenditure-reducing policy**

(2) Direct controls
Import controls: tariffs, quotas, informal controls

(3) Devaluation
Lowering the exchange rate via a formal devaluation, depreciation or downward float
→ **Expenditure-switching policies**

Figure 21.1 The '3 Ds' of deflation, direct controls and devaluation

Deflation, or a reduction in the level of aggregate demand in the economy, reduces a current account deficit because it is mainly *expenditure reducing*. By contrast, import controls and de-valuation are primarily *expenditure switching*.

> *e*xaminer's voice
>
> Make sure you understand the difference between, but also the links between, expenditure-reducing and expenditure-switching policies.

Deflation

Deflation involves using contractionary monetary and/or fiscal policy to reduce the demand for imports. For example, if the marginal propensity to import in the economy is 0.4, reducing aggregate demand by £10 billion should cause spending on imports to fall by £4 billion. This is an expenditure-reducing policy.

Although deflation is primarily an expenditure-reducing policy, it also has an expenditure-switching element. By reducing the rate of domestic price inflation relative to inflation rates in other countries, deflation increases the price competitiveness of exports and reduces that of imports.

However, in modern economies this is usually quite a small effect and the main effect of deflationary policies is to reduce aggregate demand and to depress economic activity in the domestic economy. Output and employment tend to fall rather than the price level. Unfortunately, as well as reducing the demand for imports, deflation affects the domestic economy. Falling demand for domestic output may force firms to seek export orders, so as to use spare production capacity. However, because exports are generally less profitable than domestic sales, a sound and expanding home market may be necessary for a successful export drive.

In summary, when deflating aggregate demand to achieve the external objectives of supporting the exchange rate and reducing a current account deficit, a government sacrifices the domestic economic objectives of full employment and

economic growth. For this reason, governments may choose to use expenditure-switching policies of import controls and devaluation, in preference to expenditure-reducing deflation.

Direct controls

The **direct controls** used to reduce a payments deficit are import controls. **Embargoes** and **quotas** directly prevent or reduce expenditure on imports, while **import duties** or **tariffs** discourage expenditure by raising the price of imports. Import controls do not, however, cure the underlying cause of disequilibrium, namely the uncompetitiveness of a country's goods and services. Indeed, import controls may reduce rather than increase competitiveness. Moreover, because a country essentially gains a 'beggar my neighbour' advantage at the expense of other countries, import controls tend to provoke retaliation.

Ultimately, protectionism reduces specialisation and causes world trade, world output and economic welfare all to fall. Because of this, international organisations such as the EU and the World Trade Organisation (WTO) have reduced the freedom of individual countries to impose import controls unilaterally to improve their current accounts. However the EU uses its common external tariff to provide protection for all its members.

Devaluation

The word **devaluation** is used in a number of different ways. In a strictly narrow sense, a country devalues by reducing the value of a fixed exchange rate or an adjustable peg exchange rate. (Fixed exchange rates and adjustable peg exchange rates are explained in Chapter 22.) However, the term is also used in a looser way to describe a downward float or **depreciation** of a floating exchange rate. The word 'depreciation' can also confuse. Devaluation or a downward float causes an *external* depreciation of the currency; more units of the currency are needed to buy a unit of *another* currency. Don't confuse this with an *internal* depreciation of the currency, occurring when there is inflation *within* the economy.

'Unavailability' of import controls means that a country must generally choose between *deflation* and *devaluation* if it wishes to reduce a current account deficit. As with import controls, devaluation has a mainly expenditure-switching effect. By increasing the price of imports relative to the price of exports, a successful devaluation switches domestic demand away from imports and towards home-produced goods. Similarly, overseas demand for the country's exports increases in response to the fall in export prices.

Price elasticity of demand and devaluation

The effectiveness of a devaluation in reducing a payment deficit depends to a significant extent upon the price elasticities of demand for exports and imports.

As Figure 21.2 shows, when the demands for exports and imports are both highly price elastic, a devaluation can reduce a current account deficit. Following a

> **e*xaminer's voice**
> Price elasticity of demand is explained in Chapter 3. A2 Unit 5 and Unit 6 exam papers are synoptic and may test your ability to apply knowledge of elasticity in a context such as the balance of payments and exchange rates.

devaluation, the domestic price of imports rises from P_1 to P_2, while the overseas price of exports falls from P_3 to P_4. As a result, *domestic* residents spend less on imported goods following an increase in their relative prices. At the same time, residents of *overseas* countries spend more on the country's exports, whose relative prices have fallen.

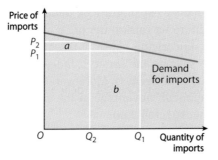
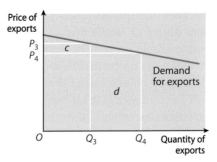

Figure 21.2 *The effect of a devaluation (or downward float) of an exchange rate on the current account of the balance of payments*

On the import side, area *b* in Figure 21.2 shows reduced expenditure on goods produced in other countries. Higher import prices mean that consumers switch to the now cheaper domestically produced substitutes. However, expenditure on the goods still being imported rises by area *a*. When demand for imports is price elastic – as in Figure 21.2 – total domestic expenditure on imports *falls* by area $(b - a)$.

In a similar way, expenditure on the country's exports *increases* by area $(d - c)$, providing overseas demand for the country's exports is price elastic. Area *d* shows increased expenditure on exports because prices of exports fall relative to prices of overseas produced substitutes. However, the foreign exchange earned by the goods exported *before* the devaluation falls by area *c*.

Overall, the current account improves by $(b - a) + (d - c)$, assuming the demand for imports and the demand for exports are both price elastic.

The Marshall–Lerner condition

It is more difficult to see what may happen to the current account when, for example, the demand for exports is price inelastic but the demand for imports is price elastic. Fortunately, the **Marshall–Lerner condition** provides a simple rule to assess whether a change in the exchange rate improves the current account. The condition states that when the *sum* of the export and import price elasticities is greater than unity (ignoring the minus sign), a fall in the exchange rate can reduce a deficit (and a rise in the exchange rate can reduce a surplus). When, however, the export and import price elasticities of demand are both highly inelastic, summing to less than unity, a fall in the exchange rate can have the perverse effect of worsening a deficit (while a revaluation might increase a surplus).

> *e*xaminer's voice
>
> Although exam questions do not require knowledge of the Marshall–Lerner condition, used relevantly, it can improve the quality of an examination answer.

Expenditure-reducing policies versus expenditure-switching policies

The Marshall–Lerner condition is a *necessary* condition, but not a *sufficient* condition, for a fall in the exchange rate to reduce a payments deficit. For a devaluation or downward float to be successful, firms in the domestic economy must have spare capacity with which they can meet the surge in demand brought about by the fall in the exchange rate. This means that expenditure-reducing deflation and expenditure-switching devaluation should best be regarded as complementary policies rather than as substitute policies for reducing a current account deficit. Deflation *alone* may be unnecessarily costly in terms of lost domestic employment and output, yet may be necessary to provide the spare capacity and conditions in which a falling exchange rate can successfully cure a payments deficit.

The J-curve

Even if the Marshall–Lerner condition is met and spare capacity exists in the economy, firms within the country may still be unable immediately to increase supply following a fall in the exchange rate. In the short run, the Marshall–Lerner condition may not hold because elasticities of demand are lower in the short run than in the long run. In these circumstances, the balance of payments may worsen before it improves. This is known as the **J-curve effect**, which is illustrated in Figure 21.3.

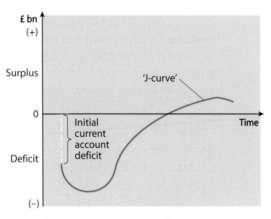

Figure 21.3 The J-curve effect

The initial worsening of the balance of payments which follows the fall in the exchange rate may, of course, reduce confidence in the idea that changing the exchange rate is the most appropriate method for reducing a payments imbalance. Falling confidence may, in turn, cause capital outflows that destabilise both the balance of payments and the exchange rate. The J-curve effect thus reduces the attractiveness of exchange rate adjustment as an instrument to correct payments disequilibrium. Even when the benefits of a falling exchange rate are realised, they may be short-lived. The increased price competitiveness produced by the devaluation is likely to be eroded as increased import prices raise the country's inflation rate.

Nevertheless, if conditions are right, a devaluation can reduce a current account deficit. Despite occurring on so-called 'Black Wednesday', the pound's devaluation in September 1992 was extremely successful, at least for a number of years. There were two main reasons for this. First, expenditure reduction in the severe recession of the early 1990s created the spare capacity that enabled successful expenditure switching following the pound's devaluation. Second, the factories built in the UK by Japanese companies such as Honda and Toyota had just come 'on stream', producing goods of a quality that people wanted, in the UK and overseas.

Does a current account surplus pose a problem?

While people readily agree that a persistent current account deficit can pose serious problems, fewer people realise that a balance of payments surplus on the current account can also lead to problems. Indeed, because a surplus is often seen as a sign of national economic virility and success, it is frequently argued that the bigger the surplus, the better must be the country's economic performance.

To the extent to which the surplus measures the competitiveness of the country's exporting industries, this is true. There are, nevertheless, several reasons why a *large* payments surplus is undesirable, although a small surplus may be a justifiable policy objective.

One country's surplus is another country's deficit

Because the balance of payments must balance for the world as a whole, it is not possible for all countries to run surpluses simultaneously. Unless countries with persistently large surpluses agree to take action to reduce their surpluses, deficit countries cannot reduce their deficits. This means that deficit countries may be forced to impose import controls from which all countries, including surplus countries, eventually suffer. In an extreme scenario, a world recession may be triggered by a resulting collapse of world trade.

At various times since the 1970s, the current account surpluses of the oil-producing countries have led to this problem, as have the Japanese and latterly the Chinese payments surpluses, which have largely matched the US trade deficit. On several occasions, the US government has faced pressure from US manufacturing and labour interests to introduce import controls and other forms of protectionism. When introduced, US protectionism undoubtedly harms world trade.

Shanghai: China's major centre for world trade

Almost without exception, non-oil-exporting developing countries also suffer chronic deficits, although these are very different from the US trade deficit. The imbalance of trade between more developed and less developed countries cannot

be reduced without the industrialised countries of the 'North' taking action to reduce surpluses that have been gained at the expense of the developing economies of the 'South'.

The 'Dutch disease' effect

The growth of the UK's oil trade surplus in the 1970s and 1980s illustrates another problem that a payments surplus can cause. Via its effects on confidence and speculation, the oil surplus, which transformed the UK's current account from deficit to surplus, attracted a huge 'hot money' inflow. The capital inflow caused the pound's exchange rate to rise to a level greatly overvalued in terms of the trading competitiveness of the UK's non-oil manufacturing industries. As a result, the UK's manufacturing industries lost world markets and suffered acutely from import competition.

Arguably, the 'Dutch disease' effect — named after an earlier, similar occurrence in the Netherlands economy following the discovery of natural gas in northern Holland — was a major cause of the early phase of deindustrialisation of the UK economy. Indeed, via the rising exchange rate, the effect of the oil trade surplus on the 'real' economy caused much of the benefit of North Sea oil revenues to be lost in financing imports and the upkeep of the unemployed.

As we have indicated, a decade later an overvalued pound also contributed to the recession at the beginning of the 1990s. However, in this case overvaluation resulted less from a 'Dutch disease effect' than from the government's deliberate decision to enter a fixed exchange rate system — the exchange rate mechanism of the European monetary system — at a 'high' rather than a 'low' exchange rate.

A balance of payments surplus is inflationary

It is often forgotten that when the exchange rate is fixed a balance of payments surplus can be an important cause of domestic inflation. This is because a balance of payments surplus is an injection of aggregate demand into the circular flow of income, which, via a multiplier effect, increases the equilibrium level of nominal or money national income. If there are substantial unemployed resources in the economy, this has the beneficial effect of reflating real output and jobs. However, if the economy is initially close to full capacity, demand-pull inflation results. (Note also that a balance of payments deficit has the opposite effect. The deficit is a leakage or withdrawal of demand from the economy, which deflates the equilibrium level of income.)

> **examiner's voice**
> Exam questions on a balance of payments surplus have been rare in recent years. This is because the UK has a current account deficit and questions are usually set on current economic problems. However, do not rule out the possibility of a question on a surplus rather than a deficit.

Policies to cure or reduce a balance of payments surplus

The policies available to a government for reducing a balance of payments surplus are the opposite of the '3 Ds' of *deflation*, *direct controls* and *devaluation* appropriate for correcting a payments deficit. The policies are the '3 Rs' of **reflation, removal of import controls** and **revaluation**.

- Reflating demand, via expansionary monetary policy or fiscal policy, increases a country's demand for imports.
- Trade can also be liberalised by removing import controls.
- There have been calls on countries with large payments surpluses, such as Japan and China, to revalue in order to reduce global payments imbalances. But because there is much less pressure on a surplus country to revalue than on a deficit country to devalue, such calls have not usually been successful. It is also worth noting that, for a revaluation to reduce a current account surplus, the Marshall–Lerner condition must be met. In addition, a 'reverse J-curve' may operate, causing the payments surplus to get bigger immediately after the revaluation, before it eventually starts to get smaller.

Summary

The balance of payments comprises all the currency flows into and out of a country within a particular time period. The current account is usually regarded as the most important part of the balance of payments, largely because it reflects the country's trading competitiveness. While the main items in the current account are the balances of trade in goods and services, net income flows are also significant. Income flows link the current account to the other main part of the balance of payments: capital flows.

Long-term direct capital flows occur when multinational corporations (MNCs) invest in capital assets such as factories and property located in other countries. Businesses invest overseas in order to make a profit. Some or all of the profit generated by outward investment can then, in future years, be remitted back to the parent company and its shareholders. In this way, a debit item in the capital flow section of the balance of payments creates a credit item in the current account, namely an investment income *inflow*. Investment income also *flows out* of the economy to overseas-based MNCs undertaking foreign direct investment (FDI) in the domestic economy. *Net* income flows are calculated by subtracting profit outflows from profit inflows.

The 'balance' item, which is always calculated for accounting purposes, must not be confused with balance of payments equilibrium.

Equilibrium occurs when the current account more or less balances over a period of years; conversely, a persistent deficit or surplus indicates disequilibrium. To reduce a persistent deficit, a government may deflate domestic demand, impose import controls, or devalue or allow market forces to float the exchange rate downward. Conversely, reflation, the relaxing of import controls and revaluation can reduce a balance of payments surplus on the current account. Deflation and reflation are respectively expenditure-reducing and expenditure-expanding policies, whereas the imposition and withdrawal of import controls and devaluation and revaluation are expenditure-switching policies.

A necessary condition for a devaluation to improve the current account is that demand for exports and imports must be sufficiently price elastic. But this on its own is not enough. Expenditure switching requires spare capacity to exist on the supply side of the economy. Moreover, the spare capacity must be able to produce goods of a quality that consumers want, and in sufficient quantity. The J-curve shows the changes in the current account in the months and possibly years following a devaluation. Likewise, in the event of a revaluation, the reverse J-curve maps the initial increase and subsequent fall in a current account surplus.

In recent years, there have been important changes in the UK balance of payments. Most significantly, the balance of trade in manufactured goods has moved from surplus into deficit, thus reversing a historical trend established when the UK became an industrialised economy. The deterioration of the balance of trade in manufactures was to some extent disguised by a large surplus in the balance of trade in oil following the development of the North Sea oil fields in the 1970s. But North Sea oil's contribution to the UK balance of payments has passed its peak, pointing to serious problems for the UK that may emerge when North Sea oil eventually runs dry.

Nevertheless, the outlook for the UK may not be too gloomy, since oil revenues have financed capital flows that have built up large UK-owned holdings of assets located in other countries. These assets will continue to yield income for their UK owners long after North Sea oil production has diminished, thereby filling the hole in the current account caused by the decline of oil revenues.

Self-testing questions

1 State and briefly explain the main items in the UK current account.

2 How have the balances of trade in goods and services changed in recent years?

3 What is a long-term capital flow?

4 Explain the link between capital flows and net income flows in the current account of the balance of payments.

5 Why do short-term capital flows take place?

6 What is the purpose of the 'balance' (or balancing) item in the balance of payments account?

7 What has happened to the UK balance of trade in manufactured goods in recent years?

8 Explain the meaning of balance of payments disequilibrium.

9 Does a current account deficit pose problems?

10 Outline the policies that may be used to reduce a payments deficit.

11 Distinguish between an expenditure-reducing and an expenditure-switching policy.

12 Explain the J-curve.

13 Why may a balance of payments surplus pose problems?

14 How may a balance of payments surplus be reduced?

Chapter 22
Exchange rates

Specification focus

Exchange rates figure briefly in the Module 2 specification in the link between monetary policy and aggregate demand for output. Exchange rates are a core topic in the international economy section of the Module 6 specification, which requires candidates to understand the links between the balance of payments and exchange rates. Knowledge and understanding of the euro is important too for the Module 4 specification covering the European Union. The Unit 6 exam may also assess understanding of the euro.

AS Module 2 The National Economy
   Main Instruments of Government Macroeconomic Policy

A2 Module 4 Working as an Economist
   The Deepening of European Integration

   Module 6 Government Policy, the National and International Economy
   The International Economy

A2 Synoptic coverage
   The Unit 6 examination may draw on knowledge, learnt at AS, about the effect of interest rate changes on the exchange rate, and thence on exports and imports in the current account of the balance of payments.

Introduction

Although domestic currencies are used to pay for internal trade within countries, imports are usually paid for in the currency of the country exporting the goods or services. An exchange rate measures how much of another currency a particular currency can buy; it is the external price of the currency quoted in terms of the other currency. Exchange rates can also be measured against gold, or against a weighted average of a sample or 'basket' of currencies. Currencies are bought and sold in the foreign exchange market, which is now an international 24/7 electronic market. On a global scale, the market never closes, and ICT-based buying and selling takes place throughout the day and night.

The chapter begins by describing different ways to measure a country's exchange rate. Having outlined the main types of exchange rate system, the chapter explains and analyses how balance of payments disequilibrium is dealt with in floating and fixed exchange rate systems. Towards the end of the chapter, the relationship between the euro and other currencies is examined.

Measuring the exchange rate

The pound's exchange rate against the dollar and euro, and the sterling index

The convention of quoting exchange rates in terms of the US dollar is of fairly recent origin. Before 1914 most exchange rates were expressed in terms of gold and only after 1945 did the dollar become the near universally accepted standard by which the external values of other currencies were measured. In recent years, in response to the changing pattern of UK trade, the pound's exchange rate is often quoted against the euro and the dollar. This is an example of **bilateral exchange rates**.

These days, the **sterling index** is also used to measure the pound's exchange rate. The sterling index, which is sometimes called the **effective exchange rate index**, does not measure the pound's external value against a particular currency. Rather it is a trade-weighted average of the pound's exchange rate against a number of leading trading currencies, calculated to reflect the importance of each currency in international trade. On 28 April 2005, the sterling index was 102.8 compared to its 1990 index of 100. This means that over the years since 1990, the sterling exchange rate had appreciated or increased in value by 2.8% when measured against the exchange rates of the UK's most important trading partners. However, as Figure 22.1 shows, over a longer period from 1975 to 2005, the pound's exchange rate fell against an average of other currencies, although there were shorter periods in which it rose.

> **examiner's voice**
>
> Data-response questions may use the sterling index to show changes in the pound's exchange rate. Alternatively, the dollar exchange rate or the euro exchange rate may be used.

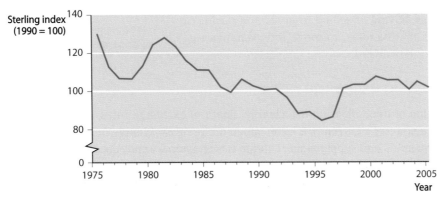

Figure 22.1 Changes in the sterling index between 1975 and 2005

The real exchange rate

The different exchange rates mentioned so far are all *nominal* exchange rates. The final measure of the exchange rate is the **real exchange rate**, which measures the rate at which home-produced goods exchange for imports, rather than the rates at which currencies themselves are traded. The real exchange rate, which is a measure of competitiveness, is calculated by the following formula:

$$\text{pound's real exchange rate} = \text{sterling index} \times \frac{\text{domestic price level}}{\text{weighted foreign price level}}$$

The different types of exchange rate system

Figure 22.2 shows the main types of exchange rate system. The two extreme types are **freely floating exchange rates** (also known as **cleanly floating exchange rates**) and rigidly **fixed exchange rates**. As shall be explained, a fixed exchange rate is the most extreme form of a **managed exchange rate**.

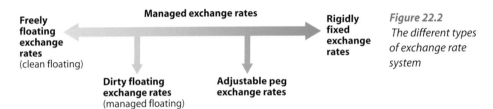

Figure 22.2
The different types of exchange rate system

The managed exchange rates that lie between the extremes of freely floating and rigidly fixed exchange rates take two main forms: **adjustable peg** and **managed floating** (or **dirty floating**) **exchange rates**. Adjustable peg exchange rates resemble fixed exchange rates in many respects, but the rate at which the exchange rate is fixed may be changed from time to time. A formal devaluation reduces the fixed exchange rate, while revaluation increases the fixed rate. As its name indicates, a managed floating exchange rate is closer to a freely floating exchange rate than to a fixed exchange rate. Market forces or supply and demand 'officially' determine the exchange rate, but the country's central bank intervenes 'unofficially' behind the scenes, buying or selling reserves and raising or lowering interest rates, to move the exchange rate upward or downward.

> **examiner's voice**
> Don't confuse exchange rate systems or regimes with particular measures of an exchange rate, such as the pound/dollar exchange rate.

Freely floating exchange rates

In a regime of freely floating (or 'cleanly' floating) exchange rates, the external value of a country's currency is determined on foreign exchange markets by the forces of demand and supply alone. Later in this chapter, we shall see that in recent years capital flows and speculation have been extremely significant in influencing the supply of and demand for a currency, and hence its exchange rate. However, we shall first simplify by assuming that a currency is demanded on foreign exchanges solely for the payment of trade and that trade flows alone determine exchange rates. We shall assume, too, that any holdings of foreign currencies surplus to the immediate requirement of paying for trade are immediately sold on the foreign exchange market.

The theory outlined in this section is called the **traditional approach** to floating exchange rates. The traditional approach, which largely ignores capital flows, contrasts with the **monetary approach**, developed in the 1950s and 1970s by the monetarist economists Milton Friedman and Harry Johnson. The monetary approach argues that capital flows, brought about by conditions in global money and financial markets, are much more important than trade flows in determining changes in exchange rates.

UK exports are priced in sterling, so overseas-based importing companies require pounds to buy them. When the exchange rate of the pound falls, UK exports become more competitive in overseas markets. The volume of UK exports increases, leading to greater overseas demand for pounds to finance the purchase of these exports. This explains the downward-sloping demand curve for pounds, which is illustrated in Figure 22.3.

But just as UK exports generate a demand for pounds on foreign exchange markets, so imports into the UK generate a supply of pounds. The explanation lies in the fact that UK trading companies generally pay for imports in foreign currencies. Importers must sell sterling on the foreign exchange market in order to purchase the foreign currencies needed to pay for the foreign currencies needed to pay for the

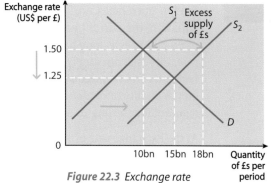

Figure 22.3 Exchange rate determination in a freely floating exchange rate system

goods they are buying. As the pound's exchange rate rises, fewer pounds are needed to buy a given quantity of foreign currency. This means that the sterling price of imports falls. UK consumers are likely to respond to the falling price of imports by increasing total spending on imports (which happens as long as the demand for imports is price elastic). A greater total quantity of sterling must be supplied on to foreign exchange markets to pay for the imports – even though the sterling price of each unit of imports has fallen. The result is the 'upward-sloping' supply curve of sterling depicted in Figure 22.3. This shows more sterling being supplied on the foreign exchange market, the higher the pound's exchange rate.

To explain the equilibrium exchange rate shown in Figure 22.3, we start by assuming the demand curve for sterling to be in position D, while the supply curve of sterling is in position S_1. Equilibrium occurs at the exchange rate £1 = $1.50. At this exchange rate, the demand for pounds equals the supply of pounds, and the money value of exports (paid in sterling) equals the money value of imports (paid in foreign currencies). Since we are assuming that exports and imports are the only items in the country's balance of payments, the balance of payments is also in equilibrium.

Note that when we ignore complications introduced by capital flows, exchange rate equilibrium implies balance of payments equilibrium on current account and vice versa. The two equilibria are just different sides of the same coin: exchange rate equilibrium is price equilibrium, whereas balance of payments equilibrium means that the quantity of the currency flowing into the country equals the quantity flowing out. Given the simplifying assumptions we have made, once the

balance of payments is in equilibrium, there is no pressure for the exchange rate to rise or fall.

Suppose, however, that some event or 'shock' disturbs the initial equilibrium — for example, an improvement in the quality of foreign-produced goods causes UK residents to increase demand for imports whatever the exchange rate. In Figure 22.3, the increase in demand for foreign exchange to pay for imports causes the supply curve of sterling to shift rightward from S_1 to S_2. (Remember, when more foreign currencies are demanded, more sterling must be supplied.) In the new situation, the current account of the balance of payments is in deficit to the tune of £8 billion — as long as the exchange rate stays at $1.50. At the $1.50 exchange rate, UK residents supply or sell £18 billion to pay for imports, but because overseas residents still demand the same quantity of UK goods (assuming that their views on the quality of UK goods relative to foreign goods has not changed), the overseas demand for sterling to pay for UK exports remains at £10 billion.

At the exchange rate of $1.50 to the pound, an excess supply of sterling of £8 billion exists. The market mechanism now comes into action to restore equilibrium — both for the exchange rate and for the balance of payments. When the excess holdings of sterling accumulated at the exchange rate of $1.50 are sold on the foreign exchange market, the pound's exchange rate falls. This increases the price competitiveness of UK exports while making imports less price competitive. The exchange rate falls until a new equilibrium exchange rate is reached at $1.25 to the pound.

Conversely, if the initial equilibrium is disturbed by an improvement in the quality of UK goods or services, the demand curve for sterling shifts rightward. This moves the current account into surplus, causing the pound's exchange rate to rise or appreciate in order to relieve the excess demand for sterling. Providing UK residents don't change their views on the relative quality of imports, the exchange rate rises until the balance of payments and exchange equilibrium are once again restored.

The advantages of floating exchange rates

It is argued that freely floating exchange rates have the following advantages.

Balance of payments equilibrium

The exchange rate (which is the external price of the currency) should move up or down to correct a payments imbalance. According to the traditional theory of exchange rates, the currency should never be overvalued or undervalued for very long. In the event of an overvalued exchange rate causing export uncompetitiveness and a payments deficit, market forces should quickly adjust towards an equilibrium exchange rate, which also achieves equilibrium in the balance of payments. Similarly, undervaluation should be quickly corrected by an upward movement of the exchange rate.

Resource allocation

If the world's resources are to be efficiently allocated between competing uses, exchange rates must be correctly valued. For efficient resource allocation in a constantly changing world, market prices must accurately reflect shifts in demand and changes in competitive and comparative advantage that result from technical progress and events such as discoveries of new mineral resources. In principle, a freely floating exchange rate should respond and adjust to these changes. By contrast, a fixed exchange rate may gradually become overvalued or undervalued, as demand or competitive and comparative advantage move against or in favour of a country's industries.

Domestic policy objectives

It is sometimes argued that when the exchange rate is freely floating, balance of payments surpluses and deficits cease to be a 'policy problem' for the government, as it is then free to pursue the domestic economic objectives of full employment and growth. Market forces 'look after' the balance of payments while governments concentrate on domestic economic policy. If, in the pursuit of domestic objectives, the inflation rate rises out of line with other countries, in a freely floating world the exchange rate simply falls to restore competitiveness.

Inflation

In much the same way, a 'responsible' country with a lower than average inflation rate should benefit from a floating exchange rate because the exchange rate insulates the country from 'importing inflation' from the rest of the world. If inflation rates are higher in the rest of the world, a fixed exchange rate causes a country to 'import' inflation through the rising prices of goods imported from high-inflation countries. By contrast, a floating exchange rate floats upward, which lowers the prices of imports, thereby preventing the import of inflation from the rest of the world.

Independent monetary policy

With a floating exchange rate, monetary policy can be used solely to achieve domestic policy objectives, such as the control of inflation. This is called an 'independent' monetary policy. By contrast, with a fixed exchange rate, interest rates may be determined by events in the outside world (and in particular by capital flows out of and into currencies), rather than by the needs of the domestic economy. To maintain a fixed exchange rate, interest rates may have to be raised to prevent it from falling. In this situation, monetary policy is no longer independent, in the sense that it can no longer be 'assigned' to pursuing purely domestic policy objectives.

The disadvantages of floating exchange rates

Freely floating exchange rates nevertheless have some disadvantages.

International trading uncertainty

It is sometimes argued that, whereas fixed exchange rates create conditions of certainty and stability in which international trade can prosper and grow, the

volatility and instability caused by floating exchange rates slow the growth of, and even destroy, international trade. In fact, 'hedging', which involves the purchase or sale of a currency in the 'forward' market 3 months in advance of the actual delivery of the currency and payment for trade, considerably reduces the trading uncertainties associated with floating exchange rates. Indeed, fixed and managed exchange rates may also cause uncertainty, especially when a currency is over-valued and a devaluation is expected.

Speculation and capital flows

The argument that a freely floating exchange rate is never overvalued or under-valued for very long depends crucially upon the main assumption of the traditional theory of exchange rates, that currencies are bought and sold on foreign exchange markets only to finance trade. This assumption means that speculation and capital flows have no influence upon exchange rates. But as the monetary theory of exchange rates argues, this is at odds with reality, ignoring a very important element of the real world. Well over 90% of currency transactions taking place on foreign exchange markets relate to capital flows and to the decisions of individuals, business corporations, financial institutions and even governments, to switch wealth portfolios between different currencies. In the short run, exchange rates are extremely vulnerable to speculative capital or 'hot money' movements into or out of currencies. Just like a fixed exchange rate, a floating exchange rate can be over-valued or undervalued and fail to reflect correctly the trading competitiveness of the country's industries.

Sterling dealers in London, shortly before currency speculation forced the pound out of Europe's exchange rate mechanism in September 1992

Cost-push inflation

Floating exchange rates often result in cost-push inflation. Suppose a country has a higher rate of inflation than its trading partners. Trading competitiveness and the current account of the balance of payments both worsen, causing the exchange rate to fall in order to restore competitiveness. This may then trigger a vicious cumulative downward spiral of ever faster inflation and exchange rate depreciation. The falling exchange rate increases import prices, which raise the rate of domestic cost-push inflation. Workers react by demanding pay rises to restore the real value of the eroded real wage. At the next stage, increased inflation erodes the export competitiveness initially won by the fall of the exchange rate, which in turn triggers a further fall in the exchange rate to recover the lost advantage. And so the process continues. The resulting downward spiral can eventually destabilise large parts of the domestic economy, causing unemployment and reducing economic growth.

Demand-pull inflation

Floating exchange rates can trigger demand-pull inflation as well as cost-push inflation. With a floating exchange rate, there is no need to deflate the domestic economy to deal with a balance of payments deficit on the current account. But suppose a large number of countries with floating exchange rates simultaneously expand aggregate demand. This can lead to excess demand on a worldwide scale, which fuels global inflation. This happened in the 1970s, when a worldwide expansion of demand created conditions in which oil and primary goods producers could raise prices and still sell in world markets. In countries such as the UK, the resulting inflation appeared to be 'import cost-push' inflation, caused by the rising cost of imported energy and raw materials. However, the true cause lay in excess demand created by the simultaneous effects of demand expansion and floating exchange rates, when world supply could not increase, at least in the short run, to meet the surge in global demand.

> **e*xaminer's voice**
>
> A2 Unit 6 exam questions may ask for analysis and evaluation of the advantages and disadvantages of floating exchange rates.

Long-term versus short-term determinants of the exchange rate

Figure 22.1 shows that the pound's exchange rate generally fell against other currencies over the three decades from the 1970s to the early 2000s. Indeed, the downward trend occurred through most of the twentieth century and has continued right up to the present day. The **purchasing power parity theory** (PPP) provides the best explanation for such *long-term* changes in exchange rates. PPP means that the prices of goods in different countries are made equal by changes in the countries' exchange rates.

Consider a situation in which a country's inflation rate is 10% higher than the inflation rates of its main competitors. The PPP theory predicts that, in this situation, the country's exchange rate falls by approximately 10%, to offset the loss of trading competitiveness caused by the higher domestic inflation rate. As a result, the purchasing power of exports over imports returns to its earlier level: that is, the

level existing before domestic inflation moved out of line with inflation rates in the rest of the world.

Although the PPP theory provides a good explanation of *long-term* changes in exchange rates (taking place over many decades), it is less useful for explaining *short-term* changes. Short-term changes in exchange rates result mainly from speculative capital flows. 'Hot money' flows cause exchange rates to 'over-shoot', in which case the currency becomes overvalued, or to 'undershoot', leading to undervaluation. However, because speculative flows tend to even out over periods longer than a few years, 'hot money' movements are less significant for explaining long-term changes in exchange rates.

> **e*xaminer's voice**
>
> Although exam questions do not require knowledge of the purchasing power parity theory, used relevantly, it should improve the quality of an examination answer.

Fixed exchange rates

With a freely floating exchange rate system, the currency's external value rises or falls to eliminate a balance of payments surplus or deficit on the current account. By contrast, with fixed exchange rates, a currency's external value remains unchanged, while the internal price level, or more usually the level of domestic economic activity and output, adjusts to eliminate balance of payments disequilibrium.

Although most exchange rates now float freely, fixed exchange rates have been important for quite long periods in the last 100 years. In a rigidly fixed system, devaluation is ruled out as a means of reducing a current account deficit. This means that deflationary policies that decrease aggregate demand have to be used to improve the current account. As a result, deflation harms the domestic economy, which explains why modern governments generally reject a return to rigidly fixed exchange rates. Governments prefer to be able to devalue, or to engineer a downward float of the currency.

The longest period of rigidly fixed exchange rates occurred in the nineteenth century and in the early years of the twentieth century. During this period, most major world currencies were fixed against gold in a system known as the **gold standard**. In addition, from 1999 until 2002, 12 EU currencies were rigidly fixed against each other in preparation for their eventual disappearance when replaced by euro notes and coins in 2002. These countries now form the eurozone. The eurozone will grow in size when the local currencies of new EU member countries are eventually replaced by the euro.

> **e*xaminer's voice**
>
> Exam questions on fixed exchange rates are less common than questions on floating exchange rates. Questions may occasionally ask for a comparison of fixed and floating exchange rates or for a discussion of whether stable exchange rates are desirable.

The advantages of fixed exchange rates

Because the advantages and disadvantages of fixed exchange rates are closely but oppositely related to those of floating rates, which have already been described in some depth, only a brief summary is presented here.

The main advantages of fixed exchange rates are:

- certainty and stability
- the anti-inflationary 'discipline' imposed on a country's domestic economic management and upon the behaviour of its workers and firms. (This is explained in greater depth later in the chapter, in the section on the relationship between fixed exchange rates and monetary policy.)

The disadvantages of fixed exchange rates

By contrast, the principal disadvantages of fixed exchange rates include:

- a possible increase in uncertainty
- continued overvaluation or undervaluation of the currency
- severe deflationary costs of lost output and unemployment for a deficit country, and importation of inflation by a surplus country
- a possible balance of payments or currency crisis in a country whose currency is overvalued
- tying up of resources in official reserves, which could be used more productively elsewhere

Managed exchange rates

An exchange rate is managed when the country's central bank actively intervenes in foreign exchange markets, buying and selling reserves and its own currency, to influence the movement of the exchange rate in a particular direction. By managing the exchange rate, a country's monetary authorities hope to achieve the stability and certainty associated with fixed exchange rates combined with a floating exchange rate's ability to avoid overvaluation and undervaluation by responding to market forces.

But critics of managed exchange rates argue that, instead of combining the advantages of both fixed and floating exchange rates with the disadvantages of neither, in practice the opposite happens. Exchange rate management too often achieves the disadvantages of uncertainty and instability combined with the ineffective and wasteful use of official reserves in frequent fruitless attempts by governments to stem speculative 'hot money' flows into or out of currencies.

As well as by maintaining a rigidly fixed exchange rate, exchange rates can be managed in two ways. These are through an adjustable peg (or fixed peg) system and by managed floating (or dirty floating).

Adjustable peg exchange rate systems

An adjustable peg exchange rate has a closer resemblance to a rigidly fixed exchange rate than to a freely floating exchange rate. Nevertheless, adjustable pegs are more flexible than rigidly fixed exchange rates. This is because the exchange rate is adjusted upward or downward from time to time by the country's central bank. An upward revaluation corrects an undervalued exchange rate, whereas a downward adjustment or devaluation is used to correct overvaluation.

Figure 22.4 illustrates devaluation of the pound in an adjustable peg exchange rate system. The exchange rate is initially fixed at a central peg of $2.00. Supply and demand then determine the day-to-day exchange rate. Providing the exchange stays between a ceiling and a floor set at the time that the central peg was set, the exchange rate is correctly valued for trade. There is no need for central bank intervention. However, the graph shows the exchange rate falling to the floor of $1.98, possibly because of a speculative capital flow against the currency. At this point the central bank intervenes, raising domestic interest rates to attract capital flows into the currency, and using reserves to support the fixed exchange rate. By selling reserves and buying its own currency, the central bank creates an artificial demand for its own currency. (A policy of buying and selling currencies to support an exchange rate is known as **exchange equalisation**. The policy operates in a similar way to buffer stock stabilisation of primary product prices.)

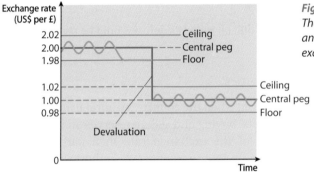

Figure 22.4
The devaluation of an adjustable peg exchange rate

Persistent support for the currency means that the exchange rate is overvalued, condemning the country to over-priced exports, under-priced imports and a current account deficit. In a rigidly fixed exchange rate system (which can be illustrated by the left-hand part of Figure 22.4), this is the end of the story. The country's government has to deflate the domestic economy and/or impose import controls, since devaluation and revaluation are not permitted in a rigidly fixed system.

However, Figure 22.4 goes on to show the authorities devaluing the exchange rate to a new central peg of $1.00 so as to correct the imbalance. This illustrates the difference between adjustable peg and rigidly fixed exchange rate systems.

examiner's voice

You can bring your knowledge of adjustable peg exchange rates into an answer on fixed exchange rates. Questions on managed exchange rates may occasionally be set, but technical terms such as 'adjustable peg' won't appear in the wording of a question.

Managed or dirty floating

In the past, fixed and adjustable peg exchange rate systems have been abandoned when the exchange rate has been allowed to float and find its own level. What happens next depends on whether the float is 'clean' or 'dirty'. Earlier sections of this chapter have already explained clean or pure floating. By contrast, 'dirty' or 'managed' floating occurs when the exchange rate is *officially* floating, in the sense that a country's monetary authorities announce that market forces are determining the exchange rate, but in fact they intervene *unofficially* behind the scenes to buy or sell their own currency to influence the exchange rate. At one extreme, 'dirty' or managed floating is simply a *smoothing operation* for a clean or freely floating exchange rate. However, at the other extreme, currency intervention may try to secure and then maintain an unofficial exchange rate target.

In the past, governments and central banks have sometimes got together to manage their exchange rates, without resorting to a full-blown adjustable peg system. The two most famous occasions were the 1985 Plaza Accord and the 1987 Louvre Accord, in which major industrial countries tried to peg their currencies within agreed target zones. Although neither accord was successful, in 2004 there was pressure to create a similar accord committing central banks to buy and prop up the US dollar.

Between 1985 and 1990, the UK government set an unofficial target for sterling which 'shadowed' the currencies in the exchange rate mechanism (ERM) of the European monetary system (EMS), particularly the Deutschmark. At the time, the UK had to choose between joining the ERM at a high or a low exchange rate. To understand why the government chose to join at a high exchange rate, we must now examine how, in the 1980s, exchange rate policy became entwined with both monetary policy and 'counter-inflation' policy.

Fixed and adjustable peg exchange rates and monetary policy

At various times in recent decades, UK governments used a high exchange rate as a policy instrument with which to control inflation. A high exchange rate reduces inflation in three different ways. In the first place, it causes the prices of imported food and consumer goods to fall. The second effect operates through falling prices of imported raw materials and energy. These reduce costs of production, which in turn reduces cost-push inflationary pressure within the domestic economy. The third effect is more subtle, since it operates through changes in human behaviour. If the exchange rate remains high, firms which raise prices by more than their international competitors suffer falling profits and even bankruptcy. At the same time, workers who push for higher wage increases than those on offer in competitor countries face the risk of unemployment. Realising it is against self-interest to behave in an inflationary way, firms and workers choose to moderate price rises and wage claims. The economist, Sir Alan Budd, argues that the pound's membership of the ERM at a high exchange rate had precisely this effect, 'bleeding' the economy of inflationary expectations between 1990 and 1992.

A high exchange rate thus disciplines or constrains domestic inflationary pressures. But if a devaluation is expected, the counter-inflationary discipline provided by the high exchange rate quickly disappears. If the government's commitment to a high

exchange rate is questioned, the credibility of counter-inflation policy may vanish. In this situation, inflationary pressures are unleashed, which reduces international competitiveness and causes the current account to deteriorate. An overvalued exchange rate leads to a 'hot money' outflow, which puts downward pressure on the exchange rate. To prevent the exchange rate from falling, the country's central bank may have to increase domestic interest rates. Higher interest rates contract or deflate aggregate demand in an economy already suffering a loss of export competitiveness brought about by the high exchange rate.

***e*xaminer's voice**
From 1985 until 1992, the exchange rate functioned as an intermediate target of monetary policy in the UK. At A2, it is important to understand the links between controlling inflation, monetary policy and the exchange rate.

Using a high exchange rate in this way to reduce domestic inflation means that monetary policy in general, and interest rates in particular, are not available to stimulate or reflate aggregate demand within the economy. Indeed, the deflationary effects of a high exchange rate and high interest rates mean that the domestic policy objectives of full employment and economic growth have to be sacrificed to the external objective of supporting the exchange rate.

The development of a single currency in the EU

The European exchange rate mechanism

From 1990 to 1992, the pound's exchange rate was managed in an adjustable peg system known as the **exchange rate mechanism** (ERM) of the **European monetary system** (EMS). In an important sense, the ERM was a precursor to the single currency, the euro.

The European Union (or European Community as it was then called) created the ERM to allow more efficient implementation of common economic policies. Before the ERM, financial assistance granted by the EU to member countries, most notably in the common agricultural policy (CAP), was sometimes distorted by fluctuating exchange rates. A relatively fixed exchange rate system within the EU could reduce or eliminate these distortions. As a result, the ERM was created as an adjustable peg exchange rate system, but not a single currency system.

The EU national currencies joining the ERM were fixed against each other, although EMS rules allowed periodic realignments (devaluations and revaluations) to take place. However, by the time the pound joined the ERM in 1990, the system had fossilised and become much more rigidly fixed. The pound entered at too high an exchange rate, but then could not be devalued. This made the overvalued pound extremely vulnerable to a speculative outward capital flow. It became a question of 'when' rather than 'if' the pound would have to leave the ERM.

A massive run on the pound occurred in September 1992, culminating on so-called 'Black Wednesday' with the pound being forced out of the ERM. Since then, the pound's exchange rate has floated. Following the pound's exit, speculators 'picked off' other ERM currencies, which left the EMS much weaker. Because of this, the European Union decided to go one significant stage beyond an adjustable peg exchange rate system, by replacing national currencies with a single currency, the euro.

European monetary union (EMU) and the euro

Just like the ERM and the EMS, the euro was created to facilitate greater economic union among EU member states. However, the euro goes a significant stage further than this. To supporters and critics alike, the single currency is a stepping stone to full monetary union between EU states and, possibly in the future, to a much fuller economic union.

Before proceeding further, it is worth noting that EMU means two different things. The *official* EU meaning is *economic* and monetary union. Defined in this way, EMU suggests that common monetary arrangements adopted by EU member countries are part of a grander scheme to integrate the national economies of member states. More *narrowly* defined, the acronym means *European* monetary union, which involves a common monetary policy applied to all EU member states adopting the euro. In the latter meaning, EMU can be interpreted simply as a step towards making the EU's single market work better and more efficiently.

Currently, the UK is *inside* the EU but *outside* the eurozone, retaining the pound as the national currency and implementing a strictly national UK monetary policy. By contrast, eurozone member countries are subject to the monetary policy implemented in Frankfurt by the European Central Bank (ECB). The pound's exchange rate floats against the euro, but some of the other non-eurozone EU currencies are more or less fixed against the euro.

The process of creating the euro and EMU began in the early 1990s, around the time the exchange rate mechanism disintegrated. The first step in the process centred on the publication of a timetable for introducing the single currency. The timetable required a European Central Bank to be established prior to the euro's introduction. In an important sense, the euro began its life in 1999 when the exchange rates of the 12 currencies eventually replaced by the euro were irrevocably fixed against each other. But in a strictly formal sense, the single currency came into operation 3 years later in 2002 when euro notes and coins replaced the 12 national currencies.

The impact of the euro upon eurozone economies

The introduction of the euro can be said to have had the following effects on the member countries of the eurozone.

- **Economic integration.** The euro has replaced national currencies such as the French franc and the German Deutschmark in the countries adopting the single currency. As noted, for supporters of greater economic integration in the EU, the single currency is a necessary step towards a much fuller economic union. In this view, monetary union and the euro enable EU firms and consumers to benefit in

future years from increased specialisation, a larger market, faster growth and higher living standards. Opponents of the euro argue that these supposed advantages are more than countered by the single currency's adverse effects.

- **Price competitiveness.** Whichever view is preferred, each member country is now 'locked in' to the single currency at the exchange rate agreed prior to entry. This means that eurozone countries have lost the freedom to lower or raise national exchange rates to correct overvaluation or undervaluation against each other. Countries that entered at too high an exchange rate face having to deflate domestic demand to restore competitiveness within the eurozone. Conversely, the countries that entered the eurozone at too low an exchange rate can reap the benefit of artificially high price competitiveness.

- **Speculation.** One of the reasons for creating the euro was to prevent national currencies of member countries being 'picked off' by international speculators, as had occurred in the early 1990s. When the euro was launched, many economists believed that the strength of eurozone economies (and the euro's potential role as a world reserve currency) would deter speculative selling or buying of the currency. Nevertheless, the euro itself is potentially vulnerable to a speculative attack. Although eurozone countries can no longer devalue or revalue against each other, the euro itself floats against the rest of the world's currencies. In 2002 and the early part of 2003, 'hot money' flowed from the euro into the dollar. This greatly increased the price competitiveness of eurozone exports in world markets. However, the direction of speculative flows reversed in the latter part of 2003 and in 2004. In these years, the euro's rising exchange rate made eurozone industries increasingly uncompetitive in world markets, particularly in the USA and in countries such as China whose currencies are fixed against the dollar.

- **Monetary policy.** Eurozone member countries can no longer implement independent monetary policies. In an important sense, national central banks such as Germany's Bundesbank and the Bank of France are now just branch banks of the European Central Bank, which sets an interest rate for the whole of the eurozone.

- **'One size fits all'.** The fact that the ECB sets an interest rate for the whole of the eurozone has led to the 'one size fits all' problem. In the 1990s, before launching the euro, the EU tried to get eurozone countries to converge their national business cycles. Without convergence, each country might be in a different phase of its business cycle. Some countries might be in recession or on the verge of recession, while others were in the recovery or boom phases of the economic cycle. Complete convergence, by contrast, means that every country is in the same phase of the business cycle. In the event, convergence has not occurred and, indeed, there is some evidence of growing *divergence* since the euro's introduction. A lack of convergence means that a high interest rate is needed to dampen demand-pull inflationary pressures in fast-growing countries such as Ireland, while low interest rates are required to stimulate economic recovery or to ward off recession in countries such as Germany. The 'one size fits all' problem stems from the fact that these requirements are mutually exclusive.

But *realpolitik* within the EU usually means that the needs of core economies, particularly Germany and France, override the requirements of peripheral countries such as Ireland and Portugal. The core economies have required a lower interest rate than peripheral countries.

- **Interest rates.** However, somewhat in conflict with the last sentence, the ECB has been criticised for being too cautious and deflationary when setting interest rates for eurozone countries. If true, this may reflect the influence in the eurozone of the German fear of high inflation, which stems from memories of the disastrous effect of German hyperinflation in the early 1920s. In the German view, interest rates must at all times be set sufficiently high to pre-empt inflationary pressures, especially those supposedly arising in 'less responsible' 'Club-Med' members of the eurozone, namely Greece, Spain, Portugal and Italy.

- **Fiscal policy.** The German view just outlined helps to explain the fiscal policy imposed on eurozone countries by the Stability and Growth Pact. To prevent expansionary fiscal policies fuelling excess demand and inflation, the Pact tried to prevent eurozone countries from increasing budget deficits to more than 3% of GDP and national debts to more than 40% of GDP. When first implemented, the Stability and Growth Pact was meant to rein in profligate fiscal policies of some of the smaller EU countries. In the outcome, the pact more or less disintegrated in 2003 and 2004, when the budget deficits and national debts of supposedly 'responsible' Germany and France began to break the pact's rules. Opponents of the Stability and Growth Pact believe that the pact has really been fighting yesterday's problem of inflation instead of the current problem of stagnation, possible deflation and unemployment. As long as it exists in its original form, the pact reduces the chance of a eurozone government successfully using expansionary fiscal policy to get out of recession or a slow-growth economic environment.

The UK, the euro and the five economic tests

In recent years, UK political parties have considered whether or not to replace the pound with the euro. In the early 2000s, the Labour government, which at the time favoured joining the euro, decided that the UK should only join if five economic tests are passed. The two main tests are **convergence** and **flexibility**, which in turn affect the other tests, namely **investment**, **employment** and the **financial sector**. By 2004, only the financial sector test (which relates to the compatibility of financial service industries in the City of London) had been completely passed — at least according to the Labour government.

If the UK does eventually decide to join the eurozone, a high degree of convergence is desirable so that the UK's business cycle can be synchronised with those of other eurozone countries. A degree of convergence with the eurozone has

examiner's voice
Don't confuse the UK government's *five economic tests*, which must supposedly be met before the political decision is taken on whether or not to join the eurozone, with the *convergence criteria* that the EU set for prospective entrants in the 1990s before the launch of the euro. The UK government's five tests do not apply for other prospective entrants, and they could of course be rejected by a Conservative government.

been taking place, but it is far from complete. However, it is unlikely that complete convergence is possible, at least for the next few years. One reason for this has already been stated, namely the fact that the economies of the 12 existing eurozone countries have themselves not converged. A second reason relates to the fact that the UK economy, with its greater ties with North America and other non-EU countries, differs significantly from other eurozone countries.

The impact of the euro upon the UK economy

If the UK eventually adopts the euro as its currency, it is likely to face the following issues.

- **Interest rates and the housing market.** For the *realpolitik* reason already explained, if the UK is booming when Germany is in recession, the ECB will be under pressure to cut interest rates to help the 'core' country, Germany. This would overheat the UK economy and exacerbate a specifically British problem related to the UK housing market. Owner-occupancy is greater in the UK than in most eurozone countries, and UK house buyers pay variable interest rates on their mortgages in contrast to the fixed interest rates common in the eurozone. Fixed rate interest rates mean that a cut in the ECB's interest rate has little effect on continental housing markets. However, if the UK were in the eurozone, the effect would be great, unleashing a spending spree amongst UK owner-occupiers suddenly benefiting from a fall in mortgage interest repayments.
- **Monetary and fiscal policy.** It follows that, if monetary policy is taken away from the Bank of England (as eurozone entry dictates), then arguably the UK should be able to use fiscal policy to manage demand. But as explained, the deflationary bias of the EU's Stability and Growth Pact currently limits the freedom of eurozone members to use fiscal policy to head off a deep recession. Unless the pact's rules are changed or the pact is abandoned, adopting the euro will significantly limit the UK's freedom to use fiscal policy to boost employment and economic growth.
- **Supply-side policies.** In terms of employment, supply-side policies adopted in the UK, but not in much of mainland Europe, mean that the UK has a more flexible labour market. For example, it is easier to hire and fire workers in the UK than in Germany. The counter-argument is that UK workers are more poorly trained than continental workers and their language skills are much worse. (To some extent, this last point is not important because English is now the international business language.) Geographical mobility of labour is poor both within the UK and across EU frontiers. However, this and similar problems, such as the poor quality of UK management, are generally intractable and not subject to quick policy fixes. These problems will remain whether or not the UK joins the euro. Euro entry may render the UK even less competitive in an enlarged eurozone or it may jolt the UK into taking serious action to improve the quality of UK workers and management.
- **Employment and investment.** Employment and investment could both be greatly affected if and when the pound disappears. Currently the pound is floating.

William Hague addresses an anti-euro rally at the Conservative Party Conference in Bournemouth, 2000

In the event of overvaluation, the exchange rate can fall to restore competitiveness, unless, of course, a 'hot money' inflow overvalues the currency. If the UK joins the euro, devaluation will no longer be available as a policy instrument to restore competitiveness. Entry at an overvalued level would condemn the UK economy to trading uncompetitively and the need for deflation. Joining at the right exchange rate is therefore essential if the UK is to benefit from euro entry. Fortunately, by 2004, 'hot money' flows had changed direction, causing the pound's exchange rate to fall against the euro. Exchange rate conditions had become more suited to the UK joining the eurozone, though both major political parties were increasingly distancing themselves from adopting the euro.

- **Politics.** Ultimately the decision to replace the pound with the euro is a *political* as well as an *economic* decision. By promising a referendum on the single currency in which the electorate may well vote 'no', the UK government is boxed in. The electorate is unlikely to support a political decision to adopt the euro, even if the economic conditions, though not perfect, eventually become more favourable.

> *e*xaminer's voice
> Examination questions may ask for evaluation of the case for and against the UK joining EMU. They may also ask for discussion of the effects on the UK of *staying out* of EMU, as an alternative to the effects of *joining* it.

Reserve currencies

Chapter 21 mentioned that the US dollar is the world's reserve currency, defined as the currency that governments and central banks outside the USA wish to hold.

Indeed, the reserve currency status of the dollar also means that individuals and companies worldwide hold the dollar as a wealth asset in preference to their national currencies.

To take on a world reserve role, a currency must be transmitted into overseas ownership. In the case of the dollar, the USA's huge balance of payments deficit on the current account has provided the main transmission mechanism, along with the willingness of governments and people worldwide to hold the dollar. To function as a reserve currency, the dollar must be 'hard' (that is, greatly in demand), but the huge balance of payments deficit that transmits dollars into overseas ownership tends to 'soften' the currency. The dollar becomes less desirable to hold, which puts downward pressure on the currency's exchange rate.

Vast overseas ownership of the dollar renders the currency vulnerable to a mass-selling panic. To some extent this happened late in 2004, encouraged in part by the US government's policy of 'benign neglect' with respect to the dollar's exchange rate. The US administration seemed to encourage the dollar's fall, hoping that, by making US goods more competitive in world markets, the problem of a growing US payments deficit would diminish.

However, two factors temper mass selling of dollars. First, a large-scale sale of dollars inevitably involves mass purchase of other currencies, such as the euro. For this to occur, dollar holders' confidence in the euro, and in the economies of eurozone countries, must exceed their doubts about the dollar and the US economy. The sheer size and hegemonic role of the US economy means that the dollar is still generally regarded as a better bet than other currencies. Second, the USA's huge current account deficit means that other countries have huge surpluses. This means that their currencies are in short supply on foreign exchange markets. This in turn means a lack of a transmission mechanism to convey the currencies into widespread overseas ownership, and into a world reserve role equalling the past role of the dollar.

Summary

The exchange rate is the *external* price of a currency. Exchange rates usually quote a currency's price against another currency, although gold and artificial currency units have sometimes been used. In recent years, index numbers have been used to measure exchange rates — for example, the sterling index, which measures the pound's exchange rate against a trade-weighted 'basket' of currencies of the major countries with which the UK trades. A distinction is also made between nominal and real exchange rates.

There are three types of exchange rate system: freely floating, fixed and managed. Free-market forces determine freely floating (or *clean* floating) exchange rates. In the absence of capital flows, currencies are sold on foreign exchange markets solely to buy overseas currencies needed to pay for imports. A current account deficit leads to excess supply of the importing country's currency. The exchange rate then falls and restores current account equilibrium. Thus, in a floating exchange rate system, free-market forces rather than government intervention determine both the exchange rate and the current account of the balance of payments. But this is over-simple. In the real world, capital inflows and outflows — particularly speculative 'hot money' flows — can lead to overvalued and undervalued exchange rates, which make the country's exports artificially expensive or artificially cheap.

Floating exchange rates have been criticised for being unstable and for promoting uncertainty. Evidence does not always support this criticism, and in any case exporters and importers can reduce uncertainty by hedging, which involves buying or selling currencies on the forward market. By contrast, an advantage of fixed exchange rates is their alleged stability. Supporters of managed and relatively fixed exchange rates argue that this stability represents a form of 'public good' shared by all, which, by reducing uncertainty, is conducive to the efficient use of the world's resources and to the growth of output and trade. They also argue that relatively fixed exchange rates impose 'rules of the game', which act as a source of external discipline on policy-makers and economic agents within countries. By imposing discipline, the exchange rate reduces inflation within countries, both by directly discouraging inflationary wage and price rises and also, but less directly, by lowering inflationary expectations. However, when speculators believe that a fixed exchange rate is over- or undervalued, and that a devaluation or revaluation is imminent, a fixed exchange

rate may be just as unstable as a floating exchange rate.

According to their supporters, managed exchange rates combine the advantages of floating and fixed exchange rates with the disadvantages of neither system. Managed exchange rates are stable, yet the possibility of devaluation or revaluation means they are unlikely to be wrongly valued for very long. By contrast, critics of managed exchange rates reach the opposite conclusion, namely that managed exchange rates combine the disadvantages of floating and fixed exchange rates with the advantages of neither system.

Until fairly recently, the exchange rates of most of the countries in the European Union were managed in the exchange rate mechanism of the European monetary system. However, most former members of the ERM (but not the UK) have replaced their national currencies with a single currency, the euro. The adoption of the euro, which is a part of the process of economic and monetary union (EMU), is meant to facilitate the adoption of common economic policies and a greater degree of economic integration among EU countries.

From 1998 until 2002, the exchange rates of the 12 countries joining the euro were irrevocably fixed against each other, but the 12 currencies floated jointly against non-eurozone currencies. Since the disappearance of the 12 national currencies in 2002, the euro has continued to float against non-eurozone currencies, including the pound. As yet, the euro has not developed into a world reserve currency. Despite the dollar's exchange rate weakening in 2004, the US currency continues to be the world's main reserve currency, although gold also continues to have a world reserve role.

Self-testing questions

1 State three ways in which a country's exchange rate can be measured.

2 Distinguish between a currency's nominal exchange rate and its real exchange rate.

3 Using a demand and supply diagram, show how a freely floating exchange rate is determined.

4 Outline the advantages and disadvantages of a floating exchange rate.

5 How may a fixed exchange rate discipline inflationary behaviour?

6 Describe two types of managed exchange rate.

7 Distinguish between 'dirty' and 'clean' floating.

8 Why has the exchange rate sometimes been targeted as a macroeconomic policy objective?

9 What was the exchange rate mechanism of the European monetary system?

10 Why did the UK leave the ERM in 1992?

11 Does the euro have a fixed or a floating exchange rate? Explain your answer.

12 Why did most members of the EU decide in the 1990s to replace their national currencies with the euro?

13 Why was convergence deemed a necessary condition for a successful eurozone?

14 Explain two possible effects on the British economy if the UK were to adopt the euro.

Part 8

Markets at work and the European Union

Chapter 23
Markets at work

Specification focus

This chapter applies concepts and theories learnt when studying AS Modules 1 and 2 to the three optional topics in the AS Module 3 specification.

AS **Module 3 Markets at Work**

The Housing Market; The Environment; The Economics of Sport and Leisure

A2 **Synoptic coverage**

The analysis and explanation of UK housing markets provided in this chapter will be useful when answering a Unit 6 exam question on UK monetary policy. Likewise, coverage of environmental economics in the chapter will add depth to an answer addressing the Module 5 topic of the impact of environmental change on economic behaviour.

Introduction

Previous chapters in this book have explored conventional microeconomic and macro-economic topics that are central to most traditional economics courses. The final two chapters are different. This chapter surveys the three optional topics assessed in the AS Unit 3 examination, while Chapter 24 covers the European Union, the case study topic in the A2 Unit 4 examination.

AS Module 3: Markets at Work contains three optional contexts, namely:
- *Option 1: The Housing Market*
- *Option 2: The Environment*
- *Option 3: The Economics of Sport and Leisure*

The Module 3 specification does not require candidates to learn any concepts, terms or theories over and above those learnt when preparing at AS for the Unit 2 and Unit 3 examinations. The specification advises that:

Provided candidates have developed a sound grasp of the economic principles specified in Markets and Market Failure and the National Economy, the information contained in the data provided in the Markets at Work questions should be enough to answer all parts of the question on the candidate's chosen option.

Nevertheless, this chapter has been written to provide candidates with basic information about the special features of each of the optional topics from which a choice has to be made.

Housing markets

The structure of housing markets

There are many different housing markets in the UK. Housing markets can be separated according to the type of property (flats, semi-detached and detached houses, etc.), but most importantly by the type of **tenure** enjoyed by the household living in the property.

Note that a household is not the same as a family. For example, a family placing an elderly grandparent in sheltered accommodation creates a new one-person household. Likewise a teenager leaving the family home to live in a flat becomes a new household.

When discussing the structure of UK housing markets, four main types of tenure can be identified. These are owner-occupation, the private rented sector and two forms of social housing: the local authority rented sector (or council housing) and the housing association sector.

Owner-occupation

In the owner-occupied sector, households own their own property, although very often the houses are mortgaged. A **mortgage** is a loan from a bank or building society, secured against the value of the house. Owner-occupiers who do not need a mortgage when buying a property are called 'cash buyers'. However, most homeowners borrow at least part of the sum needed to buy a house.

Consider a first-time buyer purchasing a £120,000 house with a £100,000 mortgage, repayable over 25 years. If the person becomes unemployed and fails to repay the loan, the bank or building society can repossess the house, leaving the person homeless. Owner-occupiers become outright owners only when mortgages have been fully repaid, usually years after the initial house purchase.

Private renting

In the private rented sector, landlords lease properties that they own to tenants. In the early part of the twentieth century, private rented accommodation was the dominant form of housing. This is no longer the case. Private renting is now relatively insignificant, although it is still important for certain groups, such as students and young earners waiting to buy a first property.

In the mid-twentieth century, the private rented sector declined for two main reasons: rent controls were imposed below the free-market level, and tenants were

granted security of tenure, which made it difficult for landlords to evict them. These controls were introduced to correct an alleged market failure, namely landlords exploiting tenants by charging excessive rents and evicting without good reason. But by making it less attractive to lease property, rent controls and security of tenure created a shortage of private rented accommodation. Arguably, government intervention that was intended to correct market failure created new government failure in the housing market.

Local authority housing

The local authority rented sector contains houses usually specially built by local government and leased at below-market rents subsidised by taxpayers. Council houses were first built after the First World War, to try to correct the market failure in the housing market which had led to low-income families living for the most part in poor-quality or slum private rented accommodation.

From 1979 onwards, UK governments, particularly Margaret Thatcher's Conservative administrations, believed that the building of 'ghetto' council estates, inhabited by very poor families with no income earner, were indicative of government failure. Government policy thus switched to reducing rather than increasing the size of the local authority housing sector.

Housing associations

The housing association sector comprises charities and other non-profit-making organisations known as Registered Social Landlords (RSLs). These combine private and public funds to provide housing for those in need on low incomes. Housing associations are the smallest sector in the housing market, but through a process of new building and the transfer of housing from local authorities, they had increased from almost zero in 1981 to over 1 million dwellings by 2000. Housing associations account for about 5% of housing, and this is set to increase.

A high proportion of tenants, who in earlier decades would have been council tenants, are accepted by housing associations on the recommendation of local authorities. By claiming housing benefit, many tenants have some or all of their rent paid by central government. RSLs are entitled to government grants to finance further house building, provided they can also raise private funding.

Regional housing markets

There is a clear 'north/south' economic divide in the UK housing market, with house prices and private rents much higher in London and the southeast than in other UK regions. Nonetheless, there are pockets of high-priced housing outside southeast England – for example, in the plusher Manchester and Leeds commuter belts, and in Edinburgh. With the average price of Greater London houses rising well above £200,000, 'millionaire' properties have proliferated in the more prosperous parts of the country. However, at the other extreme, rundown houses in declining and increasingly derelict northern manufacturing regions have sometimes sold for less than £100 – if a buyer can be found.

The factors explaining differences in regional house prices include the immobility of housing and the poor quality of housing in some locations. Supply and demand factors are also important. Supply factors include the availability of building land and the impact of planning controls. Demand factors, which relate strongly to the relative success of regional economies, include population density and growth (both of which are affected by migration between regions), and marked regional differences in personal income and wealth.

By making it difficult, if not impossible, for low-income families to move to the southeast in search of jobs, regional price differences contribute to immobility of labour. Other reasons for labour immobility include the shortage of affordable rented accommodation and the fact that many workers living in the southeast are reluctant to move outside the region. Although it is possible to buy much larger houses with the money raised from house sales in the southeast, lower regional wages and the fear of never being able to afford to move back again deters movement to lower-priced parts of the country.

*e*xaminer's voice
The 'north/south' divide in UK house prices illustrates that there are many different sub-markets within the overall UK housing market. In one sense, there are nearly as many sub-markets as there are houses, as each house is unique in some particular way — for example, location, type of building or interior decoration. Think how you might apply the concepts of barriers to entry and exit to these markets. How easy is it to buy, or for that matter to sell, a house in a particular location?

The stock of housing

To understand housing markets, it is useful to distinguish between stocks and flows. The *stock* of housing comprises all properties built in previous years that are currently used for housing. Each year, the stock rises or falls according to whether the *flow* of newly built properties added to the stock exceeds the *flow* of demolished properties and accommodation converted to other uses.

*e*xaminer's voice
The difference between a *stock* and a *flow* has been mentioned on a number of occasions in this book. The difference is very important when considering factors affecting the supply of housing. 'Nominal' and 'real' are two other important words that economists use. Make sure you understand the difference between *nominal* and *real* house prices.

The supply of new and second-hand housing

Newly built properties increase the supply of housing available for buying. Most new houses are bought from four or five large house-building companies, which account for most of the new homes built in the UK. However, the supply of housing also includes 'second-hand' houses bought from existing owner-occupiers who wish to sell.

It is worth stressing that the sale of a second-hand house generally creates a demand for another property. The seller has to buy another house to live in. However, there are exceptions. In some cases, sellers move into rented accommodation. Executor sales caused by the death of house owners provide other examples. Executor sales and house repossessions by banks lead to 'forced' sales of property. By increasing the supply of housing in already stagnant housing markets, 'forced' sales can worsen house price crashes.

The long-run rise in the price of housing

Figure 23.1 shows the long-term trend growth of house prices in the UK, covering a period from 1970 to 2005, together with the short-term cyclical fluctuations around the trend. Note that the short-term fluctuations closely follow the business cycle for the whole economy. The graph shows that, in the long term, house prices have risen in the UK, although there have also been short-term 'booms and busts'.

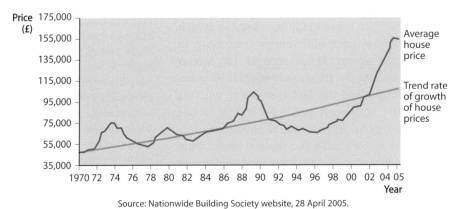

Source: Nationwide Building Society website, 28 April 2005.

Figure 23.1 Changes in house prices in the UK

In the long term, the demand for and the supply of housing have both increased (or shifted rightward), but demand has increased faster.

- The *supply* of owner-occupied housing has increased at a faster rate than overall supply because landlords have left the rental market and sold their properties for owner-occupancy. On occasion, however, when housing market conditions favour private letting, the reverse is true. The recent growth of the 'buy-to-let' market, in which cash-rich City workers spend their bonuses on properties to let, provides a topical example.
- The main causes of the long-term rightward shift of *demand* have been population growth, the growth in the number of households and real income growth. Good-quality housing is a normal good with a positive income elasticity of demand. Indeed, for many people, owner-occupied housing is a superior good with an income elasticity of demand greater than +1. By contrast, poor rented accommodation is an inferior substitute.

Short-run fluctuations in the price of housing

Figure 23.2 illustrates the main reason why house prices rise and fall in the UK. Short-run price fluctuations are caused primarily by the demand curve for housing shifting rightward or leftward along a vertical supply curve depicting the total stock of housing in the economy. A rightward shift of demand from D_1 to D_2 causes house prices to rise from P_1 to P_2. At any point in time, the total stock of housing is fixed and completely inelastic with respect to the price of housing. Factors that explain why the stock of housing is unresponsive to price changes include the general shortage of land, the effect of planning controls, which make it difficult to convert land from other uses, and the length of time taken to build a new house.

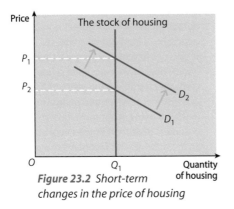

Figure 23.2 Short-term changes in the price of housing

The demand for housing

Like all consumer goods, people demand housing for the utility or welfare derived from the consumer services that houses provide. All houses provide basic shelter, but each house also combines other desirable attributes, such as location, a view, a garden, car parking and rooms suitable for work, leisure and hospitality. The demand for housing is also affected by a number of factors specific to housing markets. A house is a consumer durable good that delivers a stream of consumer services over a long period, typically a century or more. Unlike other durable goods, such as cars and television sets, which depreciate and lose value during their lives, most houses — or certainly the land on which houses are built — appreciate and gain value. This means that the demand for housing is determined not only by people's need for shelter, but also by the fact that people treat housing as a form of investment. Housing is an attractive wealth asset — indeed, the main wealth asset of many UK residents.

Far from reducing demand, a rise in house prices may therefore trigger a speculative bubble in the house market. Rising house prices drive up demand, causing a further rise in prices, with the process continuing until the bubble bursts. Rising house prices also mean that owner-occupiers already on the 'housing ladder' can gain from further price rises. For existing house owners, the value of their asset increases, but the value of their mortgage generally stays the same. Owner-occupiers benefit from **capital gains** — the difference between the price they paid for the house and its current higher market value.

In this situation, two things may happen. First, the number of 'first-time buyers' increases because young people, desperate to get on the housing ladder, try to buy before houses become unaffordable. Second, wishing to become even wealthier, existing owner-occupiers try to 'trade up' by purchasing larger properties in more desirable locations. Both these events shift the demand curve for housing rightward and fuel a further rise in house prices. During a house market boom, therefore, activity

in the housing market soars. Increases occur in both the number of people trying to sell and the number trying to buy property. However, demand rises faster than supply.

Market failure and government intervention in UK housing markets

In the nineteenth century and the early part of the twentieth century, free-market forces largely determined UK house prices. But unregulated market forces also meant that most of the population could not afford to buy a house at a price set by the market. As a result, many people rented poor-quality slum accommodation in which they were exploited by private landlords. While some economists blamed the housing market for this outcome, others argued that poverty and an unequal income distribution, not the housing market, caused the market failure.

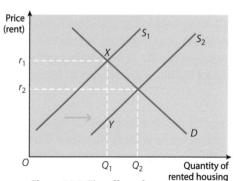

PAULA SOLLOWAY/PHOTOFUSION

Poor-quality housing may be deemed to be a demerit good

Figure 23.3 *The effect of subsiding rents in the market for rented accommodation*

Many economists argue that good-quality housing is a **merit good**, yielding external benefits for the whole community. Moreover, the long-term private benefits enjoyed by the occupiers of good-quality housing — for example, in terms of longer life expectancy and good health — are greater than the short-term private benefits they receive. If decent-quality housing is a merit good, then arguably free markets result in excessively high house prices and rents. Too few people, particularly the poor, end up living in houses of adequate quality. This leads to the case for government intervention to bring down the price of housing and to make sure that affordable rented accommodation of decent quality is available for the poor.

Figure 23.3 shows how a government might use subsidies to reduce rents. Without a subsidy, the free-market rent is r_1, and Q_1 properties are leased. But if the property owner receives a subsidy equal to the vertical distance XY, the supply curve of rented housing shifts rightward to S_2. The rent falls to r_2 and the quantity of subsidised rentals increases to Q_2.

In the UK, council house rents rather than private rents have been subsidised, although the largest part of the socially owned stock of housing has now been sold or privatised. Moreover, in recent years there has been a shift away from subsidy to the payment of housing benefit, which tops up the income of poor families and enables them to pay market rents. House-building companies may also be required to build 'affordable housing', either for rent or for sale, as a part of mixed property developments which for the most part contain more expensive housing.

Although good-quality housing is arguably a merit good, poor-quality slum housing may be deemed to be a **demerit good**. However, it is wrong to suggest that prices and rents for poor-quality housing should rise. Rather, the opposite should happen. There should be intervention to encourage private landlords to improve the quality of slum properties using both 'the carrot and the stick' (financial incentives and compulsion).

> *e*xaminer's voice
>
> Make sure you can explain why a house can be regarded both as a merit good and as a demerit good. Think also about how government intervention to correct alleged market failures in the housing market can distort the market and lead to new problems (see below).

Government failure in housing markets

The rapid deterioration of many council estates into 'sink' ghettos, where nobody wants to live, provides an example of government failure in housing markets. Reacting to this problem, which had been created by well-intended governmental provision of socially owned housing, recent UK governments have switched much of the stock of social housing to housing associations. They believe that private charitable owners stand a better chance of maintaining both the quality of the housing stock and the quality of tenants' lives.

Rent controls provide another example of possible government failure in housing markets. The effect of UK rent controls introduced in the mid-twentieth century is illustrated in Figure 23.4. Having decided that the free market rent r_1 was inequitable and excessive, the UK government imposed a rent ceiling at r_C. Landlords responded by reducing the quantity of rented houses from Q_1 to Q_3. Meanwhile, demand among prospective tenants increased to Q_2. Excess demand, or a shortage of rented housing equal to $Q_2 - Q_3$, was the inevitable result of this policy.

Landlords found that their ability to remove rented accommodation from the market depended on whether they could evict sitting tenants. In the 1960s, UK governments introduced new laws that made it almost impossible to evict a tenant legally, against the tenant's will. This led to:

- criminal activity by rogue landlords, using violence to 'persuade' tenants to leave
- property being switched from private letting as soon as tenants died or could be evicted
- almost no new properties being built for private rental and very few existing properties being switched from owner occupancy to private rental

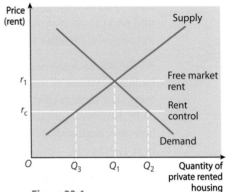

Figure 23.4
The effect of rent controls

Thus government intervention to correct a perceived market failure became the main factor creating a shortage of private rented accommodation. The shortage still persists today, despite legislation in the 1980s and 1990s to remove rent controls and to make it easier for landlords to evict tenants.

How housing markets affect and are affected by the national economy

The aggregate demand/aggregate supply (*AD/AS*) macroeconomic model drawn in Figure 23.5 can help to explain some of the ways in which UK housing markets affect the national economy.

Housing markets and aggregate demand

Economic activity in the housing market tends to affect aggregate demand rather more than aggregate supply. Consumption spending is the largest component of aggregate demand. In turn, spending on housing is the largest component of consumption, particularly if we include spending on complementary goods such as carpets, bathroom and kitchen furniture, cookers and washing machines.

Suppose the *AD* curve is initially in the position AD_1. The economy is in recession, suffering from deficient aggregate demand, with real output at y_1 well below the full

examiner's voice

It might be useful at this stage to reread the sections of Chapter 2 dealing with maximum and minimum price controls (price ceilings and price floors) and the so-called 'black' markets that can emerge when price controls are imposed and enforced.

examiner's voice

The aggregate demand/aggregate supply (*AD/AS*) macroeconomic model is the area of theory that candidates are expected to apply when answering macroeconomic questions. This applies just as much to a macro question in the Unit 3 exam as it does to a question in the Unit 2 exam on the national economy.

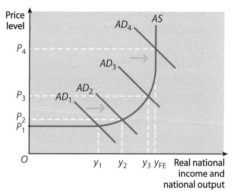

Figure 23.5 *The AD/AS model and the housing market*

employment level y_{FE}. The diagram shows that, to bring about economic recovery and end the recession, the *AD* curve must shift rightward. In the UK, spending on housing and on other consumer goods has generally led to recovery from recession.

As Figure 23.5 shows, a consumer and housing market boom can have largely beneficial effects. Output rises to y_2, thereby creating jobs and reducing unemployment, but there is relatively little inflation because the price level only rises from P_1 to P_2. However, problems may surface when spending on housing increases as the economy approaches full employment. The *AD* curve shifts rightward — for example, from AD_3 to AD_4 — but because of insufficient spare capacity in the economy, excess demand pulls up the price level from P_3 to P_4 in a demand-pull inflation.

The importance of owner-occupied housing in the UK means that 'boom and bust' in the housing market tends to promote and exacerbate 'boom and bust' in the whole economy: that is, it makes the business cycle more volatile. Owner-occupiers (but not tenants) benefit tremendously from rising house prices. They enjoy tax-free capital gains and become much wealthier. Consumption is positively related to both personal wealth and income. Wealthier households consume more, and at all levels of income the proportion of income saved falls. Indeed, when house prices are rising rapidly, owner-occupiers feel that they don't need to save to increase wealth because house price inflation is doing the job for them. Consumption is also positively related to consumer confidence. Rising house prices usually give rise to increased consumer confidence and a 'feel-good factor', further boosting consumption.

Towards the peak of an economic boom, house price inflation is usually significantly higher than general inflation. Monetary policy is then used to try to reduce house price inflation and the consumer spending spree it generates. However, excessive house price inflation has generally been restricted to the more prosperous parts of the UK, where service industries rather than manufacturing are the mainstay of the economy. Raising interest rates to control house price inflation in London and the southeast has the unfortunate effect of reducing aggregate demand in *all* regions. This leads to the problem of 'two-speed Britain'. Manufacturing regions, but not the whole economy, enter recession or teeter on the brink of recession. Regions dependent on manufacturing require low interest rates to nurture their fragile economies, but their needs are overridden by high interest rates targeted at the overheated property market in southeast England.

Not only do housing markets affect the economy, but the economy in turn affects housing markets. We have also noted how monetary policy (interest rate changes) affect housing markets and house prices. In addition, as housing has an income elasticity of demand greater than +1, economic growth leads to a larger proportionate increase in demand for owner-occupied housing, together with all the complementary goods that go with housing.

> *e*xaminer's voice
> Examination questions are likely to be set to test understanding of the links between monetary policy, housing markets, the state of aggregate demand, and 'boom' or 'bust' in the economy. The Bank of England decides on interest rate policy, taking account of conditions in housing markets, particularly the rate of house price inflation compared to general inflation and whether a difference between the two rates signals an overheated economy.

Housing markets and aggregate supply

Although housing markets affect the national economy primarily through their effect on aggregate demand, aggregate supply can also be affected. Arguably, aggregate supply, economic growth and national competitiveness in the UK have been adversely affected by:

- owner-occupancy and the lack of affordable private rented accommodation contributing to geographical immobility of labour and labour market rigidity
- the favourable tax treatment granted to housing, which has diverted savings away from productive investment in industry

As a result, the economy's *LRAS* curve has shifted rightward at a slower rate than would have been the case without these adverse effects.

Positive and negative equity, and equity withdrawal

Changes in the national economy also affect positive and negative equity. People enjoy **positive equity** when the value of their assets (the things they own) exceeds the value of their liabilities (their debts). During house market booms when house price inflation runs ahead of the general rate of inflation, owner-occupiers' positive equity increases. House values rise in real as well as in nominal terms, and at the same time owner-occupiers benefit from the fact that mortgage debt does not rise.

In these circumstances, many owner-occupiers indulge in **equity withdrawal** (equity leakage). This occurs when households remortgage their properties (that is, borrow more money secured against the now higher value of their properties) and then spend the sums borrowed on general consumption — new cars, holidays, home improvements, etc. Alternatively, many households borrow more money and increase their mortgages in order to 'trade up' to larger, more expensive properties.

Don't confuse equity withdrawal (which occurs during housing market booms) with the **negative equity** trap, which can occur in the subsequent 'bust'. This affects owner-occupiers — usually first-time buyers — who buy houses with the aid of very large mortgages at the peak of a house price boom. If house prices fall, some owner-occupiers end up with the value of their houses having fallen below the value of their mortgage debt.

In an economic downturn, incomes fall and unemployment increases. In this situation, many owner-occupiers, who are unable to make monthly mortgage repayments, try to sell their houses so as to repay the debt. But those suffering from negative equity are doubly unfortunate. Personal debt exceeds the value of the household's property. As a result, a household caught in the negative equity trap cannot use a house sale to repay all its debt. In extreme cases, a bank or building society seizes (or **repossesses**) the house that secures the mortgage, and the evicted household becomes homeless.

examiner's voice

As a general rule, exam questions do not mention terms or concepts that are not explicit in the relevant specification(s). However, good candidates can usefully bring such terms into their answer(s). Sometimes this rule is broken, as evidenced by a recent Unit 3 exam that asked for an explanation of negative equity.

The environment

Economic activity and the environment

Previous chapters, notably Chapters 9 and 13, have explained some of the ways in which economic activity affects the environment, and in which the environment affects economic activity. The coverage of these issues in this chapter is quite short, reflecting the fact that environmental externalities are explained in depth in Chapter 9, while Chapter 13 discusses how the production of national income affects economic welfare, in part through its effect on the environment. Chapter 13 also makes a brief reference to the sustainability of economic growth.

AQA Advanced Economics

Production of consumer goods and services that people want and need requires the use of raw materials, sources of energy and other primary products. If carefully used and conserved, resources such as soil fertility and fish stocks can be renewed. However, some resources, such as fossil fuels, are non-renewable resources. Literally, they are 'used up' as they are used, and cannot be replaced. This is called **resource depletion**. Between these extremes, resources such as iron and copper are non-renewable in the sense that mining reduces the total quantity of the natural resource available to be extracted in the future, but renewable in so far as recycling is possible.

Production also leads to **resource degradation** through the production and 'consumption' of **negative externalities**. Resource degradation occurs when firms (and consumers) treat the atmosphere, oceans, land, rivers and lakes as a giant waste bin in which to dump the unwanted by-products of economic activity. Depletion captures the effect of activities such as logging or mining; degradation concerns the pollution of air, water and land.

> *e*xaminer's voice
>
> At this stage, refer back to Chapter 1 and read the section on the difference between economic growth and economic development (pp. 5–6). Some sections in Chapter 13 (on measuring economic welfare) also provide useful background material for the economics of the environment.

Sustainable and unsustainable economic activity

Many economists believe that resource depletion and degradation will eventually make economic growth unsustainable, at least for most of the world's population. They argue that:

- the world's non-renewable natural resources will be exhausted
- the world's pollution problem will become so acute that the capacity for self-cleaning and regeneration will be exhausted
- as the population continues to grow, it will reach a point where humankind will destroy itself through sheer weight of numbers

Free-market economists are much more optimistic, arguing that an increased resource usage will cause the prices of raw materials and energy to rise. Rising resource prices will create incentives for people to behave differently. Consumers will economise and reduce the amount of goods and services they buy. At the same time, producers will respond to the changing relative prices of raw materials and energy by altering methods of production and by exploring the earth's crust for new supplies of minerals and fossil fuels that are uneconomic to exploit at lower relative prices.

Most economists agree that economic growth and development should be sustainable. Professor David Pearce believes sustainable economic development 'ensures that the needs of the present are met without compromising the ability of future generations to meet their own needs'. He argues that this does not mean 'no growth'; rather it recognises the limits of growth and looks for alternative ways of growing. Sustainable development probably requires a shift in the balance of how economic progress is pursued. Sustainable development means a change in consumption patterns towards environmentally more benign products, and a change in investment patterns towards augmenting environmental capital.

Consumers and the environment

For much of human history, economic activity had relatively little adverse effect on the environment. This is no longer true. Consumption cannot, of course, be separated from production. Firms deplete and degrade the environment in order to produce and sell goods to consumers. But through profligate and wasteful behaviour, consumers add to the environmental problems resulting from production.

Population growth, which creates more consumers, obviously leads to environmental problems. But population growth probably contributes less to resource depletion and degradation than income growth. Very poor people scratching a living from the earth's crust are seldom much concerned with the environmental effect of their activities, such as cutting down trees to provide fuel. However, it is richer people in high income countries, particularly the USA, who are most responsible for more environmentally destructive consumer behaviour. Per head, First World consumers use up much more fuel, timber products and other resources than inhabitants of poorer countries. Nevertheless, as incomes grow in countries such as China and India, their citizens tend to copy the wasteful consumer behaviour of richer countries, thereby worsening global environmental problems.

Other things being equal, consumers prefer to buy cheaper rather than more expensive goods. Faced, for example, with a choice between two apparently identical tables, most people buy the cheapest. But suppose the expensive table was made from timber cut from forests where conservation practices are followed, but the cheaper table is made as a result of the destruction of tropical rain forests. Why, in these circumstances, do consumers still decide to buy the cheaper table? Part of the answer lies in the fact that consumers lack sufficient information about how goods are made. But even with this information, many consumers will buy the cheaper table. All too often, consumers are short-sighted, tending to go for the immediate bargain even when knowing that their long-term interest lies in buying goods made in an environmentally responsible way. Moreover, while gaining the benefits that low prices provide, individuals personally suffer little of the environmental harm. The effects of resource depletion and degradation are spread far and wide, possibly across the whole world, with future generations suffering most of the consequences.

Consumers are also responsible for negative externalities that harm the environment. These range from the relatively trivial, such as the problem of litter, to the potentially very serious, such as the global warming caused by private motor cars and air travel. As is the case with industrial pollution, governments can use regulation and/or taxation to reduce environmentally harmful consumption externalities. Governments also try to persuade people to alter behaviour — for example,

examiner's voice

Make sure you understand the difference between resource depletion and resource degradation. The rate at which resources are depleted depends on whether they are renewable or recyclable, as well as on current and future rates of usage. For resource degradation, refer back to the coverage in Chapter 9 of negative externalities (pp. 154–59), and to Table 9.1, which shows a number of consumption (and production) externalities.

by walking and cycling, and by improving the energy efficiency of homes. But persuasion, on its own, is generally ineffective. Financial carrots and sticks may also be necessary to get people to alter lifestyles. Governments can subsidise public transport and solar power, while taxing private motor cars and fossil fuels.

Household waste and the environment

High incomes lead to high levels of consumption, which in turn lead to large amounts of waste. In much of the developed world, local government provides a rubbish collection service which, as Chapter 9 explains, is often free and financed by local taxes. But when rubbish collection is free, there is no incentive to economise in producing waste. Too much rubbish results. Charging a price for waste disposal creates the incentive to throw out less and recycle more. But charging can create new environmental problems. To avoid the charge, some households may 'free-ride' by dumping rubbish, thereby harming local environments.

In the UK, much rubbish, both household and industrial, is dumped in landfill sites. These sites fill up rapidly, so soon the UK will face the problem of what to do with the continuing flow of rubbish. With pollutants seeping into ground water or entering the atmosphere, landfill also poses problems for future generations. Recently, the UK government decided to tax the use of official landfill sites. Unfortunately, this led to 'cowboy' practices such as 'fly-tipping' rubbish on farm land and quiet rural roads. In a similar way, motorists harm the environment by dumping old cars in city streets.

Rubbish collection provided by the council may create new problems, such as eyesore pollution

These examples illustrate the **law of unintended consequences**. Governments introduce regulations or taxes in order to improve the environment and to correct alleged market failures. Unfortunately, government intervention triggers consequences that the policy-makers had not foreseen, which, if sufficiently harmful,

render the policy ineffective. Free-market economists believe that the resulting problems of government failure are worse than the market failures that governments try to correct.

Recycling

Incineration or burning rubbish is an alternative to landfill. By producing electricity, waste incineration marginally reduces the use of fossil fuels, but it also pollutes the atmosphere, not least through the emission of harmful dioxin chemicals. Recycling waste is a more environmentally sustainable option. Firms want to be seen as 'green' and 'environmentally friendly'. Sometimes this is little more than a cynical marketing exercise, but many firms now use recycled raw materials such as glass and paper. Automobile companies such as BMW now build cars with a high percentage of recyclable parts. Governments promote recycling by providing facilities such as bottle banks and by requiring manufacturers to make their products recyclable. In the future, manufacturers may be required by law to take back goods such as cars and television sets once these goods have reached the end of their economic lives.

Sometimes, however, recycling produces new problems. In the 1990s, German households recycled paper so enthusiastically that, because of an oversupply of paper, the market collapsed and recycling companies went out of business. For a time, paper banks went unemptied and Germans were unable to recycle books and newspapers.

Shopping and the environment

Seventy years ago, few people owned cars or refrigerators, and household freezers had not yet been developed. In the UK, most households shopped daily for food and groceries at local shops close to where they lived. People walked to the local shops or travelled by bus or tram. Food was largely supplied by local farmers. Shopping was not generally a 'leisure activity', as it often is today. Incomes were lower and mostly spent on essentials.

The modern pattern of shopping is very different. Out-of-town shopping malls have sprung up, dominated by large retail chains owned by multinational corporations. High streets and malls contain identical shops in every town and city. High rents have forced out small local shops, although attempts are being made to revive local shops to try to reverse the decline of local communities and environments.

The change in the pattern of shopping has had a significant environmental impact, both locally and globally. Food retailing is dominated by a handful of supermarket chains, which for the most part do not buy from local farmers. Instead, their supply chains extend across the world. Shoppers drive to the huge out-of-town stores and retail complexes, buying goods that have already been transported by truck or plane over hundreds or thousands of miles. Bubble packs and other methods of

> ### examiner's voice
>
> Refer back to Chapter 9 (p. 151) and read about rubbish as an example of a public 'bad'. Just like public *goods*, public *bads* create a 'free-rider' problem, which stems from the issue of non-excludability.

packaging add to the problem of household and industrial waste. Although benefiting from substantial economies of scale, the large supermarket chains have been accused of destroying the rural economy in the UK. Critics claim that supermarkets use monopoly power to pay rock-bottom prices to UK farmers, which eventually drives many out of business.

So, while modern retailing undoubtedly contributes significantly to high material living standards, it is also harming the environment and local communities. Are the environmental costs a price worth paying for the material benefits that modern retailing delivers?

Transport and the environment

Over the last century, humankind has benefited enormously from developments in road and air transport. Private ownership of cars has been a great personal liberator, enabling ordinary people to enjoy freedom of movement unimaginable for most of human history. But as Chapter 9 explains, the use of motor vehicles has created the twin problems of carbon pollution and road congestion. Besides contributing to resource depletion by running down the earth's stock of fossil fuels, motor vehicles are partly responsible for the emission of greenhouse gases and the resulting problem of **global warming** also described in Chapter 9.

Unfortunately, it is now recognised that general emission of pollutants by motor vehicles, manufacturing processes and particularly by aeroplanes is responsible for another very serious problem. This is called **global dimming**. Partly through their effect on cloud cover, atmospheric pollutants cause the sun's radiation to bounce back into space, thus dimming the amount of radiation reaching the earth's surface. On first sight, global *dimming* seems quite benign because it counters the process of global warming. However, global dimming carries the extremely gloomy message that successful reduction in general atmospheric pollution greatly speeds up the process of global warming caused specifically by greenhouse gases. Even if left unchecked, global dimming will have its own devastating effects, largely through causing drought and disrupting monsoon weather patterns.

Road building and an integrated transport policy

Road construction firms and many motorists believe that more roads should be built, particularly motorways, bypasses and ring roads round towns. But road building encourages even more car use, until eventually new roads are just as congested as the old roads that they were built to relieve. Economists generally accept the need for *some* extra road building, particularly to improve access to more remote parts of the country. However, they believe that road building on its own is not the solution to traffic congestion. Instead, they argue for an **integrated transport policy**, in which investment in rail and bus services improves public transport to an extent sufficient to attract private motorists from their cars. But as the experience of recent Labour governments has shown, implementing an integrated transport policy in a densely populated country is not easy. Indeed, transport *disintegration* rather than *integration* may occur.

Providing *more* public transport cannot by itself reduce traffic congestion. This is most obvious in the case of bus travel. Buses compete with other vehicles for road space. On congested roads, bus journeys are slow and unreliable. In these circumstances, few motorists are willing to abandon cars and to travel by bus instead. For motorists to switch to public transport on a large scale, private car use must be made much more difficult, particularly in congested areas and at congested times of day.

As is the case with other market failures, regulation, taxation and subsidy are the main policy instruments that UK governments have used to deter car use. Parking restrictions and pedestrian zones are forms of regulation used to relieve congestion in town centres. Motorists are taxed in three main ways: at the time of purchase, by the annual vehicle tax and by a tax on fuel. The first has little effect on car use. As new cars are taxed at exactly the same rate of VAT as other consumer goods, the tax system does not increase car prices relative to the prices of other goods. As with the annual vehicle tax, VAT taxes car *ownership* but not car *use.* By contrast, fuel taxes may deter car use because the more the car is driven, the greater is the total tax paid.

To deter car use, UK governments have recently switched the structure of motoring taxation away from car ownership and the annual vehicle tax towards higher fuel taxes. But in practice, this has had little or no effect on car use. The income elasticity of demand for private motoring is high, but the price elasticity of demand is low. Although fuel tax is levied at a rate of well over 100 per cent, low price elasticity of demand means that the tax would have to be very much higher to bring about a significant reduction in demand for car travel. Meanwhile, the high income elasticity of demand, together with continuously rising personal incomes and a fall in the real cost of motoring, mean that demand for private motoring has significantly increased.

Apart from their political impracticality, higher fuel taxes are a blunt instrument, raising the price of car use for *all* motorists, and not just those driving on congested roads. Fuel tax falls particularly heavily on low-income motorists living in remote rural areas, who tend to be more dependent on their cars than people living in big cities. Rural motorists often have to drive longer distances, yet lack a public transport alternative. Thus, by taxing the rural poor more heavily than the urban rich, higher fuel taxes have adverse distributional effects on people's real incomes.

Road pricing

For political and economic reasons, government sentiment has recently swung away from ever-higher fuel taxation toward the idea of road pricing. One form of road pricing already widely used in the UK is charging for parking. Tolls are also charged for using bridges and tunnels. But motorists are hardly ever charged for driving along ordinary roads.

The main economic argument *against* road pricing relates to the public good properties that roads sometimes possess. Before the recent development of electronic road pricing, roads other than motorways were generally non-excludable. It is impractical to locate barriers or toll gates at every point of access or exit on an ordinary road. *Uncongested* roads are also non-rival (or non-diminishable). An extra motorist driving on an almost empty road does not add to road congestion in any significant sense. As with all public goods, there is a case for *not charging a price* for the use of an uncongested road. Provided the road remains uncongested, the allocatively efficient amount of road use is the amount that motorists choose when granted free access. However, as soon as a road becomes congested, there is a case for road pricing. The case for road pricing is analysed in Chapter 9.

If and when road pricing is introduced on any scale in the UK, motorists will probably be charged for driving into city centres, and also according to the time of day when journeys are made. (The London congestion charge, introduced in 2003, is based on these principles.) Besides being politically unpopular, road pricing may contribute to the further decline of inner-city shopping areas and to the growth of out-of-town retail parks. Road pricing may also simply shift congestion to new areas where road use is currently free. Similarly, if tolls are introduced on UK motorways, they may shift traffic back on to roads through towns and villages that the motorways were built to relieve. (Tolls have recently been introduced on a section of privately-owned motorway, designed to reduce congestion on the M6.)

On the plus side, road pricing may create a more allocatively efficient division of transport between rail and road. Rail use creates fewer negative externalities than road use. Without road pricing, road use is too cheap compared to rail travel. As a result, too many people travel by road and too few by rail. In theory, road pricing can correct this resource misallocation, although some economists argue that rail subsidies are needed as well, to create 'correct' (that is, allocatively efficient) *relative* prices of road and rail.

*e*xaminer's voice
The theoretical explanation of road pricing in Chapter 9 is of A2 standard. By all means refer back to the explanation (pp. 158–59), but remember it is more advanced than that required at AS.

The national economy and the environment

There are two main reasons why governments want to maintain and improve the quality of the environment. In the first place, the environment contributes significantly to people's standard of living and economic welfare. The second reason stems from the fact that the environment affects sustainability of economic activity. Humankind's ability to produce and consume goods and services in the future will depend in large part upon how we treat the environment now.

Figure 23.6 shows the main trade-off facing governments with respect to the conflict between macroeconomic and environmental objectives, namely the trade-off between the two policy

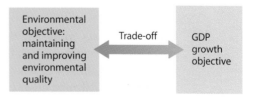

Figure 23.6 The trade-off between maintaining and improving environmental quality and maximising the economy's growth rate

objectives of maintaining and improving environmental quality, and maximising the economy's growth rate, measured by GDP growth. This conflict is explained in some depth in Chapter 13, so no further details are provided in this chapter.

The pursuit of environmental objectives can also affect a government's ability to achieve full employment, control inflation and reduce a balance of payments deficit.

*e*xaminer's voice

Chapter 12 provides examples of other trade-offs and conflicts facing a government's economic policy-makers. However, this is the most relevant trade-off for the environment option in Module 3.

Employment

There are a number of ways in which the pursuit of environmental objectives might *destroy* jobs:

- Assuming a slower growth rate, fewer workers are needed than with a high growth rate.
- The need to comply with environmental regulations and pay pollution taxes internalises previously external costs of production. Businesses incur costs of production previously left as externalities on third parties. Compliance costs might also destroy jobs, particularly if competitors in other countries are not similarly regulated and taxed.
- Jobs may be lost through **environmental dumping**. This occurs when multinational companies evade environmental regulations and taxes by relocating polluting or dirty activities in countries with laxer environmental policies. Environmental dumping creates employment in poorer countries, albeit in dirty jobs, at the expense of employment in developed countries.

However, environmental regulation can also *create* jobs, thereby lessening the conflict between environmental and employment objectives:

- Richer nations place greater value on the quality of the environment. Jobs are then created, producing goods and services to meet increased demand for environmental quality. The production of organically grown food provides an example.
- Manufacturing firms in countries, such as Sweden and Germany, with the most demanding environmental regulations, gain a competitive advantage in producing the new technologies designed to meet new, tougher environmental laws and standards. As other countries adopt similar standards, export demand creates jobs in the countries and firms leading the development of clean technology.

Inflation

By raising costs of production, environmental regulations and taxes might contribute to cost-push inflation. The pursuit of environmental objectives may affect the inflation rate in other ways. Arguably, by allowing retailers to benefit from economies of scale and other improvements in productive efficiency, the growth of out-of-town shopping centres and superstores has reduced inflationary pressures. However, the UK government has decided to limit any further out-of town development, having accepted the argument that shopping centres and superstores damage the environment, both inside and outside the urban areas that the stores serve.

Balance of payments

Many of the factors already mentioned will also affect a country's trading position. The increased business costs that environmental regulations and pollution taxes bring about are likely to reduce international competitiveness and worsen the balance of payments on the current account. Likewise, via the process of environmental dumping, multinational companies relocate production in poor countries, and then import finished goods or components from these countries. Not only does this penalise 'virtuous' companies that decide to remain at home, but it makes it harder to raise environmental standards. As a result, countries may use protectionism to defend themselves against what they see as 'unfair' imports. This could degenerate into a form of environmental 'imperialism' in which rich countries ban imports from poor countries, using environmental arguments to cover their own inefficiencies.

Sport and leisure markets

The demand for sport and leisure

Leisure activities are what people choose to do in their leisure time. Defined very broadly, **leisure time** includes all the hours not spent working to earn income or studying. In a narrower and perhaps more accurate definition, time spent sleeping and performing household and personal chores should be excluded.

examiner's voice
Make sure you understand the difference between 'leisure time' and 'leisure activities'.

Some people, such as the unemployed and old people, have a large amount of leisure time — but without very much income. As a result, many leisure activities are not available to the 'time-rich, but money-poor'; the activities are simply too expensive. Indeed, many unemployed people would probably prefer more income (and thus a job) and less leisure time, in order to be able to exercise an **effective demand** (desire backed up by an ability to pay) for leisure activities.

At the other extreme, some people enjoy very little leisure time because they work very long hours. People who are 'money-rich, but time-poor' — for example, those with highly paid City jobs — are often willing to pay large sums of money to enjoy intensively the small amount of leisure time that they can squeeze out of a day or weekend.

There are, of course, many leisure activities that are either completely free or virtually free. These include reading a library book, watching television, listening to the radio and going for a walk. But many other leisure activities are only available for those who are prepared to pay. Many of these are only available for the better-off.

Leisure time is generally considered a **normal good** (a good for which demand increases as income increases). Most people, unless their income comes from other sources, must work in order to afford the various leisure activities they wish to undertake. High wage rates often encourage people to work longer at the expense of leisure time. However, there are exceptions, and for many people there will come

a point beyond which they will prefer to enjoy leisure time rather than to work longer hours. On the other hand, many highly paid people enjoy working. Very high hourly wage or salary rates do not necessarily mean that people with high incomes work very short hours in order to enjoy lots of leisure time. For a person in work, an extra hour of leisure time can mean giving up an hour's pay. The hour's pay is the **opportunity cost** and the price of the extra hour of leisure time. The higher the hourly wage rate, the greater is the opportunity cost of an extra hour of leisure time.

The demand for particular leisure activities

Different leisure activities are **substitutes** for each other (as are working for pay and enjoying leisure time). A rise in the price of one leisure activity will tend to reduce demand for that activity, as people switch their demand to other substitute forms of enjoying leisure time that are now relatively cheaper. When demand for a particular leisure activity such as the cinema is highly price elastic, an increase in cinema prices results in a more than proportionate fall in demand. People switch to close substitutes, such as hiring a video or watching a film on television, or to completely different leisure activities.

> *e*xaminer's voice
>
> Cross elasticity of demand is an important concept to use when explaining and analysing the demand for different leisure activities.

The extent to which different leisure activities are substitutes for each other is measured by **cross elasticity of demand**. A cross elasticity of demand of +0.4 for video hire with respect to cinema prices indicates that a 10% increase in cinema prices results in a 4% increase in the demand for videos. Although inelastic (that is, less than 1), this figure indicates that going to the cinema and hiring a video are quite close substitutes.

However, consider the case of two football clubs, say Manchester United and Liverpool. For certain floating supporters, the two clubs may be close substitutes, with the supporters switching towards whichever team is more successful. But 'true fans' stay completely loyal to one club, regardless of its success or lack of success. For the 'true fan', both price elasticity and cross elasticity of demand with respect to the prices charged by rival clubs can be highly inelastic. Indeed, price and cross inelasticity may extend beyond prices charged to see games, to **complementary goods** such as replica football shirts and other sports merchandising.

Income elasticity of demand for leisure activities

Although, for most people, *leisure time* is a normal good, the same is not true for all *leisure activities*. For some people, a leisure activity such as eating at a fast-food restaurant is an inferior good with a negative income elasticity of demand. But at the other extreme, there are many leisure activities for which demand increases at a faster rate than income. A luxury holiday is an example.

Participation, spectator and elite leisure activities

Leisure activities can be divided into those in which people take part and those for which the general public are spectators. For many leisure activities, including sports such as football and tennis, people do both. Some mass-participation leisure activities, such as walking or jogging, are free or virtually free. So are some forms of spectating, such as watching a televised rugby game or watching sport in the local park.

Participation and spectator leisure activities can be further divided into elite and non-elite categories.

- An elite activity may be classified in one of two ways: first, on the basis of cost or the price charged to participate or watch others participating in the activity; and second, on the basis of few people having the talent or aptitude to excel when participating in the activity. Sailing and yachting are sometimes elite in both senses: skill required and expense of participating.
- At the other extreme, the mass-participation sport of angling — which claims to be the UK's most popular participation sport — is generally non-elite: virtually anyone can participate at relatively little cost, providing they are willing to give up the time required.

The supply of sport and leisure

When considering the supply of sport and leisure activities, it is useful to distinguish between an initial decision to build a sport and leisure facility, such as a fitness centre, and the subsequent decision on how the facility should be used. Once in use, the facility provides a continuing stream of sport or leisure services.

With regard to the first decision, some facilities, such as a temporary open-air theatre, may be quite easy and cheap to provide, but others, such as a super stadium capable of hosting a World Cup football final or major athletics events, are very expensive to construct. Indeed, as recent aborted attempts to build a national athletics stadium in England show, very few 'super facilities' are successfully completed. This is partly because it is very difficult to run sports stadiums and theatres profitably. Construction is usually financed with borrowed funds, on which interest has to be paid. Once complete and up-and-running, large sport and leisure facilities require expensive maintenance and periodic refurbishment. To make a profit, costly facilities require constant use to generate a flow of sales revenue from the box office. Some sports facilities, such as soccer stadiums, are used only once a fortnight, and even then not throughout the year. It may be impossible to run such a facility profitably, particularly when the supply of the 'product' that spectators are paying to see (for example, a Premiership football team) leads to huge wage costs in addition to the costs of running the stadium.

The more a sport or leisure facility — however big or small — can be used continuously throughout the day, week and year, the greater is the chance of making a profit. In the case of major spectator sports, stadium use can be increased by:

- ground sharing (for example, AC Milan and Inter-Milan at the San Siro stadium)
- using the stadium for more than one sport (for instance, soccer and rugby)

- incorporating hotels, banqueting and conference suites into the stadium (as at Chelsea Football Club)
- incorporating other revenue earners into the stadium (for example, a shop selling club merchandise or a club museum)

But even with better facility usage, it may still be impossible to make a profit from running sports stadiums, theatres and opera houses. Increasingly, the only way leading professional sports clubs can make a profit is by selling rights to televise the sport. When this happens, the 'supply' of an event such as a Premiership football match may be controlled by television companies such as Sky, rather than by sports administrators.

Sport and leisure pricing

One way in which the providers of sport and leisure facilities can increase revenue is by charging different prices, both for different events available at the facility and to different customers. Here are some examples:

- Football clubs charge higher prices for 'big games' — for example, against a top club or a local rival. Likewise some theatres charge different prices for different plays or shows.
- Sports fans and theatre-goers are charged different prices for seats in different parts of the stadium or theatre. Some seats provide a better view than others, so the quality of the 'product' varies according to where the seat is located. Customers are prepared to pay more for a high-quality view and comfort than for lower quality.
- Lower prices for children and old-age pensioners provide an example of price discrimination in sports and leisure events and facility use.
- Lower prices are sometimes offered for frequent users, as in season ticket pricing.
- London theatres also use a form of 'standby' pricing, similar to that used by airlines. Theatre-goers can buy tickets at very low prices a few hours before a show, providing there are unsold tickets available. Since the show is being provided anyway, it is better from the theatre's point of view to sell a ticket at a very low price than to have an empty seat in the theatre.

The Criterion theatre has a pricing structure for various different circumstances that enables it to maximise profits

> ### examiner's voice
> While price discrimination provides a reason for the different prices charged for many sport and leisure activities, the theory of price discrimination (explained in Chapter 6) is an A2 rather than an AS topic.

Figure 23.7 introduces another way in which sport and leisure industries address the problem of unused capacity. The diagram shows the number of rooms occupied in a hotel on different days of the week *assuming that the same price is charged for a room throughout the week.* 'Peak' demand occurs in the middle of the week (largely because of business demand), with the 'off-peak' at the weekend. The hotel could improve room utilisation by reducing weekend prices to attract families and other tourists. This will lead to more even demand through the week, enabling better use of capacity. Likewise, lower prices may be charged in the 'off-peak' winter season than in the summer, although for winter-sport hotels, 'peak' and 'off-peak' seasons are reversed.

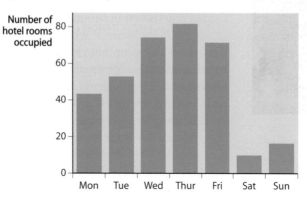

Figure 23.7 Hotel-room occupancy on different weekdays

Commercial, government and voluntary sector supply

The government and the voluntary sectors, as well as the private sector, supply sport and leisure facilities and services. In part, this results from the difficulty of providing many sport and leisure activities commercially at a profit. Another reason stems from the fact that many sport and leisure activities are judged to be merit goods. Historically, many sports were first provided by the voluntary sector, through the medium of sports clubs. In the 1960s and 1970s, government took a much larger role in the UK, increasing public subsidies for sport and encouraging active participation. More recently, however, private provision has grown fastest.

To explain the relative importance of commercial, government and voluntary sector supply of sport and leisure activities, it is useful to distinguish between **collective consumption goods**, **private good substitutes** for collective goods, and **pure private goods**.

It can be argued that consumers look first to the public sector or government sector for the provision of collective goods such as parks and clean beaches and bathing areas. When consumers become dissatisfied with the level and quality of government provision, the voluntary and commercial sectors begin to replace government provision. Government provision works best when the good or service provided is fairly uniform. The more private and less collective the good, the more likely is additional output to be provided by the commercial sector. Individual consumers have little influence with regard to the key elements of a collectively provided sport or leisure service, such as quality, form, type and time of availability.

Desire for individual control increases with income, so as a country gets richer, the commercial sector provides for the needs of the high-income consumers who are prepared to pay more for a specialised or customised service. Thus the commercial sector provides exclusive health and fitness centres, which offer a greater range of services and facilities than local authority-run centres can provide.

part 8

Competition and monopoly in sport and leisure markets

Leisure markets often contain a number of segments or sub-markets, some of which are highly competitive, while others contain very few firms or suppliers. For example, there are thousands of different holiday resorts and travel agents in the travel industry, particularly in the global travel market. However, one or two very large companies, such as Thomson Travel Group (a subsidiary of the European company Preussag AG, the world's largest travel company), dominate significant segments of the market, such as the package holiday industry. Internet-based competition is now reducing the size of traditional travel markets and the market power of their dominant firms.

examiner's voice

The AS specifications require an introductory knowledge of competitive markets and monopoly. The detailed theoretical explanations and analysis set out in Chapters 5 and 6 of perfect competition, monopoly and oligopoly are not required for the AS exams.

Some professional sports, such as football and snooker, provide an interesting mix of competition and monopoly. Football clubs and teams usually compete in a league. Their purpose is to win the league and to be generally successful from year to year. In a conventional market, driving out rivals and becoming a monopoly is the ultimate sign of success. However, if a football club bankrupts its rivals, there is no one to play against. If Manchester United, Arsenal or Chelsea always wins the Premiership, the league becomes boring and fans begin to lose interest. Scottish football, where Celtic and Rangers dominate, has already suffered this problem, although the two leading teams are still well supported. The top teams could seek to solve the problem by abandoning the league and joining a new European super league, where competition might be stiffer and the 'market' more interesting for fans.

Football clubs try to purchase success by buying top players from other clubs in the transfer market. But this contributes to the problem just described. Some sports impose special rules and regulations on member clubs to reduce the chance of one club or a handful of clubs dominating the competition. Under a system known as the draft, American football (the NFL) recruits young players from US universities and colleges. The best players graduating from US universities are drafted into the clubs that performed poorly in the previous season. As a result, it is rare for a club to dominate the NFL for more than a year or two.

Voluntary associations of clubs were the original founders of many of today's professional sports leagues. Member clubs usually continue to decide league rules and regulations — and the extent to which the league is 'competitive' in a business sense. Sports leagues are often 'anti-competitive', erecting entry barriers to prevent or deter new clubs joining the league. In the 1970s, the spread of colour television transformed snooker from an unfashionable UK sport into a 'big-money' televised sport. Fearing competition from younger players attracted into the game by the prospect of big money, established snooker players used the sport's rules to prevent emerging players from entering televised money-spinning competitions such as the

World Snooker Championship. The barriers have now been removed and young players dominate the game.

Market failure and sport and leisure activities

Some sport and leisure activities have **public good** properties. Crowd behaviour provides a good example. A crowded theatre or soccer stadium creates 'atmosphere', which members of the crowd generally enjoy. But at the other extreme, overcrowding and hooligan behaviour generated by the anonymity that the crowd provides have **'public bad'** properties, reducing the welfare of most members of the crowd. International sporting success can also be regarded as a public good, since it is impossible to prevent people from benefiting from the feeling of national well-being that such success generates. In a similar way, when a local soccer team starts playing well and winning all its matches, productivity and performance noticeably improve in local factories and offices.

Anti-social 'leisure' pursuits, such as graffiti 'art' and football hooliganism, are also demerit goods. More usually, however, sport and leisure activities are merit goods rather than demerit goods. When sports facilities are readily available, juvenile crime and anti-social behaviour rapidly fall. Participant sports also involve physical exercise, which makes people healthier and lengthens their lives. But when merit goods, such as sports playing fields, are provided solely through the market, the market may fail in the sense that too few people consume and enjoy the benefits.

There are many examples of positive and negative externalities generated by sport and leisure activities. **Positive externalities** are generated by sporting activities in public parks, and by beautiful coastal or mountain views. People enjoy watching the sport or the beautiful view without having to pay for their pleasure. Examples of **negative externalities** include dropped litter and traffic congestion caused by travelling to and from leisure activities and sports events.

The national economy, the environment, sport and leisure

By improving public health, reducing crime and enhancing a sense of national well-being, government support for sports and leisure activities can have desirable effects on the national economy. Labour productivity may increase and absenteeism from work may reduce, thus freeing resources for alternative and more productive uses elsewhere in the economy.

Spending on large sport and leisure facilities, such as a large new football or rugby stadium, is a form of investment that increases aggregate supply. Investment spending is also an important component of aggregate demand and can shift an economy's aggregate demand curve rightward. The spending can also have important multiplier effects, both at a national level and in terms of a regional multiplier, stimulating the local economy around a new sports facility. The new soccer stadiums built for Arsenal and Manchester City and Cardiff's Millennium Stadium (built by the Welsh rugby authorities but used for other sports and pop concerts) provide examples of major sports investments. On match days, the

part 8

Millennium Stadium stimulates trade in the scores of pubs and bars in central Cardiff where the stadium is situated, but on the cost side, general retail trade has suffered. Some 'mega' projects, most notoriously the Millennium Dome, have turned out to be 'white elephants', unable to provide useful services without continuous subsidy.

All the projects just mentioned are located on inner-city or brownfield sites. Sometimes major sport and leisure facilities are built instead on greenfield sites, on the edge of cities and close to motorways and airports. This minimises traffic congestion on match days, but like out-of-town retail parks and shopping malls, opponents of such schemes claim they have an adverse effect on the environment.

Leisure activities unrelated to conventional team sports such as soccer and rugby also have an environmental impact. Arguably, the 'off-road' use of mountain bicycles, motor bikes and four-wheel drive vehicles contributes significantly to soil erosion and to general degradation of common land and other rural land. Even relatively benign leisure activities such as rambling can have similar adverse effects if too many people visit open spaces such as the Lake District or Richmond Park in London.

Similar and perhaps more serious problems are increasing globally as international tourism grows. High incomes in the world's richer countries and the fall in the real price of air travel are two factors promoting the growth of international tourism. Of course, poor Third World countries want international tourists to visit them. Tourism creates jobs for local people, it earns vital hard currency and it contributes to the development process. But international tourism also creates many problems, such as the destruction of local cultures as hamburger joints, nightclubs, casinos and other forms of 'cultural imperialism' take over local economies. Many visitors to Ibiza and Nepal are completely ignorant of and unsympathetic to local traditions. Local beauty spots are destroyed and crime proliferates as tourism takes over.

Summary

This chapter has covered the three topic options in AS Module 3: Markets at Work. When opening the Unit 3 examination paper, candidates face three questions to choose from. However, the extra choice in the Unit 3 examination is largely illusory, at least for most candidates. The reason for this is simple. Teachers seldom prepare candidates to answer questions on all three options. Some schools and colleges concentrate on only one option, others on two of the three options. In previous examinations, the Housing Market option has

been the most popular. The Environment option has been the second most popular option. Relatively few schools and colleges have prepared candidates for Option 3: The Economics of Sport and Leisure.

You might, of course, have read the whole of Chapter 23 out of general interest in order to turn yourself into a better economist. On the other hand, time and revision constraints might have led you to focus on just one or possibly two of the three options. Whatever your strategy and the reasons for your choice, make sure you are comfortable with, and confident about, the main themes covered in the section of the chapter you decide to use.

Options 1 and 3 explain how markets function, covering market structure, demand and supply, and pricing in the housing and sport and leisure markets. Market failures and government failures are also explained, together with how the national economy affects housing and sport and leisure markets, and how the markets also affect the national economy. Option 2 is somewhat different: there is similar emphasis on interaction between the environment and the macro economy, but option 2 focuses mostly on relationships between the environment and market and government failures, rather than on how particular markets operate.

Self-testing questions

1 What is a mortgage?

2 Distinguish between an owner-occupier, a landlord and a tenant.

3 Relate the terms 'stock' and 'flow' to the supply of housing.

4 Explain the main reason for changes in average house prices in the UK.

5 How has owner-occupancy affected labour mobility in the UK?

6 How do house prices affect monetary policy in the UK?

7 Distinguish between resource depletion and resource degradation, and between sustainable and unsustainable economic growth.

8 Explain two ways in which consumers adversely affect the environment.

9 Compare good and bad effects of retailing and transport on the environment.

10 How may the interaction between global dimming and global warming affect the environment and economic activity?

11 Outline various forms of road pricing that might be introduced.

12 How may the pursuit of standard macroeconomic objectives affect a government's ability to achieve its main environmental objectives?

13 Distinguish between leisure time and a leisure activity.

14 Outline the factors affecting the supply of a particular sport or leisure activity.

15 Why would a soccer club charge different prices for tickets for different games?

16 What can happen in a competitive sport if one team becomes too dominant?

17 How may the construction of a major sports stadium affect national and regional economies?

Chapter 24
The European Union

Specification focus

This chapter surveys a number of the topics which could appear in the Unit 4W examination paper on the European Union. The chapter is also useful for studying topics in other AS and A2 specifications that require knowledge and understanding of the European Union and European economic problems, policies and issues.

AS Module 1 Markets and Market Failure
Government Intervention in the Market

Module 2 The National Economy
The preamble states that candidates should be aware that the performance of the UK economy is influenced by its membership of the European Union.

A2 Module 4W Case Study on the European Union

Module 5 Business Economics and the Distribution of Income
Government Intervention in the Market

Module 6 Government Policy, the National and International Economy
The preamble states that developments in the UK economy should be seen in the context of the UK's membership of the European Union.
The International Economy

A2 Synoptic coverage
The Unit 4 case study question can cover all aspects of the AS and A2 (Modules 5 and 6) specifications, but in the context of the European Union.

Introduction

This final chapter is for candidates preparing for AQA Module 4: Working as an Economist. For this module, candidates are assessed by means of a case study on the European Union (EU), or by coursework. Before you start reading this chapter, check whether you are preparing for the case study or for coursework. The content of the chapter will still be useful even if you are doing coursework, because knowledge of the EU is necessary for answering examination questions on topics such as the common agricultural policy (CAP) and the single currency (the euro) on other AQA unit exam papers.

The chapter begins by considering the special features of the case study examination paper which differentiate it from the other AQA economics exam papers. A brief history of the European Union (EU) then follows, together with an explanation of how the EU has developed from a customs union into a fuller single market, and thence on to a partial monetary union.

The main part of the chapter surveys the EU's common economic policies. These policies may, of course, form a stepping stone to eventual full economic union. The final sections of the chapter wind up with brief surveys of the arguably poor recent economic performance of the EU economy, and EU fiscal policy in the context of the EU's Stability and Growth Pact.

Special features of the Unit 4W case study examination paper

The Unit 4 case study examination tests exactly the same skills as the coursework option. As the title 'Working as an Economist' indicates, these skills are largely **investigative skills**. The case study question requires candidates to prepare a report on a particular EU-related topic, such as EU enlargement or monetary policy, with the report addressed to the client commissioning the report. Although clients could include an EU commissioner, a UK government department or a pressure group, the nature of the client is not usually very relevant to the report. The report must inform and give advice to the client, before making a justified recommendation on a course of action that the client should undertake on the basis of the advice given.

The maximum mark for the report is 84. Up to 10 marks are awarded for knowledge, 20 marks for application, 20 marks for analysis and 30 marks for evaluation. The first three skills require candidates to draw on information contained in the data in the case study, before using appropriate economic theories to address the issues posed by the different parts of the question. Evaluation, which includes the skill of commenting critically on the data (for example, detecting possible bias and omissions in the data sources), can be undertaken in two rather different ways. Many candidates restrict their evaluation to the final part of the report, usually under their final heading 'My justified recommendation'. However, the best answers also display the skill of evaluating arguments as they are introduced in the main body of the report. Such candidates explain whether a particular argument is significant and widely applicable, or whether it is relatively trivial, and relevant only in special, rather limited circumstances.

Up to 4 marks are also awarded for quality of language, which covers the use of English and reasonably accurate spelling. In past examinations, many of the best answers (which have typically been at least four pages long) have been presented in the style of a formal business report. Although the examination does not require this approach, past AQA Examination Reports have recommended that candidates divide their answers into separate sections, with the title of the sections following the 'bullet point' topic headings in the wording of the question. The Examination Report for the June 2004 examination also advises that the European Union should not be treated as a separate topic area to be bolted on to the rest of the A2 course. Rather the EU should act as a continuous context for teaching the content of Modules 5 and 6, and as a focus of further investigations undertaken by students.

The following topics may form the scenario for a Unit 4W examination, although the data and the question may, of course, encompass more than one of these topics:

- EU enlargement
- the single currency (the euro)
- the EU as a trading bloc (customs union)
- EU regional problems and regional policy
- the common agricultural policy (CAP)
- EU employment and unemployment
- EU competition policy
- the common fisheries policy (CFP)
- inflation in the EU
- economic growth problems
- EU fiscal policy (including tax harmonisation and the Stability and Growth Pact)
- transport problems in the EU
- EU monetary policy and Economic and Monetary Union (EMU)

*e*xaminer's voice

The Module 4W specification provides the following topic headings for organising your study of the European Union: Deepening and Widening of European Integration; The Regional Dimension of the EU; The Reform of the EU; Economic Problems — the European Dimension; Globalisation and the EU; EU Aspects of Global Problems.

The first seven of these topics are ranked in the order of topics appearing in the first seven ECN 4W examination papers, between January 2002 and January 2005. Until quite recently, candidates could generally expect that the topic covered by the next examination had not been set in a previous examination. (The one exception was the euro, which appeared in the AQA specimen examination paper as well as in the January 2003 examination.) But with seven of the eleven topics having appeared in questions (up to and including the January 2005 examination paper), candidates are now advised to expect the reappearance of earlier topics, as well as questions on topics so far unexamined.

Another feature of the Unit 4W examination, which differentiates the paper from other AQA exams, is worth noting. A significant proportion of the marks are awarded for **application** and **analysis** of the information in the case study extracts. Candidates who do not make use of this information and who do not make constant references to the extracts do not score high marks, however much knowledge is stored in their heads about the EU. In past exams, candidates who entered the exam room possessing little knowledge of the EU have often done better than those who spent hours preparing for Paper 4W, since lack of knowledge has forced students to make use of the data. In addition, to earn marks for evaluation, candidates must be prepared to criticise the data, particularly in terms of bias and omission. As the mark schemes currently stand, candidates' marks are restricted unless they comment on and — if relevant — criticise the data sources.

Origins and history of the EU

Why was the EU created?

To answer this question, a little knowledge is needed of events in European history in the 80 years or so between the 1870s and the EU's creation (as the EEC) in the late 1950s. France had long been a major European power. However, Germany did not exist as a separate state until the unification of Prussia with a large number of smaller separate states in 1871. German unification meant that two more or less equally sized countries now faced each other across the river Rhine, a natural barrier that has always separated France from its neighbours to the east. But as well as being a natural barrier, by the 1870s the Rhine was fast becoming a major transport route. This was the time when both France and Germany were industrialising and developing steel industries, the output of which was fed into both countries' arms industries.

*e**xaminer's voice**

The exam will not test detailed historical knowledge. Nevertheless, to understand how the EU functions today (and over the 10 years before your exam) it is useful to know how the EU came into being and about its early years.

The parliament of the European Union in Brussels

*e**xaminer's voice**

Many candidates answering the case study question on the EU have no understanding of its geography. You should build up a basic knowledge of the EU's *geography* as well as its *history*.

The map in Figure 24.1 shows that in the period of nineteenth- and early twentieth-century industrialisation, iron ore (the raw material for steel making) was mined in Lorraine in eastern France. Because coal (the source of energy used to make steel) was mined in the Ruhr region of northern Germany, the two commodities travelled

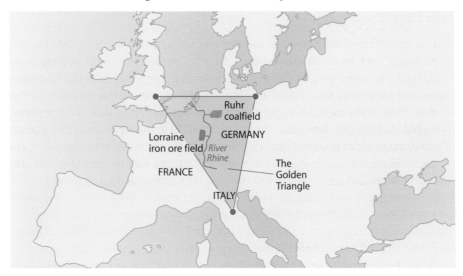

Figure 24.1 *Rhineland Europe and Europe's Golden Triangle*

in opposite directions along the Rhine, so that steel could be manufactured in both Germany and France. But as well as being the main transport route between the industrial regions of both countries, the Rhine became a source of international conflict. Steel is important for arms production, and Germany and France both wanted to increase their military strength while reducing that of their rival. The desire to control the Rhine and the industrial resources close to its banks thus led to war between Germany and France. Between 1870 and 1940, Germany invaded France on three occasions, in each case incorporating the industrial regions of eastern France into an expanded Germany. On one occasion, soon after the end of the First World War, France invaded Germany. It took over part of the German Rhineland, including the Ruhr coalfield, using the excuse that Germany had failed to pay reparations for Germany's earlier invasion of France.

Shortly after 1945, realising how repeated military aggression had damaged both countries, the new leaders of France and Germany decided that the Rhine must become a source of peace and unity, rather than a continuing cause of damaging military conflict. In 1951, the six countries that were eventually to form the EEC signed the Treaty of Paris, which set up the **European Coal and Steel Community (ECSC)**. The aim of the ECSC was to promote free trade in coal, iron ore and iron and steel products between Germany, France and Italy, and also the smaller Benelux countries (Belgium, the Netherlands and Luxembourg).

The EU's early years: the EEC

The ECSC was a precursor of the **European Economic Community (EEC)**, which was established by the Treaty of Rome in 1957. The EEC (which changed its name to the **European Community** in 1986, and to the **European Union** in 1993) began its life in 1958. (The European Community still exists, as one of the *pillars* of the EU. The acronym 'EC' is now more often used for the **European Commission** rather than for the European Community. The commission is the European Union's main executive body, forming and implementing EU policies.)

France and West Germany were the most important of the six countries that formed the EEC in 1958 (the other countries being Italy and the Benelux countries). The reasons why France and Germany agreed to form the EEC were partly economic and partly political. The economic reasons stemmed from the benefits that all the member countries believed they could achieve from creating a large area of internal free trade, similar to the ECSC, but covering trade in a range of goods much wider than just coal, iron and steel. Politically, West Germany sought protection from a re-emergence of fascism and Nazism within Germany, and also from the communist bloc countries to the east. France, by contrast, wanted a stable and economically successful Germany to protect France from German invasion. This could best be achieved by both countries trading freely with each other. On the economic front, France was willing to create free trade in manufactured goods (which would mostly benefit Germany), provided small French farms could be protected by a common external tariff from the competition of more efficient New World farmers in countries *outside* the EEC. Germany readily agreed to the creation of a protectionist common agricultural policy (CAP) as the quid pro quo of free trade in manufactured goods *within* the EEC.

The EU's core region: the Golden Triangle (or Golden Banana)

In the 1950s, western Europe was recovering from war damage. Much of the capital stock had been destroyed or damaged by bombing during the Second World War, and by the failure to replace machines and buildings that had been worn out during the war. The recovery process, which started *before* the EEC was created, greatly accelerated when the Community was formed. One European region, initially known as the **Golden Triangle** (and now called the **Golden Banana** because of the shape of the Rhine valley, which is central to the region), especially benefited. This triangle, with its corners in southern England, northern Germany and northern Italy, straddled the EEC's core or heartland, which, as we have noted, centres on the Rhine valley. For western European countries, the river Rhine had previously been a source of division, aggression and war. However, with the creation of the EEC, the Rhine symbolised how cross-border free trade between the Benelux countries, Germany and France could benefit all the countries bordering or close to the great river. Of course, at this time the United Kingdom was not a member of the EEC, but the UK's decision to join the Community in 1973 stems from its desire to share the economic benefits that were enjoyed by the Community's six original states.

The regions lying outside the Golden Triangle or Banana, mostly located in countries that at later dates joined the Community, are sometimes called the EU's peripheral regions. We shall come across the relationship between the **core** and the **peripheral regions** later in this chapter, in the section on EU regional problems and regional policy.

EU enlargement

By 2004, the European Union had grown from six original members to 15 member countries. The EU-6 became the EU-9 in 1973 when the UK, Ireland and Denmark joined the then EEC. Greece joined in 1981 and the EU-10 became the EU-12 when Spain and Portugal joined in 1986 (and the EEC became the European Community). The next stage of enlargement occurred in 1995, when Austria, Sweden and Finland joined to form the EU-15.

Then as now, Switzerland and Norway were the only two significant *western* European countries *outside* the European Union. However, Norway (but not Switzerland) is a member of the European Economic Area (EEA), which was formed in 1992. Before 2004, the central and east European countries that joined the Union on 1 May 2004 were EEA member states. Since 2004, the EEA has continued to exist because Norway, Iceland and Liechtenstein still desire to be a part of the EU's internal market, without assuming full EU membership responsibilities. EEA membership gives these countries the right to be consulted by the European Commission during the formulation of Community legislation, but not the right to a voice in decision making, which is reserved exclusively for member states.

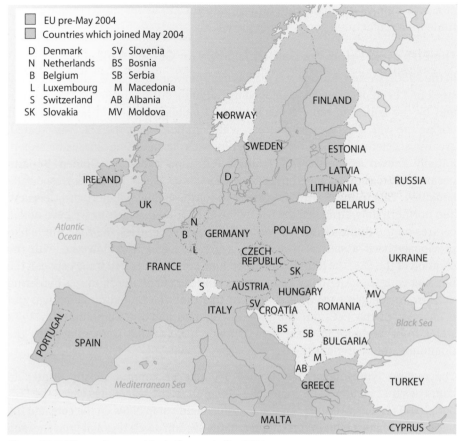

Figure 24.2 EU member countries before and after 2004

examiner's voice

Exam questions can be set on the effect of enlargement on existing EU member states, and on the economic performance of the new entrants or accession countries.

Figure 24.2 shows the 15 member countries that formed the EU in 2003, together with the ten new members (or accession countries) that joined the Union on 1 May 2004 to form the EU-25. The dates at which all the 25 countries joined the EU are shown in more detail in Table 24.1. The table also shows how each country added to GDP at the time it joined the enlarged community.

Table 24.1 European enlargement: a summary of key dates

Enlargement date	Countries joining	Population % addition	GDP (PPP) % addition	GDP per head, entrants as % of existing average
1973	Britain, Denmark, Ireland	33.4	31.9	95.5
1981	Greece	3.7	1.8	48.4
1986	Portugal, Spain	17.8	11.0	62.2
1995	Austria, Finland, Sweden	6.3	6.5	103.6
2004	Cyprus, Czech Republic, Estonia, Hungary, Latvia, Lithuania, Malta, Poland, Slovakia, Slovenia	19.6	9.1	46.5

Source: *The Economist*, 29 April 2004.

Proposed further enlargement of the EU

Enlargement of the European Union is not yet complete. As Figure 24.3 shows, Turkey, Bulgaria, Croatia and Romania have applied for membership. Turkey's application is especially interesting. Its population, at 63 million, is larger than that of any current EU country apart from Germany (UK population is around 60 million). Perhaps more significant is the fact that Turkey's cultural differences provide a bridge between European civilisation, which is largely Christian in origin, and the Islamic civilisations of the Middle East.

Figure 24.3 Current EU member countries and proposed members, 2005

The countries just listed are likely to form the next group of accession countries. Other eastern European countries, particularly the Ukraine, may also eventually apply for membership. First, though, these countries must establish their democratic credentials.

*e*xaminer's voice

An examination question has already been set on 'first wave' enlargement, which was completed in 2004. You should consider (a) looking backward to evaluate the success or failure of the 'first wave' and (b) looking forward to the proposed 'second wave' enlargement illustrated in Figure 24.3.

EU population

Before the EU was enlarged in 2004, the 15 member countries covered an area roughly one-third the size of the USA. However, the EU-15's population was greater than that of the USA (380 million as against 295 million). Indeed, the EU population was the third largest in the world, after China and India, accounting for some 6% of the total world population. In 2004, the ten accession countries added a further 74 million people, taking the EU-25 population to over 454 million.

National populations within the EU-25 range considerably in size. At one extreme are countries such as Malta and Luxembourg, with populations of less than half a million. At the other end of the range is Germany, with a population of over 82 million.

Before the 1990s, **natural increase** (the difference between births and deaths) was the major factor contributing to population growth. But after 1990, **net migration** into the EU replaced natural growth as the major cause of a rising population in EU-25 countries. Workers migrating into the EU from other countries mostly go to the richer EU-15 countries, there being little or no inward migration to the poorer new member states. Indeed, the ten entrant countries are losing young workers, who choose to migrate *within* the EU to better-paid jobs in western Europe. Figures 24.4 and 24.5 summarise some of the main changes in EU population in recent years.

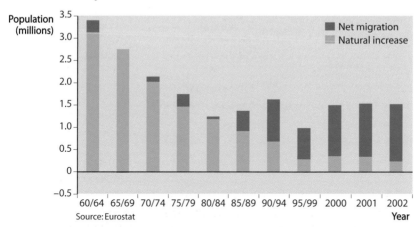

Figure 24.4 The contribution of natural increase and net migration to EU population growth, 1960–2002

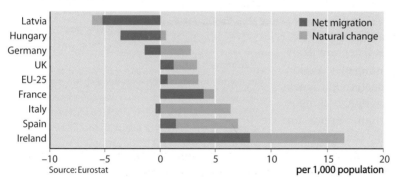

Figure 24.5 The rate of population change in selected EU countries, 2002

The EU as a trading bloc

Types of trading bloc

When imposing tariffs or liberalising trade, a country can act unilaterally, bilaterally or multilaterally. **Unilateral** action occurs when a country acts on its own, **bilateral** action involves joint action and agreement with one other country, while **multilateral** action requires agreement with a number of other countries. Preference areas, free trade areas, customs unions and common markets are all examples of **multilateral trading blocs**.

- **Preference areas.** Member countries agree to levy reduced or preferential tariffs on certain trade, as in the EU's Association Agreements with certain developing countries. When the Commonwealth functioned as a preferential area, cheap food produced by Commonwealth countries entered the UK market tariff-free, in return for similar preferences being given to UK exports of manufactured goods.

- **Free trade areas.** Member countries abolish tariffs on mutual trade, but each partner determines its own tariff on trade with non-partner countries.

- **Customs unions.** A customs union also creates intra-union free trade, but takes away members' freedom to set their own tariffs against non-member states. Instead, all members of the customs union impose a common external tariff on trade with non-members.

- **Common markets.** A customs union can develop into a full common market by creating free internal trade in services as well as in goods. Free mobility of capital and labour is also required, which means that there must be additional provisions to encourage trade and integration through the harmonisation of trading standards and practices.

Figure 24.6 illustrates the main difference between a customs union and a free trade area, and also the way in which the two forms of trading bloc are similar. The similarity lies in the fact that both organisations have internal free trade, at least in goods, though not necessarily in services. The difference lies in the way tariffs are set against imports from non-member states. Members of a free trade area are free to set their own tariffs against non-members, but members of a customs union lose this freedom and have to abide by an external tariff common to all member states.

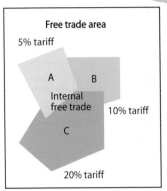

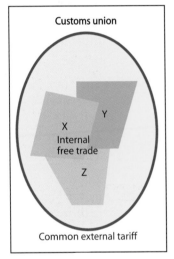

Figure 24.6 The difference between a free trade area and a customs union

examiner's voice
Knowledge of free trade areas and customs unions may be needed in order to answer a Unit 6 question on the international economy, as well as to answer a Unit 4W question on trading blocs.

The rules of origin problem

Members of a free trade area face the problem that imports may enter the area via the country with the lowest external tariff. Once inside the free trade area, the

goods may then be re-exported tariff-free into other member countries, thereby avoiding the higher import duties imposed by these countries. To prevent this happening, complex **rules of origin** tend to govern intra-area trade to ensure that free trade refers only to goods genuinely produced within the free trade area.

A slightly different problem occurs in a customs union such as the EU. To prevent non-member countries (such as Japan and China) manufacturing goods *within* the EU from raw materials and components imported from *outside* the Union, the EU insists that, for a good to qualify for internal free trade, most of the good's value must originate within the Union. This has led to Japanese companies such as Toyota and Sony locating car and TV manufacturing plants *inside* the EU, with components being supplied by other factories located in the EU. As a result, over 70% of the value of many Japanese branded product originates within the European Union and qualifies for internal free trade across EU national frontiers.

Development of the EU as a trade bloc

The European Union started life as a **customs union**, which since 1993 has developed one stage further into a more or less full **common market**. Prior to entering the EEC in 1973, the UK had been a member of a **free trade area** (the **European Free Trade Association** or **EFTA**) and also of a **preference area** (the Commonwealth).

The Treaty of Rome, which created the EEC in the late 1950s, envisaged that free movement of goods between member countries would be followed over a period of 12 years by free trade in services and free movement of capital and labour. When all this was accomplished, the Community would be a full common market. However, these events did not happen, at least in the period before the signing of a new Community treaty, the **Single European Act (SEA)** of 1986. There were a number of reasons why member countries dragged their feet in creating a full common market. To take one example, West Germany feared that its financial service firms would be unable to compete in a Community-wide financial market with the accession of the UK in 1973.

But having established agreement between member countries, the SEA set out a 6-year timetable, to be completed on 31 December 1992, after which a more or less full common market would operate. The words 'more or less full' are actually quite significant. Although there is supposed to be internal free trade in both goods and services within the EU, these freedoms are not complete. An inability to decide on, and then to impose, uniform standards relating to goods, and distortions created by member governments favouring local suppliers, are two reasons why this is so. National governments still prevent foreign arms suppliers from competing in the supply of weapons, and the EU lacks a Community-wide energy market. Competition is also discouraged in protected national energy markets from gas and electricity supply companies located in other member countries.

examiner's voice

Make sure you understand that the European Union (or EEC as it was) started life as a customs union, before the 1986 Single European Act turned it (in 1993) into a more or less complete common market.

The EU as an economic and monetary union

In the early 1970s, the UK's decision to join the EEC meant leaving a free trade area and joining a customs union that already possessed a number of common economic policies. Indeed, the fact that the word 'economic' is central to the European Union's original name clearly indicates that the EU's founding fathers intended to develop the economic nature of the organisation well beyond a mere trading bloc.

UK residents who support the United Kingdom's continued membership of the EU are known as **europhiles**, while those who want the country to withdraw membership are known as **europhobes** or **eurosceptics**. Some, but not all, eurosceptics would be happy for the UK to remain an EU member, but only if the Union were to restrict its role to that of a glorified free trade area. However, for europhiles, rolling back the clock in this way is completely unrealistic. To gain the benefits of free trade that the EU's huge internal market provides, their view is that the UK must accept the extra baggage of common economic policies. For a europhile, the UK government should work actively *within* the EU to make the common economic policies work.

Over the 50 or so years since its inception, the EU has introduced a number of common economic policies. Of these, the **common agricultural policy** or **CAP**, which began in 1962, is by far the most important (and expensive). Other common policies include the **common fisheries policy**, the **EU competition policy** and the **EU regional policy**. There was also an early attempt to introduce a common tax policy, centring on the introduction of VAT as the EEC's main expenditure tax. But because different member countries continue to levy their own national rates of VAT, **tax harmonisation** has not been developed much further. Nonetheless, the creation in the late 1990s of the **Stability and Growth Pact** to constrain or limit government spending and borrowing in eurozone countries has been a (so far largely unsuccessful) attempt to impose a **common fiscal policy**.

In the early 1990s, the **Treaty of the European Union (Maastricht Treaty)** began the process that eventually created **monetary union** (at least for the **eurozone** countries), and a single currency (the **euro**), which replaced national currencies such as the French franc and the German Deutschmark.

Monetary union was considered necessary for two reasons. In the first place, although the Single European Act had eventually created almost complete internal free trade in goods and services, the need to exchange national currencies to conduct this trade led to transaction costs. A single currency was thus deemed necessary to complete the single market. In the second place, upward and downward movements of EU national currencies led to undervalued and overvalued exchange rates within the trading bloc. Exchange rate fluctuations artificially increased the competitiveness of those countries benefiting from a falling exchange rate, while reducing the competitiveness of countries

> *e**xaminer's voice**
> At this stage, it would be useful to refer back to Chapter 22's coverage of the single European currency, or euro.

whose exchange rates were rising. Monetary union would create a level playing field for all member countries.

However, as Chapter 22 explains, monetary union is not complete. Of the EU-15 countries, only 12 are currently eurozone countries, though the ten accession countries that joined the EU in 2004 will also eventually convert to the single currency.

The EU as a possible future political union

The European Union has always possessed common political institutions, namely the **European Commission (EC)**, the **Council of Ministers**, the **European Council** and the **European Parliament**. In the strictly economic sphere, the European Commission, which acts as the EU's civil service and main executive body, implements the EU's common economic policies. Individual commissioners, chosen from the different EU countries, are responsible for agriculture, fisheries, competition and the EU's other economic policies.

Currently, the EU lacks a **political constitution**. Europhiles cautiously support further degrees of political integration, but eurosceptics fear that a federalist conspiracy exists, which so far has succeeded in reducing the sovereignty and power of the EU's nation states.

The EU could, in principle, develop into a full **political union**. But for this political project to come about, the national governments and populations of all the member states must also support such a venture. At the time of writing, this seems highly unlikely. In the UK, for example, europhobes and eurosceptics are likely to outvote europhiles on this issue.

A political union is the ultimate form of integration between countries. Separate national political institutions and local laws can still exist, but these are submerged below overarching and much more powerful institutions and legal frameworks covering the whole of the union. Nevertheless, several degrees of integration can exist, federal and non-federal. For example, in the USA, the states have substantial powers of taxation, whereas UK local government has few such powers (though Scotland now has some ability to raise its own taxes). If the EU ever develops into a full political union, it would probably resemble the USA, which is a federation of 50 member states. If the EU eventually becomes a United States of Europe, its member countries will function much as New Jersey and California do within the federal American system.

e*xaminer's voice*

Although examination questions will not be set on the topic of possible eventual EU political union, you should be broadly aware of the functions of the EU's existing political institutions, particularly the role of the European Commission, which implements and to some extent initiates EU economic policies. However, you must at all times avoid descending into an anti-European (or, indeed, a pro-European) rant. Your job when writing your report is to advise and to recommend. You should avoid being too polemical.

The EU, trade creation and trade diversion

The extent to which membership of a trading bloc is advantageous, both for the country involved and for the welfare of people throughout the world, depends on whether the trading bloc is trade creating or trade diverting. **Trade creation** increases the total volume of international trade because the growth of internal free trade among members exceeds any loss of trade with non-members brought about by tariffs protecting the trading bloc. **Trade diversion** refers to changes in the pattern of international trade when trade that used to take place with non-members diverts into trade between members.

examiner's voice

Make sure you understand the meaning of trade creation and trade diversion. They can sometimes be used when answering a Unit 6 question on patterns of trade and the effects of protectionism. It may also be useful to apply the theory of an optimal tariff (explained in Chapter 20) to the EU as a customs union and common market.

If the trade-creating benefits of joining a customs union such as the EU exceed any loss of trade resulting from trade diversion, there is a net welfare gain. However, countries *within* the union receive most of the gain, whereas countries *outside* the union suffer a welfare loss. In the case of the EU, this means that already-rich countries grow wealthier while already-poor developing countries suffer the effect of the common external tariff and agricultural levies protecting EU members. To some extent, special access given to trade from developing countries can reduce this adverse effect.

Defenders of the EU's trade policies argue that customs unions are a **second-best solution** to the need to create international trade, given the fact that the **first-best solution** (completely free trade between all the world's nations) has proved impossible to achieve in the modern world. For the EU, the extent to which this argument is true depends on whether the Union is *outward-looking* or *inward-looking*, which in turn depends on the extent to which the EU is protectionist. A low common external tariff supports the pro-free trade case, but a high tariff wall provides evidence of a 'beggar my neighbour' desire to gain at the expense of others. (At this stage, you should refer back to the coverage in Chapter 20 of the welfare gains and losses that result from tariffs, and optimal tariff theory.)

Trade creation, trade diversion and UK membership of the EU

As trade creation is a major potential advantage of joining a customs union such as the EU, the loss of the benefits of trade creation must also be a potential disadvantage of leaving. Before joining the EEC in 1973, the UK bought food from countries such as the USA, New Zealand and Jamaica. Had the food bought from these sources been more expensive than EU-produced food, the country's decision to join the Community would have resulted in **trade-creating benefits** of membership if, following entry in 1973, it could now obtain these goods from cheaper sources in EU member countries.

There is some evidence that, as far as some manufactured goods are concerned (for example, cars), the UK has benefited from the trade-creating advantages of EU

membership. But this is not true for many agricultural imports, for which the UK has suffered the **trade-diverting disadvantages** of membership. This has involved a shift from a low-cost source outside the EU (which is now subject to a tariff) to a high-cost source within the EU. Since EU entry in 1973, in real terms the UK consumer has had to pay much higher prices for food than was the case before entry.

However, whether or not, for the UK, the trade-diverting disadvantages of EU membership exceed the trade-creating benefits, there is little doubt that the UK would lose tariff-free access to the huge EU market if it ever decided to leave. Supporters of leaving the EU claim that the UK could negotiate tariff-free access in the same way that non-members such as Norway have done. However, Norway is a small country that has never been a member of the EU. It is unlikely that Germany, France and other EU countries would be willing to grant the UK similar privileged access if it decided to leave the EU.

The common agricultural policy (CAP)

Article 39 of the Treaty of Rome called for the creation of a common policy for agriculture. The objectives of the policy were:

- to stabilise agricultural markets
- to raise agricultural productivity
- to increase farm income
- to assure the availability of supplies

The CAP, adopted in the 1960s, was based on a system of **price support** backed up by **variable import levies**, **intervention buying**, **export refunds** and a **structural policy**. The CAP is funded through the **European Agricultural Guidance and Guarantee Fund (EAGGF)**.

As we noted earlier, the basic *raison d'être* of the original EEC was to end for ever the possibility of another war between France and Germany by binding the two countries together economically. The bargain was that the industrial markets of the Community members would be opened to the Germans as long as French farmers were protected in a highly regulated common agricultural market. Their own French market had long been protected in this way. It was therefore inevitable from the beginning that the CAP would be cast in the mould of former French agricultural policy, which shared many features with that of pre- and postwar German agricultural policy — both were highly protectionist.

For social and political reasons, the CAP's main objective was to raise farmers' incomes above free-market levels, which were regarded as being too low. To achieve this, the CAP established a free internal market in which the prices of many farm products would be supported by a **buffer stock scheme**. This scheme involved a system of **export subsidies** and a system of **variable import levies** designed to prevent undercutting of the **target price** set for Community farmers.

However, the CAP damaged the interests of consumers and taxpayers in the EU, and imposed severe burdens on farmers in the developing world, as well as in more developed countries such as New Zealand. Over the years, the common farm product prices of the CAP have tended to be supported at roughly twice world market levels. Consequently, families in the EU have had to bear a double burden of both higher food prices and higher taxes, both of which result from the CAP's support-buying and export subsidies, which keep EU prices high.

Reform of the common agricultural policy

In its early days, the common agricultural policy's main activity was to subsidise production of basic foodstuffs in the interests of self-sufficiency. Over the years, however, the policy of self-sufficiency in key foodstuffs at all times began to produce excessive surpluses, creating beef and butter mountains, and milk and wine lakes. This led to calls to reform the CAP. The reforms that have been introduced have generally removed overproduction and excess supply, and have cut the funding required to support the purchase of buffer stocks, which previously accounted for nearly 70% of the EU budget. The CAP now takes well under half of the total EU budget. This is because the EU has expanded other policies outside the field of agriculture and has deliberately curbed CAP spending. At the same time, the range of activities funded from the budget for agriculture has expanded to include rural development and the environment. Less than 1% of all public expenditure in the EU now goes on support for EU farmers.

As a part of the EU's **Agenda 2000**, rural development became the second pillar of the EU's agricultural policy, alongside farming. Agenda 2000 also responded to fears that more intensive farming and animal husbandry were to blame for 'mad cow disease', dioxin in milk, artificial hormones in meat and other food-related health scares. High on the Agenda 2000 list of priorities were environmentally sound production methods, high standards of animal welfare, and food safety and quality.

In 2003, the EU announced a fundamental reform of the common agricultural policy to change the way the EU supports its farm sector. The CAP is now geared more towards consumers and taxpayers, while giving EU farmers the freedom to produce what the market wants. In future, the vast majority of subsidies will be paid independently from the volume of production. The EU argues that severing the link between subsidies and production will make EU farmers more competitive and market-orientated, while providing necessary income stability for farmers. More money will be available to farmers for environmental, quality or animal welfare programmes by reducing direct payments for bigger farms.

The main elements of the 2003 reforms are:

- a single farm payment for EU farmers, largely unconnected to the amount of food farmers produce

- this payment is linked to the respect of environmental, food safety, animal and plant health and animal welfare standards, as well as the requirement to keep all farmland in good agricultural and environmental condition
- a reduction in direct payments for bigger farms to finance the new rural development policy
- a mechanism for financial discipline to ensure that the farm budget, fixed until 2013, is not overshot
- cuts in the prices that the EU pays for products such as butter and milk

examiner's voice

A case study question might require you to write a report, advising how, on the basis of the information in the extracts, the CAP might be further reformed. Alternatively, it might ask for an evaluation of the reforms currently being implemented.

The different elements of the reform came into force in 2004 and 2005, with the single farm payment starting in 2005.

The common fisheries policy

Fisheries and fish farming account for approximately 1% of the EU gross national product and are an important source of jobs in areas where there are few alternatives to fisheries. These industries also supply products to the EU market, which

is the world's third largest fishing power after China and Peru. Nevertheless, the EU remains the world's largest importer of fish, with an annual trade deficit of € 7 billion. There are around 100,000 vessels in the EU fishing fleet, although the number is declining.

Whereas the CAP has the problem of dealing with overproduction of food, the **common fisheries policy (CFP)** faces the opposite problem of overfishing and the consequent scarcity of fish stocks and falling fish catches. The CFP aims to

Despite having around 100,000 fishing vessels, the EU remains a net importer of fish

protect scarce fish resources to ensure that EU fishing fleets can stay in business. Its policy objectives are to ensure a fair standard of living for the fishing community, to stabilise markets, and to ensure the availability of fish supplies and that the supplies reach consumers at reasonable prices.

Figure 24.7 shows how catches of cod have declined in recent years in one of the EU's main fishing grounds, the North Sea, which lies between the east coast of the UK and mainland Europe. This decline results from perhaps the most serious problem facing the CFP, namely the **tragedy of the commons**. The tragedy stems from the fact that the world's oceans form a huge common area in which, for the most part, anyone can fish. Overfishing was not a problem when catching technology was simple and fish were plentiful. At this time, an extra fishing boat had no noticeable effect on fish stocks, and consequently on the catches of other fishermen. But as the number of fishing boats increased and fishing technology improved, fish stocks started to decline. This can be explained by the fact that fisherman receive all the proceeds from the sale of the fish that they catch. But at the same time, a fisherman suffers almost no loss from his own contribution to the depletion of fish stocks. Adding together his gain and his loss, the fisherman concludes rationally that the only sensible course is to fish as much as possible. But this is the conclusion reached by each and every fisherman. This is the tragedy: freedom to fish eventually brings ruin to all. Fishermen are locked into a system that compels them to catch as many fish as possible, in a world where fish stocks are limited.

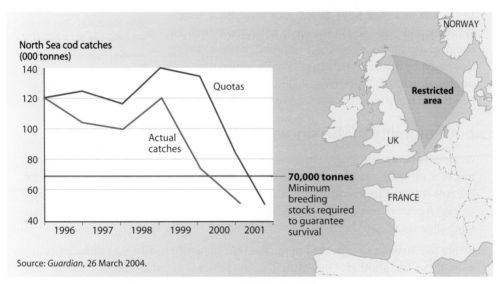

Source: *Guardian*, 26 March 2004.

Figure 24.7 The decline of cod catches in the North Sea

Since 1973, the CAP has tried to introduce Community-wide protective measures, including quotas, to deal with the reduction of fish stocks in Europe's coastal waters. The quota and conservation policy was last reformed in 2003. The new reforms are trying to reduce the amount of fishing taking place in EU waters, so as to make the management of fish stocks sustainable. The measures fix annual total allowable catches (TACs) on the basis of fish stocks. Accompanying measures encourage the reduction of the fishing fleet, including decommissioning vessels if appropriate, while trying to prevent adverse social and economic effects on fishing communities. Measures have also been taken to make fish farming sustainable. In the past, as Figure 24.7 shows, quotas were generally set too high, at a level above the actual total size of fish catches. It remains to be seen whether the 2003 reforms will be any more effective.

The CFP also operates through the European Union's structural policies, designed to achieve orderly change as the EU's industries adapt to changing demand and supply conditions. The **fisheries structural policy** is designed to help the fisheries and aquaculture sectors to adapt their equipment, facilities and production

processes to market requirements and the constraints imposed by scarce resources. The **Financial Instrument for Fisheries Guidance (FIFG)**, established in 1993, provides financial assistance for restructuring of the EU fleet by granting aid for scrapping, exporting and converting fishing vessels, and for modernisation. The main thrust of financial aid is to support the reduction rather than the growth of the total EU fishing fleet.

The CFP faces criticism from two main sources. On the one hand, scientists and environmentalists claim that the policy does not go far enough in reducing total fish catches, and that soon fish stocks, particularly in the North Sea, will have fallen to a level from which recovery is impossible. On the other hand, the fishermen themselves claim that their livelihoods are being destroyed by the CFP's existing controls, which they feel are too draconian, bureaucratic and insensitive to the needs and traditions of local fishing communities.

examiner's voice
Candidates are not expected to possess much prior knowledge of the common fisheries policy. This means that most of the information needed to answer a question would be provided in the case study extracts.

Labour mobility in the single market: the Bosman case

As already noted, the Single European Act has tried to create completely free labour mobility within the single market. In theory, though not always in practice, workers are free to move from country to country within the EU member states in search of jobs. A good example of the impact of the law is provided by the case of a Belgian footballer, Jean-Marc Bosman.

Before the Bosman case in the European Court of Justice in 1996, a footballer could only move to another club with the agreement of both clubs. Usually this agreement was only reached after the setting of a transfer fee, whereby the buying club actually purchased the player from the selling club. This applied regardless of whether or not the player's contract with the selling club had ended. Hence, out-of-contract players were not allowed to sign a contract with a new team until a transfer fee had been paid, or they had been granted a free transfer.

The Bosman case arose because Jean-Marc Bosman's contract with Belgian club side RFC Liège had run out and he wanted to be transferred to French club Dunkerque. Liège, however, refused to let Bosman leave without the payment of a transfer fee, which Dunkerque was unwilling to pay. Bosman claimed that as an EU citizen, he possessed the right to freedom of movement within the European Union if he wished to find work (under Article 48 of the Treaty of Rome). The transfer system prevented him exercising his right to freedom of movement and Bosman argued that the system should be changed so that players who were out of contract with their club could move to another club without the payment of a transfer fee.

The European Court of Justice found in favour of Bosman and against RFC Liège, the Belgian Football Association and the Union of European Football Associations (UEFA). The court decided that transfer fees for out-of-contract players were illegal where a player was moving *between* one EU nation and another. (Later, the right of an out-of-contract player to move to a new club was extended to movements *within* a single EU country.)

The Bosman case has affected football throughout the EU. Clubs now need to sign players for longer contracts than before; otherwise they will risk losing their players on free transfers. And because out-of-contract players are so sought after, the players can demand higher wages and move to the club that offers the best wages. The Bosman case increased 'player power' considerably. Now, as in all other industries, the best workers (in this case, star footballers) have control over their own career, and the ability to demand wages that reflect their skills. However, Jean-Marc Bosman received little personal benefit. At the time of the case, Bosman was approaching the end of his playing career and, as the names of his clubs indicate, Bosman was not the world's most talented footballer.

> **examiner's voice**
> You need to understand why it was necessary to make capital and labour completely mobile to create a full common market. The Bosman case provides an interesting example of how labour was made more mobile in a professional sport. However, has complete labour mobility been achieved in all of the EU's labour markets?

EU competition policy

The Bosman case is also relevant for EU competition law because, then and now, football clubs often try to implement collective cartel agreements that reduce the extent to which competition takes place in sports markets.

The EU Competition Commissioner has said that the *raison d'être* of the internal market is to allow firms to compete on a level playing field in all the member states. He argues that competition promotes economic success, safeguarding the interests of European consumers and ensuring that European undertakings, goods and services are competitive on the world market.

The main aim of EU competition policy is to establish 'a system ensuring that competition in the internal market is not distorted'. To achieve this aim, the policy tries:

- to ensure that healthy competition is not hindered by anti-competitive practices on the part of companies or national authorities (**restrictive agreements** and **concerted practices**)
- to prevent one or more undertakings from improperly exploiting their economic power over weaker companies (**abuse of a dominant position**)
- to prevent the governments of member states from distorting competition (**state aid**)

Although EU competition policy takes precedence over the national policy of member states, the principle of subsidiarity (which has already been mentioned in Chapter 8 in the context of UK competition policy) means that EU policy is activated only when firms adversely affect or distort trade between member states. However, EU competition law is also

> **examiner's voice**
> To understand EU competition policy, you first need to know about UK national competition policy, which is described and explained in Chapter 8. Knowledge of EU merger policy and policy toward cartels may also be useful when answering a Unit 5 question on the effectiveness of competition policy.

applied to agreements or conduct of parties established outside the European Union if such agreements or conduct restrict competition in the common market and affect intra-EU trade.

EU law prohibits restrictive agreements and concerted practices with an anti-competitive object or effect on the market, and abuse of a dominant position. A **restrictive agreement** is an agreement between undertakings whose objective is to limit or eliminate competition between them in order to increase the prices and profits of the undertakings concerned without producing any objective counter-balancing advantages. In practice, these agreements usually entail: price fixing; production quotas; sharing markets, customers or geographical areas; bid rigging; or a combination of these practices. Such agreements are bad for consumers and society as a whole, since the undertakings involved set prices higher than they would in conditions of free competition.

A **concerted practice** is a step below a restrictive agreement. It involves coordination among firms which falls short of an agreement proper. A concerted practice may take the form of direct or indirect contact between undertakings whose object or effect is either to influence market behaviour or to let each other know what conduct they intend to adopt in the future. Certain types of agreement are almost always prohibited. These are:

- horizontal or vertical agreements that fix prices directly or indirectly
- agreements on conditions of sale
- agreements to partition market segments, to reduce prices or to prohibit, restrict or, on the contrary, promote imports or exports
- agreements on production or delivery quotas
- agreements on investments
- joint sales offices
- market-sharing agreements
- agreements conferring exclusive rights to public service contracts
- agreements leading to discrimination against other trading parties
- collective boycotts
- voluntary restraints (agreements not to engage in certain types of competitive behaviour)

EU competition law also states that 'any abuse by one or more undertakings of a dominant position within the common market or in a substantial part of it shall be prohibited as incompatible with the common market in so far as it may affect trade between member states'. Such abuse may consist in:

- directly or indirectly imposing unfair prices or other unfair trading conditions
- limiting production, markets or technical development to the detriment of consumers
- applying dissimilar conditions to equivalent transactions with other trading parties
- making the conclusion of contracts subject to acceptance by the other parties of supplementary obligations that have no connection with the subject matter of such contracts

Company mergers and takeovers can create or strengthen a dominant position, which may give rise to abuse. This risk has justified advance vetting of mergers by the EU authorities. A merger or 'concentration' exists where a firm acquires exclusive control of another firm, or of a firm that it previously controlled jointly with another firm, or where several firms take control of a firm or create a new one.

The merger directive, 2004

In 2005, the EU countries finally ratified a new merger directive to enable takeovers and mergers to take place across national frontiers in the Union. Before the directive came into force, some EU countries prohibited cross-border mergers. As a result, the EU's merger rules were a hotchpotch of national law and regulation. In many EU countries there was no clear legal way in which a firm could combine with another in a different EU country. Big firms could merge, at great legal expense, but smaller firms were at a disadvantage. As a result, cross-frontier takeovers and mergers have been far less common in the EU than in America.

The European Commission had long argued in favour of more cross-border mergers to create more competitive markets throughout the European Union. But before 2005, agreement on the proposed merger directive was held up by a controversy over workers' representation on company boards. Germany wanted the German system of labour relations known as *mitbestimmung* to be upheld in cross-border mergers. *Mitbestimmung*, 'co-determination', means that workers are represented on German company boards and participate in decision-making. For many decades after the Second World War, co-determination gave German business peaceful labour relations. However, the exposure to international competition has turned *mitbestimmung* into an anachronism and an obstacle to Germany's own restructuring.

The 12 members of the EU-15 that refuse to give their workers the same rights as German workers refused to accept the German proposal. A compromise was eventually agreed in November 2004, which was ratified by the European parliament in May 2005. Germany agreed to water down its demands on workers' rights, though employee participation can still be granted in cases where at least a third of employees of the combined group enjoyed such rights before the merger. Critics of the merger directive argue that even in this watered-down form, cross-border mergers within the EU will still be less common than those in America.

examiner's voice
The 2004 merger directive is an example of a recent and relatively controversial EU policy initiative that could be part of the scenario for a future case study question on competition policy.

EU regional problems and regional policy

More than a third of the EU's budget is currently allocated to regional policy. The policy tries to help lagging regions to catch up, restructure declining industrial regions, diversify the economies of rural areas with declining agriculture and revitalise declining neighbourhoods in the cities. Job creation is the policy's main concern, although the further aim is to strengthen the economic, social and territorial 'cohesion' of the Union.

Regional policy was not, however, a significant part of the common policies imple- mented in the early years of the European Union. Although policies such as the common agricultural policy and the common fisheries policy were intended to help the poorer regions of the EU, these policies were not very effective in reducing regional disparities. The common fisheries policy may, for example, have harmed UK fishing communities by opening previously protected UK fishing waters to overfishing by Spanish trawlers. Arguably, this is an example of an EU policy contributing to regional problems rather than reducing them.

EU regional policy supplements rather than replaces the national regional policies of member states. It is *additional* or an *'add-on'* to national policy. (Don't confuse this principle of **additionality** with the principle of **subsidiarity** that is central to EU competition policy. Subsidiarity means leaving policy as much as possible to member states, with the European Commission intervening only when an EU-wide problem or issue is involved.)

*e*xaminer's voice
Make sure you understand the difference between *subsidiarity* (in EU competition policy) and *additionality* (in EU regional policy).

There are two main regional problems in the EU:

- **'Rust-belt' regional problems.** These are the regional problems that much of the northern and western UK suffered before and after joining the EU in 1973. These problems occurred in nineteenth-century industrial areas where the old, previously 'staple' industries became uncompetitive. Some of these industries went into terminal decline as they lost out to new goods produced elsewhere in the world. Other industries have suffered, not because demand for their products had disappeared, but because countries such as China have gained a competi- tive advantage. When this happens, as a part of the globalisation process, multi- national companies move production overseas. Industries affected include coal, steel, shipbuilding, heavy engineering and textile industries manufacturing cotton and woollen fabrics.
- **Remote, peripheral agricultural areas that were never industrialised.** As the name implies, the peripheral regions are remote and are located away from the EU core region. Until recently, peripheral regions also suffered from poor transport links with the rest of the EU. Before the UK joined the EU in 1973, southern Italy and areas of France, such as Brittany, were the main peripheral regions. These regions had little or no manufacturing, agricultural holdings were small and farmed by poor peasants, and soils were often infertile. When the UK joined the EU, many of the rural areas in Cornwall, Wales and Scotland fell into this category. More recently, and on a significantly greater scale, much of the territory of the ten new members of the EU-25 is currently occupied by poor farming communities.

Some 'rust-belt' areas of Belgium, Germany and France, such as the Lille region in northern France, have benefited from closeness to the EU core or 'Golden Banana'. Good infrastructure provision (motorways and fast trains) by national governments has helped these regions adapt and change their economies. By contrast, the UK's 'rust-belt' industries are remote from the EU central core (though not usually as remote as the UK's peripheral agricultural areas), and the UK's general failure to improve its motorways and trains has not helped its traditional manufacturing regions.

The EU areas most helped by regional policy have been those closest to the EU core. Southern France and coastal Spain and other parts of the 'Club-Med' member states have also benefited, but this may be due less to regional policy than to the growth of tourism and people's desire, as they grow richer, to move to the sun. But good communications, which are partly the result of EU regional policy, have helped in this respect. It is also worth noting that some small EU countries, notably Ireland, have done very well out of EU membership and EU regional aid. Consequently, their regional problems have reduced or disappeared.

As with UK national regional policy, two views can be taken of EU regional policy:

- The **free-market, anti-government view** regards regional problems as the result of *too much* government intervention preventing market forces from automatically reducing regional disparities. According to this view, the purpose of government should be to create conditions in which markets can function efficiently. In these conditions, capital is attracted by the low wage rates paid in previously depressed regions. At the same time, labour moves in the opposite direction in search of jobs and higher wage rates. If governments prevent this happening — for example, by insisting on the same wage rate for the same work in all regions — the regional problems persist and can even get worse. Free-market economists therefore argue that regional policy is unnecessary, raises taxes and reduces market-orientated flexibility.

- The **interventionist or Keynesian view** argues that regional disparities are a problem of **market failure** rather than **government failure**. Keynesian economists have traditionally believed that well-chosen intervention can reduce regional problems. They argue that relying solely on market forces and the price mechanism drains declining regions of younger people and adds to social costs of congestion in the areas to which people migrate. By triggering positive regional multiplier effects, 'smart' interventionist regional policies can have the opposite effect, building competitive advantage in previously declining regions.

Despite their differences, free-market and Keynesian economists generally agree that regional policy should build new **infrastructure** (for example, motorways and high-speed railways) to provide the external economies that private sector businesses need. Many also agree that creating conditions in which **indigenous businesses** can grow is more important than attracting branch factories owned by multinational companies into the regions. In the case of an indigenous business, the owner and the business's employees live locally and spend much of their incomes within the region.

Finally, it is important to note that, for EU regional policy to be successful, wealth and high incomes have to be generated *somewhere* in the EU. If, by contrast, the *whole* of the EU becomes unsuccessful, it will fail to generate the extra resources that regional policy transfers to the poorer parts of the Union. But with **globalisation** and

part 8

the transfer of manufacturing and services such as call centres to India and China, the EU may become less and less capable of producing the wherewithal needed for a successful regional policy. The recent and comparatively poor economic performance of the EU makes this a possibility.

Key dates in EU regional policy

In 1957 the preamble to the Treaty of Rome referred to the need 'to strengthen the unity of the 6 economies that formed the EEC to ensure their harmonious development by reducing the differences existing among the various regions and the backwardness of the less-favoured regions'. This was followed in 1958 by the setting up of the **European Social Fund (ESF)**, along with the **European Agricultural Guidance and Guarantee Fund (EAGGF)**. Nearly 20 years later in 1975, the **European Regional Development Fund (ERDF)** was established to redistribute part of the member states' budget contributions to the poorest regions in the European Community.

Regional policy was further developed in 1986 by the **cohesion policy** set up by the Single European Act. The cohesion policy was initially designed to offset the burden of the single market for the southern countries and other less-favoured regions. After 1989, the EU's **Structural Funds** (previously known as **Solidarity Funds**) were strengthened. The Treaty of the European Union, which came into force in 1993, then designated regional cohesion as one of the main objectives of the EU, alongside economic and monetary union and the single market. The treaty established the **Cohesion Fund** to support environmental and transport projects in the least prosperous member states. In 1999 the Structural Funds and operation of the Cohesion Fund were reformed. In 2000, the European Council meeting in Lisbon adopted a strategy to try to make the EU 'the most competitive and dynamic knowledge-based economy in the world by the year 2010'. But as we have seen in the context of EU merger policy, the Lisbon strategy may be having the opposite effect.

EU transport problems and transport policy

The European Commission believes that the 'ability to move people and goods quickly, efficiently and cheaply is a central tenet of the EU's goal for a dynamic economy and cohesive society'. The transport sector generates 10% of EU wealth measured by gross domestic product (GDP), equivalent to about €1 trillion a year. It provides more than 10 million jobs.

The removal of barriers to cross-border trade and travel has increased the volume of long-distance goods and passenger transport. Growing prosperity has led to a spectacular rise in car use — a phenomenon being repeated in the new member states that joined the EU in 2004.

The constant growth in mobility is putting severe strains on the EU's transport systems. The main result is congestion. The European Commission states that daily traffic jams affect 10% of the EU's motorway network, while 20% of the rail network suffers from bottlenecks. At 16 of the EU's main airports, 30% of flights are delayed for more than 15 minutes. Congestion on roads and at airports increases pollution, adding an estimated 6% to EU fuel consumption.

The commission has drawn up a strategy for dealing with congestion, while seeking to deliver quality transport services for its citizens that are safe, reliable and efficient. Although many aspects of transport policy come under national governments, it makes sense for the European single market to have a single transport infrastructure. One of the main effects of the Single European Act was to open national transport markets across the EU to competition, particularly in the road and air sectors and, to a lesser extent, for rail. As a result, trucks can operate in countries other than their own, so that they no longer return empty on international journeys. The liberalisation of air travel has brought more competition and lower fares as well as an increase of 30% in connections between member states since 1993. In March 2003, a first package of measures to liberalise rail infrastructure took effect, opening about 70–80% of rail freight traffic over main lines to competition.

The EU aims to improve the European transport network

The EU also promotes major transport infrastructure projects, known as **Trans-European Networks (TENs)**. In 2003 the TENs programme was extended to include the ten states joining the EU in 2004. Among the priority TENs projects are:

- the removal of bottlenecks on the main east–west inland waterway linking the Rhine, Main and Danube
- a programme to regulate traffic on the busy shipping lanes off the EU coasts
- several north–south and east–west rail upgrades

Liberalisation alone has not been able to solve several deep-seated problems, including congestion and pollution and the dominance of road over other forms of transport. Another problem is the fragmentation of transport systems, with poor links to outlying regions and the lack of good connections between regional and national networks. Road haulage now carries 44% of all goods transported in the EU, against 41% by short-sea shipping routes, 8% by rail and 4% by inland waterways. The imbalance is more marked for passenger transport, where road (largely car) transport accounts for 79% against rail's 6% and 5% by air. Shifting goods and passengers from roads to less polluting forms of transport is now a key factor for a sustainable transport policy. Another factor is the ability to integrate different modes of transport by combining road–rail, sea–rail and rail–air elements.

In democratic market economies, the switch from road to rail cannot be imposed by EU or national law. The EU argues that it is best done through a process of incentives, such as targeted investments in other transport modes so that they can handle the overflow, and pricing schemes that reflect the real cost of road use and which encourage a 'natural' migration from roads to alternative forms of

transport. The purpose is to have fewer long-distance passengers or goods travelling by road and more by rail, and to replace some short-haul passenger flights by rail journeys. Infrastructure charging also supports the idea of paying for pollution caused. The transport sector is responsible for about 28% of all EU emissions of CO_2, the main greenhouse gas. Road transport alone accounts for 84% of this total. Better fuel efficiency, the use of alternative fuels and fuel taxation are measures being introduced by EU member countries.

In 2001, the EU's White Paper on transport set goals for each sector, some of which are now being implemented. These include increasing compulsory rest periods for drivers of heavy trucks from 8 to 9 hours and limiting the total driving time per week to 56 hours. Other White Paper targets seek to:

- improve train speeds to reverse the decline in rail's share of passenger and freight transport
- reduce flight delays by creating an integrated European air traffic control structure, and regulate airline slot allocations at airports
- invest more in maritime and inland waterways, and improve port services and maritime safety standards
- mix modes of transport to offer greater efficiency, less congestion, lower costs and cleaner air, and introduce integrated ticketing and baggage handling for dual-mode journeys

Macroeconomic performance in the EU

Table 24.2 shows changes over the period 1995–2004 in four key macroeconomic indicators for EU-15 countries, the 12 eurozone countries, the UK, the USA and Japan.

The main points to note are as follows:

- The UK has generally enjoyed a faster growth rate than the EU-15 and the eurozone. The UK is, of course, a member of the EU-15, but not of the eurozone 12. US growth has been even higher, but Japan, by contrast, has generally suffered low and sometimes negative growth, which reflects a lack of aggregate demand and recessionary conditions in a previously 'miracle' economy.
- Since 1998, employment growth has been faster in the EU-15 and the eurozone than in the UK. However, unemployment rates continue to be much higher in many of the continental countries, especially Germany and France. The faster rate of employment growth in these countries may therefore simply reflect the fact that a larger percentage of the working population has been unemployed and therefore available to be drawn into jobs. Full employment in the more prosperous parts of the UK means that, in the short term, employment can only grow through internal and external migration, and through attracting groups such as homemakers and the elderly into the economically active labour force.

examiner's voice

Unit 6 examination questions often include data showing the recent (and sometimes the projected future) performance of the UK, the eurozone, the USA and Japan. Such questions reflect the importance of international economics in Module 6: Government Policy, the National and International Economy.

	EU-15	Eurozone	UK	USA	Japan
Real GDP annual growth rate (%)					
1995	2.4	2.2	2.9	2.5	2.0
1996	1.6	1.4	2.8	3.7	3.4
1997	2.5	2.3	3.3	4.5	1.8
1998	2.9	2.9	3.1	4.2	−1.0
1999	2.9	2.8	2.9	4.4	−0.1
2000	3.6	3.5	3.9	3.7	2.4
2001	1.7	1.6	2.3	0.8	0.2
2002	1.0	0.9	1.8	1.9	−0.3
2003	0.8	0.5	2.2	3.0	1.4
2004	2.2	2.0	3.0	4.4	2.6
Total annual employment growth rate (%)					
1995	0.8	0.6	1.2	1.9	0.1
1996	0.3	0.2	0.9	2.0	0.4
1997	0.9	0.9	1.8	2.2	1.0
1998	1.8	1.8	1.0	2.4	−0.7
1999	1.7	1.8	1.4	2.2	−0.8
2000	2.0	2.2	1.2	2.2	−0.1
2001	1.3	1.4	0.8	−0.1	−0.6
2002	0.5	0.5	0.8	−0.8	−1.4
2003	0.3	0.1	0.9	0.0	−0.2
2004	N/A	N/A	N/A	N/A	N/A
Total unemployment rate (%)					
1995	10.0	10.5	8.5	5.6	3.1
1996	10.1	10.7	8.0	5.4	3.4
1997	9.8	10.6	6.9	4.9	3.4
1998	9.3	10.0	6.2	4.5	4.1
1999	8.5	9.1	5.9	4.2	4.7
2000	7.6	8.2	5.4	4.0	4.7
2001	7.2	7.8	5.0	4.8	5.0
2002	7.6	8.2	5.1	5.8	5.4
2003	7.9	8.7	4.9	6.0	5.3
2004	8.0	8.8	4.7	5.5	4.7
Inflation rate (annual change in harmonised index of consumer prices)					
1995	2.8	2.6	2.7	2.8	−0.1
1996	2.4	2.3	2.5	3.0	0.1
1997	1.7	1.7	1.8	2.3	1.8
1998	1.3	1.2	1.6	1.6	0.6
1999	1.2	1.1	1.3	2.2	−0.3
2000	1.9	2.1	0.8	3.4	−0.7
2001	2.2	2.3	1.2	2.8	−0.7
2002	2.1	2.3	1.3	1.6	−0.9
2003	2.0	2.1	1.4	2.3	−0.3
2004	1.9	2.1	1.3	3.0	−0.6

Source: Eurostat

Table 24.2 Selected macroeconomic performance indicators: EU-15, eurozone 12, UK, USA and Japan, 1995–2004

- The UK has benefited from the largest and longest-lasting fall in unemployment. Unemployment also fell in the eurozone, but in each year the unemployment rate has been significantly higher there than in the UK. Indeed, the eurozone unemployment rate began to increase again after 2001 whereas, after a minor blip, the UK rate continued to fall — at least until the end of 2004.

- The inflation rate has generally been low, and within the acceptable range set by the relevant monetary authority in all the countries and economic areas shown in the table. However, in recent years the UK has been slightly more successful in reducing inflation than the EU-15 taken as a whole, and the eurozone 12.

Taken together, the data series in Table 24.2 show that EU macroeconomic performance has generally been poorer than the performance of the US economy. UK performance has generally been better than that of the eurozone countries, but not as good as that of the USA. For the whole of the 1990s and early 2000s, Japan has been a special case, largely because Japanese residents generally fail to spend money in their own country.

> *e**xaminer's voice**
>
> Beware of falling into the trap of arguing that economic performance in mainland Europe, and in the eurozone in particular, is in all respects worse than UK economic performance. In west Germany and France, workers are generally better looked after by their governments, welfare provision is more generous, holidays are longer, and standards of living are often higher than for most people living in the UK. However, the UK's higher recent growth rate means that UK living standards are catching up, though greater UK income inequality means that low-paid British workers receive few of the benefits.

'Old Europe', 'New Europe' and different models of capitalism

To understand why the US and UK economies have generally performed better than the eurozone countries, it is useful to divide European countries into the countries of **'Old Europe'** and **'New Europe'**. (This distinction was first made by Donald Rumsfeld, the neo-conservative US defense secretary, when complaining in 2003 about the French and German refusal to join in the US and UK invasion of Iraq.) Old Europe centres on the EU-6 countries which created the EEC in 1957–58. By contrast, New Europe refers to the ten accession states that joined the EU in 2004. These countries are mostly located in central Europe.

To some extent, Old Europe and New Europe reflect two quite different models of capitalism and the market economy. The Old European countries have adopted or been influenced by the German **social-market economic model**. By contrast, central European countries seem much more willing to adopt the **Anglo-American model** of capitalism, which, as the name indicates, forms the basis of the market economy in the UK and the USA.

The Anglo-American model can best be understood in terms of the dictum, 'the business of business is business'. In this model, the role of the state in the economy is minimised and as much as possible is left to markets and the pursuit of self-interest. The model's good points are flexible labour and product markets, low

It is worth repeating advice stated early in the chapter that analytical and evaluation skills and use of data are more important than detailed technical knowledge of the EU when answering the case study question in the Unit 4 examination. By all means learn about all the topics listed on page 474, but make sure to be selective in how you use your knowledge. For the examination, relevant and accurate use of economic theories presented in earlier chapters of this book is more important than factual knowledge of the European Union.

Self-testing questions

1 What was the European Coal and Steel Community?

2 Outline a political reason for the creation of the European Economic Community.

3 Describe briefly the enlargement of the European Union since 1958.

4 Explain the similarities of, but also the differences between, a free trade area and a customs union.

5 What is the difference between trade creation and trade diversion?

6 How might the EU benefit from setting an optimal common external tariff (see Chapter 20)?

7 Explain the difference between a customs union and a common market.

8 What are the objectives of the common agricultural policy (CAP)?

9 Why has it been necessary to reform the CAP?

10 Apply the concept of a buffer stock policy (see Chapter 2) to the CAP.

11 Summarise the 2003 reforms of the CAP.

12 What is the main difference between the CAP and the common fisheries policy?

13 Explain how European fisheries illustrate the 'tragedy of the commons'.

14 Distinguish between 'subsidiarity' in the EU's competition policy and 'additionality' in the EU's regional policy.

15 What is the EU merger directive?

16 What has been the effect of the European Court of Justice's ruling in the Bosman case?

17 Why does the EU need a transport policy?

18 What is eurosclerosis?

19 What is the purpose of tax harmonisation?

20 What is the Stability and Growth Pact, and why has it failed?

Index

A

abatement costs   157
absolute advantage   384–385
accelerator principle   271–273
Advisory Conciliation and Arbitration
   Service (ACAS)   204
Agenda 2000   487
aggregate demand   252, 277
   components of   252
   deficient aggregate demand   267
aggregate supply   278–285
   long-run   281
   short-run   278
agricultural prices   27–32
alternative investment market   115
alternative theories of the firm   117–119
   economic natural selection   118
   managerial theories   117
   organisational/behavioural theories
      117
Anglo-American model of capitalism
   500
automatic stabilisers   243, 351–352
autonomous consumption   258
average propensity to consume   256
average propensity to save   256

B

balance of payments   see Chapter 21
   balance of payments equilibrium   412
   balance of trade in services   407–408
   balancing item   412
   capital flows   409–412
   current account   405–408
   current account surplus   418–419
   external equilibrium   412
   hot money   410
   long-term capital flows   409
   net income flows   408
   short-term capital flows   410
   structure of the UK balance of payments
      405–412
bank deposits   323
bank lending   331
   qualitative controls   331
   quantitative controls   331
bank money   325
Bank of England   329, 334
barriers to entry   95–97
barter   322
benefit principle   362
boom   241
Bosman case   490–491
Budget Day   357
budget deficit   269, 351
   cyclical   352
   structural   353
Budget Report   357
buffer stock policy   29
business cycle   238, 272–273

C

capital deepening   384
capital gains   449
capital gains tax   340
capital goods   3
capitalism   7
capital spending   357
capital widening   384
carbon taxes   157
cartel agreements   97
central bank   323
circular flow of income   252
claimant count   290
closed economy   252
Code for Fiscal Stability   357
collective bargaining   284, 298
command economy   6–7
   command mechanism   6
commercialisation   377
commodity money   322
common agricultural policy (CAP)
   31–32, 483, 486–488
   buffer stock scheme   487
   export subsidies   487
   variable import levies   487
common fisheries policy   483, 488–490
   tragedy of the commons   488

common markets   481
community charge   341
companies   104
comparative advantage   385–387
Competition Commission   126
competition policy   123–132
competitive advantage   388
complementary goods   24, 43
composite demand   43
congestion   158
consumer goods   3
consumer prices index (CPI)   300
consumer sovereignty   80
consumer surplus   78, 90
consumption   256
consumption theory   262
contestable market theory   129
contractualisation   137, 376
contractual saving   261
corporation tax   340
cost–benefit analysis   169–170
  value judgements   174
cost-plus pricing   87
cost-push inflation   286
costs   52–55
  average total cost   54
  average variable cost   54
  fixed cost   52
  long-run cost   57–60
  marginal cost   54
  variable cost   53
council tax   341
credit cards   325
cross elasticity of demand   43, 464
cross-subsidy   92–93
crowding in   354–355
crowding out   270, 353–354
  financial   354
  resource   353
current spending   357
customs unions   481
cyclical fluctuations   238
  long cycles   238

D
deficit financing   215
deflation   299, 414–415
deflationary policy   300

deindustrialisation   12–15, 206, 296
demand curve   18
  shifts of demand   23
demand-deficient unemployment   213
demand-pull inflation   269, 279, 286, 330
demerit goods   163–165, 451
  demerit goods and externalities   164
  demerit goods and the informational problem   165
  value judgements   165
dependency culture   348
dependency theory   394
deposit money   324
  demand deposits   324
  sight deposits   324
depreciation   415
deregulation   9, 128, 139–141, 377
  financial markets   379
  free-market revival   140
  theory of contestable markets   140
devaluation   414–415
different wage levels   193
direct investment   409
direct taxes   342
discounting the future   172
discretionary demand management   334
discretionary fiscal policy   269
diseconomies of scale   57
disequilibrium   253
disinflationary policy   300
distribution of income   262
division of labour   383–389
double coincidence of wants   322
Dutch disease effect   419

E
earnings trap   361
economic cycle   239
  long cycles   244
economic development   5
economic efficiency   73–76
  allocative efficiency   75
  cost efficiency   73
  dynamic efficiency   76
  monopoly and economic efficiency   77

perfect competition and economic
   efficiency   76
productive efficiency   73
technical efficiency   73
X-efficiency   74
economic growth   5, 237–249
long-run economic growth   237
long-run growth rate   239
neoclassical growth theory   245
new growth theory   245
short-run economic growth   237
sustainable economic growth   6, 248
economic liberalisation   137–145
economic problem   3
economic systems   3
economic welfare   78, 230–237
economies of scale   57, 69, 105–109
economies of concentration   109
economies of disintegration   109
economies of increased dimensions   106
economies of information   109
economies of massed resources   107
economies of vertically linked processes
   107
external economies of scale   109
financial or capital-raising economies
   of scale   108
firm-level economies of scale   108
indivisibilities   106
internal economies of scale   105
learning effects   109
managerial economies of scale   107
marketing economies   108
multi-plant economies of scale   107
plant-level economies of scale   106
risk-bearing economies of scale   108
volume economies   106
El Niño effect   241
embargoes   415
endogenous growth theory   245
enterprise economy   369
environment   454–463
economic activity   454–455
environmental dumping   462
national economy   461–463
equilibrium price   19–21
disequilibrium   19
equilibrium   19

equilibrium wage rate   189, 192
equity   362
equity leakage   454
equity withdrawal   454
EU competition policy   483, 491–493
merger directive, 2004   493
EU enlargement   477–480
EU population   480
EU regional policy   483, 494–496
additionality   494
Cohesion Fund   496
cohesion policy   496
European Agricultural Guidance and
   Guarantee Fund (EAGGF)   496
European Regional Development Fund
   (ERDF)   496
European Social Fund (ESF)   496
Solidarity Funds   496
Structural Funds   496
subsidiarity   494
EU regional problems   493–496
euro   435–439
economic tests   437–438
eurocurrency market   412
eurodollars   411
**European Agricultural Guidance and
Guarantee Fund (EAGGF)**   486
European Central Bank (ECB)   435
**European Coal and Steel Community
(ECSC)**   476
European Commission   476, 484
European Community   476
**European Economic Community
(EEC)**   476
European monetary system (EMS)   434
European monetary union (EMU)   435
European Union   476, see Chapter 24
Council of Ministers   484
EU fiscal policy   502
European Council   484
European Parliament   484
Golden Banana   477
Maastricht Treaty   483
New Europe   500
Old Europe   500
political union   484
Single European Act (SEA)   482
Stability and Growth Pact   503–504